ISBN 978-1-5278-0871-3
PIBN 10904113

CATHOLIC RECORD SOCIETY

MISCELLANEA · IX

LONDON
1914
PRINTED PRIVATELY FOR THE SOCIETY
AT THE MERCAT PRESS
EDINBURGH

Mother [illegible]

From [illegible]

CATHOLIC RECORD SOCIETY

MISCELLANEA · IX

LONDON
1914
PRINTED PRIVATELY FOR THE SOCIETY
AT THE MERCAT PRESS
EDINBURGH

This Volume is
Issued to the Members for 1912-13
Being the First for the Year

TABLE OF CONTENTS

ILLUSTRATIONS

Portraits

Inset Pedigrees

Inset Slip

No. I

ANNALS OF THE ENGLISH COLLEGE, SEVILLE

WITH AN ACCOUNT OF FOUR OTHER FOUNDATIONS FROM 1589 TO 1595, AN UNFINISHED MEMOIR, WRITTEN BY FATHER ROBERT PERSONS, S. J., IN 1610.

CONTRIBUTED BY THE REV. J. H. POLLEN, S. J.

This memoir, though not dated, must clearly have been written between the receipt of Father Price's letter (mentioned below) of 1st March 1610, and the author's death 16th April following. It will therefore be one of his latest compositions. His object was perhaps to continue a history of the Seminaries, of which a 'Relation' was written in English about 1593 (*C.R.S.* v, 259 *n*), though no copy of it is at present known. The Seminary of Seville may be said to live on in that of Valladolid, with which Bishop Challoner united it about 1770.

ANNALES SEMINARII SEU COLLEGII ANGLORUM HISPALENSIS AB ANNO 1591

Stonyhurst MSS., *Collectanea P.*, ff. 344 sqq., a copy made by Father Christopher Grene, while he was in the English College Rome, about the year 1680. The Original, he says, was Persons's autograph, but this has now apparently perished. For facility of reference a summary of each section is here added in square brackets.

[§ 1.—The Invitation, 1590.

When the English Seminary of Valladolid was founded in 1589, Father Persons sent priests to almost all parts of Spain to beg for alms. Fathers John Cecil and William Warford, who had visited Andalusia, gave Father Persons a glowing account of the prospects of founding a seminary at Seville, and Father Bartolomeo Perez, then Jesuit Provincial at that place, warmly urged its cause.]

Collegium seu Seminarium Anglorum, quod in præclarissima civitate Hispalensi ad Anglicani regni remedium reductionemque ab heresi summa Dei bonitate altissimaque providentia institutum est, initium habuit ab anno 1592, quanquam biennio fere ante, aut etiam triennio, occasio huic negotio præbita est, hac quam dicam ratione.

Cum anno 1589* eadem Dei Providentia Anglicanæ gentis Seminarium Pinciæ seu Vallisoleti in Provincia Castellana coep-

* MS. in error has 1592.

tum fuisset,* nullis tamen reditibus vel annuis censibus firmatum, P. Robertus Personius Anglus Soc. Jesu Sacerdos, qui ei rei præfuerat, nonnullos dimiserat per omnes fere Hispaniarum provincias sacerdotes Anglicanæ nationis, qui subsidium pecuniarum alendo Seminario Pinciano procurarent.

In Boeticam vero provinciam venerunt duo Joannes Cecilius† et Gulielmus Warfordus‡ præclara virtutis laude ornati, qui præter subsidia non contemnenda eleemosynarum, spem quoque P. Personio fecerunt posse in civitate Hispalensi Seminarium commodissime constitui, cum propter potentiam divitiasque civitatis, liberalitatem civium, tum etiam ob maximam portus opportunitatem, ex quo sacerdotes Seminariorum absolutis iam studiis tu-

* The very interesting history of the foundation of the college of Valladolid, was written at the time by Father Persons, in a *Relation* sent to Cardinal Allen, 14 September, 1589 (see letter *n.* 5 below). It is not identical with the *Informacion* about Seminaries in general written by Persons, ' en Valladolid á primero de Setiembre de 1589,' which is printed at the end of his *Relacion de algunos martyrios*, Madrid, 1590. (British Museum, 4902, aaa, 54). Persons' *Relation* is alluded to in the curious *Relacion de un Sacerdote Ingles . . . de la venida de su Magestad [Philip II] al colegio de los Ingleses*, Madrid 1592. (British Museum, 811, c. 13), and this is abbreviated in D. Yepes, *Historia particular de la persecucion de Inglaterra*, Madrid, 1599, pp. 746-764. Persons' Relation seems also to have been used by H. More, *Historia Provinciae Anglicanae*, St Omers, 1660, pp. 156-159. Father John Blackfan, one of the first students, wrote in 1620 an independent account, *Annales Collegii S. Albani in oppido Valesoleti*, privately printed, London, ex typ. Manresana 1899. See also F. Sacchini, *Historia Societatis Jesu*, Pars v. Rome, 1661, pp. 461-463. Tierney-Dodd, ii, 177 n, and Ap. 375. A. Bellesheim, *W. Cardinal Allen, und die Englischen Seminare auf dem Festlande*, Mainz, 1885, pp. 181-185, 237-239; A. O. Meyer, *England und die Katholische Kirche unter Elizabeth*, Rome 1911, pp. 99-100, 304. T. A. Dunne, *The first years of St Alban's. College Valladolid*, in the *Ushaw Magazine* for March and July, 1906. The Register of the College has been preserved, a transcript of it was in the possession of the late Bishop Goss.

† John Cecil, of Trinity College Oxford, then of Rheims, and Rome, was a brilliant scholar and at first gave promise of becoming a leader in the English Church. Unfortunately he was also vain, and, when the hour of trial came, wanting in principle. When arrested in England, he obtained his liberty by offering to disclose the plans of Catholics, though he refused to give such information as would lead directly to the execution of priests. This led to his living a double life, which we can see (now that the state papers are open to inspection) was not always honourable. From time to time there were sinister rumours against him, but he seemed to live them down. He was trusted by the Catholics of Scotland (*Spanish Calendar*, 1586-1603, p. 615), and a strong letter in his commendation was written by Father Creswell, 30 July 1595 (Vatican Archives, fondo Borghese iii, 124; g. 20). For the rest of his career see the *Dictionary of National Biography*.

When this paper was written in 1610, there was no doubt that this duplicity was a matter of the past, and so Father Persons, though he had knowledge of sundry things to Cecil's discredit (Tierney III., Ap., 157; V., 10, 11, Ap. 14-20), is content to mention only such as would tend to his favour. Cecil when first arrested gave in personal descriptions of some here mentioned—'Blunt and Roberts, men of reasonable stature, the [second] much beard, the other little, clerkish. Dudley and Younger, the [first] of middle stature, flaxen, the other tall and black. Walford and Almonde are both of reasonable stature, and of hair flaxen, somewhat reddish.' (*Dom. El.* 238, 179; 239, 13).

‡ William Warneford, Warford or Walford, see Foley, *Records* vii, 815 and *Dict. Nat. Biog. s.v.*, and *Acts of English Martyrs*, 1891, 249 sq.

tissime in Angliam ad lucrandas animas pro Seminariorum instituto, missionumque ratione transmitti possent.

Itaque summopere P. Personio persuadebant ut quam citissime Hispalim advolaret, rem omnem sine dubio ex sententia effecturus; idipsum literis creberrimis affirmabat Bartholomæus Perez* qui eo tempore Præpositus erat Provinciæ Bæticæ pro Societate Jesu, vir magnis ornamentis literarum ac pietatis leloque animarum plenus, et in Seminaria Anglicana mirifice affectus, ex eo tempore quo Romæ eorum instituta fructusque cognoverat; unde quibuscunque modis poterat (poterat autem pluribus) Seminarii huius Hispalensis erectioni favebat.

[§ 2.—Father Persons's Visit.

Father Persons therefore came at the end of the year, but for various reason the plan of foundation could not then be realised. Neither house, nor funds, nor scholars could be provided satisfactorily, and it did not seem prudent to commence a fresh seminary until that of Valladolid was better founded. Father Persons too was occupied in preaching to the English galley-slaves at Puerto S. Maria, of whom he converted ninety-three, and obtained their liberty.]

Hac invitatione speque allectus venit Hispalim Personius ad finem anni 1590,† adductis secum 4 sacerdotibus, ad missionem Anglicanam paratis, qui erant Joannes Fixerus, Jacobus Youngerus, Richardus Bluntus, et Richardus Dudlæus. Hac tamen vice (ut sunt Dei opera, quo maiora eo pluribus difficultatibus ut plurimum obsepta) principium Seminario dari non potuit, tum quod Personius magnam partem hyemis apud portum S. Mariæ‡ consumere coactus est, in reducendis ab hæresi nonnullis Anglis qui in triremibus regiis captivi detinebantur (nonaginta autem et tres reducti sunt et ab utraque servitute tum animi tum corporis liberati)§ tum vero quia tam exiguo illo tempore quo Pinciani Seminarii necessitas P. Personii absentiam tolerabat, neque domus commoda Hispali conquiri potuit, neque copia alumnorum ad studia, neque alimenta ad sustentationem, neque coetera rei tantæ necessaria comparari posse videbantur.

* Bartolomeo, Perez S.J., see Sommervogel, *Bibliothèque d. l. C. d. Jésus*, VI. 515. There are several of his letters, as Dec. 2 and 27, 1592, extant in foreign Jesuit archives (Epp. Hisp. xxx.) which show how sincere a friend to the English Seminary he was. Before the start was made there had been opposition. Father Estevan de Hojeda in particular wrote from Seville to Aquaviva on the 19th of April, and again on the 2nd of July—asking him to make Persons wait, as there was so much begging going on. But the General seems to have decided in Persons' favour, so Father Perez's course was clear.

† Persons left Madrid on the 5th or 6th of November, and was at Valladolid 12th November. See his letters below.

‡ Puerto S. Maria lies on the north side of Cadiz Harbour some twenty-five miles from Seville.

‖ Father Persons eventually won the freedom of this considerable number of prisoners, by a very strong letter (Seville, 4th April, 1591) to Don Juan de Idiaquez, (of which a translation is printed by Knox, *Letters of Cardinal Allen*, Introd., 113-115), insisting that the Spanish ministers should trust the English.

[§ 3.—The Twelve Apostles.

Meantime twelve lately ordained priests were dispatched to England, of whom the last sent John Brushford was taken and cast into prison, where he died.]

Omnis itaque cogitatio de Seminario Hispalensi instituendo in aliud tempus rejecta est, quo Seminarii Pinciani vires validiores et firmiores essent, et coetera paratiora ad hoc opus prosequendum. In præsenti tamen nonnulla constituta fuerunt quæ plurimum videbantur interesse ad causam Catholicam sublevandam, quorum primum erat ut duodecim sacerdotes (et omen quidem videbatur in numero) zelo divinæ gloriæ accensi in Anglicanam messim mitterentur: hi erant* Joannes Cecilius; Gulielmus Warfordus; Joannes Robertius; Oliverius Almannus; Jacobus Youngerus; Thomas Salowaius; Joannes Fixerus; N. Rochus; Richardus Bluntus; Franc. Lokwodus; Rich. Dudlæus et novissimus omnium Joannes Brushfordus, cui prima tamen mercedis sors tributa videtur, quando sociis omnibus secure Angliam ingressis ipse solus in portu Anglicano captus et in carcerem coniectus, post anni unius tolerantiam qua fidem catholicam fortiter confessus est felicissime moritur.

[§ 4.—The Foundation of a Residence at S. Lúcar.

The old church of the English, St. George's, had become very dilapidated. It was now ceded to the English at Father Persons's request, John Cecil having first solicited the grant. Persons (as visitor) appointed four English chaplains, Thomas Stillington, D.D., Martin Array, George Ambler, William Seburne, and he also obtained money from the King of Spain and the Duke of Medina Sidonia to rebuild the church.]

Alterum quod hoc tempore perfectum est, fuit translatio regiminis et possessionis Ecclesiæ et domus S. Georgii Anglorum in civitate S[ti] Lucar (quæ prius penes mercatores Anglicanos erat) ad sacerdotes quosdam nationis Anglicanæ qui in Seminariis instituti fuerant, ut majori diligentia cultum divinum in eadem procurarent. Nam cum, deficiente iam numero zeloque et magna etiam ex parte pietate Catholica, istiusmodi mercatorum (quorum multi iam in Anglia reversi fuerant† ut hæresim liberius calvinianam

* For these names see the catalogue of Seville students below.

† The English at St Lúcar de Barrameda still formed a Catholic community in 1754. In that year they sent in a petition to the Pope, which gave the following account of their history. Founded in 1517, chaplains being appointed by the bishops of London, Winchester and Exeter, the patronage was made over in 1591 to Cardinal Allen, who named Father Persons as visitor. This was confirmed by a brief of Clement VIII, 5th March 1592. The Jesuit Provincial continued to hold that office till 1666, when in consequence of diminished revenues, etc, Cardinal Howard appointed a Dominican visitor, and this was confirmed by a bull of Innocent XII, 23rd Dec. 1691. On 2nd June 1696 the same cardinal appointed the Archbishop. of Seville visitor, and things went well after an Englishman, Don Francis Malbrank, rebuilt the church for 11,000 pais. Now (1754) the colony was alarmed at a rumour that the Jesuits wanted to obtain a renovation of the brief of Clement VIII. The signatories are John Price, *Proposito*, Richard Butler,

amplecterentur) ecclesia hæc domusque S. Georgii in egestatem maximam pervenissent, ita ut ruinæ iam proximæ esse viderentur, factum est, procurante eodem P. Personio (quod Joannes etiam Cecilius antea sollicitaverat),* ut ius omne istius Ecclesiæ ac domus per ipsos confratres et mercatores, ad dictorum sacerdotum ius ac possessionem transferretur. Quod et perfectum est instrumento publico, die 29 mensis Aprilis anno D. 1591, cuius instrumenti copia in collegii huius nostri archivio reposita est.

Ad huius ergo Ecclesiæ domusque S. Georgii gubernationem advocavit P. Personius e Seminario Valesoletano D. Thomam Stillingtonum,† S. Theol. Doctorem, quem eiusdem ecclesiæ præpositum curavit fieri, cum antea in Seminario Rhemensi Theologiam prælegisset: evocavit etiam ex civitate Toletana Martinum de Aray ‡ et ex Seminario Pinciano Georgium§ Amblerum sacerdotes Anglos, qui primi Residentiæ S. Lucar facti sunt Capellani, postea vero Gulielmum etiam Seburnum ‖ ex civitate Ulissiponensi (ubi

Hyacinth Butler, James Lynch, Lawrence Carter (?), Thomas Power, Robert Fleming, Samuel Eyre, Robert Walsh, Thomas Beeson (? Begson), Peter Stranger, Ales Macnamara, Francis Britchell, Dom. H. French, Peter Pritchard, John Brukdale, Dom. Terry, Peter Langton, Gerald Barry, Anthony Butler, Francis Matthew, Thomas Wadding, Nicholas Langton, Thomas Power, Rafaele Pinchinony, Maurizio Lucas, Thomas Cantillon, Thomas Walsh, Thomas Laich, Henry Seix, John Poold, Edward Hall. This document is still preserved in the English College, Rome (Scritture XLIV). with a Spanish translation. The college also possesses a copy of the grant of indulgences to the church, hospital and college of St Lúcar for the feasts of St Thomas and St George. Granted in 1598. (*Chronologia Monumentorum*, f. 197.

John Cecil gives his account of these proceedings in his *Discovery of the errors etc. committed by William Criton Priest and Professed Jesuit* (? Paris) 1599, p. 19, but with characteristic vainglory claims the lion's share in the foundation not only of the residence of St Lúcar, but also of all the seminaries in Spain.

† Thomas Stillington is described in English College Register as of the archdiocese of York. He had been a scholar at Rome (1580-1584), (Foley VI, iii, 144) and took his doctorate there. He returned to Rheims 22nd October 1584, and there was put to teach 'cases' till 1589, when Dr Barrett sent him with the second batch of Rheims students, to commence the new seminary at Valladolid. But as it was found more convenient that the scholars there should go to the neighbouring school of the Jesuits, Stillington found himself with little to do, and so would have been glad of the post Father Persons found for him. He seems to have been there in 1596 (Knox, *Douay Diaries*, p. 375.) See also *Domestic Calendar Additional*, 1580-1625, p. 314. He died in 1597. A. Jessopp. *Letters of H. Walpole*, p. 49.

‡ Martin Array of the diocese of Carlisle was one of the first scholars of the English College Rome, *Cath. Rec. Soc.* ii. 87 seq. Then going on to the English Mission he worked for some time under the name Cotton, and was more than once made prisoner, *Ibid*, 250, 275, and Morris *Troubles*, ii, 164-166, He was probably now in Spain because England had become too hot for him. He returned to Rome in company with Father Persons, 1596-1597, Foley vi, 568, and in 1598, he acted as procurator for the Archpriest Blackwell, during the first Appeal.

§ George Ambler, of the arch-diocese of York, had already finished his course at Rheims, and was returning to England (Knox, *Douay Diaries*, p. 226), when he came to Spain to complete his ecclesiastical training.

‖ Probably the Rheims priest William Seborne, of the diocese of Hereford, who had been ordained in 1583 (*Douay Diary*). In placing four chaplains at this church Father Persons must have been making a provision well in excess of the needs of

pro tempore residebat) ad idem munus advocavit, effecitque apud maiestatem regiam, ut duo millia aureorum tribuerentur per ipsum Regem ad ædificium domus et ecclesiæ reficiendum, et ad alia de novo exædificanda, præter nonnullas eleemosinas ab ipso etiam Excellentissimo Duce de Medina Sidoniæ procuratas, cuius principis ope ac favore præcipuaque auctoritate (cum dominus sit temporalis eiusdem civitatis S. Lucar*) stabilita fuit ac sustenata hæc sacerdotum Anglorum residentia, quæ cœpit, ut dixi, anno D. 1591.

[§ 5.—The Foundation of the College.

After the very successful entertainment of Philip II at the new College at Valladolid, 2nd August 1592, Persons went to Seville. He had obtained letters of commendation from the king, and from many of the nobles, and the foundation was accomplished in two months. List of the principal benefactors and of the first scholars. The first house was taken in the Calle San Lorenzo, then a larger one in the Calle S. Magdalena, then after three years, one in the Cal de las Armas, finally in the Calle de la Sierpe.]

Anno vero sequenti, hoc est 1592, compositis iam et constitutis utcumque Seminarii valesoletani rebus (cuius anni mense Augusto piissimus rex Philippus Hispaniarum 2s cum unico filio Philippo Principe ac Elizabetha Infanta Seminarium illud vallesoletanum ingressus honorificentissime visitaverat†) idem P. Personius 2° Hispalim, literis regiis ac præcipuorum in aula principum commendatione adiutus, ut Seminarium Anglicanum hac in civitate Hispalensi constitueret, quod Deo propitiante ita brevi confectum est ut intra duorum mensium spatium satis ampla jam extaret familia in optimi Collegii formam redacta.

Præcipui autem huius operis ab initio fautores et auctores fuere Illustrissimus Dns Rodricus de Castro Archiepiscopus Hispalensis,‡

the English colony: but we see from his letter to Barrett, that he contemplated giving newly ordained priests a year or two for leading a clerical life in a Catholic country, before they returned to England, where they would have to live in lay attire and among lay folk, almost altogether deprived of the support of their fellow-priests, *Hatfield Calender*, iv, 69.

* The town of Medina Sidonia lies some thirty-five miles south-east of St Lúcar de Barrameda.

† The *Relacion* of this visit is mentioned above *n.* 1. Verses had been written for the occasion in ten languages, but the Spanish Edition only quotes the Spanish, Latin and Italian. The collection however seems to be still extant in MS. in the Biblioteca Nacionale, Madrid, M. 158, Sommervogel, *s.v.*, Valladolid, A.

‡ On comparison of this part of Father Persons's paper with the letter addressed to him about Seville by Father John Price, 1st March 1610 (Stonyhurst MS. Anglia A. iii. 9, printed in Tierney's Dodd, ii, Ap. 376) it is clear that Persons has followed his local informant with but few variations for the names and other details here given, his own memory being probably slow after the lapse of so many years. The blanks, which he here left in his MS. and which Father Grene has faithfully imitated, are probably due to Price having given the titles of the Spanish grandees summarily, whereas Persons wanted to give them in full; and for this would probably desire to consult some Spanish courtier. Over the first name he has made a curious slip. Father Price enumerated the favourers of this work as 'the cardinal then living, Don Rodrigo de Castro, the assistant that then was, Don

Illus[mi] Duces [blank in MS.], Ill[mi] Marchiones de Priego et de Ayemonte, Ill[mæ] Marchionissæ de Tarifa et de Alcala, et inter magnates præcipue contulit Rev[mus] D. Franciscus Sarmentus de Mendoça Episcopus giennensis,* vir summæ eruditiones ac pietatis, qui statim ut de his duobus Seminariis Anglicis intellexerat mille aureos eleemosynæ annuæ eisdem attribuit, dum viveret, et ad duos etiam post mortem annos, mortuus autem est piissime, uti vixerat, anno D. 1595.

Atque hæc de Nobilitate Boetica quæ ab initio Seminario Anglo-Hispalensi munifice contribuit. Ex equestri vero ordine, nec non plebeio, plurimi fuerunt, quorum nomina perlongum fuisset hic attexere, et pluris interest ut in libro vitæ ob egregiam pietatem quam in hoc inscribantur catalogo. In primis tamen fuerunt quantum memoria repetere possum D. franciscus de Caravajal [5 lines left blank in MS.]† et alii nonnulli qui vel annua fere vel menstrua alendis collegialibus tribuebant subsidia.

Neque minor enituit ordinis Ecclesiastici amor pietasque in hoc tam pio opere omni ratione promovendo, inter quos ut paucos e multis percurramus in primis fuerunt D. franciscus Blancus [four lines left blank in MS.].‡

Primus Seminario huic Rector datus est ex Societate P. franciscus Peralta § vir magna charitate morum suavitate &—— Minister autem ei adiunctus est ex natione Anglicana P. Carolus

Francisco de Carvajal and the Conde de Priego' (Tierney, Ap. 376) and meant the Cardinal Archbishop of Seville, Don Rodrigo de Castro, (1582-1601—Gams), the Bishop auxiliary Don Francisco de Carvahal (translated in 1604 to Coria—Gams), and Conde de Priego. But Persons whose sight was now very bad, read the list wrong. Perhaps as the reader will see, he combined the names *with the title which followed.* At all events he does not see that de Carvajal was a bishop. The blank which follows was clearly meant to have been filled in with Father Price's names, 'the dukes and duchesses of Arios, of Vejar, of Sesa.'

* Francis Sarmiento de Mendoza bishop of Jaen, of good repute, both as a priest and as a writer, was one of the most respected men in the church of Spain.

† This blank should probably have contained the names which Father Price enumerates thus, 'Secular gentlemen of the cabildo (?Corporation) don Juan Vincentelo, don Juan de Arguijo, Juan Antonio del Alcazar, and Miguel de Xaurigui.'

‡ This blank would similarly have contained the following:—'The apostolic inquisitors don Francisco Blanco, don Juan Capata, don Juan de Valdes;—divers canons of the Cathedral church, don Bernardino Rodriguez, don Alonzo Colomal, don Francisco de Ribera, the doctors Vahamonte, Pacheco, Santander y Asoca, all of great learning and singular piety.'

§ Father Francis de Peralta (1554-1622) deserves a place in our English Catholic biographies, for he spent most of the active years of his life in the management of the English College of Seville, in which he eventually died 7th January 1622 (or 1621—Sommervogel). He wrote in Spanish, accounts of the deaths of two students Egerton and Waller (see below), which were published in Latin in the *Litteræ Annuæ* of 1596, and in Spanish in Yepez, p. 852. He also published accounts of Doña Luysa de Carvahal, etc.—Seville, 1614, and of the martyrdoms of the Ven. MM. Atkinson, Thulis and Wrennol—Seville, 1616, and composed in MS. à life of Father Weston.

Tancardus* Soc. Jes. Sacerdos, qui optime Seminarii huius principia moderati sunt &——.† His ergo initiis coeptum est Seminarium hoc Hispalense die 25 Novembris D. Catharinæ virgini sacrato, anno ut iam dictum est 1592 et prima domus conductitia fuit in platea S. Laurentii.

Alumni qui simul cum patribus Personio et Cresswello primi appulerunt fuere Joannes Worthingtonus, [Georgius] Chamberlanus, Thomas Egertonus, et franciscus feltonus; post duorum autem mensium spatium alia domus amplior conducta fuit ad habitationem Seminarii in platea S. Magdalenæ, in qua manserunt per triennii fere spatium, quoad coemptis et resarcitis novis et amplioribus ædibus, in platea quam de armis vocant, ad eas transmigrarunt.

Atque hæc in universum dicta sint de principio atque prima erectione Seminarii Anglo-Hispalensis, nunc autem quæ singulatim quoque anno acciderint breviter etiam attingenda mihi videntur.

[§ 6.—The Feast of St Thomas, 1592.

A sufficient number of students having arrived from Valladolid and elsewhere, many of the townspeople came to visit an institution previously unknown to them. On the 29th of December therefore, when the college chapel was solemnly opened, an academic display was given. Emblems and verses on many subjects adorned the walls of the inner hall, Canon Caloma (afterwards Bishop of Barcelona) sang the mass in the presence of the Cardinal Archbishop, and a great gathering of dignitaries. Thomas Egerton welcomed the cardinal at his arrival, John Worthington preached in Latin on St. Thomas, and deeply touched all present by his reference to the vocation of the Seminarists. After mass four of the students took the college oath, of receiving the priesthood and returning to England. George Chamberlain explained its meaning in a short Spanish speech, which affected deeply all that were present.]

Cum institutum iam esset collegium—cumque bene magna iam studiosorum Anglorum manus partim ex Seminario vallisoletano partim aliunde confluxisset, plurimi ex omnium hominum ordine rei novitate moti—visendi ac percunctandi causa ad domum nostram veniebant,‡ quibus ut commodius satisfieret, et ut Collegii institutum finisque omnibus magis innotesceret—expedire videbatur ut exercitia nonnulla literaria tum de pietate tum etiam de literis haberentur, quod factum est maximo hominum concursu atque gratulatione.

Die 29 Decembris præclarissimo X[ti] martyri Thomæ Cantuariensi

* An account of Father Charles Tancard or Tancred is given in Foley vii., 761, who believes him to have come from Boroughbridge, Yorks.

† This sign is that which Father Grene uses for his own omissions.

‡ It must be remembered that the institution of Seminaries for clergy students was then an innovation in the Church, and that there were as yet hardly any in Spain. The account of the visit paid by Philip II mentioned above (note 1), dwells on the great interest taken by the courtiers in the details of this orderly religious life. The horarium for the day attracted special attention, and is reproduced in full. The oath of the mission, of which mention is made below, had been first suggested by Father Persons, *C. R. S.* ii, 87.

sacrâ, factum est primum sacrum solomne in ipsa Collegii capella, addito etiam atrio interiori et in Ecclesiæ formam pro illa die composito, variisque linguis ex omni genere carminum emblematumque ornato. Missam cantabat Ill. D. Alumnus de Columna Canonicus Ecclesiæ Cathedralis, interfuerunt sacro Ill^{mus} Card. Archiepiscopus, Ill^{mus} D. Assistens, civitatis senatores, doctores, praelati ordinum religiosorum; viri graves doctique plurimi.

Ex alumnis Thomas Egertonus oratione latina ingredientem Cardinalem excepit, Joannes Worthingtonus concionatus latine infra sacrum ipsum, luculenter peroravit de vita et laudibus S. Thomæ Cantuariensis,* quæ omnia cum ad præsentem statum conditionemque temporum hominumque et præcipue sociorum suorum, qui pro instituti sui ratione in Angliam ad Martyrii coronam ingressuri erant, [spectabant], audientium animos mirifice commovit.

Absoluto sacro quattuor alumni iuramentum publice præstiterunt iuxta formam instituti Seminariorum, quod ut melius ab omnibus intelligeretur Georgius Chamberlainus† sermone quodam brevi sed eleganti et ad motus animorum efficaci lingua Hispanica totius negotii rationem explicavit: quo facto vix dici potest quanta omnium satisfactione imo plane admiratione discessum sit.

[§ 7.—A Defence of Theology, 1593.

On the 20th of February 1593, Richard Walpole and Henry Floyd, priests, defended conclusions in universal theology, which had been printed, for a whole day in the college hall, FF. Melchior de Castro and Ignatius Yañes, lecturers at the Jesuit College of St Hermenegild presiding, the one in the morning the other in the afternoon. There was a large attendance of learned and of religious men, who greatly praised the defendants, especially Walpole. Three days later he became a Jesuit, while Henry Floyd left with Persons for Lisbon, to return in due time to England.]

Paucis deinde interiectis diebus aliud quoddam exercitium literarium et illud quidem peregregium magisque ad ingeniorum acumen, maturitatemque in literis experiundum quam antecedens exhibitum est. Die enim 20mo febr. Sacerdotes duo alumni Richardus Walpolus et Henricus Floydus‡ conclusiones ex universa Theologia decerptas proeloque divulgatas publice in Collegii atrio per diem

* Father Grene notes here that this speech may be read in his *Collectanea P.* fol. 273-280 now at Stonyhurst. At that place Fr. Grene says the speech was 'composita a Personio, scripta ab Henrico Walpole.' This future martyr had just arrived from Flanders, and his brother Richard from Rome. After a short time Henry went to Valladolid. Jessopp—*One Generation of a Norfolk House*, 1878, p. 167.

† George Chamberlain, *see*, *Dict. Nat. Biog.*, Gillow etc. He also made the farewell speech to King Philip at Valladolid, printed Yepez p. 763. See also the Register below.

‡ Richard Walpole became eventually the Prefect of all the English Houses in Spain. Jessopp, *One Generation of a Norfolk House* and Foley vii. 810. Henry Floyd, as also his younger brother John, Cambridgeshire men, eventually entered the Society, and Henry played a distinguished part in the affairs of the English Catholics. Foley mistakenly states that he was not yet a priest, vii. 268.

integrum, præsidente mane P. Melchiore de Castro, vesperi autem Jgnazio de Yañes* prælectoribus Collegii Societatis S. Hermenigildi cum maxima omnium approbatione exhibuerunt. Ad quam publicam disputationem cum omnis fere ordo religiosorum doctorumque hominum concurrisset, singularem defensoribus laudem præcipue vero Walpolo tribuerunt, qui tertio abinde die Soc. Jesu ingressus est. P. Floydus vero Ulyssiponem una cum P. Personio ad missionem Anglicanam suo tempore capessendam discessit.

[§ 8.—The Residence of Lisbon.

Father Persons had founded a residence for priests, with the assistance of the Cardinal Archduke Albert, viceroy of Portugal; the Count of Alegra, the Archbishop of Lisbon, and the Duke of Braganza. Many of the Portuguese nobility had suggested and offered to help in the foundation either of a seminary or of a residence at Lisbon. Father Persons chose the latter for various reasons, especially because an Irish College had already been begun there. William Seburn was appointed provost, John Richards and Henry Floyd chaplains. The Duke contributed an annual pension of one hundred gold crowns.]

Sed cum ibi navigandi commoditas non statim daretur, commoratus est nonnihil in ea civitate, ut residentiæ cuiusdam assisteret, quam P. Personius iis ipsis diebus Ulissippone instituerat, auxilio, gratia et eleemosynis Serenissimi Archiducis Cardinalis Austriaci, qui viceregio munere per universum Lusitaniæ regnum fungebatur, et Illust^{mi} comitis de porto alegre qui ei præcipuus a conciliariis erat, Illustrissimorum item virorum D. Antonii Archiepiscopi Ulissipponensis et Theodosii Ducis Bragantini, qui omnes ceterique multi ex nobilitate Lusitanica P. Personio authores et adiutores fuerunt, ut vel Seminarium iuventutis Anglicanæ, ut Vallisoleti et Hispali factum erat, Ulissipone quoque erigeret, vel saltem residentiam aliquam sacerdotum Anglorum ea ipsa in civitate ob portus commoditatem institueret, qui adventantes scholares ad alia Seminaria hospitio acciperent, eosque deinde, qui absolutis studiis in Angliam reverterentur, eodem genere charitatis prosequerentur.

Elegit vero Personius potius ut Residentia fieret quam Seminarium, tum quia civitas Ulissipponensis longe dissita est a reliquis duobus erectis iam Seminariis, iterque valde devium et impeditum habet, eoque fiebat ut P. Personius adesse Seminarii initiis et progressui prout necessarium videbatur non posset, tum etiam vel præcipue quia fieri ibi coeperat Seminarium quoddam Hibernorum, cui fortasse incommodum nonnullum attulisset Seminarum Anglorum in eadem civitate. Residentia itaque Sacerdotum instituta † est, cui prepositus datus est Gulielmus

* F.F. Melchior de Castro, and Ignatius Yañez, distinguished professors, are both commemorated by Sommervogel ii. 866; viii. 1357.

† The Residence of Lisbon was subsequently changed and enlarged into a college by the generosity of Don Pietro Coutinho. It then passed into the charge of the

Seburnus vir multæ pietatis etc. Socii vero pro capellanio assignati fuerunt Joannes Richardus* et Henricus Floydus Sacerdotes & ——. Atque hoc fuit initium Residentiae Anglicæ Ulissipponensis, cuius sustentationi — Dux Bragantinus pensionem annuam aureorum centum pro suo in Anglos amore constituit.

[§ 9.—St. Omers.

The persecution of Catholics was then extremely violent in England, and it had been decided that their children, especially those of the upper class, should be placed under heretical masters from their early years, to be brought up in Calvinism. Father Persons betook himself to the king, and setting before him the extreme wickedness of the measure obtained the institution of yet another seminary at St. Omers, with the grant of 2000 gold crowns yearly, its government to be by the Society. When Father Aquaviva's consent had been given, the seminary was started in very brief space, Father William Flack, who diligently urged the matter in person, and Father William Holt, who was then in Brussels, giving assistance.

Thomas More and William Reyner, priests, were sent to England from the College of Seville.]

Hoc eodem fere tempore ingressi sunt Societatem iuvenes Angli duo Joannes Colinus et Arthurus Hocus ut coadiutores temporales fierent——Valde sæviebat in Anglia persecutio hoc tempore contra catholicos, ubi inter cætera constitutum fuerat† ut filioli deinceps parentum catholicorum præsertim nobilium a teneris annis præceptoribus traderentur hereticis pestilentissima hæresi Calviniana imbuendi: cuius rei indignitate impietateque motus P. Personius ad aulam regiam statim se contulit, scelerisque immanitatem Majestati regiæ aperuit, obtinuitque commiserante

Secular clergy, and papal approbation was given 22nd September 1622, (Tierney, V. 263). Students arrived from Douay 14th Nov. 1628, and the institution still flourishes.

* John Richards was a priest of the Roman College, who had been sent to Valladolid as a preparation for England.

† Father Persons does not specify when this constitution, or decree, or proclamation was promulgated, and thus we cannot say for certain what it was, nor can we assign a certain date for Father Persons obtaining a promise from the King. The first diploma of King Philip was dated 13th March 1593 (Appendix no. 18 below). though it may have been promised earlier. The settlement at St Omers, however, had begun perhaps a year before.

This college grew out of the smaller school at Eu in Normandy, instituted by Persons's agency in 1582 (*C. R. S.*, I. 31, and *n*). In 1590 the school was still there, see Appendix no. 12. But in 1592 various circumstances, principally the prevalence of war in France, induced the President of Rheims, Dr Barrett, to think of removing it to St Omers. The municipal records of St Omers show that he made three applications to the 'magistrat' for leave to settle. The two first are undated, the third, of 18th September 1592, shows that he, had already purchased a house, opposite to the Walloon Jesuit College, the classes of which the scholars were to attend, and the fathers were to 'veiller sur lesdits Anglois.' They were not to be more than 15 in number, under the direction of 'pères venerables.' St Omers MS.—*Deliberations des Magistrats*, 1592, M., and *Liasse*, 241, n. 1. The migration from Eu was probably made soon after.

rege tantæ calamitati, ut aliud adhuc Seminarium puerorum Anglorum Audomaropoli in Belgio institueretur—eoque seminario attribuit pientissimus Rex duo millia aureorum in singulos annos, iussitque ut penes Soc. Jesu esset Seminarii regimen.* Quod cum R. P. Claudius Præp. Genl[is] admisisset,† brevissimo tempore Seminarii principia posita fuere; ad quam rem multum profuit P. Gul. Flacci industria et præsentia—et P. Gulielmus Holt qui Bruxellis agebat &——.

Hoc eodom anno ex alumnis missi sunt in Angliam Sacerdote P. Thomas Morus et Gulielmus Reynerus.

[§ 10.—Annals of the College of Seville for 1594.

On the 15th of May Pope Clement VIII expedited the apostolic letters to confirm the privileges of the College. In October Father Persons, having been ill of fever, came to Seville for change of air, and brought with him three students. Other new comers were the brothers John and Thomas Knatchbull. Thomas Bruscoe and Henry Sheratt were sent to England; William Ball, priest, died in April.]

Ad 15 diem Maii huius anni—Clemens viii literis Apostolicis confirmationem et privilegia huius Seminarii Hispalensis expedivit.‡

Mense Octobri P. Personius quartana febri Valisoleti correptus, tum mutandi aeris tum ob valetudinem, tum negotiorum etiam causa Hispalim venit, secumque duxit tres alumnos——. Præter plures qui Valisoletano venerunt, venerunt alii duo Joannes et Thomas Knatchbulli fratres: missi in Angliam duo, P. Thomas Brusco et

* The foundation deed of St Omers, confirming the grant of 2,000 crowns pension, has just been printed with notes in the *Stonyhurst Magazine*, 1911 (xii, 348-355.) It is dated at Brussels, 6th May 1594, but was of course preceded by many preliminaries. We do not know when the first application was made, but the first royal answer giving a pension of 1920 crowns, bore date 13th March 1592, (below Appendix n. 18). This it appears was taken to St Omers by Father Flack in April. But the officials in Flanders 'made delay,' and on 17th July 1593, Persons wrote to the general to say that he had new orders from the king about St Omers. These letters were received by Henry Walpole, the martyr, in August, and a copy of them carried by him to Flanders(*C. R. S.* v. 254. A. Jessopp, *Letters of Henry Walpole*, p. 48.) Here he and Father Flack presented the new letters at Brussels, 27th September, (*Diary of the Walloon Jesuits.* MS. St Omers.) Again it would seem that delays were made (*C. R. S.*, v. 225), from Appendix 18 it appears that Father Persons had returned once more to the king early in 1594, and had received a yet ampler grant, making the pension 2,000 crowns instead of 1,920, and appointing a very sure source from which they might be drawn. The foundation deed of the following May shows the grant in its final and permanent form.

† We see from the previous notes that the course of the foundation at St Omers was long and complicated, and hence the delay in the consent of Father General Aquaviva, which the text suggests. He wrote to the Provincial of Flanders, Father Manare, on the 31st of July 1593, that both he and Cardinal Allen were under the impression that the plan would come to nothing. It does not appear when the general's approval was given. It was not until 23rd November 1593, that FF. Flack and Smith took charge of the new seminary *Diary of the Walloon Jesuits*, MS. St Omer *Les Jesuites anglais à Saint Omer*, Difficulté's avec le Magistrat à l'occasion de lear premier établissement—A communication by M. l'abbé O. Bled to the *Bulletin de la Société des Antiquaires de la Morinie, vol. viii, p.* 547.

‡ There is an original parchment exemplar of this brief at the English College, Rome.

P. Henr. Seratus: mortuus unus P. Gul. Balus mense Aprili.*

[§ 11.—Annals for 1595.

In March the house in the Cal de las Armas was bought at a cost of over 5000 crowns. Anne de Spinosa gave 7000 to build the church, her brothers 6000 more.]

Mense Martio empta domus—in platea armorum—Expensa fuerunt in domo reparanda et accommodanda plusquam quinque millia aureorum &——†.

Anna de Spinosa dedit 7 millia aureorum ad ecclesiam ædificandam—et eius fratres alia sex millia.‡

Father Grene concludes his copy with the words,—Hucusque ex autographo Personii.

CATALOGUS ALUMNORUM, QUI A PRIMA SEMINARII ANGLO-HISPALENSIS FUNDATIONE IN EO VIXERUNT

From the original document, Stonyhurst MSS. *Anglia* A. ii., *n.* 15. The first fourteen entries are in Father Persons' own hand.

In primo Anglorum adventu, anno 1591, cum nondum seminarium

* It will be noticed that many of these names are missing from the Register. Neither the three youths who came with Persons, nor the two Knatchbulls, nor William Ball, nor Thomas Bruscoe appear. The history of the latter is thus given by Fr. Blackfan, p. 50. 'Leaving Rome with Fr. Campion in the year 1580, and reaching England almost simultaneously with him, he was also captured then, and lay some eight years in prison, and was all but worn out by extreme torments. Finally having been freed by a wonderful intervention of providence, he passed two years with friends and relatives in gathering fresh strength and nerve for new combats. Then he came courageously to this college [Valladolid], to finish the studies which he had begun at Rome. Now, leaving in the college the sweet odour of his good life, he set forth to work in the English vineyard, in which he still works strenuously until the present time' [1620].

Of William Ball some further details are given in the *Litteræ Annuæ S.J., pro* 1594, 1595 (Neapoli, 1604) p. 569. He had come from England bringing six youths with him, and died regretting that he was not suffering martyrdom.

Father Henry Walpole, writing to Seville, 2nd August 1593, commends himself to Mr Knatchbull, who may have been the father of John and Thomas (Jessopp, *Letters of H. Walpole*, p. 46.)

† The signs of omission, which Father Grene here makes in such numbers, point to abbreviations, which may be due to his having read the same matter in the *Litteræ Annuæ* (Naples 1604). Referring to them, I find the following particulars. Three were sent to England in 1595, and amongst others two brothers came, of whom the eldest was only fifteen. The father, condemned for harbouring a priest, had died after eight years incarceration ; the mother had given birth to the children in prison. They are described as singularly good, and universal favourites. But unfortunately as they were alive, their names are omitted. On the feast of St. Hyacinth the scholars had given a literary display, and at Christmas, they had composed and acted a tragi-comedy, *Anglia lapsa resurgens*, which had greatly pleased the visitors. The King had given money to buy a house and garden ; and the Duke of Medina Sidonia, asked by Persons to give a supply of water, gave twice the quantity requested. So some could be used 'ad ornamentum.'

‡ These details are taken from Fr. Price's letter, mentioned above, which also contains further information, as to the furnishing and solemn opening of the church. Father Price, however, owing to some writer's slip, leaves it uncertain whether the eventual address was Cal de las Armas, or Calle de la Sierpe.

fundaretur, sed domum tantum conductitiam haberent, juxta ecclesiam Divi Andreæ, ut in Annalibus habetur, hi sequentes sacerdotes in uno eodemque convictu fuerunt, et omnes paulo post ad Angliam missi.

1°. Joannes Cecilius, comitatus Salopiensis, ætatis annorum 30, qui Romæ theologiæ studium absolverat, sacrosque ordines susceperat; missus est in Angliam mense Aprili 1591; ex quâ in Scotiam migravit, ibique strenue laboravit; reversus in Hispaniam, anno 1593: et iterum in Scotiam; et deinde iterato in Hispaniam, anno 1595, unde et Romam, negotiorum publicorum causa à rege destinatus.*

2°. Gulielmus Warfordus, Bristoliensis, Romæ presbyter ordinatus, et una cum patre Cecilio in Angliam missus, post trium annorum fructuosos in Domini vineâ labores, Romam se contulis, ut in societatem Jèsu reciperetur; quod et factum est anno 1594.†

3°. Joannes Robertsius, Romæ etiam ordinatus, profectus in Angliam eodem tempore, ibique laborat.‡

4°. Oliverius Almanus, Oxoniensis Romæ presbyter factus, eodem tempore una cum aliis ad missionem Anglicanam discessit.§

* See above note.

† See above, note 3. He died in Valladolid, 3rd November 1608.

‡ This John Roberts is to be distinguished from his better known namesake the martyr, whose entry in the Valladolid Catalogue is as follows: Johannes Ruperti, admissus in hoc collegium, 18° Octobris anno 1598, diocesis Bangorensis in Wallia, ingressus est ordinem Benedictinorum. Vide *Annales domesticos* p. 65 [*i.e.*, Blackfan, p. 87], ubi martyr occubuit sub finem decembris, *i.e.*, 10° Decembris, 1610. The Roberts of 1592, was the son of Laurence Roberts of Killimarsh. He was admitted to Caius College, Cambridge, in 1576, and he went to Rheims in 1583, and was sent in the same year to Rome, (Foley vi, 161, who however confuses him with the martyr), see also J. Morris, *John Gerard* (1881) p. 74. He is mentioned in the general memorial from the secular clergy, sent to Rome in favour of the Archpriest, 8th November 1598, as sure to sign if he could be met with. (Stonyhurst, *Collectanea P.* f. 570). We infer from the last clause that he led a very retired life. He had also probably, like most other priests in England, changed his name. Similar causes account for the great difficulty in tracing the subsequent careers of all the priests here named.

§ Alman (also Almande, and Almonde) Oliver. His college course 1581 etc., may be followed from the Rheims and Roman registers—*Douay Diaries*, 179, 185, Foley vi, 153, 552. After his return he kept in 'the South parts' (Foley vi, 743), and is said to have been with Mr Wynchcombe in Berkshire, (Foley i, 381, but the year must be 1592, not 1591), under the name Henwiche. He has been sometimes (Challoner, Foley) erroneously considered the brother of John Almond, the martyr, or even identified with him. The latter however came from South Allerton, near Liverpool, and was several years Oliver's junior. In 1598 Oliver Almond wrote to Dr Bagshaw, in favour of a peaceful solution of the 'Wisbech stirs' Law, *Archpriest Controversy*, p 21, but the editor is mistaken in identifying him with Richard Parker, the assistant to the Archpriest Blackwell. The college careers of the two, show that they were quite distinct persons. Later on he seems to have been a prisoner, for in 1620 he presented a fine chalice to the church of the English College, Rome, about which Father Grene writes: 'Oliverius Almondus (lib. rub. *n.* 114) dedit calicem argenteum affabre factum templo hujus collegii, qui adhuc (hoc anno 1666) super alios omnes existimatur, cum hac inscriptione in fundo seu sub pede, OLIVERIUS ALMÓNDUS, olim hujus collegii alumnus, hunc calicem Sanctissimae Trinitati, Beatae Mariae, et Sancto Thomae Cantuariensi episcopo, & Martyri, e vinculis propter fidem consecravit et dedit A.D 1620.'

5°. Jacobus Youngerus, Dunelmensis, sacro presbyterii ordine Romæ suscepto, hinc quoque in Angliam missus, post multos labores carceresque perpessos rediit in Belgium, et theologiam prælegit in seminario Duaceno.*

6°. Thomas Salovayus in seminario Vallesoletano presbyter factus, in Angliam quoque missus eodem tempore.†

7°. Joannes Fisherus, Southamptoniensis, Romæ ordinatus, eodem tempore ad Angliam missus, et post duos annos Ulissiponem revertitur.‡

8°. Nicholaus Rochus, in Hispaniis ad ordines sacros promotus, eodem anno, in Angliam profectus.§

9°. Ricardus Bluntus, sacerdos multis ornamentis tum literarum, tum etiam virtutis, præditus, eodem anno 1591 ad Angliam destinatus magno animarum fructu ibi laborat.‖

10°. Francisus Lockwodus, eodem tempore missus.¶

* James Younger (also Young, *alias* Dingley and Christopher) born about 1563. His college career may be traced from 1581, in the *Douay Diaries* p. 183, 193, Foley vi, 158, 508, 554. After leaving Valladolid he with Fixter, Blunt and Dudley, had a special audience with Philip II, of which an account may be found in the *Relacion de un Sacerdote Ingles*, see above *n.* 1. Younger was captured after a year in England, when he lost heart, communicated to the persecuting government a great many details about priests and Catholics, and was eventually liberated on the condition that he should supply the government with useful information. This was not honourable, but it does not prove him to have been a 'spy' and 'apostate,' as Brother Foley and others have thought. He also offered 'to displace' Persons. But this only meant turning him out of his place, not murdering him, *Domestic Calendar*, 1591-1594. There is as yet no indication that Younger went on giving information, when once set free; nor is it proved that the informations which he gave when in prison did any great harm to his co-religionists, though they may have done so. After liberation he went to Douay, and there became a D.D., and was lecturing at the college in 1596, *Douay Diaries* 374. See also *Acts of English Martyrs*, p. 98, etc.

† Thomas Saloway, is called Salway and Saulway in the *Douay Diaries.* He was of the Diocese of Worcester, went to Rheims, probably very young, in 1583, and came to Spain after completing his course. Father Blackfan in 1619 writes of him and Lockwood, 'usque nunc strenuam navant operam in messe illa,' *Annales*, p. 47.

‡ John Fixter, *alias* Wilson, came to England with Cecil, and took a share, no doubt at Cecil's instigation, in the discreditable informations, which his colleague gave against Catholics. He stayed in England for a year, then returned to Lisbon, where he was in 1597 (T. Birch, *Memoirs of Queen Elizabeth*, 1754, p. 127,) and still in touch with John Cecil. He 'died in Spain' before 1602, W.C. *Reply to Father Persons libel*, p. 70: his discreditable conduct having, its eems, come to light.

§ Nicholas Rook, seems to be a mistake for Henry Rook, diocese of Oxford, who was at Douay with the Thomas Salway and others of the first colony who came to Spain in 1589, and is called Henry Rook by Father Blackfan, *Annales*, pp. 40, 43, at the time of his arrival and departure.

‖ Richard Blunt, entered the society in 1596, and eventually became the first provincial of the English Province. In that office he had important parts to play in the varying fortunes of the Catholics during the revival under Queen Henrietta Maria, in the affairs of the bishop of Chalcedon, and in the missions of Panzani, Conn and Rosetti, etc.

¶ Francis Lockwood, a Yorkshireman, had been ordained at Rheims, in 1588. *Douay Diaries*, p. 14. Father Blackfan in 1619 (*Annales*, p. 47) says of him conjointly with Saloway, that they were working strenuously in England.

11°. Ricardus Dudleus, eodem tempore missus, de cujus laboribus multa laude dignissima scribuntur.*

12°. Joannes Brushfordus qui omnium novissime eodem anno missus, captus est in portu, et carceri traditus, ubi etiam moritur.†

In secundo vero Anglorum adventu, anno 1592, cum jam seminarium fundaretur, sequentes habuit, vel alumnos vel convictores.

13°. Gulielmus Reynerus, Dioc. Lincolniensis, Romæ sacris ordinibus susceptis, Hispalim venit, anno 1592, ut inde in Angliam mitteretur, quod et factum est eodem anno.‡

14°. Henricus Floydus, Dioc. Nordovicensis, Vallesoleti sacris initiatus, post conclusiones theologicas in seminario hoc publicè sustentatas Ulissiponem mittitur ut inde in Angliam discederet.§

(15°) Joannes Worthingtonus, Lancastrensis, ætatis 19, admissus anno 1592, 25 Novembris. Studuit Dialecticæ.‖

(16°) Thomas Egertonus, Cestrensis, anno ætatis 20. Studuerat Dialecticis: admissus in hoc Collegium anno 1592, 25 Novembris.¶

(17°) Georgius Chamberlaynus, Oxoniensis, ætatis 16, admissus 1592, 25 Novembris. Studuit Dialecticæ.**

* Richard Dudley, son and heir of Edmund Dudley of Yanworth, Westmorland, had studied law in London, but abandoning his inheritance went to Rheims in 1583, thence to Rome, Valladolid and Seville. He worked at first on the Border (Cecil to Allen, R.O., *Scotland*, iv. 4). In 1595 his reputation stood so high that he was called upon to arbitrate in 'the stirs' of Wisbech. In 1602 he was in London, passing under the name of Walgrave, and though arrested, had so many friends that he got off. *Cardinal Allen's Letters*, p. 204; Foley, *Records*, i. 29, vi. 160.

† John Brushford, of the diocese of Exeter, was received at the English Hospice Rome, 14th June 1581, then entered the college, and was sent to England a priest in 1585. But he afterwards left the country again and went to Verdun to join the Jesuits, but his health broke down, and he had to leave. From thence he seems to have gone to Spain, arriving there 8th October 1590. This appears from the statements of one Gilbert Laton, a very suspicious character, against whom Brushford perhaps filed an information (*Domestic Calendar*, 1593, p. 322). Brushford eventually died in Wisbech, about 1593.

‡ William Rainer (or Reyner), born about 1546, had been a student of the college at Rome 1586-1589, and was afterwards a D.D., a writer and a member of Arras College. Dodd, ii. 379.

§ Henry Floyd, one of the original three who set out from Rheims for Valladolid in 1587. After his return to England he was received into the Society in 1599. Many papers regarding his troubles and adventures, are gathered by Foley i. 503-513. See also Blackfan, 48.

‖ John Worthington, of the Blainsco family, and nephew of the third President of Douay, became eventually a Jesuit, and a missioner in his native county. Foley vii. 865.

¶ Thomas Egerton died in the college, and his obituary notice written by Father Peralta, was printed at Seville in Spanish, and in Latin in the Annual letters.

** George Chamberlain, of Sherborne, Oxfordshire, and future bishop of Ypres. It has already been seen that, young though he was, he had been twice chosen as spokesman on important occasions, and had greatly touched his hearers. The same great gifts and charm of character were conspicuous in him in after life. Gillow i. 458; *Dict. Nat. Biog.*, x. 1; Blackfan, p. 45.

(18°) Franciscus Feltonus, Londinensis, ætatis 16, admissus anno 1592, 25 Novembris. Studuit Rhetoricæ.*

(19°) Pater Ricardus Walpolus, Norfolciensis, ætatis 28. Postquam in reliquis tribus seminariis, Rhemensi, Romano et Pinciano studia absolvisset, huc appulit, 27 Novembris, et post conclusiones in hoc collegio publicè de universâ theologiâ habitas, ingressus est societatem Jesu, mense Februario anno sequentis.†

(20°) Robertus Gualterus, Cantius, ætatis 21, admissus anno 1592, 27 Novembris. Studuit Dialecticæ. Mortuus est piissime in hoc collegio, mense Septembri, 1593.‡

(21°) Gulielmus Houseus, Buckinghamiensis, ætatis 19, admissus 1592, 27 Novembris. Studuit Dialecticæ.

(22°) Ludovicus Griffidius, Carnarvoniensis, ætatis 21, admissus 1592, 27 Novembris. Studuit Dialecticæ.

(23°) Lawrentius Hammonus, Londinensis, ætatis 17, admissus 1592, 29 Novembris. Studuit Rhetoricæ.

(24°) Pater Thomas Morus, Eboracensis, ætatis 25, profectus in Angliam anno 1593.§

(25°) Georgius Blomerus, Oxoniensis, ætatis 20. Dimissus a seminario anno 1593.

(26°) Thomas Stukeleyus, Devoniensis, ætatis 23. Dimissus anno 1593.

(27°) Gulielmus Wilsonus, Cestrensis, ætatis 21, admissus anno 1592, 29 Novembris. Studuit Dialecticæ.

(28°) Thomas Urmstonus, Lancastrensis, ætatis 20, mortuus anno 1593, admissus anno 1592, 29 Novembris. Studuit Dialecticæ.

(29°) Gulielmus Medcalfus, Lancastrensis, ætatis 23, admissus anno 1592, 12 Septembris.||

(30°) Joannes Sparchfordus, Salopiensis, ætatis 26, sacris ordinibus initiatus anno 1593, admissus eodem anno mense Februarii. Studuit sacræ theologiæ.

(31°) Augustinus Stukeleyus, Devoniensis ætatis 18, admissus anno 1593, mense Februarii. Studuit Rhetoricæ.

(32°) Thomas Benstead, Nordovicensis, ætatis 19, admissus anno 1593, mense Februarii. Studuit Rhetoricæ.¶

* One would like to know whether Francis Felton was not some relation of Blessed John Felton, and the Venerable Thomas Felton his son, of Bermondsey Abbey.

† Richard Walpole. See Foley, vii. 809.

‡ Robert (?) Waller. The Annual Letters for 1594 (p. 569), add that he was a good Greek scholar, twenty-four years of age, and died wishing for the pains of martyrdom.

§ Thomas More, great-grandson of the martyr, and afterwards agent for the English Clergy at Rome and in Madrid, when he took part in the negotiations for the Spanish match, etc. Gillow, v. 117, *Dict. Nat. Biog.*

|| William Medcalfe, after ordination went to the English College, Rome in 1597, and shortly after became a Jesuit; but died in his novitiate. (Foley, vi, 202.)

¶ The Ven. Thomas Benstead, *alias* Hunt, was eventually martyred at Lincoln in July 1600 He is the protomartyr of the college. The Register of St. Alban's Valladolid gives 12th November 1592, as the date of his leaving them for Seville. Father Blackfan gives the date of his martyrdom as March, *Annales*, p. 60.

(33°) Thomas Worseleus, Lancastrensis, ætatis 21, admissus anno 1593, mense Februarii. Studuit Rhetoricæ.

(34°) Henricus Sherrattus, Lancastrensis, ætatis 25, sacris ordinibus initiatus, anno 1593, profectus in Angliam anno 1595, admissus anno 1593, mense Februarii. Studuit theologiæ.

(35°) Gualterus Morganus, Monmuthicensis, ætatis 18, admissus anno 1593, mense Februarii. Studuit Rhetoricæ.

(36°) Joannes Middletonus, Eboracensis, ætatis 38, admissus anno 1594, mense Decembris. Studuit sacræ Theologiæ.

(37°) Pater Gulielmus Davisius, Salopiensis, ætatis 57, admissus anno 1595, mense Maii. Studuit sacræ Theologiæ.*

(38°) Joannes Evanus, Carnarvoniensis, ætatis 19, admissus anno 1595 mense Maii. Studuit Rhetoricæ.

(39°) Joannes Halleus, Norfolciensis, ætatis 21, admissus anno 1595, mense Maii. Studuit Rhetoricæ.

(40°) Thomas Holmus, Lancastrensis, ætatis 18, admissus anno 1595, mense Maii. Studuit Rhetoricæ.

(41°) Edoardus Huttonus, Dunelmensis, ætatis 18, mortuus anno 1595, admissus anno 1595, mense Junii. Studuit Rhetoricæ.

(42°) Edmundus Canon, Essexiensis, ætatis 17, admissus anno 1595, mense Junii. Studuit Rhetoricæ.

(43°) Ricardus Homfredus, Cornubiensis, ætatis 17, admissus anno 1595, mense Julii. Studuit Rhetoricæ.

APPENDIX

LETTERS OF FATHER PERSONS ABOUT THE FOUNDATION OF THE SPANISH SEMINARIES—1589-1594

The following letters, or extracts of letters, are preserved by Father Christopher Grene, S.J., in his *Collectanea P.*, now at Stonyhurst. The Originals at the time of copying (about 1680) were in the English College, Rome; and have now perished, it is to be feared. Father Grene habitually made extracts, indicating omissions by the sign '&——.' His annotations he makes sometimes in the margin, sometimes, when using Latin, inserts them into the text. They are here put at the foot of the page, with his initials C. G.

I

(*Col. P.*, f. 479.) Personius ad [Creswellum] Rectorem Collegii Anglicani de Urbe. Complutum (Alcala) 28 Aprilis, 1589.

If f. Gibbons † and Charles come ‡ I shall help myself by one of

* The prefix 'Pater,' seems to show that he was a priest before entering. He migrated to the English College, Rome in 1600, and became choir-master there, as well as teacher of 'cases of conscience.' On the 10th September 1603, the Pope gave him the usual scholar's 'viaticum,' and he returned to the English mission. Foley, vi, 226.

† 'Fr. Richard Gibbons.'—C.G. See Foley vii, 299.

‡ 'Intelligit, uti videtur, Charles Tancard.'—C.G. See Foley vii, 761.

them &——. The Provincial also of Andaluzia f. Bartolomeo Perez will receave willingly them from Sicily,* as before I wrott yt you should sollicit; and the two niew visitors,† of all these four Provinces are very well contented to receave two at least of our countrymen in every province &——. I have bin this month in Alcala almost under hands of Phisicians; but now I hope within 3 or 4 daies to be well, and to returne to Madrid &——

2

(*Ibid.*) Idem ad Eundem, 24 Junii 1589.

Touching your schollers in the end of this sommer I could be content you sent either all or the principall of them this way——. All things goe wel here, though slowly. I know not how the affaires of the Society goe there, for that none write to me of it, and so I know not whether anything be further to be dealt heer with 101‡ or noe, with whome they tell me yt I may perchance speake ere many dais. These distractions of Portugal§, and some indisposition of the K's person, have hindred all other businesse heer for this month past. I pray you sollicit the dispatch of those four of ours in Sicily for Andaluzia &——. The rest you will understand by my good Cardinal ‖ &—— Jun 24 1589.

You know the hand.

3

(*Col. P.*, f. 479 and 484.) Idem ad Eundem, Madrito, 22 Julii, 1589.

P.C. It is not for want of health—Our friends be arrived hither, as you may see by this hand in perfect health.¶ I have sent the relation of the successe of the English army to my L. Cardinal. Upon the 13th of this month I had very gratious audience of his majesty. I have also obteined of the K. letters in favour of the niew seminary to be founded at Valladolid, as also of other noblemen, who all greatly do favour yt enterprize, God prosper it to his honour. I am likewise to goe shortly to Valladd about the founding of the saide seminary.

4

(*Col. P.*, f. 479.) F. Charles Tancard from Madrid, 22 July 1589, to F. Martial in Rome, narrat se feliciter pervenisse Madritum cum sociis, et mittendum se (Alcala) Complutum.

* 'Nostros intelligit Anglos [e Societate] qui tum Sicilia morabantur.'—C.G.

† 'De his visitatoribus, vide *Annales Soc.*'—C. G.—That is Sacchini, *Historia Soc. Jesu* 1561, vol. v, p. 458.

‡ 'Videtur significari hoc numero Rex Hispaniæ.'—C.G.

§ An English army of 20,000 men invaded Portugal in May. But the expedition was mismanaged, decimated by disease, and by 4 June was on its way home.

‖ Cardinal Allen.

¶ 'Gulielmus Flaccus erat in hac scribenda Personii amanuensis.'—C.G. See Foley, vii, 261.

F. Persons in the postcript addeth a few lines thus :—

My little father I most hartily salute you & all your good chickens there, you know whome I meane, etc.*

5

(*Col. P.*, f. 484.) Idem [Persons] ad Eundem [Creswell] Vallisoleto, 14 Septembris, 1589.

I wrott to you by the last ordinary, since which we have nothing more then this, that the Seminary niewly begunn is now setled, albeit not without great adoe, as you shal understand by a certain *Relation*, which I send to my L. Cardinal.† I intend to depart to-morrow morning towards the court, and from thence to Madrid, there to dispatch some businesse, and see what further good may be done amongst good folkes for the better sustentation and help of this our Seminary &——. Charles [Tancard] is att Alcala to end his Divinity. William flack is to be heer in Valld[d] for Minister in the Engl. Seminary; and f. Gibbons, who goeth with me from hence to Madrid, shal from thence goe into Portugal, &——

6

(*Col. .P*, f. 498.) Ad Creswellum Rectorem Coll. Ang. de Urbe. Madrito, 11 Novembris, 1589.

Aliquid scribit de Seminario Vallisoletano, quod adhuc satis tenuem habet fundationem, et de modo agendi P. Creswelli non admodum grato, de quo alias sæpe, de viaticis &——(parvi momenti).

7

(*Ibid*) Ad eundem. 9 Decembris. Toledo.

I have bin these 9 or 10 daies in Toledo. F. Thomas Warcop ‡ dyed att Alicante the same day that he landed there. Since the last ordinary I spake againe with the king about our affaires of the Society, and what successe I had you shall easily learn at the Casa.§ I pray you faile not to send me an authentical copye of the constitutions of your college there. We have a family of about 20 persons in our Seminary of Valladolid, and noe lawes or con-titutions as yet &—— And if y[e] point might be procured, which I wrot to you before, to witt that the head government as well of this Seminary as of others might be in our Cardinal, I think it would be good &——. God already beginneth to help this Seminary diverse waies, though hitherto the K. hath not given but 100 crownes, &——

* P. Martialis hoc ipso die obiit Romæ (Morus p. 21). Eo venerat initio anni 1585.—C.G.

† On the *Relation*, see above, note.

‡ Thomas Warcop, one of the Jesuits summoned from Sicily.—See Foley vii. 814.

§ That is the Casa Professa, Rome.

Monsieur Rivière
Temporal Father, for 55 years, of Poor Clares, Gravelines
From the painting, Ursuline Convent, Greenwich

To face p. 25

As for the pension granted to the Seminary of S[t] Omers, after long toyle and much contradiction made, as well by—,*as also by the President, &——, God almighty hath given us as good a dispatch, as we could desire for. In the steede of 1920 ducats which the King assigned us before, upon uncertaine licences for the maintenance of 16 schollers, now the King hath appointed 2,000 crownes of gold to be setled, payd and receaved of the first and surest money of the passaportes of all kinde of merchandize that enter att Gravelin: which passaports are rented in that towne for the present at above 10,000 crownes a year, and if at any time they should faile, it is setled upon the surest and readiest rent that the king hath in Flanders. All this is granted by the King, and the minute given to the secretarie to be drawn out, wherein the matter is earnestly commended to Ernestus: and besides this three other letters are written by the King to the Bishop, Governor and Magistrates of S Omers, to protect and favour the seminary as a thing principally esteemed and loved by his Majesty. Order also is given to pay presently all arrerages from the date of the King's first letters, which are of the 13 of March, 1593, &——which shall goe also by the next extraordinary.

* We can hardly doubt that the name, here represented by a dash, is that of Cardinal Allen. We have seen (p. 21 *n.* †) that up to the time of writing, the cardinal did not expect that the proposed college would succeed. Moreover no other name but his, could well be expected to precede that of President Barrett's. See Father More, 'Alano praeterea Cardinali et Barretto Praesidi Duaceno non arridebat hoc novum pene in conspectu domicilium; alio enim avertendum juventutem et subsidia verebantur, et suum isto non exonerandum sed evacuandam seminarium.'—*Historia Provinciae Anglicanae*, 1660, p. 162. For Allen's anxiety about the Douay Seminary at this time, see *Letters of Cardinal Allen*, p. 358.

8

(*Ibid.*) Idem ad eundem, Madrito, 7 Januarii, 1590.

I pray you pay to f. Thomas Wright* in Genua ten crownes.† I pray you remembr to procure from Praga all yt may be had of f. Campian's doings, whereof I wrot to you before——&——. I hope by this day our L[d] Cardinal is Arch Bishop of Machlen‡ &——. The story of the martyrs we shal print here, if it like us § &——

9

(*Col. P.* f. 498). Ad P[m] Creswellum, Vallisoleto, 24 Junii, 1590.

I repose myself a little now after a most painful winter past in Madrid, though here also there want not labour enough—in building &—.More concerning this house you may reade in my lre to Dr Barret, which I pray you send to him—Præsens Rector parum idoneus ‖ &——.

10

Many other letters off Persons this yeare are about matters concerning the Seminary of Valld. privileges to be obtained at Rome for it &—de re pecuniaria &—*Viz.* of feb. 3 and 24; April 28 Madrito, in qua multa de collegio erigendo in Lusitania, Hispali &—; Id Maii in qua apparet quod P. Thomas Wrytus habitabat tunc Genuæ &——.

11

(*Col. P.* f 500). Ad P[m] Creswellum, Vallisoleto, 22 Julii 1590.

I remaine here in Vall[d] since the 15 of June, and am soe to doe until about the 15 of August, when I am to returne to Madrid, though—many—do make great instance y[t] I goe presently to Sevil for the great hope there is given of a Seminary alsoe—; but t'is impossible to attend to so many things together——The present maintenance of this Sem[ry] wil amount to 2500 △

12

(*Ibid.*) Idem ad eundem, Vallisoleto, 23 Julii.

Expectat pro illo Seminario oraut 30 alumnos Rhemis aut Augius [Eu] &—ut in aliis literis scripsenat.

Niew Rector Juan Lopez Maçana a most worthy man &—.2 f. Roderico Cabredo Confessour and most affectionat to our nation —the habitation fit for 30 &——.

* Thomas Wright, a brilliant but somewhat unstable man. He eventually left the Society, was taken up by Essex, converted W. Alabaster, was imprisoned and banished. In 1611 he had some repute as a preacher in Belgium.—Foley vii. 1460. Jessopp, *Letters of H. Walpole*, 1873, p. 55. Dodd confuses him with his contemporary, Thomas Wright, Dean of Courtrai, for whom see *Dict. Nat. Biog.*

† 'Plurima de re pecuniaria hic omitto.'—C.G.

‡ For the nomination of Cardinal Allen to the see of Malines *see* Knox, *Letters of Cardinal Allen*, Introd. cxv.-cxvii.

§ The *Relacion de algunos martyrios*, see above *n.* 1.

‖ Apparently Father Pedro de Gusman, who resigned at this time, and died 27th December following—Blackfan, p. 43.

No. II

REGISTERS OF THE ENGLISH POOR CLARES AT GRAVELINES, INCLUDING THOSE WHO FOUNDED FILIATIONS AT AIRE, DUNKIRK AND ROUEN, 1608-1837

CONTRIBUTED BY WILLIAM MARTIN HUNNYBUN, M.A.

ANNOTATED BY JOSEPH GILLOW

The convent of Poor Clares at Gravelines owed its origin to the zeal of Mrs Mary Ward, a person of good family, who went abroad to St. Omers in 1607 intending to embrace a religious life. Having made her wish known to the Jesuit Fathers established in that town, they recommended her to the French Convent of the Order of St. Clare. Not having any portion she was unable to become a choir nun and entered upon her probation as a lay sister. She remained in this position for nine months and was frequently sent to solicit alms for the convent. In one of her charitable journeys she heard of certain lands at Gravelines bequeathed by a pious person for the site of a monastery. She begged the Fathers of the Society to employ their influence to procure it for the founding of a convent of Poor Clares, for the use of the English. They were successful in this through the friendship of the Bishop of St. Omers and the Abbot of St. Bertins. In consequence of the promising aspect of affairs Mrs Ward left the French House and set out for Brussels, in order to obtain from the Archduke, who was ruler of the Netherlands, in which country Gravelines was then situated, the necessary permission for carrying out the good work. She interested several English gentlemen who resided at Brussels and obtained the powerful assistance of the Infanta, who admired her zeal and pious perseverance. Leave to found the convent was granted on two conditions: (1) that it should be under the ordinary jurisdiction of the Bishop of the Diocese and (2) that it should be in no way chargeable to the inhabitants of Gravelines.

The approbation of the Pope, Paul V, was next obtained, who by his brief instructed the Bishop of St. Omers to take charge of the convent and afford due assistance in temporal as well as spiritual matters to the religious who should begin the work.

Mrs Ward, having so far succeeded, collected together a considerable number of English gentlewomen, who were desirous of embracing this strict way of life and procured the Bishop's authority for taking out of the French Convent of St. Omers, called the Archer's House, such English nuns as had been professed in it. The Abbess refusing her consent, the Bishop was appealed to, and by his authority Mary Gough, who was appointed Superior of the new establishment, Sisters Clare Fowler, Lucy

Darell and Ann Campion, all English ladies of good birth, together with two lay sisters, left the convent and took possession of a house that the Poor Clares had temporarily taken at St. Omers. Here they were joined by many young women who had heard of the proposed foundation and left Great Britain and Ireland to become Religious. Mary Ward having accomplished her pious work, retired again into the ranks of the humble lay sisters.

On the 14th of September 1609, the English Poor Clares were conveyed to Gravelines and took possession of their house there. It being too small and in too ruinous a state for the due performance of their religious exercises, they set about building a more suitable one. This, by the portions of some of their religious and the assistance of friends, was finished in 1611, much of the manual labour being carried out by the nuns themselves. The church was erected by the generosity of one of the Gage family, some of whom were resident in the town. As soon as the religious were able to carry out the strict observance of their Rule, the election of officers, presided over by the Provincial of the Friars Minor, took place. All the votes were given for Madame Gough, as abbess, and they elected as vicaress and councillor, Sister Ann Brooke; 1st portress and councillor, Sister Gage, in religion called Colette of St. Andrew; 2nd portress and councillor, Sister Frances of St John Walleston; sacristan and councillor, Agnes of St John Knightley; Procurator, Sister Frances of St Dominie Havers; infirmarian and councillor, Sister Clare of St John Tyldesley; and councillors only, Sisters Clare of St John Fowler, Ann Tholward and Lucy Darell. The Abbess reserved to herself the offices of Novice mistress and of choir mistress.

For some years, under the Abbesses Gough and Gage the convent suffered much from pecuniary difficulties, but with the accession of Elizabeth Tyldesley, called Sister Clare Mary Ann, these difficulties were removed and the convent was in a very flourishing state.

In 1619 the number of professed nuns had so much increased that it was resolved that a filiation should be made at Aire in the province of Artois. It was called the Convent of the 'Immaculate Conception of our beloved Lady.' Eleven religious, bix., Dorothy Knightley, Catherine Bentley, Grace Pennington, Mildred Alcock, Margaret and Elizabeth Crisp, Frances Philipson, Mary Goolding, Elizabeth, Dorothy, and Ann Radcliffe left Gravelines for Aire, having as Abbess, Catherine Keynes, and as Vicaress, Helen Parker.

Again in 1625 the Convent of Nazareth possessed such a considerable number of nuns that the Abbess Tyldesley determined to found a new house at Dunkirk under the title of 'Convent of Bethleem of English Poor Clares.' This new Convent was unable to receive novices, and the nuns at first proposed only to open school. Eleanor Dillon was chosen Superior and with her went four Irish sisters, Martha Chevers, Alice Nugent, Mary Dowdel and Cecily Dillon. In 1629 these nuns left for Ireland where they founded two houses of Poor Clares This new convent was scarcely established when, owing to the fault of the chaplain, a revolution broke out in the Mother House. Without any reason he deposed Abbess Tyldesley and chose in her place Sister Margaret Radcliffe.

The nuns were divided into two camps and there was no happiness or peace in the Convent. This state of things was put an end to by a great misfortune which befell the Convent. A fire broke out and in a very short time the granary, three dormitories, the refectory and the novitiate were burnt to the ground; but none of the nuns or their pupils were hurt. The governor of the town came to condole with the Religious and was much surprised when he was told of the unhappy changes which had taken place in the convent. A few days after the Provincial of the English Jesuits of Watten sent the Guardian of St Omer to visit the Poor Clares. They were fully aware of the illegality of their position and desired to be released from it. He proposed a new election, which was gladly received and the same day Abbess Tyldesley was re-established in office. The chaplain was sent to the English College at Douai and Sister Margaret Radcliffe, together with ten other religious, to the house at Dunkirk.

The ravages caused by the fire were fully repaired the next year and the nuns were consoled by a brief from Pope Urban VIII, full of affection and compassion for their troubles and sympathy for the courage these holy women had at all times displayed.

Fresh troubles arose and the poor Clares in order to put an end to interference obtained from Pope Urban VIII a brief which placed the Convent of Gravelines under the jurisdiction of the Bishop of St Omers.

Three or four years later the venerable Abbess desired to found another house to relieve the crowded state of the Convent at Gravelines. The town of Rouen seemed the most suitable for her purpose; but, unhappily, France was then at war with Spain and the Abbess found her work suddenly stopped. The town of Gravelines was besieged by the French and the nuns and their pupils found the peace, they had enjoyed for seventeen years, disturbed during the forty-three days the siege lasted. The French general-in-chief visited the convent and the thanksgiving for the taking of the town by the French was sung in the convent chapel, the parish church being almost destroyed during the bombardments.

When quiet was again established thirteen nuns started for Rouen, having as their head Mrs Mary Taylor, in religion Mary of St Frances, as Abbess, and Margaret Bedingfeld, in religion Sister Margaret Ignatius as Vicaress, together with Sisters Winefride Giffard, Helen Bradshaw, Ann Prow, Elizabeth Sternhold, Elizabeth Browne, Ann Perkins, Ann Yates, Margaret Sternhold, Elizabeth Salisbury, Elizabeth Hone, Mary Peterson, Elizabeth Martin and Eleanor Bradshaigh. The new convent received the name of 'Convent of Jesus-Mary-Joseph of English Poor Clares of Rouen, Normandy.' In 1650 it was legally recognised by letters patent granted by Louis XIV.

In 1652 Gravelines was again beleaguered, and after a siege, which lasted sixty-nine days, was again taken by the Spaniards.

During the first month of the rule of Louisa Taylor, who succeeded Madame Tyldesley as Abbess, the convent met with a terrible catastrophe. The powder magazine of the fortress caught fire and the explosion caused great damage to the town and the fortifications. The convent only separated from the fortress by the Place Royale, was much injured, but none of the nuns or pupils were hurt, though they were much terrified by the sad event and some had to leave the ruined convent for a time to recover from the shock and until the dilapidated buildings were restored. Scarcely were these works finished when war once more broke out between Spain and France, and Gravelines was again attacked. The poor nuns suffered great anxiety and fear for many days, but, on August 30, Gravelines surrendered. About this time William Warren, a native of Canterbury, a young ecclesiastic, aged 28 years, favourably known as a preacher and director, was attached to the Convent of Nazareth as Confessor.

Under the government of Madame Taylor the convent adopted the reform of St Colette and its constitutions. Up to then the Poor Clares of Gravelines were not cloistered. The chancel of the chapel was in consequence separated from the choir by an iron grille, which was opened only to allow of the altar being arranged.

Ann Bedingfeld, in religion Anne Bonaventure, was 5th Abbess, and during her prelacy two notable novices entered—Lady Warner, by birth Ann Trevor Hanmer, and her sister-in-law Elizabeth Warner. The former had become a convert with her husband, Sir John Warner, and both embraced the religious state, he joining the Society of Jesus and she becoming a poor Clare. They made their religious profession on the same day in the Chapel of the Convent at Gravelines.

In 1662 Louis XIV visited the Convent at Gravelines and again in 1670 and 1671. Madame Bedingfeld obtained from the king, at his first visit, an endowment for the convent of 1,200 livres, and at his last visit a further endowment of 280 livres, to be paid annually from the royal treasury. A further favour was granted by the French government permitting a full discharge from any payment of good passing to or from England through any of the ports and free carriage of letters addressed to or sent by the Poor English Clares of Nazareth.

From 1731 to 1740 no novices were received at the convent, probably owing to the fact that the time of persecution in England had partly passed and also that the number of Catholic families diminished daily, owing to the progress of Protestantism. This caused much pecuniary distress to the Convent, owing to the loss of patrons. But from 1740 to 1750 this state of things improved and 13 novices were received.

Several years passed with perfect tranquillity in the Convent of Nazareth and in 1760 the census made by the town showed that the community consisted of 30 nuns. However in 1762 the nuns were much disturbed by the decree of the Parliament of Paris, banishing the English as well as the French Jesuits from France.

The Convent prospered from 1783-1789 when the revolution broke out and a time of trouble, deceptions, misfortunes and irreligion began, and a decree of the States General, sanctioned by the king (Louis XVI) suspended the taking of monastic vows in all monasteries whether of men or women. Many religious orders protested against these laws and finally the National Assembly decreed that exception should be made for schools and nuns of foreign nations. So the Poor English Clares of Graveline were safe and their house remained open. The public troubles did not diminish the number of the French and English pupils. In 1791 the Municipality forbad the religious to teach English and their chapel was closed to the public.

The great revolutionary storm did not trouble the Poor Clares until the 12th October 1793 when the popular Assembly of Gravelines ordered that rigorous measures should be at once taken against the ci-devant Poor Clares. At four o'clock in the evening soldiers were placed as sentinels at all the gates of the Convent; and the papers and property of the nuns was seized. Five days later the two communities of Benedictines and Poor Clares from Dunkirk were brought prisoners to the Convent, consisting in all of forty-two persons, making the whole number of prisoners seventy-seven. A few days after this Commissioners arrived and effaced all pictures and tokens of religion, royalty or nobility, both within and without the enclosure, and likewise secured all the sacred vessels, ornaments, and vestments, shut and sealed up the chapel and sacristy. For eighteen months the three communities were confined together and suffered many privations and afflictions, particularly from the want of fuel in a very severe winter. They were reduced to the necessity of cutting up the cupboards and wainscoting of the house and even the trees of the garden to obtain firing. They were allowed only a very small sum daily amounting to about twopence of English money.

At length they were declared at liberty; but seeing no prospect of an end to their miseries where they were, they petitioned for passports to return to England, which were granted. Before leaving Gravelines the nuns appeared before the municipal authorities and stated that they left Gravelines with much regret; grateful for all the kindness shown them during the time they had resided there. They further declared their firm intention of returning when the war between France and England was ended. They placed their property in the hands of a Procurator and refused to renounce any of the rights they had acquired by their long residence in the town and left with confidence, under the protection of the laws and the municipality, the little property they had purchased with their small means. Two days later, on 26th April 1795, they gave fullest power to Robert Murdoch, a merchant at Dunkirk, to manage their property during their absence and claimed the value of their furniture which had been sold.

On 29th April they left Gravelines, sailing the next day from Calais and reached London on May 3.

On arriving in England they met with a warm reception from many persons, but to the Duchess of Buckingham and her worthy chaplain they were principally indebted for their support in London. At a later date she received them at her house at Gosfield in Essex. Afterwards they removed to Coxside near Plymouth, and thence to Clare Lodge near Catterick, but finally settled at a house at Gosfield, lent them by the Duchess and where they could live in a manner suitable to their monastic statutes. The venerable Abbess Keith, who had suffered many troubles during her stay in England, was taken ill and died at Gosfield in 1799. Her successor, Madame Penswick, also died there in 1813.

On the 2nd of December 1814, the English Poor Clares embarked for Calais where many friends met them and on the 6th of that month they reached Gravelines. The community consisted of Madame Martin, Abbess, Elizabeth Trump, Catherine Lee, Ann Meynell, Jane Green and two sisters from the former convent of Poor Clares at Dunkirk. The inhabitants gave them a most noble welcome and they went at once to their chapel, where they found the altar and ornaments of the choir in as good order as if they had never left the convent. In spite of great pecuniary difficulties the Abbess succeeded in carrying out the necessary repairs to the convent and by 1816 the community was in a state of prosperity.

Gradually the number of nuns at the Convent of Gravelines diminished, death and the decreasing number of pupils and novices rendering its position very precarious. The loss of M. Rivière, who for fifty-five years had been their temporal father and had been able to save by his noble disinterestedness and ability the greater part of the property of the nuns, while other religious communities had been completely or almost completely robbed of their goods, was a most severe blow and was soon followed by the death of the Abbess Martin.

Four years after the death of Madame Martin the number of nuns was reduced to four. The school had scarcely any pupils and no religious vocations offered. Abbess Cullen at last laid their difficulties before the Poor Clares at Plymouth and towards the spring of 1833 three English nuns left that convent and started for Gravelines, accompanied by their chaplain. When they reached the convent they found that one of the nuns had left and that there remained only the Abbess Cullen and Sisters Latham and Page. The new sisters could not accustom themselves to their new surroundings, and two of them after some months returned to England, while the third who wished to accompany them was prevented by illness. Gravelines did not please the English chaplain and one day, when least expected, he said farewell to the Abbess and left.

The community of Gravelines was now truly a house of mourning. Of the four nuns who remained two were constantly ill. Sister Latham only remained in good health, and she resolved, with the consent of the Abbess, to write to the Poor Clares at Scorton Hall and ask them to come to their help, offering very advantageous terms of filiation. In 1834 six nuns from Scorton joined the convent, and signed an agreement by which they obliged themselves to follow faithfully the rules of the community. The leading spirit among them was Sister Frances Summers, who guided the others in all their difficulties with great firmness and ability. Unhappily three months after reaching Gravelines her health was completely ruined and she died after a short illness. The nuns from Scorton lost heart and perceived the uselessness of their efforts to sustain the convent. The death of the chaplain, M. Louvel, was the final blow, and taking a desperate resolution, they took leave of Madame Cullen and Sister Latham, and all five returned to Scorton Hall, without waiting for the end of the time they had agreed to stay.

The convent showed a picture of complete desolation, the few pupils left the school and Sister Latham could no longer carry on the labours of the house, her duties as a Religious and teach her classes. With one Sister confined to her bed by acute suffering, and the other exhausted by her various duties, the end was near. They were not however in pecuniary need, having, besides the produce of their garden, a yearly income of about £100, which was rent paid by the tenants of their rural properties.

M. l'Abbé Gobrecht, who after the death of M. Louvel, had been appointed Confessor to the nuns, often discussed the situation with the two Poor Clares, as to the best means of replacing the nuns who had left. He feared that unless some steps were taken to ally themselves to a religious body, by the death of the two owners of the property, it would fall, by French law, into the hands of the State. He proposed to associate them with the Ursuline Nuns of Boulogne-sur-mer and thought this would offer more guarantee of stability, than again seeking subjects from the English convents of Poor Clares, who already had tried more than once to establish themselves at Gravelines and had failed.

The Poor Clares approved of his suggestion and, at their request, he made a journey to Boulogne and offered the Ursulines there to transfer to them under certain conditions the convent of Nazareth and the property belonging to it. Legal difficulties arose, but were overcome and three French nuns came to Gravelines and obtained permission to open a home of their order. The Abbess, Madame Cullen, never knew the result of these negotiations, she died in January 1838, while they were still pending. By the death of the Abbess Cullen, Sister Latham was the only remaining English Poor Clare at Gravelines; in fact the Convent of Poor Clares existed no longer. It had lasted for 229 years and 296 pious women had lived the hard and severe life of the order within its walls.

Although Madame Latham's constitution seemed utterly ruined by the adverse events of the last eight long and disastrous years, under the loving care and sympathy of the Ursuline nuns, she recovered her health, but she longed to return to her native country and as perfect liberty of action was left her she left Gravelines and returned to her family at Liverpool in 1839. Ten years later, when her health was completely restored, she came back and passed eight days with the nuns. She found the convent and school flourishing, but the recollection of what had been saddened her and she returned again to England and the last English Poor Clare of Gravelines died in 1857 at Liverpool.

Mr Gillow, who has supplied the important notes of the nuns' families, and of four of the chaplains, in which the registers are deficient, has also kindly added, from his valuable collections, some particulars of other chaplains or visitors at the Convent, whose names do not appear in the text.

W. M. H.

THIS BOOK CONTAINETH THE NAMES, AGES, AND TIMES OF PROFESSIONS, OF ALL THE RELIGIOUS, THAT HAVE BEEN RECEAVED IN THIS CONVENT OF NAZARETH OF THE POOR CLARES ERECTED IN THE TOWN OF GRAVELING, TOGEATHER ALSO WITH THE DAY AND YEAR OF THEIR DECEASE. AND FIRST MENTION IS MADE OF ALL THOSE WHO FOR THE BEGINNING AND ESTABLISHING OF THE SAID MONASTARY BY VERTUE OF OBEDIENCE WEAR TAKEN OUT OF THE CONVENT OF THE POOR CLARES IN THE TOWN OF SAINT OMERS. ANNO DOMINI

ONE THOUSAND SIX HUNDRED AND EIGHT THE 7TH DAY OF NOVEMBER

(1) Sister **Margarett Fowler,** now Call'd Sister Clare of S[t] John; Sister **Mary Goudge,** now named Sister Mary of S[t] Stephen, and Sister **Elizabeth Darrell,** now call'd Sister Lucy of S[t] John, with two lay sisters, the one being of the French nation: call'd Sister **Antonettte of S[t] John,** and the other of the English, called Sis[r] **Ann Campion,** by Commandment & Vertue of Holy Obedience: were taken forth of the Convent of the poor Clares situated in the town of Siant Omers: to begin this Convent in Graveline of our English nation, of all which number Sister Mary Goudge was Publickly Elected Abbeyss on the 28th day of December, and remained from that time with the above named Religious enclosed in a secular house of S[t] Omers, lent unto them by the Lord Bishop of the sayde Town, till the 15th of Sep[r] 1609—& then she came to this Town of Graveline accompanied with the aforesaid Religious & two more Lay Sisters novices, the one named Sis[r] **Ellen Burton,** now call'd Sis[r] Clare of S[t] Stephen, & the other Sis[r] **Frances Courtes,** now call'd Sis[r] Frances of S[t] Thomas, with eight young Ladys ready to receive the Habit, whose names are hereafter specified, and the 4th day of April following 1610 by Vertue of Holy Obedience Sister **Ann Brooke,** since call'd Sis[r] Ann of S[t] John, with Sis[r] **Ann Tholward,** since call'd Sis[r] Ann of S[t] Frances, was transported from the afore mentioned Convent of the Poor Clares in S[t] Omers unto this in Graveline: so that the number of all those who weare taken out of the sayde Convent for founding of this: were 7, five Enclosed Sisters, and two Lay Sisters whose names were before specified.

(2) These five following Bills are of the five Religious that came forth from S[t] Omers to begin this Convent.

S[t] Omers, 1[st.]
In the Convent of the poor Clares of S[t] Omers Anno Domini 1593 made her holy Profession Sister Clare John, alias **Fowler,** (*) being aged 19 years. Anno Domini 1656 the 20th of June in our Poor Convent of Nazareth of English Poor Clares in Graveline is most happily Deceased, strengthened with all the Rights of our holy Moth[r] the Church, our most Venerable & Dearly beloved Moth[r] Jubilarion Sis[r] Clare John, alias Fowler, the 82nd years of her Age and 63rd of her holy Profession, having Religiously spent 17 years in the convent of poor Clares at S[t] Omers & was one of the first who came forth with our R[d] Moth[r] Foundress to begin

* Margaret Fowler was a near relative to the eminent Catholic printer and exile, John Fowler, whose wife was Alice, daughter of John Harris, secretary to Sir Thomas More

this Monistary where she Lived a most holy Life in the perfect & strict observance of our Holy Rule and Constitution without the least Dispensation, even Several years after her being a Jubilarion, ever Conserving (3) her first fervour even to the end. Serving us for a Modell to form us in the due & true Spirit of our Vocation: & Singular in all Virtues, particularly in the Misprise and Contempt of her self, true Simplicity, Obedience, and Austerity, being never Satiated in her desires of Suffering for the Love of God: with an humble Conformity to his divine Will, even to her last breath, which she has Rendered most Sweetly unto her heavenly Spouse after a Violent feaver of 7 days space, Sustained with great Patience, and tranquillity, for whose Soul we humbly beg your Suffrages of Charity. Requiescat in Pace.

(4) St Omers 2nd.

Anno Domini 1596 in the Convent of the poor Clares of St Omers Sis^r.^ Mary Stephen **Goudge** made her Holy Profession being aged of 19 years.*

Anno Domini 1613 the 23rd of November in our Convent of the poor Clares in Graveline is happily departed this life after haveing Receiv'd all the Rites of our holy Moth^r^ the Church. Our Rev^d^ and well beloved Moth^r^ Abbess, Sist^r^ Mary Stephen, alias Goudge aged 36 years, 17 whereof she has faithfully served God in our Holy Order, liveing a Life more Angelicall than human, 12 years in the Convent of the poor Clares of St Omers, whence being called by Holy Obedience to begin this our Convent in Graveling, she humbly obeyd & submitted herself to take the chardge upon her, wherein she comported herself & exercised the Office of Abbess very worthily, prudently, humbly, and charitably ye term of 5 years. Supporting with admirable fortitude & constancy many Oppositions and Difficulties for ye defence of Holy Poverty. All which she surmounted by the assistance of Divine grace, with great vertue and Prudence, founding us in ye strict observance of our Holy Rule, for which all Glory to God unto whom we crave y^r^ H- Prayers of Charity for the happy repose of her soul. Requiescat in Pace.

(5) St Omers ye 3^d.^

Anno Domini 1596 in the Convent of the poor Clares of St Omers was receiv'd Sis^r^ Ann **Brooke** the 18th of Feb^ry^ aged of 33, where she lived 14 and 3 in this †

* Mary Goudge, Goffe, or Gough, was elected the first abbess of Gravelines, Dec. 28, 1608. She was daughter of Thomas Gough, of The Marsh, co. Salop, Esq., by his second wife Margaret, daughter of Edward Lloyd, of Coesmere, in the same county, Esq., both families of great antiquity, as evidenced by the various Visitations of Salop.

† Daughter of John Brooke, of Madeley, co. Salop, Esq., and his wife, Anne, daughter of Francis Shirley, of Shirley and Staunton Harrold, co. Leicester, Esq., by Dorothy, daughter of John Giffard, of Chillington, co. Stafford, Esq. She was sister to Sir Basil Brooke, of Madeley Court, Knt.

Anno Domini 1613 the 24th day of October in our Convent of the poor Clares of Nazareth in Graveline has happily yealded her soul to God, Strengthened with all ye Rights of our Holy Moth^r ye Church. Sister Ann Brook being aged of 50 years, 17 of which she most prayseably Lived in H. Religion, imploying ye greatest part therein in Serving & assisting the Sick, which she performed with exceeding great Compassion, Charity & Edification to all, and 2 years before her Death was Chosen first Vicaress of y^s Monastery, besides the aforesaid Vertues wherein she was a Mirour to all, she gave and left us Singular Example of her great Prudence, humility, and Conversation most Sweeti for the happyest repose of whose Soul we humbly beg your Prayers of Charity. Requiescat in Pace.

(6) St Omers 4.
Anno Domini 1605 was received in the Convent of the poor Clares of St Omers, Sis^r Lucy **Darrell** the 27th day of Decemb^r aged of 19 years where she Lived 4 & 7 in this Convent.*

Anno Domini 1613 the 23rd of Novemb^r in our Convent of the poor Clares of Graveline is happily Departed forth of this Life, haveing receiv'd all ye rights of our H. Mother ye Church, our most dear and well beloved Sis^r Lucy Darrell being aged 27 years of Age, haveing Lived in our Holy Order the space of 9 years in great purity and holiness of Life, especially she hath been to us a perfect Pattern of Humility, Patience and the fear of God, for the rest of whose Soul we humbly request the Suffrages of your Devout Prayers of Charity. Requiescat in Pace.

(7) St Omers 5.
Anno Domini 1596 was receiv'd in ye Convent of ye poor Clares of St Omers. Sister Ann **THolward** the 4th day of Octob^r where she lived 14 and 3 in this Convent.

Anno Domini 1613 the 26th of Novemb^r in our Convent of the poor Clares of Graveline hath Rendred her Soul to her Createur our Most D^r and well beloved Sister Ann THolward, having received all ye rights of our holy Moth^r the Church. Aged of 44 years haveing Laudably Lived in our H. Order the space of 17 years, and left us many Examples of her Vertues. Particularly of Singular Humility, Devotion & Piety. For the rest of whose Soul we humbly Crave your Prayers of Charity. Requiescat in Pace.

(8) These five Religious are of the Irish Nation; who made here their Holy Profession, and went afterwards to found in Ireland.

Anno Domini 1622 the 8th day of 7ber made her holy Holy Pro-

* Daughter of Thomas Darell, of Scotney Castle, co. Kent, Esq.

fession Sis^{r} Ellenor **Dillon**, now call'd Sister Mary of St Joseph, being aged of 21 years, and in the year 1626 the 20th of May was taken out to begin a House of ye same Nation granted in the Town of Dunkerk in Flanders, where she exercised the Office of Superior and also at Newport where they after settled for a year or 2 and professed 2 of their own Nation and then wear Translated into Ireland.

Item the same Day and year made also her holy Profession Sis^{r} Cecily **Dillon**, now call'd Sis^{r} Cecily of St Frances, being aged of 19 years, and in ye same year & day was takein forth to begin a house of ye same Nation in Dunkerk, and from thence after a year removed to Newport, and in the ye year 1629 wear by ye Irish Friars transported into Ireland where she was established Abbess.*

(9) Anno Domini 1620 the 25th of Dec: made her Holy Profession Sister Martha **Chevers**, now Call'd Sister Martha Mariana of ye Irish Nation, being aged of 21 years, & in the year 1626 the 20th of May was taken forth to assist in founding of a house for the same Nation, first begun in Dunkerk in Flanders, & after removed with others that wear here received for the ame end to Newport & thence to Ireland. †

Anno Domini 1625 the 6th of May, Sis^{r} Alse **Nugent** now Call'd Sis^{r} Magdalin of St Clare, made her H. Profession being Aged of 24 years of ye Irish Nation, and the same year the 20th of May went out to accompany those that have been formerly mentioned of the same Nation.

Anno Domini 1625 the 6th of May made her ho: profession, Sis^{r} Mary **Dowdel** now Call'd Sis^{r} Mary Peters, being Aged of 19 years and the same year the 20th of May weare taken out to accompany those that have been formerly mention'd of the same Nation.

(10) Aire 1st

These following are the Names of all those that have been Professed in this House, as well those that went out to begin the Convents of Rouen, Dunkerk, and Aire, as those that are dead and living in this House.

Anno Domini 1610 the 3rd of Novr made her H. Profession

* Eleanor and Cecily were daughters of Sir Theobald Dillon, first Viscount Dillon, of Costello-Gallen, co. Sligo, by Eleanor, daughter of Sir Edward Tuite, of Tuitestown, co. Westmeath, Knt.

† Of the ancient family of Chevers of Ballyhaly and Macetown, of whom Edward Chevers, of Macetown, co. Meath, was created by James II. Viscount Mount-Leinster, co. Carlow, in 1689.

Sis[r] Ellen **Parker,** now Call'd Sis[r] Mary of S[t] Bernard Aged of 29 years. The year of our Lord 1639 the 8th day of Decemb[r] in our Convent of the English poor Clares in Aire is happily Departed this Life our R[d] Moth[r], S[i] Mary Parker y[e] 58th year of her Age and the 29th of her Profession in ho: Religion, haveing Laudably exercised y[e] office of Moth[r] Vicaress the space of 20 years with great Edification and Vertue, being very Exemplar in Regular Observance, and also in humility, Charity, Devotion, and a holy Innocent Life, who hath borne a long Infirmaty with great Patience, being Strengthen'd with the Sacraments of our ho: Moth: ye Church, hath Sweetly yealded her Spirit to her Immortal Spouse, whom she hath faithfully served, for the Repose of her Soul, we earnestly intreat your Holy Suffrages of Charity. Requiescat in Pacé.*

(11) Item the same Day and Year made her holy Profession Sister Timothy **Walleston,** now Call'd Sister Frances of St John, being aged of 28 years.

Anno Domini 1632 the 21st of March in our Convent of English poor Clares in Graveline is happily departed this Life, Strengthened with all the Rights of our ho: Moth: the Church, our dearly beloved Sister Frances of S[t] john, alias Walleston, the 55th of her Adge, and the 23rd of her being in the holy Religion, all which she Consumated in the Regular and Strict observance of our holy Rule and Institute most assiduous in Prayer, and Singular in Conformity in all things to the Will of Alm[ty] God, and most Exemplar in the Contempt and disesteem of herself, and all things of this Life. Of all things she gave us most particular and especial testimony in this her last Sickness, for the perfect rest of her Soul we humbly crave the help of your ho: Pray[rs.] Requiescat in Pacé.

(12) Item the same Day and Year made also her holy Profession Sister Elizabeth **Tildesly:** now Call'd Sis[r] Clare Mary Ann: being aged of 24 years. †

In the year of our Lord 1654 the 17th of Feb[ry] in our afflicted Convent of the English poor Clares of Graveline is happily deceased this Life, Strengthened wth the Rights of our Holy Moth[r] the Church, Our Venerable and most D[r] Moth[r] Abbess, Sis[r] Clare Marie Ann alias Tildesly the 68th year of her Age and 44 of her holy Profession, being one of the first that received the holly Habit in this Convent, which she has governed in quality of Abbess the Space of 39 years very Laudably and peaceably,

* Daughter of Edward Parker, Lord Morley, by Elizabeth, only daughter and heiress of William Stanley, Baron Monteagle.

† Daughter of Thomas Tyldesley, of Morleys Hall and Myerscough Lodge, co. Lancaster, Esq., by Elizabeth, daughter of Christopher Anderton, of Lostock Hall, co. Lancaster, Esq. She was baptized at Church Town, Garstang, Nov. 30, 1585. Her nephew, Sir Thomas Tyldesley, was the famous royalist general who was slain at the battle of Wigan-lane in 1651.

Emery Walker Ph. sc.

Mother Elizabeth Clare Mary Ann Tyldesley
3rd Abbess of Poor Clares, Gravelines
From the painting, Ursuline Convent, Greenwich

To face p. 36

(16) Item the same Day and Year made also her H: Profession Sister Mary **Giffard** now Call'd Sis[r] Mary of S[t] Magda: Aged of 19 years.*

Anno Domini 1633 the 20th of Decemb[r] in our Monastery of the English poor Clares of Nazareth in Graveline happily ended this Mortality, our Dearly beloved Sister Sis[r] Mary Giffard the 43[d] of her Age and y[e] 24th of her Holy Profession, being one of y[e] 1st that entred into this Ho ly House, she lived with Singular and great example of Zeal in the Divine honour and Service, particularly in y[e] Choir, Charity and Love towards her neighbours wth perseverant affection, applying her self to all that might advance her in the State of her Perfection. Most assiduous in Prayers & Devotion to the Glorious Virgin, & in her last Sickness Left us a great example of her Patience & Resignation, for whose soul we humbly crave your holy Prayers of Charity. Requiescat in Pace.

(17) Item the same Day and Year made her Holy Profession Sis[r] Susanna **Gage**, since Call'd Sis[r] Collet of S[t] Andrew Aged 18 years and was Canonically chosen Abbess of y[e] Convent the 15th Day of December.

Anno Domini 1615 the 7th of May, in our poor Convent of the poor Clares in Graveline is happily Departed this Life Strengthened with all the Rights of our Ho: Moth[r] the Church Our Venerable and most Dearly beloved Moth[r] Abbess, Sis[r] Collet Gage, aged of 23 years, having served God in our Holy order the space of 6 wherein she prudently exercised the Office of Abbess one year and a half and was indued with a Singular Sweetness of Conversation, profound Humility, and Charity, but above all she had a most assured Confidence in the Divine Providence and Goodness of God, and in the time of her Sickness, left us many examples of her Admirable Patience and Resignation to the Divine will, for the Repose of her Soul we humbly crave y[e] holy Suffrages and Prayers of Charity. Requiescat in Pace.

(18) Aire 3rd

Item the same Day & year also made her holy Profession Sis[r] Catherine **Bentley**, now Call'd Sister Magdalin of S[t] Austin, aged 18 years.

Anno Domini 1659 the 1st of Jully in our Convent of English poor Clares in Aire hath happily rendred her Soul to her Heavenly Spouse fortifyde with all the Rights of our holy Moth[r] the Church. Our Rev[d] and most D[r] Moth[r] Vicaress. S[tr] Magdalin of S[t] Austin the 68 year of her Age, and 50 of her

* Daughter of John Gifford, Esq., M.D., of London, by Catherine, daughter of John Legat, of Hornchurch, co. Essex, Esq. Her nephew, Henry Gifford, of Burstall, co. Leicester, was created a baronet in 1660.

Mother Susanna Collet Gaye
2nd Abbess of Poor Clares, Gravelines
From the painting, Ursuline Convent, Greenwich

To face p. 38.

holy Profession, haveing been very vertuous, Charitable, and Devout. For the happy rest of whose Soul we humbly crave your Prayers of Charity. Requiescat in Pace.

(19) Anno Domini 1611 the 3rd Day of May made her holy Profession, Sisr Ann **Bentley**, now Call'd Sisr Angela of St Anthony, aged of 22 years.

The year of our Lord 1656 the 27 of June in our Convent of Nazareth of English poor Clares in Graveline is happily departed this Life Strengthened with all the rights of our holy Mothr ye Church. Our Venerable and Dearly beloved Sister. Sisr Angela of St Anthony, otherwise Bentley, the 67th year of her Age and 46 of her Profession unto holy Religion which time she spent very fervently in the true Observance of her holy Rule, haveing Supported the space of 30 Years a Continual infirmaty & great deafness with an admirable Patience and tranquillity of mind, and perfect Resignation to the Divine Will. She was insatiable in her zeal of God's honour & the Conversion of England, which she demanded perseverently by her Prayers. She was very particularly Devoted to Our Bd Saviour, Passion, & unto Our Bd Lady. For the Repose of her Soul we humbly beg your Suffrages and Prayers of Charity. Requiescat in Pace.

(20) Item the same Day and Year also made her holy Profession Sisr Frances **Havers** now Call'd Sisr Frances of St Dominick being aged of 30 years.*

The Year of Our Lord 1647 the 9th day of April in our Convent of Nazareth of English poor Clares in Graveline, is happily deceas'd. Strengthened with all ye Rights of our holy Mother the Church Our Dearly Beloved Sister, Sisr Frances of St Dominick, alias Havers, aged of 66 years and ye 36 of her holy Profession the which she hath faithfully imployed in the Divine Service to the great Edification of all our Community, haveing exercised diverse of the principle Offices in our Convent with a Singular humility and eminent Charity, being a great Lover of Poverty, and ye Contempt of herself, and in her last Sickness wch was very painful she has left us special examples of Patience, and Conformity to the Divine Will. We humbly beg the happy assistance of your Holy Sacrifices & Prayers for the Repose of her Soul. Requiescat in Pace.

(21) Aire 4.

Anno Domini 1612 the 3rd day of July made her Holy Profession

* Daughter of Thomas Havers, of Thelton Hall, co. Norfolk, steward to the Duke of Norfolk, by Elizabeth, daughter of William Dale, of Doyke (?), co. Suffolk, Esq.

Sis[r] Margaret Ratcliffe, now Call'd Sister Margaret of S[t] Paul, being Aged of 27 years.*

Anno Domini 1654 the 26th of Aug[t] in our Convent of the Immaculate Conception of our B[d] Lady of English poor Clares in Aire, is happily departed this Life. Our Venerable D[r] Sister, Sis[r] Margaret of S[t] Paul haveing left us great Examples of the perfect practice of all Virtues, Namely of a Singular Devotion, very assiduous in the well Spending of her time, and in gitting of humble work. Constantly exercising herself in humility and abjection of herself for the Love of her heavenly Spouse Jesus. Yet least there may be anything w[ch] may detain her Soul from the perfect injoying him, we humbly crave y[r] ho: Prayers of Charity. Requiescat in Pace.

(22) Anno Domini 1613 the 7th day of Octob[r] made her holy Profession Sis[r] Philip **Alcock** now called Sis[r] Philip Mary being aged of 18 years.

Anno Domini 1667 the 27th of Aug[st] at 8 of y[e] clock in the Morning: in our Convent of English poor Clares in Graveline, is most happily deceas'd this life strengthened with the Rights of our holy Mother the Church, Our Venerable D[r] Moth[r] Jubilarion Sis[r] Mary Philip alias Alcock the 73 years of her Age and 55 since her entrance into holy Religion, all which time she spent most laudably in the Vertues most suitable to her Vocation, like to a true Child of our Foundress, by her humility, misprise of herself, and great esteem of others, being so Submissive as a Novice altho she was the Eldest in the house, our good God who knew her vertues was pleased to give her a tryal thereof by long and painful Sickness, and pains, the which she did Support with great Resignation to the Will of God, we humbly crave y[r] holy Prayers and Suffrages for the Repose of her Soul. Requiescat in Pace.

(23) Aire 5.
Upon the same Day and Year made also her ho: Profession Sister Grace **Penengton,** now Call'd Sis[r] Catherine of S[t] Frances being aged of 24 years.†

Anno Domini 1638 the 17th of Oct[br] in our Convent of y[e] English Poor Clares in Aire, hath happily rendered her Soul into the

* Second daughter of Sir Francis Radcliffe, of Dilston, co. Northumberland, and Derwentwater, co. Cumberland, 1st Bart., by Isabel, daughter of Sir Ralph Grey, of Chillingham, co. Northumberland, Knt. She was sent in 1629 to found the convent at Aire in Artois, of which she was first Abbess.

† Daughter of John Penington, of Penington, co. Lancaster, and Muncaster, co. Cumberland, Esq., by a daughter of Sir George Radcliffe, of Dilston and Derwentwater, Knt. Her brother, Sir John Pennington, of Muncaster, Knt., was ancestor of his namesake who was created Baron Muncaster, in the peerage of Ireland, in 1783.

hands of her Creator, Our most D[r] and well beloved Sis[r] Catherine of S[t] Frances the 50th Year of her Age and of her Profession the 25, haveing Prayseable lived in the observance of our Holy Rule with the Exercise of many Vertues, and in particular of Obedience, Charity, Humility, and a great Love to the Holy Vocation and Religion, the which after having Supported with great Resignation to the Divine Will, Many Pains and Infirmatys many Years, and with an admirable patience in her last sickness very painful and troublesome, in the end being strengthened with the Sacraments of the Church, have happily changed this Mortal Life for the Immortal, we require for the Repose of her Soul, your holy Prayers. Requiescat in Pace.

(24) Aire 6.

Item the same Day & Year made also her holy Profession Sister Mildred **Alcock** now Call'd Sis[r] Mildred Archangel being aged of 18 years.

Anno Domini 1652 the 4th of December in our Monastery of the Immaculate Conception of our B[d] Lady of English poor Clares in Aire, is departed this Life our D[r] Sister Mildred Archangel, Strengthened with all the Rights of our Holy Moth[r] the Church, She has left us very rare Examples of Humility, Patience, & Sweetness in Conversation which render'd her very pleasing to all, but above all to Alm[ty] God whom we hope she now enjoys, but fear lest anything detains her Repose, we humbly crave the assistance of your Holy Prayers for the Love of God. Requiescat in Pace.

(25) Aire 7.

Item the same Day & Year made also her ho: Professi: Sister Margaret **Crisp**, now call'd Sis[r] Margaret of S[t] Clare, being aged of 17 years.*

Anno Domini 1661 the 21st of March in our Convent of the Immaculate Conception of our B[d] Lady of English poor Clares in Aire is most happily departed, furnished with all the Rights of our Holy Moth[r] the Church our Dearly beloved Sister, Sis[r] Margaret of S[t] Clare, she haveing left us Examples of a Solid Vertue, and of a special devotion to all the holy Saints, omitting no endeavours for the augmentation of their honour, & that others might be in like manner devoted to them, whose Sweet Society we hope she now enjoys. Yet humbly crave your Holy Prayers lest there may be any thing which may detain her. Requiescat in Pace.

(26) Aire 8.

Item the same Day & Year made also her holy Profession.

* Daughter of John Crispe, of Ore, Esq., by Mary, daughter and coheiress of John Gage, of Firle, co. Sussex, Esq.

Sis[r] Catherine **Keynes**, now call'd Sis[r] Catherine of S[t] Clare, being aged 24 years.*

Anno Domini 1646 the 20th of Nov[r] in our Convent of English poor Clares in Aire is happily departed this Life, fortify'd wth the Rights of our holy Moth[r] y[e] Church, our most D[r] & well beloved Moth[r] Sis[r] Catherine of S[t] Clare, the 57 Year of her Age, and 33rd of her holy Profession. Having Laudably lived in the Observance of our holy Rule & performed the Office of Portress, Mistress of the Novices, & Abbess with exampler Vertue and Content of our Community, being Indued with a Singular Devotion, Sweetness, Humility, and very great Patience in a long and most Grievous Infirmity, for the happy Repose of her Soul, we humbly Crave y[r] Holy Prayers of Charity. Requiescat in Pace.

(27) Item the same Day and Year made also holy Profession Sister Isabelle **Witheral**, now Call'd Sis[r] Elizabeth of S[t] Magdalin being aged of 22 Years.

Anno Domini 1618 the 8th of Octob[r] in our Convent of the poor Clares in Graveline is happily deceas'd strengthened with all the Rights of our holy Moth[r] the Church, Our most D[r] and well beloved Sister, Sis[r] Elizabeth of S[t] Magdalin aged of 28 Years, 6 of w[ch] she has lived Laudably in our holy Order, endued with all vertues, particularly perfect Obedience, Humility, & Devotion. As also with very great patience which she has shewed in a painfull & Long Sickness wherewith it pleased God to visitt her with, Many other good Examples of a perfect Zealatrice of her Vocation: for the Repose of whose Soul we humbly crave your Prayers of Charity. Requiescat in Pace.

(28) Item the same Day and Year made also her holy Profession Sis[r] Mary **Cotten**, now Call'd Sis[r] Mary of S[t] Joseph, being aged 22 Years.†

Anno Domini 1641 the 26th of Jan[ry] in Our Convent of Nazareth of English poor Clares in Graveline, is most happily departed, furnished with the Rights of our holy Mother the Church, Our most D[r] & well beloved Sister, Sis[r]. Mary Joseph Cotten the 48th of her Age and the 27th of her holy Profession. All which time she spent most fervently in the Zealous Observance of her holy Vocation, being most humble, Obedient, & Charitable. For her soul, happy rest. We humbly crave the assistance of Y[r]. holy Prayers. Requiescat in Pace.

(29) Anno Domini 1614 the 12th of Ap[l] made her holy Profession, Sis[r] Jane **Alcock**, now Call'd Sis[r] Barbara of S[t] Martin, being aged of 20 Years.

* Daughter of Edward Keynes, of Compton Pauncefoot, co. Somerset, Esq., of which family were many noted Jesuits.

† The Cottons were lords of the manors of Warblington and Bedhampton, co Hants., and were distinguished for their sufferings for the Faith.

Anno Domini 1629 the 25th of March in our Convent of the English poor Clares in Graveline, is happily Deceas'd, our Dearly beloved Sister, Sisr Barbara of St Martin alias Alcock, aged of 36 years. Haveing virtuously lived in our holy Order the space of 16 years, & left us very singular examples of her Charity to all, & great Patience in many sicknesses and pains. Which she endured with special Resignation & Conformity to the divine will, and perticularly this last, wherein after having received all the Rights of our holy Mothr the Church, she yielded her Soul to her Creator, for the happiest repose of her Soul, we humbly and instantly crave the assistance of yr Holy Suffrages through Charity. Requiescat in Pace.

(30) Item the same Day & Year made also her holy Profession, Sister Mary **Haywood**, now Call'd Sisr Mary of St Peter being aged of 24 Years.*

Anno Domini 1661 the 8th of Sepr the feast of our Bd Ladyes Glorious Nativity, in our Convent of Nazareth of English poor Clares in Graveline is most happily deceas'd. Strengthened with the Rights of our holy Mothr the Church, Our Venerable most Dearly beloved Sister, Sisr Mary Peter Alias Haywood, the 72 year of her Age and 48 since her entry into holy Religion, most part of which she was always infirm & sustained many long and greivous Sicknesses with great patience & Conformity to the Divine will, especially this last year, a true Purgatory unto her: which she had begg'd dureing her Life to Suffer in this world, wherein she has left us Singular Examples of all vertues, particularly a profound Knowledge of herself, Humility, Obedience and Contrite Tears, for ye Speedyest repose of her Soul, we humbly crave your Prayers of Charity. Requiescat in Pace.

(31) Rouen I.

Anno Domini 1614 the 7th of Octobr made her holy Profession Sister Mary **Taylor**, now Call'd Str Mary of St Frances being aged of 17 years.

Anno Domini 1658 in our Convent of Jesus, Mary, Joseph of English poor Clares of Rouen, Normandy, the 8th of Decembr furnished with all the Rights of our holy Mothr ye Church is most happily departed, our most Venerable and Dearly beloved Mothr Abbess, Sr Mary Frances alias Taylor, the 62d year of her Age & of her Profession ye 44th after haveing lived with exemplar Edification in our Convent of Graveline, who after being Mistress of Novices 7 years, and Vicaress 18, was by Holy Obedience sent with 14 Religious to the Town of Rouen, Nakedly depending upon God's Providence, and there on reposed as on a firm Pillar, by the

* Niece of FF. Elizaeus and Jasper Heywood, S.J., and grand-daughter of John Heywood (or Haywood), the famous epigrammatist.

help of which she Establish'd to the wonder of all the beholders this Convent, and made herself our Foundress, not only for the temporal Fabricque, but for our best foundation in true & Solid Vertue, in the Zeal of which she Consumed her Corporall forces, haveing thereby sustained many long and painfull Sicknesses, but Chiefly ye 2 last Years of her Life, which Consumed & dryed up her Body and Bowells like a Carkass, and thus wth admirable Patience, joying to see ye wall of her body broken in Pieces. For the Speedyest repose of her Soul we crave your Prayers of Charity. Requiescat in Pace.

(32) Item the same Day & Year made also her Ho: Profession, Sis^r^ Margarett **Croock,** now Call'd Sis^r^ Margarett of St Martha, Aged 23 Years.

Anno Domini 1664 the 24th of March in our Convent of English poor Clares in Graveline is most happily Deceased Strengthened wth ye Rights of our Holy Mother the Church, our Venerable & Dr Mother Jubilarian, Sis^r^ Margarett Martha alias Crook, the 51 Year of her being Religious, which time she has most fervently spent in the Constant practice of those Vertues Conformable to her Vocation. Particularly Devout Prayer, Humility, holy Simplicity and Obedience with Singular Respect & Confidence in her Superiour, her Patience & Conformity to ye Divine Will was during 15 Years of Continual Infirmity most remarkable, but above all her last Sickness which was very Sensible and Sharp, and gave a happy Period to her Languishing desires to be wth God, for whose Speedyest enjoying his Holy Vision, wee humbly crave your Suffrages of Charity. Requiescat in Pace.

(33) Anno Domini 1615 made her Holy Profession Sis^r^ Elizabeth **Thwaytes,** now Call'd Sister Collet Clare the 1st day of June, being Aged of 22 years.*

Anno Domini 1675 the 22nd of Feb^ry^ in our Convent of Nazareth of English poor Clares in Graveline, is happily deceased, Strengthened wth ye Rights of our Holy Moth^r^ ye Church, Our Venerable & Dear Mother, Sister Collet Clare Thwaytes, the 83rd year of her Age, & 61 of her holy Profession, by whose Deprivation we have lost a Burning torche y^t^ gave us all light in the practice of all Virtues, namely of a Singular Sweetness of Conversation for during the whole time of her Life the Peace of her Soul was never alter'd for any accident. Notwithstanding she exercized the Office of Portress, M^rs^ of Novices, & lastly Vicaress 24 years; & with so great a Satisfaction y^t^ she gained the hearts of her Community, & seculars who were Edify'd at her aspect, uttering wth out intermission vocall asperations to Jesus, Maria,

* Daughter of William Thwaites, of Long Marston, co. York, Esq., by Eleanor, daughter of Philip, 3rd Lord Wharton, and his wife, the Lady Francis Clifford, daughter of Henry, 2nd Earl of Cumberland.

as long as her tongue could move during her last Sickness, haveing been bedrid ye space of 15 months, wch she sustained wth Singular patience & Resignation in all her great pains, being as Submissive to her Infirmarions who had been her Novices as to her Superiours, to whom she even had so high a Respect; even to the least exterior duty: as if she had been a Novice. We humbly crave y^r^ holy Prayers of Charity. Requiescat in Pace.

(34) Anno Domini 1616 the 11th of Jan^ry^ made her H: Profession Sis^r^ Martha **James**, now Call'd Sis. Martha Mary being Aged 22 years.

Anno Domini 1625 the 3rd of Octr in our Convent of the poor Clares in Graveline is happily Departed this Life haveing receiv'd all the Rights of our Holy Mother the Church, Our Dr Sister Martha Mary, being a true Zelatrice of Holy Poverty, Austerity and Humility, & Singularly endued with the Contempt of herself, and Love towards her neighbour which Vertues she hath exemplarly exercised & faithfully laboured in the Service of the Holy Community to our great Edification the term of 11 years wch she has lived in our Holy Order, and deceas'd the 32nd of her Age, for the Repose of whose Soul we humbly crave the assistance of your Holy Prayers. Requiescat in Pace.

(35) Item the same Day and year made her Holy Profession, Sis^r^ Elizabeth **Taylor** now Call'd Sis^r^ Elizab: of St Andrew, being Aged of 20 years.

Anno Domini 1664 the 1st of Apr^l^ in our Convent of Nazareth of English poor Clares in Graveline is most happily deceas'd furnish'd with all ye Rights of our Holy Mother the Church, Our Venerable Dear Sis^r^ Eliz: of St Andrew the 70th year of her Age, & 50th of being Religious, wch time she hath employ'd in faithful Service to the Monastery, till deprived by Infirmatys of her forces for exteriour Labours. She addicted herself most Seriously to Prayer and interiour Exercises to unite herself to her heavenly Spouse, to whose hands finally rendering the Same, we Crave for her y^r^ Charitable Suffrages. Requiescat in Pace.

Anno Domini 1616 13th day of Jully made her Holy Profession Sis^r^ Ann **Clark**, now Call'd Sis^r^ Ann Didacus, being aged of 19 years.

Anno Domini 1664 the 13th day of June, in our Convent of English poor Clares in Graveline, is happily departed furnish'd wth all ye Rites of our Holy Moth^r^ ye Church, Our Dearly beloved Sister, Sis^r^ Ann of St Didacus (alias Clark), the 69th Year of her Age and 49 of her Holy Profession haveing ever retained an assiduous Application to Holy Pray^r^ and Zeal for Religious Observances being some Years before her Death detained wth a

Languishing Infirmaty & Paulsey, wch bereaved her of the use of her Members. She exercised so great Patience therein & Conformity to the Divine Will as she left us Singular Examples of these Vertues, we humbly crave y^r Holy Prayers of Charity for the Repose of her Soul. Requiescat in Pace.

(37) Item the same Day and Year made also her H. Profession Sister Rosamonde **Poole**, now Call'd Sis^r Ellen of St Bernardine being Aged 28 Years.

Anno Domini 1654 the 9th of Jan^ry In our Conv^t of Nazareth of English poor Clares in Graveline is happily departed this Life, furnished wth all the Rites of our Holy Moth^r the Church, Our Dearly Beloved Sister, Sis^r Ellen Bernard the 62 year of her Age and 30 of her Holy Profession. She Lived with Singular, and great Examples of Piety & Zeal in the Divine Service humility and Charity, and Love to her Neighbour, applying herself to all that might advance her in the perfection of her estate, most assiduous in Prayer and Devotion to the Glorious Virgin, and in her last Sickness left us great Examples of her Patience and Resignation, for whose Soul we humbly Crave your Holy Prayers of Charity. Requiescat in Pace.

(38) Aire 9.

Anno Domini 1617 the 5th of Jan^ry made her holy Profession Sis^r Mary **Goolding**, now Call'd Sis^r Mary of Jesus, being Aged of 22 years.

Anno Domini 1661 the 26th of Feb^ry in our Convent of the Immaculate Conception of our B^d Lady in Aire is most happily departed this Life our Most D^r S^r, Sis^r Mary of Jesus, haveing given us all great Edification by her Vertious Examples, Chiefly of an Admirable patience, Perseverance and assiduousness in Prayer, being ever very Zealous of All: God, honour & Glory, and hath as I confide received the reward of all her Fidelities to him, yet since his Divine Judgments are inscrutable, and fear least anything may detain her, I humbly crave y^r Holy Prayers for the Love of God. Requiscat in Pace.

(39) Aire 10.

Item the same Day and Year made her Holy Profession Sis^r Elizabeth **Radcliff**, now Call'd Sister Barbara of St Collet Aged of 28 years.*

Anno Domini 1645 the 31st of March in our Convent of English poor Clares in Aire is happily departed out of the miseries of this Mortal Life, being fortified wth ye Sacraments of our Holy Mother

* Third daughter of Sir Francis Radcliffe, of Dilston and Derwentwater, 1st Bart., and aunt of Francis, 1st Earl of Derwentwater. She was sent in 1621 with her sister Margaret to direct the convent of the English Franciscan nuns at Brussels.

ye Church, Our Dr Sister, Sis^{r} Elizabeth Radcliffe the 56th year of her Age and the 28th of her holy Profession having laudably lived in the Observance of our Holy Rule with an exemplar Vertue, being very humble, Charitable and Devout, being a Zealous Lover of Holy Poverty, & very patient & resigned in a long & greevious Sickness, we humbly crave y^{r} good Prayers for her soul's happy Repose. Requiescat in Pace.

(40) Item the same Day and Year made her holy Profession Sis^{r} Frances **Yates**, now Call'd Sis^{r} Frances of St Clare being Aged of 20 years.*

Anno Domini 1625 the 28th of Jan^{ry} in our Convent of poor Clares in Graveline is happily departed this Life, Strengthened with all ye Rights of our holy Moth: the Church, Our most D^{r} and well beloved Sis^{r} Frances Yates, after a painful Sickness sustained by her wth great patience & Conformity to the Divine Will, wch Vertues she truly practiced during the Course of her Life, as also a most prompt Obedience, Interior and Exteriour Recollection & was truly zealous of all perfection. She was 28 years of Age & Lived 9 in our holy Order, for the perfect Repose of her Soul, we humbly Crave your holy Prayers of Charity. Requiescat in Pace.

(41) Item the same Day & Year made her holy Profession Sis^{r} Bridget **Ann**, now Call'd Sis^{r} Bridgett of St Stephen, being Aged of 21 years.†

Anno Domini 1693 the 22nd of Decemb^{r} in our Monastery of Nazareth of English poor Clares in Graveline has happily ended this Life our Dearly beloved Sis^{r}, Sis^{r} Bridget Ann, strengthened with all the Rites of our holy Moth^{r} ye Church, ye 38th year of her age & ye 18th of her being in Religion. She was truly zealous of the perfection of her Vocation, most eminent in Holy Poverty, humility, neglect of herself and all temporal things. Infatigable in all works of Charity, and of Singular Patience & Conformity to the Divine Will in Sufferance, for the true happiness of her Soul we humbly crave your holy Prayers of Charity. Requiescat in Pace.

(42) Rouen 2.

Anno Domini 1618 the 4th day of March made her Holy Profession

* Daughter of Thomas Yate (or Yates), of Lyford, co. Berks, Esq., by Mary, daughter of Francis Tregian, of Golden, co. Cornwall, Esq., and his wife Mary, eldest daughter of Charles, 7th Lord Stourton. Her mother was born in prison, where her grandfather was kept for twenty-eight years on account of his faith (*vide* account of his imprisonment, *Morris, Troubles of our Catholic Forefathers, First Series, pp.* 65-140).

Daughter of George Anne, of Frickley Hall, co. York, Esq., by Margaret, daughter and co-heiress of Richard Fenton, of Burghwallis Hall, in the same county, Esq.

Sis^r^ Ann **Prow,** now Call'd Sis^r^ Ann of St Raphael, being Aged of 28 Years.

Anno Domini 1671 the 29th of Sepr in our Convent of Jesus Maria, Joseph, of English poor Clares in Rouen, is most happily Deceas'd this Life strengthened wth all ye Rights of our holy Moth^r^ ye Church, Our Venerable Moth^r^ Jubilarion, Sis^r^ Ann Raphael alias Prow, the 81st Year of her Age & of her being in Religion the 53^d^ whereof she spent 27 years in our Dr Convent of Graveline in infatigable Labours both here and there for ye service of ye holy Religion she was most faithful & exemplar in ye observance of all Religious Disciplin, & when her forces were by her regular Duties & great Age exhausted she spent ye rest of her Life in Continual Dolours & has now finish'd her Course wth a Lingring & sharpe sickness, wch she endur'd wth Singular Patience to ye edification of us all. We most humbly recomend the speedye rest of her Soul to y^r^ Holy Prayers of Charity. Requiescat in Pace.

(43) Aire 11.
Item, the same Day made also her Holy Profession, Sis^r^ Frances **Phillipson** now Call'd Sis^r^ Frances of St Bonaventure, being Aged of 20 Years.

Anno Domini 1661 the 21st of March in our Convent of the Immaculate Conception of English Poor Clares in Aire is most piously deceased our Dr Sis^r^, Sis^r^ Frances of St Bonaventure alias Phillipson, haveing left us great Edification by her Diligence & fervour in the well performance of the Divine Office as well by Night as by Day, and I hope ere now hath receiv'd the Crown of all her other Vertues, yet the Judgments of God being uncertain, I humbly beg your holy Prayers of Charity for the repose of her Soul. Requiescat in Pace.

(44) Rouen 3^d^.
Item the same Day & Year made her Holy Profession Sis^r^ Elizabeth **Rayner,** now Call'd Sis^r^ Mary Gabriel being Aged of 28 Years.

Anno Domini 1647 the 23^d^ of July in our poor Exile of Jesus, Maria, Joseph, in Rouen of the English poor Clares, is happily deceased with all ye Rights of the holy Church, our most Dr Sister, Sister Mary Gabriel, the 58th year of her Age, and the 30th since her entrance into ye holy Religion, and the 3^d^ of her exile from her Dr Monastery of Graveline. Whence with 15 nuns she was sent by Holy Obedience to help their urgent necessitys by reason of the afflictions of our poor Country, to live here upon God's providence, in the one & the other place she spent her Life as a true Zelatress of her Holy Profession and Continual observance, a great Lover of Holy Poverty and perseverantly Labouring for ye Service of ho: Religion & Concluded ye last Year for ye space of 9 months with a most Sharp & Dolorous sickness, wch she endured wth admirable Conformity to the Divine Will; for ye repose of her Soul wee humbly crave y^r holy Prayers. Requiescat in Pace.

(45) Rouen 4th.

Anno Domini 1619 the 6th of March made her Holy Profession Sister Magdaline **Brown**, now Call'd Sister Magdaline Clare, being Aged 16 Years.*

Anno Domini 1639 in our Convent of Jesus, Mary Joseph of the English poor Clares in Rouen in Normandy is this 10th of Decemb^r happily departed this Life strength'd with all the Rights of our holy Mother the Catholic Church, our Venerable & Dearly beloved Sister, Sister Magdalene Clare (alias Brown) the 57th Year of her Age and ye 41 of her holy Profession. Whereof she spent 27 years in our Dr Convent at Graveline where she endured many painful infirmatys with singular patience, underwent many hard Labours for the holy Religion & since her coming to Rouen hath wth infatigable Labour assisted in the care of the building of this House, & 12 years was Portress, she all her life suffer'd much wth an infirm body without ever attending to it, or sparing herself from ye Exercises of ye Holy Religion; being a great Lover & Practiser of Austerity, Poverty, and ye Zeale of her Holy Profession, for what yet Remain in her Soul to be purified, I humbly crave y^r holy Prayers of Charity. Requiescat in Pace.

(46) Item the same Day & Year made also her Holy Profession Sister Dorothy **Yaxlee**, now Call'd Sis^r Ursula of St Bernard, being Aged of 18 Years.

Anno Domini 1653 the 21st of April in this our Convent of English poor Clares in Graveline is happily departed this Life Strengthened with all ye Rights of our Holy Mother the Church, our Dearly beloved Sister, Sis^r Ursula Bernard, the 52th Year of her age & the 35th year of her Profession, she was a great Lover of holy Poverty, Contempt & Neglect of herself, & Singular for Conformity to the Divine Will & Patience, in her last Sickness, which was very sharpe & painfull, for the speedy Repose of whose Soul I humbly crave your Holy Suffrages & Prayers of Charity. Requiescat in Pace.

(47) Item the same Day & Year made also her Holy Profession, Sister Dorothy **Carlton** now Call'd Sister Dorothy Joseph Aged of 17 Years.

Anno Domini 1625 the 20th of Jan^ry in our Convent of poor

* Daughter of Sir Henry Browne, of Kiddington, co. Oxon, younger son of Anthony, first Viscount Montagu, by his second wife, Magdalen, daughter of William, 3rd Lord Dacre of Gillesland. Her mother was Anne, daughter of Sir William Catesby, of Ashby St Legers, co. Northampton, Knt.

Clares in Graveline, is happily Departed this Life, our most Dear and well beloved Sister, Sist[r] Dorothy Joseph Carlton, Aged of 23 haveing Lived Laudably in our holy Order the space of 7 years, most exemplar in all Religious observances, particularly indued with great Devotion, Obedience, Humility, and Sweetness of Conversation, for the Repose of whose Soul we humbly crave your Prayers of Charity. Requiescat in Pace.

(48) Anno Domini 1619 the 22nd of Jully, Sis[r] Mary **Cape**, now Call'd Sister Mary Collett, made her Holy Profession, being Aged of 16 Years.

Anno Dominio 1639 the 30th of March in our Convent of Nazareth of poor Clares in Graveline is happily deceased, being administered with all y[e] Rights of our holy Mother the Church, our Dearly beloved Sister Mary Cape, now Call'd Sist[r] Mary Collet, the 36th year of her Age, have served most fervently our Lord in this our holy Religion, 21 Years, in Singular Innocency & purity of Soul, strict Obedience, with all Religious Observance, and most assiduous in holy Prayer, & interiour exercises; her sickness was long & painfull, wherein she left rare examples of Patience, humility, and intire Resignation to the Divine will, for the repose of her Soul, we humbly crave the assistance of your holy Prayers. Requiescat in Pace.

(49) Aire 12.
The same Day & Year made also her holy Profession Sister Dorothy **Radcliffe**, now Call'd Sis[r] Dorothy Frances Bruno, Aged of 25 Years.*

Anno Domini 1639 the 22[d] of Sep[r] in our Convent of poor Clares in Aire is most happily deceased administred with all y[e] rights of our holy Mother y[e] Church our dearly beloved Sister Frances Bruno alias Radcliffe, y[e] 45th Year of her Age, and y[e] 20th Since her Ho: Profession, have lived in holy Religion with great vertue, and Edification, being very exemplar in y[e] Love and exercise of holy Poverty, also very humble, Devout, and patient in a long and painfull Sickness, which she hath Suported many Years with a perfect resignation to the Divine will, for the repose of whose Soul we humbly crave the assistance of your holy Prayers, Requiescat in Pace.

(50) Aire 13.
The same Day & Year made also her holy Profession Sister Elizabeth **Crisp**, now call'd Sis[r] Mary Stephen being Aged of 20 Years.†

Anno Domini 1637 the 9th of Ap[l] in our Convent of poor Clares

* Fifth daughter of Sir Francis Radcliffe, and sister of Elizabeth above.

† Sister of Margaret Crispe above.

in Aire, is happily deceased our Dearly beloved Sister Mary Stephen (alias Crisp) ye 38th Year of her Age, and ye 18th since her holy Profession, haveing Lived laudably in ye holy Religion, and endowed wth many vertues, principally wth a sweet Conversation & Charity, sparing no paines, having exercised ye Office Several Years of Dispenceer, and that of Mistress of Novices these last 3 Years wth much vertue, haveing Edified us by her humility and patience as well in her Life as in her last Sickness, wch she supported wth great resignation to ye Divine will, & being fortifyed wth ye Sacraments of our holy Moth^r^ ye Church, happily render'd her Soul to her Creature, for ye repose of whose Soul we humbly crave ye Prayers of Charity. Requiescat in Pace.

(51) Aire 14.
The same Day & Year made also her holy Profession Sister Ann **Radclyffe,** now Call'd Sis^r^ Clare Benedict being Aged of 24 Years.*

Anno Domini 1639 the 30th of Novr in our Convent of poor Clares in Aire, is happily departed this Life furnish'd with the Rights of our holy Mother the Church, our Dearly Beloved Sister Clare Benedict Radclyffe, Aged of 44 & 20 since her holy Profession, haveing Lived in holy Religion wth great Virtue and Edification, being very Zealous in ye observance of Poverty, very humble & Obedient & of a most sweet mild conversation, haveing suported with great Resignation a long & tedious Sickness which makes us Confide she already receives ye reward of her Fidelity in God's Services but as ye Judgments of God are inscrutable, I most humbly beg the assistance of y^r^ holy Prayers for the repose of her Soul. Requiescat in Pace.

(52) Anno Domini 1619 the 29th of Decemb^r^, made her Ho: Profession, Sis^r^. Anno Sanford, now Call'd Sis^r^ Ann Teresa, being Aged of 28 Years.†

Anno Domini 1637 the 21st of Nov: in our Convent of Nazareth of English poor Clares in Graveline, is happily departed this Life, Strengthened wth ye rights of our Holy Mother ye Church, our Dearly beloved Sister, Sister Ann Teresa Sanford, being Aged of 46 & 18 since her entrance into the holy Religion, she was very eminent in Charity, Infatigable in all paines, & humble Labours, a great Zelatrix of holy Poverty & assiduous in holy Prayer, of wch Vertues she has left us rare Examples, for the happy rest of whose Soul, we humbly Crave your holy Prayers of Charity. Requiescat in Pace.

* Sixth daughter of Sir Francis Radcliffe, and sister of Elizabeth and Dorothy above.

† Daughter of Humphrey Sandford, of the Isle of Rossall, co. Salop, Esq., by Jane, daughter of Edward Giffard, of Whiteladies, co. Stafford, Esq., and his wife Frances, eldest daughter and heiress of Bartholomew Skerne, of London, Esq.

(53) Anno Domini 1620 the 22nd of July made her holy Profession, Sis^{r} Grace **Evele**, now Call'd Sis^{r} Winifrid Madgelin, being Aged of 25 Years.

Anno Domini 1635 the 25th of March, being Good Friday, in our Convent of Nazareth of poor Clares in Graveline, is most happily deceased our Dear Sister Winifred Magdalin, the 40th year of her Age, & 14th since her holy Profession, being administered wth the holy Sacraments of the Church, she was most assiduous & fervent in Prayer: & singular in the guift of tears & Contrition, wth a Strong Confidence in God; & in the Passion of our B^{d} Saviour which she particularly manifested in her last Sickness, by her extraordinary Patience, Devotion, and Conformity to the Divine Will, for the happy rest of whose soul we humbly crave the assistance of your holy Prayers. Requiescat in Pace.

(54) Aire 15.

The same Day & Year made also her Ho: Profession Sis^{r} Elizabeth **Evelinge**, now Call'd Sister Catherine Magdalin being Aged of 23 Years.

Anno Domini 1668 ye 23rd of Septr the 72nd of her Age & of her Religious Profession the 50th in our Convent of the Immaculate Conception of our B^{d} Lady of ye poor Clares in Aire. Amongst the Prayers & tears of her Children, not without a great want: being left of her, haveing been ye Example of all sortes of Vertues, especially of a remarkable Patience in her long Infirmaties, has piously Slept in our Lord, fortified with ye Sacraments of our Holy Mother ye Church, the Venerable Mother, Sister Catherine Magdalin Evelinge,—for 25 years a most deserving Abbess; who haveing wth great praise Discharged ye office of Portress, & M^{rs} of Novices, for ye admirable guifts of her Soul, also a more polish'd way of writing above her Sex, prefer'd at Length to ye Government of the above sayed Convent, and hath peacefully governed the same not with Less prudence, than general Satisfaction of all, leaving behind her a great Example of a most perfect Poverty, which she delighted in. She was most Loveing & tender to all: & very austere to her self, that she may Enjoy the reward of all her good workes, we humbly crave the assistance of y^{r} Prayers of Charity. Requiescat in Pace

(55) Aire 16.

The same Day and Year made also her Holy Profession, Sister Rose **Evelinge**, now Call'd Sister Agnes Joseph being Aged of 18.

Anno Domini 1654 the 4th of Octob^{r} in our Convent of the Immaculate Conception of our B^{d} Lady of poor Clares in Aire, is most piously departed this Life, our Dear Sister Agnes Joseph Evelinge, the 52nd year of her Age, and 34 since her entrance to Religion, haveing left us great Examples of a perfect Charity, ever makeing the best of all, which gives us reason to hope she is now in the Injoying the Divine Vision of God, but for feare there may be any spot yet to detain her, I most humbly Crave your most holy Prayers (for the Love of God) for the Repose of her Soul. Requiescat in Pace.

(56) Aire 17.

The same Day & Year made also her holy Profession Sis^{r} Mary **Perkins,** now Called Sis^{r} Mary of St John Evangelist being Aged of 23 years.

Anno Domini 1639 the 18th of Sepr in our Convent of Poor Clares in Aire is happily deceas'd, Comforted with ye Sacraments of our Holy Mother ye Church, our Dearly Beloved Sister, Sister Mary of St John Evangelist Perkins, the 42nd year of her Age & ye 19th since her holy Profession, haveing Lived in the true Observance of our holy Rule, being indued wth a great humility, Charity, Austerity, and a most tedious Sickness, for ye Repose of her Soul we humbly beg y^{r} Prayers of Charity. Requiescat in Pace.

(57) Rouen 5th.

The same Day & Year made also her holy Profession; Sis^{r} Ann **Perkins,** now Call'd Sis^{r} Lucy Clare the 16th year of her Age.

Anno Domini 1658 in our Convent of Jesus, Mary, Joseph of poor Clares in Rouen, the 31st of March, is most happily departed this Life: furnished with all ye Rights of our Mother the Church. Our Dearly Beloved Sister, Sis^{r} Lucy Clare Perkins the 55th Year of her Age, and the 39 since her entrance into the holy Religion, haveing Lived therein very Religiously all her Life. We humbly crave, and earnestly recommend her unto y^{r} holy Suffrages for ye speedy rest of her Soul. Requiescat in Pace.

(58) The same Day and Year made also her holy Profession Sister Martha **Moris** now Call'd Sis^{r} Cicily Austin being Aged 16 Years.

Anno Domini 1663 the 16th of July in our Convent of Nazareth of poor Clares in Graveline, is happily departed this Life, furnished with ye rights of our holy Mother ye Church, Our Most Dearly beloved Sister, Sis^{r} Cicily Austin Moris, the 59th year of her Age & of her Religious Profession ye 43rd—wch time she hath spent in the true Spirit of her Vocation, by an humble patience & total Contempt of her self and adhering to God by holy Prayer & exercise of ye Divine presence, whereof she was particularly favoured by his goodness peaceably consumating her Life by a short, but most painful sickness, with a Singular meekness and Conformity to the Divine Will, for whose speedy rest we most humbly crave y^{r} Suffrages & Prayers of Charity. Requiescat in Pace.

(59) Anno Domini 1621 the 3rd of May made her holy Profession

Sis^r Elizabeth **Tilliard,** now Call'd Sis^r Collet Gertrude being Aged of 18 Years.

Anno Dni. 1630 the 4th of March in our Convent of Poor Clares of Nazareth in Graveline is happily deceased administered with ye Rights of our holy Mother ye Church, our D^r beloved Sis^r, Sis^r Collet Gertrude Tilliard, ye 27th Year of her Age, & ye 10th since her holy Profession. She Lived most vertuously, & was indeed in a most particular Manner with all which in humaine sight might render her agreeable to God & Man, & Singularly she had in practice Obedience, Humility, & a general perseverant Sweetness in Conversation which accompanied her to the last, with an exceeding patience during all y^t time of her Sickness. for the happy repose of her Soul we most humbly & instantly Crave the assistance of your holy Prayers of Charity. Requiescat in Pace.

(60) Aire 18

The same Day & Year made also her holy Profession, Sis^r Mary **Pickford** now Call'd Sis^r Mary Hierome being Aged of 22 Years.*

Anno Domini 1660 the 20th of May in our Convent of Poor Clares in Aire, of the Immaculate Conception of our B^d Lady is most happily departed this Life, our Dearly Beloved Sister, Sister Mary Hierome Pickford Aged of 61 Years & 39 since her Profession. She hath left us great Edification by her Singular patience, by her Supporting of Sufferances, for which I Confide she now Enjoys the reward, but fearing there may be any thing that may hinder her Speedy Felicity, I humbly beg the assistance of your holy Prayers. Requiescat in Pace.

(61) Anno Domini 1621 the 13th of June, made her holy Profession Sis^r Eliz **Alcock** now Call'd Sis^r Ursula Frances, the 33rd Year of her Age.†

Anno Dni. 1658 the 1st of Sepr in our Convent of Poor Clares in Graveline, of Nazareth, is happily departed this Life, furnish'd with ye Rights of our holy Mother ye Church, our Dearly beloved Sister Ursula Frances Alcock the 70th Year of her Age & 37th of her holy Profession, haveing been Profest 9 years before of ye 3rd Order of our ho: Fath^r, Serving during that time our Community

* Probably sister of the Rev. Edward Pickford *alias* Daniel, D.D., president of the English College at Lisbon, and Fr. John Jerome Pickford *alias* Daniel, O.S.F.

† Daughter of Thomas Alcock, of Frowton, co. Kent., Esq., by Dorothy, one of the six daughters and co-heiresses of John Gage, of Firle Place, co. Sussex, Esq., by Margaret, third daughter of William Shelley, of Michelgrove, co. Sussex, Esq. Upon the death of her grandfather, John Gage, no less than fifteen manors devolved upon his nephew and namesake, John Gage, who was created a baronet in 1622. She was sister to Mary, Mildred, and Jane Alcock above.

Domina Anna broune Abbatissa et fondatrix huius
conuentus de Betlehem Dunkercæ, obijt 29 Martij 1665,
ætatis 65° professionis 45° et prælaturæ suæ 15°,
Dilecta Deo, et hominibus cuius memoria in benedictione est

Emery Walker Ph. sc.

Mother Anne Ludovick Browne
Abbess of Poor Clares, Dunkirk
From the painting Ursuline Convent, Greenwich

Cath. Rec. Soc.

To face p. 55

in Nature of an extern lay Sister. Notwithstanding she was Grand Child to Mr Gage one of ye Chiefest founders of this our Convent, who gave her a fortune equal to her other Sisters he placed here, but she rather Choose for ye above mention'd term of 9 years to serve our Community as an out Sister & both then & ever Since her entrance until her decripied Years hath Indefatigably employed her forces with humility, Zeal & fervour for the profit of our Monastery, to whom she was a most beneficial member, & of a most Edifying & exemplar life, for when for Age & infirmaty she was forced to cease her Corporal Labours, she applyed her self with new fervour to Prayer and to all Enteriour Exercises that might make her more pleasing to her heavenly Spouse, Suporting with humble Submission to his divine will those Indispositions & infirmatys that attends Old Age. Which makes us Confide that she is already in ye full fruition of Eternal happiness, but as the Judgments of God are inscrutable I Confide you will allow for the assistance of her Soul your Prayers & Suffrages. Requiescat in Pace.

(62) Dunquerque 1.

Anno Dni 1621 the 22nd of Augt made her Holy Profession Sister Ann **Browne**, now Call'd Sis^{r} Anne of St Ludovick being Aged of 19 years.*

Anno Domini 1665 ye 29th of March being Palm Sunday in our Convent of Bethlem of poor Clares in Dunquerque is happily departed this Life to receive as we hope ye Palme of Victorie our R^{d} & Dr Moth^{r} Abess Sis^{r} Anne Ludovick Browne, administered wth ye rights of our holy Mother ye Church aged of 63 Years, & professed 44, haveing Lived 32 of them in our Dr Convent of Graveline, from whence she was sent by holy obedience wth some other Religious to found our Convent in Dunquerque wch she hath by ye most divine assistance most happily ended, after having Laboured for ye space of 13 Years & sustain'd many Crosses, she was adorned wth a most eminent Charity, a most firm Confidence in ye divine Providence, & a most profound humility, & a most admirable patience particularly in ye suporting of a lingering infirmaty for 16 Years, her last Sickness was long & painful, but Suported wth angelical resignation, we humbly crave ye assistance of y^{r} holy Prayers for ye repose of her Soul. Requiescat in Pace.

(63) Rouen 6.

The same Day & Year made also her holy Profession, Sis^{r}

* One of the two daughters and only children by his first wife of Sir Henry Browne of Kiddington, and sister of Magdalen above. Sir Henry married secondly Mary, daughter of Sir Philip Hungate, of Saxton, co. York, Bart., and was father of Sir Peter. whose son Henry was created a baronet in 1659.

Anne **Yeates**, now call'd Sis[r] Anne Clare, being Aged of 18 Years.*

Anno Döm: 1667 the 24th of Jany in our Convent of Jesus, Maria Joseph, of poor Clares in Rouen is most happily departed this Life administered with ye rights of our holy Moth[r] ye Church, our Dearly beloved Sis[r] Anne Clare Yeates, Aged 65 & ye 47th since her Profession, which she made in our Dear Convent at Graveline from whence she was sent by holy Obedience for the beginning of this Convent, where she has left us great examples for our Edification by her Religious comportment singular sweetness, pietie & devotion, And hath finished her happy course by sustaining a most painfull sickness with great Patience & intire Conformity to ye will of God. We most humbly crave the assistance of your Prayers & Suffrages for the Repose of her Soul. Requiescat in Pace.

(64) Aire 19.

The same Day & Year made her holy Profession Sis[r] Mary **Evelinge**, now Call'd Sis[r] Marie Alexious being Aged of 17 Years.

Anno Doñi 1657 the 6th day of Ap[l] in our Convent of Poor Clares in Aire of y[e] Immaculate Conception of our B[d] Lady is happily departed this life, our Dearly beloved Sister, Sis[r] Mary Alexious Evelinge, having receiv'd y[e] Sacraments of our holy Moth[r] the Church, being aged of 53 and 35 since her holy Profession, she hath left us much edified by her strict observance of Silence, & holy Poverty, which she Cherish'd like a true Child of our holy Father. I Confide she now injoys y[e] reward of her fidelity, but as the judgments of God are secreet: I most humbly beg y[r] Assistance of your Prayers and Suffrages. Requiescat in Pace.

(65) Aire 20.

The same Day & Year made also her Profession Sister Elizabeth **Kerton**, now Call'd Sis[r] Frances Magdalin, being Aged of 18 Years.

Anno Doñi 1671 the 29th of Ap[l] in our Convent of the Immaculate Conception of our B[d] Lady in Aire, of poor Clares, is happily departed this Life administred with the Sacraments of our holy Mother y[e] Church, our D[r] beloved Sister Frances Magdalen Kerton, being Aged of 68 and 50 since her holy Profession, haveing left us an example of most prompt obedience; in which she excell'd, which makes us hope she hath received her reward in heaven, but since y[e] Judgments of God are inscrutable, & not to be failing in my duty to her I most humbly beg the assistance of your Suffrages and Sacrifices. Requiescat in Pace.

* Daughter of Thomas Yate (or Yates), of Lyford, and sister of Frances above.

(66) The same Day and Year made also her Profession, Sis[r] Mary **Morris**, now Call'd Sister Mary Clare aged of 16.

Anno Doni 1661 the 3[d] of Octob[r] in our Convent of poor Clares in Graveline of Nazareth is most happily departed this Life, our D[r] Sister Mary Clare Morris, Strengthened with all the rights of our holy Mother y[e] Church, being Aged of 57 and of her Profession 42, haveing ever since her entrance into y[e] holy Religion been very exact in the strict observance of our holy Rule; giving us great example of humility, abjection, patience, holy Recolection & Silence, hardly ever speaking an unnecesary word, being also most exemplar in holy poverty, for the happy rest of whose Soul we most humbly beg the assistance of your Prayers and Suffrages. Requiescat in Pace.

(67) Dunquerque 2nd.

Anno Domi: 1622 the 8th day of Sep[r], Sis[r] Elizabeth **Berington** now Call'd Sis[r] Eliz: Magdalin made her Profession, being Aged of 19 Years.*

Anno Dmni: the 12th of May 1666 in our Convent of Bethlem of poor Clares in Dunquerque is happily departed this Life, furnish'd with all y[e] Rights of our holy Mother y[e] Church, Our dearly & well beloved R[d] Moth[r] Vicaress Sis[r] Elizabeth Magdalin Berington, the 68th year of her Age, and y[e] 44th since her holy Profession, haveing Lived very Exemplarly 33 Years in our Convent at Graveline, & exercised several offices very laudably, particularly that of Mistress of Novices. And from thence was sent by holy Obedience to assist at y[e] foundation of y[e] poor Convent. Where she hath acquited herself of y[e] Office of Vicaress with great humility, prudence, & Zeal of Regular observance, & hath left us rare examples of singular patience during a long & painful sickness, where of she dyed most sweetly, amongst y[e] teares & prayers of her Comunity, who craves in all humility the Prayers & Suffrages of y[e] Community for y[e] Repose of her Soul. Requiescat in Pace.

(68) The same Day & Year made also her holy Profession Sis[r] Margaret **Poole**, now Call'd Sis[r] Clare Margaret, being aged of 19 years.

Anno Domi 1659 the 22nd of July in our Convent of Naz[th] of poor Clares in Graveline is happily departed this Life, Administred with all the Sacraments of our holy Moth[r] y[e] Church, our dearly beloved Sister, Sister Clare Margaret Poole, the 44th Year of her Age and the 28th since her entrance to Religion, during which time she hath ever exercised her self in the fervent exercises of Religious discipline, true humility, & holy poverty, & in all

* Daughter of William Berington, of Winsley Hall, co. Hereford, Esq., by Eleanor, daughter and heiress of Richard Goodman, chief-yeoman of the buttery to Queen Elizabeth.

conform'd her self to ye spirit of her Vocation. Most particularly testify'd in her last Sickness, which was long & very painful, for whose speediest rest we humbly crave the assistance of y^r Prayers. Requiescat in Pace.

(69) The same Day & Year made also her holy Profession Sis^r Constance **Coufaud** now Call'd Sis^r Catherine of St Dominick. Aged of 22 Years.*

Anno Domi: 1664 the 17th of Novr is happily Departed this Life, furnish'd wth y^e rights of our holy $Moth^r$ y^e Church, in our Convent of Nazareth of poor Clares in Graveline, Our Dr Sister Catherine Dominick Confand y^e 65th Year of her Age, & 42 since her Profession, during which time she render'd her self very assiduous in y^e practice of those vertues suting to her State. Chiefly zeal for y^e Divine honour. The 16 last Years of her Life she was afflicted with Appoplexical fitts, & other very sensible paines, and interiour sufferance, which she sustain'd with exemplar patience, & Conformity to ye Divine Will. For ye speedy repose of her Soul we humbly crave y^r Prayers of Charity. Requiescat in Pace.

(70) Rouen 7.

Anno Dmi 1623 ye 15th of .Sis^r Margaret **Sternhold**, now Call'd Sis^r Mary Winifrid made her holy Profession, Aged of 26 Years.

Anno Dmi 1674 the 22^d of Jan^{ry} in our Convent of Jesus, Mary, Joseph of poor Clares in Rouen, is most happily departed this Life, Strengthened with the Rights of our holy Mother ye Church, our Vene: Mother Jubilarion, Sis^r Margaret Winifred Sternhold, the 77 year of her Age & 52 since her Profession, haveing spent 22 Years in our Dr Convent of Graveline in Indifatigable Labours for ye Service of ye Comunity, & both their and here was Indifatigable in ye observance of all regular Disciplin. A great Lover of holy Poverty, & ye Contempt of her self, ever seeking & disireing ye worst of all things for her own use, treating her body with great Rigour & Austerity, but was most Charitable to others, her last Sickness was sharp & painful, which she suffer'd wth an Invincible patience & Conformity to ye Divine will without ye least Complaint, concealing as much as she cou'd her Sufferances, wch had ever been her practise, we most humbly intreat ye assistance of y^r prayers for ye repose of her Soul. Requiescat in Pace.

(71) Anno Dmi: 1624 ye 28th of May made her holy Profession being aged of 17 Years, Sis^r Mary **Carlton**, now call'd Sister Mary Bonaventure.

* Daughter of William Cuffaud, of Cuffaud, in the parish of Basing, co. Southampton, Esq., by Mary, daughter of Sir Geoffrey Pole, of Lordington, co. Sussex, Knt., brother of Reginald, Cardinal Pole.

Anno Dmi: 1669 ye 8th of Augt in this our Convent of Naz: of Poor Clares in Graveline is happily departed this Life furnish'd wth all ye rights of our holy Moth^r^ the Church, our Dearly beloved Sis^r^, Sis^r^ Mary Bonaven: Carlton ye 60 Year of her Age, & 42 since her holy Profession, which she hath spent wth great fidelity in ye Service of holy Religion, where unto she was a most profitable Member, chiefly for her zeal of Religious Disciplin Educating her Novices in ye strick observance of our holy Rule, Constitutions, & Cerimonies, rendering her self a true observer of wch she instructed her Young in her Submission & Respect to her Superiors, as well as her humble & affable Comportment was Singular to all, the hopes of her present felicity moderates ye loss we have sustained by ye death of so Sufficient a Member, which with all Ernestness I Commend to y^r^ Prayers for Charity. Requiescat in Pace.

(72) Rouen 8.

The same day & year made also her holy Profession Sis^r^ Margaret **Bedingfield**, now Call'd Sis^r^ Margaret Ignatia, being Aged of 19 Years.*

Anno Dmi: 1670 the 6th of March in our Convent of Jesus, Mary, Joseph of poor Clares in Rouen, is most happily departed this Life amidst ye Prayers & tears of her most afflicted Children, our most Venerable & Dr Mother Abb: Sis^r^ Margaret Ignatia Bedingfield, the 66 year of her Age & 46th of her holy Profession, 20 whereof she most praysably lived in our Convent of Graveline, & was sent by holy Obedience from Retice wth 14 other Religious to begin this our Convent at Rouen ye year 1644, & was Chosen Vicaress ye same year for ye assistance of our R^d^ Moth^r^ Foundress, after whose death she was Cannonically Elected Abbess which charge she exercised eleven years in ye perfect practise of all vertues sutable there unto, her Compation and Charitie to others was so Singular y^t^ we may say of her (as of holy Job) y^t^ mercy hath grown with her from her Infancy. She being Continually solicitous to do good to all, & Comfort those she saw afflicted, by Resigneing them (73) to the Divine Will, of which she gave us all rare example in her own person, in all ye accidents of y^s^ Life, that she had even naturalized her self there unto so perfectly y^t^ she wou'd say in occations y^t^ she cou'd finde no opposition to any Sufferance comeing from ye hand of God, & had always in her Mouth these words *Fiat Voluntas tua*, the like may be said of her humility & neglect of her self, with a perfect disengagement from all things in this world, in fine all vertues seem'd to be practis'd by her above ye common, which gives us great hopes of her present felicitie, yet if any thing remaines in her Soul to be purified, we humbly beg ye assistance of y^r^ prayers of Charitie. Requiescat in Pace.

* Second daughter of Francis Bedingfeld, of Redlingfield, co. Suffolk, Esq., by Katherine, daughter of Sir John Fortescue, chancellor of the exchequer. Her ten sisters likewise became nuns.

(74) The same day and year also made her holy Profession Sis[r] Ann **Wright**, now Call'd Sis[r] Ann of the Conception, being Aged of 22 Years.*

Anno Dmi 1633 the 9th of Jan[ry] in our Convent of Naz[th] of poor Clares in Graveline is happily departed this life, strengthened wth y[e] Rights of our holy Moth[r] the Church, our dearly beloved Sir[r], Sis[r] Ann of y[e] Concep[n] Wright, y[e] 29th Year of her Age, & y[e] 7th since her Profession, being truly Zealous of her Vocation, strict in holy Obedience, retired & devout, during her Sickness w[ch] was both long & teadious, giving us great example of patience and resignation to y[e] will of God, for the happy rest of her Soul, we humbly beg y[e] help of your Prayers for Charity, for y[e] love of God. Requiescat in Pace.

(75) Anno Dmi 1625 the 13th of June made her holy Profes[n] Sis[r] Ann **Giffard**, now Call'd Sis[r] Agatha Frances, being Aged of 19.†

Anno Dmi 1633 the 8th of Ap[l] in our Convent of poor Clares in Graveline, happily enjoy'd the change of mortality, to immortality, furnish'd wth all the rights of our holy Moth[r] the Church, our dearly beloved Sister, Sis[r] Agatha Frances Gifford, Aged 29 & 8 years since her ho: Profession, the divine mercy had Singularly indued her with a faithful Co-operation to y[e] spirit of her vocation & the vertues suiting unto it, as a most profound humility, mildness, devotion, & holy poverty, wherein till her death she left us most Singular & practical examples, for y[e] full releasment of what may yet detain her Soul, we most humbly beg the assistance of y[r] holy Prayers. Requiescat in Pace.

(76) Anno Dmi 1625 the twenty-fifth of Decemb[r] Sis[r] Eugenia **Jerningham** made her Profession being Aged of 16 Years, now Call'd Sis[r] Clare Eugenia.

Anno Dmi 1680 the 23[d] of Oct[r] in our Convent of Naz: of poor Clares in Graveline is happily departed this Life strengthened with all y[e] Rights of our holy Mot: y[e] Church, our Ven: Moth[r] Jub[n] Sis[r] Clare Eugenia Jerningham, y[e] 70th year of her Age & 55 since her holy Profess[n] w[ch] time she hath spent in an exact observance of our holy Rule & Constitutions, being most exemplar for her Zeal for y[e] divine Office from whence either Night nor day she very seldom dispens'd wth her self, and even

* Daughter of John Wright, of Kelvedon Hall, co Essex, Esq., by his first wife Anne, daughter of Sir Edward Sulyard, of Wetherden, co. Suffolk, Knt.

† Daughter of Thomas Gifford, Esq. (son of John Gifford, of London, and Dunton Walet, co. Essex, Esq., M.D.), who acquired Burstall, co. Leicester, in right of his wife Anne, daughter and heiress of Gregory Brookesby, of Burstall, Esq. Her sister Mary married George Neville, 10th Lord Abergavenny, and her brother Henry Gifford was created a baronet in 1660.

to her death, & altho she was ye Eldest in ye house yet by her humility she esteem'd her self as ye youngest, employing her self in all servil exercises. She was Singular in Charity by giving wth much content her assistance to any one & no less had she for y^{e} Soules in purgatory, for whose Sollasé & releasment she was a faithful advocate, her Confidence in God, & devotion was great towards y^{e} B^{d} Sacraments. for her speedy enjoying of eternal felicity, we humbly beg y^{e} assistance of y^{e} Prayers. Requiescat in Pace.

(77) Rouen y^{e} 9$^{th.}$

Anno Dñi: 1626 the 29th of June Sis^{r} Eliz: **Sallisbury** now Call'd Sis^{r} Eliz: Peter, made her Profession being aged of 26 years.

Anno Dñi 1661 the 20th of Sepr in our Convent of Jesus, Mary, Joseph of English poor Clares in Rouén, is most happily departed this Life, Strengthened wth all ye Rights of our holy Moth^{r} ye Church, our Dr Sis , Sis^{r} Elizabeth Peter Sallisbury ye 64 year of her Age, & 36 of her Profession, of which she spent 19 years in our Dr Convent of Graveline, and both here & there hath left us Singular Edification of vertue, namely a strict Observance of holy Poverty, & an exact fidelity in ye least observance of our holy Religion, praising God with great fidelity & affection night & day in the Choir, without exception, or Consideration of her weak, little, & tender body, wth by her Love to God made her also to go thorough with joy & Courage ye austerities of our holy Rule, & that her last & painful Sickness wch Singular patience & conformity to ye Divine will, we humbly crave ye assistance of your Prayers of Charitie for ye repose of her Soul.. Requiescat in Pace.

(78) The same day & year made also her Profession Sis^{r} Ann **Standish**, now Call'd Sis^{r} Ann Laurence being aged of 19 years.*

Anno Dñi 1664 the 29th of Decemb^{r} in our Convent of poor Clares in Graveline is happily departed this Life, Strengthened with all the Sacram^{ts} of our holy Mother the Church, our Dr Sister, Sister Ann Laurence Standish the 58th Year of her age & 39 of her being Religious, which time she spent in faithful Service to the holy Religion, not admitting dispensations from Laborious toile & regular observance, till some months before her death: tho' she was afflicted with a Cancer in her breast, to her extream torment which Marterdom she Indured wth invincible patience & serenity, & sweetly rendered her Soul, for whoes happy rest we humbly crave the assistance of y^{r} Prayers and Suffrages. Requiescat in Pace.

* Daughter of Thurstan Standish, of Burgh Hall, and Gatehurst in Shevington, in the parish of Standish, co. Lancaster, Esq., by Elizabeth, daughter of Thomas Anderton, of Chorley, Esq.

(79) The same Day & Year made also her holy Professn Sisr Luysia **Taylor**, now Call'd Sister Luysia Clare aged 16 years.

Anno Dñi 1667 the 27th of Augt in our Convent of Naz: of English poor Clares in Graveline is most happily departed this Life, Strengthen'd wth ye Sacramts of our holy Mothr ye Church at 7 o'clock in ye Morning, our most Rd & Dr Mothr Abbess, Sisr Luysia Clare Taylor, the 58 Year of her Age, and 43 of her holy Profession the 10th day of her Sickness, wch was a Violent feaver, accompany'd with grivious paines, indured with admirable patience & Conformity to ye divine Will, amidst ye tears & prayers of her afflicted children, whom she left truly Desolate, but enrich'd by the examples we retain of her Vertues, chiefly a profound humility, perseverant sweetness in her Conversation, a general Charity towards all, wch sbe exercised in several offices, haveing been several terms Portress, Mistress of Novices, and finally being chosen Abbess, she bore ye burden thereof with Indifatigable pains for ye good of Religion, & every member thereof 14 Years, ever haveing a Singular Confidence in God; in our Bd Lady & ye assistance of ye Soules in Purgatory, for whose Relief she was most peculiar devoted, our loss in her deprivation is unspeakable, for ye speediest rest of her Soul, we humbly beg ye Assistance of yr Prayers and Suffrages. Requiescat in Pace.

(80) Anno Dñi (1626) the 12th of Augst made her holy Profession Sis: Dorothy **Giffard**, now Call'd Sisr Dorothy Joseph Aged 22 Years.*

Anno Dñi 1673 the 18th of Febry in our Convent of English poor Clares of Nazareth in Graveline, is happily departed this Life, Strengthen'd wth all the Sacraments of our holy Mother the Church, our Dearly beloved Sister, Sisr Dorothy Joseph Giffard, Aged of 69 and yr 48th of her holy Profession, haveing serv'd as an exampler modell of vertues, suting to her Vocation, namely a great neglect of her self, sweetness in Conversation, & an assiduous well spending of her time, haveing exercised very Laudably for several Years the office of Infirmarion, finally a Singular patience & conformitie to ye divine will in frequent Sicknesses, principally in this her last, we humbly crave ye assistance of yr good Prayers of Charity for the speedyest rest of her Soul. Requiescat in Pace.

(81) Anno Dñi (1629) the 26th of July made her holy Profession Sisr Alice **Abbott** now Call'd Sisr Martha Clare, Aged of 36 Years.

Anno Dñi 1632 the 20th of Novr in our Convent of English poor Clares of Nazareth in Graveline is happily departed ye Life

* Second daughter of Peter Giffard, of Chillington Hall, co. Stafford. Esq., by Frances, daughter of Walter Fowler, of St Thomas' Priory, co. Stafford, Esq.

Emery Walker ph. sc.

Mother Luysia Clare Taylor
4th Abbess of Poor Clares, Gravelines
From the painting, Ursuline Convent, Greenwich

To face p. 62

strengthened wth all y^e^ rights of our holy Moth^r^ ye Church, our Dr Sister, Sis^r^ Martha Clare Abbott, ye 40th Year of her Age, & 14th of her being Religious, 10 years of which she spent in serving our Comun : in quality of an extern Lay Sister, being Professt of ye 3^d^ Order of our holy Father St Francis. She was very devout, & had a great Confidence in ye divine mercyes, & in a long & painful Sickness, hath much edified us by her patience, we humbly crave your Prayers of Charitie for ye repose of her Soul. Requiescat in Pace.

(82) Anno Dñi 1629 the 4th of Decemb^r^ made her Profession Sister Mary **Crooke,** now Call'd Sis^r^ Mary Frances being aged of 49 Years.

Anno Dñi 1650 the 25th of March in our Convent, of English poor Clares of Nazareth in Graveline, is most happily departed this Life Strengthened with all the Rights of our holy Mother the Church, our Dr Sister, Sister Mary Frances Crooke the 70th year of her age & year 21st of her Profession, a poor Clare, haveing been professed 9 years before of ye 3^d^ order of our holy Father S Francis, an extern Lay Sister, & in that quality served our Convent with great fidelity and humility, as well when she was an out Sister, as since her entrance into our Convent; with great zeal aplying her self to Laborious and hard Labour, haveing a great Contempt of her self, & a great Love of holy Silence, Consumating her Life by a painfull Sickness, for ye Speediest rest of her Soul, we humbly beg the Assistance of your holy Prayers. Requiescat in Pace.

(83) Anno Dñi 1630 the 9th of Augt made her holy Professi: Sister Ursula **Gifford,** now Call'd Sis^r^ Ursula **Collet,** being aged of 23 years.*

Anno Dñi 1688 the 4th of March in our Convent of Nazareth of English poor Clares in Graveline, is happily departed this Life, Strengthened with all ye Sacraments of our holy Mother ye Church, our Venerable Jubilarion Sis^r^ Ursula Collett Gifford, ye 81st Year of her Age & ye 59th since her Entrance into ye holy Religion, she hath left us much edified by her fidelity in the practise of those vertues most suitable to her holy Vocation, which she ever had a high esteem of, she was very mild, humble & sweet in her Comportment & Conversation, gratefull for any service renderd her, most Respectful to Superiors, and Constant to her Devotions, reciting notwithstanding her Infirmaties, and great age the divine Office daily untill 5 days before her death. We most humbly beg ye assistance of y^r^ holy Prayers for the happy rest of her Soul. Requiescat in Pace.

(84) Rouen 10.

The same Day & Year made also her holy Profession, Sis^r^ Eliza-

* Fourth daughter of Peter Giffard and sister of Dorothy above.

beth **Hone**, now Call'd Sis[r] Frances Clare, being Aged of 26 years.

Anno Dñi: 1672 the 20th of February in our Convent of Jesus, Mary, Joseph of English poor Clares in Rouen is most happily Departed this Life, furnish'd with all the Rights of our holy Moth[r] ye Church, our Dr Sis[r] Sister Frances Clare Hone, the 70th Year of her Age, & ye 43 since her Profession, 15 of which she spent in our Dear Convent of Graveline very exemplarly, from whence she was sent by Holy Obedience with 14 others y[e] Year 1644 to begin our Convent at Rouen, for y[e] best establishment of which, she ever aplyed her self with a Constant Zeale to y[e] Last moment of her Life, & as God had from y[e] 1st begining presented her with a Singular grace in her Vocation, highly to esteem all that was to his Service so did she faithfully cooperate on her part to render her self in things most pleasing to his Divine Majesty, & hath left us a most admirable example of Obedience, a vertue she most highly esteemed, saying it was y[e] secure way to Salvation. Her humility, was no less exemplar, which made her ever seek the worst & poorest of all things, being ever ready to take all faultes upon her self and to Excuse others, most sweet & mild in Conversation. (85) Charitable and compationate to all, and in y[e] Sharp trials of Interiour and Exterior Suffrances by which God was pleased to try her, was most patient, & sweetly Resigned to the Divine Will, but as y[e] Judgments of God are unknown, lest anything may detaine her Speedy rest, I humbly crave ye assistance of your holy Prayers and Suffrages. Requiescat in Pace.

(86) The same Day & Year made also her holy Profession Sis[r] Elizabeth **Bradshagh**, now Call'd Sis[r] Elizabeth Clare the 19th year of her Age.*

Anno Dñi: 1639 the 17th of Feb[ry] in our Convent of Nazareth of English poor Clares in Graveline, is most happily departed this Life, Strengthened with the Rights of our holy Mother ye Church, our Dr Sister, Sister Elizabeth Clare Bradshagh, ye 28th Year of her Age, & 10th since her entrance into holy Religion, wherein she served our Lord wth Singular Innocency & purity of heart, Zeal, & fervour of Religious discipline. And her own advancement in all true Virtue, & in her last Sickness left us great examples of patience & Conformity to ye Divine Will, for ye happy rest of her Soul we most humbly crave the assistance of y[r] Prayers & Suffrages of Charity. Requiescat in Pace.

(87) Anno Dñi 1630 the 19th of Augt made her holy Profession Sis[r] Ann **Bradshagh**, now Call'd Sis[r] Mary Anna, being aged of 18 Years.†

* Third daughter of Roger Bradshaigh, of The Haigh, co. Lancaster, Esq., by Anne, daughter of Christopher Anderton, of Lostock Hall, co. Lancaster, Esq.

† Fourth daughter of Roger Bradshaigh and sister of Elizabeth above.

Emery Walker Ph. sc.

Sister Elizabeth Clare Bradshaigh
Poor Clare of Gravelines
From a photograph of the painting at Haigh Hall, Wigan,
kindly supplied by the Earl of Crawford and Balcarres

To face p. 64

Emery Walker Ph.sc.

Sister Mary Ann Collet Bradshaigh
Poor Clare of Gravelines
From a photograph of the painting at Haigh Hall, Wigan
kindly supplied by the Earl of Crawford and Balcarres

To face p. 65.

Anno Dñi 1666 the 18th of Sepr in our Convent of Naz: of English poor Clares in Graveline, is most happily departed this Life, furnish'd with all ye Rights of our holy Mother ye Church, our Dr Sister, Sisr Collett, Mary Ann Bradshagh, the 55th Year of her Age, & 37 of her holy Profession, all which time she most laudably spent in ye true and constant practice of those vertues most sutable to her holy Vocation, being most exact in holy Obedience & in all other Observances, even to ye least Cerimony of our holy Religion, to which she hath ever been a most beneficial Member, by her great Zeal, prudence & Charity, a patron of patience by her humble Conformity to ye divine Will, in Suporting above the space of 20 years most painfull Infirmaties, for the Speediest rest of whose Soul we humbly beg ye assistance of yr holy Prayers. Requiescat in Pace.

(88) The same Day & Year made also her holy Profession, Sister Dorothy **Anderton**, now Call'd Sisr. Dorothy Ignatia Aged of 24 Years.*

Anno Dñi 1658 the 14th of July in our Convent of English poor Clares of Nazareth in Graveline is happily Departed this Life Strengthened with ye Sacraments of our holy Mother ye Church, our Dr Sister, Sisr Dorothy Ignatia Anderton, ye 57th Year of her Age, & 29th of her holy Profession, she hath given us great example of abjection & holy Poverty, with a totall neglect of her self treating her body with great Austeritie, & in her last Sickness exerciseing great patience, & Conformity to the divine Will, for her Speedy enjoying of Everlasting Glorie, We most humbly entreat the assistance of your Prayer & Suffrages. Requiescat in in Pace.

(87) The same Day & Year made also her holy Profession, Sister Barbera **Hobert**, now Call'd Sisr Barbara Xaveria, being Aged of 20 Years.

Anno Dñi: 1663 the 24th of Augst in our Convent of Naz: of English poor Clares in Graveline, is happily Departed this Life, furnish'd with all ye rights of our holy Mother ye Church our Dr Sister, Sisr Barbara Xaveria Hobert, ye 53d Year of her Age & 38th of her Profession, during which time she hath given us great example of abjection, & holy Poverty, with a great zeale of ye strict observance of regular disciplin & exercised in her last Sickness, (which was tedious and painful) Singular Patience & Conformity to ye Divine Will, for ye happiest rest of whose Soul we humbly beg ye assistance of yr Prayers. Requiescat in Pace.

(90) Anno Dñi 1632 ye 26th Sepr made her Profession Sister

* Eldest daughter of Roger Anderton, of Birchley Hall, co. Lancaster, Esq., by Anne, daughter of Edward Stanford, of Perry Hall, co. Stafford, Esq., and first cousin to Elizabeth and Anne Bradshaigh above.

Elizabeth **Giffard**, now Call'd Sis^{r} Elizabeth Frances Aged of 17 Years.*

Anno Dñi 1668 ye 28th of Ap^{l} in our Convent of Naz: of English poor Clares in Graveline is most happily departed y^{s}. life administred with all the Rights of our holy Mother ye Church, our Dr Sister, Sis^{r} Elizabeth Frances Gifford, ye 52^{d} Year of her Age & 33^{d} of her holy Profession, haveing for several yeares exercised her self in humble & toylesome Labours, to ye great service of holy Religion, after which being withheld by a Languishing painfull Infirmity, she adicted her self to long Prayers, to which she renderd her self indispensable, notwithstanding her great indispositions, her patience and Conformity to ye divine will was Singular in her last Sickness, we humbly crave ye assistance of your Prayers, & Suffrages for ye repose of her Soul. Requiescat in Pace.

(91) The same day & Year made also her holy Profession Sister Catherine **Carrelton,** now Call'd Sis^{r} Catherine Joseph, being Aged of 24 Years.

Anno Dñi 1654 the 26th of Jully is most happily deceased y^{s} Life furnished with ye Rights of our holy Moth^{r} ye Church, our Dr Sister, Sister Catherine Joseph Carrelton ye 46th Year of her Age, & ye 22nd of her Profession, poor Clare of our Convent of poor Clares of Naz: in Graveline, who by divine disposition, & our Ld Bishop's Obedience, was one y^{t} was refuged wth our R^{d} Moth^{r} Vicaress, and 2 more of our Dr Sisters in ye Convent of ye Penitent Capucinesses in St Omers, upon ye sad accident of Ruine of our Convent, by ye blowing up of ye Maggasine, where she hath happily attain'd to ye end of her Pilgrimage, to ye great edification of that holy family whose Charity to her and ye rest is inexpressible, consumating her Life in true & solid vertue, which she hath practiced ever since her entrance into holy Religion, particularly Zeale for her own perfection, and punctuality of Religious discipline, exact obedience, & great Love of holy poverty, leaving also Singular examples of patience & Conformity to ye divine will in her last Sickness, for ye happy repose of whose Soul, we humbly crave ye assistance of y^{r} Suffrages & Prayers. Requiescat in Pace.

(92) Rouen 11th.

Anno Dñi: 1633 the 4th of Octob^{r} made her holy Profession, Sister Winifred **Giffard,** now Call'd Sis^{r} Winifred Clare, aged of 16 years.†

Anno Dñi: 1706 the 23^{d} of Nov: in our Convent of Jesus,

* Sixth daughter of Peter Giffard and sister of Dorothy and Ursula above.

† Seventh daughter of Peter Giffard and sister of Dorothy, Ursula, and Elizabeth above.

Maria, Joseph, of English poor Clares in Rouen, is most happily departed this Life, furnish'd with all y[e] Rights of our holy Moth[r] y[e] Church, our most Venerable most Rev[d] & dearly beloved Moth[r] Abbess, Sister Winifred Clare Giffard, 3[d] Abbess of this Convent, the 90th year of her Age & 75 since her entrance into Religion, 12 whereof she spent in our D[r] Convent of Graveline, in an exact Regularity, & in y[e] practise of all Religious vertues, particularly Silence, recollection & abstraction, & was by holy Obedience sent with 14 more to begin this Monistary, for y[e] accomplishment of which, she underwent many Difficulties, giving great assistance to our Venerable Moth[r] foundress, who Imploy'd her in y[e] chief Offices of y[e] house, after whose death she was chosen Vicaress, which Office she perform'd wth great Charity, & Zeal for Religious Observance for 11 years, after which she was chosen Abbess, governing with Singular Zeale, Charity, & prudence as long as Age & Infirmity permitted her, (93) Her Confidence in divine providence was no less admirable than y[e] aversion she had for y[e] praise & applauses of Men saying that poor Clares ought neither to be known, nor spoken of, her devotion to y[e] holy Sacraments made her during y[e] long term of her Superiority to receive daily that most delicious food, saying she drew strength from y[e] same, to support that heavy Burden, which to y[e] general Satisfaction of her Communitie she laudably exercised 31 years, deposeing her self 5 years before her death. Nothwithstanding y[e] Opposition of her Religious, who were at last Oblig'd to acquiesce, her Age and infirmities not permiting her Longer to undergoe y[e] fatigue of that charge, her patience, humility, sweetness, and submission with which she bore her continual infirmities was admirable, in fine being ripe for heaven, some weeks before her death, she fell into a dropsy, which soon led her to her long desired home, having with Singular piety & presence received her Creator, she sweetly slept in our Lord to live eternally. Requiescat in Pace.

(94) Dunquerque 3[rd.]

Anno Dni: (1633) ye 4th of Octob[r] Sr Mary **Clarke**, now Call'd Sist[r] Mary Evangelist made her Profession, Aged of 18 Years.

Ann Dñi (1685) ye 25th of Feb[ry] in our Convent of Bethlem of English poor Clares in Dunquerque is most happily departed this Life, Strengthened with ye rights of our holy Mother ye Church, our most Venerable Moth[r] Jubilarion Sr Mary Evangelist Clarke ye 70th year of her Age & 53 since her entrance into Religion, she was one of the first y[t] was sent from our Convent of Graveline for y[e] foundation of this our Convent at Dunquerque, in which she took great pains, & has left us a true Example of ye practise of all sorts of Solid Vertues, in which she grounded her Novices, have suported with an Admirable Patience this her last Sickness, which was long & sharp, for the happy Repose of whose Soul we most humbly beg ye Assistance of y^r^ Prayers & Suffrages. Requiescat in Pace.

(95) Anno Dñi: (1634) the 22nd of Augt Sis^r^ Elizabeth **Marcher**, now Call'd Sis^r^ Eliz: Joseph, made her holy Profession Aged of 24 years.

Anno Dñi: (1682) the 23rd of Sepr in our Convent of Nazareth of English poor Clares in Graveline is most happily departed this life strengthend with all the Rights of our holy Mother ye Church, our Dear Sis^r^, Sister Eliz: Joseph Marcher, the 77 year of her Age & 49 since her entrance into ye holy Religion, imploying the long term thereof in ye exact Observance of our Rule, not dispenseing with her self neither for Age, nor Infirmities from conventual Observance, untill 5 months before her death, which time her Dr Spouse was pleased to trye her fidelity, haveing by a Palsey taken from her ye use of her Limbs, & speech, which Visitation she suported wth Admirable patience, & resignation to ye divine Will. She was one of so great Prayer y^t^ nothwithstanding the imployments of dispenser & sick mother, which for several years she very laudably exercised. She found daily time to spend several hours therein. She was very humble, Obedient, & Submissive to Superiors, to whom she ever bore a Dutiful Respect, if there remains yet any defects to be purged, ye assistance of y^r^ Prayers is humbly requested. Requiescat in Pace.

(96) Anno Dñi (1635) the 22nd of Augt Sis^r^ Catharine **Victor**, now Call'd Sis^r^ Cath: Clare made her Profession, Aged 23 years.*

Anno Dñi: (1662) the 8th of Jan^ry^ in our Convent of English poor Clares of Naz: in Graveline, is happily departed this Life, strengthened with the Rights of our holy Mother ye Church, our D^r^ & beloved Sister, Sis^r^ Catherine Clare Victor, ye 50th Year of her Age, & 27th of her Profession, all which time she hath spent in continual labours & left us Singular examples of ye true Spirit of our holy Foundress, treating her poor Body, as if she had been Insensible to Suffrances, & ended her Pilgrimage as she Lived in a total Conformity, & abandoning her self to ye Divine Will & holy Obedience. She hath exercised several Offices to the General content of all the Community. Principaly that of M^rs^ of Novices, & that of Sick Mother, for several years, Exerciseing it with singular Charity & happily ended her Course in the same employ to receive as we hope ye eternal reward of her Labours which that she may the sooner injoy, the Assistance of your Prayers is humbly intreated. Requiescat in Pace.

* Daughter of Edward Victor, of Cornwall, and sister of the Rev. Francis Victor *alias* Bishop and Williams, archdeacon of the Chapter, who died in 1683, and Sr. Frances Victor, a Bridgettine nun of Syon, who died at Lisbon in 1681.

(97) Rouen 12.

Anno Dñi: (1636) ye 6th of Jan^ry^ Sr Mary **Paterston,** now Call'd Sis^r^ Mary Magdalen, made her holy Profession, being Aged of 19 Years.

Anno Dñi: (1656) in our Convent of Jesus, Maria, Joseph of English poor Clares in Rouen upon ye 7^t^ of July, is happily departed this Life. Strengthened with the rights of our holy Mother ye Church, our Dr Sister, Sis^r^ Mary Magdalen Paterston, ye 40th year of her Age & ye 21st of her Profession, as Alm^ty^ God had in ye beginning given her a Singular grace to esteem highly all that was to his holy will & service, so did she therewith wholy Cooperate to ye end of her Life in Innocency & Purity of heart tho she was of weak forces, yet Indispensably underwent ye rigor of Regular Observance, till her last Sickness, which virtue she had ever practised all her Life, for the speedy repose of her Soul, we humbly beg the Assistance of y^r^ holy Prayers. Requiescat in Pace.

(98) Anno Dñi: (1636) the 26th of Jully Sis^r^ Ann **Wesby,** now Called Sis^r^ Ann Frances, made her Profession being Aged of 20 years.*

Anno Dñi: (1655) the 16th of Aug^st^ in our Convent of English poor Clares of Nazareth in Graveline, is most happily departed this Life, Strengthened wth all the Rights of our holy Moth^r^ ye Church, our Dearly beloved Sister, Sis^r^ Ann Frances Wesby, ye 39th year of her Age, & ye 19th of her Profession, which time she hath spent with great fervour in ye exact observance of her Rule haveing been very exemplar in ye Virtue of Obedience, & Mortification, & of a very peaceful, sweet Conversation, & Singular Compationate to all. She Supported a long & tedious Sickness with an Invincible Patience, we humbly request of Charity ye Assistance of y^r^ Prayers & Suffrages, for ye Repose of her Soul. Requiescat in Pace.

(99) Anno Dñi: (1637) the 2nd of Aug^st^ Sis^r^ Frances **Gerard,** now Call'd Sis^r^ Frances Collett, made her holy Profession, being Aged of 17 years.†

Anno Dñi: (1661) the 19th of Aug^st^ in our Convent of Nazareth of English poor Clares in Graveline is most happily Departed this Life, Strengthened with the Rights of our holy Moth^r^ ye Church our Dr Sister, Sis^r^ Frances Collet Gerard, ye 43rd Year of her Age & ye 26th of her Profession, all which time she hath spent in ye strict observance of our holy Rule, having rendered singular

* Daughter of Thomas Westby, of Mowbreck Hall and Burn Hall, co. Lancaster, and Westby, co. York, Esq., by Perpetua, daughter of Edward Norreys, of Speke Hall, co. Lancaster, Esq.

† Youngest daughter of Sir Thomas Gerard, of Bryn Hall, co. Lancaster, Knt. and 2nd Bart., by Frances, daughter of Sir Richard Molyneux, of Sefton, 1st Viscount Molyneux of Maryborough in Ireland.

Service to holy Religion, by her humble & faithful Labours. She exercised for several Years the Office of Dispenseer with great fervour & Charity; in which she died as a Lamb, as she had lived, for whose happiest rest we humbly beg y[r] Prayers & Suffrages. Requiescat in Pace.

(100) Anno Dñi: (1637) the 2nd of July, Sis[r] Mary **Grovel**, now Call'd Sis[r] Mary Paul, made her holy Profession, being Aged 16th Years.

Anno Dñi: (1666) the 11th of Sepr in our Convent of Nazareth of English poor Clares in Graveline is happily departed this Life, Strengthened with ye Rights of our holy Mother ye Church, our Dearly Beloved Sister, Sister Mary Paul Grovel, the 45th Year of her Age, and the 30th since her Entrance into the holy Religion. She was of a most Sweet Innocent conversation, taking great delight to speake of God, his Saints, & of virtue, but above all y[e] Immaculate Virgin, y[e] Moth[r] of God, to whom she was ever Devoted in a most particular Manner, & above all to y[e] Mistery of her spotless conception, being a great Lover of y[e] Virtue of purity, & we hope her devotion was very acceptable to this Clement Virgin, it having pleased her D[r]. Spouse to take her out of this world upon a Saturday within his B[d] Mothers octave of her Nativity, as her humble Client, had frequently wisht & desired, y[t] she may speedely obtain y[e] recompence of her fidelity in her services y[r] Prayers & Suffrages are most humbly supplicated. Requiescat in Pace.

(101) The same Day & Year made also her Profession, Sist[r] Dorothy **Draycott**, now Call'd Sis[r] Dorothy Peter being Aged of 18th Years.*

Anno Dñi: (1683) the 15th of Novemb[r] in our Convent of Naz: of English poor Clares in Graveline is happily departed y[s] Life, Strengthened with all ye rights of our holy Mother ye Church, our Dr Sis[r], Sister Dorothy Peter Draycott ye 66th Year of her Age & ye 48th since her Entrance into holy Religion which time she spent in y[e] Study of Virtues most Suitable to her Vocation. As a great neglect of her self-esteem of Regular Observance, not exempting her self Night, nor Day from y[e] Community, nothwithstanding her continual infirmities, which were great, yet suffer'd in silence with much patience, & resignation to y[e] Divine will, whose Soul we humbly commend to y[r] holy Prayers & Suffrages. Requiescat in Pace.

* Daughter of Alban Draycott, of Paynesley, co. Stafford, Esq., who obtained his christian name through his being born in prison at St. Alban's, where his father suffered much for the faith. Her mother was Ellen, most probably daughter of Richard Parker, of Audley, co. Stafford, Esq. Many of the family were secular priests, Benedictines, Jesuits, and nuns, and some of them used the *alias* of Parker.

(102) Rouen 13.

Anno Dñi: (1638) the 8th of Sepr Sister Elizabeth **Martin**, now Call'd Sistr Mary Anna Clare, made her Profession, being Aged of 29 Years.

Anno Dni: (1686) the 15th of Augt is happily departed this Life, furnish'd with all the Rights of our holy Mother the Church, in ye Convent of English poor Clares in Rouen our Dearly beloved Sister, Sister Mary Ann Clare, otherwise Martin, ye 77th Year of her Age, & 49th since her entrance to ye holy Religion, 7 of which she spent in our Convent of Graveline, from whence she was sent with 14 more by holy obedience for ye founding of our Convent at Rouen, & in both places hath left great examples of a most exact Obedience, and all other Virtues, patiently supporting many Infirmities without ye least relaxation of fervour, notwithstanding her feeble body, faithfully Imploying her time to ye very last & most happily gave up her soul to her Creator, whom I hope she now enjoys. Yet fearing any humaine frailty may detain her, I most humbly crave yr Suffrages of Charity. Requiescat in Pace.

(103) Anno Dni: (1639) the 12th of Augt Sisr Margaret **Blundell** now Call'd Sistr Margarett Clare, made her Profession, being Aged of 17 Years.*

Anno Dni (1647) the 9th of Janry in our Convent of English poor Clares of Naz: in Graveline is most happily departed this Life strengthened with all ye rights of our holy Mothr ye Church our Dr Sister, Sister Margarett Clare Blundell, Aged of 24 Years, & ye 8th of her Profession, which she hath spent very vertuously. Singularly loving her vocation, & ye true observance thereof, & ever had a most peculiar devotion to our Bd Lady, perseverantly languishing till the last to make herself more pleasing to her, & her Dr Son, for the speediest, and happiest, rest of whose Soul, we humbly crave ye assistance of your holy Prayers & Suffrages of Charity. Requiescat in Pace.

(104) Anno Dni: (1640) the 25th of March, Sisr Christina **Morley** now Call'd Sisr Christina of ye holy Cross, made her Profession, being Aged of 18 Years.

Anno Dni: (1679) the 24th of Novr in our Convent of English poor Clares of Naz: in Graveline is happily departed this Life, strengthened with ye rights of our holy Mothr ye Church, our Dr Sister Christina of ye holy Cross Morley, ye 58 Year cf her Age & the 40th since her holy Profession. She hath from her first entrance to ye Religion been an exampler model to us of an exact observer of those virtues most suitable to her vocation, particularly of a most profound humility, contempt of herself & silent tendance to her own perfection, having the latter years of her life suffer'd

* Daughter of Nicholas Blundell, of Crosby Hall, co. Lancaster, Esq., by Jane, daughter of Roger Bradshaigh, of The Haigh, co. Lancaster, Esq.

with much virtue & resignation many painful & languishing infirmities, but principally in her last sickness, her patience was admirable, supporting her her Agony, which was violent, & of 4 days endurance & suported by her wth humble submition to ye divine Will, having her judgment to ye last. We humbly crave ye assistance of y[r] holy Prayers & suffrages for ye happy Repose of her Soul. Requiescat in Pace.

(105) Dunquerque ye 4th.

Anno Dñi: (1640) ye 12th of Augt Sist[r] Ann **Blundell** now Call'd Sis[r] Clare Collett, made her holy Profession, being Aged of 16 Years.*

Anno Dñi: the (1667) the 26th of Jan[ry] in our Convent of Bethleme of English poor Clares in Dunkerk, is most happily departed y[s] Life, strengthened wth all y[e] rights of our holy Mother the Church. Amongst y[e] prayers and tears of her Desolate Children. Our most Rev[d] & D[r] Moth[r] Abbess Sist[r] Clare Collett Blundell, y[e] 43[d] Year of her Age, & 27th of her holy Profession, having lived very exemplary 13 Years in our D[r] Convent at Graveline, and from thence sent to assist in y[e] foundation of this Convent, & hath exercised y[e] Office of Mistress of Novices, divers Years, & y[t] of Abbess 2 Years. W[th] much charity, humility, & zeal of Gods glory & Y[e] good of our Convent, not desisting from toyle night, nor day. She was Singular for her love of poverty & devotion to y[e] Holy Sacrament, & to y[e] Sacred Virgin Mary, Moth[r] of God, for Whose sake, wth y[t] of her B[d] Sons, we humbly beg a participation in y[r] Prayers, & Suffrages for y[e] repose of her Soul. Requiescat in Pace.

(106) Anno Dñi: (1640) the 12th of Aug[t] Sis[r] Ann **Beddingfield**, now Called Sis[r] Ann Bonaventure, made her Profession, being Aged of 17 Years.†

Anno Dñi: (1697) the 17th of Nov[r] in this our Convent of Naz: of English poor Clares in Graveline is happily departed this Life. Strengthened with all y[e] rights of our holy Mother y[e] Church, our most venerable & most R[d] D[r] Mother Abbess, Sis[r] Ann Bonaventure Beddingfield, amidst y[e] tears, & Prayers of her most afflicted Children (who cannot Sufficiently bewail her deprivation) having render'd herself all, in all, to each till attayned to y[e] 74th Year of her Age, & 58th of her Religious Profession, & 30th of her Government in qualitie of Abbess, during which term she admitted 63 to y[e] holy Profession, & notwithstanding her great Age and infirmities. We looked upon her as an exemplar model, & incitement to y[e] practise of all solid Virtues, as humility, charity, conformity to the Divine Will & great Confidence in God, with an

* Daughter of Nicholas Blundell and sister of Margaret above.

† Born 1623, tenth daughter of Francis Bedingfeld, and sister of Margaret above. She was elected 5th abbess of the convent in Sept., 1667.

admirable equality in all events, prosperous, & adverse. Her maternal tenderness was to all singular, & no less her affability, & sueetness to y[e] winning of Respect, as well from externs, as her Community, her prudence in Governing was excelling, by an assiduous attendance to our (107) Convent's Concernes, (but not to give intermission to regular observance) wherein as long as she enjoyed health, she was indispensable. Day & Night, constantly assisting at y[e] divine Office, which was to her an Incomparable delight, Time was so precious to her, that rarely she gave herself release from some actual imployment, according to her forces, finally what was of a most particular remark she never when allowed, even from her first entrance into Religion abstained from refectionating herself with the delicious banquet of her Soul's food, which she ever held to be y[e] sole support in all occurence, as did evidence her prudent & Charitable proceedings in all her undertakings & concernes, her particular devotion to our B[d] Lady was very remarkable. but especially in her last Sickness, with no less cause of amaisement than imitation, under whose protection we may Confidently believe she was securely shrouded from all hindrance to her speedy enjoyment of a B[d] eternity, but since y[e] Judgments of God are inscrutable, I humbly crave y[e] assistance of y[r] prayers and Suffrages. Requiescat in Pace.

(108) Dunkerk y[e] 5th

The same Day & Year, made also her Profession Sis[r] Mary **Roochwoode**, now Call'd Sis[r] Mary Collet, aged of 17 Years.*

Anno Dñi: (1676) the 24th of June, in our Convent of English Poor Clares of Bethlem in Dunkerk is happily departed this life, strengthened with all y[e] rights of our holy Mother y[e] Church, our R[d] & D[r] Moth[r] Abbess, Sis[r] Mary Collet Roochwoode, y[e] 52[d] year of her Age, & y[e] 37th of her Entrance into Religion, of which she spent 15 in our Convent at Graveline from whence she was sent to assist in y[e] foundation of our poor Convent in Dunkerk where she exercised very laudably the Office of Mistress of Novices, & afterwards that of Abbess, with great humility, prudence, charity, & tender compassion towards all, having always a perseverant Confidence in y[e] Divine Providence, in y[e] great labours, & heavy Crosses she sustained y[e] 10 years of her being Abbess, having renderd her Sueet Soul into ye hands of her Creator amongst ye prayers, & tears of her afflicted children, remaining Orphelines by ye privation of so worthy, & dear a Supe[r] whose Soul we humbly recommend to y[r] holy Prayers and Suffrages. Requiescat in Pace.

(109) Rouen 14[th.]

Anno Dñi: (1640) the 8th of Sepr made her holy Profess:

* Born 17 Nov. 1623, eldest daughter of Sir Robert Rookwood, of Stanningfield and Coldham Hall, co. Suffolk, Knt., by Mary, daughter of Sir Robert Townsend, of Ludlow. She was third abbess of Dunkirk.

Sis[r] Ellen **Bradgshagh**, now Call'd Sis[r] Mary Ignatia, being Aged of 21 Years.*

Anno Dñi: (1673) the 28th of Dec[r] in our Convent of Jesus, Mary, Joseph of English Poor Clares in Rouen is most happily departed y[s] life strengthened wth all the Rights of our holy Mother y[e] Church, our most R[d] Moth: Vicaress, Sis[r] Mary Ignatia Bradgshagh, y[e] 55th Year of her Age, & 34th since her entrance into holy Religion whereof she spent 5 in our Convent at Graveline & both there, & here, hath left singular examples of piety, virtue, & Zeal of Religious observance to y[e] last moment of her life, being most indefatigable in all y[t] was for y[e] service of y[e] Holy Religion, & for her own advancement, & others in perfection. She was sueet, & humble in Conversation, & most Charitable to all, but y[t] which gave y[e] greatest luster to her vertues, was her high esteem, & practise of holy Obedience, wth a most singular conformity to ye divine will wch was remarkable in her last Sickness wch was of 10 Months, wch she bore wth infinite patience, for whose speedy enjoyment of eternal bliss, y[r] Prayers are most humbly craved. Requiescat in Pace.

(110) Rouen 15th

Anno Dñi (1640) the 8th of Sepr Sis[r] Ellenor **Bradgshagh**, now call'd Sis[r] Cecily Frances, made her Profession being Aged of 18 Years.†

Anno Domi: (1650) the 12th of Aug[st] the feast of our Glorious Mother St Clare, in our Convent of Jesus, Mary, Joseph of English Poor Clares in Rouen, is happily departed y[s] Life administred wth all y[e] rights of our holy Moth[r] y[e] Church our D[r] Sister, Sis[r] Cecily Frances Bradgshagh, y[e] 28th Year of her Age & 10th since her Profession, she hath ever been a true singular, & constant example of all Religious Observances, & y[e] love of her Profession, very particular in y[e] virtue of Holy Obedience, Poverty, & Prayer, in conserving her 1st fervour, innocency & piety, to y[e] edification of all she rendered up her Soul to her Creator, wth y[e] same fervour, & tranquillity, she ever lived, for y[e] full release of w[t] humain frailty may have contracted, we humbly crave y[r] prayers of Charity. Requiescat in Pace.

(111) The same day & year made also her holy Profession, Sis[r] Ann **Walton**, now Call'd Sis[r] Ann Joachim, being Aged of 20 Years.‡

* Sixth daughter of Roger Bradshaigh and sister of Elizabeth and Anne above.

† Daughter of James Bradshaigh, of The Haigh, co. Lancaster, Esq., by Anne, daughter of Sir William Norreys, of Speke Hall, co. Lancaster, K.B. Her brother, Sir Roger Bradshaigh, Knt., was brought up a Protestant by his guardian, James Stanley, 7th Earl of Derby, and was created a baronet, 17 Nov. 1679.

‡ Daughter of William Walton, of Little Walton Hall, co. Lancaster, Esq., by Dorothy, daughter of Christopher Anderton, of Horwich Hall, in the same county, Esq.

Anno Dni: (1677) in our Convent of Naz: of English Poor Clares in Graveline, the 10th of Nov: is most happily departed this Life, Strengthened wth all the rights of our holy Mothr ye Church our Dr Sister, Sisr Ann Joachim Walton, ye 59th Year of her Age, & 37th since her Profession. She hath left us an excellent example of conformity to ye divine will having supported with invincible patience a continual deafness for 30 years, as also a lingering & tedious Consumption, during ye long trial thereof, she demonstrated her fervent love to her heavenly Spouse by a punctual fidelity in all regular observance, not admitting dispensations notwithstanding her great infirmities, she was a true lover of poverty, & strict observer of Silence, we hope she already enjoys ye reward of her Sufferances but as ye Judgments of God are secret, I wth humility, beg ye assistance of yr prayers, for ye repose of her Soul. Requiescat in Pace.

(112) Dunkerk ye 6th

Anno Dñi: (1643) the 3rd of May Sr Eliz: **Clifton**, now Call'd Sisr Mary Joseph, made her Profession, Aged of 19 Years.*

Anno Dñi: (1678) the 5th of July in our Convent of Bethelem of English Poor Clares of Dunkerk is happily departed ys Life, furnish'd wth all ye rights of our Holy Mothr ye Church, our Dr Sister, Sisr Mary Joseph Clifton the 56th year of her Age, & of her Profession ye 36th 11 of which she spent in our Convent of Graveline, from whence she was sent by holy Obedience to help in our Convent of Dunkerk, in both places she left us a Singular example of those virtues most Correspondant to her Vocation, particularly a profound humility, a great neglect of herself, fervour & zeal of regular observance, & a perseverance in Prayer, in which Almty God was pleased much to favour her, wch gives us hopes of her present happiness, yet not to be failing in my duty. I humbly implore ye assistance of yr prayers for ye cancelling of what human frailty may have contracted. Requiescat in Pace.

(113) The same day and year made also her Profession, Sisr Dorothy **Clifton**, now call'd Sisr Dorothy Frances, aged of 18 years.†

Anno Dñi: (1677) the 16th of June is happily departed this life in our Convent of English poor Clares of Nazareth in Graveline, our Dr Sister, Sisr Dorothy Frances Clifton, Aged of 53 years, & of her Profession 34, having exercised very laudably several Offices, as that of Portress, Mrs of ye Choir, & lastly yt of Mistress of Novices, for ye space of 9 Years, notwithstanding her great infirmities which she sustained wth great patience & resignation,

* Daughter of Thomas Clifton, of Westby Hall and Clifton Hall, co. Lancaster, Esq., by Ann, daughter and co-heiress of Sir Cuthbert Halsall, of Halsall Hall and Clifton Hall, the latter estate being thus restored to the Clifton family. Her brother, Sir Thomas Clifton, was created a baronet 2 March 1660-1.

† Daughter of Thomas Clifton and sister of Elizabeth above.

she was very admirable for Charity, endeavoring to hide & excuse ye faults of all, & ever had a singular Confidence in God, & devotion to ye Holy Sacrament, no Corporal infirmity detaining her from nourishing her soul wth that delicious Banquet, which she receiv'd with much devotion, but some hours before her death, which we Confidently, Confide was precious in ye sight of God, but being his Judgments are secret, your Prayers are humbly supplicated for ye repose of her Soul. Requiescat in Pace.

(114) Anno Dñi: (1646) the 3rd of Novr made her holy Profession, Sis^{r} Eliza **Lone**, now Call'd Sister Teresa Joseph, being aged of 22 Years.

Anno Dni: (1675) the 16th of March is happily departed this Life furnish'd wth all ye Rights of our holy Moth^{r} the Church, in our Convent of Naz: in Graveline of English Poor Clares, our Dr Sis^{r}, Sister Teresa Joseph Lone, ye 51st Year of her Age, & the 33rd since her entrance into ye holy Religion, which times he hath spent in an assiduous tendance to all sorts of virtues, namely humility, making herself an Abject in ye house of God for his Love, & so rigid to her Body, that she consumed it in ye strict observance of our Holy Rule, being indispensably observant in ye least ceremony of our Convent, we most humbly beg for the Love of God ye Prayers & Suffrages for ye repose of her Soul, Requiescat in Pace.

(115) Dunkerk ye 7th

The same day & year made also her holy Profession Sister Ann **Anderton**, now Call'd Sis^{r} Ann Clare being Aged 20.*

Anno Dni: (1664) the last day of Novr in our Convent cf Bethlem in Dunkerk of English Poor Clares is most happily departed this Life, Strengthened with all ye Rights of our holy Moth^{r} ye Church our Dr Sis^{r} Sister Anne Clare Anderton, the 38th Year of her Age, & ye 18th since her entrance into Religion, wherein she hath much edified us by her true desire to answer to her holy vocation, for which she had a very peculiar Love, & esteem, for the speediest rest of her Soul we humbly & earnestly crave the assistance of y^{r} Prayers & Suffrages of Charity. Requiescat in Pace:

(116) The same Day & Year made also her Holy Profession Sis^{r} Ann **Berington**, now Call'd Sister Ann Michel aged of 20 Years.

Anno Dni (1687) the 29th of May in our Convent of Naz: in Graveline of English poor Clares is most happily departed this Life, furnished with all ye rights of our holy Mother ye Church, our Dr Sister, Sis^{r} Anne Michel Berington, the 61st Year of her Age, & 40th since her entrance into holy Religion, during which

* Second daughter of Roger Anderton, and sister of Dorothy above. She was sent in 1652 to found the convent at Dunkirk.

time, she hath much edified us by her Humility, Obedience, & Respective submission to her Superiors, she was indispensable in her fidelity to ye Choir, never absenting herself night nor day from the divine office, excepting for extremity of sickness. She was Singularly devout to our B^d^ Lady, & to her holy Mother, whose Sacristin she was. Keeping with great neatness her Altar, her patient supporting long & tedious infirmities without relaxation to Regular observance, hath much edify'd us. that her soul may speedily enjoy eternal bliss, we beg most humbly y^r^ Prayers & Suffrages. Requiescat in Pace.

(117) Dunkerk ye 8th

Anno Dom: (1646) the 21st of 9^ber^ made her ho: Profess, Sis^r^ Frances **Roochwood,** now Call'd Sis^r^ Clare Frances, being Aged of 21 Years.*

Anno Dni: 1692 the 5th of Octr in our Conv^t.^ of Bethlem in Dunkerk of English poor Clares is most piously deceas'd our Venerable & Dearly beloved Moth^r^ Abbess, Sister Clare Frances Roockwood administred wth all ye rights of our holy Mother ye Church. Aged of 67 years, & of her Religious profession 47 after having spent 10 Years in our Conv^t^ at Graveline, she was sent by Holy Obedience to Dunkerk & deserveth to be number'd amongst the chief foundresses of this monastery, having built no small part of this Conv^t^ & of 48 Religious now living in it giving the Veil to 39 of them, she bore ye office of Vicaress 7 Years, wth y^t^ prudence that she was thought worthy to succeed her Sister of happy memory in ye Office of Abbess, in which being placed, we may truly say she Governed in solicitude, providing wth all her forces for ye profit of her Monastery, wch she ruled 16 entire Years wth very great courage of mind, in Religion she adopted in herself ye name of Clare, truly imitating her glorious moth^r^ St Clare, in her devotion to ye most Holy Sacrament of ye Alter, exhorting all under her charge, to ye reception there of, both living and dying, she was a very great edification to us all, leaving us great examples of patience, & conformity to ye divine will, desiring to be desolved & to be wth Christ. yet least any thing should detain her speedy felicity we beg ye assistance of y^r^ Prayers & Suffrages. Requiescat in Pace.

Anno Dni: (1647) the 3rd of Novr made her holy Profess^n^ Sis^r^ Eliz: **Anderton,** now Call'd Sis^r^ Winifrid Frances being aged of 18 years.†

Anno Dni: (1700) the 23rd of Ap^l^ in our Conv^t^ of Naz: of English Poor Clares in Graveline, is happily departed this Life, our Ven: Moth^r^ Jub^rn^ Sis^r^ Winifred Frances Anderton, the 73rd Year

* Second daughter of Sir Robert Rookwood and sister of Mary above.

† Third daughter of Roger. Anderton and sister of Dorothy and Anne above.

of her Age & 54th of her holy Profession, all which time she render'd herself a Constant example of Regular discipline & strict observance of our Holy Rule, particularly animating us to a zealous practice of holy poverty, obedience, respect & submission to Superiors, Silence Recollection, & prayer, in which she was most assiduous & singularly devoted to ye Royal prophet David, to whose honour she employed her thoughts & much time in reciting ye Psalms, so yt her conversation seem'd to be more divine yn human, being seldom heard to speak an unnecessary word, her perseverant mortified pious Life, was finished by a happy death, of no other sickness yn a pure decay of nature, tho' t'was so sudden yt she enjoy'd not those helps she might have had, wherefore I ye more earnestly crave for her ye assistance of yr holy Prayers & Suffrages of Charity. Requiescat in Pace.

(119) Anno Dni: (1648) the 3d of Novr made her holy Profession Sisr Mary **Anderton**, now Call'd Sisr Mary Euphrasia, being Aged of 18 Years.*

Anno Dni: (1683) the 31st of Oct: in our Convt of Naz: of English poor Clares in Graveline, is most happily departed this Life furnish'd wth all ye rights of our holy Mother ye Church. Our Ven: Mothr Vicaress, Sisr Mary Euphrasia Anderton, the 52d Year of her age & 34th of her Profession, having exercised several Offices to ye general satisfaction of all ye Community, dying in that of Vicaress wch she exercised very laudably 7 Years, Animating our Community by word & example to ye strict observance of our Rule & Constitutions, her example serving us as a light to guide ourselves by in the practice of all other virtues, particularly of Humility, Poverty, Mortification & in a great contempt of herself, in yt degree as if she had been insensible, the tender feeling she had of our Bd Saviours bitter passion, inviting her to the imitation thereof, caused her wth a generous courage to embrace all afflictions both interiour & exteriour having always in her mouth these sacred words of her divine Master, *Fiat Voluntas tua* the hopes she is already in ye full enjoyment of Eternal bliss, moderates our grief for ye loss we sustain in her, whose virtues & deserts made her no less amiable to externes than to our own Community. I humbly beg ye Assis: of yr Prayers for ye repose of her Soul. Requiescat in Pace.

(120) Anno Dni: (1649) the 6th of March, made her holy Profession Sisr Dorothy Collett **Standford**, Aged of 20 Years.†

Anno Dni: (1679) the 23rd of May in our Convt of Naz: of English poor Clares in Graveline is happily departed this life,

* Fourth daughter of Roger Anderton and sister of Dorothy, Anne, and Elizabeth above.

† Second daughter of William Stanford, of Perry Hall, co. Stafford, Esq., by Dorothy, daughter of Sir John Peshall, of Horsley Hall, co. Stafford, 1st Bart. She was first cousin to the Andertons above.

administred with all ye rights of our Holy Moth^{r} ye Church, our Dr Sister, Sister Dorothy Collett Standford. the 50th year of her age and 30th of her Profession, since which time she hath given us an example of an ardent love to God, & her Neighbour, never being satiated in her desire for ye perfectionating herself, & for ye advancement of God's glory, & ye Salvation of Souls, which made her with much alacrity, altho of a tender constitution to imploy herself in ye most servile works of our Convent, until some few years before her death, that her heavenly spouse was pleased to visit her by continual infirmities, wch she bore wth no less fervour, than patience, we humbly crave ye assistance of y^{r} Prayers for ye repose of her Soul. Requiescat in Pace.

(121) Ano: Dni: 1649 ye 3^{d} of Nov: Sis^{r} Frances Dominick **Norton**, now Call'd Sis Frances Dominick made her holy Profession being Aged of 18 Years.

Anno Doi: (1660) the 16th of June in our Convent of Naz: of English poor Clares in Graveline is most happily departed this Life, our Dr Sister, Sis: Frances Dominick Norton, ye 29th Year of her Age & ye 12th since her Entrance into Holy Religion, having been administred with ye rights of our holy Moth^{r} ye Church. She exercised her self in those virtues most suitable to her Vocation, chiefly Obedience, in which she was very singular, Almighty God being pleased to try her fidelity by interiour Sufferances she rendered herself very faithful still combating manfully against herself. She finally ended her Life with great Calmness of Mind, & confidence in God Whose Soul we humbly recommend to your Prayers of Charity. Requiescat in Pace.

(122) Anno: Dni: (1652) the 13th of Ap^{l} made her holy Profession Sis^{r} Frances **Towers**, now Call'd Sis^{r} Frances of ye holy Cross, being Aged of 21 Years.

Anno Dni: (1684) the 18th of June in our Convent of Naz: of English Poor Clares in Graveline, is happily departed this Life, administered with all ye rights of our holy Moth^{r} ye Church, our Dr Sister, Sister Frances of ye Holy Cross Towers, ye 53rd Year of her Age, & ye 32nd since her holy Profession, having spent several years in Continual Labours for the Service of ye Communitie, until our Lord was pleased to give her ye trial of long & painful infirmities which she bore with singular patience & resignation, & was greatly devoted to ye Infancy of our sweet Saviour, & to ye Holy Sacrament, we most humbly crave y^{r} most holy Prayers for the repose of her Soul. Requiescat in Pace.

(123) Anno Dni: (1652) the 25th of Decemb^{r} Sister Alice **Marcer**, now Call'd Sister Clare Joseph made her holy Profession, being Aged of 28 Years.

Anno Dni: (1669) the 17th of Dec: in our Conv^{t} of English Poor Clares of Naz: in Graveline is most happily departed this Life strengthened wth the rights of our holy Moth^{r} ye Church our Dr Sis^{r}, Sis^{r} Clare Joseph Marcer, the 48th year of her Age & 19th of her Holy Profession, She faithfully & zealously spent her first Years in toylsome labours, till detained by infirmities, wch notwithstanding, she permitted not of any dispensations to assiduously imploying her forces for the service of holy Religion. She was very exemplar for patience, & neglect of herself, for ye repose of her Soul, we humbly beg ye assistance of y^{r} prayers of Charity. Requiescat in Pace.

(124) Anno Dni: (1654) the 13th of June, made her ho: Profess: Sister Elen **Roulenston**, now Call'd Sis^{r} Elen Frances, being aged of 28 years.

Anno: Dni: (1678) the 4th of June, in our Convent of Naz: of English Poor Clares in Graveline is most happily departed this Life, strengthened with all ye rights of our holy Moth^{r} ye Church, our Dr Sister, Sis^{r} Ellen Frances Roulenston, the 61st year of her Age, & 33rd since her entrance into ye holy Religion, during which time she has been most faithful to God, ye holy Religion, & to her own Soul, to enrich it with all such Virtues as might make it pleasing to her heavenly Spouse, joyning to her most humble & servile imployments, most fervent & affectionated prayers, leaving us much edified at her holy Life, & happy death, whose Soul we humbly recomend to y^{r} Prayers & Suffrages. Requiescat in Pace.

(125) The same Year & Day, made also her holy Profession Sister Elizabeth **Unsworth**, now Call'd Sis Martha Alexs: being Aged of 23 Years.*

Anno Dni: (1700) the 5th of Jan^{ry} in our Conv^{t} of Naz: of English Poor Clares in Graveline, is most happily departed this Life, strengthened wth all ye rights of our holy Moth: ye Church, of Dr Sister, Sis^{r} Martha Alexious Unsworth the 69th Year of her Age, & 46th since her Entrance into Religion, which time she faithfully imploy'd in all humble Labours suitable to her Vocation, always being ready to load herself, whom she call'd ye Ass of ye Convent wth each ones burdens of Laborious works, till ye last 7 Years of her Life, that God was pleased to try her wth Continual Corporal Infirmities, & interiour Suffrances, all wch she supported wth great patience, & Resignation to ye divine will, persevering in an ardent devotion to ye Imaculate Virgin Mother of God, & to ye B^{d} Sacram^{t} she receiv'd with joy & thanksgivin the Doct^{rs} advertisem^{t} to prepare for death, as having long Languish'd after ye embracements of her heavenly Spouse, wch y^{t} she may be ye sooner in possession of y^{r} Prayers of Charity are most humbly intreated. Requiescat in Pace.

* Of the Lancashire family of Unsworth.

(126) Anno: Dni (1655) the 25th of March, made her ho: Profession, Sisr Ann **Finch**, now Call'd Sisr Matilda of ye Passion being Aged of 21 Years.

Anno Dni: (1693) the 30th of Novr in our Convent of Naz: of English Poor Clares in Graveline is most happily departed this Life, Strengthened with all ye rights of our holy Mothr ye Church, our Dr Sister, Sister Matilda of ye Passion Finch ye 42nd Year since her entrance into ye holy Religion, & ye 62nd of her Age, during which she has left us great examples of a Singular fervour, & love of God, great devotion to ye Holy Sacrament, & to ye Sacred Passion, spending daily nothwithstanding her Continual Infirmitys, several hours of mental Prayer, her fervour giving her forces to deprive herself of her rest to hearken to ye voice of her Beloved in ye holy Sacrament, & to give to him by her feverous recital of ye Divine Office, & Singing his Praises, the Charming agreeable voyce he had given her which she employed totally to his honour, as she did all her Corporal forces, breathing out her Soul with the same fervour she lived, which we recommend to your Prayers of Charity. Requiescat in Pace.

(127) The same day & year, made also her Profession, Sisr Eliz: **Lewes**, now Call'd Sisr Ignatia Joseph, being Aged 19 Years.

Anno Dni: (1705) the 30th of Sepr in our Convent of Naz: of English Poor Clares at Graveline, is happily departed this Life, fortified with all ye rights of our holy Mothr the Church our Venerable & Dr Mothr Vicaress & Sisr Ignatia Joseph Lewis Jubilarian, Aged of 70 years, & 52 since her entrance into Religion, where she has exercised the Principal Offices of ye house, to ye General Satisfaction of all, Namely yt of Vicaress, the space of 16 years, at different times, in this, as well as others, she truly might be esteem'd a Model of wt we all ought to aim at for her Obedience & Respect to Superiours was remarkable, her Charity was both universal, & particular for she was observed always, if (possible), immediately to Oblige those from whom she'd reciev'd any Mortification, or unkindness, her Prayers were devout, & Constant, as was her Regularity to Conventual Assemblys, which neither her Age, or delicate Constitution excused her from this unrelented fervour, made her unweariedly spend hours before her hidden God in ye holy Sacrament who I hope unveiled she now enjoys; after those fervent aspirations which she made all ye time of her Sickness till her happy death, but as ye Judgments of God are impenetrable I humbly beg yr holy prayers of Charity. Requiescat in Pace.

(128) Anno Dni: (1657) Sisr Mary **Boothe**, now Call'd Sisr Mary Frances, made her holy Profession ye 4th of Octobr being Aged of 17 Years.*

* Daughter of Richard Booth, of Woolston-cum-Poulton, co. Lancaster, yeoman, and sister of the Rev. Edward Booth, baptized 15 Dec. 1639, by the venerable martyr, Dom. Edward Ambrose Barlow, O.S.B., whose name he used as an *alias* throughout his ecclesiastical career.

Anno Dni: (1659) the 16th of Apl in our Convent of Naz: of English Poor Clares in Graveline is most happily departed this Life, Strengthened wth all ye rights of our holy Mother ye Church, our Dr Sister, Sister Mary Frances Boothe, the 19th Year of her Age, & 2nd of her holy Profession, ye greatest part of which she passed in a most painful & sharp Sickness with a Constant conformity to the divine Will, she was of a most Singular Candour, & purity of Soul, devout & Obedient, for whose Speediest repose we humbly crave ye assistance of yr Prayers for Charity. Requiescat in Pace.

(129) Anno: Dni: (1658) Sister Mary **Allote,** now Call'd Sister Mary Magdalen upon ye 4th of Octobr made her holy Profession, being Aged 69 Years Old.

Anno: Dni (1674) the 31st of March in our Convt of English Poor Clares in Graveline, is most happily departed ys life, furnish'd wth ye rights of our holy Mother ye Church, our Dr Sister, Sistr Mary Magdalen Allote, aged of (84) & professed 15 Years, having faithfully, & indefatigably served our Convt in quality of extern Servant, ye space of 39 having receiv'd our holy habit. She employed ye remainder of her Life in a constant devotion, rendering her Life conformable to her Name, spending her time in ye Choir, in a quiet repose of most perseverant prayer, rarely dispensed wth herself from vocal Prayer, even during Manual works, she was indued wth a general Charity to her Neighbour a great respect to her Superior, & ye Comunity, she silently supported ye incomodities of Old Age & ever had a great devotion to our Bd Lady, & to her good Angel, I humbly beg ye assistance of yr Prayers for ye repose of her Soul. Requiescat in Pace.

(130) Anno: Dni (1659) the 2nd of July, Sisr Ann **Jump,** now call'd Sister Ann Frances, made her Profession, being Aged of 24 Years.*

Anno Dni: (1677) the 22nd of March in our Convt of Naz: of English Poor Clares in Graveline, is happily departed ys life, administred wth all the Sacraments of our holy Mothr ye Church, our Dr Sister, Sister Ann Frances Jump, the 43rd year of her Age, & 18th since her holy Profession, all which time she spent in a constant fidelity to God, & infatigable Labours for ye service of Religion, making herself an abject in ye house of God for his Love. She was of a sweet peaceable humour, & indeavour'd to hide her Virtues, by a silent tendance to her own perfection, living amongst us in humility & obscurity, the more to imitate her heavenly spouse, in whose embracement she may ye sooner be in possession, yr Prayers & Suffrages are most humbly Supplicated. Requiescat in Pace.

* Of the yeomanry family of Jump of Hesketh Bank, co. Lancaster (*vide C.R.S.*, vi, 101).

(131) Anno Dni: (1661) Sister Margarett **Clifton**, now Call'd Sister Mary of Nazareth (y[e] 24th of June) made her holy Profession, being Aged of 23 Years.*

Anno: Dni (1702) the 11th of March in our Convent of Naz: of English Poor Clares in Graveline, is most happily departed this Life, strengthened w[t] all the Rights of our holy Moth[r] y[e] Church, our D[r] Sister, Sister Mary of Nazareth alias Clifton, the 64th Year of her Age & 42 since her entrance into y[e] holy Religion, w[ch] time she hath spent in a zealous, & true observance of our Holy Rule, leaving us most particularly Edified at her Obedience, humility, holy Simplicity, & Respect to Superiors. She had a strong Confidence in Divine Providence, a tender devotion to y[e] holy Sacrament: & a deep sense of Alm[ty] God's goodness, which carried her on in a solid joy, to a true contempt of all terrestrial things, for her Soul's speedy fruition of Eternal bliss. I humbly crave y[r] Prayers & Suffrages of Charity. Requiescat in Pace.

(132) Anno: Dni: (1661) the 24th of June Sister Marg[t] **Batte**, now Call'd Sist[r] Margeret Clare, made her Profession being Aged of 39 Years.

Anno: Dni: (1700) the first of Jan[ry] in our Convent of Naz: of English Poor Clares in Graveline is most happily departed this Life, our D[r] Sister, Sist[r] Marg[t] Clare Batte, y[e] 79th Year of her Age, & 40th since her holy Profession, strengthened wth all y[e] rights of our holy Mother y[e] Church, all w[ch] time, she spent in y[e] strict observance of our Holy Rule, & constitutions, & Constant service to y[e] Religion, 20 Years with incomparable Charity, she performed y[e] Office of Apothicary, & was never more Cheerful, & content, than when she cou'd by any means solace or ease y[e] sick, & infirm, her great humility was accompanied wth a perfect Obedience, Submission, & respect to Superiours, high esteem of her holy Vocation: & singular devotion to our B[d] Lady, her perseverant virtuous Life was finish'd by a most happy sueet death, for her Souls full fruition of eternal glory. I humbly crave of Charity y[r] holy Prayers & Suffrages. Requiescat in Pace.

(133) The same day & Year made also her holy Profession Sister Eliz: **Ashton**, now Call'd Sist[r] Rosalia Franc: the 36th Year of her Age.†

Anno Dni: (1679) the 23rd of Nov: in our Conv[t] of Naz: of English Poor Clares in Graveline, is most happily departed y[s] Life. Strengthened wth y[e] rights of our holy Mother y[e] Church, our D[r] Sister, Sister Rosalia Frances Ashton, y[e] 56th Year of her Age, &

* Daughter of Thomas Clifton, and sister of Elizabeth and Dorothy above.

† Daughter of Henry Ashton, of Littlewood Hall, co. Lancaster, gent., by Julian, daughter of William Elston, of Higher Brockholes Hall, in the same county, gent.

26th since her Profession, which time she hath spent in y[e] continual service of y[e] sick in which duty she did acquit herself with so general a Charity, that y[e] examples she hath left us during so many years of Charitable employment, hath no less edified us, than her other virtues, namely her prompt Obedience to y[e] very inclination of her Superiour, & Charity in hiding & excusing y[e] faults of others, she was very assiduous, & intense in Prayer, as also in y[e] exercise of y[e] presence of God, we humbly crave y[e] assistance of y[r] Prayers for y[e] speedy repose of her Soul. Requiescat in Pace.

(134) Anno Dni: (1662) the 1st of Jan[ry] Sister Dorothy **Butler** now Call'd Sist[r] Magdalen of Bethlem made her Profession, being Aged of 19 Years.*

Anno Dni: (1687) the 12th of Jan[ry] in our Conv[t] of Naz: of English Poor Clares in Graveline, is happily departed y[s] life, strengthened wth y[e] rights of our holy Mother y[e] Church our D[r] Sister, Sister Magdalen of Bethlem Butler, the 44th Year of her Age, & 25th since her Profession, she was a great Lover of holy Poverty, most faithfully performing all things under her charge, most zealous for Alm[ty] Gods honour & glory, by y[e] service she render'd y[e] Choir, both in Singing, & well performance of the Divine Office, most constantly coming both day & night, but above all she was most singularly eminent for her devotion to our B[d] Lady, for whose honour she omitted nothing, & by whose mediation we may believe she obtained so happy a death which she was most resigned to, although but 2 days Sick & all her life had an extraordinary apprehension of, we most humbly crave y[e] assistance of y[r] Prayers & Suffrages for y[e] repose of her Soul. Requiescat in Pace.

(136) Anno Dni: (1662) the 1st of Jan[ry] made her Profession Sis[r] Susana **Jump**, now Call'd Sis[r] Mary Joseph y[e] 23[d] Year of her Age.†

Anno Dni: (1705) the 2[d] of Feb[ry] in our Conv[t] of Naz: of English Poor Clares in Graveline is most happily departed y[s] Life, fortified wth all the Rights of our holy Moth[r] y[e] Church, our D[r] Sis[r], Sister Mary Joseph Jump, y[e] 69th Year of her Age, & 46th since her Entrance into holy Religion which time she spent wth unrelented fervour & fidelity, in y[e] strict observance of our holy Rule, and service of y[e] holy Community, emploing her forces in y[e] most toylsome Labours, & Constant Charitable Offices towards y[e] sick & infirm, whom she tenderly compationated, her Love for holy Poverty, & great neglect of herself, scarce ever permited

* Daughter of Henry Butler, of Rawcliffe Hall, co. Lancaster, Esq., by his third wife, Elizabeth Grimston, of the family seated at Grimston Garth, co. York.

† Sister of Ann Jump above.

her to accept of anything new, nor even w[t] was necessay, thro' humility contenting her self wth others worn Clothes, y[e] too Latter Years of her Life, Alm[ty] God was pleased to visit her wth frequent violent sicknesses, & lastly a lingering Consumption, w[ch] for 9 months, confined her to y[e] Infirmary, during w[ch] tryals she gave us rare examples of patience, mortification, & an entire Conformity to y[e] divine Will. I humbly beg y[r] pray[rs] of Charity for her Soul's speedy rest. Requiescat in Pace.

(137) Anno: Dni: (1663) the 3[d] of May Sister Ann **Clifton**, now Call'd Sis[r] Clare, Mary, Ann made Profession being Aged 16 Years.*

Anno: Dni: (1722) the 5th of Decem[r] in our Conv[t] of Naz: of English Poor Clares in Graveline, most happily quitted this mortal exile, strengthened wth y[e] Sacraments of our holy Mother y[e] Church, our Venerable Moth[r] Jubilarian, Sister Clare Mary Ann Clifton, y[e] 75th of her Age & 60th since her Entrance into holy Religion; notwithstanding her great Age, her perseverant fervour made her constant at y[e] Divine Office. Night & day, she gave us Edification by her esteem, & regard to holy poverty, careful in y[e] use of every little thing, y[t] nothing might be wasted, her Ardent Love for y[e] Infant Jesus, put her into such transports of Joy about y[e] time of Christmass, y[t] she cou'd not forbear shewing it by her exterior comportment, she had also a tender love for his B[d] Mother, & was a chief promotress of devotion in her honour, especially y[e] Rosary & Scapular, but humain frailty being great. I humbly request y[r] prayers of Charity. Requiescat in Pace.

(138) The same day, & Year, made also her Profess[n] Sister Mary **Plaisington**, now Call'd Sis[r] Mary Frances the 26th Year of her age.†

Anno Dni: (1672) the 31st of July in our Conv[t] of Naz: of English Poor Clares in Graveline, is most happily departed this Life, strengthened wth all y[e] Sacraments of our holy Mother y[e] Church, our D[r] Sister, Sist[r] Mary Frances Plaisington, the 48th Year of her Age & y[e] 20th since her entrance into Religion, w[ch] time she spent in a Continual tendance to all sortes of virtues, & to y[e] punctual observance of our holy Rule, she exercised several offi es to y[e] general satisfaction of y[e] Comunitie, as y[t] of Vicaress 6 years, & as long a term of Mistress of Novices, educating her

* Daughter of Thomas Clifton and sister of Elizabeth, Dorothy, and Margaret above.

† Daughter of Robert Plesington, of Dimples Hall, Esq., by Alice, daughter of Lawrence Rawstorne, of Newhall, and his wife Holcroft, daughter of Robert Hesketh, of Rufford Hall, all in the county of Lancaster. Her brother, the Venerable John Plesington, was martyred for his priesthood in 1679.

young in ye true spirit of their Vocation, she was insatiable in her desire of Perfection, wch made her wth heroical Courage overcome all repugnance of Nature, treating her body as well in Sickness, as in health, as if she had been insensible, she was very assiduous in Prayer, most humble, & Obedient, in fine, wee may say wth truth y^{t} all virtues shined in her, whose soul we confide receives ye reward already of ye same yet fearing anything may detain her, allow her of Charity ye succour of y^{r} Prayers. Requiescat in Pace.

(139) The same day & year made also her holy Profession Sister Grace **Plesington**, now Call'd, Sis^{r} Grace of ye Holy Ghost, aged of 25 years.*

Anno: Dni: (1706) the 3rd of Sepr in our Conv^{t} of Naz: of English Poor Clares in Graveline is piously decease'd, fortified with all ye rights of our Holy Moth: the Church, our Dr Sister, Sis^{r} Grace of ye Ho: Ghost Pleasington, Aged of 68 Years, Profess'd 42 during wch time she hath faithfully corresponded wth ye dutys of her state, & call to perfection, ever solicitously seeking & joyfully embracing any occasion or Employs of Contempt & practicing H: Poverty in all things wch was no less Edifying, than her Obedience, submission & Respect to Superiour, Love to ye holy Sacrament & fidelity to God both day & night. Notwithstanding many indispositions wch might lawfully have excused her, this fervour of Spirit, doubtless made her cry out wth pleasure, w^{n} ye Doctor told her ye news of her aproaching death, *Lætatus sum in his que dicta sunt Mihi in Domum Domini ibimus*, where I hope she is now enjoying ye reward of her perseverant virtue, yet lest any thing may retard her bliss, we humbly crave y^{r} usual Prayers & Suffrages. Requiescat in Pace.

(140) Anno Dni: (1664) the 12th of Augt Sister Mary **Williamson**, now Call'd Sister Mary Collett made her holy Profession, Aged of 24 Years.

Anno: Dni: (1668) the 9th of June in our Conv^{t} of Naz: of English Poor Clares in Graveline, is most happily departed this Life, Strengthened wth all ye Sacraments of our holy Mother ye Church, our Dr Sis^{r}, Sister, Mary Collet Williamson, the 28th year of her Age & 5th since her Entrance into holy Religion, wch time she hath spent in ye true observance of our holy Rule, & constitutions, leaving great examples of an entire conformity to ye divine Will, of Obedience, humility, & sueetness of conversation, & patience, particularly in her last sickness, which was Languishing & painful, for ye speediest rest of whose Soul, we humbly beg ye assistance of your Prayers & Suffrages. Requiescat in Pace.

(141) Anno: Dni: (1664) the 21st of Octr made her holy

* Sister of Mary Plesington above

Profession, Sis^r^ Eliz: **Finch**, now Cali'd Sis^r^ Anne Clare, Aged of 27 Years.

Anno Dni: (1689) the 14th of March, in our Conv^t^ of Naz: of English Poor Clares in Graveline, is happily departed y^s^ Life, Strengthened wth all the Rights of our holy Moth^r^ ye Church, our Dr Sis^r^, Sis^r^ Ann Clare Finch, the 53rd Year of her Age, & ye 26th since her entrance into holy Religion. She ever had a singular love to her vocation, & to the virtue of purity, she was most severe & rigid to herself, treating her body wth out mercy, still inventing occasions to Mortify herself, as well in diet, as all other occasions, & did wth humble submission and patience cheerfully bear ye incommodities of long & painful infirmities, principally of a great incommodity in her sight, wch for several years Obliged her to leave her Breviary, to her great affliction, wch made her redouble her Mental, & vocal Prayers, in wch she was most indispensable, as also in her Submission in all events to ye divine will, for ye speediest rest of her Soul, we humbly beg ye assistance of y^r^ Prayers. Requiescat in Pace.

(142) Anno Dni: (1665) the 6th of July, made her holy Profession Sis^r^ Alice **Blundell**, now Call'd Sister Luisa Clare aged of 16 years.*

Anno Dni: (1720) the 14th of June in our Conv^t^ of English Poor Clares in Graveline, is happily deceas'd strengthened wth all ye rights of our holy Moth^r^ ye Church, our Venerable Moth^r^ Jubilari: Sis^r^ Lucia Clare Blundell aged 71 professed 56. She much Edified us wth her fervour & fidelity in ye observance of our holy Rule, & wth much Wisdom, Prudence, & Charity acquitted herself of several Offices, was most assiduous in Prayer spending all spare moments in ye Choir, as her centre, had a tender Devotion to ye holy Family, & ye SS.^ts^ of our holy Order, & most exemplar in her esteem, Love, & practice of H. Poverty, her pious Life, was follow'd wth as happy a death that nothing may stop her wish'd for felicity, we humbly request y^r^ accustomed Charity for ye Repose of her Soul. Requiescat in Pace.

(143) The same Year & day made also her holy Professi: Sis^r^ Henrieta Maria **Cannell**, now Call'd Sister Mary of ye Assumption ye 20th Year of her Age.†

Anno Dni: (1704) the 29th of Decr in y^s^ our Conv^t^ of Naz: of English Poor Clares in Graveline fortified wth all ye rights of our ho: Moth^r^ ye Church is happily departed this Life our most D^r^ & R^d^ Mother Abbess, Sis^r^ Mary Assumption Cannel amidst ye prayers, & tears of her afflicted Children the 60th Year of her Age, & 41 of

* Daughter of William Blundell, of Crosby Hall, co. Lancaster, Esq., by Anne, daughter of Sir Thomas Haggerston, of Haggerston Castle, co. Northumberland, 1st. Bart.

† She was elected 6th abbess in Nov. 1697.

her Profession, 7 of Prelacie, & 9th day of her Sickness, which was a Continual fever, & Violent Catarrh upon her breast which she supported wth admirable patience & Conformity to ye divine will, persevering to ye end in her accustomed practice of Mortification, Charity, Compassion, & aimable sweetness, wch drew a Respect as well from externs as her own Community, 28 of which receiv'd from her ye first principles of Religion, wch during ye 9 years she was Mistress of Novices she with an unwearied Zeal inculcated unto them, sparing no pains for there advancement in perfection, giving them in all occasions example of a profound humility, Prudence, & a Generous Courage, bearing all Crosses wth equality, Joy, & Alacrity, her devotion to her good Angel & (144) ye Immaculate Virgin Mary, questionless obtained her a presence of spirit even to the last moment, which she seem'd to make the best use of, but the judgments of God being inscrutable I humbly crave ye assistance of your prayers & Suffrages for the Speedy Repose of her Soul. Requiescat in Pace.

(145) The same day & Year made also her holy Profession Sisr Margarett **Mollineux,** now Call'd Sistr Angela of ye Ascension, being Aged of 19.*

Anno Dni: (1720) the 2nd of Feb: in our Convt of Nazareth of English Poor Clares in Graveline, is most happily deceased, our Ven: Mothr Jubilarian Sisr Angela of ye Ascension Mollineux, Aged of 74 & 55 Years since her entrance into holy Religion, which time she spent in a most examplar Regularity in all Religious dutys, great & small, Constantly following ye Cömunity with so great a fervour and Recollection & abstraction, that it was evident she placed her chief comfort, & satisfaction, in interiour conversation wth God, being a great lover of Prayer, singularly devoted to our Bd Lady, & most strict in ye observance of Silence, having been remarkable for having spent ye whole Lent wth out speaking to any one, & when in ye Office of Sick Mother, she exercised it wth all ye Charity imaginable, sparing no pains nor Labour night nor day, for ye service of ye sick, her humility, & humble opinion of herself was very edifying, & also her Charity, & patience in supportation of Infirmities. She receiv'd the Viaticum most devoutly, but her last Sickness being a dropsical humour wch mounting suddenly to her Stomach, allow'd not time for ye holy Oyles. I therefore crave more earnestly yr holy Prayrs for ye repose of her Soul. Requiescat in Pace.

(146) The same Day & Year made also her Profession, Sister Catherine **Mollineux,** now Call'd Sister Catherine Joseph, being aged of 17 Years.†

* Fifth daughter of John Molyneux, of Alt Grange and New Hall, co. Lancaster, Esq., by Margaret, daughter of John Whalley, of Orrell, in the same county, gent.

† Fourth daughter of John Molyneux and sister of Catherine above.

Anno Dni: (1688) the 20th of Decemb^{r} in our Conv^{t} of Naz: of English Poor Clares in Graveline, is most happily departed y^{s} Life, our Dr Sis^{r} Cathe: Joseph Mollineux. Strengthened wth all ye rights of our holy Moth^{r} ye Church, the 40th Year of her Age, & 25th since her entry into Religion, during which time she hath left us much Edified, our Dr Lord having been pleased to give her ye tryal of several years of languishing infirmities, wch she bore wth great patience. Resignation, & alacrity. she was most Compassionate to all & ready to help any in necessity according to her power, she imployed her voice both in Reading & Singing in ye Choir wth fervour & fidelity. that nothing may retard her speedy singing amongst the Choir of Angels. I most humbly crave ye assistance of your Prayers for Charity. Requiescat in Pace.

(147) Anno Dni: (1666) the 15th of Augt made her holy Profession, Sister Ellen **Wilkerson**, now call'd Sist^{r} Beatrice of ye Holy Sacrament, Aged of 20.*

Anno Dni: (1693) the 3rd of Dec: in our Conv^{t} of Naz: of English Poor Clares in Graveline is most happily departed y^{s} life administred wth ye rights of our Holy Moth^{r} ye Church, our Dr Sist^{r}, Sist^{r} Beatrice of ye ho: Sacrament Wilkerson, the 47th Year of her Age, & 28th since her entrance into holy Religion wch time she hath faithfully employ'd in ye Service of God, & ye Community, by her great Labours, & faithful Complyance in all Religious observances, she had a singular esteem of her holy Vocation, & contempt of the world, faithfully imploying her time either in working, or long Prayer, & I hope will now offer them up for us, yet least anything shou'd detain her Speedy felicity, be pleased of Charity to afford her your holy Prayers. Requiescat in Pace.

(148) The same day & year made also her holy Profession Sis^{r} Frances **Radische**, now Call'd Sis^{r} Frances Ignatia Aged of 31 Years.

Anno Dni: (1693) the 3rd of Dec: in our Convent of Naz: of English Poor Clares in Graveline, is most happily departed ye life administered wth ye rights of her holy Moth^{r} ye Church, our Dr Sister, Sister Frances Ignatia Radische, ye 57th year of her age & ye 28th since her entrance into holy Religion which time she hath faithfully exercised in ye service of God, spending her forces in 2 terms of Sick Mother & 12 years that of Portress to ye great satisfaction of all, being most charitable to all, depriving herself both the rest, & all commodities to pleasure or accomodate any one, she was most mortified to herself, treating her body wth all imaginable rigour, consummating her life & forces in ye service

* Probably cousin to Margaret and Catherine Molyneux and sister to Fr. Thomas Wilkinson *alias* Molyneux, S.J., who was cast into Morpeth gaol during the Oates Plot ferment and poisoned by the prison surgeon, and died a confessor of the faith, 12 Jan. 1681, aged 43.

of our Community, to whom she had ever been a most beneficial member, having notwithstanding a sharp fever, of w[ch] she dyed, performed her employment of Infirmarian until y[e] Morning she received her Viaticum, dying three days after finishing her life wth admirable patience & conformity to y[e] divine will. Languishing to be dissolved & to enjoy her spouse & to y[e] end nothing may retard her happiness, I most humbly crave y[e] assistance of y[r] Prayers of Charity. Requiescat in Pace.

(149) Anno Dni: (1667) the 1st of Nov: Sis[r] Trever **Warner**, now call'd Sis[r] Clare of Jesus, made her holy Profession being Aged of 31 Years.*

Anno Dni: (1670) the 26th of Jan[ry] in our Conv[t] of Naz: of English Poor Clares in Graveline, is most happily departed y[s] Life, our D[r] Sister, Sis[r] Clare of Jesus Warner, y[e] 35th Year of her Age, & 4th since her entrance into Religion, leaving us amongst other virtues, a great & rare example of humility, & singular contempt of y[e] world, for being a Lady of quality, & having a husband & Children, whom she dearly loved, wth other worldly advantages, no sooner was she converted to y[e] Catholic faith; but with a most generous, & heroical Resolution, scarce heard of, she left all to hear Gods call, in a poor & humble Religious State of Life, & though we have reason to believe she now receives y[e] eternal reward promised to those that leave all for Gods sake: yet we humbly beg y[e] charitable assistance of y[r] prayers for y[e] speedy repose of her Soul. Requiescat in Pace.

(150) The same day & year made also her holy Profession, Sis[r] Eliz: **Warner**, now Call'd Sis[r] Mary Clare, being aged of 25 years.†

* Lady Trevor Warner, born 20 April 1636, wife of Sir John Warner, of Parham, co. Suffolk, created a baronet 16 July 1660, was daughter of Sir Thomas Hanmer, of Hanmer Hall, co. Flint, 1st Bart., and was christened Trevor after her godfather, Baron Trevor. She was married in London to John Warner on 7 June 1659, by Dr John Warner, Bishop of Rochester, and had two daughters, Catherine born 1660, and Susan born 1662, who both eventually became Benedictine nuns at Dunkirk. Lady Warner and her sister-in-law, Elizabeth Warner, were received into the church on 23 June, and Sir John on 6 July 1664. Thereupon Sir John and Lady Warner agreed to separate and consecrate the remainder of their lives to religion. Sir John entered the Society of Jesus in 1665, and was professed of the three vows in 1667. Under the decretals, *De conversione conjugum*, respecting the admission of married persons into religion by mutual consent, Lady Warner could not otherwise have been professed a Poor Clare as she wished, it being necessary that both should take solemn vows in an approved religious order. 'The Life of Lady Warner' was written by Fr. Edward Scarisbrick *alias* Neville, S.J., and printed at St Omer in 1691 embellished with her portrait; 2nd edition, to which is added an "Abridgment of the Life of her sister-in-law, Mrs Elizabeth Warner, in Religion Sister Mary Clare," London 1692; 3rd edition, London 1696; 1769; and 1858.

† Born 24 May 1641, daughter of Francis Warner, of Parham, Esq., by Elizabeth, daughter of Sir John Rous, of Henham, co. Suffolk, Knt. She was sister to Sir John Warner, Bart., and an Abridgment of her Life was published as above.

Anno Dni: (1681) the 28th of Feb: in our Convt of Naz: of English Poor Clares in Graveline, is most happily departed this Life, our dearly beloved Sister, Sistr Mary Clare Warner, ye 39th Year of her Age, & 14th since her profession, Strengthened wth all ye Sacraments of our holy Mother the Church, having ever since her entrance into holy Religion, made it her business to attend to Correspond to her holy vocation, by a great disessteem of all that might hinder her from ye same & a extraordinary attention to prayer, never having slackened from her 1st fervour, wch made her tho of a weak Constitution go through ye rigour of our Rule without ye least dispensation, & most punctually exact in ye least cerimony of our holy Religion, as having a most high esteem of holy Obedience, I Confide she is now in ye full possession of ye happiness yt attended so virtuous a Life, however not to fail in my duty, I commend her Soul to yr holy Prayers & Suffrages. Requiescat in Pace.

(151) The same day & year made her holy Profession Sister Frances **Shelton**, now Call'd Sisr Frances Joseph the 26th Year of her Age.

Anno Dni: (1687) the 1st of July in our Convt of English Poor Clares of Naz: in Graveline, is most happily departed this Life, Strengthened wth the Rights of our holy Mother ye Church, our Dr Sisr, Sister Frances Joseph Shelton, ye 47th year of her Age, & 21st since her entrance into holy Religion, which time she hath spent most fervently in ye true Observance of our holy Rule, being most constant to ye Choir day & night. Notwithstanding her great & constant infirmities, she was of a quiet peaceable humour, & exact in all religious observances, very obedient & humble: delighting for ye love of God to make herself an abject in his house, I humbly crave ye assistance of yr holy Prayers & Suffrages for ye speediest rest of her Soul. Requiescat in Pace.

(152) Anno Dni: (1669) the 28th of May Sisr Jane **Reynolds,** now call'd Sisr Collet Gertrude made her holy Profession being aged of 18 Years.

Anno Dni: (1708) the 23d of Nov: in our Convent of Graveline of English Poor Clares has happily quitted ys mortal exile, our Dr. Sisr, Sisr Collet Gertrude Reynolds, aged of 58 & 41 since her Entrance into holy Religion, after having receiv'd all ye Rights of our holy Mothr ye Church. Wth a great sense of devotion, tho' her sickness was extremely violent, as well as long, which she bore wth an admirable patience, & singular piety the sharpness of her pains, not giving ye least interruption to her continued aspirations, & conformity to ye divine will, and in ye office of dispenseer, & infirmarian she was very singular in her indefatigable Labours, & her general Charity & compassion to all, wch qualities tho very infirm herself, she never ceas'd to exercise, or spared any pains in doing Charities for others, tho she was always careful to be as little troublesome in her own illness as possible, notwithstanding suffer'd abundantly in sensible pains, & lameness, her ardent devotion to our Bd Lady, & ye Angel Gabriel doubtless stood pouerful intercessors for her, yet not to be failing in our duty humbly crave yr holy Prayers for ye repose of her soul. Requiescat in Pace.

(153) The same day & year made her holy Profession Sister Catherine Frances **Fox**, now call'd Sisr Catherine Frances. Aged of 27 Years.

Anno Dni: (1709) the 28th of Janry in our Convt of Naz: of English Poor Clares in Graveline, is most happily reposed in our Lord, our most Dr Sistr, Sistr Catherine Frances Fox, the 66th Year of her Age, and 41 since her entrance into holy Religion, since which she hath been both constantly exact, & fervent in the observance of our holy Rule, in its strictest rigor, adjoyning thereunto a continual mortification ever choosing ye worst of all things, both in Clothes, & diet, notwithstanding she was most compassionate, & considerate of others, evidenced in ye universal Charity she shew'd to all ye 9 years she was dispenseer, & near as long Mrs of Novices, in which office she dyed, expressing in her last sickness her accustomed zeal for ye good of Religion particularly for her own young, to whom, as well as to us all, she gave a most perfect example of a profound humility, contempt of herself, & ye world, intensness in Prayer, & respect during ye time of it wch was both long & even continual wch made her a pattern of piety, as well as prudence, regretted by all, yet since ye Judgments of God are impenetrable. I beg yr usual help for ye repose of her soul. Requiescat in Pace.

(154) Anno: Dni: (1670) ye 24th of June made her holy Profession Sistr Eliz: **Collingwood**, now call'd Sistr Eliz: Clare aged of 32 years.*

Anno: Dni: (1716) ye 17th of Octobr in our Convent of Naz: of English Poor Clares in Graveline is most happily reposed in our Lord, Sisr Eliz: Clare Collingwood, ye 79th Year of her Age, & 47th of her entrance into ye holy Religion. She was so addicted to piety, even whilst she was secular, yt it was frequently perceiv'd by one yt lay wth her, yt she rose in ye night to pray, & wou'd Continue a long time in yt holy occupation, if not interrupted, by percieving her Companion awaken wch she diserning her humility made her hasten to bed for fear any appearance of virtue

* Daughter of Cuthbert Collingwood, of Dalden, co. Durham, and Eslington, co. Northumberland, Esq., and sister of Fr. Thomas Collingwood, S.J., and Dom Roger Anselm Collingwood, O.S.B. Her nephew, George Collingwood, of Eslington Hall, married Catherine, daughter of Henry Brown, 5th Viscount Montagu, and was executed at Liverpool, 25 Feb. 1716, for having joined the Chevalier de St George.

might be seen in her, as she was ingenious to hide her Sanctity in y[e] world, so was she no less apprehensive of y[e] Moth of Vanity in Religion, ever shuning y[e] applause of Creatures, & fearing nothing more y[n] their Praises. God Alm: was pleased to try her wth great aridities, depriving her of all sensible Comfort in his divine service, notwithstanding she was always most assiduous, & intense in Prayer, & no less exemplar in her nearness in holy Poverty & fidelity in the performance of all Religious dutys, particularly of Regularity, having never been seen to come too late to any assembly of y[e] Community. She dy'd of a pure decay of Nature w[ch] made her slip so Suddenly from us y[t] she was deprived of y[e] benefit of being anointed, but had receiv'd her viaticum, so we do confide does already enjoy y[e] reward of her virtue, but y[e] Judgm[ts] of God being inscrutable y[r] accustom'd Charity is most humbly intreated for y[e] rest of her soul. Requiescat in Pace.

(155) Anno: Dni: (1670) the 8th of Decemb[r] Sist[r] Eliz: **Bell**, now call'd Sist[r] Mary Collet made her Profession, being aged of 26 years.

Anno: Dni: (1705) the 9th of March in our Conv[t] of Naz: of English Poor Clares in Graveline fortified with all y[e] rights of our holy Moth[r] y[e] Church, & wth presence of Spirit even to y[e] last moment our D[r] Sister, Sist[r] Mary Collet Bell render'd her soul to her Creator, Aged of 60 years, & 35 since her entrance into holy Religion, having wth fidelity applyed herself to y[e] acquisition of all virtues y[t] cou'd render her most perfect in our state w[ch] she hath left us a lively example of, as seeking her own abjection, assiduity in Prayer, silence, & retiredness, a general Compassion, & Charity to all, ever excusing y[e] absent, & interpretating all in y[e] best sense, her mortification in diet was remarkable, as well as y[e] custody she had over her senses, chiefly her Eyes, w[ch] she seem'd only to use for necessity, nor was her holy industry less, to turn of any thing that might redown'd to her own prayse, or discover her Sufferances, w[ch] she ever concealed as much as possible, w[ch] her last Sickness proved, never speaking of it till 3 days before her death, tho it was y[e] 6th of a violent fever, w[ch] y[e] Doct[r] declared mortal at first sight, her consumated virtue joyn'd to a strong confidence in y[e] Immaculate Moth[r] of God. I hope merited a speedy reward, yet since y[e] best actions must pass a strict examing, I beg y[r] usual charity for y[e] repose of her Soul. Requiescat in Pace.

(156) Anno: Dni: (1671) the 26th of July Sis[r] Mary **Blundell** now call'd Sis[r] Mary Bonaventure made her holy Profession, Aged of 17 Years.*

Anno: Dni: (1690) the 16th of Jan[ry] in our Conv[t] of Naz: of English Poor Clares in Graveline, is most happily departed y[s] life

* Daughter of William Blundell and sister of Alice above.

strengthened wth all ye rights of our holy Moth^{r} ye Church, our Dr Sister, Sister Mary Bonaventure Blundell, the 36th Year of her Age, & 20th since her entrance into Religion, during wch time she much Edified us by her Religious comportment, & high esteem of her holy vocation, she was very compassionate & charitable, willing to assist all, never giving refusal to any, y^{t} required her service, during ye three last years of her life she suffer'd much, by a lingering Consumption particularly ye last 7 months of her life y^{t} she was confined to her Bed wth admirable patience & resignation to ye Divine Will, & Singular silence wthout complaint wch was her practise ever to silence her own indisposition, she was very intense in Prayer, singularly devote to ye ever B^{d} Mother of God, who no doubt obtain'd her so happy a death. most sweetly & quietly rendering her soul wth joyned hands into those of her Creator, y^{t} nothing may retard her speedy happiness, we earnestly crave ye assistance of y^{r} holy Prayers. Requiescat in Pace.

(157) Anno: Dni: (1672) the 12th of June, Sist^{r} Eliz: **Tempest,** now call'd Sis^{r} Frances Clare, made her holy Profession, Aged of 20 Years.*

Anno: Dni: (1694) the 8th of Augt in our Conv^{t} of Naz: of English Poor Clares in Graveline, is most happily departed this Life, Strengthened wth all ye rights of our holy Moth^{r} ye Church, our Dr Sister, Sist^{r} Frances Clare Tempest the 43rd Year of her Age & 24th since her entrance into Religion, she has left us great proofs of solid virtue, by a serious tendance to perfection, & interiour Recollection, ever w^{n} not hinder'd by obedience, & conventual cerimonies, retaining her first fervour, she was a model to us of modisty, & all Religious observances, & made as peaceable & sweet an end as one might expect after so exemplar a Life, wch gives us great hopes of her present felicity, for fear notwithstanding there may remain anything yet to purify, we humbly crave ye assistance of y^{r} Prayers & Suffrages. Requiescat in Pace.

(158) Anno: Dni: (1672) ye 8th of Decr Sis^{r} Mary **Heyes** now Call'd Sis^{r} Margaret Ignatia made her holy Profession. Aged of 24 Years.

Anno: Dni: (1700) the 19th of March in our Conv^{t} of Naz: of English Poor Clares in Graveline is happily departed y^{s} Life, Strengthened wth all ye rights of our holy Moth^{r} ye Church, our Dr Sister, Sis^{r} Margaret Ignatia Heyes, the 53rd Year of her Age, & 29th since her entrance into holy Religion, she hath left us much edified at her humility, & contempt of herself, & high esteem of her Holy Vocation, she was most Charitable, & compassionate,

* Daughter of Stephen Tempest, of Broughton Hall, co. York, Esq., by Susan, daughter and co-heiress of William Oglethorpe, of Roundhay Grange, co. York, Esq.

Indefatigable in all humble Labours, till ye Alm^{ty} was pleas'd to visit her wth a painful Lingering Consumption, the which she suffer'd wth much patience, & entire conformity to ye Divine Will during ye 7 months she was confined to her Chamber, she frequently animated by her words, & example, to a strong Confidence in God, & to rejoyce in our happy state, for her Soul's speedy possession of her heavenly Spouse, whom incessantly she Languished after, I humbly crave y^{r} holy Prayers & Suffrages of Charity. Requiescat in Pace.

(159) Anno: Dni: (1672) the 8th of Decemb^{r} made her holy Profession, Sister Mary **Masey**, now call'd Sister Mary Anna Clare, Aged 17 Years.

Anno: Dni: (1697) the 4th of November in our Conv^{t} of Naz: of English Poor Clares in Graveline is most happily departed y^{s} Life strengthened wth all ye Sacraments of our holy Moth^{r} ye Church, our Dr Sis^{r}, Sis^{r} Mary Anna Clare Masey, ye 43^{d} Year of her Age, & 26th since her entrance into holy Religion, wch time she spent wth great fervour, & zeal in ye true observance of our holy Rule, being a great Lover of holy poverty, silent suffering, respect & submission to superiours, fidelity in ye performance of all thing committed to her Charge, devote to our B^{d} Lady, whose Sacristin she was 11 years, & above all her Singular Charity to ye Sick, for whose service and solace, she cheerfully sacrificed her Rest, time & forces, even to ye prejudice of her own health, as was most evident, ye 2 latter years of her life she wth a most filial respect, and compassion tended our Dr R^{d} Moth^{r} Abbess of happy Memory Moth^{r} Ann Bonaventure, 13 days before whose death, she sweetly finish'd her Life, have suffer'd with great patience, & conformity to ye divine Will a violent fever for 10 days. We humbly beg ye help of y^{r} prayers for ye speediest rest of her soul. Requiescat in Pace.

(160) Anno: Dom: (1673) the 2^{d} of Feb: Sister Anne **Cannell** now call'd Sis^{r} Ann Clare, Aged of 19 Years, made her Profession.

Anno: Dni: (1721) the 26th of June in our Conv^{t} of Naz: of English Poor Clares in Graveline, most happily quitted y^{s} mortal exile, administred wth all ye Rites of our holy Moth^{r} ye Church, our Dr Sister, Sister Ann Clare Cannell, ye 67th Year of her Age & 49th since her Entrance into holy Religion, wch time she hath spent in an unrelented fervour, great intenseness in Prayer, & interiour Recollection and a fervent Love of God, being as one dead to all things of this world, desirous to be unseparably united to her heavenly spouse whose celestial Vision we hope she now enjoys, but least any thing shou'd detain her, your accustomed Charity is most humbly requested for the repose of her Soul. Requiescat in Pace.

(161) Anno: Dni: (1675) the 21st of Nov: Sister Ellen **French,** now call'd Sisr Ellen Clare, made her Professi: Aged of 17 Years.

Anno: Dni: (1700) the 2d of Feb: is happily departed this Life, strengthened wth all ye rights of our Mother ye Church, in our Convent of Naz: of English Poor Clares in Graveline, our Dr Sister, Sistr Ellen Clare French ye 44th year of her Age, & ye 27th since her entrance into Religion, all which time she seriously applyed her self to ye acquisition of those virtues most suitable to her vocation, & most particularly edified us at her prompt Obedience, respect, & submission to superiours, silently suffering ye many incommodities of an infirm body wth a Cheerful equal temper. She was generally Charitable to all, never refusing her assistance to any in wt she was able, she was very devout to ye most holy Sacramt of ye Alter, and to our Bd Lady, and in all accourances had a strong Confidence in God, & Conformity to his Holy Will, for her Soul's speediest repose I humbly crave yr holy Prayers & Suffrages of Charity. Requiescat in Pace.

(162) Anno: Dni: (1674) the 26th of July Sisr Eliz: **Dandy** now call'd Sisr Eliz: Frances made her holy Profession, Aged of 23 years.

Anno: Dni: (1713) the 21st of Apl in our Convent of English Poor Clares of Naz: in Graveline, is happily departed this Life, our Dr Sister, Sisr Elizabeth Frances Dandy, Aged of 63 & 40 since her entrance into Religion, 30 whereof Almty God tryed her by painful infirmities, wt unabled her to comply wth her vocation of Lay Sister, she applied herself to perseverant prayer; & to ye performance of wch service her infirmities permitted her to render, being singular Charitable to All, but most mortified to her self, concealing for several years a Cancer she had in her breast, even until her death from knowledge, as much as she cou'd, even ye dolour it caused her, willingly & joyfully supporting ye same for Love of her heavenly spouse. Languishing to be dissolved to enjoy him Eternally, wch that she speedily may do, be pleased to afford her ye assistance of yr holy Prayers. Requiescat in Pace.

(163) Anno: Dni: (1676) the 6th of March Sistr Margarett **Richerson,** now call'd Sistr Margaret Winifred, made her Profession, Aged of 23 years.

Anno: Dni: (1728) ye 10th of Janry in our Convt of Naz: of English Poor Clares in Graveline, is most happily deceased, our Dr Sistr, Sistr Margaret Winifred Richerson, administred wth all ye rights of our holy Mothr ye Church Aged of 66 & 43 since her entrance into holy Religion her Assiduity to ye gaining of perfection from her 1st entrance continued to her dying day, & was particularly exemplar in ye observance of Silence, being careful not to speak wh a sign wou'd serve, & so punctual in all regular observances, y[t] she was never seen to come too late to any, her Love, Respect, & obedience to Super[rs] was very singular, as also her devotion to S[t] John Evang[t] whose Spirit she endeavour'd to acquire, by a general Love to all, and in her care w[n] Mistress of Novices, her cheerful supportation of sharp & long illnesses was very edifying, in her last sickness she was attacked wth an asthma, w[ch] she was frequently subject too, & tho y[e] Doct[r] did not apprehend her in present danger, yet she found, & knew herself so near death, y[t] y[e] whole Night before she dyed, did not dare to sleep in y[e] least, telling her tender in y[e] morning, she apprehended, she shou'd never waken more in y[s] world, & dye before she had received her God, y[e] Viaticum was brought to her, betwixt 6 & 7 of y[e] clock in y[e] morning, and she dyed before they had finish'd annointing her. I humbly beg y[r] prayers for y[e] speediest repose of her soul. Requiescat in Pace.

(164) The same day & year made also her holy Profession, Sister Mary **Hensby**, now call'd Sist[r] Mary of Immaculate Conception, being 22 years.

Anno: Dni: (1698) y[e] 3[d] of May in our Conv[t] of Naz: of English Poor Clares in Graveline, is happily departed y[s] life, strengthened wth y[e] rights of our holy Moth[r] y[e] Church our D[r] Sister, Sist[r] Mary of y[e] Immaculate Conception Hensby, Aged of 45 & 23 since her entrance into holy Religion, since which time she much edified us by her prompt Obedience, love for holy poverty, recollection and equality of temper, Assiduity in prayer, Ardent devotion to y[e] holy Sacrament, & exact observance of Regular discipline, supporting wth great patience, & Conformity to y[e] divine will, many Infirmities, & sharp tryalls, her humility taught her to conceal ingeniously several talents & endowments she was advantaged with all & to require as if ignorant y[e] directions of others. I hope ere this she enjoys y[e] reward of her pious Life, yet it being y[e] divine will to surprise her wth a Sudden death, we y[e] more ernestly recommend her to y[r] holy prayers & Suffrages. Requiescat in Pace.

(165) Anno: Dni: (1677) the 21st of Novem: Sis: Eliz: **Gerard,** now call'd Sist[r] Mary of y[e] Passion, made holy Professi: being Aged of 17 Years.*

Anno: Dni: (1728) the 9th of March in our Convent of Naz: of English Poor Clares in Graveline, strengthened wth all y[e] rights of our holy Mother y[e] Church is happily departed y[s] Life, our D[r] Beloved Sister, Sister Mary of y[e] Passion Gerard Jubilarian, Aged of 69 & 52 since her entrance into holy Religion. She has

* Daughter of Sir William Gerard, of Bryn Hall, co. Lancaster, 4th Bart., by Anne, daughter of Sir John Preston, of Preston Patrick and Under Levens halls, co. Westmoreland, and of the Manor of Furness, co. Lancaster, 1st Bart.

G

much edified us wth her piety, devotion, & example in Conventual dutys, & little serviceable actions, nothwithstanding her weak constitution & age; even showing in her beheaviour an angelical Innocency, & primitive fervour, which doubtly has obtained her a great reward, yet least any thing shou'd retard her speedy enjoyment of it, I humbly beg y[r] accustom'd prayers. Requiescat in Pace.

(166) The same day & year made also her Profession, Sist[r] Isabella **Ashton,** now call'd Sist[r] Collet Clare being Aged of 19 Years.*

Anno Dni: (1692) the 16th of Nov[r] in our Convent of Naz: of English Poor Clares in Graveline, is most happily departed y[s] life, Strengthened wth all y[e] rights of our holy Mother y[e] Church, our D[r] Sister, Sister Collet Clare Ashton y[e] 35th Year of her Age & y[e] 16th since her entry into holy Religion, during all w[ch] time she has left us much edified at her humility, and sweetness, retaining y[e] same Respect, & willing Complyance to all, as if she were a Novice. She was very singular for silence, tending to herself, & to her Obedience seeking her own Mortification, esteeming her self a Miserable Sinner, w[ch] made her during Life, but most especially during a long & tedious Consumption to apprehend death, w[ch] our D[r] Lord was pleased so to sweeten, by giving all things y[t] might render her happy, in such manner that gives us great hopes of her already happiness, yet for fear anything may yet remain to be purified, y[r] Prayers we most humbly crave. Requiescat in Pace.

(167) Anno: Dni: (1678) the 29th of March Sis[r] Eliz: **Beazer,** now call'd Sis[r] Teresa Benedict made her holy Profession being Aged of 24 Years.

Anno: Dni: (1711) the 9th of July in our Conv[t] of Naz: of English Poor Clares in Graveline, is happily deceased fortified wth y[e] Sacraments, our D[r] Sist[r], Sist[r] Teresa Ben: Beazer, Aged of 58th & 35th since her entrance into our ho: Ord[r] having before her admittance here, spent 8 years under y[e] Rule of S[t] Benedict at Ypres, from whence she came, unwilling to be exposed to y[e] distraction of a new beginning. She brought along wth her, y[e] true broken spirit of Religion, w[ch] she daily improved by her constant & exact Obedience, & Respect to Superiours, fidelity to God, preventing goodness & civility to all, to w[ch] was added a most extraordinary patience, in several great & painful infirmities, w[ch] made her condemn'd by y[e] Doctors several years & kept us astonish'd how she cou'd persevere to do so many little services for holy Religion, & as y[s] was esteem'd a kind of miracle, so was

* Daughter of Roger Ashton, of Littlewood Hall, co. Lancaster, Esq., by Elizabeth, daughter of Richard Depdale, of Stratford-upon-Avon, co. Warwick, gent. She was niece of Elizabeth Ashton above.

ye restoration of her speech, wch she had lost 7 years, as we have reason to believe was obtained by prayer, the fervour in wch she dyed, we hope speedily merited her a plentiful experience of ye divine Mercy, notwithstanding, humbly recomend her Soul's speedy rest, unto y^r^ holy Prayers. Requiescat in Pace.

(168) Anno: Dni: (1680) the 6^h^ of Jan: Sist^r^ Marget **Ratlife**, now call'd Sist^r^ Mary of Jesus, made her holy Profession, aged of 38 years.

Anno Dni: (1693) the 2nd of Decr in our Conv^t^ of Naz: of English Poor Clares in Graveline is most happily departed y^s^ life, strengthened wth all ye rights of our holy Moth^r^ ye Church, our Dr Sister, Sist^r^ Mary of Jesus Ratlife, Aged ot 51 and 13 Years since her entrance into holy Religion, having left us much edified at her Virtue, chiefly her fervour, & fidelity to God, & the holy Religion, by her exact practise & observance of all religious Ceremonies, notwithstanding her Infirmities, wch she bore wth great silence, patience, & resignation to ye divine will, endeavoring in all things to make herself more pleasing to her heavenly Spouse, seeking in all things her own Mortification, & to live in humility as an abject in his house, whose soul we most humbly recommend to y^r^ holy Prayers. Requiescat in Pace.

(169) The same Day & Year made also her holy Profession Sister Margarett **Culchett**, now call'd Sister Margarett of ye holy Ghost, being aged of 29 Years.*

Anno: Dni: (1682) the 12th of Jan^ry^ in our Conv^t^ of Naz: of English Poor Clares in Graveline, is most happily departed y^s^ Life, Strengthened wth all ye rights of our holy Moth^r^ ye Church, our D^r^. Sis^r^, Sister Margarett of ye holy Ghost Culchett, ye 37th year of her Age, & 4th since her entry into ye holy Religion, which time she has spent in ye strict Observance of our holy Rule, & of such virtues as might make her more pleasing to her heavenly Spouse, bearing wth Silence, & humble Submission to ye divine will, all difficultys, & repugnance of Nature, being much addicted to Prayer, & as one deaf & dumb to all things of y^s^ world, wch makes us hope she is gone to ye nuptial feast of ye Lamb, more Loaden wth virtues than Years, but as ye Judgm^ts^ of God are hidden I must humbly beg y^r^ prayers for her speedy enjoying of eternal bliss. Requiescat in Pace.

(170) Anno: Dni: (1681) the 3rd of May, Sis^r^ Margarett **Meredith**, now call'd Sis^r^ Clare Margarett made her Profession, being of 29 Years.

Anno: Dni: (1708) the 24th of July in our Conv^t^ of Naz: of English Poor Clares in Graveline, most happily quitted this mortal

* Daughter of Thomas Culcheth, of Culcheth Hall, co. Lancaster, Esq., by Anne, daughter of James Bradshaigh, of The Haigh, Esq., and sister of Sir Roger Bradshaigh, 1st Bart.

exile, our Dr Sister, Sister Clare Margarett Meredith, the 56th Year of her Age, & 30th since her entrance into holy Religion, where she wth out ye least relaxation, prouv'd her self a perseverant pattern of virtue, & fervour to ye last moment of her Life, which seem'd to be but one continual act of ye Love of God, wch cou'd not possibly but receive a daily increase by constant application to ye divine presence, her great abstraction exact Silence, contempt of ye world, fidelity to all religious duties, holy simplicity, Obedience, to Suprs her silent sufferance was no less remarkable, for she had certainly dropt down dead in some assembly, had not her Illness been discover'd by her looks, & occasion'd her being sent to ye Infirmary, where wth a most earnest & Languishing desire she expected her last hour, & enjoyment of her God, wch yt nothing may retard, I humbly request yr accustom'd prayers & Suffrages. Requiescat in Pace.

(171) Anno: Dni: (1682) the 21st of Novr Sisr Elizabeth **Widdrington**, now call'd Sisr Mary Ignatia, made her Profession, being aged of 29 Years.*

Anno: Dni: (1713) the 4th of March is happily departed ys Life in our Convt of Naz: of English Poor Clares in Graveline, our Dr Sister, Sisr Mary Ignatia Widdrington, administered wth all ye rights of our holy Mother ye Church, aged of 60 Years, & 32 of Religion, since which she has been constantly exact, & fervent in ye punctual observance of our holy Rule & Constitutions, bearing wth patience, & great Courage many Sicknesses, never admitting of dispensations, but in time of greatest extremities, nor abstaining from nourishing her Soul wth ye Sacrament of ye holy Eucharist, tho ever so ill, her fervour giving her forces for ye same, having a great Devotion to ye ho: Sacramt, to our Bd Lady, St Joseph, & ye Souls in Purgatory from whom she was a Constant Benefactrice, by her Continual prayers for their relief, which if she now stands in need of your prayers for her Speedy Enjoyment of Eternal bliss is most humbly Intreated. Requiescat in Pace.

(172) Anno: Dni: (1684) ye 6th of Janry Sister Margaret **Culcheth**, now call'd Sistr Dorothy Joseph aged 25 made her holy Profession.†

Anno: Dni: (1724) ye 11th of Novr in our Convt of Naz: of English Poor Clares in Graveline, is most happily deceas'd our Dr Sister, Sistr Dorothy Joseph Culcheth, administred wth all ye rights of our holy Mother ye Church, Aged of 66 & 42 since her

* Daughter and co-heiress of Sir Edward Widdrington, of Cartington, co Northumberland, Bart., by Catherine Charleton, of Hesleyside, in the same county. Her sister Mary married Sir Edward Charleton, of Hesleyside, Bart.

† Dorothy Culcheth was sister of Margaret Culcheth above. There is apparently some confusion in the text.

Entrance into holy Religion, all which time she has been most Indefatigable in her laborious vocation never admitting of any release, placing her perfection chiefly in delighting herself in all humble works, which she performed wth y[e] greatest fidelity imaginable. She was ever ready & even preventing to assist any who wanted her help, her grounded interior humility was also manifested by y[e] mean opinion she had of herself, even reputing herself y[e] least & most undeserving in y[e] house, her great esteem, & love to holy Poverty, gave her a constant watchfullness to hinder the least thing from being wasted. She had a Singular Devotion to our B[d] Lady & S[t] Joseph, who undoubtedly obtained her y[e] courage & patience wth which she bore her last Sickness, we humble request for her y[r] accustom'd Charity. Requiescat in Pace.

(173) The same day & year made also her holy Profession Sist[r] Catherine **Copland,** now call'd Sis[r] Catherine Magdalin y[e] 44th Year of her Age.*

Anno: Dni: (1691) the 5th of March, in our Conv[t] of Naz: of English Poor Clares in Graveline, is most happily departed this Life, Strengthened wth all the Sacraments of our holy Mother y[e] Church, our D[r] Sis[r], Sis[r] Catherine Magdalen Copland, y[e] 51st Year of her Age, & 7th since her profession, having served our Convent in quality of extern Servant 9 Years, & both then, & since her coming to Religion employed her forces most infatigably in y[e] Service of y[e] holy Community, who were much Edified at her virtues, namely her humility, patience, mortification, & assiduity in Prayer, studying still how to please her heavenly Spouse, & render herself more agreeable in his divine sight, whose sweet embracements we confide she now enjoys, but if any thing remains yet to purify, we humbly crave, she may receive the assistance of y[r] holy Prayers. Requiescat in Pace.

(174) Anno: Dni: (1684) the 12th of Aug[t] Sis[r] Jane **Whittingham,** now call'd Sis[r] Mary Frances made her Profession, being aged of 24 years.†

Anno: Dni: (1722) the 9th of March in our Conv[t] of English Poor Clares of Naz: in Graveline, is most happily departed y[s] Life, Strengthened wth all the Sacraments of our holy Moth[r] y[e] Church, our D[r] Sister, Sis[r] Mary Frances Whittingham, y[e] 62[d] of her Age & 38th since her Profession, she was ever a most Laborious, & serviceable member, one of a great devotion & tenderness, but it pleased God to visit her for several years before she dyed w[th]

* Daughter of Robert Copeland, of Dolphin Lee in Bulk, co. Lancaster, gent., and Catherine his wife.

† Daughter of Thomas Whittingham, of Whittingham Hall, co. Lancaster, Esq., by Anne, daughter of Henry Ogle, of Notts, Esq. She was grand-daughter of Godfrey Whittingham, of Whittingham Hall and Ashley Hall, Esq., by his first wife Isabel, daughter of Sir John Vavasour, of Spaldington Hall, co. York, Knt.

many particular interiour Sufferances, which she bore with much patience, & great Edification to us all, that she may ye more; speedily enjoy her eternal reward, y^{r} Prayers are humbly requested. Requiescat in Pace.

(175) Anno: Dni: (1685) ye 25th of March, Sis^{r} Eliz: **Shaftoe,** now call'd Sis^{r} Mary of ye Incarnation made her holy Profession, being of 19 Years.*

Anno: Domini (1743) ye 3^{d} of May in our Conv^{t} of Naz: of English Poor Clares in Graveline, is happily departed y^{s} life, strengthened wth all ye rights of our holy Moth^{r} ye Church, our Ven: Moth^{r} Jubilarian, Sis^{r} Mary Incarnation Shaftoe aged of 78 & 61 since her entrance into holy Religion, from which time she has been a constant example of unrelented ferv^{r} piety, & devotion, joyn'd to a great intenseness in Prayer, in which she daily spent many hours, & has ever been most remarkable for her devotion to ye Holy Sacram^{t} making ye Choir her constant center, & with an astonishing fervour refresh'd her soul with y^{t} heavenly food, w^{n} scarse able to get out of her bed. Respect, Obedience to Sup^{rrs} was ever her darling virtue, wch she wth unweary'd endeavours inculcated into her Novices during ye three terms she laudably exercised y^{t} Office, wherein she gave them example of all Religious virtues, particularly of Silence, & abstraction from all things of y^{s} world. She sustained many infirmitys wth admirable patience, chiefly her last wch was a Violent fever of 20 days & Catarrh, her tender devotion to our B^{d} Lady was also peculiar, who doubtless assisted her, in her happy death, having render'd up her soul wth perfect tranquillity, & presence of mind, & I now confide is enjoying ye only object of her affections, but not to be wanting in our duty humbly crave y^{r} accustomed Cha: for her. Requiescat in Pace.

(176) Anno: Dni: (1685) ye 1st of 7^{ber} Sister Ellen **Lasley,** now call'd Sister Ellen Bernard made her holy Profession being aged of 41 years.

Anno: Dni: (1703) the 9th of June in our Conv^{t} of Naz: of English Poor Clares in Graveline is most happily departed ye life, furnish'd with all ye rights of our holy Moth^{r} ye Church, our Dr Sister Sister, Ellen Bernard Lasley, Lay Sister, the 59th Year of her Age, & 19th since her holy Profession, all which time she has spent in

* Daughter of John Shaftoe, of Bavington Hall and Fenwick Hall, co. Northumberland, Esq., by Frances, daughter of Edward Fenwick of Stanton, co. Northumberland, Esq. Her father and three brothers, William, Edward, and John, and her nephew John, joined the Chevalier de St George, and were all taken prisoners at Preston, where her brother Captain John was shot by sentence of court-martial. Her brother William married 24 June 1695, Elizabeth, daughter of Thomas Riddell, of Swinburne Castle, co. Northumberland, Esq., was attainted of high treason like his father, brothers, and son John, and died in exile at Brussels. William's younger son, Dom William Benedict Shaftoe, O.S.B., died at Lisbon in 1742.

a faithful Complyance wth her holy vocation, rendering herself a most Edifying member by her diligent employing each moment thereof in ye service of holy Religion, perseverantly joining prayer with Labour, & never making a reply to what was required of her, she was most Respectful to Sup^{rs} & so exemplar in all virtues suitable to her state y^{t} she at her death merited ye Elogium from her Conf^{r} that her greatest imperfections might serve for example of virtue for others to practice, but ye Judgm^{ts} of God being inscrutable, I humbly crave for her y^{r} prayers of Charity. Requiescat in Pace.

(177) Anno: Dni: (1686) ye 10th of June, Sis^{r} Frances **Crane,** now call'd Sis^{r} Frances of ye holy Ghost, made her holy Profession aged of 18 Years.*

Anno: Dni: (1699) the 14th of Sepr in our Conv^{t} of Naz of English Poor Clares in Graveline, is most happily departed y^{s} Life, strengthened wth ye Sacraments of our holy Mother ye Church, our Dr Sister, Sister Frances of ye Holy Ghost Crane, aged 32 & 14 since her entrance into holy Religion, during which time she much edified us by her general charity to all, she being extremly compassionate, & to ye utmost of her power helpful to any she saw in any sort of affliction, she was insatiable in her endeavours to solace ye Souls in Purgatory, & most ardently devoted to ye adorable Sacrament of ye Alter, she lived & dyed a large sharer of ye Cross. Alm^{ty} God being pleased to try her wth great aridities, interiour suffrances, & almost continual Corporal infirmities, lastly most violent Convulsions, wch deprived her of her speech, and sences, & two days after of Life, for her Soul's speedy repose I humbly crave y^{r} holy Prayers. Requiescat in Pace.

(178) Anno: Dni: (1686) the 26th of July, Sister Bridgett **Wesbye,** now call'd Sis^{r} Bridget Clare, made her holy Profession, aged of 20 Years.†

Anno: Dni: (1741) the 2^{d} of July in our Conv^{t} of Naz: of English Poor Clares in Graveline, is most happily deceas'd, strengthened wth all ye Rites of our holy Mother ye Church, our Venerable, & Dr Moth^{r} Jubilarian Sister Bridget Clare Westbye, aged of 75 Years, & 56 since her Entrance into holy Religion. which time she fervent spent in acquiring all virtues suitable to her vocation, chiefly a constant tendance to her own interiour, & ye surmounting of whatever might render her less pleasing to Alm^{ty} God, her Charity, & humility was singular, read'ly assisting

* Daughter of Francis Crane, of Woodrising Hall, co. Norfolk, Esq., by Mary, daughter of William, first Lord Widdrington, of Widdrington Castle, Northumberland.

† Daughter of Thomas Westby, of Mowbreck Hall and Burn Hall, co. Lancaster, and Westby, co. York, Esq., by Bridget, daughter of Thomas Clifton, of Clifton Hall, Lytham Hall and Westby Hall, co. Lancaster, Esq. and sister of Sir Thomas Clifton, Bart.

any one who stood in need of help, even in the most abject employs, never declining any thing of that Nature, notwithstanding her age & infirmities, which she supported wth great Courage, & Patience, admitting no dispensation from y^e constant observance of our holy Rule, & fervent performance of y^e Divine Office day & night, y^e peculiar devotion she always had to St Joseph doubtless obtained her y^e singular tranquillity, & peace of mind during 6 months Languishing decay of nature & daily expectation of death, y^e $Judgm^{ts}$ of God being unknown, I earnestly request y^r accustom'd Charity for y^e repose of her Soul. Requiescat in Pace.

(179) Anno: Dni: (1687) the 20th of May, Sis^r Jane **Widdrington**, now call'd Sister Mary Antony made her Profession being aged of 17 Years.*

Anno Dni: (1749) the 12th of Augt in our $Conv^t$ of English Poor Clares in Graveline, is most happily deceas'd, our D^r & Venerable Mo^r Jub^n Sister Mary Antony Widdrington, aged eighty. & 64 since her Entrance into holy Religion, during wch she was remarkably Austere to herself, & indulgent to others, & most exemplar in her unrelented fervour, wch carried her on notwithstanding her great age to keep ye morning watch ye space of 24 years in wch she cou'd not be prevail'd upon to desist, till a month before her death, & spent great part of ye night in prayer w^n not hinder'd wth ye sick, for whom her zeal & charity was indefatigable night & day, & no less General to all who were in need of her assistance, preventing every one in serving them in all y^t was most disgustful & abject, in wch her humility was very peculiar. Consumating her Life, & forces in ye service of our Community, to whom she had ever been a most beneficial member, her Respect & submission to Sup^{rs} was equally edifying, as was also her tender devotion to ye Passion, & to our B^d Lady, her last illness was a decay of Nature, in wch 7 days before she expired she cou'd not swallow any nourishment to sustain her, wch she sufferd to y^e last wth singular patience & sweetness, & gives us all reason to hope she now enjoys eternal Recompense, yet y^e $Judgm^{ts}$ of God being inscrutable we humbly intreat y^r Charitable Prayers: Requiescat in Pace.

(180) The same Day & Year made also her holy Profession Sister Catherine **Fitzwilliams**, now call'd Sis^r Catherine Clare, y^e 18th year of her Age.

Anno: Dni: (1700) the 8th of Novr in our $Conv^t$ of Naz: of English Poor Clares in Graveline, is most happily departed y^s life, strengthened wth y^e $Sacram^{ts}$ of our holy Mo^r y^e Church, our Dr Sister, $Sist^r$ Cath: Clare Fitzwilliams, Aged of 30 years, &

* Daughter of William, second Lord Widdrington, of Widdrington Castle, by Elizabeth, daughter and heiress of Sir Peregrine Bertie, of Evedon, co. Lincoln, Knt., younger son of Robert, first Earl of Lindsey.

13 since her entrance into ho: Religion, wch time she has spent in a fervent pursuit of all solide virtues, most conformable to her holy vocation and strict observance of our holy Rule, & Constitutions, wth generous courage and cheerfulness breaking through all difficultys wch any ways opposed her perfection, complyance wth her duty & Obedience to Superiours, in wch virtue she was particularly exemplar. As also in ye practice of holy poverty, and Sisterly Charity, wch was generally experienced by all in those three years she was sick mother, & 3 months she was 1st Portress, in wch office she dyed of a most painful fever, wch for ye space of 10 days she supported wth great patience, & Conformity to ye divine Will. I humbly recomend her souls speedy rest to y^{r} holy Prayers and Suffrages of Charity. Requiescat in Pace.

(181) The same Day & Year made also her holy Profession Sist^{r} Ann Norris, now call'd Sist^{r} Anna Maria Aged of 17 years.

Anno Dni: (1743) ye 19th of March, in our Conv^{t} of Naze: of English Poor Clares in Graveline, is most happily deceas'd our D^{r} & Ven: Mo^{r} Jub^{n} Sis^{r} Anna Maria Norris, Aged of 75 & 57 since her entrance into holy Religion, during wch time she has been a constant example of fervour, & Regularity, ever showing a great esteem, & Value w^{rs} zeal. for ye exact Observance of our holy Rule, & all customs & Ceremonys of holy Religion, particularly during ye 2 terms of her being Vicaress; she was also remarkable in her general goodness, & Charity, wch made her Aimable to all, her devotion to our B^{d} Lady, & ye holy family was very singular & no less edifying was her patience, & cheerful supportation of a painful Rheumatism, & Lingering decay, but her unrelented fervour gave her courage to assist at ye Divine Office w^{n} scarce able to walk, & was at Vespres ye day before she dy'd, assisting there wth her usual fervour, & devotion, ye next morning being risen wth design to Communicate she was seiz'd with an apoplectic fit, wch depriv'd her of ye benefits, but recover'd her senses so far as to make her Confession. Rec^{d} ye Extreme Unction, & sweetly render'd up her soul about 9 o'clock at night, y^{t} nothing may retar'd her speedy enjoyment of Eternal bliss. I humbly beg y^{r} accustomed Prayers. Requiescat in Pace.

(182) The same day and year made also her holy Profession Sis^{r} Catherine **Bryers,** now call'd Sis^{r} Cath: Teresa being aged of 17 years.*

* Daughter of Robert Bryers (or Breers) of Walton Hall, in the parish of Walton-on-the-Hill, co. Lancaster, Esq., by his first wife Mary, daughter of John Molyneux, of Newhall, West Derby, co. Lancaster, Esq. Her brother, the Rev. Lawrence Breers, formerly a professor at Douay College, died in London 14 Nov. 1744. His *Douay Dictates* and his *Formula of Pontifical Oath* taken by him at Douay 12 May, 1686, are now at Old Hall College.

Anno Dni: (1713) ye 19th of Novr in our Convt of Naz: of English Poor Clares in Graveline, is most happily quitted ys Mortal Exile our Dr Sister, Sisr Catherine Teresa Bryers, Aged of 44 & 28 since her entrance into holy Religion, in whch she gave us a constant example of devotion to our Bd Lady, & Angel Guardian, whose little Alter she wth great respect adorned and kept most neatly for several years, very faithful to Religious dutys, & exact to Ceremonys, and tho her health was very weak, and unconstant, yet her fervour gave her Courage to Keep ye Larum, and call ye Community to Matins 15 years, together her Ingenuity was very distinguishing, as well as her Complyance in makeing use of it, for ye Service of any that beg'd her assistance this Charity made her never Idle, wch Joyn'd to her fidelity to God I hope obtained her a speedy injoymt of him, yet least any thing shou'd be wanting, I beg yr prayers for her Soul's Repose. Requiescat in Pace.

(183) Anno: Dni: (1687) ye 20th of May made her ho: Prof: Sisr Mary **Blackett**, now call'd Sisr Mary of ye ho: Ghost aged of 30 years.

Anno: Dni: (1693) ye 28th of Novr in our Convt of Naz: of English Poor Clares in Graveline, is most happily departed this Life, admistered wth all ye Sacraments of ye Church, our Dr Sister, Sistr Mary of Holy Ghost Blackett, ye 38th Year of her Age, & 8th since her entry into ye holy Religion, wch time she hath spent wth great fervour, Love, & fidelity to God, & ye holy Religion, by her constant labours, & exactitude in regular discipline having a most high esteem of her holy vocation, & great tendance to prayer, & to her own perfection, Languishing to enjoy her God, as appeared by her expressions of joy, when ye last Sacraments was ordained her, which she receiv'd with great devotion, & immediately after sweetly rendering up her Soul to her Creator, for whose Speediest enjoying of Eternal Bliss, we humbly crave yr holy Prayers. Requiescat in Pace.

(184) Anno: Dni: (1687) the 6th of Decembr Sisr Hanna **Seacome**, now call'd Sisr Agnes Joseph, made her holy Profession being aged of 18 years.

Anno: Dni: (1736) the 5th of July in our Convt of Naz: of English Poor Clares in Graveline, is most happily departed ys life, our Dr Sister, Sister Agnes Joseph Seacome ye 67th Year of her age, & 50th since her entrance into ye holy Religion. Almty God was pleased to favour her in a peculiar manner by her conversion to ye Catholic faith, withstanding wth great Courage & Constancy ye many endeavours yt were us'd by her Parents and Relations to draw her from it. She also gave great marks of ye high esteem she had of her holy vocation to Religion by a singular exactness in Religious Customs & Ceremonies, & an humble carriage, & greatful comportment, during ye many years Almty God was pleas'd to afflict her wth sharp illnesses, wch we hope has merited her an Everlasting Crown, but ye Judgments of God being secret we earnestly entreat y^{r} accustom'd prayers for ye repose of her Soul. Requiescat in Pace.

(185) The same day & year, made her ho: Profession Sis^{r} Ann **Clifton**, now call'd Sis^{r} Ann Frances, being Aged of 18 Years.*

Anno: Dni: (1702) in y^{s} our Conv^{t} of Naz: of English Poor Clares in Graveline, ye 28th of Feb^{ry} is most happily departed this Life strengthened wth all ye rites of our holy Mother ye Church our Dr Sister, Sister Ann Fran^{s} Clifton, Aged of 32 Years, & 15 since her entrance into holy Religion, wch time she spent wth great fervour in ye exact observance of our holy Rule, wth admirable courage patience, & fortitude of mind, sustaining, & surmounting many sharp pains & Languishing illnesses, & unless w^{n} confined to her bed, scarce ever dispensed wth herself night or day from ye Divine Office, notwithstanding her Office of Infirmarian wch she exercised wth great compassion, & general Charity to all. She was most assiduous in Prayer, & particularly devoted to ye Holy Sacram^{t} & our B^{d} Lady had a high esteem of her holy Vocation wch she particularly exprest at her death, showing by her perfect Conformity, & joy of Spirit, rather to be going to Celebrate ye nuptials of her Spouse, y^{n} to pay ye tribute to Justice, her most sweet & happy death gives assured hopes of her speedy Possession of Eternal glory, but ye Judgm^{ts} of God being inscrutable, I beg for her y^{r} holy Prayers of Charity. Requiescat in Pace.

(186) The same day & year made also her holy Profession Sist^{r} Ellen **Gerard**, now call'd Sist^{r} Winifred Magdalin, being aged of 19 Years.†

Anno: Dni: (1696) ye 5th of Janu^{ry} in our Conv^{t} of Naz: of English Poor Clares in Graveline, is most happily departed y^{s} life, strengthened wth ye rights of our holy Moth^{r} ye Church, our Dr Sister, Sister Winifred Magdalen Gerard, aged of 27 & 9 since her entrance into Religion, wherein she has much edified us by her serious tendance to herself, a prompt Obedience to ye very inclination of her Sup^{r} a sweet condescendance, compassion, & charity to her Sisters, nearness in holy Silence, great contempt of ye world & high esteem of her holy Vocation, wch she expresst in a most particular manner at ye hour of her death, as also her

* Daughter of Gervase Clifton, of Westby, gent., younger son of Sir Cuthbert Clifton, of Westby and Lytham, Knt., by his second wife, Dorothy, daughter of Sir Thomas Smith, of Wotton Wawen, co. Warwick. Her mother was Dorothy, daughter of Hamlet Mascy, of Rixton Hall. co. Lancaster, Esq., by Dorothy, daughter of Roger Bradshaigh, of The Haigh.

† Daughter of Sir William Gerard, of Bryn Hall, co. Lancaster, 4th Bart., by Anne, daughter of Sir John Preston, of Preston Patrick and Under Levens, co. Westmoreland, and the Manor of Furness, co. Lancaster, first Bart.

desire to dye, to enjoy her God, y[t] nothing may hinder her speedy possession of y[t] happiness, I humbly beg y[e] assistance of y[r] holy Prayers. Requiescat in Pace.

(187) The same day & year made also her holy Profession Sister Margaret **Osbaldeston**, now call'd Sister Teresa Joseph, aged of 21 Years.*

Anno: Dni: (1730) y[e] 1st of Feb[ry] in our Conv[t] of Naz: of English Poor Clares in Graveline is most happily departed, fortified wth all y[e] rights of our holy Moth[r] y[e] Church, our D[r] Sister, Sis[r] Teresa Joseph Osbaldeston, y[e] 64th Year of her Age, & 43rd since her entrance into holy Religion, during which time she has given us great examples of humility, ever Embracing y[e] most abject, & Laborious Employments, was remarkable for her Respect & Obedience to Sup[rs] had a strong confidence in God, & ever expresst a great Love for her holy Vocation, dyed wth great sentiments of piety, being present to herself to y[e] last w[ch] makes us confide she already Enjoys y[e] reward of her good works, but y[e] Judgments of God being inscrutable, we humbly request the assistance of y[r] holy prayers, for y[e] repose of her Soul. Requiescat in Pace.

(188) Anno: Dni: (1688) y[e] 6th of July, Sis[r] Eliz: **Briers** now call'd Sist[r] Mary Euphrasia, made her Profession being aged of 17 Years.†

Anno: Dni: (1730) y[e] 1st of Nov[r] in our Conv[t] of Naz: of English Poor Clares in Graveline is most happily departed y[s] Life, fortified wth all y[e] Rites of our holy Moth[r] y[e] Church, our D[r] Sister, Sister Mary Euphrasia Briers, y[e] 68th year of her Age & 43[d] since her Entrance into holy Religion, during w[ch] time she has much Edified us by her constant fervour, & assidiousness to y[e] Divine Office day & night, was remarkable for her patience, supporting many painfull infirmities, particularly y[e] stone, & Gout, her tender Devotion to our B[d] Lady, & S[t] John Baptist, has we Confide made them very powerful Intercessors for her, but y[t] nothing may retard her speedy Enjoyment of Eternal happiness, I humbly request y[r] Prayers of Charitie. Requiescat in Pace.

(189) Anno: Dni: (1688) y[e] 27th of Decemb[r] Sister Dorothy **Fettyplace**, now call'd Sister Mary Teresa, made her holy Profession, being Aged of 22 Years.‡

* Daughter of John Osbaldeston, of Sunderland Hall in Balderstone, co. Lancaster, Esq., by Anne, daughter of Richard Blackburne, of The Hill, in Goosnargh, co. Lancaster, Esq.

† Daughter of Robert Bryers (or Breers) and sister of Catherine above.

‡ Daughter of Bartholomew Fettiplace, of Swyncombe, co. Oxon, Esq., by Mary, daughter and heiress of William Englefield, fourth son of Sir Francis Englefield, of Englefield, co. Berks, and Wotton Basset, co. Wilts, 1st Bart. Her grandfather, Francis Fettiplace, of Swyncombe, married Dorothy, daughter of Thomas Yate, of Lyford, co. Dorset, Esq.

Anno: Dni: (1705) ye 20th of May in our Conv^t^ of Naz: of English Poor Clares in Graveline, sweetly Reposed in our Lord, fortified wth all ye rights of our holy Moth^r^ ye Church, our tenderly beloved Sister, Sister Mary Teresa Fettyplace, ye 38th Year of her Age, & 17th since her entrance into holy Rgligion, during wch time she was neve perceiv'd wth reflection either in word or sign to have given trouble to any one, nor was her virtue less inventive in excusing her neighbour, wch made her not only conceal w^t^ ever mortification she met wth from them, but found means of praise even in their imperfections, this charitable practice, joyn'd to an unchangeable sweet, mild temper made her pious conversation coveted by all, & consequently generally amongst us, a mean opinion of herself. Obedience, & respect to Sup^rs^ seem'd to be her particular character, to wch was added a perfect conformity to ye Divine Will, & a singular devotion to ye Immaculate Mother of God, by who's intercession she doubtless obtained so remarkeable a patience in her frequent Sicknesses, & incisions, wch ye remedys of her infirmities obliged her to, thus being refin'd in ye furnace of both Corporal, & spiritual Suffrances I hope was crown'd immediately wth an immortal recompense yet since ye Judgm^ts^ of God are secretes to us, I humbly request in her soul's behalf y^r^ Suffrages & Prayers. Requiescat in Pace.

(190) Anno: Dni: (1689) the 5th of June made her ho: Profession, Sis^r^ Jane **Gee**, now call'd Sis^r^ Frances Xaveria, being Aged of 18 Years.

Anno Dni: (1723) ye 17th of Octr furnish'd wth all ye rights of our holy Moth^r^ ye Church, render'd up her Soul in our Conv^t^ of English Poor Clares in Graveline our Dr Sister, Sister Frances Xaveria Gee, ye 52^d^ Year of her Age, & 36th since her entrance into holy Religion, during which time she gave us great Edification, by an humble carriage, ever seeking after humble, & abject works, & expressing continually much Comfort, & Content in her happy call to Religion, ye last Year of her Life she underwent a painful Consumption without ye least sign of impatience, & dyed with great Confidence in Gods Mercies, we humbly crave for her y^r^ accustom'd Charity. Requiescat in Pace.

(191) Anno: Dni: (1689) ye 25th of Novr Sister Anne **Smythe**, now call'd Sis^r^ Ann of ye Presentation, made her holy Profession, being Aged of 17 Years.*

Anno: Dni (1728) ye 22nd of Feb^ry^ in our Conv^t^ of Naz: of English Poor Clares in Graveline, is happily departed this Life, strengthened wth all ye rights of our holy Moth^r^ ye Church, our Dr Sister, Sis^r^ Anne of ye Presentation Smythe, ye 56th Year of her age

* Daughter of Sir Edward Smythe, of Eshe Hall, co. Durham, 1st Bart., by Mary, daughter and co-heiress of Sir Richard Lee, of Langley and Acton Burnell, co. Salop, 2nd Bart.

& 39th since her entrance into holy Religion she was Replenish'd with a most solid & perfect Religious Spirit, which she particularly signaliz'd in ye Office of Mrs of Novices, zealously instilling into her Young whatever cou'd conduce to their perfection. Inciting them by her own example to ye practice of a punctual Obedience, Respect & submission to Suprs also exactness to all regular customs & ceremonies as far as her health wd permit, & gave us all great example of Piety in her Cheerful, & couragious supportation of many sicknesses, yt nothing may retard her speedy possession of Eternal happiness, I humbly beg yr accustom'd Charity. Requiescat in Pace.

(192) Anno Dni: (1690) ye 1st of Janry made her holy Profession Sisr Eliz: **Seacum**, now call'd Sisr Clare Frances, being aged of 16 Years.

Anno Dni: (1716) the 25th of Janry in our Convt of Nazar: of English Poor Clares in Graveline is happily departed ys Life fortified wth all ye rights of our holy Mothr ye Church, our Dr Sister, Sister Clare Frances Seacome, Aged of 42, & 27 since her entrance into holy Religion. She was prevented wth grace in a most particular manner, even from her Childhood, which occasion'd her conversion to ye catholic faith, & remained constant in it, notwithstanding all ye caresses, & ill treatment of her parents at 12 years old, doubtless 'twas ye same grace yt made her lead so holy a Life in Religion, being ever most exact in all Re: Observances, Obedient to Suprs & a great Lover of holy poverty, wch was joyn'd to a serious tendance to herself, & constant practise of Interior mortification but of all virtues she seem'd to shine most in that of conformity to ye divine will, bearing ye most sensible Crosses wth an heroic patience, wch we confide has before this obtaind her an Eternal reward, but ye judgments of God being inscrutable, I beg ye assistance of yr holy prayers for her speedy repose. Requiescat in Pace.

(193) The same day & Year made also her ho. Profession Sisr Ann **Copley**, now call'd Ann of ye Nativity being Aged of 20 Years.*

Anno Dmini (1718) ye 4th of Sepr in our Convt of Naz: of English Poor Clares in Graveline is happily deceased, adminstered wth all ye rights of our holy Mother ye Church, our Dr Sister, Anne of ye Nativity Copley, aged of 50 years, & ye 30th since her entrance into ye holy Religion, where she has been a great example of fervour, having no regard to her tender Constitution, placing her chief Satisfaction in ye strict Observance of our holy Rule, till by Infirmities a few Years before her death, was forc't to admit of

* Of the ancient Catholic family of Gatton, co. Surrey, and probably daughter of Roger Copley and his wife Anne. Bro. Foley, *Records S.J.*, vi., 471, says that her three sisters were nuns, the eldest a Canoness, and two Benedictines at Dunkirk.

some Dispensations, so great a lover of Regularity, & follow: ye Comunity, that notwithstanding ye lameness she was often subject to, could not be prevailed wth to be absent from assisting at ye Divine Office both day & night, to wch she had a peculiar devotion, & at all other times as far as holy Obedience permitted her, made ye Choir her chiefest place of residence. She supported wth a great deal of Courage, & entire resignation her last Sickness of a fever & vomiting, that nothing may retard her speedy enjoyment of Alm^{ty} God I humbly request y^e assistance of y^r prayers & suffrages. Requiescat in Pace.

(194) The same day & year made also her holy Profession Sistee Mary **Rape**, now Call'd $S^{t\,r}$ Mary Clare, y^e 19th Year of her Agr.

Anno Dni: (1709) the 6th of Feb^{ry} in our $Conv^t$ of Naz: of English Poor Clares in Graveline, y^e 38th Year of her Age, & 21st since her Entrance into Ho: Religion has most edifyingly render'd her pious Soul, our D^r $Sist^r$ Mary Clare Rape, after a Violent fever of 20 days, wch she Supported wth a most extraordinary patience & Resignation to y^e divine will wch as it were by force raised her above y^e terror & usual apprehensions she had of death, expressing when drawing nigh that hour the wonderful effect she then found in her Soul, by her former interiour Suffrances, wch she ever bore wth great sweetness & Silence, as well as many corporal infirmities, wch to ye sensible increase of her mortification render'd her unable for ye duties of her Laborious Vocation, tho she constantly endeavour'd to supply it by her fidelity in whatever Obedience she was put to, being always observ'd to employ her time profitably, & to benefit by all contradictions she met with. bearing them with a Singular Mildness, which also appeared in her virtuous Conversation in which you might discern her being guided by an interiour spirit; wch doubtless made her actions most pleasing to Almighty God, who that she may speedily enjoy, I humbly intreat y^r accustom'd charity. Requiescat in Pace.

(195) Anno: Dni: (1690) the 16th of Ap^l Sis^r Ann **Dempster** now call'd $Sist^r$ Ann Laurance made her Profession being aged of 24 Years.

Anno: Dni: (1708) the 10th of Novr in our $Conv^t$ of Naz: of English Poor Clares in Graveline is happily slept in our Lord, our Dr Sister, Sis^r Ann Laurence Dempster, Aged of 43 & 20 since her entrance into holy Religion: tho by Violence of Convulsions was incapable of Confessin or Viaticeum, yet by an instinct some hours before, had disposed herself by all sorts of acts proper for a dying person, for she was ill of a fever, but not thought in danger, her last, as well as many other great Sicknesses, she supported wth very remarkable patience, & resignation, chiefly a most consuming & painful Rheumatism, which reduced her to a perfect Anatomy, she recover'd of it, but never so, as to be able to quit ye Infirmary, where she gave most constant proofs of her peaceful spirit, tendance to her self Recollection, & nere Concience, thus joyn'd to her continual infirmities, we hope has helpt her to an Immortal Crown: but since human frailty is great, I ernestly request your usual prayers & Suffrages for ye repose of her Soul. Requiescat in Pace.

(196) The same Day & Year made also her holy Profess: Sis^r^ Margarett **Shaftoe** now call'd Sis^r^ Clare of the Holy Sacrament, being Aged of 18 Years.*

Anno: Domini: (1713) the 7th of June in our Conv^t^ of Naz: of English Poor Clares in Graveline has joyfully & sweetly return'd her Soul to her Creator our most Dr Sister, Sister Clare of ye Holy Sacrament Shaftoe, Aged of 42 & ye 24th since her entrance with ye holy Religion, during which t'was evident by her humble devout & recollected comportment, y^t^ she was perseverant in ye pursuit of virtue & made her increase of perfection her sole buissiness, being most particularly exemplar in silence, retirement, tendance to her self & devotion to ye Holy Eucharist from wch she doubtless receiv'd such a strength of spirit as made her wth an astonishing patience & perfect Conformity support ye cruel pains of a Cancer in her bowels wch reduced her to a very Anatomy, yet her unchangable sweetness, was both ours & ye Doct^rs^ wonder especially ye month she lived after ye last Sacraments, for he said her Suffrances was inconceivable to any but ye Allm^ty^ whom I hope she speedily enjoy'd, yet not to neglect our duty, I humbly request y^r^ accustom'd Succour. Requiescat in Pace.

(197) Anno: Dni: (1690) the 8th of Sepr Sister Mary **Blundell** now call'd Sister Mary Bonaventure made her holy Profession being of 17 years.†

Anno: Domini (1719) ye 22nd of May in our conv^t^ of Naz: of English Poor Clares in Graveline has quitted y^s^ mortal Exile, our Dr Sister, Sister Mary Bonaventure Blundell, Vicaress ye 46th year of her age & 30th since her entrance into holy Religion, from her Childhood she had a pent to virtue, a tender devotion to our holy Fath: St Francis, & to all ye Saints of our holy Order, wth a thirsty desire of following their footsteps, wch from ye day she took ye habit she signaliz'd, placing her study & delight in ye practice of their virtues, chiefly by a Respect & submission

* Daughter of John Shaftoe and sister of Elizabeth above.

† Daughter of William Blundell, of Crosby Hall, co. Lancaster, Esq., by Mary, daughter of Rowland Eyre, of Hassop Hall, co. Derby, Esq. Her brother Nicholas succeeded to the estates, married Frances, daughter of Marmaduke, 2nd Lord Langdale, and left two daughters and co-heiresses, the younger of whom, Frances, eventually became sole heiress, and, having married Henry Peppard, Esq., was succeeded in the estates by her son Nicholas who assumed the name of Blundell.

to Sup^{rs}, Assiduity, & intenseness in prayer, holy poverty was her darling virtue, wch appeared in her Clothes, & throughout all her actions, in whatever employments she was in, tho of distraction, she appear'd wth an interiour recollection, & performd all dutys wth ye greatest fidelity imaginable as was manifest ye 6 years she was Choir Mistress, & was ever a pattern of Regularity, a little after she was Chosen Vicaress it pleas'd God to visit her with a sharp sickness in wch her patient & silent supportation of suffrances was most edifying, as was her always pious conversation, w^{n} her health permitted her to return to ye Com^{ty} she made it her study to give all manner of satisfaction, wch caused her being so suddenly snatch'd from us, generally regretted, she was seiz'd upon wth an appoplectic fit, blood gushing out of her mouth, & gave us only time to administer ye holy Oyles, wch makes us, tho her Life was a daily preparation for death earnestly petition y^{r} holy prayers for her speedy enjoyment of eternal glory. Requiescat in Pace.

(198) The same Day & Year also made her holy Profession Sister Catherine **Busby,** now call'd Sis^{r} Cath: Eugenia being Aged of 23 years.*

Anno: Dni: (1743) the 19th of Octr in our Conv^{t} of Naz: of English Poor Clares in Graveline, is most happily deceas'd our Ven: Moth^{r} Jub^{n} Sister Catherine Eugenia Busby, Aged of 77 & 55 since her entrance into Holy Religion, during which time she has exceedingly edified us by her silent & patient Supportation of many sharp & tedious Sicknesses, notwithstanding she has been a very serviceable member, performing several employments, as y^{t} of Dispencier, Infirm^{n} & Sacristin, & was very remarkable for ye well spending of her time, employing her self either in reading or working with her needle till ab^{t} a week before her death, this joyn'd to her constant devotion to our B^{d} Lady, & St John Baptist doubtless obtained her so happy an end, she receiv'd all ye Rites of ye Church wth perfect presence of Spirit tranquillity & peace of mind y^{t} nothing may retard her speedy enjoyment of Alm^{ty} God. I earnestly petition y^{r} H: Prayers & Suffrages. Requiescat in Pace.

(199) The same day & year made also her holy Profession Sister Mary **Mollineux** now call'd Sister Mary Evangelist being aged of 17 years.†

* Of the family of Busby, of Coddington, co. Oxon, and probably sister of Fr. John Busby *alias* Brown, S.J., and niece of Fr. George Busby *alias* Brown, S.J. Two of her relatives, Teresa and Anne Busby, were nuns at the English convent at Brussels, O.S.D., the latter being superioress.

† Daughter of Richard Molyneux, of New Hall in West Derby, co. Lancaster, Esq., by Elizabeth, daughter of Robert Harrington, of Huyton Hey, co. Lancaster, Esq., through which marriage the Huyton estates eventually passed to the Molyneux family.

Anno: Dni: (1728) y^e 6th of March is happily departed y^s Life, in our $Conv^t$ of Naz: of English Poor Clares in Graveline our Dr Sister, Sister Mary Evangelist Mollineux, administred wth all y^e Rites of our ho: $Moth^r$ y^e Church y^e 55th year of her age 38 since her entrance into holy Religion, wch time she has spent in y^e fervent pursuit of all virtues most conformable to her holy Vocation, namely Love, respect, Obedience, & Submission to Sup^{rs} & has left us much edified at her admirable courage, & fortitude of mind where wth she surmounted most continual & Languishing Infirmities, her sweetness, patience, & conformity to ye will of God, was not less remarkable in a blindness wch she supported for many years wth out ever being heard to complain, she enjoy'd a perfect presence of mind, & not a quarter before her death desired ye Father y^t assisted her to dye to joyn wth her in saying the *Te Deum* in thanksgiven to Alm^{ty} God for all ye Crosses & Sufferances it had pleased him to send her, & render'd up her last breath in most affectionate acts, but human frailty being great, beg y^e assistance of y^r H Prayers for y^e repose of her soul. Requiescat in Pace.

(200) Anno: Dni: (1691) the 6th of Feb^{ry} Sis^r Mary Magda: Bagnall, now Call'd Sis^r Mary Magdalen made her holy Profession being Aged of 18 Years.*

Anno: Dni: (1709) the 8th of June in our $Conv^t$ of Naz: of English Poor Clares in Graveline is piously deceas'd Our most Dr Sister, Sister Mary Magdalen Bagnall, Aged of 37 & 19 since her entrance into y^e Holy Religion, where she has evidenc'd herself an Example of unrelax'd fervour, Intenseness, & fidelity to Prayer, an habitual interiôur union wth God, wch particularly appear'd in a painful, & Lingering Consumption of 2 years, wch she supported wth an unparallel'd Courage & Cheerfulness, but chiefly her last Sickness, in which her unchangeable Sweetness was most remarkable, as well as her presence of Spirit, which next to an application to her own interiour, she employ'd in taking notice of each particular, & expressing her kindness to ye Community, to whom a little before she dyed she bid her last farewell, & confest her thoughts were so taken up in conserving her patience, & union wth God, y^t it banisht all apprehensions in any kind, y^s disposition gives us hopes of her present felicity, but not to be failing in my duty, humbly beg y^r prayers. Requiescat in Pace.

* Daughter of Dudley Bagenal, of Dunleckney Manor, co. Carlow, Esq., by Anne, 2nd daughter of Edward Butler, of Ballyragget, co. Kilkenny, Esq. Her father, who accompanied James II. into exile and was an officer at his court, died at Bruges in 1712. He was son of Colonel Walter Bagenal, of Dunleckney Manor (born 1614, who was executed by Cromwell at Kilkenny in 1652), by his wife, Elizabeth daughter of Christopher Roper, 2nd Lord Teynham. Her elder sister, Ann, in 1692 married Sir Gervase Clifton, of Clifton, co. Notts, 4th Bart., after whose death in 1731 she became the wife of William Blackburne, Esq., and died in 1734.

Emery Walker Ph.sc.

Mother Catharine Dominic Bagnall
7th Abbess of Poor Clares, Gravelines
From the painting, Ursuline Convent, Greenwich

To face p. 115

(201) The same Day & Year made also her holy Profession, Sister Catherine Bagnall, now Call'd Sister Cath: Dominick being Aged of 17 Years.*

Anno: Dni: (1736) in this our Convent of Naz: of English Poor Clares in Graveline the 8th of Ap[l] most sweetly & piously rendered her Soul to her Creator amidst ye tears & prayers of her afflicted Children, strengthen'd wth ye Rites of our holy Moth[r] ye Church, our most Venerable & Dearly beloved Mother Catherine Bagnall, in ye 63rd Year of her Age, & 47 of her Religious Profession, & 31 of her Government in quality of Abbess. She was endow'd wth Singular advantages of nature, & grace wch renderd her amiable to all she conversed with. Indifatigable in her assiduity for ye Community's advancement Spiritual, & temporal Great was her faith, & confidence in Almty God, & invincible her Courage & patience in Cross Events, ye Singular Devotion she had to ye Passion of our Bd Saviour doubtless Strengthen'd her to Support wth [illegible] Continual Infirmities, she [illegible] examples of Mortification, most particularly in her diet, her Maternal tenderness & Compassion for ye Sick was no less extraordinary, having no regard to her own health to give them any ease or Solace. She was seiz'd on Mandy Thursday wth her last Sickness; yet wou'd not omit Serving at ye Table, & washing ye feet, from whence she was Constrain'd to take her bed, Employing her last 11 days continual fever, in fervent & repeated Aspirations to Almighty God, which did not hinder her taking particular notice of each person of her Community, & giving them her blessing, till she was not able to lift up her hand, her great Devotion to St Frances Xaverious (by whom she had (202) often been favour'd), doubtless obtain'd that unalterable Sweetness & presence of Spirit to the last moment, so Saintly a Death, gives us all reason to hope she's now in the enjoyment of a happy Eternity; but not to be failing in our Duty, we humbly Request ye accustom'd Prayers. Requiescat in Pace.

(203) Anno: Dni: (1692) the 8t of Sep[r] Sister Ann Newsham now Call'd Sister Ann Didacus made her holy Profession being aged of 26 Years.†

* Sister of Mary Bagenal above. She was elected 7th Abbess in Jan. 1705. The following is extracted from a letter from the spy Le Brun (Capt. J. Ogilvie) to the Duke of Mar, dated from Dunkirk, 10 Aug. 1717 (*The King's Stuart Papers, Hist. MS. Comm.*):—'I doubt not you know who is Lady Abbess there [Gravelines]. She is the sister of Bagnall that is with Mr. Whytlye (Ormonde) and she knows every step Mr Whytlye takes, and you can judge what secretaries nuns are, but more particularly my Lady Abbess, who can keep nothing longer than she can find an occasion to tell it. Everybody knows this that knows her.'

† Probably a grand-daughter of Richard Newsham (or Newsam) of Forton, gent., one of the purchasers of the Manor of Forton, co. Lancaster, in 1643-4, whose will was proved in 1672. He was second son of William Newsam, of Forton, gent., second son of Robert Newsam, of Newsam Hall in Plumpton, co. Lancaster, Esq., by Elizabeth, daughter of Capt. Sherburne, of Greenhalgh Castle (*vide C.R.S.*, vi., 172).

(201) The same Day & Year made also her holy Profession, Sister Catherine **Bagnall**, now Call'd Sister Cath: Dominick being Aged of 17 Years.*

Anno: Dni: (1736) in this our Convent of Naz: of English Poor Clares in Graveline the 8th of Apl most sweetly & piously rendered her Soul to her Creator, amidst ye tears & prayers of her afflicted Children, strengthen'd wth ye Rites of our holy Mothr ye Church, our most Venerable & Dearly beloved Mother Catherine Bagnall, in ye 63rd Year of her Age, & 47 of her Religious Profession, & 31 of her Government in quality of Abbess. She was endow'd wth Singular advantages of nature, & grace wch renderd her amiable to all she conversed with. Indifatigable in her assiduity for ye Community's advancement Spiritual, & temporal. Great was her faith, & confidence in Almty God, & invincible her Courage & patience in Cross Events, ye Singular Devotion she had to ye Passion of our Bd. Saviour doubtless Strengthen'd her to Support wth remarkable patience & serenity Continuul Infirmities, she likewise great examples of Mortification, most particularly in her diet, her Maternal tenderness & Compassion for ye Sick was no less extraordinary, having no regard to her own health to give them any ease or Solace. She was seiz'd on Mandy Thursday wth her last Sickness; yet wou'd not omit Serving at ye Table, & washing ye feet, from whence she was Constrain'd to take her bed, Employing her last 11 days continual fever, in fervent & repeated Aspirations to Almighty God, which did not hinder her taking particular notice of each person of her Community, & giving them her blessing, till she was not able to lift up her hand, her great Devotion to St Frances Xaverious (by whom she had (202) often been favour'd), doubtless obtain'd that unalterable Sweetness & presence of Spirit to the last moment, so Saintly a Death, gives us all reason to hope she's now in the enjoyment of a happy Eternity; but not to be failing in our Duty, we humbly Request yr accustom'd Prayers. Requiescat in Pace.

(203) Anno: Dni: (1692) the 8t of Sepr Sister Ann **Newsham** now Call'd Sister Ann Didacus made her holy Profession being aged of 26 Years.†

* Sister of Mary Bagenal above. She was elected 7th Abbess in Jan. 1705. The following is extracted from a letter from the spy Le Brun (Capt. J. Ogilvie) to the Duke of Mar, dated from Dunkirk, 10 Aug. 1717 (*The King's Stuart Papers, Hist. MS. Comm.*) :—'I doubt not you know who is Lady Abbess there [Gravelines]. She is the sister of Bagnall that is with Mr Whytlye (Ormonde) and she knows every step Mr Whytlye takes, and you can judge what secretaries nuns are, but more particularly my Lady Abbess, who can keep nothing longer than she can find an occasion to tell it. Everybody knows this that knows her.'

† Probably a grand-daughter of Richard Newsham (or Newsam) of Forton, gent., one of the purchasers of the Manor of Forton, co. Lancaster, in 1643-4, whose will was proved in 1672. He was second son of William Newsam, of Forton, gent., second son of Robert Newsam, of Newsam Hall in Plumpton, co. Lancaster, Esq., by Elizabeth, daughter of Capt. Sherburne, of Greenhalgh Castle (*vide C.R.S.*, vi., 172).

Anno: Dni: (1719) the 16th of July in our Convent of Naz: of English Poor Clares in Graveline, is most happily deceased our Dr Sistr Ann Didacus Newsham, strengthened wth all ye Rights of our holy Mothr ye Church, being aged of 43 Years, 28 since her entrance into ye holy Religion, wch time she has spent in a great tendency to her own perfection, & fidelity in acquitting herself of wt ever was enjoyned her by holy Obedience in her laborious Vocation, she made it her endeavour to acquire ye Spirit of our holy Rule, was much addicted to prayer, & particular devoted to her Patron Saint Didacus, & most remarkable in ye imitation of him, in the practice of ye virtue of holy Simplicity, her last Sickness was a painful Catarrh, she made a most holy & edifying end, I humbly Petition yr accustomed Charity for ye repose of her Soul. Requiescat in Pace.

(204) Anno: Dni: (1693) the 25th of Novr Sistr Margarett **Blundell**, now Call'd Sistr Clare Collet made her holy Profession, being Aged of 19 Years.*

Anno: Dni: (1709) the 10th of Febry in our Convt of Naz: of English Poor Clares in Graveline, has happily rendered her sweet & pious Soul, our Dr Sisr Clare Collet Blundell, ye 34th Year of her Age & 16th since her entrance into ho: Religion, leaving all in a general affliction for ye loss of so Virtuous & substantial a member, as equally beloved as esteem'd for her deserts, & true piety, being a most solid Example of a constant tendance to herself & zeal for ye increase of her own perfection, therefore abhor'd & shun'd nothing more than distracted occassions, notwithstanding wn ordered by H Obedience, performed them wth a remarkable fidelity, & quietness, taken care never to give mortification to any, being of so mild & sweet temper yt she seem'd even insensible of ye provocations she met wth, & so Charitable to hide them wn she cou'd, & tho of a most weak & tender Constitution was so exemplary Compassionate yt she often ventur'd all things beyond her Strength to help any she saw in Suffrance or affliction, & always preventing in any humble or serviceable action, proceeding from that vile opinion she had of herself, which doubtless also, made her Confidence (205) more strong in ye mercies of God, Who she languisht so much to Enjoy, & expresst it just a moment before she dyed, being in full presence of Spirit, yt that nothing may deprive her of this, I humbly beg yr usual relief for her Soul. Requiescat in Pace.

(206) The same Day & Year made also her holy Profession Sister Mary **Frankland**, now call'd Sister Mary Bruno being Aged of 21 Years.

Anno: Dni: (1725) the 24th of March in our Convt of Naz: of English Poor Clares in Graveline is happily departed this Life, our

* Daughter of William Blundell and sister of Margaret above.

Dr Sister, Sis^{r} Mary Bruno Frankland, ye 50th Year of her Age, 29th since her entrance into holy Religion, she ever had so great an esteem of her vocation, y^{t} she often said no Contradiction or Cross w^{t} ever could lessen her gratitude to Alm^{ty} God for calling her to so happy a state, & used a faithful Violence to ye gaining of perfection, she was very Charitable, & compassionate in ye tend ance of ye Sick, much devoted to our B^{d} Lady & St Bruno, who doubtless obtained her to be so well disposed for death for the speediest repose of her Soul, we humbly crave y^{r} accustomed Charity. Requiescat in Pace.

(207) Anno: Dni: (1695) the 25th of Nov: Eliz: **Allbot** now call'd Sis^{r} Mary of ye Holy Ghost, made her ho: Profession being Aged of 26th Years.

Anno: Dni: (1707) the 25th of June in our Conv^{t} of Naz: of English Poor Clares in Graveline is happily dead in our Lord, fortify'd wth ye rights of our Holy Moth^{r} ye Church, our Dr Sister, Sist^{r} Mary of the Holy Ghost Allbot ye 39th Year of her Age, & 11th of her holy Profession, since which she has faithfully Comply'd with her Laborious Vocation, employing ye extent of her strength in ye H: Community's Service, neither was her fidelity less towards God, for no wearyness nor Infirmity of body seemd sufficient to make her omit her prayer or lessen her fervour in it, as well as her devotion to ye Immaculate Mother of God, her patience resignation, & desire of death in her last Sickness, gives us great hopes of her present happiness, but since we are all Ignorant of ye Judgments of God, we humbly beg ye usual assistance for her speedy repose. Requiescat in Pace.

(208) Anno: Dni: (1696) the 17th of May made her holy Profession, Sister Catherine **Price** now call'd Sister Catherine Xaveria, being Aged of 20 Years.

Anno: Dni: (1751) ye 25th of July in our Conv^{t} of Naz: of English Poor Clares in Graveline has quitted this mortal exile administered wth all ye Rights of our holy Moth^{r} ye Church, our Ven: & Dr Moth^{r} Jub^{rn} Catherine Xaveria Price, aged 75, 56 since her entrance into holy Religion wch time she has spent in ye pursuit & practice of those virtues most suitable to her state, fervent Love of All: God & was endow'd wth remarkable piety from her Infancy, her tender compassion for the sick, of which she gave singular proofs, during ye time of her being Infirmarian, was no less Edifying thinking nothing too much y^{t} cou'd conduce to their ease, or relief, & has left us a great example of Conformity to ye Divine Will in her patient Supportation of many years painful & sharp Infirmities, & bore her last sickness wch was a Dropsy & Violent fever wth heroic patience, as she was most particularly devoted to our B^{d} Lady, S: Xaveria & her good angel, we don't doubt both they have been powerfull Intercessors to obtain her a speedy enjoyment of eternal rest, but not to be failing in our duty, humbly request her y^r accustomed Prayers of Charity. Requiescat in Pace.

(209) The same day & year made also her holy Profession Sis^r Mary **Talbot**, now Call'd Sis^r Mary of Jesus, being Aged of 19 Years.*

Anno: Dni: (1717) the 5th of Feb^ry in our Conv^t of Naz: of English Poor Clares in Graveline is most happily deceas'd furnish'd wth all ye Rights of our H: Moth^r ye Church, our Dr Sister, Sis^r Mary of Jesus Talbot, being Aged of 40 & 21 since her entrance into holy Religion, she was very patient in her supportation of Continual Infirmities, often express'd a great gratitude for her Vocation, she had also a tender Devotion to St Austin by whose mediation wee have reason to believe she obtain'd so happy & resign'd a death, we humbly beg your usual Charity for ye Speedyest repose of her Soul. Requiescat in Pace.

(210) The same day & Year made also her H. Profession Sister Mary **Clifton**, now call'd Sist^r Mary Stephen being aged of 17 Years.†

Anno: Dni: (1729) the 6th of Decemb^r in our Conv^t of Naz: of English Poor Clares in Graveline is most happily departed this Life, fortify'd wth all ye Rites of our ho: Moth^r ye Church, our Dr Sister, Sis^r Mary Stephen Clifton, ye 51st Year of her Age, & 34th of her H: Profes^n since wch time she has been very fervent in embracing of humble & Laborious work's, & w^n Infirmarian gave herself to ye attendance of ye Sick wth ye greatest compassion & tenderness Immaginable. She has also left us great marks of her undaunted Courage & patience in ye Supportation of a painful cancer, & other Infirmities for some years before her death, her great Love to her H. Vocation joyn'd to a strong Confidence in God, & constant devotion to our B^d Lady, & ye Angel Gabriel, doubtless was powerful in obtaining her so happy an end, & we hope a speedy fruition of Eternal bliss, yet ye Judgm^ts of God being inscrutable, we humbly request y^r accustom'd Prayers of Charity. Requiescat in Pace.

(211) Anno: Dni: (1696) the 24th of June, Sister Mary **Fletcher**,

* Daughter of Gilbert Talbot, 2nd son of John, 10th Earl of Shrewsbury, and his countess Mary, daughter of Sir Francis Fortescue, K.B., of Seldon Hill, co. Bucks. Her brother, Fr. Gilbert Talbot *alias* Grey, S.J., born 11 Jan. 1672-3, *de jure* 13th Earl of Shrewsbury, died in 1733.

† Daughter of James Clifton, of Ward's House in Salwick, gent. younger brother of Sir Thomas Clifton, Bart., of Clifton, Westby, Lytham, and Salwick halls. Her mother was Anne Brent, of Larkstoke, co. Gloucester (*vide C.R.S.*, vi., 194).

now call'd Sis^{r} Mary Baptist, made her holy Profession, being aged of 24 Years.*

Anno: Dni: (1724) on ye 19th of Jan^{ry} render'd up her Soul, Sister Mary Baptist Fletcher, aged of 52 & 29 since her entrance into holy Religion, which time she spent in ye humble work's of a Lay sister, with great neatness, & fidelity, & during her Infirm Life, which was several years before her death. She was ever employ'd in something or other for the Service of Religion, her last sickness was painful & violent, which she bore with a great deal of Resignation, & dyed perfectly present to herself, her hands joyn'd, uttering most holy Aspirations to God, we humbly crave for her y^{r} accustomed Charity. Requiescat in Pace.

(212) Anno: Dni: (1697) Sister Ann **Golden**, now Call'd Sis^{r} Ann Winifried made her H. Profession ye 27th of Decemb^{r} being Aged of 19 Years.†

Anno: Dni: (1711) the 10th of June in our Conv^{t} of Naz: of English Poor Clares in Graveline is happily deceas'd our Dr Sister, Sist^{r} Ann Winifrid Golden the 33rd Year of her Age & 15th of her holy Profession during wch time she has been a perseverant example of fervour, & Regularity, particularly in ye Choir. Obedience, Respect, & submission to Superiours, most Laborious in giving her strength for ye service of holy Religion, which joyn'd to her Sweet practises of Mortification, was esteem'd by all to Shorten her Life; but gives us reason to hope it gain'd her an ample reward in Heaven. Yet ye Judgments of God being unknown to us, I earnestly beg your Prayers for her Soul. Requiescat in Pace.

(213) Anno: Dni: (1699) the 2nd of Feb^{ry} Sis^{r} Jane **Frankland**, now Call'd Sister Mary of ye Angels, made her Profession being Aged of 32 Years.

Anno: Dni: (1728) the 11th of March, in our Conv^{t} of Naz: of English Poor Clares in Graveline, is departed this Life, fortified wth all ye Sacraments of our holy Moth^{r} ye Church, our Dr Sister, Sist^{r} Mary of ye Angels Frankland ye 65th Year of her Age & 30th since her entrance into holy Religion, she ever expresst a Singular content, & Love to her holy vocation, a confidence in ye mercys of God: she courageously supported many Long & tedious Infirmities, wch never hindered her from fervently employing to ye extent of her forces her agreeable voice in Singing,

* Daughter of Thomas Fletcher, of Denton's Green in Windle, co. Lancaster, gent. (*vide C.R.S.*, vi., 202). Of her niece Mary, born in 1719, daughter of Richard Fletcher, of Denton's Green, a curious account of a miraculous cure from a serious disease in 1768, through the application of the relic of the hand of the Ven. Martyr Fr. Edmund Arrowsmith, is related in Foley's *Records, S.J., ii.*

† Daughter of John Golden, of Southworth Hall, co. Lancaster, gent., son of Richard Golden, of Winwick Hall, gent., by Anne, daughter of John Hawarden, of Fenistrete, co. Lancaster, gent. (*vide C.R.S.*, vi., 106).

& reciting ye Divine Office wch we hope has already merited her ye possession of eternal happyness, but ye Judgments of God being unknown I humbly petition for her yr usual Prayers. Requiescat in Pace.

(214) Anno: Dni: (1699) the 26th of July made her holy Profession Sister Mary **Fox**, now Call'd Sistr Mary Nicolas, being Aged of 27 Years.

Anno: Dni: (1749) the 29th of Sepr has happily quitted this Mortal Exile, fortify'd wth ye Extrem Unction, our Dr Sister, & Ven Mothr Jubn Sisr Mary Nicolas Fox, aged 78 & 52 since her entrance into holy Religion, wch time she has faithfully spent in ye pursuit of all virtues most suitable to her holy Vocation, Chiefly Regularity, Retirement, Devotion, & Recollection, & was no Less Remarkable in Respect, & Submission to Superiours, having rendered Religion much Service in Several Employments, & Exercis'd the Office of Vicaress 11 years. All: God was pleas'd to afflict her wth great infirmitys several years before her death, Particularly wth Appoplectic, & palsical fitts, wch in a Manner depriv'd her of her speech, being unable for ye most part to articulate, or make herself understood, but by signs, wch she supported wth singular patience & Resignation, as also her last Sickness, her great devotion to our Bd Lady & St Micheael, doubtless obtain'd her so happy a death, wth perfect presence of mind, till half an hour before she expir'd, not being able to swallow several days before; depriv'd her of ye benefit of her Viaticum, we ye more earnestly entreat yr accustom'd Prayers of Charity. Requiescat in Pace.

(215) Anno: Dni: (1699) the 8th of Decembr Sister Cath: **Willson**, now call'd Sister Mary Michael made her H Profession being aged of 25 Years.

Anno: Dni: (1705) the 30th of July in our Convt of Naz: of English Poor Clares in Graveline, is happily departed this Life, fortify'd wth all ye Rites of our H Mothr ye Church, our Dr Sister, Sistr Mary Michael Willson, Aged of 32 & ye 7th since her entrance into H Religion, during which time she faithfully employ'd ye extent of her forces in duly acquitting herself of her Laborious Vocation, wch she had a sincere desire of, seeking in all things her own contempt, & abjection, her actions being animated wth an interior Spirit, wch tho she endeavour'd to conceal, yet her pious discourse constantly shew'd it, & discover'd she placed her perfection in hidden virtue, thus fidelity, & application in her ordinary actions Joyn'd to a sweet & peaceable temper, wth a strong Confidence in ye divine mercys kept her in a great equality during Life, & I hope meritted an immediate possession of her God, but since humain frailty is great, earnestly crave yr holy Prayers for ye rest of her soul. Requiescat in Pace.

(216) The same Day & Year made her holy Profession Sister Margaret **Ross**, now call'd Sis[r] Frances Clare being aged of 22 Years.

Anno: Dni: (1719) the 28th of June, in our Conv[t] of Nazareth of English Poor Clares in Graveline is happily departed this Life strengthened wth all y[e] rights of our holy Moth[r] y[e] Church, our D[r] Sister, Sist[r] Frances Clare Ross, y[e] 42nd Year of her Age, & 21 since her Entrance into y[e] holy Religion. She faithfully employ'd her strength in y[e] Service of holy Religion, by y[e] Laborious humble works of a Lay Sister, to y[e] extent of her forces, till it pleased God to try her wth long & painful infirmities, being most part of y[e] time confin'd to y[e] Infirmary, her last Sickness was a Lingering Consumption, whereof she most happily died, wth a great deal of Resignation, Allacrity, & Confidence in God, y[t] nothing may retard her speedy enjoyment of him. I humbly crave your holy Prayers & Suffrages of Charity. Requiescat in Pace.

(217) Anno: Dni: (1702) the 17th of May Sister Ann **Blundell**, now call'd Sister Mary Anna Joseph, made her ho: Profession, being aged of 30 Years.*

Anno: Dni: (1719) the 8th of Octob[r] in our Conv[t] of Naz: of English Poor Clares in Graveline is happily deceased, our D[r] Sister Mary Anna Joseph Blundell being aged of 48 & 19 years since her entrance into y[e] holy Religion, who tho of a very infirm Constitution yet by her piety, & fidelity to Religious Observance, as far as health wou'd permit her has been an Examplar Member. She was very Submissive, & Respectful to Superiours, Singularly Charitable, & serviceable to all, doing many hidden & humble actions wth a silent tendance to her own perfection, & supported her all most continual Infirmitys wth an Edifying patience, & conformity to y[e] divine will, we humbly entreat y[r] accustomed Prayers of Charity for y[e] speediest Repose of her Soul. Requiescat in Pace.

(218) Anno: Dni: (1703) the 3rd of May, Sister Catherine **Garbot**, now call'd Sister Mary Victoria, made her holy Profession being aged of 22 Years.

Anno: Dni: (1749) the 18th of June, in our Convent of Naz: of English Poor Clares in Graveline is happily deceas'd, strengthened wth all y[e] Rights of our holy Moth: y[e] Church, our D[r] Sister Mary Victoria Garbot aged 68 Profest 46, who from her coming to our House at 5 years old, & since her entrance into holy Religion, has much Edified us by her Innocency of Life, Mildness, Devotion, & piety, & no Less distinguish'd herself in Obedience, Submission, & Respect to Superiours. All: God was pleased to try her wth great Infirmities several years before her death, being confin'd to her Chamber 21 years wth a Goutish Rheumatisme, w[ch] entirely

* Daughter of William Blundell and sister of Mary above.

contracted all her Sinews, unable to help herself. She suffer'd wth Exemplar patience, Cheerfulness, & Conformity to ye divine will. Gratitude to ye Community made her petition y^{t} they might not be charg'd w^{h} ye usual Prayers for her, after her decease, having as she said, been so great a Burden to them in her Sickness, nevertheless to Comply wth our duty we humbly entreat them for ye speedy Repose of her Soul. Requiescat in Pace.

(219) Anno: Dni: (1703) the 15th of Augt made her holy Profess: Sister Bridget **Stockley,** now call'd Sist^{r} Winifrid Magdalen being aged of 23 years.

Anno: Dni: (1734) the 25th of Decemb^{r} in our Conv^{t} of Naz: of English Poor Clares in Graveline, is most happily departed this Life, our Dr Sister, Sist^{r} Winefrid Magdalen Stockley, Aged of 54 & 32 since her Entrance into holy Religion, her last Sickness, was a Catarrh, took her off more Suddenly than was expected, & only left time for ye Extrem unction, but her pious Life gives us just reason to hope that she was not found unprepared, & that our loss is her gain. She was particular for interiour Recollection, & union wth God, 'twas easy to discern by her discourse ye comfort she found in that pious entertain, as also in her call to Religion, expressing in all occasions her contempt of ye World & Love to her holy Vocation, her Singular Devotion to our B^{d} Lady, & good Angel has we dont doubt made them powerful intercessors for her, but that nothing may retard her Enjoyment of Eternal Bliss, I humbly request for her y^{r} accustom'd Prayers of Charity. Requiescat in Pace.

(220) Anno: Dni: (1704) the 28th of May made her holy Profession, Sister Mary **Gerard,** now call'd Sister Paschalis, aged of 22 years.*

Anno: Dni: (1735) the 26th of Ap^{l} in our Convent of Naz: of English Poor Clares in Graveline, is happily Departed y^{s} Life. strengthened wth all ye Rights of our holy Moth^{r} ye Church, our Dr Sister Mary Paschalis Gerard, Aged of 54 Years, & 32 since her entrance into holy Religion, during wch time she has given us Singular Example of her Patience, not only in her last Sickness, but also in ye Supportation of many other infirmities in wch she not only shew'd her Courage, but fervour, & was not less remarkable for her Charity to ye Sick never Sparing herself in any thing that cou'd be of Comfort, or Solace to them, & even most faithful in the performance of any works appointed her by holy Obedience, & always ready to prevent those whom she perceived to stand in need of help, her particular Devo: to ye Passion, & strong Confidence in ye mercies of All: God, has I hope already

* Daughter of Sir William Gerard, of Bryn Hall, co Lancaster, 5th Bart., by Mary, second daughter and eventual sole heiress of John Cantsfield, of Robert Hall and Cantsfield Hall, co. Lancaster, Esq.

obtained for her a lasting happiness, but ye Judg^ts^ of God being inscrutable. I humbly request for her y^r^ usual assistance for her speedy Repose. Requiescat in Pace.

(221) Anno: Dni: (1704) the 19th of Augt made her H: Profession, Sis^r^ Grace **Turner**, now cali'd Sis^r^ Winifred Frances Aged being of 19 years.

Anno: Dni: (1725) the 21^s^ of Nov: in our Conv^t^ of Naz: of English Poor Clares in Graveline, is happily departed Sister Winifred Frances Turner, ye 39th Year of her Age, & 20th since her Entrance into H. Religion night nor day she never spar'd her self, but spent her forces in some Laborious work or other for ye assistance of ye needy, & sick, she was ever prompt in executing Sup^rs^ Orders, & shew'd a Continual endeavour for perfection, gave marks of a singular patience in many painful Infirmities, particularly ye last 6 Months of a Consumption, most devoutly resigning to w^t^ ever cou'd befall her, either to body or mind, & a week before her death was heard Constantly to whisper to herself our B^d^ Lady will be kind to me, a quarter before she dy'd she rejoyced to hear ye Doct^r^ hold she cou'd not last out ye day, t'was ye feast of ye Presentation of our B^d^ Lady, whose Mediation doubtless obtained her so happy a death, & under whose protection we have reason to hope she'l enjoy an endless felicity, assisted by y^r^ holy Prayers wch I humbly petition for her Soul. Requiescat in Pace.

(222) Anno: Dni: (1705) the 25th of March made her holy Profession, Sister Elizabeth **Perkins**, now call'd Sist^r^ Barbara Delphina, Aged of 22 years.*

Anno: Dni: (1728) the 3^d^ of March, in our Convent of Naz: of English Poor Clares in Graveline, is happily departed this Life our Dr Sister, Sis^r^ Barbara Delphina Perkins, fortified wth all ye Rights of our ho: Moth^r^ ye Church, Aged of 45 & 26 since her entrance into holy Religion she has very much edified us by her unrelented fervor in ye observance of Regular duties, & patient & Couragious Supportation of continual sharp Infirmities. She often expresst a constant gratitude towards All: God for her conversion to ye Catholic faith, & vocation to holy Religion, her strong Confidence in ye mercies of God, during her last Sickness, wee hope has purchas'd her a speedy injoyment of Eternal Bliss, but least anything shou'd detain her. I humbly beg y^r^ accustomed Charity for her Soul's speediest rest. Requiescat in Pace.

(223) Anno: Dni: (1706) the 13^h^ of June, made her holy Pro-

* Daughter of Francis Perkins, of Ufton Court, co. Berks, Esq., by Anne, daughter of Richard Perkins, of Beenham, and his wife Anne, third daughter of John Eyston, of Leigh Farm, co. Berks, gent.

fession, Sister Tecla **Pople**, now call'd Sis[r] Mary Tecla, being Aged of 23 Years.

Anno: Dni: (1744) the 23[d] of Sep[r] in our Convent of Naz: of English Poor Clares in Graveline, is happily deceas'd, our D[r] Sister, Sist[r] Mary Tecla Pople, being Aged of 62 & 39 since her Entrance into holy Religion, having before that time serv'd 7 Years in y[e] Extern Quarters, w[h] a Constant & great fidelity, w[ch] she improv'd & Continu'd, after her entrance, by her care of w[t] ever Holy Obedience Committed to her charge in her Laborious Vocation. She was very devout, & often express'd great joy & Comfort in hearing of spiritual things, she endur'd w[h] much patience many sharp pains, & long illness, & tho her death was sudden, we Confide it was not unprovided, but not having had y[e] benefit of y[e] Sacraments, makes me wth more instance crave y[r] holy Prayers & Suffrages of Charity for y[e] Repose of her Soul. Requiescat in Pace.

(224) Anno: Dni: (1706) y[e] 3[d] of Decemb[r] made her ho: Professi: Sister Mary **Baynes,** now call'd Sist[r] Mary Joseph being Aged of 54 Years.

Anno: Dni: (1718) the 24th of Octob[r] in our Conv[t] of Naz: of English Poor Clares in Graveline, is happily deceas'd our D[r] Sister, Sist[r] Mary Joseph Baynes, administred wth all the Rights of our holy Mot[r] y[e] Church, Aged of 67 & 13th since her entrance into y[e] holy Religion, she served us in the Extern quarters for y[e] space of 22 Years wth y[e] greatest care & fidelity imaginable, making y[e] Convents Interest her own, & on account she had spent her forces in the Communities Service, they complyed wth her pious request of admitting her amongst them to end her days, & after her entrance was very Serviceable as far as her Strength wou'd permit, she encreased her tendance to perfection & was much addicted to prayer, very humble & submisive & often expressed a great Love & esteem of her Vocation, suffer'd her last long & painful Sickness wth a great deal of patience, spending y[e] Night before she died in most devout acts, & Aspirations, that she may y[e] more speedily enjoy y[e] happy reward of her Labours, I humbly crave y[e] assistance of y[r] holy Prayers. Requiescat in Pace.

(225) Anno: Dni: (1707) the 15th of Aug[t] made her ho: Profession, Sist[r] Winifred Clare **Newton,** now call'd Sist[r] Winnifred Clare Aged of 19 Years.*

Anno: Dni: (1738) the 13th of Sep[r] in our Conv[r] of Naz: of English Poor Clares in Graveline, is most Piously deceas'd fortify'd wth all y[e] Rites of our holy Mo[r] y[e] Church our D[r] Sister, Sister Winifred Clare Newton, y[e] 57th Year of her Age, & 32[d] since her

* Daughter of John Newton of Irnham, co. Lincoln, Esq., by his first wife Elizabeth, daughter of William Braylsford, of Wallow, co. Notts, Esq. She was born 16 Nov. 1688, and was aunt to FF. William and Baptist Edward Newton, S.J.

entrance into ye holy Religion, she has much edified as by her patient & Couragious Supportation of a Lingering & sickly Life, yet very serviceable in many occasions to ye holy Religion, often more than her weak forces wou'd permit, particularly in regard of the Music, of wch she had ye care for many years, her fervour in that was very extraordinary, never sparing her Voice w^n it was in her power to give ye least help, not even when in a Condition to have kept her Bed, her last illness was a Violent fever y^r carry'd her off in a few days, suffering much wth a great deal of courage, & patience, her death was most happy & edifying, wch doubtless was an effect of ye tender Devotion she bore to ye ever B^d Virgin. Acknowledging she had obtain'd her many favours, & said some time before her death, she should dye either on a Saturday, or on one of her feasts, wch was verify'd, sweetly rendering her Soul to her Creator on a Saturday, & in ye Octave of ye Nativity, y^t nothing may retard her speedy enjoyment of Eternal Happyness, I humby entreat ye assistance of your holy Prayers. Requiescat in Pace.

(226) Anno: Dni: (1707) the 8th of Sepr made her holy Profession, Sister Ann **Gerard**, now call'd S^tr Ann Xaveria Aged of 19 Years.*

Anno: Dni: (1741) the 7th of Jan^ry in y^s our Conv^t of English Poor Clares of Naz: in Graveline, is happily departed fortified wth all ye Rites of our holy Mo^r ye Church, our Dr Sister, Sister Ann Xaveria Gerard, being Ag'd of 53 & 34 since her entrance into ye holy Religion, she was endow'd wth a true Religious Spirit, had a Singular Value & esteem of her Vocation, ever showing a real Disengagement & Contempt of ye world, & love to holy Poverty. Remarkable in her fervour & strict observance of our Holy Rule, Particularly in fidelity to ye divine office as far as her health, & Obedience wou'd permit, having Render'd ye H Relig^n much service in several of ye chief employments, namely y^t of Portress for many Years, where she exercis'd in a particular manner her great Charity to ye Commun^ty as well as Respect, & Submission to Sup^rs, a Singular Conformity to ye Divine Will was ever apparent in her, as was her Sweet Cheerful Supportation of Infirmities wch she bore wth an Edifying patience & courage, her holy & Virtuous Life was follow'd by a most happy death, being present to herself to ye last moment. Sweetly rendering up her soul wth a Singular peace & tranquillity, but ye Judgmen^ts of God being Secret, we humbly beg y^r H. Prayers for the repose of her Soul. Requiescat in Pace.

(227) Anno: Dni: (1707) the 3rd of Decemb^r made her holy Profession Sister Mary **Harrington**, now call'd Sis^r Mary Gregorie, Aged of 21 Years.†

* Daughter of Sir William Gerard, 5th Bart., and sister of Mary above.

† Daughter of John Harrington, of Huyton Hey and Aigburth Hall, co.

Anno: Dni: (1715) the 27th of Decr in our Convt of Naz: of English Poor Clares in Graveline is most happily departed ys Life our Dr Sister, Sisr Mary Gregorie Harrington, Aged of 29 & 10 since her entrance into holy Religion, who's patience was very exemplar, bearing a great deafness, & an ulcer in her breast, wth a constant alacuity during ye space of 7 years or 8 being ever Serviceable to others in Embracing of many humble actions & was ever exact in Regular Observances as far as her health wou'd permit, her habitual illness being more fatal yn ye Doctr apprehended, snatch'd her from us before their was time for ye administration of ye holy Sacraments, notwithstanding we Confide her great Confidence in God joyn'd wth a Singular Innocence, & desire Speedily of Enjoying his divine presence has already obtained her a lasting happyness, but the Judgmts of God being inscrutable, I beg yr usual assistance for her speedy repose. Requiescat in Pace.

(228) Anno: Dni: 1710 ye 26th of July made her holy Profession Sisr Mary **Whitmore** now call'd Sisr Mary Clare being aged of 26 Years.

Anno: Dni: (1742) the 23d of Janry in our Convt of Naz: of English Poor Clares in Graveline, is most happily departed ys Life, Strengthened wth all ye Sacraments of our holy Mother ye Church, our Dr Sister, Sistr Mary Clare Whitmore, ye 57th Year of her Age & 32d since her Entrance into holy Religion, she has ever most faithfully acquitted herself of her Laborious Vocation of which she always shew'd a Singular Value & Esteem, & constant tendance to her own Perfection, by her practice of Silence, Prayer, & Interiour Recollection, Respect, & Submission to Suprs remarkable for her Love of ho: Poverty, & great exactness in all Religious observances, joyn'd to a Cheerful & Courageous Supportation of many painful Infirmitys & ever had a Peculiar tender Devotion to ye SSts of our Holy Order, who doubtless were very powerful in Obtaining for her so happy & Edyfying a death, rendering up her Soul to her heavenly Spouse wth great peace & tranquillity, yt nothing may retard her speedy enjoymt of eternal bliss, we humbly request yr usual Charity. Requiescat in Pace.

(229) Anno: Dni: 1711 the 15th of Augt made her holy Profession, Sisr Elizabeth **Gerard**, now call'd Sisr Bibiana Clare, Aged of 18 Years.*

Anno: Dni: (1717) the 6th of Decemr in our Convt of Naz: of English Poor Clares in Graveline, is happily departed ys Life,

Lancaster, Esq., by Dorothy, daughter and heiress of . . . Tarleton, of Aigburth Hall, Esq. Upon the death of her brother Charles, in 1720, the Harrington estates passed to the Molyneux family of New Hall. Her sister Margaret was a Benedictine nun at Cambrai.

* Daughter of Sir William Gerard, 5th Bart., and sister of Mary and Anne above.

fortified wth all Rites of our holy Moth^{r} ye Church our Dr Sister, Sis^{r} Bibiana Clare Gerard, ye 25th year of her Age, & 7th since her entrance into ho: Religion she was endowed wth a great Capacity, of a Cheerful sweet temper, wch render'd her affable to all, from her Infancy much addicted to piety, Conformity to ye divine will was apparently ever her darling Virtue, & was most Singular in her last Sickness, shewing no other Concern, or desire y^{n} ye Administration of ye last Sacramen^{ts} wch she herself requested of ye Doctor, her Respect, Submission, & punctuality to Superiours Orders in ye frequent occasions she was in, was most remarkable she plac'd her whole perfection in Virtues most Conformable to her state, & in a few Years compleated her Crown, rendering our loss, her gain, w^{n} y^{t} she may speedily enjoy, we humbly crave your Suffrages & Prayers. Requiescat in Pace.

(230) Anno: Dni: (1711) the 25th of March, made her holy Profession, Sister Eliz: **Elphenston**, now call'd Sis^{r} Mary Bernard, Aged of 23 Years.

Anno: Dni: (1760) ye 25th of Feb^{ry} in our Conv^{t} of Naz: of English Poor Clares in Graveline, is happily departed this Life, Strengthened with ye Rites of our holy Mother ye Church, our Dr Sister, Sister Mary Bernard Elpheston, ye 72nd Year of her Age, & 50th since her entrance into Holy Religion. She was of a good family, & a Convert, prevented wth grace in her call to our Holy Order, several Years before she knew the true faith, was much devoted to our holy Father St Francis, & follow'd his Example in her humble & Laborious Vocation, in wch she faithfully Comply'd wth all y^{t} was Appointed her by H: Obedience, & was ever a most Serviceable Member, All^{ty} God was pleas'd to try her with many Infirmities some years before her death, which she supported wth an Agreeable Cheerfulness, & Patience, no less Edifying, than ye 20 days of her last Sickness, wch was a Dropsy & Complication of Illnesses, & Suffer'd so much y^{t} we Confide in ye Mercys of God ye same will stand for her Purgatory, yet if any things remains to cancel, I beg y^{r} holy Prayers of Charity. Requiescat in Pace.

(231) Anno: Dni: (1712) the 28th of Augt made her holy Profession, Sister Margaret **Aughton**, now call'd Sister Clare Margaret Aged 41 Years.

Anno: Dni: (1719) the 7th of Augt in our Conv^{t} of Naz: of English Poor Clares in Graveline, is happily deceased, our Dr Sister, Sister Clare Margaret Aughton, fortified wth all Sacraments of our ho: Moth^{r} ye Church, ye 48th Year of her Age, & 7th since her entrance into holy Religion. She made it her daily endeavours to give an encrease to ye good fund of Virtue she brought wth her, & much Edified us by her great devotion, Love, & Respect to Superiours, great fidelity in her tendance of ye Sick w[ch] she was often employ'd in. She was seized on wth an appoplexy, yet happily regain'd her perfect senses for so long a time as she made her Confession, receiv'd her Viaticum, then her illness redoubling she finish'd her Life as we have reason to hope for a happy Eternity, for y[e] speediest enjoyment of which we humbly entreat y[r] accustomed Charity for her Soul. Requiescat in Pace.

(232) Anno Domini (1712) Mrs Ann **Tristram**, now Call'd Sis[r] Ann Joseph, made her holy Profession, on y[e] 27th of Decemb[r] being Aged 22 years.*

Anno: Dni: (1761) y[e] 22[d] of Feb[ry] in our Conv[t] of Naz: of English Poor Clares in Graveline, is happily deceas'd strengthened wth all y[e] Rights of our holy Moth[r] y[e] Church our D[r] Sister, Sister Ann Joseph Tristram, Jubilarian, Aged 71, she, from her Entrance ever retained her 1st fervour, most Exemplar in her constancy night & day in assisting at y[e] Divine Office, & no less Indefatigable in her Labours for y[e] Service of y[e] Community, & equally Remarkable in humility & Charity during y[e] 18 years at different times y[t] she exercised y[e] Office of Vicaress, which carried her on, notwithstanding her Age to keep y[e] Alarum till seized wth her last Sickness of 20 days fever, w[ch] wth violence of y[e] Scurvey reduc'd her body into Soares, she Supported all these tryals wth Edifing patience & Resignation to y[e] Divine Will, yet least any thing remains to cancel. I humbly entreat y[r] Prayers of Charity for her speedy Repose. Requiescat in Pace.

(233) Anno Domini (1715) y[e] 8th of Sep[r] made her holy Profession Sis[r] Catherine **Smythe**, now call'd Sis[r] Cath: Clare being Aged of 17 years.

Anno Dni: (1772) in our Conv[t] of Naz: of English Poor Clares in Graveline, y[e] 30th of March, it pleasd Alm[ty] God to call to himself our D[r] & Ven: Moth[r] Jub: Sis[r] Catherine Clare Symthe, administered wth all y[e] Rights of our holy Moth[r] y[e] Church, Aged 74 & 58 since her Entrance into holy Religion, having supported for some years Ilnesses, & Infirmities of her Age wth Extraordinary Sweetness & patience, she had a long painful Agony, sensible to y[e] End Rendering up her pious Soul into y[e] hands of her Creator of a totall decay, she was very pious, & Endow'd wth a most humble & Religious Spirit, had a great Confidence in y[e] infinite Mercies of Alm[ty] God, joyn'd to an entire Conformity to his Adorable Will was a most Capable & Serviceable Member, & rendered great Service to our Comunity by faithfully employing her talent w[ch] was Gifted wth in y[e] french tongue, & exercised Several Offices, giving us great Example of Edification, by her fidelity zeal & Exactitude in all duties, Especially y[e] 12 years of her being Portress, in w[ch] her general

* Daughter of Mr Tristram, of Ince Blundell, co. Lancaster, yeoman.

Charity was most remarkable, as no less her Respectful & punctual Submission, & Obediencc to ye least Orders of Sup^{rs} was always grateful for Charities done her, all wch we confide has already purchased her an Immortal Crown, but as all Virtues are attended wth frailtys, wee earnestly entreat y^{r} holy Pray^{rs}. Requiescat in Pace.

(234) Anno: Dmin: (1716) ye 6th of Jan^{ry} made her holy Profession Sis^{r} Isabel **Clifton**, now call'd Sis^{r} Mary Magdalen, being Aged of 16 Years.*

Anno Domn: (1775) ye 26th of June, in our Conv^{t} of Naz: of English Poor Clares in Graveline, is most happily deceas'd administered wth all ye Rights of our holy Moth^{r} ye Church, being perfectly present to herself, our Dear Moth^{r} Jub^{n} Sis^{r} Mary Magdalen Clifton, Aged 76 & 60 since her Entrance into holy Religion, wch time she spent in ye practice of those Virtues suiting her holy Vocation, ever tending to her own Perfection, she was a very Beneficial Member, & rendered great Service by her strong and agreeable Voice both for reading & Singing, wch she faithfully employd in ye Service of God, & was ever constant at ye Divine Office, both night & day till it pleased God to afflict her wth almost a total blindness for several Years, wch she supported wth great patience, & Conformity to ye divine will, was Respectful to Sup^{rs} & most remarkable for her Singular great devotion to our Lord's Passion, & to ye most Holy Sacrament of ye Altar, Continuing to refresh her Soul wth ye heavenly food till ye end of her Life, her Charitable Devotion for ye poor Souls in Purgatory was no less remarkable in assisting them by offering all her Prayers & Suffrances for their relief, & procuring them all ye Prayers she could, & doubt not but they have been Powerful Intercessors for her. Yet lest any thing shou'd retard her speedy enjoyment of Eternal happiness, we most humbly entreat y^{r} accustom'd Pray^{rs} & Suffrages for her Soul's speediest rest & repose. Requiescat in Pace.

(235) Anno Domin: (1716) ye 3^{d} of May made her ho: Profession Sis^{r} Ann **Elsum**, now Call'd Sis^{r} Ann Ludovic Aged of 20 y^{rs}.

Anno Doni: (1736) ye 31st of March in our Conv^{t} of Naz: of English Poor Clares in Graveline, is happily departed y^{s} Life our Dr Sis^{r}, Sister Ann Ludovic Elsum, being Aged of 42 & 21 since her Entrance into holy Religion: she was ever Assiduous in her tendance to perfection, exact & fervent in the Observance of Regular Duties; had a peculiar Devotion to the Divine Office, faithful in ye spending of her time for her own Spiritual advance-

* Daughter of Thomas Clifton, of Fairsnape in Bleasdale, Esq., who succeeded his uncle Sir Thomas Clifton, Bart., to the Clifton, Westby, Salwick and Lytham estates. Her mother was Eleanor Alethea, daughter of Richard Walmesley, of Dunkenhalgh, co. Lancaster, Esq.

ment, & ye Service of ye holy Comunity giving much Satisfaction ye three years she was Cutting house Sister, by her general Charity, & well performance of y^t^ duty, she was always Charitable in her Conversation, & so Innocently Merry, y^t^ rendered her Company agreeably Edifying, her last Sickness was Violent, & deprived her of presence of Spirit, so could not have ye benefit of her Viaticum, tho had been at holy Communion the day she fell ill, that nothing may retard her speedy happiness, we earnestly request your holy Prayers of Charity. Requiescat in Pace.

(236) The same day and year made also her holy Profession Sister Margret **Fisher,** now call'd Sister Mary Austen being Aged of 20 years.

Anno Domi: 1722 ye 7th of May in our Conv^t^ of Naz: of English Poor Clares in Graveline is happily departed this Life, our Dr Sister, Sis^r^ Mary Austen Fisher, administer'd wth ye Rights of our holy Moth^r^ ye Church, being Aged of 27 years, & 7 since her Entrance into holy Religion, which time she has faithfully spent in acquiring the true Spirit of our Holy Rule, & Understanding & practice of Solid devotion, joyned to an humble Obedience, & Submision to Superiours, which with her Silent Sufferings (tho her time was short, we hope has merited an immortal Crown, that nothing may put a stop thereunto, I humbly request y^r^ usual Charity for her Soul. Requiescat in Pace.

(237) The same day & year made also her holy Profession Sis^r^ Alice Ecceleston, now call'd Sis^r^ Mary Didacus being Aged of 23 years.

Anno Domini (1736) ye 19th of Feb^ry^ in our Conv^t^ of Naz: of English Poor Clares in Graveline is happily departed this Life, our Dr Sis^r^, Sis^r^ Mary Didacus Eccleston, administered wth ye Rites of our ho: Moth^r^ ye Church, being Aged of 43 & 21 since her entrance into holy Religion, having left us much Edified at her humility & Contempt of herself showing ye lest show of Singularity, ever having a great esteem of her Laborious Vocation, fervently preventing in all Occasions, & imploying ye extent of her forces in the holy Comunity's Service, much addicted to Prayer, & a Silent tendance to her own perfection endeavouring to hide as much as possible anything y^t^ might redown'd to her praise, tho we cou'd not but remark her constant patience, & Conformity to ye Divine Will in her frequent Illnesses, & Infirmities which joyn'd to an Angelical Interiour, gives us hopes she is now in ye enjoym^t^ of her Celestial Spouse, but ye Judgments of God being Secret, we humbly entreat the assistance of your holy Prayers. Requiescat in Pace.

(238) Anno Domi: (1716) the 12th of July made her holy Profession Sister Hellen **Hodson,** now call'd Sister Ignatia Frances Aged of 26 years.

Anno: Domini, (1759) the 5th of Decembr in our Convt of Naz: of English Poor Clares in Graveline, is happily Departed ys Life our Dr Sister, Sister Ignatia Frances Hodson, administered wth all ye Rites of our holy Mothr ye Church being Aged of 71 & 45 since her entrance into holy Religion, all wch time she has spent in unrelented fervour in ye Constant pursuit & practice of All Solid Virtues, & in ye strict Observance of our holy Rule & Constitutions, never Dispensing wth herself Night, nor Day from ye Divine Office, & other Observances. Notwithstanding her Laborious Employments in wch she was Indefatigable for ye Service of ye Community, & no less remarkable in Securing to herself all humble Actions, her last Sickness was a violent fever which she Suffered with singular Patience admitting of no Solace, she could possibly avoid, yet as ye Judgments of God are Inscrutable, we humbly request yr Prayers of Charity for ye repose of her Soul. Requiescat in Pace.

(239) Anno Domini (1716) the 15th of Octobr made her holy Profession Sister Briget **Petre,** now Call'd Sister Clare Stanislaus being Aged of 19 years.*

Anno Domini (1747) ye 14th of Apl in our Convt of Naz: of English Poor Clares in Graveline, is most happily departed ys Life, our Dr Sister, Sisr Clare Stanislaus Petre, Aged of 51 & 32 since her Entrance into ye holy Religion; having ever show'd a Singular regard for her holy Vocation; & Comply'd with ye same as far as her weak Constitution wou'd permit, she was endow'd wth many qualifications wch render'd her a most Capable Member, & her Zeal for ye honour of Allmty God made her often strive above wt she was able to assist ye Choir with her Music, & was no less remarkable for many other Virtues wth which she has left us much Edify'd, particularly in her patient Supportation of a Lingering Decay, of wch she dy'd, Entirely present to herself to ye last, answering to all ye Recommendations, & Receiving all ye Rites of our holy Mothr ye Church wth Singular Devotion, Confidence, & Conformity to ye Divine Will, which gives us all reason to Confide that our Loss has been her gain; & yt our Bd Lady, & St Joseph to whom she was most particularly devoted have been powerful Intercessors for her, but as ye Judgmts of God are Impenetrable, not to be failing in our Duty, we humbly request for her your accustomed Prayers of Charity. Requiescat in Pace.

(240) The same day & year made also her holy Profession Mrs Hellen **Petre,** now call'd Sister Mary Felix Aged 17.†

* Daughter of Joseph Petre, of Fithlers, co. Essex, Esq., by his first wife Catherine, daughter of Sir William Andrews, of Denton and Downham, co. Essex, 2nd Bart., and his wife Helen, daughter and heiress of Edward Attslow, of Downham Hall, co. Essex, Esq.

† Sister of Bridget Petre above. Her brother Francis Petre became

Anno: Dni: (1779) the 20th of June in our Convent of Nazareth of English Poor Clares in Graveline, Amidst ye Sighs, tears, & Prayers of her most Afflicted Children, is most happily deceas'd, strengthened wth all ye Sacraments of our holy Mother ye Church, our most Revd, most Venerable, & most Dearly beloved Mothr Abbess Sisr Mary Felix Petre Jubn in ye 80th year of her Age, & 64 since her entrance into holy Religion, 43 years of which she, in quality of Abbess governed this Monastary wth Singular prudence, affability, & Mildness, leaving us truly desolate orphelines by ye privation of ye tenderest & most Compationate of Mothers, whom we never can Sufficiently bewail, tho greatly enrich'd by ye examples we retain of her Virtues, never relenting from her 1st fervour, but daily tended to her own perfection & ye constant practice of all Virtues suitable to her holy Vocation, her tender Charity to poor distresst People extended to all in need addresst to her, which gain'd her ye Love and Respect of each one, in so much, yt we her disconsolate Children cou'd not discern on whom her Charitable assistance extended most, & that with so much dexterity, & goodness that we was blesst under her prudent Government & maternal care wch made us Obey, drawn by these attracts. more for Love, than any other motive, making each ones necessity ye Subject of her Concern, Comforting us in all tryals to ye utmost of her power. She ever had a Singular Love & Zeal for Allmty God's honour & glory, & ye advancement of her Community in perfection, was most tenderly devoted to ye Passion & death of our Bd (241) Saviour, & often power'd forth her Soul in ye Contemplation of him in y most Bd Sacrament of ye Altar, from wch she never abstain'd receiving, till Age & infirmities depriv'd her of so frequent a Support, all spare hours she spent in ye Choir, drawing down, ye we have all reason to believe many favours both spiritual & temporal upon us all: wch doubtless gave her yt strong Confidence in Divine Providence, being admirably gifted wth equality of temper in all events both prosperous & adverse, she Likewise frequently experienc'd ye powerful protection of our Bd Lady, & St Joseph invoking them in all necessity for ye good & advancement of this our Monastery, being never wearied in Imploring Succour thro ye powerful Intercession of all y holy Saints: in which our holy Father, & holy Mother, were not ye least solicited, she being Indefatigable in all yt cou'd render us happy, our only hope in so sensible a separation is, that our loss is her gain. A pure decay of Nature gave ye fatal stroke, being perfectly sensible to ye last moment, giving us all her Blessing a few minutes before she expired, sweetly gave up her Soul into ye hands of her Creator, to live as we have all reason to hope Eternally, but as ye greatest virtues are attended wth human frailtys, lest anything shou'd retard ye happy En-

Bishop of the Northern Vicariate, and was the last male survivor of the Fithlers branch of the Petre family.

Emery Walker Ph. sc.

Mother Helen Mary Felix Petre
8th Abbess of Poor Clares, Gravelines
From the painting, Ursuline Convent, Greenwich

To face p. 132

joyement of her heavenly Spouse, I earnestly recomend her Sweet Soul to y^{r} usual Prayers & Suffrages. Requiescat in Pace.

The following is written on a loose sheet, fastened over page 241.

In the Year of Our Lord 1779, on the 20th day of June after receiving the last Sacraments of the Church, died the Venerable and Reverend Mother Abbess.

S. Mary Felix Petre de Fithlers Abbess of the English Poor Clares of Gravelines in the 80th year of her age & 64th of her Profession having governed that Monastery during 43 years, she fled from the corruptions of the Age at an early time of Life & took the solemn Vows of Religion; in the Exact performance of which she became a Model of the most Eminent Virtue. It is hard to say which was most Conspicuous, her Humility in Obeying or her affability in Commanding, but surely we need no greater elogium of her Merit, than the tears of her Religious Sisters, & the Blessing of the Poor, who Equally regret her as a mother & a friend. As her Life was spent in the steady practice of Virtue, & for a long course of years had been tending to perfection, we humbly hope she will meet the Reward prepared for the Just, but as all her Virtues & all her failings must stand before that God in whose sight the heavens are Unclean, we earnestly Entreat your prayers that he may spare his Servant & bring her Speedily to a place of Eternal Rest.

(242) The same day & year made also her Holy Profession Mrs Hellen **Anderton**, now call'd Sis^{r} Mary Teresa being Aged of 16 Years.*

Anno: Domi: (1765) the 29th of May in our Conv^{t} of Naz: of English Poor Clares in Graveline, is happily departed y^{s} Life, fortified wth all ye Rites of our holy Mother the Church, our Dr Sist^{r}. Sist^{r} Mary Teresa Anderton Jub: Aged 66 & 50 since her Entrance into holy Religion, Coming to us a Young Widow, was a beneficial Member, & has left us Singularly Edified by her assiduous tendance to her own perfection, Zeal, Love of Regularity, and Exactitude in ye Observances of all Religious Duties, her obedience, Respect, & Submission to Sup^{rs} was no less Remarkable than her constant fervour & fidelitie in Assisting at ye Divine Office, till it pleased God to afflict her wth a Complication of Infirmities, joyn'd to a total Blindness, wch confin'd her to a Room Several Years before she died, & Supported ye same wth agreeable Cheerfulness, & perfect Resignation to ye will of Allm^{ty} God, her last sickness was a Lingering decay of nature, wch she bore with Edifying patience, & sweetly render'd up her Soul to God: whom she long before desired to Enjoy, that nothing

* Daughter of Hugh Anderton, of Euxton Hall, co. Lancaster, Esq., by Catherine, daughter of Francis Trappes, of Nidd Hall, co. York, Esq.

may Retard her wish'd for felicity I humbly Request y[r] usual Charity for y[e] repose of her Soul. Requiescat in Pace.

(243) Anno: Dni: 1718 y[e] 6th of Feb[ry] made her holy Profession Mrs Mary **Leckonby,** now call'd Sis[r] Mary Aloysia being Aged of 17 Years.*

Anno: Domini 1751 y[e] 9th of June in our Conv[t] of Naz[th] of English poor Clares in Graveline is most happily departed y[s] Life Strengthened wth y[e] Rites of our ho: Moth[r] y[e] Church our D[r] Sister, Sis[r] Mary Aloysia Leckonby, Aged of 52 & 34 since her entrance into holy Religion, during which time she has much Edify'd us with her Love for Regular Observance, Remarkable fidelity in y[e] Several Employments she exercis'd, particularly in y[t] of Vicaress, & Sacristin, & general Charity to every one during her care of y[e] Linen, & woollen, she Singular Candor of Life, love for her holy Vocation, & Complyance wth y[e] same as far as her health wou'd permit was no less Edifying than her Respect & Submission to Sup[rs] as well as her patient Supportation of many Infirmities, her Entire Conformity to y[e] divine will, & Strong Confidence in his mercys joyn'd to her particular devotion to our B[d] Lady & S[t] Joseph has already we hope made our loss her gain but y[e] Judgm[ts] of God being Inscrutable, not to be failing in our duty, most humbly request y[r] prayers of Charity for her. Requiescat in Pace.

(244) The same day & year made also her holy Profession, Mrs Mary **Petre,** now call'd Sist Mary Xaveria Aged of 22 Years.†

Anno: Dni: (1724) y[e] 8th of Jan[ry] in our Conv[t] of Naz: of English Poor Clares in Graveline, is happily departed this Life administer'd wth y[e] Rights of our holy Moth[r] y[e] Church our D[r] Sister, Sist[r] Mary Xaveria Petre, Aged of 28 & 7 since her entry into holy Religion, w[ch] time she has spent most holily in great fervour & exactness, tending wholy to y[e] perfectionating of her own Soul, never minding or speaking of w[t] did not touch her own Obedience, never seen Idle, her most Religious Exteriour & Sweet gravity, gain'd y[e] Affection of every one, & made her much regretted, her death, like her Life was most devout, & ended with Affectionate Acts to God & his most B[d] Mother, expressing great joy at y[e] thoughts that she shou'd enjoy y[e] Beatifical Vision, lest any ways human frailty shou'd detain her, we humbly request y[r] Accustomed Charity. Requiescat in Pace.

* Daughter of Thomas Leckonby, of Liverpool, younger son of Richard Leckonby, of Leckonby House, Great Eccleston, and of the Demesne of Elswick, co. Lancaster, Esq., by Anne, daughter of William Hesketh, of Maynes Hall, Esq. (*vide C.R.S.*, vi., 166, and correct accordingly).

† Daughter of Joseph Petre, and sister of Bridget and Helen above.

(245) The same day & year made also her holy Profession, Mrs Rebecca **Pigott**, now call'd Sist^{r} Mary Benedict being Aged of 18.*

Anno Dni: (1771) ye 27th of Sepr in our Conv^{t} of Naz: of English Poor Clares in Graveline, is piously deceas'd in our Lord, Administered wth ye Rites of our holy Moth^{r} ye Church our Dr Sister, Sist^{r} Mary Benedict Pigott Jub^{n} Aged 71 & 54 since her entrance into holy Religion, Allm^{ty} God was pleas'd to trye her fervent Love towards him by many Infirmities, Several Years being Confined to a Room by lameness wch she Supported wth Edifying Patience, as also ye deprivation of Speech, for near five Years, by an Attack of Palsie, wch she also bore wth all Cheerfulness under so great an affliction, ye same Increasing much upon her, caused her to suffer extreme pain, Especially ye two last Months of her Life, being sensible to ye last Moment, our loss in her was general, Allm^{ty} God having endow'd her with most extraordinary talents & Ingenuity for all sorts of Curious Works, wch she faithfully improved for ye Service of ye Comunity, never loosing her time, exact in all Religious Duties, & constant tendance to her own perfection, wch remarkable fervour & fidelity in ye Constant recital of ye Divine Office till ye loss of her Speech, in wch her vertue Appear'd most Singular by her perfect resignation to ye ho will of God: being most zealous for his honour & glory, all wch gives us reason to hope she has already Completed her Crown, but ye Judgm^{ts} of God being inscrutable & human frailty great. I humbly request y^{r} accustom'd Prayers of Charity. Requiescat in Pace.

(246) Anno: Domi: (1718) the 12th of Novr made her holy Profession Mrs Ann **Tarlton,** now call'd Sis^{r} Mary Alexia being Aged of 24.†

Anno: Dni: (1722) the 17th of Augt in our Conv^{t} of Naz: of English Poor Clares in Graveline, is happily departed y^{s} Life, our Dr Sister, Sis^{r} Mary Alexia Tarlton, fortified wth all ye Rites of our holy Moth^{r} ye Church, ye 27th Year of her Age, & 4th since her entrance into H: Religion, during wch time, she faithfully imploy'd her forces in her Laborious Vocation, was remarkable for her Charity, as well in speaking advantagiously of every one, as assisting those y^{t} desired her help in any occasion, she was very Respectful, & submissive to Sup^{rs} had a great Confidence in ye mercies of God, & resignation to ye divine will, wch gives us hopes she now enjoys ye reward of her labours, but ye Judg^{ts} of God being inscrutable we humbly beg ye assistance of y^{r} holy Prayers for ye repose of her Soul. Requiescat in Pace.

* Daughter of Nathaniel Pigott, of the Manor of Bodingham, co. Essex, and of the Inner Temple, the eminent barrister-at-law, by his wife Rebecca.

† Cousin of Sister Mary Harrington above.

(247) Anno Domini (1719) the 10th of June made her holy Profession, Sister Ann **Clifton**, now call'd Sister Clare Bernardine being Aged of 17 years.*

Anno: Domini: (1721) the 26th of June, in our Convt of Naz: of English Poor Clares in Graveline is happily departed ys Life, strengthened wth all ye Rites of our H Mothr the Church, our Dr Sister, Sister Clare Bernardine Clifton the 19th Year of her Age, & 3d since her entrance into the Holy Religion; she has left us much Edified by her Conformity to ye divine will, patient & Cheerful Supportation & a long & painful Infirmity wch for several Months confin'd her to her bed, she expresst a great gratitude for her Vocation, & often said that no Sufferances, or Crosses cou'd ever lessen it, she was perfectly present to herself to ye last moment, & dyed with a great Confidence in ye mercies of God, whose vision we hope she now enjoys, but his Judgments being inscrutable we humbly beg the assistance of yr Holy Prayers for her speedy repose. Requiescat in Pace.

(248) Anno: Domini (1719) the 10th of Octobr Mrs Phéebé **Jackson**, now Call'd Sistr Mary Joseph made her holy Profession, being Aged of 22.

Anno: Domini (1739) the 7th of March in our Convt of Naz: of English Poor Clares in Graveline, is most happily departed ys Life our Dr Sister, Sister Mary Joseph Jackson fortify'd with all ye Rites of our holy Mothr ye Church, ye 42d Year of her Age, & 21st since her entrance into the Holy Religion, which time she has spent in unrelented fervour & Gratitude to Alm: God for her call to the Catholic faith, & Religious Vocation: punctually exact to all Religious duties & Ceremonies, much addicted to Prayrs & interiour Recollection, most Obedient to Suprrs, & the Six Years she, as Infirmarian, was remarkable for her Charity & tenderness to ye Sick, never sparing herself Night or Day, in any thing that might be a Solace to them Notwithstanding her weak health & Constitution, being Inclin'd to a Consumption of wch she dy'd, it pleased Almty God to Afflict her with many Interiour Sufferings, & Conflicts, for a considerable time: which lasted till a little before she expir'd, she having made it her petition to live & dye wth our Bd Savr on ye Cross, gives us reason to believe they were ye effect of her Request, & yt as she has been a Large Sharer of ye Cross, he doubtless will make her partaker of Glory, which yt she may ye more speedily enjoy we humbly beg yr accustom'd Charity. Requiescat in Pace.

(249) Anno: Dom: (1719) the 27th of Decembr Mrs Ann **Watterton** now call'd Sister Clare Regis made her holy Profession being Aged of 20.*

* Daughter of Thomas Clifton and sister of Isabel above.

† Daughter of Charles Waterton, of Walton Hall, co. York, Esq., by

Anno: Dom: (1768) the 1st of May in our Conv[t] of Naz: of English Poor Clares in Graveline is most happily deceas'd our D[r] Sister, Sister Clare Regis Watterton Jub[n] Aged 69 & 50 since her Entrance into holy Religion, administered wth Extremunction she had weak health & had Continued Infirmities, but a very fervent Good Religious & a Serviceable Member, always employing her time in y[e] Service of y[e] Comunity, & a great Lover of holy Poverty, she gave us great Examples of Edification, by her great Zeal for Alm[ty] God's honour & glory, & Service in y[e] Choir in y[e] well performance of y[e] Divine Office, w[ch] she assisted at Night & Day, Even when unable, & never slackened from her 1st fervour, much addicted to Praying, & Reading even while at work, w[ch] was most Edifying as was no Less y[e] fine acts she was heard to make often of perfect Resignation & Conformity to y[e] will of Alm[ty] God, who Afflicted her with many sharp Ilnesses, & depriv'd us of her by a Violent Vomiting, joyn'd to an Impostum in her head, & Suffer'd much, we Confide in y[e] mercies of God the same will stand for her Purgatory, yet lest anything shou'd remain to cancel, we humbly request y[r] usual Charity for her. Requiescat in Pace.

(250) Anno: Dom: (1720) the 8th of Decemb[r] made her ho: Profess[n] M[rs] Mary **Ingilby** now call'd Sis[r] Mary Catherine being Aged of 21.*

Anno Dom: (1742) the 20th of June in our Conv[t] of Naz: of English Poor Clares in Graveline is most happily departed y[s] Life our D[r] Sister, Sister Mary Catherine Ingilby y[e] 44th Year of her Age & 23[d] since her entrance into holy Religion, who has left us singular examples of an unrelented fervor, & humility in embracing all humble & Laborious works, most Assiduous to Prayer, & Constant to y[e] Divine Office Day & Night, having Kept y[e] Alarum for calling to Matins the space of 20 Years to y[e] general Satisfaction of y[e] Comunity Notwithstanding her poor Sight, almost to a Blindness, w[ch] she had for Several Years, Supporting y[e] same wth an Admirable Sweetness & Patience placing her delight & Perfection in a general Charity & Service to y[e] Holy Comunity, & each in particular to y[e] extent of her Ability, not having regard to her own Infirmities, Ingeniously hiding her pains w[n] ever she cou'd, that of her stomach w[ch] was habitual, was often most violent, & took her off more sudden than was Expected by y[e] Doct[r] who did not hold her in danger till a few hours before she expir'd, a Sudden Vomiting seiz'd her, which deprived her of y[e] Benefit of her Viaticum, & makes us more Earnestly request y[r] Prayers of Charity for ye Speedy repose of her Soul. Requiescat in Pace.

Anne, daughter of Sir William Gerard, of Bryn Hall, co. Lancaster, 4th Bart. She was sister to Fr. Thomas Waterton, S.J.

* Daughter of Columbus Ingleby, of Clapdale Hall and Austwick Hall, co York, Esq.

(251) Anno: Dôm: (1721) the 2nd of Ap[l] made her ho: Profess[n] Mrs Jane **Clifton** now call'd Sis[r] Mary of ye Assumption being Aged of 19.*

Anno: Dom: (1760) the 27th of Ap[l] in our Conv[t] of Naz: of English Poor Clares in Graveline is happily departed our Dr Sister, Sis[r] Mary Assumption Clifton y[e] 58th year of her Age & y[e] 40th since her Entrance into Ho: Religion being fortify'd wth y[e] Rights of our holy Moth[r] y[e] Church. She was a very Capable member, & Serviceable from her entrance. Remarkable in fervour & Devotion, & y[e] practice of all virtues suiting her State, never Idle, very Compassionate, & Charitable, & in y[e] frequent occasions she was in, & y[e] 9 Years she was Portress her Respect & Submission to Superiours was very apparent, her patience, & perfect Resignation in her last Sickness, wch was a Catarrh, & fever, joyn'd to a Goutish humour in her stomach, was most Edifying, & gives us all reason to hope she now enjoys Eternal reward, as ye Judgments of God are Inscrutable, I humbly intreat y[r] Prayers of Charity for her Soul's Speedy rest. Requiescat in Pace.

(252) Anno: Dôm: (1721) the 1st of May made her holy Profession Sis[r] Ann **Ingilby**, now Call'd Sis[r] Clare Ignatia being Aged of 19 Years.†

Anno: Dôm: (1736) the 16th of Jan[ry] in our Conv[t] of Naz: of English Poor Clares in Graveline is most happily departed y[s] Life our Dr Sister, Sis[r] Clare Ignatia Ingilby being Aged of 35 & in Religion 16 leaving us all much Edyfied at her patient, & Silent Suffering, during three years most painful & Lingering Consumption, wore her away to an Anatomie, yet Notwithstanding her heroic Courage kept her from y[e] Infirmary till 3 weeks before she dy'd, her serenity & mildness of temper was ever most remarkable; as was her Submission, & Respect to Superiours, never making y[e] least show of difficulty in w[t] was required either from them or others, tho sometimes happening to be more than her weak forces wou'd allow of. Her Extraordinary Devotion to S[t] Ignatius doubtless obtain'd her y[e] perfect Resignation, Tranquillity, & peace of mind, w[ch] she gave us most signal proofs of at y[e] hour of her death, w[ch] tho in some manner sudden, yet allow'd time for her Viaticum, wch she rec[d] wth much Devotion & Piety, but being doubtful of her having y[e] benefit of y[e] holy Oyles, we y[e] more Earnestly Petition y[e] assistance of y[r] holy Prayers for y[e] repose of her Soul. Requiescat in Pace.

(253) Anno: Dôm: (1722) y[e] 25th of Aug[st] made her holy Pro-

* Daughter of Cuthbert Clifton, gent. (son of James, younger brother of Sir Thomas Clifton, Bart., of Clifton, Westby, and Salwick, co. Lancaster), by Dorothy, daughter of William Winckley, of Banister Hall, gent. (*vide C.R.S.*, vi., 194). She was sister to FF. James and Thomas Clifton, S.J.

† Daughter of Columbus Ingleby and sister of Mary above.

fession Sister Margaret **Cram** now call'd Sis[r] Marg[t] Winifrid Aged of 19 Years.

Anno: Dôm: (1740) ye 26th of Decemb[r] in our Conv[t] of Naz: of English Poor Clares in Graveline, is most happily departed y[s] Life, our Dr Sister Margarett Winifred Cram, fortified wth all ye Rites of our ho: Moth[r] ye Church being Aged of 37 & in Religion 19 she has much Edifyed us wth her Singular patience in a long & tedious Consumption & most violent inward pains, never expressing other Concern than that she was unable to comply with her Laborious Vocation most Serviceable as far as great Infirmities wou'd permit, much addicted to Silence & prayer, & ever assiduous in tending to her own perfection, which gives us reason to hope she's in y[e] Enjoyment of Eternal Bliss, but y[e] Judgments of God being unknown we humbly crave y[r] accustom'd Charity for y[e] repose of her Soul. Requiescat in Pace.

(254) The same day & Year made also her holy Profession, Sis[r] Mary **Merry,** now call'd Sis[r] Mary Frances being Aged of 25 Years.*

Anno: Dom: (1724) the 13th of Jan[ry] furnis'd wth all y[e] Rights of y[e] holy Church render'd up her Soul, Sis[r] Mary Frances Alias Merry y[e] 28th Year of her Age, & 3rd of her entrance into holy Religion during which time she extremly Edified us by a constant Mortification over herself in all things, prompt and ready in Obeying, never repining to do Laborious & Abject employments, tho far above her tender & weak Constitution, in her Constant hard Works she never seemed impatient, or out of y[e] presence of God, & in y[e] same Cheerful Devotion she bore her 15 days last Violent Sickness, in y[e] height of pains Singing y[e] praises of her God, whose vision y[t] she may sooner enjoy y[r] accustomed Charity is humbly requested. Requiescat in Pace.

(255) Anno: Dom: (1723) the 6th of Jan[ry] made her holy Profession Sis[r] Ann **Smithson,** now call'd Sis[r] Mary Anna being Aged of 39 Years.†

Anno: Domi: (1750) y[e] 21st of March in our Conv[t] of Naz: of English Poor Clares in Graveline is happily deceas'd fortified wth all y[e] Rights of our holy Moth[r] y[e] Church; our D[r] Sister, Sister Mary Anna Smithson, y[e] 66th Year of her Age, & 29th since her Entrance into holy Religion, during w[ch] time her devotion, singular Candor; & Innocency joyn'd to her natural sweet temper, render'd her aimiable to all, & has also left us much Edified by

* Daughter of Gilbert Merry, of Kniveton, co. Derby, gent.

† Daughter of Sir Hugh Smithson, of Stanwick, co. York, 3rd Bart., by Elizabeth, daughter of Marmaduke, 2nd Lord Langdale. Her three sisters were also nuns, yet her father conformed to the Anglican Establishment after the unsuccessful Rising in favour of the legitimate heir to the throne in 1715, and died in 1729. His grandson and namesake, Sir Hugh Smithson, 4th Bart., was created Duke of Northumberland in 1766.

her faithful spending of her time in all y^{t} her health permitted her, her patience was most remarkable in ye large share she had of ye Cross, being wth ye Rheumatisme, unable for several years before her death to walk, but by ye help of Crutches, ye 16th last Months of her Life, her Sufferances was unexpressible, wth Violence of ye Scurvy, wch roted her foot & Leg to ye Knee, all which she Supported wth an unchangeable Mildness & Cheerfulness, gives us all Reason to hope she had her Purgatory in this world, yet as ye greatest Sanctity is Requisite to appear Spotless at ye divine tribunal of Alm^{ty} God we humbly entreat y^{r} Accustom'd Prayers of Charity. Requiescat in Pace.

(256) Anno Dom: 1723 the first of May made her holy Profession Sister Catherine **Wingate,** now call'd Sister Catherine Frances being Aged of 17 Years.

Anno Dom: (1745) the 5th of Novr in our Conv^{t} of Naz: of English Poor Clares in Graveline is most happily departed this Life fortify'd wth all ye Sacram^{ts} of our Holy Moth^{r} ye Church, our Dr Sister Catherine Frances Wingate Aged of 39 & 23 since her entrance into holy Religion, to wch she has ever been a most serviceable member, never sparing herself in any employment & has sustained for some years a Violent dropsy wth an unpaiell'd Courage & patience, her Sufferances these 10 last Months has been inexplicable, but endured wth a perfect Resignation to ye Will of God. She employ'd the little intervals her sharp pains allow'd her in serving each one to ye utmost of her power, having been always remarkable for good Nature, Charity, & Innocency of Life, this joyn'd to a strong Confidence in ye Mercies of ye Alm: makes us hope she now Enjoys ye reward of her fervent Life & Sufferances, but not to be failing in our duty y^{r} Prayers are humbly requested for her repose. Requiescat in Pace.

(257) Anno: Dom: (1723) the 29th of June made her holy Profession Sister Mary **Hilton** now call'd Sis^{r} Mary Bonaventure being Aged of 25 Years.

Anno: Dom: (1736) the 31st of March in our Conv^{t} of Naz: of English Poor Clares, is most happily departed y^{s} Life fortifiy'd wth all ye Sacraments of our holy Moth^{r} ye Church; our Dr Sister, Sist^{r} Mary Bonaventure Hilton, Aged of 38 & 14 since her Entrance into holy Religion, which time she has faithfully employ'd in her Laborious Vocation, of wch had a great esteem, ever retaining her Primitive fervour, most remarkable preventing & Charitable, always ready to help any one that stood in need of assistance, her fidelity to God was not less exemplar, being much given to Prayer & the pursuit of those Virtues suitable to her State, particularly a great humility, & Contempt of herself, Patient & Cheerful Supportation of habitual Infirmities, joyn'd to a strong Confidence in ye mercy's of God, & singular Devotion to our B^{d} Lady doubtless obtain'd her so happy a death, but ye Judgts of God being secret I humbly entreat ye assistance of yr H. Prayers for ye repose of her Soul. Requiescat in Pace.

(258) Anno: Domi: (1724) on ye 4th of Febry made her holy Profession Sisr Emerientiana **Park,** now call'd Sisr Mary Colett, ag'd of 19 years.

Anno: Dom: (1777) the 4th of Augt in our Convt of Naz: of English Poor Clares in Graveline is most happily deceas'd administered, wth the Rites of our Ho Mothr ye Church our Dr Sisr, Sisr Mary Colett Park, Aged 72 & 55 since Entrance into holy Religion, wch time she most faithfully Comply'd wth her Laborious Vocation, never sparing herself Night or Day to assist any one who stood in need of her help, particularly ye Sick, to whom she was Generally Charitable, & faithfull in all appointments of holy Obedience Rendered great service to our Community. Striving to do all she cou'd till ye last eighteen days of her Life, tho she was for some Months before taken wth an illness in her Stomach & great pains in her bowels yt proceeded from an Impostum in ye Liver which carried her off, supporting ye same wth ye greatest patience, & Mildness, was very grateful for every thing that was done for her, expressing ye same a little before she died, being perfectly sensible till ye last Moment. she was always pious & fervent, remarkable in frequent Visits to ye Bd Sacrament, to which she was Singularly devoted, as also to our Bd Lady, St Petre, & her good Angel, whose little Altar she Constantly visited every Night, we doubt not but they have proved powerful Intercessors for her, but ye Judgmts of God being inscrutable, I humbly beg yr good Prayers for her. Requiescat in Pace.

(259) Anno: Domini (1725) the 1st of May made her holy Profession, Sisr Ann **Clifton,** now call'd Sisr Ann Bonaventure, Aged of 17 Years.*

Anno Dom: (1762) ye 22d of Decr in our Convt of Naz: of English Poor Clares in Graveline, has happily quitted ys Mortal Exile, fortified wth all ye Rites of our ho: Mothr ye Church, our Dr Sister, Sisr Ann Bonaventure Clifton Aged 57 & 39 since her Entrance into holy Religion, having sustained for many Years long and many painful Infirmities wth Edifying patience and Conformity to God's Holy Will, notwithstanding had been a very Serviceable Member, & Exercis'd several Offices, in wch her Obedience, Respect, & Submission to her Suprs was most remarkable, as was no less her fidelity, & great Exactitude in all customs of holy Religion, constantly tending to her own perfection, & most fervent in ye performance of ye Divine Office, both day & night, as her forces wou'd permit. A great Lover of ho: Poverty, it pleas'd

* Daughter of Cuthbert Clifton and sister of Jane above.

Al: God to visit her wth many interiour Suffrances, & Conflicts, joyn'd to an Asthma for many Years, her death was unexpectedly sudden, yet gave time for ye Sacram^ts. Her great devotion to St Cath: of Siena, of whom she had receiv'd Extraordinary favours in her Life, doubtless obtain'd her y^t tranquillity & peace of mind wth wch she rendered up her Soul, present to ye last Moment, saying it was ye happyest day she ever had, but as ye Judgm^ts of God, are unknown, we most humbly beg y^r accustom'd Charity for her Soul's speedy Rest. Requiescat in Pace.

(260) The same Day & Year made also her ho: Profession Sis^r Ann **Leckenby,** now call'd Sis^r Ann Winifrid being Aged of 18 Years.*

Anno: Dom: (1756) the 25th of May in our Conv^t of Naz: of English Poor Clares in Graveline is happily departed y^s Life our Dr Sister, Sis^r Ann Winifred Leckonby, aged 50 & 33 since her Entrance into holy Religion, which time she has spent in ye pursuit of those Virtues most suitable to her State, & faithful Complyance wth All appointments of holy Obedience, she has Left us a great Example of Silence, & patient Supportation of many Infirmities, no less Edifying in her Conformity to ye Divine Will in ye different attacks she had of a Palsy some Years before her death, ye same illness depriv'd us of her in a few hours, & prevented her having ye benefit of ye holy Viaticum; she was always singularly devoted to our B^d Lady, & St Austen, & make no doubt but their Intercession was very powerful in her favour, but ye Judgm^ts of God being inscrutable, we humbly Request for her y^r accustom'd Prayers of Charity. Requiescat in Pace.

(261) The same day & Year made her holy Profession, Sis^r Jane **Waring,** now call'd Sis^r Mary Frances Aged of 27 years.

Anno: Dom: 1739 the 16th of Sepr in our Conv^t of Naz: of English Poor Clares in Graveline is most happily deceas'd our Dr Sister, Sis^r Mary Frances Waring, fortified wth all ye Rites of our ho: Moth^r ye Church, aged of 41 & 15 since her Entrance into holy Religion. Alm: God was pleas'd to take her from us after a Violent fever of 15 days, much regretted by all, having always comply'd wth Singular fidelity to her Laborious Vocation, ever most Charitable and preventing to all, who any ways stood in need of her assistance, Remarkable for her Love to ho: poverty wch appear'd in all her Actions, as a true Child of our holy Fath^r St Francis, to whom she had a peculiar Devotion, who undoubtedly gave her his particular assistance at ye hour of her

* Daughter of William Leckonby, of Leckonby House in Great Eccleston and the Demesne of Elswick, Esq., by Anne, daughter of Thomas Hothersall, of Hothersall Hall, co. Lancaster, Esq., and sister and co-heiress of John Hothersall, Esq.

death. She departing this Life upon ye Eve of his sacred Stigmates, & we hope has already obtain'd her ye reward of her Labours, yet lest any thing shou'd retard her happyness, we humbly crave y^{r} accustomed Charity for ye repose of her Soul. Requiescat in Pace.

(262) Anno: Dom: (1725) ye 6th of Jan^{ry} made her holy Profession, Sis^{r} Margaret **Wells**, now call'd Sister Hellen Bernard, being Aged of 31 years.*

Anno: Dom: (1750) ye 24th of Decem^{r} in our Conv^{t} of Naz: of English Poor Clares in Graveline is most happily departed this Life, our Dr Sister, Sist^{r} Hellen Bernard Wells, being ag'd 55 & 25 since her entrance into holy Religion, she was ever endow'd wth singular piety & indefatigable in her endeavours to ye pursuit of Perfection, on all occasions expresst her gratitude to Allm: God for her happy call to Religion, in wch state she acquitted her self of her Laborious Vocation to ye utmost of her health, wch was no less Edyfying y^{n} her readiness to help every one, & patient supportation, & conformity to ye divine will in many painful Infirmities for some Years before her death, wch tho sudden as only to allow time for Extremunction, have just reason to confide y^{t} she was'nt found unprepar'd, her remarkable devotion to our B^{d} Lady, strong confidence in All: God, & tender devotion to ye mystery of his H. Infancy, gives us all reason to Confide y^{t} his calling her to himself ye Eve of ye feast, was to joyn wth ye Angels in their praises to him, yet as ye Judgements of God are inscrutable not to be failing in our duty, humbly request y^{r} prayers of Charity for her. Requiescat in Pace.

(263) Anno: Dom: (1726) ye 24th of Sepr made her holy Profession Sis^{r} Frances **Berington**, now call'd Sis^{r} Clare Frances Xaveria, Aged of 18 Years.

Anno: Dom: (1747) ye 25th of July in our Conv^{t} of Naz: of English Poor Clares in Graveline, is most happily departed y^{s} Life, strengthened wth all the Rites of our holy Mo: ye Church, our Dr Sis^{r} Sister Clare Frances Berington, ye 39th Year of her Age & 22nd since her Entrance into ho: Religion, to which she has been a most Serviceable member as far as her health wou'd allow, & as constant in her Endeavours for all virtues most Suitable to her state, her Respect & Submission to Supp^{rs} was no less remarkable than her patient Supportation, & Conformity to ye Divine Will particularly ye last Year of her Life, during ye sharp pains wth wch it pleas'd Alm: God to afflict her, she was present to herself to ye last, & we have all reason to Confide y^{t} her Singular Devotion to our B^{d} Lady, & St Joseph made them powerful Intercessors in her favour, but as ye Judgm^{ts} of God are Impenetrable y^{t} nothing may

* Of the notable Catholic family of Wells of Brambridge, co. Southampton.

retard her speedy Enjoym[t] of Eternal Bliss. I humbly Request y[r] usual Charity for her Requiescat in Pace.

(264) Anno: Dom: (1727) y[e] 14th of July made her holy Profession. Sister Catherine **Winckley**, now call'd Sister Catherine Joseph being ag'd of 19.*

Anno: Dom: (1749) y[e] 27th of Nov[r] in our Conv[t] of Naz: of English Poor Clares in Graveline is happily deceas'd fortify'd wth all y[e] Rites of our holy moth: y[e] Church, our D[r] Sister Sis[r] Catherine Joseph Winckley, Ag'd 42 & 23 since entrance into holy Religion, who has left us much Edified by her assiduous tendance to her own perfection, great Innocency of Life, true Religious Spirit, fervour & great exactitude in all duties of Customs & Ceremonies of holy Religion, as far as her health permitted her w[ch] was very apparent y[e] six years she exercised y[e] office of Choir Mistress, to y[e] general Satisfaction of the Community, her fidelity in all appointm[ts] of Obedience was not less Exemplar, as was also her patience in Suffering several Years habitual infirmities, her great devotion to St Joseph, & ye Saints of our holy Order, has we hope already purchased her ye Enjoym[t] of their Company, tho' to Comply wth our duty we humbly Request y[r] prayers of Charity. Requiescat in Pacè.

(265) Anno: Dom: (1727) ye 12th of Augt made her ho: Profession Sister Julia **Clifton**, now Call'd Sister Clementina Clare Clifton, being aged of 17.

Anno: Dom: (1756) ye 23rd of Ap[l] in our Conv[t] of Naz: of English Poor Clares in Graveline, has most happily quitted y[s] mortal Exile, fortified wth all y[e] Rites of our ho: Moth[r] y[e] Church, our D[r] Sister, Sist[r] Clementina Clare Clifton, ag'd 47 & 30 since her entrance into ho: Religion, she has left us much Edified wth her fidelity in her different employs, as well as in y[e] many Virtues she practis'd, her fervour & courage was no less Exemplar than her patience & silent supportation of many Infirmities, y[e] same was most remarkable in her last Sickness, w[ch] was a Catarrh, and deprived us of her in a few days, y[e] sweetness and tranquillity wth w[ch] She expir'd, joyn'd to her perfect Conformity to y[e] Divine Will, & strong Confidence in y[e] mercies of Alm: God gives us just reason to Confide y[t] S[t] Francis Xaveria, & S[t] Allexius to whom she was Singularly devoted, were powerful intercessors in her favour, but not to be failing in our duty to her, we humbly request y[e] accustom'd prayers of Charity for her. Requiescat in Pace.

(266) Anno: Dom: y[e] same day & year made her ho: Profession

* Daughter of Edward Winckley, of Banister Hall, co. Lancaster, Esq. (*vide C.R.S.*, vi., 151). She had previously been at York Bar convent, where she had been sent to school in 1715.

Sis^{r} Mary **Hull**, now call'd Sis Mary Dominic being aged 25.*

Anno: Dom: (1757) ye 15th of May in our Conv^{t} of Naz: of English Poor Clares in Graveline, has most happily quitted y^{s} mortal Exile: strengthened wth all ye Rites of our ho: moth^{r} ye Church, our Dr Sister, Sis^{r} Mary Dominic Hull aged of 55 & 31 since her entrance into ho: Religion, wch time she has spent in a faithful Compliance wth her Laborious Vocation, remarkably Charitable in her tendance of ye sick, & very patient in ye Supportation of many Infirmities, no less Edifying in her Silent tendance to perfection, & gratitude to Alm^{ty} God for her Call in Religion, she was singularly devoted to our B^{d} Lady, & St Joseph, whom no doubt not were very powerful in their Intercession for her obtaining so happy an End, but ye Judgm^{ts} of God being inscrutable, we humbly request for her speedy Repose y^{r} accustomed Prayers of Charity. Requiescat in Pace.

(267) Anno: Dom: (1727) the 3rd of Decr made her holy Profession Sister Ann **Bloome**, now call'd Sister Mary Ignatia Aged of 25 Years.

Anno: Dom: (1756) the 24th of Feb^{ry} in our Conv^{t} of Naz: of English Poor Clares in Graveline, is most happily departed y^{s} Life, our Dr Sister, Sist^{r} Mary Ignatia Bloome, strengthened wth all ye Rites of our ho: Moth^{r} ye Church, aged of 54 & 30 since her entrance into holy Religion, wch time she has spent in a due Complyance wth her Laborious Vocation, as far as her health wou'd permit, & most Edifying in her Couragious & patient Supportation of several Years Lingering Consumption, & other Infirmities, & most remarkable for Silent tendance to herself. She frequently expresst a great sense of Gratitude to All: God for her call to ye Catholic faith, & to a Religious state, her strong confidence in God, joyn'd to her singular devotion to our B^{d} Lady, St Joseph, & our holy Father. We dont doubt but was very powerful in her favour but not to be failing in our duty, we humbly request y^{r} Prayers of Charity for ye speedy repose of her Soul. Requiescat in Pace.

(268) Anno: Dom: (1731) the 29th of Sepr made her holy Profession Sister Catherine **Hodshon**, now call'd Sister Catherine Austin being aged of 25.†

Anno: Dom: (1771) ye 25th of May in our Conv^{t} of Naz: of English Poor Clares in Graveline is piously deceas'd in our Lord,

* Daughter of William Hull, of Maynes in Little Singleton, co. Lancaster, a tenant-farmer under the Hesketh. Her father died in 1707, and her mother, Elizabeth Hull, went to reside at Grimsargh, and made a return as a Catholic non-juror in 1717.

Daughter of Ralph Hodgson, of Lintz, co. Durham, Esq., by Mary, daughter of Thomas Killingbeck, of Methley, co. York, Esq.

administered wth all y[e] Rites of our holy Moth[r] y[e] Church our D[r] Sister, Sis[r] Catherine Austin Hodshon, Aged 65 & 43 since her entrance into holy Religion, w[ch] time she spent in a great tendance to her own perfection, & gave us singular example of Edification by a holy fear & love of All: God, wth a strong Confidence in his infinite mercies, & was most pious & fervent in all her Religioue duties, as far as her health wou'd permit, & was a most Serviceabls member, her Respect, & Obedience, & Submission to Sup[rs] wae no less Remarkable, than her fidelity in y[e] several Offices shs exercis'd in our Comunitie. She had a Complication of Ilnesses, w[ch] she Linger'd wth many Years, her last sickness was a violent fever w[ch] she supported wth Singular patience & silence, her devotion to our B[d] Lady, S[t] Michael, & S[t] Austin, doubtless obtain'd her y[t] sweetness & tranquility wth w[ch] she render'd up her Soul to All: God, who was pleas'd to Sweeten all her Apprehension of y[e] next world at this her last hour, present to herself till y[e] last moment, gives us all reason to hope she is in y[e] enjoyment of Eternal Bliss, yet y[t] nothing may retard her, we Earnestly beg y[r] accustomed prayers of Charity. Requiescat in Pace.

(269) The same day & Year made also her holy Profession S[tr] Ann **Hussy**, now call'd Sister Mary Xaveria, being aged of 17.*

Anno: Domini (1780) the 20th of Jan[ry] has most happily & piously render'd her Soul to her Creator our D[r] Sister, Sister Mary Xaveria Hussy, aged of 66 years, & 49 since her Entrance into Holy Religion, after a Life of great pain & Sufferings, particularly these 15 last years, w[ch] time she has been Confined to her Chair by a total Rheumatism, w[ch] in a manner deprived her of y[e] use of her Limbs. She bore the same wth an Edifying Cheerfulness, & Conformity to y[e] Divine Will, having ever been remarkable for Ardnet devotion, & Charity towards all, her firm Confidence in y[e] Mercies & merits of our good God, her tender Devotion to our B[d] Lady, S Joseph, & S[t] Xaverious doubtless Obtain'd her so happy a death have: a short time before she Expired expresst her entire Conformity to God's Will in all Events, & her gratitude to y[e] Comunity for their tender care of her, being doubtful of her having benefited by y[e] H Oyles, we more Earnestly Intreat y[r] H Prayers for her speedy rest. Requiescat in Pace.

(270) Anno Domini (1738) y[e] 29th of Dec[r] made her holy Profession Sis[r] Elizabeth **Orde,** now call'd Sister Felix Joseph, being Aged of 25 Years.

Anno: Dom: (1769) y[e] 28th of Decem[r] in our Conv[t] of Naz: of English Poor Clares in Graveline, is most happily departed y[s] Life Strengthened wth all y[e] Rites of our H. Moth: y[e] Church, our

* Daughter of George Hussey, of Marnhull, co. Dorset, Esq., by his second wife Grace, daughter of Sir Lewis Dive, of Bromham, co. Bedford, Knt.

Dr Sis^r^, Sis^r^ Felix Joseph Orde, Aged 57 & 32 since her entrance into ho: Religion, who was a Convert to ye Catholic faith, & ever Expresst her gratitude to All: God for ye same, & for his Singular goodness in having also call'd her to holy Religion, in wch her exactitude in Religious duties was very exemplar, as was her Assiduous tendance to ye Divine Office both Night & day, & ever had a great Love for holy Poverty, she was of a most affable & Cheerful temper, agreeable Company, her last Sickness was a Lingering decay & dropsy in her breast, wch wore her to skin & bone, & Supported ye same wth great courage, & perfect conformity to ye will of All: God, in whom she ever had a great confidencc in his Infinite mercys, was most particularly devoted to our B^d^ Lady, St Joseph, St Paul, her good Angel, & ye good thief who were undoubtedly powerful Intercessors for obtaining for her so fine a death, receiving ye last Sacram^ts^ wth ye greatest sentiments of devotion, & perfectly present to her self to ye last moment endeavouring as long as she was able to embrace her Crucifix, wch she did just before she Expired, yet human frailty being great, & ye Judgm^ts^ of God inscrutable, not to be failing in our duty, most humbly request y^r^ accustom'd Prayers of Charity for her. Requiescat in Pace.

(271) Anno: Dom: (1740) ye 6th of Feb: made her holy Profession Sister Jane **Anne**, now call'd Sis^r^ Mary Joseph being Aged of 19 years.*

Anno: Dom: (1753) ye 8th of May in our Conv^t^ of Naz: of English Poor Clares in Graveline, is most happily departed y^s^ Life strengthened wth all ye Rites of our holy Moth^r^ ye Church, our Dr Sis^r^, Sist^r^ Mary Joseph Anne Aged 32 & 15 since her entrance into holy Religion, who has ever been Constant in ye pursuit of those Virtues suitable to her state, most fervent in assisting at ye Divine Office both night & day, to ye extent of w^t^ her health wou'd allow, no less Edifying for her Religious Comportment, than for her Remarkable patient & Couragious supportation of an inward decay, Continuing in Employ of Infirmarian till ye night before she dy'd, but tho her death was more sudden than was Expected, we have all reason to Confide y^t^ she was found duly prepar'd, & that y^t^ our B^d^ Lady & St Joseph, to whom she was Singularly devoted, were powerful Intercessors in Obtaining for her that peace & entire Conformity to ye divine will, with which she quitted this Mortal Exile, yet human frailty being great, & ye Judgments of God inscrutable, not to be failing in our duty, we humbly request y^r^ accustom'd prayers of Charity for her. Requiescat in Pace.

* Daughter of Marmaduke Anne, of Frickley Hall, co. York, Esq., by Elizabeth, daughter of Robert Plumpton, of Plumpton Hall, co. York, Esq. Her paternal grandmother, the wife of Michael Anne, was the Hon. Jane Langdale, daughter of Marmaduke, 2nd Lord Langdale.

(272) Anno: Dom: (1741) the 1st of Jan: made her holy Profession Sister Elizabeth **Barlow,** now call'd Sisr Frances Clare being Aged of 23.*

Anno Domini (1794) ye 20th of May in our Convent of Nazareth of Poor Clares in Graveline, administered with all the Sacrements of our holy Mother the Church has happily quitted this mortal exile our Dr Sister, Sister Frances Clare Barlow, Aged 74 in Religion 53, which time she spent in a faithful Compliance with her Laborious Vocation, she was one of a very Innocent & pious life, a great lover of holy Poverty, & most exact in all the Customs, & Ceremonies of holy Religion, she was very examplar in the due & faithful performance of all appointments of holy Obedience, very respectful & submissive to Superiours, she Suffer'd with great patience the inconveniences of many Corporal Infirmities. Her pious & virtuous Life was ended by a most happy Death, quietly rendering up her Soul to her heavenly Spouse, whose presence we hope she is now enjoying, yet not to be failing in our Duty humbly crave for her yr accustom'd prayers of Charity. Requiescat in Pace.

(273) The same day and year made also her holy Profession, Sister Dorothy Joseph **Boardman,** now call'd Sisr Dorothy Joseph being aged of 24 years.

Anno: Dom: (1781) the 12th of Apl in our Convt of Naz: of English Poor Clares in Graveline, is happily departed this Life fortified with all ye Rights of our H Mothr ye Church, our Dr Sister, Sistr Dorothy Joseph Boardman, aged 64 & 42 since her Entrance into holy Religion, wch time she spent in a fervent Complyance wth her Laborious vocation, never sparing herself night, nor day, wn in her power to help any one, most Respectful, & prompt in executing all appointments of holy Obedience, never refusing help at all common works, often wth prejudice to her health, having Suffer'd many years most acute pains, caused by habitual Infirmities, all wch she sustained wth heroic patience, her Love & esteem of holy Poverty, made her careful in seeing nothing wasted or spoilt, so yt we may justly say was a true Imitation of our ho: Father St Francis, to whom she ever had a Singular Devotion, adorning his Altar wth all care & neatness, she was seiz'd on ye 9th with a violent cold fit, followed wth a sharp fever, & expired upon ye 12th, it being Maundy Thursday, her Devotion to ye Bd Sacrament gave her fervour often to nourish her Soul wth yt delicious food, had a great Compassion for ye poor Suffering Souls in Purgatory, whom she charitably assisted in all occasions, by offering all her Prayers & Sufferances for their relief, thus joyn'd

* Daughter of Anthony Barlow, of Barlow Hall, co. Lancaster, Esq., by Magdalen, daughter of Sir Edward Golding, of Colston-Bassett, co. Notts, 1st Bart. and his wife Eleanor, daughter of John Throckmorton, of Coughton, co. Warwick, Esq.

to a strong Confidence in ye powerful intercession of our B^{d} Lady doubtless obtained her so peaceful & quiet a death, but ye Judgm^{ts} of God being inscrutable, we most earnestly beg y^{r} good Prayers for her Soul's speedy rest. Requiescat in Pace.

Anno: Dom: 1741 the 2nd of Feb^{ry} made her holy Profession Sister Margaret **Hothersel,** now call'd Sis^{r} Mary Austin, being Aged of 29 years.*

Anno: Dom: 1765 the 13th of Ap^{l} in our Conv^{t} of Naz: of English Poor Clares in Graveline is most happily departed this Life, furnish'd with all ye Rites of our holy Moth^{r} ye Church our Dr Sister, Sister Mary Austin Hothersel, Aged 53 & 25 since her entrance into holy Religion, after having lingered some years & sufferd much with Singular patience & Silence many Infirmities, joyn'd to a Dropsy, which Carried her of, she gave us great Examples of Edification by her fidelity & fervour in assisting at ye divine office night & day even when she was unable, her great Devotion, & frequent Visits to the B^{d} Sacrament was no less Exemplar, lest any thing shou'd retard her Eternal happiness we humbly crave the Assistance of your Charitable Prayers and Suffrages for the Repose of her Soul. Requiescat in Pace.

(275) Anno: Dom: (1741) the 19th of March made her ho: Profession Sist^{r} Margaret **Hunter,** now call'd Sis^{r} Mary Francis being Aged of 26 Years.

Anno: Dom: (1769) the 5th of Novr in our Conv^{t} of Naz: of English Poor Clares in Graveline, is most happily departed y^{s} Life furnis'd wth all ye Rites of our ho: Moth^{r} ye Church, our R^{d} Moth^{r} Vic: Sis^{r} Mary Frances Hunter, aged 56, & 30 since her entrance into ho: Religion, after having given us a great Example of Unrelented fervour in ye Costant observance of all Regular duties, particularly y^{t} of ho: Silence; she exercis'd Several Offices in ye Community, & dyed in y^{t} of Vic: was remarkable for her zeal, & assiduous Constant attendance to ye Divine Office both Night & day, not absenting herself w^{n} judged unfit by ye Doct^{r}, was most mortified in her diet, & much Edified us by her heroic Patience, & perfect Conformity to ye Will of God in her last Sickness, wch was a painful Cancer wch she woud fain have Conceal'd, ever expressing y^{t} it was ye will of God she should Suffer, not admitting any Solace but when constrain'd by an absolute Unability, & was most devoted to ye B^{d} Sacrament, wch she receiv'd frequently in her last Sickness, & fasted to Communicate wth ye rest of ye Community but three days before her death, every one Esteeming her dying; in wch her fervour & Love of God was Edifying, all wch we hope thro ye merits of our B^{d} Saviour will Speedily bring her to ye fruition of eternal

* Daughter of Thomas Hothersall, of Hothersall Hall, co. Lancaster, Esq.

happiness, yet not to be failing in our duty, we most humbly entreat y[r] accustom'd Prayers for her soul. Requiescat in Pace.

(276) Anno: Dom: (1742) y[e] 25th of March made her holy Profession Sis[r] Jane **Throckmorton**, now call'd Sis[r] Clare Joseph being aged of 21 Years.*

Anno: Dom: (1773) the 22nd of Nov: in our Conv[t] of Naz: of English Poor Clares in Graveline, is most happily deceas'd, Administered wth all y[e] Rites of our holy Mother y[e] Church, our D[r] Sis[r] Sister Clare Joseph Throckmorton Aged 52 & 33 since her entrance into holy Religion, from w[ch] time she lived an Exemplar humble Religious Life wth Piety, fervour, & Love of her holy Vocation, & notwithstanding her weak health, having had sharp Illnesses rendered great service to our Communitie, was singularly devoted to our B[d] Lady, & S[t] Joseph, much Edifyed us by her Silent Supportation of her last Sickness of y[e] small Pox, w[ch] carry'd her off on y tenth day, & was several days unable to Swallow any thing, in w[ch] time she was a perfect model of Patience, Resignation, & Conformity to Alm[ty] God's Holy Will, & was so perfectly sensible that w[n] scarce able to speak, desired a Continuation of holy & pious discourses, in w[ch] she seem'd to have y[e] greatest Comfort, y[e] same we hope has obtain'd her y[e] enjoyment of her Divine Spouse, but not to be failing in our Duty, we humbly request y[r] Accustom'd Prayers & Suffrages for her. Requiescat in Pace.

(277) Anno: Dom: (1742) ye 31st of July made her ho: Professi[n] Sist[r] Elizabeth **Chantrill**, now call'd Sister Ann Clare being Aged of 22.

Décédée

(278) Anno: Dom: (1744) ye 8th of Sepr made her ho: Professi[n] Sist[r] Mary **Haggerston**, now call'd Sis[r] Mary Clare being Aged of 19 years.†

Anno: Dom: (1773) ye 15th of Nov: in our Conv[t] of Naz: of English Poor Clares in Graveline, is most happily deceas'd Administered wth all y[e] Rites of our ho: Moth[r] y[e] Church, our D[r] Sist[r] Mary Clare Haggerston, Aged 53 & 30 since her entrance into holy Religion, in w[ch] she has ever been in all Respects a most

* Daughter of Sir Robert Throckmorton, of Coughton Court, co. Warwick, and Weston-under-Wood, co. Bucks, 4th Bart., by Lady Theresa Herbert, daughter of William, Marquess of Powis, and his wife Mary, daughter and co-heiress of Sir Thomas Preston, of the Manor of Furness, co. Lancaster, 3rd Bart.

† Daughter of William, second but eldest surviving son of Sir Thomas Haggerston, of Haggerston Castle, co. Northumberland, 2nd Bart. Her mother was Anne, daughter of Sir Philip Constable, of Everingham Hall, co. York, 3rd Bart:, through whom the Constable estates passed to her nephew William Haggerston Constable, second son of Sir Carnaby Haggerston, 3rd Bart.

beneficial & serviceable a member, & a true good Religious, was Indefatigable in ye different employs she was in, never sparing her self for ye Service of ye Community, & ever show'd her Love of her Vocation, by a faithful & most fervent tendance to all those duties Suitable to her Calling, wth Respect & Submission to Sup^rs^ & has left us greatly Edified by her peaceful Religious Comportment during ye ten Years of her being Portress, Notwithstanding ye hardships of times wch she met with, all wch she bore wth Remarkable Cheerfulness, patience, & perfect Resignation to ye H will of God, wch she continued to give most Edifying proofs of, during her last Sickness, wch was ye small Pox & depriv'd us of her in twelve days, ye two last, she had a most Violent fever, but was present to herself, making fervent acts of ye love of God, & desire of being dissolved & enjoying him, as also to our B^d^ Lady to whom she was particularly devoted, all wch we Confide has obtain'd her ye reward of her Labours, & fervent Life, but not to be failing in our duty we humbly request y^r^ accustom'd Prayers, & Suffrages for her repose. Requiescat in Pace.

(279) Anno: Dom: (1744) ye 21st of Nov: made her holy Profession Sister Catherine **Duddell**, now call'd Sister Coecilia Joseph being aged of 18 years.

Anno: Dom: 1783 the first of June In our Convent of Nazareth of English Poor Clares in Graveline is happily deceased fortified with all the Sacraments of our holy Mother the Church our Dr Sister, Sister Coecilia Joseph Duddell aged 56 and 39 since her Entrance into holy Religion having left us much Edified by the Singular fervor and zeal with which she was animated in whatever Related to the Honour and glory of God, which appeared in faithfully and Indefatigably Employing to his Divine Service the natural strong Voice he had Endowed her with, both for the Choir & Singing, which Rendered her a most Serviceable member, notwithstanding the many Corporal Infirmities she laboured under, which to her great Mortification hindered her the latter Part of her Life from following the holy Community, which Inability she Endeavoured to Supply by the well spending of her time in what ever she was able, for the Benefit of holy Religion, scarce ever being seen Idle, she had a great Love for Holy Poverty, was tenderly devoted to our B^d^ Lady, St Joseph, and St Francis Xaverius, who doubtless obtained for her the grace to support with Patience & Resignation her last Illness, which was very long and violent; but has as I hope thro the Merits of our B^d^ Saviour purchased her an Everlasting Crown, but human frailty being great and the Judgements of God secret, I Earnestly Crave y^r^ Prayers of Charity for ye Speedy Repose of her Soul. Requiescat in Pace.

Anno: Dom: (1746) ye 24th of Sepr made her holy Profession Sis^r^ Ann **Swift**, now call'd Sist^r^ Mary Winefrid, Aged 27.

Anno: Dom: (1778) the 14th of Sepr in our Convt of Naz: of English Poor Clares in Graveline, is most happily departed this Life strengthend wth all ye Sacraments of our holy Mother ye Church, our Dr Sister, Sistr Mary Winefrid Swift, the 60th year of her Age & 33d since her Entrance into holy Religion all which time she faithfully employ'd in the Laborious Vocation & often expresst a Singular content & Love towards Allm God for her call to Religion, she was very Charitable in helping any one in Necessity, most Respectful & Submissive to Suprs, ever prompt in Executing their Orders, much devoted to our Bd Lady, St Joseph, & St Winefrid, who doubtless obtaind her courage & patience to Suffer for many Years great & sharp pains in her head wth remarkable Cheerfulness, the two last years of her life, All: God was pleas'd to afflict her wth ye Gout & Rheumatism wch was ye more sensible as she much desired to show her gratitude to ye Community by her humble works, wch gratitude made her always content wth whatever was given her, her great Compassion for ye poor Souls in Purgatory, made her a constant Benefactress, by her constant Prayers for their relief, Wch if she now stands in need of, yr Prayers for her Soules Speedy rest is most humbly craved. Requiescat in Pace.

(281) Anno: Dom: (1749) the 2d of July made her holy Profession, Sisr Elizabeth **Tichbourn,** now call'd Sisr Teresa Joseph Aged 20.*

Anno: Dom: (1765) ye 31st of July in our Convt of Naz: of English Poor Clares in Graveline, is most happily departed this Life fortify'd wth all ye rites of our holy Mothr ye Church our Dr Sister, Sisr Teresa Joseph Tichbourne aged 38 & 17 since her entrance into holy Religion, after 8 days Sickness, wch was esteem'd a Dropsy in her breast, joyn'd to a strong & continual fever, in wch her patience, & silent Supportation of ye same was most Edifying, she was of an Innocent, peaceful Life, & was remarkable for her particular general Charity to every one, wth all humility & Contempt of herself, her Love, & carefulness in holy Poverty, was no less Remarkable being a true Child of our holy Fathr St Francis, to whom she ever had a singular devotion, also to ye Passion of our Bd Saviour, wch doubtless obtain'd her that Confidence in God but yt nothing may retard her speedy enjoyment of Eternal bliss, I humbly request yr usual Charity for the Repose of her Soul. Requiescat in Pace.

(282) Anno: Dom: (1750) the 2d of July made her holy Profession Sisr Mary **Bullstrode,** now call'd Sister Mary Clementina, Aged 23, two years Novice.†

* Daughter of Benjamin Tichborne, Esq., and his wife Elizabeth Sturdy, of Hants.

† Daughter of Sir Joseph Bulstrode, knighted by James II. in exile at St Germains, younger son of Sir Richard Bulstrode, Knt., envoy of Charles II.

Anno: Dom: 1799 the 17th of April, in our Community of English Poor Clares, (formerly of Graveline) has piously slept in our Lord our Dr Str Sister Mary Clementina Bullstrode Jubilarian, aged 72 & 51 since her entrance into holy Religion, which time she has spent in a faithful tendance to her own perfection, & the acquirement of those Virtues most suiting her holy Vocation, of which she had a great esteem, was remarkable for the silent supportation of many painful Infirmities, never complaining of them while able to conceal them, render'd our Comunity much service with her music in the acquiring of which she was indefatigable was very patient & resigned to the will of All: God in the Crosses, he was pleas'd to send her, particularly those he visited her with towards the end of her life, which were many & very afflicting, she was much devoted to our Bd Lady & St Joseph, who have doubtless proved powerful intercessors in her favor, her Death was more sudden than Expected & only gave time for the Extreem Unction, yet tho' sudden we have all reason to think was not unprepared for, the Judgments of God being secret, we request for her your prayers of Charity. Requiescat in Pace.

(283) Anno: Dom: (1750) the 27th of Novr made her holy profession, Sisr Mary **Moody,** now call'd Sisr Mary [Catherine Aged 31.

Anno Domini 1794 the 6th of January in our Convent of Naz: of English Poor Clares in Graveline, has happily quitted this Mortal Exile fortified with all the Sacrements of our holy Mother ye Church our Dr Sister Mary Catherine Moody aged 75 & 44 since her Entrance into Religion which she spent in a faithful Compliance with her Laborious vocation, ever remarkable for the well spending her time scarce ever being seen Idle, even when Confin'd to a Room, was always willing to help any who stood in need of assistance, she had a great Love of holy Poverty join'd to a particular Devotion to our Bd Lady, St Joseph & our holy Father, and the Long Supportation of a Violent & painful illness During which she made Continually fine Acts, has we hope purchased her the repose, she aspired after, but the Judgements of God being secret & humain frailty great, we humbly request your usual prayers for her Soul. Requiescat in Pace.

(284) Anno Dom (1751) the 6th of June made her holy Profession Sisr. Dorothy **Hanford,** now call'd Sisr Dorothy Maria Aged 20, two Years Novice.*

and James II. at Brussels. Her brother James was canon of Seclin in Flanders.

*Daughter of Edward Hanford, of Redmarley, co. Worcester, Esq., second son of Walter Hanford, of Woollashall, co. Worcester, Esq., by Frances, daughter of Sir Henry Compton, of Hartpury Court, co. Gloucester, Knt. Her mother was Frances, daughter of Robert Hornyold, of Blackmore Park, co. Worcester, Esq., by Bridget, daughter of Anthony Windsor Esq.

Anno: Dom: (1761) the 6th of Decr in our Convt of Naz: of English Poor Clares in Graveline, is most happily deceas'd fortify'd wth all ye Rites of our holy Mothr ye Church our Dr Sister, Sisr Dorothy Maria Hanford, Aged 30 & 12 since her entrance into holy Religion, during wch time she much edified us in her fidelity in different employs, joyn'd to her Sweet & Aimiable temper, peaceful Inoffensive, ever pious & fervently tending to her own Perfection, & was equally remarkable for her general goodness & Charity, experienc'd by all, in ye six Years she was Infirmarian, always ready to help any one that stood in need of her Assistance. Expressing a great Comfort in never having been absent from any one at their last breath during yt time, wch joyn'd to her great Sufferance of a Lingering Consumption she supported wth an Edifying patience, & resignation to ye divine will gives us all reason to hope she Completed her Crown in a short time, least any thing may retard her speedy enjoyment of Eternal Bliss, I humbly Request yr usual Charity for her.. Requiescat in Pace.

(285) The same day & Year made also her holy Profession Sister Ann **Burrell** now call'd Sisr Ann Xaveria Aged 20, two Years Novice.

Anno Dom: 1783 the 19th of November in this our Convent of Nazareth of English Poor Clares in Graveline is happily departed this Life strengthen'd with ye Sacrament of Extreme Onction our Dr Sister Str Anne Xaveria Burrell aged 52 and 34 since her Entrance into H Religion, having left us great Example of an Unrelented fervor which seemed always upon the Encrease, very zealous for Regular Observance, and Scrupulously Exact to the Minutest Customs and Ceremonies of holy Religion, most punctual in assisting at ye Divine Office both Day and Night that it Evidently appeared she placed her Perfection in ye faithful Observance of our H. Rule; remarkable for her Charity towards her Neighbour ever Endeavouring to hide and Excuse the faults of Others, and assist any who stood in need of her Help especially the sick for whose solace she often deprived herself of her Rest, had a strong Confidence in God, and greatly devoted to our Bd Lady, St Frances Xaveria and St Alexius who I doubt not have been Powerful Intercessors in her favour, but as human frailty is great and the Judgments of God secret lest any thing shou'd remain yet to be Cancelled I humbly Crave your Prayers of Charity for the speediest Repose of her Soul. Requiescat in Pace.

(286) The same day & Year made also her holy Profession Sisr Catherine **Manby**, now call'd Sisr Clementina Stanislaus Aged 18 two Years Novice.*

* Daughter of Francis Manby, of Downsell Hall, co. Essex, Esq., eldest son and heir of Sir Thomas Manby, of the same, Knt., by his first wife

Anno Domini 1795 the 8th of Jan^{ry} in our Convent of English poor Clares of Nazareth, inGraveline administer'd with all the rites of our Holy Mth the Church, has most happily quitted this Mortal exile, our Dr Sister, Sister Clementina Stanislaus Manby, Aged 62 & 43 since her entrance into holy Religion, which time she faithfully spent in the service of our Community, was very remarkable for the well spending of her time, scarce ever sèen Idle when able to apply herself to any thing. She was very pious, & often express'd her gratitude to All: God, for her call to Religion was very grateful for Charities done her, & particular in praying for those that render'd her service, it pleased God to afflict her with a long & painful Infirmities, which Confin'd her to the Infirmary some years before her Death, her patient supportation of Interior, & Corporal sufferances join'd to the perfect resignation & tranquillity with which she prepared herself for her last passage, has we hope obtain'd her the rest she aspired after, yet, the Judgments of God, being secret, & human frailty great, humbly request for her, the assistance of your prayers of Charity. Requiescat in Pace.

(287) Anno: Dom: (1752) the 29th of June made her holy Profession Sis^{r} Mary **Hodshon** now call'd Sis^{r} Mary Agnes Aged 20.*

Anno Domini 1782 ye 19th of June in this our Convent of Nazareth of English Poor Clares in Graveline is happily departed this Life strengthen'd with all ye Sacraments of our holy Mother ye Church our d^{r} Sister, S^{tr} Mary Agnes Hodshon aged 50 & 31 since her Entrance into H. Religion having left us great Subject of Edification by the remarkable Sweetness, Patience & Conformity to ye holy Will of God with which she bore for some years before her Death most acute and lingering Pains, very faithful in ye managing and well spending of her time for ye service of ye H: Com^{ty} particularly devoted to ye B^{d} Eucharist which appeared in her Constant and frequent Visits to ye B^{d} Sacrament never omitting ye same but in Extremity of Illness; her Strong Confidence in ye Passion & Merits of our B^{d} Saviour, joined to her tender Devotion to our B^{d} Lady & St Peter, has I hope pleaded Powerfully in her Behalf; but as the Judgements of God are unknown to us, and human frailty being great, not to be failing in our Duty, I humbly intreat your Prayers of Charity for ye Speediest Repose of her Soul. Requiescat in Pace.

Juliana, daughter and co-heiress of Sir George Selby, of White House, co. Durham, and of Dawley, co. Middlesex, Bart., and his wife Mary, daughter of Richard, 1st Viscount Molyneux.

* Daughter of Ralph Hodgson, Esq., of Lintz Hall, co. Durham, Esq., and sister of Ralph Hodgson, of the same, Esq., who married Catherine, daughter of Roger Strickland, of Catterick Hall, and of Richmond, co. York, Esq., by Catherine, daughter of Simon Scrope, of Danby Hall, co. York, Esq.

(289) Anno: Dom: (1755) the 15th of Augt made her holy Profession Sisr Mary **Falkner**, now call'd Sis Mary Felicité Aged of 24 Years.

Décédée

(290) Anno: Dom: (1756) the 24th of Sepr made her holy Profession Sister Mary **Routledge** now call'd Sister Mary Joseph Aged of 25 Years.

Anno Domini, 1794 ye 9th of May in our Convent of English Poor Clares of Naz: in Graveline, has happily slept in our Lord our Dr Str, Sister Mary Joseph Routledge, Aged 63 and 39, since her entrance into religion, which time she has faithfully employ'd in a fervent Compliance with her Laborious Vocation, was very remarkable for the well spending of her time, never sparing herself when in her power to render service to the holy religion, she was a great lover of holy poverty, always endeavouring to put every thing to use & advantage. Her respect & Submission to Superiours, were very Singular, her Devotion to the most Holy Sacrement, of the Altar, gave her fervour often to refresh her Soul with that most delicious food, she had a high esteem of her holy Vocation, for which she often express'd her gratitude to Al: God, she was much devoted to our Bd Lady, & St Joseph, who doubtless obtain'd her the great Confidence she had in the mercies of God, no less examplar was her patient Supportation of Corporal infirmities, she gave us great examples of Resignation to the divine will, particularly during her last Illness, which was a decay & dropsy in her breast, which taking her off more suddenly than was Expected, she was depriv'd of the last sacrements, her pious & virtuous life gives us reason to hope she is in the enjoyment of Eternal Bliss, yet not to be failing in our duty request for her, your accustom'd prayers of Charity. Requiescat in Pace.

(291) Anno: Dom: (1758) the 21st of Nov: made her holy Profession Sisr Hellen **Barrow**, now call'd Sister Hellen Joseph Aged of 26 Years.*

Anno: Dom: (1763) the 7th of Janry in our Convent of Naz: of English Poor Clares in Graveline is happily deceas'd in our Lord, our Dr Sister, Sisr Hellen Joseph Barrow, Lay Sister, being of 31 & 5 since her Entrance into holy Religion, she was one of an Innocent, pious Life, fervent & a great fidelity in all Appointments of holy Obedience as far as her health permitted, she Suffer'd much Several Months wth a Lingering Consumption & particularly ye last eight days of her life, in wch her patience was most edifying, as was ye Acts she made wth perfect presence of mind till ye last Moment, but as ye Judgmts of Allmty God are Inscrutable,

* Daughter of Edward Barrow, of Westby, co. Lancaster, yeoman, and his wife Anne Hall, and sister of the Rev. John Barrow and FF. Richard and Joseph Barrow, S.J.

we most humbly intreat y^{r} Prayers & Suffrages for ye Repose of her soul. Requiescat in Pace.

(292) Anno Dom: (1760) ye 29th of June made her holy Profession Sis^{r} Ann **Clifton,** now call'd Sis^{r} Anna Maria Aged of 18 years.*

Decedee.

(293) Anno Dom: (1761) the 30th of Augt made her holy Profession Sis^{r} Catherine **Lee,** now call'd S^{tr} Catherine Alexia Aged of 21 years.

Anno Dom 1828 Jan^{ry} 21 in our Convent of Nazareth of English Poor Clares in Graveline happily departed this life strengthened with all the Holy Sacrements our dear Sister, S^{tr} Catherine Alexia Lee aged 88 and 67 since her entry into Holy religion. Requiescat in Pace.

(294) Anno: Dom: (1763) the 7th of Novr made her ho: Profess^{n} Sis^{r} Dorothy **Hoole,** now call'd Sis^{r} Dorothy Clare, Aged of 38 years.†

Anno Dom: 1792 ye 20th of February in our Convent of Nazareth of English Poor Clares in Graveline is happily deceased strengthen'd with all ye Sacre^{ts} of our H. Mother the Church our d^{r} Sister, S^{tr} Dorothy Clare Hoole aged 67 and in ye 30th since her entrance into holy Religion having served in the Extern Quarter with great fidelity for the space of 17 years and after her Entrance into H. Religion was no less serviceable in her Laborious Vocation for a Lay Sister in which she persever'd with great fervor till about two years before her Death, when she was reduced to a most lingering condition which she bore in silence & tranquillity, this joined to her fervent Preparation for Death gives us great hopes she is already in the Enjoym^{t} of her heavenly Spouse whom she ardently desired to be united to, was tenderly devoted to our B^{d} Lady & St Jos: but the Characteristic Virtue seem'd to be obedience and it may be said that she Expired in ye almost actual Exercise of it wch gives us no small room to Confide that she has obtain'd the Victory promised to the Obedient, but human frailty being great lest anything sh^{d} yet remain to be Cancelled I humbly intreat your usual Prayers of Charity. Requiescat in Pace.

(295) Anno: Dom: (1764) the 28th of May made her holy Profession Sis^{r} Ann **Penswick,**‡ now call'd S^{tr} Mary Victoria aged of 18 years.

* Daughter of one of the younger branches of the Cliftons, of Westby, co. Lancaster.

Of the Hoole family of Elswick, co. Lancaster (*vide C.R.S.* vi. 166).

Daughter of Randal Penswick, of Great Eccleston, and sister of Thomas Penswick, steward to the Gerards of Bryn, co. Lancaster. She was aunt to Bishop Thomas Penswick, V.A.—N.D., the Rev. John Penswick, and

Décédée à Gosfield en Angleterre Juillet 1813 dans lés fonctions d'Abbesse depuis 1799.

(296) Anno: Dom: (1764) the 27th of Novr made her holy Profession Sis^{r} Elizabeth **Jump**, now call'd Sis^{r} Clare Frances aged of 18 years.*

Anno Dom 1823 Octr in our Convent of Nazareth of English Poor Clares in Graveline happily departed this life strengthened with the sacrement of Extreme Onction our Dear Sister, S^{tr} Elizabeth Clare Frances Jump age 77, and 59 since her entry into Holy Religion. Requiescat in Pace.

(297) Anno: Dom: (1765) the 28th of May made her holy Profession Sis^{r} Clementina **Johnson**, now call'd Sis^{r} Clementina Clare, aged of 17 years.†

Anno Dom 1793 ye 16th of May in our Convent of Nazareth of English Poor Clares in Graveline, has piously quitted this Mortal Exile fortified wth all the Sacraments of our Holy Mother the Church, our Most Rev^{d} & Dearly beloved Mother Abbess; Sister Clementina Clare Johnson ye 45th year of age & 28th of her Holy Profession, amidst ye tears & prayers of her truly afflicted Children whom she has left in the deepest trouble & distress as we can never sufficiently lament the loss of so worthy a Superior. Almighty God had endow'd her wth an Extraordinary Capacity wth other gifts both of nature & grace wch she faithfully Improved for ye Benefit & Advantage of ye Com^{ty} to whom she gave general Satisfaction the space of 14 years wch she Govern'd us wth so much prudence, sweetness & affability that Endear'd her to us, for we never fail'd to find in her a tender Mother & an aff^{ate} Friend, wch visibly appear'd when she could solace or Comfort us under any Pressure or affliction, by this Charitable & Compassionate Disposition she was easily moved wth a feeling sense of ye Sufferings of others & Inclined her to attend to ye necessities of every poor Person that address'd to her (297) *bis* whom she always relieved as far as Circumstances would allow often repeating that we should never want while we could help poor distress'd People, her Confidence in ye Fatherly Care of Divine Providence was very great wch seem'd to Increase in times of the greatest Necessities. She always show'd an Unwearied Sollicitude for ye Benefit of the

Randal Penswick, who succeeded his father as agent to the Gerards. She succeeded the Abbess Emilia Keith in Jan., 1799, as 11th abbess of the convent then settled at Gosfield, in Essex, where she died at the age of 67.

* Daughter of William Jump, of Hesketh Bank, co. Lancaster, gent., by Katherine, daughter of Alexander Parker, of Bradkirk Hall, and of Gray's Inn, barrister-at-law, by Dorothy, daughter of Thomas Westby, of Mowbreck Hall, co. Lancaster, Esq.

† Daughter of Mr Johnson, of Lea, co. Lancaster, and a relative of the Abbess Penswick, William Penswick, of Great Eccleston, having married Grace Johnson, of Lea. She was elected 9th abbess, 8 Oct. 1799.

Com^{ty} being most Indefatigable never sparing her Pains where she had ye least Prospect of Procuring them any advantage, often to ye Prejudice of her own health by her Close Application to ye affairs of ye Convent in wch her Activity Joined to her deliberate Cool reflection of mind & forecast wth an Unalterable serenity and Composure wch no Cross event could ever change was very remarkable. Her Cheerful Mild temper wth so Many other Amiable qualifications render'd her not only a Comfort to her Com^{ty} but affable and agreeable to all she Conversed wth. In short she was Universally beloved & Esteemed & we were truly happy: when Almighty God was Pleased to deprive us of her, especially in these distressing times wch adds much to our severe Cross and makes our loss Irreparable. Her last Illness was a Continual Vomiting wth other Bilious Complaints wch terminated in an Imposthume in her stomach, she suffered much during the space of five Months wth her Usual (297) *ter* Peace and tranquillity & Edified us greatly by an Uncommon Patience & Resignation to the Holy Will of God, ever grateful for every thing done for her, was always thoughtful and attentive to each one of ye Com^{ty}, often Expressing her tender Concern for us all, this Join'd to the many other virtues wch she has left so great Examples of, makes so lasting an Impression on us that no time or Circumstance will ever be able to Efface, however this reflection Comforts us, that while we lament our loss, she is thro ye Merits of our Blessed Saviour's bitter Death and Passion (in wch she ever Placed her entire hopes & Confidence ye Intercession of our B^{d} Lady, St Joseph, & our H. Mth St Clare) gone to receive from his hands ye reward of those Virtues wch he alone can sufficiently Prize, and is now in ye Eternal Enjoyment of that happiness promised to ye meek & humble of Heart, but as the Judgments of God are Unknown to us and ye greatest Purity required in all those that are to follow ye Lamb where-ever he goes, not be failing in our Duty, Earnestly request the Charitable assistance of your fervent Prayers. Requiescat in Pace.

(298) Anno: Dom: (1767) the 21st of Octr made her holy Profession Sis^{r} Emilia **Keith**, now call'd Sis^{r} Mary Austin Aged of 30 years.*

(298) Anno Domini 1799 ye 4th of Jan^{ry} in our Community of

* She was elected 10th abbess in May 1793, and, on the 12th of the following October, the convent was seized by the revolutionists, and guards put in charge. Five days later, the two communities of Poor Clares and Benedictines of Dunkirk, consisting in all of 42 persons, were brought prisoners to this convent, thus increasing the number at Gravelines to seventy-seven prisoners. Thus they remained until they obtained permission to return to England, when the abbess and the rest of the community were released and left the convent at Gravelines on 29 April, 1798, sailed from Calais on the following day, arrived in London on 3rd May, and through the munificenec of the Duchess of Buckingham, who placed her house at their disposal, were re-established at Gosfield, in Essex.

English poor Clares (formerly of Graveline) has piously quitted this mortal exile fortified with all the rights of our holy mother the Church, our Rev[d] & Dear M[th] Abbess, Mary Austin Keith, the 61st year of her age, 31st since her entrance into holy Religion, & 6th of her Government in quality of Abbess, she was a Convert to the Catholic faith, & ever express'd her Gratitude to Almighty God for the same, as also for her Call to holy Religion, having a high esteem of her holy vocation, & ever seem'd to place her Perfection in the practice of those Virtues that might render her most pleasing to her heavenly Spouse, particularly in obedience & submission to Superiours, which she also endeavour'd to inculcate into her Novices, the three years she was mistress; her resignation to the divine will was also remarkable in the heavy Cross's it pleased Almighty God to visit her with, those especially that preceded & follow'd our quitting our D[r] Convent at Graveline, which were many & very great, she was also remarkable for speaking well of the absent & was generally Charitable to all, as far as her weak health wou'd permit, she was greatly devoted to S[t] Austin & S[t] Francis de Sales, who were no doubt powerful advocates in her favor & procured her the tranquillity & resignation with which she met Death of which she had always had a great dread, till her last sickness, when it pleas'd her heavenly Spouse to sweeten it to her in a wonderful manner, her last Illness which was long & painfull she supported with edifying patience, which join'd to her other Virtues has, we Confide obtain'd her a happy Eternity but as the Judgments of God are secret & not to be failing in our duty, we humbly request for her your accustom'd prayers. Requiescat in Pace.

[*In pencil*] Died at Gosfield in England Jan. 4th 1799.

Anno Dom 1799 y[e] 4th of Jan[ry] in our Comunity of English Poor Clares formerly of Graveline fortified with all the rights of our holy Mo[r] ye Church Departed this mortal life our R[d] Mo[r] Abbess Mary Austin Keith aged 61 & 31 since her entrance into Religion & 6 of her government in quality of Abbess, she was a Convert to the Catholic faith & ever shew'd her Gratitude to God for her Conversion as well as for her call to Religion by the practice. Requiescat in Pace.

[Note that the longer obituary memoir is given with the profession after it, which is followed by a shorter memoir. The original is adhered to.]

(299) Anno: Dom: (1769) the 19th of March made her holy Profession Sis[r] Lydia **Nihell**, now call'd Sis[r] Catherine Joseph, being Aged of 20 years.*

Anno Domini 1794 y[e] 29th of December in our Convent of English Poor Clares of Nazareth in Graveline, Strengthened with all the Sacrements of our Holy Mother the Church has most happily quitted

* Sister of Fr. Edward Nihill, S.J.

this mortal exile our D^{r} S^{tr}, Sister Catherine Joseph Nihell aged 46 and 27 since her entrance into holy Religion, she was ever Innocently & piously inclined & much addicted to prayer, a great lover of holy Poverty, & very Charitable in helping any one that stood in need of her assistance, she has left us much edified at her patient supportation of the many inconveniences attending a sickly life, her patience & Conformity to the divine will was particularly remarkable during her last Illness, which was a lingering & painful decay, which confin'd her to a Room some Months before her Death, which time she faithfully spent in preparing for her last passage, her pious life was ended by a most happy & Edifying Death, being present to herself to the last, St Joseph, to whom she was tenderly devoted, doubtless obtain'd her the peace, and tranquillity with which she render'd up her Soul to her heavenly Spouse for her speedy enjoyment of Eternal Bliss, I humbly crave for her your accustom'd prayers of Charity. Requiescat in Pace.

(300) The same day & Year, made her holy Profession Sis^{r} Ann **Mennell**, now call'd Sis^{r} Ann Joseph Aged of 21 Years.*

Anno Dom. 1825 March 4th in our Convent of Nazareth of English Poor Clares in Graveline happily departed this life strengthened with the sacrements of Extreme Onction our Dear Sister Ann Joseph Mennel aged 77 and 56 since her entry into Holy religion. Requiescat in Pace.

(301) Anno: Dom: (1770) the 16th of July, made her holy Profession Sis^{r} Ann **Jump**, now call'd Sis^{r} Ann Teresa Aged of 21 Years, Novice 4 Years.†

Décédée

(302) Anno: Dom: (1775) the 14th of Sepr made her holy Profession, Sis^{r} Jane **Fairbrother**, now call'd Sister Mary Teresa Aged of 20 Years.

Décédée

(303) Anno: Dom: (1781) the 14th of March made her holy Profession, Sis^{r} Jane **Green**, now call'd Sis^{r} Winefred Clare Aged of 31 Years.‡

Anno Dom 1827 Octr 31st in our Convent of Nazareth of English Poor Clares in Graveline happily departed this life strengthened with all the holy Sacrements our dear Sister, S^{tr} Jane Winifred

* Daughter of Roger Meynell, of Kilvington Hall, co. York, Esq., by Barbara Anne, daughter of Thomas William Selby, of Biddleston Hall, co. Northumberland, Esq.

† Sister of Catherine Jump above.

‡ Daughter of Francis Greene, of Liverpool, gent., by Elizabeth daughter and eventual co-heiress of Cuthbert Clifton, of Salwick, gent., and his wife Dorothy Winckley. She was sister to Fr. Francis Greene, S.J.

Clare Green aged 77 and since her holy profession, 46 Years. Requiescat in Pace.

(304) Anno Domini 1784 the Seventh of November made her holy Profession Sis[tr] Frances **Todd,** now called S[tr] Mary Frances being aged of twenty three Years.

Anno Domini, 1797 y[e] 1st of January in our Community of English Poor Clares (formerly of Graveline) has happily changed (as we have all reason to think) this mortal life for a better, administer'd with all the Rights of our Holy Mother the Church our D[r] Sister, Sister Mary Frances Todd, in the 35th Year of her Age and 13 since her Entrance into holy Religion, which time she has spent in a faithful tendance to her own perfection, and the acquiring those Virtues that might render her most pleasing to her heavenly Spouse, was from her Enfancy much enclined to Piety, had a great esteem of her holy Vocation, and often expressed her Gratitude to Almighty God, for the same, she was a great lover of holy Poverty and Remarkable for General Charity towards all who stood in need of her Assistance which was evident the 6 years she was Infirmarian, during which time she never spared herself night nor Day for the Comfort or Solace of any one under her care, she was greatly devoted to our Holy Father & S[t] Aloysius, who were doubtless powerful intercessors in her favor, in obtaining her so happy a Death, her last Illness was a lingering and painfull Consumption, which she supported with patience and resignation to the Divine Will was perfectly Sensible to the last, and has we Confidently hope receiv'd the reward of her Virtuous and pious life, yet not to be failing in our Duty, humbly request for her your accustom'd prayers. Requiescat in Pace.

(305) Anno Dom: 1786 y[e] 25th of May made her holy Profession S[tr] Ann **Worsick,** now Called Sister Ann Didacus, Aged of 22 years & a half.*

Anno Dom: 1797, y[e] 4th of April in our Community of English Poor Clares, (formerly of Graveline) has happily slept in our Lord, our D[r] S[tr], Sister Ann Didacus Worsick, aged 33 years, & 12 since her Entrance into holy Religion, which time she has spent in a faithful Compliance with her Laborious Vocation as far as her weak health wou'd permit. She was much addicted to prayer, & a silent tendance to her own perfection, was of a quiet peaceful temper a great lover of holy poverty, & much devoted to S[t] Joseph & S[t] Teresa, who, I hope have proved powerful intercessors in her favor, her virtuous & pious life join'd to her silent & patient Supportation of

* Daughter of Alexander Worswick, of Lancaster, and cousin to Alexander Worswick, of Leighton Hall, co. Lancaster, Esq., son of Thomas Worswick, of Lancaster, banker, and his wife Alice, daughter of Robert Gillow, of Lancaster, Esq.

Emery Walker Ph. sc.

Mother Mary Aloysia Martin
12th Abbess of Poor Clares, Gravelines
From the painting, Ursuline Convent, Greenwich

To face p. 163

frequent & painful Ilness's, particularly her last, which was long & violent, has I hope obtained her, the enjoyment of her heavenly spouse, after whom she ardently languished, but the Judgments of God being inscrutable & human frailty great I humbly entreat for her your prayers of Charity. Requiescat in Pace.

(306) Anno Dom: 1788 ye 29th of June made her holy Profession S^{tr} Mary **Martin** now called S^{tr} Mary Aloysia aged of 18 years and 8 months.

Anno Dom 1829 Jan^{ry} 22nd in our Convent of Nazareth of English Poor Clares in Graveline happily departed this life strengthened with all the sacrements of our holy Church Our Dear Sister, S^{tr} Mary Aloysia Martin aged 58 & 40 since her entry into H. Religion. Requiescat in Pace.

(307) Anno Domini 1816 the 17th of Septem^{r} made her Holy Profession S^{tr} Margaret **Darrel** now Called Sister Dorothy Clare being aged 61.*

Anno Dom 1829 Jan^{ry} 15th in our Convent of Nazareth of English Poor Clares in Graveline happily departed this life strengthened with all the holy Sacrements our Dear Sister S^{tr} Margeret Dorothey Clare Darrel aged 73, and, 12, since her entry into our Holy Order. Requiescat in Pace.

(308) Anno Dom: 1857 ye 21st Novr made her Holy Profession Sister Margaret **Cullen** now Called S^{tr} Mary Xaveria, being aged 46 & 9 months.

Anno Dom 1838 Jan^{ry} 19 in our Convent of Nazareth of English Poor Clares in Graveline happily departed this life strengthened with all the holy Sacrements, our Dear Sister Margaret Cullen, called in religion, Sister Mary, Xaveria, aged 67, and 21 since her entry into Holy religion. Requiescat in Pace.

(309) Anno Domini 1819 the 20th of May made her holy Profession S^{tr} Juliana **Page**, now called Sister Aloysia Clare, being aged 31.

Partie de Gravelines pour l'Angleterre.

(310) Anno Domini 1819 the 26th of July made her holy Profession S^{tr} Mary Ann **Thompson** now called Sister Ann Aloysia being aged of 22.

Partie de Gravelines pour l'Angleterre,

(311) Anno Domini 1829 the 9th of September made her holy

* Daughter of Philip Darell, of Calehill, co. Kent, Esq., by Mary, daughter of Robert Constantine, Esq.

profession Sister Jane **Latham*** now called Sister Jane Francis Xavera being aged 48.

Partie de Gravelines pour l'Angleterre y décédée en 1858.

A List of our Dear Sisters whose deaths have been neglected to be registerd.

Sister Elizabeth Ann, Clare Chantrell.
Sister Ann, Mary, Clifton, (p.).
Sister Ann, Victoria, Penswic, (p.).
Sister Ann, Teresa, Jump, (p.).
Sister Jane Mary Teresa Fairbrother, (p.).

Requiescat in Pace.

[Memoirs of the Chaplains]

Anno: Dom: (1701) At our Conv[t] of English Poor Clares of Naz: in Graveline, y[e] 19th of Nov[r] happily departed this life our Ven: & Rev[d] Father Confessor, Mr William **Warren**,† having receiv'd All y[e] Rites of our holy moth[r] y[e] Church, Aged (70) 43 whereof he most Charitably spent in quality of Conf[r] to y[e] general Satisfaction

* She eventually withdrew to her relations in Liverpool, where she was living in 1857, and was the last of the community.

† Son of John Warren and his wife Anne Downes, born at Canterbury, co. Kent, in 1631; converted at the age of 19; educated at St Omer's College, whence he went to the English College at Rome in 1651; was ordained priest 17 Dec. 1656, left the College 24 April 1658, to be confessor to the Poor Clares at Gravelines, and so continued till his death 19 Nov. 1701, aged 70. He wrote—(1) 'Devotions to Saint Joseph, spouse of Blessed Mary, Virgin Mother of our Lord. With Life and Miracles of that glorious Saint. Written in French by the R.F. Paul de Barrie, of the Society of Jesus, and now Englished,' *s.l.*, 1663, 16mo., title, preface, and errata 4ff, pp. 250; (2) 'A Pious Collection of severall profitable directions fitted for the English Poor Clares in Graveling in order to the better observance of their institute. Very usefull and profiable for all religious women.' Doway, Mairesse, (1684), 18mo, pp. 182; (3) 'Some Reflections upon the Prerogatives, Power, and Protection of St Joseph, Spouse of the Blessed and ever Immaculate Virgin Mary, Mother of God. With several Devotions to the said most glorious Patriarch.' Printed in the year 1710, 12mo., title, preface, &c., 12 pp., pp. 226, besides frontispiece of St Joseph and Child Jesus. The author in his preface states that his work was mainly drawn from 'Pious Remarks upon the Life of St Joseph. Translated from the French of R.F. Paul de Barrie, S.J.,' all the copies of the second English edition of which were brought up. M. Raymond de Bertrand, in his 'Histoire du Convent des Pauvres Clarisses Anglaises de Gravelines,' Dunkerque, 1857, implies (p. 104) that Mr Warren wrote his 'Reflections' about the same period as his 'Pious Collections,' hence the 1710 edition was either a posthumous or second edition. M. de Bertrand (p. 103 *ibid.*) erroneously credits Mr Warren with *A Method of Conversing with God*, 'La première édition tirée à un petit nombre d'exemplaires ne suffisant pas aux demandes des amateurs, il se vit dans la nécessité d'en faire imprimer une seconde au format in-18,' hence 'The Second Edition. Translated out of French by J. W. of the Society of Jesus,' London, Tho. Hales. 1692, 12mo., pp. 135, besides title and dedication, signed J.W., to the Rev. Mother Ann Bedingfield, Abbess of the English Poor Clares at Graveling, A 1-4, pp. 135; s.l., 1778, 12mo., pp. 71; Liège, 1789, 12mo., pp. 143—but this work was by Fr. John Warren, S.J., who refers to his relations in the convent in the preface.

of ye whole Community, no less afflicted at ye loss of so tender a Father, than Edified at his Singular & Exemplar Life, full of Zeal in promoting ye perfection of all & each particular soul Committed to his fatherly Charge, never sparing himself in any occasion that might conduce to their comfort, or advance their spiritual progress, either by his Virtuous Sermons, or other Writings, wch are conserved to future memory, he was so general a Father to all, that none ever noted him to be Singular to any, the whole course of his Life was so Austerly managed, & thoroughly mortified, that neither Acquaintance of friends, or any such like impediments interupted his regular hours, his patience, Charity, & Compassion to all was so remarkable, that he deservedly became a pattern to all those of his Profession who knew him, as one endow'd wth all virtues suitable to his sacred Character, ye wch we Confide will throu: ye infinite merits of our B^d^ Redeemer purchase him an Eternal Reward, but since ye Judgm^ts^ of God are Inscrutable we humbly request y^r^ Charity in giving him a remembrance in y^r^ Sacrifices, & Prayers. Requiescat in Pace.

(469) Jesus, Maria, Francis, Clara.

In ye Year of our Lord (1733) ye 24th of Feb^ry^ happily departed this Life at ye monastery of English Poor Clares call'd Naz: at Graveline, having receiv'd ye Rites of our holy Moth^r^ ye Church, the R^d^ Mr Gervace **Brickbeck,** Conf^r^ of ye said monastery in ye 56th year of his Age, 22 of which he had most Laudably, & Charitably spent in that imployment, he died much regretted by ye whole Community as well for ye Paternal Affection he had for all, as for ye Edifying examples of his Life & virtues, there Appear'd in him a singular Zeal for promoting ye perfection of all, & every one Committed to his care; neither did he ever spare himself in any thing by wch he cou'd Comfort or help them, show'd himself in such manner a common Father to all, that he never was seen to Incline wth a Singular propention to any one, his patience towards all was admirable, his Charity, & Comiseration such y^t^ no Virtue necessary for that Imployment seem'd to be wanting in him, tho' we confide y^t^ all these good Qualities throu: ye infinite merits of our Dr Redeemer will procure him a happy Immortality, yet because ye Judgm^ts^ of God are Inscrutable, we for Charity's sake Earnestly beg ye assistance of y^r^ holy Sacrifices & Prayers. Requiescat in Pace.*

* Gervase Birkbeck, who had used the *aliases* of Catterick and Poole at St Omer's and Rome, was a younger son of Thomas Birkbeck, of Hornby Hall, co. Westmoreland, Esq., and his wife Margaret, daughter of John Catterick, of Carleton, co. York, Esq., and niece of the venerable martyr Edmund Catterick. His paternal grandfather, Henry Birkbeck, of Hornby Hall, married Ellen, daughter of George Pole (or Poole), of Wakebridge, co. Derby, Esq., and sister of Fr. Anthony Pole, S.J., hence the *alias* of Poole adopted by Gervase Birkbeck. He studied at St Omer's College, and entered the Society at Watten under the name of Catterick, 7 Sept. 1698, returned to England in delicate health in 1701, but resumed his studies at the English

(470) Jesus, Maria, Franciscus, Clara.

In y[e] year of our Lord (1756) the 2[d] of Aug[t] struck wth an Appoplexy having receiv'd y[e] Sacrament of Extreme Unction, died at our Conv[t] of Naz: in Graveline at y[e] Age of 41, the R[d] M[r] Tho[s] **Binyon** Priest, who having finish'd wth Credit his higher Studies of Divinitie, in y[e] English College of Rome, undertook y[e] direction of y[e] English Clarisses here, w[ch] for y[e] space of 17 years he perform'd with so much prudence, Charity, & Zeal, y[t] must always leave his name in Benediction, he was constant & Assiduous in what concern'd Allmighty Gods Service, Generous at y[e] Poor, in long & repeated pains & sufferings the most Accute, remarkably patient, in Charitable functions to his neighbour ever to Call, y[r] holy Prayers & Sacrifices we humbly implore that he may Rest in peace. Requiescat in Pace.*

(471) Jesus, Maria, Franciscus, Clara.

In the year of our Lord 1794 y[e] 29th of December has happily departed this Life having received the Extreem Unction, (depriv'd of the other rites of our Holy Mother the Church, by an Appoplexy) at our Convent of English Poor Clares at Graveline, the R[d] M[r] Anthony **Lowe**, Aged 62, Confessor of this our Convent, which Office he faithfully perform'd the space of 36 years to the great Satisfaction of our Com[ty], who much lament the loss of so good a Father. He was of a most Charitable disposition, ever ready to help poor distressed people, this Inclination, caused him often to Inconvenience himself, rather than refuse his assistance to those who craved it, his piety & great Confidence in God, were no less singular, than his perfect Conformity to the divine will, which doubtless enabled him to sustain with Cheerfullness & patience the many afflictions it pleased God to visit him with, in particular those attending an Ill state of health, as also the deprivation of all spiritual help during the 18 months he was Confined by the rulers of those troublesome times, which space he spent, as we have all reason to think in fervent preparation for his last hour, which tho' sudden, we hope was not unprovided for, but as the greatest purity is requisite for those that appear at the Tribunal of an impartial Judge, I humbly crave for the repose of his Soul, the assistance of your prayers for Charity. Requiescat in Pace.†

College at Rome, where he was admitted 8 Nov. 1708, and was ordained priest 20 Dec. 1710. He left the college to be confessor to the Poor Clares at Gravelines on 19 April 1711, and so continued till his death as above. In the diary of the college at Rome he is put down as aged about 33 in 1708. He was brother to Fr. Edward Birkbeck *alias* Poole, S.J., and a relative of Fr. Gervase Pole (or Poole), S.J., and Bro. Gervase Pole, S.J., after one of whom he was no doubt named.

* Thomas Benyon, son of William Benyon, of Ince, co. Lancaster, yeoman, and his wife Mary Bradshaw, having been confirmed by Bishop Witham, was sent to the English College at Rome; where he was admitted 17 Aug. 1732, aged 17, was ordained priest 14 March 1739, and left the college to become confessor at Gravelines, in which office he died as above.

†Anthony Lowe, born (according to the diary of the English College at

[ADDED MEMOIRS OF OTHER CHAPLAINS]

From time to time the following notes have been made with respect to confessors at Gravelines which may help to fill up gaps in the list:—

The Rev. William Cape appears to have been here when at the request of Fr. Christopher Davenport, O.S.F., he translated from the French—'The Chronicle and Institution of the Order of the Seraphicall Father St Francis,' St Omer, John Heigham, 1618, dedicated to 'the Englishe Poore Clares in Gravelinge.'

Fr. Arthur Francis Bell, O.S.F., the venerable martyr who suffered at Tyburn in 1643, was appointed Confessor here in 1622 and continued as such till 1623.

Rev. Robert Rookwood, son of Edward Rookwood, of Euston, co. Suffolk, Esq., by Elizabeth, daughter of William Brown, of Elsing, co. Norfolk, Esq., younger brother of Anthony, 1st Viscount Montagu. Until twenty-eight years of age he lived the life of a country gentleman, when, by the advice of a Jesuit father, he set out for St Omer's, but on his way was arrested at Gravesend with his companions, brought before the Bishop of London, and committed to Newgate. After seventeen weeks imprisonment he made his escape, and so reached St Omer's College, whence he went to Rome and was admitted into the English College under the *alias* of Rawley, October 3, 1620, aged 32. There he was ordained priest on Holy Innocents, 1621, and left the College to be Confessor at Gravelines, September 21, 1626. Thus he remained till 1648 when he accompanied the nuns who left Gravelines to found a new convent at Rouen, and there continued Confessor till his death, November 12, 1668—(*Foley, Records S.J., vols. i., iii., and vi.*)

Rev. Thomas Jenison *alias* Francis Gray, son of John Jenison, of Walworth, co. Durham, Esq., by Mary, daughter of Sir Thomas Gerard, of The Bryn, co. Lancaster, Knt., in which county he was born in 1603. He was admitted into the English College at Rome, November 6, 1633, aged 30, and was ordained priest, March 22, 1637. On the following October 15th, he left for Piacenza, where for about six months he was *socius* to the procurator of the college. Subsequently he became Confessor at Gravelines, possibly when Mr Rookwood left for Rouen in 1648.

Rev. James Tomlinson *alias* Greene, son of James Tomlinson, of Winmarleigh, by Jane, daughter of Thomas Greene, of Bowers House in Little Nateby, co. Lancaster, Gent., was admitted into the English College at Rome April 24, 1694, aged 21 was ordained priest December 21, 1697, and left the college April 1, 1701, to assist the Rev. William Warren at Gravelines, whom he succeeded as Confessor upon his death in the following November. He seems to have left in or before April, 1711.

According to Bro. Foley (*Records S.J.*) and Dr Oliver (*Collections, p.* 370) several Jesuits served as confessors at Gravelines, but it is most probable that they were not resident chaplains, being only occasional or extraordinary confessors. Foley (*vii* 864) says that Fr. Thomas Worsley *alias* Hervey, S.J.,

Rome) 19 March 1734, was son of Samuel Lowe and Alice Spencer, protestants, of London. After the death of his father, his mother having re-married a Catholic, was received into the Church, and brought up her son Anthony a Catholic. He was sent to Rome, but on his voyage the vessel was attacked by the Algerians, and in the fight prior to capture, young Lowe was wounded, and detained a prisoner for eleven months. From this wound he remained lame for the rest of his life. Upon his release, he proceeded to the English College at Rome, where he was admitted 9 June 1749. There he was ordained priest, 18 Feb. 1758, and on the following 10 April was sent to be confessor at Gravelines, where he passed the remainder of his career as above.

was confessor to the nuns here during the latter part of his life, which ended at Liège at the age of 74 in 1671. Again Foley says (*vii,* 395) that the venerable martyr, William Ireland *alias* Ironmonger, S.J., was for several years confessor to the Poor Clares at Gravelines prior to his going to the English mission in 1677. He suffered at Ayburn two years later. Dr Oliver says that Fr. John Panting, S.J., was confessor in or after 1761 till 1766. At that period he was minister at Watten.—J. G.]

[*These pages, A-C, are from a loose sheet in MSS. Book*]

(A) The Requiem Table of Nuns from the year 1758 to 1788.

Nuns deceased

1759, Decr 5th, S Ignatia Frances Hodson, Q,
1760, Feb. 25th, S. Mary Bernard Elphinstone, L.
1760, April 27th, S. Mary Assumption Clifton, Q.
1761, Feb. 22^d^, S. Anne Joseph Tristram Jub., Q.
1761, Decr 6th, S. Dorothy Maria Hanford, Q.
1762, Dec: 22^d^, S. Anne Bonaventure Clifton, Q.
1763, Jan. 7th, S. Helen Joseph Barrow, L.
1765, Ap. 13th, S. Mary Austen Hothersel, Q.
1765, May 29th, S. Mary Teresa Anderton, Q.
1765, July 31st, S. Teresa Joseph Tichbourne, Q.
1768, May 1st, S. Clare Regis Wotterton, Q.
1769, Nov. 5th, S. Mary Frances Hunter, Q.
1769, Dec. 28th, S. Felix Joseph Orde, Q.
1772, March 30th, S. Cath. Clare Symthe Jub, Q.
1771, May, 25th S. Cath. Austen Hodshon, Q.
1771, Sept. 27, S. Mary Benedict Pigot Jub. Q.
1773, Nov. 15th, S. Mary Clare Haggerston, Q.
1773, Nov. 22^d^, S. Clare Joseph Throckmorton, Q.
1775, June 26th, S. Mary Magdalen Clifton Jub Q.
1777, Aug. 4th, S. Mary Colet Parks Jub, L.
1778, Sept. 14th, S. Mary Winifrid Swift, L.
1779, June 20th, S. Mary Felix Petre Abbess Jub, Q.
1780, Jan. 20th, S. Mary Xaveria Hussey, Q.

(B) Requiem Table continued

1781, Ap. 12th, S. Dorothy Joseph Boardman, L.
1782, June 19th, S. Mary Agnes Hodshon, Q.
1783, June 1st, S. Cecil Joseph Duddel, Q.
1783, Novr 19th, S. Anne Xaveria Burrell, Q.

The Profession Calendar from the Year 1758 to 1788.

Nuns Professed

1758, Nov. 21st, S. Helen Joseph Barrow, L.
1760, June 29th, S. Anna Maria Clifton, Q.
1761, Augt 30th, S. Cath: Alexia Lee, L.
1763, Nov. 7th, S. Dorothy Clare Hoole, L.
1764, May 28th, S. Mary Victoria Penswick, Q.

1764, Nov. 27th, S. Clare Frances Jump, Q.
1765, May 28th, S. Clementina Clare Johnson, Abbess.
1767, Octob. 21st, S. Mary Austen Keith, Q.
1769, March 19th, S. Cath: Joseph Nihell, Q.
1769, March 19th, S. Ann Joseph Mennell, L.
1770, July 16th, S. Anne Teresa Jump, Q.
1775, Sept. 14th, S. Mary Teresa Fairbrother, Q.
1781, March 14th, S. Winifred Clare Green, L.
1784, Nov. 7th, S. Mary Frances Todd, Q.
1786, May 25th, S. Anne Didacus Worsick, L.
1788, June 29th, S. Mary Aloysia Martin, Q.

Catalogue of the decased

Quire Nuns	22
Lay Sisters	5

Number Professed

Quire Nuns	10
Lay Sisters	6

(C) Profession Calendar of Quire Nuns from 1750 now in being, viz in 1788

1750, July 2nd, Aged 23, S. Mary Clementina Bulstrode.
1751, June 6th, S. Clemtina: Stanislaus Manby, aged 18.
1755, Augt 15th, Aged 24, S. Mary Felicity Falkner.
1760, June 29th, Aged 18, S. Anna Maria Clifton.
1764, May 28th, Aged 18, S. Mary Victoria Penswick.
1764, Novr 27th, Aged 18, S. Clare Frances Jump.
1765, May 28th, Aged 17, S. Clemtina Clare Johnson Abbess.
1767, Oct. 21st, Aged 30, S. Mary Austen Keith.
1769, March 19th, S. Catherine Joseph Nihell.
1770, July 16th, Aged 21, S. Anne Teresa Jump.
1775, Septr 14th, Aged 20, S. Mary Teresa Fairbrother.
1784, Novr 7th, Aged 23, S. Mary Frances Todd.
1788, June 29th, Aged 18, S. Mary Aloysia Martin.

Profession Calendar of Lay-Sisters from 1741, now existing, viz in 1788

1741, Janry 1s, Aged 22, S. Frances Clare Barlow.
1742, July 31st. Aged 22, S. Anne Clare Chantrill.
1750, Novr 27th, Aged 22, S. Mary Cathe, Moody.
1756, Septr 24th, Aged 25, S. Mary Joseph Routledge.
1761, Augt 30th, Aged 20, S. Cathe Alexia Lee.
1763, Novr 7th, Aged 38, S. Dorothy Clare Hoole.
1769, March 19th, S. Anne Joseph Mennel aged.
1781, March 14th, Aged 31, S. Winifred Clare Green
1786, May 25th, Aged 22, Anne Didacus Worsick.

JANUARY

(443)	1	(304) (132)
	2	
	3	
	4	(298) (296)
		(186) (125)
	5	(283)
	7	(285) (291) (226)
	8	(286) (244) (96)
	9	(103) (74) (37)
	10	(163)
	11	
	12	(169 (134)
	13	(254)
	14	
	15	(307)
(444)	16	(252) (156)
	17	
	18	
	19	(211)
	20	(269) (47)
	21	(293)
	22	(306) (70)
	23	(228)
	24	(63)
	25	(192)
	26	(28) (149) (105)
	27	
	28	(153) (40)
	29	
	30	
	31	

FEBRUARY

(445)	1	(187)
	2	(161) (145) (136)
	3	
	4	
	5	(209)
	6	(194)
	7	
	8	
	9	
	10	(204)
	11	
	12	
	13	
	14	
	15	
(446)	16	
	17	(86) (12)
	18	(80)
	19	(237)
	20	(294) (84)
	21	(94)
	22	(232) (191) (33)
	23	
	24	(469) (267)
	25	(230)
	26	(38)
	27	
	28	(185) (150)
	29	

MARCH

(447)	1	
	2	
	3	(222)
	4	(300) (171) (83) (59)
	5	(173)
	6	(199) (72)
	7	
	8	
	9	(174) (165) (155)
	10	
	11	(213) (131)
	12	
	13	(248)
	14	(141)
	15	
	16	(114)
448)	17	(248)
	18	
	19	(181) (158)
	20	
	21	(255) (43) (25) (11)
	22	(130)
	23	
	24	(206) (32)
	25	(29) (82) (53)
	26	
	27	
	28	(14)
	29	(62)
	30	(233) (48)
	31	(257) (235) (129) (57) (39)

APRIL

(449)	1	(35)
	2	
	3	
	4	(305)
	5	
	6	(64)
	7	
	8	(201) (75)
	9	(50) (20)
	10	
	11	
	12	(273)
	13	(274)
	14	(239)
	15	
(450)	16	(128)
	17	(282)
	18	
	19	
	20	
	21	(162) (46)
	22	
	23	(265) (118)
	24	
	25	
	26	(220)
	27	(251)
	28	(90)
	29	(65)
	30	

MAY

(451)	1	(249)
	2	
	3	(175) (164)
	4	
	5	
	6	
	7	(236) (17)
	8	(271)
	9	(290)
	10	
	11	
	12	(67)
	13	
	14	
	15	(266)
	16	(297)
(452)	17	
	18	
	19	
	20	(272) (189) (60)
	21	
	22	(197)
	23	(120)
	24	
	25	(268) (260)
	26	
	27	
	28	
	29	(242) (116)
	30	
	31	

JUNE

(453)	1	(279)
	2	
	3	
	4	(124)
	5	
	6	
	7	(196)
	8	(200)
	9	(140) (253) (176)
	10	(212)
	11	
	12	
	13	(36)
	14	(142)
	15	
	16	(121) (113)
(454)	17	
	18	(218) (122)
	19	(287)
	20	(85) (250) (240) (2)
	21	
	22	
	23	
	24	(108)
	25	(207)
	26	(247) (234) (160)
	27	(19)
	28	(216)
	29	
	30	

JULY

(455)	1	(151) (18)
	2	(178)
	3	
	4	
	5	(184) (112)
	6	
	7	(97)
	8	
	9	(167)
	10	
	11	
	12	
	13	
	14	(88)
	15	
(456)	16	(203) (58)
	17	
	18	
	19	
	20	
	21	
	22	(68)
	23	(44)
	24	(170)
	25	(263) (208)
	26	(91)
	27	
	28	
	29	
	30	(215)
	31	(281) (138)

AUGUST

(457)	1	
	2	(470)
	3	
	4	258)
	5	
	6	
	7	(231)
	8	(157) (71)
	9	
	10	
	11	
	12	(179) (110)
	13	
	14	
	15	(102)
(458)	16	(98)
	17	(246)
	18	
	19	(99)
	20	
	21	
	22	
	23	
	24	(89)
	25	
	26	(21)
	27	(79) (22)
	28	
	29	
	30	
	31	

SEPTEMBER

(459)	1	(61)
	2	
	3	(139)
	4	(193)
	5	
	6	
	7	
	8	(30)
	9	
	10	
	11	(100)
	12	
	13	(225)
	14	(280) (177)
	15	
(460)	16	(261)
	17	
	18	(87) (56)
	19	
	20	(77)
	21	
	22	(49)
	23	(223) (95) (54)
	24	
	25	
	26	
	27	(245)
	28	
	29	(214) (42)
	30	(127)

OCTOBER

(461)	1	(296)
	2	
	3	(66) (34)
	4	(55)
	5	(117)
	6	
	7	
	8	(217) (27
	9	
	10	(15)
	11	
	12	
	13	
	14	
	15	
(462)	16	
	17	(190) (154) (23)
	18	
	19	(198)
	20	
	21	
	22	
	23	(76)
	24	(224) (5)
	25	
	26	
	27	
	28	
	29	
	30	
	31	(303) (119)

NOVEMBER

(463)	1	(188)
	2	
	3	
	4	(159)
	5	(275) (256)
	6	
	7	
	8	(180)
	9	
	10	(195) (111)
	11	(172)
	12	
	13	
	14	
	15	(278) (101)
Lost	16	(166)
	17	(69) (106)
	18	
	19	(182)
	20	(26) (81)
	21	(52) (221)
	22	(41) (276)
	23	(2) (6) (92) (133) (135) (136)
	24	(104)
	25	
	26	(7)
	27	(264)
	28	(183)
	29	
	30	(51) (115) (126)

DECEMBER

Lost	1	
	2	(168)
	3	(147) (148)
	4	(24)
	5	(137) (238)
	6	(210) (229) (284)
	7	
	8	(10) (31)
	9	
	10	(45)
	11	
	12	
	13	
	14	
	15	
(466)	16	
	17	(123)
	18	
	19	(295)
	20	(146) (16)
	21	
	22	(259) (41)
	23	
	24	(262)
	25	(219)
	26	(253)
	27	(227)
	28	(270) (109)
	29	(299) (471) (143) (78)
	30	
	31	

[In the original Calendar there are no November deaths after Novr 15, and page (466) begins with 16 December, this would account for 31 days not recorded. They are supplied here. W. H. M.]

(467) Memento mei Coecilia Joseph finish'd in ye Year of our Lord 1781

[pencil note] Catherine Duddell no. 279

MEMORIAL OF PUPIL

(480) Anno Domini 1787 In our Convent of English Poor Clares of Nazareth at Graveline is happily departed this Life strengthen'd with ye Extreme Unction Mifs Mary Joseph Sophia Castrique from Dunkirk ye 6th of June in the 14th year of her Age, Buried on ye following Day by our R^d F^r Confessor under ye first Window in the Young Cloyster. No bells but our own wch were Rung ye same as for a Nun, the Service was performed in our Church by ye gentlemen of ye Parish. Requiescat in Pace.

No. III

THE REGISTER BOOK OF PROFESSIONS, ETC., OF THE ENGLISH BENEDICTINE NUNS AT BRUSSELS AND WINCHESTER, NOW AT EAST BERGHOLT. 1598-1856

CONTRIBUTED BY THE LADY ABBESS AND COMMUNITY OF ST MARY'S ABBEY, EAST BERGHOLT

EDITED BY JOSEPH S. HANSOM

The Register Book is of substantial paper, 11×8 inches, and is well bound in brown leather. The first twenty pages of Registers are margined all round in red ink. The writing is very clear, with few corrections or erasures, the ink being still fresh. This part includes all the first registers down to the year 1682, and is evidently a fair copy from some earlier writing. Then follow six pages in a large sloping hand continued until 1717, the ink being quite brown. Four pages follow in neat copper-plate bringing the register down to 1768. The remaining seven pages complete the Winchester Register and are penned by the same hand. The last entry at Winchester is 4th November 1856. In the original, but not reproduced here, are fifteen more pages of modern Registers since the Community moved to East Bergholt. Preceding the Registers are thirty-seven pages of financial affairs of the Community.

The spellings are seldom beyond easy recognition. The names in religion of the nuns are usually given, and it is thought that no changes were made from the baptismal names in several of the earlier ones. Where there is evidence to the contrary, the baptismal names are supplied in foot notes. This is important to fix the positions in families. The paternal names are often well known as those of prominent Catholic families. There are however cases of mixed marriages, temporisers, &c. Some foot notes help to clear the ground in cases. The years of profession, in the margins, have been removed to the head line of each register.

REGISTER

The Booke of the ages, together with the years and dayes of the entrance, Cloathing and Profession of the Religious women of the English Monasterie of the Assumption of our Blessed Ladie of the holie Order of Sainct Benedict begun in Bruxells the 11th of July in the year of our Lord 1598.

Date of Profession

1580 **Lady Joanna Berkely**

The 14th of September in the year of our Lord 1580. Our Rt Revd Ladie & Abbesse, the Lady Jone Barkley, Daughter of Sir John Barkley of Beverston in the Countie of Glocester, was received into the Monasterie of St Peeteers of the holie Order of St Benedict at Reames in France. The 12th of November in the same year she was invested with the holie Habitt of St Benedict. The 6th of December in the year of our Lord 1581, she made her Profession at the age of 25.

And in the yeare of our Lord 1598 by advice of the Revd **Father William Holt** of the Societie of Jesus, My **Ladie Marie Percey**, procured **Madam Barkleys** coming from France into Bruxells to be first Abbesse of this Monasterie of the holie Order of St Benedict, dedicated unto the Assumption of our Blessed Ladie, which the **Ladie Marie Percey** was then beginning accompanied by **Mrs Dorothy Arundell** & her sister **Mrs Gertrude Arundell**. At the same time came from Rome the R^d Priest, **Mr Robert Chambers**, who was chosen for Confessarious of the Monasterie. **Mrs Elizabeth Tichburne** then served this holie companie, & was afterwards a Convers Sister. The 11th of July Madam Barkley, Ladie Marie Percey & and the two Mrs Arundells tooke possession of this house, which was purchased of **Sr Roland Longinus** Esquire, & **Vicont of Winnoxe Bergues**, and all Solemnities and Rights performed The first payment was made by the Ladie Marie Percey upon the 14th of July according to a contract passed between the Lady Marie Percey and the Vicont with both their signatures the 18th of Aprill the same year. The first payment was 1500 flo; The whole purchase of the house came to ten thousand and five hundred florens which house is cituated in the city of Bruxells, in a street called Hietegatts. In the year 1599 the 14 of November, Madam Barkley received her Benediction at the hands of the R^t Honble & R^t R^d the **Lord Mathias Hovius Archbishop of Machline** & was made Abbesse of the English Monasterie of the Assumption of our Blessed Ladie of the holie Order of St Benedict in Bruxells, being received and acknowledged in the church by all these whose names followeth. **The Ladie Marie Percey, Mrs Dorothy Arundell Mrs Gertrude Arundell Mrs Elizabeth Cansfield**, after called, D. Anne, **Mrs Frances Gawen, Mrs Elizabeth Southcott Mrs Margarett Thomson** after called D. Winifride, **Mrs Margaret Smith** after called D. Renata, **Mrs Elizabeth Tichburn** after called S^tr Scholastica, **Mrs Margaret Whitecars** after called S^tr Martha, **Mrs Cibille Banks** after called S^tr Benedict, **Mrs Elizabeth Clayton** after called S^tr Catharine. All which rendring their obedience, acknowledged her for their lawfull Superiour. Died 1616.

1600 **Ladie Marie Percey**

Dame Marie Persey, Daughter to the R^t Honble the Lord Thomas Persey,* Earle of Northumberland, entered this Mon-

* The Blessed Thomas Percy, seventh earl, martyred at York 22 Aug. 1572, refusing to accept his life at the cost of his religion. He married

asterie the 11th of July in the year of our Lord 1598, was invested with the holie Habitt of St Benedict the 21 of November in the year of our Lord 1599, & made her Profession the 21 of November 1600, at the age of 31. Died 1642.

1600 **Dame Dorothy Arundell**

Dame Dorothy Arundell Daughter of Sir Jhon Arundell of Lanhern in the Countie of Cornwell, entred this Monasterie the 11th of July in the year of our Lord 1598, was Invested with the holie Habitt of St Benedict the 21 of November in the year of our Lord 1599, and made her Profession the 21 of November in the year of our Lord 1600, at the age of 40. Died 1613.

1600 **Dame Gertrude Arundell**

Dame Gertrude Arundell, Daughter of Sir Jhon Arundell of Lanhern in the Countie of Cornwell, entred this Monasterie the 11th of July in the year of our Lord 1598, was Invested with the holie Habitt of St Benedict, the 21 of November in the year of our Lord 1599, & made her Profession on the 21 of November in the year of our Lord 1600 at the age of 29. Died 1636.

1600 **Dame Anne Cansfield**

Dame Anne Cansfild,* Daughter of Thomas Cansfild of Roberts Hall, in the Countie of Lancaster, Esquire, was received into the Monasterie the 4th of November in the year of our Lord 1598, was Invested with the holie Habitt of St Benedict the 21 of November in the year of our Lord 1599, & made her Profession the 21 of November in the year of our Lord 1600, at the age of 24. Died 1611.

1600 **Dame Francis Gawine**

Dame Francis Gawine, Daughter of Thomas Gawine of Norrington† in Willshire, Esquire, was received into the Monasterie the 26 of September in the year of our Lord 1599, was Invested with the holy Habitt of St Benedict the 21 of November in the year of our Lord 1599, and made her Profession the 21 of November in the year of our Lord 1600, at the age of 24. Died 1640.‡

Anne Somerset, daughter of the second earl of Worcester. Their daughter Mary became the second abbess.

* Dame Anne Cansfield's baptismal name was Elizabeth. The residence is Robert Hall, registers of which are printed in *C.R.S.* Vol. iv.

† Thomas Gawen, of Norrington, Wilts, was a strong 'popish recusant,' and married Catharine, dau. of Sir Edward Waldegrave, K.G., of Stanninghall, Norfolk. His son Thomas Gawen was of Horsington, Wincanton, Somerset, in 1623 (*Harl. Soc.*, xi., 39).

‡ In 1622 she was sent to the foundation at Cambray.

1600 **Dame Elizabeth Southcot**

Dame Elizabeth Southcot Daughter of Jhon Southcot* of Wittum in the Countie of Essex Esquire was received into the Monasterie the 26 of September in the yeare of our Lord 1599, was Invested with the holie Habitt of St Benedict the 21 of November 1599 and made her profession the 21 of November in the yeare of our Lord 1600, at the age of 20. Died 1631.

1600 **Dame Winifred Thomson**

Dame Wenefred Thomson Daughter of Jhon Thomson† of Brodwell in the Countie of Oxford Esquire, was received into the Monasterie the 10 of Aprill in the yeare of our Lord 1599, invested with the holie Habitt of St Benedict the 21 of November Ano 1599 & made her Profession the 21 of November Ano 1600 at the age of 26. Died 1613.

1600 **Dame Renata Smith**

Dame Renata Smith‡ Daughter of Mr Jhon Smith in Yorke, was received into the Monasterie the 10 of Aprill Ano 1599, Invested with the holie Habitt of St Benedict the 21 of November Ano 1599, made her Profession the 21 of November Ano 1600 at the age of 26. Died 1613.

1603 **Dame Mary Watson**

Dame Marie Watsone Daughter of Roland Watsone of Portingam in the Countie of Shrowsberie Esquire, was received into the Monasterie the 14 of Januarie Ano 1601, Invested with the holie Habitt of St Benedict the 22 of July Ano 1602, and made her Profession the 6 of August Ano 1603 at the age of 20. Died 1630.

1603 **Dame Ursula Huicke**

Dame Ursula Huicke Daughter of Mr Christofer Huicke§ in

* In the Visitation 1634 (*Harl. Soc.*, xiii., 492), John Southcote of Witham, Essex, mar. Magdalen, dau. of Sir Edward Waldegrave of Hever Castle, Kent. His father was John Southcote, Judge of the Queen's Bench; bur. at Witham, 1585 (Foss's *Judges*).

† John Thompson of Broadwell was a recusant at liberty in 1592, who died after seven years imprisonment in Gloucester. His son Francis Thompson *alias* Yates was a Jesuit. Dame Winefride's baptismal name was Margaret. (Mrs Bryan Stapleton, *Oxfordshire Missions.*)

‡ Dame Renata Smith was baptized Margaret Winifride. Another Dame Renata Smith appears later, being one of the Smythes of Eshe, herein spelt 'Smith.' Although a name in religion, it may shew a connection with the York family.

§ The *Freemen's Roll of York* (*Surtees Soc.*, cii., 22) gives under 22 Eliz., or 1579-80—'Xpoferus Hewike, marcer, fil. Thomæ Hewike, wax-chandler.' He was senior chamberlain of the city within two years. Under 24 Hen. viii., or 1532-3, there is 'Thomas Hewet, wax-chandler, fil. Willelmi Hewet, parisshe clerk' (*Ibid.* xcvi., 252). It suggests that Hewet may be a

Yorke was received into the Monastery the 14 of Januarie An° 1601, invested with the holie Habitt of St Benedict the 22 July An° 1602, and made her Profession the 6 of August An° 1603, at the age of 33. Died 1638.

1603 **Dame Agnes Lenthall**

Dame Agnes Lenthall* Daughter of Jhon Lenthall of Lacheford in the Countie of Oxford Esquire was received into the Monasterie the 1 of September An° 1601, Invested with the holie Habitt of St Benedict the 22 of July An° 1602, & made her Profession the 6 of August An° 1603, at the age of 21.

1603 **Dame Agatha Wiseman**

Dame Agatha Wiseman† Daughter of Sir William Wiseman of Bardox in the Countie of Essex and of Jane daughter of Sir Edmund Huddleston, was received into the Monasterie the 22 of March An° 1602, Invested with the holie Habitt of St Benedict the 22 of July An° 1602, & made her Profession the 6 of August An° 1603, at the age of 18. Died 1647.

1605 **Dame Eugenia Poulton**

Dame Eugenea Poulton Daughter of Ferdinand Poulton of Barton in the Countie of Buckingam Esquire, & of Catherine daughter of William Jackman of Wing Bucks, was received into the Monasterie the 21 of March An° 1603, Invested with the holie Habitt of St Benedict the 10 of Februarie An° 1604, and made her Profession the 12 of May 1605 at the age of 24. Died 1645 at Ghent.

1605 **Dame Clare Curson**

Dame Clare Curson‡ Daughter of Sr Francis Curson of Waterperrie in the Countie of Oxford, was received into the Monasterie the 15 of August An° 1603 Invested with the holie Habitt of St Benedict the 10 of Februarie An° 1604 & made her Profession the 12 of May An° 1605 at the age of 26. Died 1626.

1605 **Dame Barbara Leeke**

Dame Barbara Leeke Daughter of Jhon Leeke of Newwork upon Trent in the Countie of Derby Esq., was received into the

corruption of Hewick, instead of a diminutive of Hugh, as writers tell us. Heworth, near the walls of York, is however more likely. More cognate to our purpose however is that John Hewett, *alias* Weldon or Savell, venerable martyr in 1588, may be a relation of Dame Ursula Hewicke in the text. His father was also freeman of York (Gillow, *Dict. Eng. Caths.*, iii., 294).

* Dame Agnes Lenthall became fifth abbess, and died in 1651.

† Baptized Winefride. A pedigree describes her as a nun 'in France,' which must be an error for Flanders? Bardox is Broadoaks, Braddox, &c. (*C.R.S.*, ix.)

‡ Baptized Elizabeth.

Monasterie the 15 of August in the yeare of our Lord 1603, Invested with the holie Habitt of S Benedict the 10 of Februarie, An° 1604, & made her Profession the 12 of May An° 1605 at the age of 30. Died 1647.

1608 **Dame Anastasia Morgan**

Dame Anastatia Morgan Daughter of Edward Morgan of Pettie Coye in the Countie of Monmorth Esquire, was received into the Monasterie the 15 of August An° 1605, Invested with the holie Habitt of S[t] Benedict the 23 of Aprill An° 1607 and made her Profession the 29 of Aprill An° 1608 at the age of 31. Died 1646.

1608 **Dame Helen Dolman**

Dame Helen Dolman* Daughter of S[r] Robert Dolman of Poclinton in the Countie of Yorke, was received into the Monasterie the 23 of March An° 1605, Invested with the holie Habitt of S[t] Benedict the 23 of Aprill An° 1607, & made her Profession on the 29 of Aprill An° 1608 at the age of 22. Died 1648.

1608 **Dame Marie Gage**

Dame Marie Gage Daughter of Edward Gage of Furle in the Countie of Sussex Esquire, was received into the Monasterie the 23 of September An° 1605, Invested with the holie Habitt of S[t] Benedict the 23 of Aprill An° : 1607, & made her Profession the 29 of Aprill An° 1608 at the age of 22. Died 1614.

1608 **Dame Marie Persons**

Dame Marie Persons Daughter of Mr George Persons of Netherstone† in the Countie of Somerset was received into the Monasterie the 27 of June An° 1605, Invested with the holie Habitt of S[t] Benedict the 23 of Aprill An° 1607 & made her Profession on the 29 of Aprill An°. 1608 at the age of 18. Died 1642.

1608 **Dame Potentiana Deacon**

Dame Potentiana Deacon Daughter of Mr Jhon Deacon of Argaston‡ in the Countie of Midlesex (who leaving the world became a Religious man of the holie order of Carthusians) was received into the Monasterie the 11 of July An° 1606, Invested with the holie Habitt of S[t] Benedict the 23 of Aprill An° 1607 &

* The daughters of Sir Robert Dolman of Pocklington, by his wife, Eleanor, dau. of Sir William Mallory of Studley, who are not accounted for by marriage, are—Elizabeth, Ursula and Grissell (Foster's *Visitations*, 86.)

† This is evidently George, brother of Fr. Robert Persons, S.J., who was born at Nether-Stowey (*C.R.S.*, ii).

‡ Possibly Haggerstone.

made her Profession the 29 of Aprill An° 1608, at the age of 32. Died 1644 Cambray.

1610 **Dame Scholastica Smith**

Dame Scholastica Smith Daughter of George Smith of Ashbie in the Countie of Lester Esquire, was received into the Monasterie the 15 of June An° 1607, Invested with the holie Habitt of St Benedict the 5 of August An° 1608 & made her Profession the 2 of Februarie An° 1610 at the age of 26. Died 1660.

1611 **Dame Magdalen Digbye**

Dame Magdalen Digbye Daughter of Everead Digbye * of Goters in the Countie of Buckingham Esquire, was received into the Monasterie the 5 of July An° 1608, Invested with the holie Habitt of St Benedict the 29 of December An° 1609 & made her Profession the 11 of Januarie An° 1611 at the age of 22. Died 1659.

1611 **Dame Lucy Knatchbull**

Dame Lucy Knatchbull Daughter of Renold Knatchbull of Saltwood Castle in the Countie of Kent Esquire, was received into the Monasterie the 5 of July 1608, Invested with the holie Habitt of S^t^. Benedict the 29 of December An° 1609 & made her Profession the 11 of Januarie An° 1611 at the age of 22. Died 1629 Ghent.

1611 **Dame Martha Colford**

Dame Martha Colford Daughter of Mr Gabriell Colford of Caufstock in the Countie of Essex, was received in the Monasterie the 17 of December An° 1608, Invested with the holie Habitt of St Benedict the 29 of December An° 1609, and made her Profession ye 11 of Januarie An° 1611, at the age of 19. Died 1634.

1612 **Dame Cecilia Atslow**

Dame Cecilia Atslow, Daughter of Edward Atslow† of Dowham in Essex, Esquire, was received into the Monasterie, the 22 of November An° 1609, Invested with the holie Habitt of St Benedict the 22 of July An° 1611, & made her Profession the 22 of July An° 1612, at the age of 26. Died 1640.

1612 **Dame Anne Ingleby**

Dame Anne Ingleby, Daughter of Mr David Ingleby‡ in Yorkshire,

* His eldest son Sir Everard Digby (knighted 1603), of Drystoke, Rutland. mar. Mary d. and h. of William Mulshoe of Gothurst (now Gayhurst), Bucks (*Harl. Soc.*, lviii, 40). He was involved by Catesby in the Gunpowder Plot.

† Edward Atslow, of Downham, and his wife, Frances, d. of John Wingfield, of Suffolk, with a son and two daughters (all married) appear in the Visitation of 1634 (*Harl. Soc.*, xiii, 337).

‡ Sir William Ingleby, of Ripley, had a second son, David. (*Yorks.*

was received into the Monasterie the 29 of June An° 1610, Invested with the holie Habitt of S[t] Benedict the 22 of July An° 1611, and made her Profession the 22 of July An° 1612, at the age of 19. Died 1626.

1612 Dame Benedict Hawkins

Dame Benedict Hawkins, Daughter of S[r] Thomas Hawkins of Nash in the Countie of Kent, was received into the Monasterie the 22 of July An° 1610, Invested with the holie Habitt of S[t] Benedict the 22 of July An° 1611, & made her Profession the 22 of July An° 1612, at the age of 25. Died 1661.

1612 Dame Alexia Blanchard

Dame Alexia Blanchard,* Daughter of Henerie Blanchard of Priers Court, in Barkshire, Esquire, was received into the Monasterie the 22 of July An° 1610, Invested with the holie Habitt of S[t] Benedict the 22 of July An° 1611, & made her Profession the 22 of July An° 1612, at the age of 30. Died 1652.

1612 Dame Margaret Curson

Dame Margarett Curson, Daughter of S[r] Francis Curson, of Waterppery, in the Countie of Oxford, was received into the Monasterie 30 of September An° 1610, Invested with the holie Habitt of S[t] Benedict the 22 of July An° 1611, & made her Profession the 22 of July An° 1612. Died 1659.

1612 Dame Catharine Paston

Dame Catherine Paston, Daughter of Edward Paston of Thorpe, in the Countie of Norfolke, Esquire, was received into the Monasterie the 3 of September An° 1611, Invested with the holie Habitt of S[t] Benedict the 5 of October An° 1612, & made her Profession the 6 of October An° 1613, at the age of 20. Died 1640.

1615 Dame Elizabeth Rookwood

Dame Elizabeth Rookwood, Daughter of Edward Rookwood, of Eustoun, in the Countie of Suffolke, Esquire, was received into the Monasterie the 23 of October 1610, Invested with the holie Habitt of S[t] Benedict the 5 of October An° 1612, & made her Profession the 24 of Februarie An° 1615, at the age of 33. Died 1631.

Visitation, 1563 and 1585). He may have had no male issue, as the estates went in a younger line. Another son was the Ven. Francis Ingleby, priest and martyr.

* In the Visitation of 1623 (*Harl. Soc.*, lvi, 72), Henry Blanchard, J.P., by his wife Mary, dau. of Richard Bruning, of Wymering, Hants, had a daughter, Dorothea, who 'cæpit velā Castitatis.' He was buried at Chieveley, in which parish is Prior's Court House. Dame Alexia became the fourth abbess.

1615 Dame Wenefrid Tresham

Dame Wenefrid Tresham, Daughter of Francis Tresham,* of Russhum, in the Countie of Northamton, Esquire, was received into the Monasterie the 8 of September An° 1609, Invested with the holie Habitt of St Benedict the 8 of September An° 1614, & made her Profession the 15 of September An° 1615, at the age of 17. Died 1665.

1615 Dame Renata Smith

Dame Renata Smith, Daughter of Mr George Smith, of Eshe,† in the Countie of Durhame, was received into the Monasterie the 10 of September An° 1612, Invested with the holie Habitt of St. Benedict, the 8 of September An° 1614, & made her Profession the 15 of September An° 1615 at the ageof 20 Died 1644.

1616 Dame Marie Vavasour

Dame Marie Vavasour‡ Daughter of William Vavasour, of Haslewood Esquire in the Countie of Yorke, & of Anne, daughter of Sir Thomas Manners was received into the Monasterie the 3 of September An° 1611. Invested with the holie Habitt of St Benedict the 4 of October An° 1615, & made her Profession the 5 of October Ano 1616, at the age of 16. Died 1676.

1616 Dame Christina Lovell

Dame Christina Lovell Daughter of Sr Robert Lovell of Martine Abbie in the Countie of Surrey was received into the Monasterie the 4 of October An° 1614, Invested with the holie Habitt of St Benedict, the 4 of October An° 1615, & made her Profession the 5 of October An° 1616 at the age of 19. Died 1639.

1616 Dame Marie Philipps

Dame Marie Philipps Daughter of Mr Peter Philipps was received into the Monasterie the 4 of November Ano 1614. Invested with the holie Habitt of St Benedict, the 4 of October An° 1615, & made her Profession the 5 of October An° 1616, at the age of 20. Died 1654.

1617 Dame Columba Gage

Dame Columba Gage Daughter of Mr Robert Gage of Haling, in the Countie of Surrey was received into the Monasterie the 24 of July An° 1615, Invested with the holie Habitt of St Benedict the 15 of September An° 1616, & made her Profession the 28 of Sep. An° 1617, at the age of 52. Died 1641.

* Francis Tresham, of Rushton, drawn into the Gunpowder Plot by Catesby. Dame Winefride Tresham's baptismal name was Lucy.

† Smythe of Eshe.

‡ Dame Mary Vavasour became the fifth abbess.

1617 Dame Aurea James

Dame Aurea James Daughter of S[r] Henrie James of Rumden in the Countie of Kent was received into the Monasterie, the 3 of September An° 1615, Invested with the holie Habitt of S[t] Benedict, the 11 of September An° 1616, & made her Profession the 28 of September An° 1617 at the age of 21. Died 1669.

1617 Dame Teresa Gage

Dame Teresa Gage, Daughter of M[r] Edward Gage, of y[e] house of Furle in the Countie of Sussex, was received into the Monasterie, the 10 of Februarie An° 1615, Invested with the holie Habitt of S[t] Benedict the 29 of September An° 1616, & made her Profession the 2 of October An° 1617, at the age of 26. Died 1654.

1619 Dame Etheldred Smith

Dame Etheldred Smith Daughter of M[r] George Smith of Eshe in ye Countie of Durhame, was received into ye Monasterie ye 8 of September 1616, Invested with the holie Habitt of S[t] Benedict, ye 4 of Januarie 1618, & made her Profession ye 14 of Aprill 1619, at the age of 21. Died 1666, at Paris.

1619 Dame Dorothy Manock

Dame Dorothy Manock Daughter of William Manock* of Giffers Hall in the Countie of Suffock Esquire, was received into ye Monasterie ye 12 of November 1616, Invested with the holie Habit of S[t] Benedict, y[e] 4 of Januarie 1618 & made her Profession y[e] 14 of Aprill 1619, at y[e] age of 27. Died 1635.

1619 Dame Marie Kempe

Dame Marie Kempe Daughter of John Kempe† of Pentlow Hall in Essex, Esquire, was received into ye Monasterie the 14 of December 1616, Invested with the holie Habit of S[t] Benedict the 18 of Januarie 1618, and made her Profession the 14 of Aprill 1619 at the age of 23. Died 1657.

1619 Dame Placida Brooke

Dame Placida Brooke‡ Daughter of M[r] Robert Brooke in Hartfordshire was received into the Monasterie the 14 of December 1616, Invested with y[e] holie Habit of S[t] Benedict y[e] 18 of Januarie 1618, and made her Profession y[e] 14 of April 1619 at the age of 23. Died 1626.

* Mannock of Gifford's Hall.

† There is said to be a fine monument in Pentlow church to George Kempe, *ob.* 1606, his son John and Eleanor his wife, with four sons and ten daughters kneeling (*Kelly's P.O. Dir.*).

‡ Baptized Alice.

1619. **Dame Catharine Bond**

Dame Catharine Bond Daughter of Mr William Bond in London was received into ye Monasterie the first of August 1617, Invested with ye holie Habitt of St Benedict the 14 of September 1618, & made her Profession the 15 of September 1619 at ye age of 20. Died 1655.

1619 **Dame Marie Roper**

Dame Marie Roper Daughter of ye Lord Christopher Roper Baron of Tencham* in ye Countie of Kent was received, into ye Monasterie ye 12 of September An° 1617, Invested with ye holy Habit of St Benedict the 14 of September 1618, & made her Profession the 10th of November 1619, at ye age of 21. Died 1650 at Ghent.

1620 **Dame Marie Wintour**

Dame Marie Wintour Daughter of Sr Edward Wintour of Lidnie in ye Countie of Shrosberie† was received into ye Monasterie ye 15 of August An° 1618, Invested with ye holy Habit of St Benedict ye 13 of October 1619, & made her Profession ye 25 of October 1620 at the age of 16. Died 1630.

1620 **Dame Flavia Langdale**

Dame Flavia Langdale Daughter of William Langdale of Lenthrope‡ in the Countie of Yorke Esq. was received into ye Monasterie the 3 of September An° 1618, Invested with ye holie Habit of St Benedict the 13 of October 1619, and made her Profession ye 25 of October 1620 at the age of 20. Died 1672.

1621 **Dame Vivina Yaxley**

Dame Vivina Yaxley Daughter of Henerie Yaxley of Yaxley in the Countie of Suffolk Esq.: was received into ye Monastery ye 22 of October An° 1618, Invested with ye holy Habit of St Benedict the 3 of May 1620, and made her Profession ye 9 of May 1621, at ye age of 22. Died 1654.

1622 **Dame Brigit Draycott**

Dame Brigit Draycott Daughter of John Draycott of Peinseley in ye Countie of Stafford Esq.: was received into ye Monasterie the 24 of September 1616, Invested with the holy Habit of St Benedict the 18 of April An° 1621, & made her Profession ye 19 of June 1622 at ye age of 18. Died 1654.

* Daughter of Christopher, second Lord Teynham of Linstead in Kent.

† More likely Lidney or Lydney in co. Gloucester, where the Wintours had an estate.

‡ Baptized Joyce. The only unmarried daughter given in the Visitation, 1612 (J. Foster's, p. 129).

1624 **Dame Mechtilda Trentham**

Dame Mechtilda Trentham Daughter of Francis Trentham of Trent in y[e] Countie of Stafford Esq.: was received into ye Monasterie ye 24 of October An[o] 1620, Invested with ye holy Habit of S[t] Benedict ye 25 of September 1622 & made her Profession ye 14 of Januarie 1624 at ye age of 24. Died 1670.

1624 **Dame Christina Paris**

Dame Christina Paris Daughter of Philipe Paris of Linther* in the Countie of Cambridge Esq.: was Invested with the holy Habit of S[t] Benedict ye first of May An[o] 1623 and made her Profession ye 5 of May 1624 at the age of 18. Died 1646.

1624 **Dame Marie Eure**

Dame Marie Eure Daughter of the Lord William Eure of Malton in the Countie of York Baron† was Invested with ye holy Habit of S[t] Benedict ye 27 of August An[o] 1623 & made her Profession the 24 of November 1624 at ye age of 19. Died 1635.

1624 **Dame Francisca Paston**

Dame Francisca Paston Daughter of Edward Paston of Thorpe in ye Countie of Norfolke Esq.: was invested with ye holy Habit of S[t] Benedict the 27 of August An[o] 1623 & made her Profession the 24 of November An[o] 1624 at ye age of 20. Died 1652.

1624 **Dame Apolonia Waldegrave**

Dame Apolonia Waldegrave Daughter of S[r] Nicholas Waldegrave of Borle† in ye Countie of Essex was Invested with ye holy Habit of S[t] Benedict ye 12 of September An[o] 1623 & made her Profession the 24 of November An[o] 1624 at y[e] age of 22. Died 1638.

1625 **Dame Constantia Penruddocke**

Dame Constantia Penruddocke Daughter of S[r] Thomas Penruddocke of Sallesberie in y[e] Countie of Wiltshire was Invested with ye holy Habit of S[t] Benedict y[e] 12 of September An[o] 1623, & made her Profession ye 8 day of March An[o] 1625 at ye age of 24. Died 1672.

1627 **Dame Lucie Pershall**

Dame Lucie Pershall Daughter of S[r] John Pershall of Horselet in ye Countie of Stafford Baronett was received into ye Monasterie

* In the Visitation of 1619 there appear eight daughters of Philip Parris of Little Linton by his wife Margaret, dau. of Charles Waldegrave of Stanninghall, Norfolk,—Frances, Elizabeth, Eleanor, Dorothy, Anne, Jerony-my, Margaret and Mary (*Harl. Soc.*, xli, 37).

† Her mother was Lucy, eldest daughter of Sir Andrew Noel of Dalby and Brook, a gentleman high in favour with Queen Elizabeth.

the 24 of October An° 1620, Invested with ye holy Habit of St Benedict ye 11 of September 1625 & made her Profession ye 21 of Januarie 1627 at ye age of 18. Died 1637.

1627 Dame Marina Draycott

Dame Marina Draycott* Daughter of John Draycott of Peinsley in ye Countie of Stafford Esq. was received into ye Monasterie ye 3 of June An° 1624, Invested with ye holy Habit of St Benedict the 11 of September 1625 & made her Profession ye 21 of Januarie 1627 at ye age of 19. Died 1673.

1644 Dame Barbara Melchiora Campbell

Dame Barbara Melchiora Campbell Daughter of the Lord Archibald Campbell Earle of Arguile in Scotland was received into the Monasterie the 14 of June An° 1628, Invested with ye holy Habit of St Benedict the 29 of December 1642 & made her Profession ye 6 of Januarie 1644 at the age of 19. Died 1688.

1652 Dame Gertrude Blount

Dame Gertrud Blount Daughter of Mr Miles Blount of Orltun in ye Countie of Heryford was received into ye Monasterie the 10 of May An° 1650, Invested with ye holy Habit of St Benedict ye 13 of November 1650, & made her Profession ye 13 of November 1652 at ye age of 36. Died 1682.

1655 Dame Anne Forster

Dame Anne Forster Daughter of Henerie Forster of Cobdock-hall† in ye Countie of Suffolke Esq. was received into ye Monasterie ye 29 of September An° 1652. Invested with ye holy Habit of St Benedict ye 5 of October 1653, & made her Profession ye 25 of April 1655 at ye age of 19. Died 1717.

1655 Dame Placida Forster

Dame Placida‡ Forster Daughter of Henerie Forster of Cobdock-hall in ye Countie of Suffolke Esq. was received into ye Monasterie ye 29 of September An° 1652, Invested with ye holy Habit of St Benedict ye 31 of May An° 1654, and made her Profession ye 1 of June 1655 at ye age of 16. Died 1714.

1655 Dame Dorothy Blundell

Dame Dorothy Blundell§ Daughter of Robert Blundell of Ince-

* Dame Marina Draycote was prioress in 1668.

† Dame Anne Forster became the sixth abbess. Copdock Hall, in the parish of that name, became a farm house.

‡ Baptized Etheldreda.

§ Dame Dorothy Blundell was seventh abbess.

blundell in ye Countie of Lancaster Esq. was received into ye Monasterie ye 18 of July An° 1653. Invested with ye holy Habit of S[t] Benedict ye 31 of May An° 1654 & made her Profession ye 1 of June An° 1655 at ye age of 19. Died 1713.

1655 **Dame Maura Blundell**

Dame Maura* Blundell Daughter of Robert Blundell of Inceblundell in y[e] Countie of Lancaster Esq. was received into ye Monasterie ye 18 of July An° 1653. Invested with ye holy Habit of S[t] Benedict ye 31 of May 1654 & made her Profession the 1 of June 1655 at ye age of 18. Died 1690.

1656 **Dame Marie Gwillyms**

Dame Marie Gwillyms Daughter of M[r] William Gwillyms of Bailypitt in y[e] Countie of Munmouth was received into ye Monasterie y[e] 4 of October An° 1653. Invested with ye holy Habit of S[t] Benedict ye 14 of September 1655 & made her Profession y[e] 13 of November 1656 at y[e] age of 27. Died 1696.

1657 **Dame Hilda Russell**

Dame Hilda Russell Daughter of John Russell of little Malvern in y[e] Countie of Worcester Esq. was received into ye Monasterie the 24 of June An° 1655. Invested with ye holy Habit of S[t] Benedict ye 11 of July 1656, & made her Profession ye 26 of August An° 1657 at ye age of 25. Died 1700.

1657 **Dame Mildred Russell**

Dame Mildred Russell† Daughter of John Russell of little Malvern in ye Countie of Worcester Esq. was received into ye Monasterie the 24 of June An° 1655. Invested with ye holy Habit of S[t] Benedict ye 11 of July 1656, and made her Profession y[e] 26 of August An° 1657 at ye age of 19. Died 1712.

1658 **Dame Joseph Dallyson**

Dame Joseph Dallyson Daughter of S[r] Charles Dallyson‡ of Lissington in ye Countie of Lincolne was received into ye Monasterie ye 21 of July An° 1656. Invested with ye holy Habit of S[t] Benedict ye 27 of August 1657, & made her Profession ye 24 of November 1658 at ye age of 24. Died 1703.

* Baptized Margaret.

† Baptized Helen.

‡ Sir Charles Dalison (Recorder of Lincoln, 1636, knighted 1642 and serjeant-at-law 1664), by his wife Elizabeth, d. and coh. of Robert Smith of Lincoln, had in 1668 (? in his will) five daughters not married—Bridget (Dame Joseph), Martha (the next nun), Mary, Sarah and Decima, besides Susanna, bapt. 1644 (*Harl. Soc.*, l, 287-8).

1658 Dame Martha Dallyson

Dame Martha Dallyson Daughter of Sr Charles Dallyson of Lissington in ye Countie of Lincolne was received into ye Monasterie ye 21 of July An° 1656, Invested with ye holy Habit of St Benedict ye 27 of August 1657 & made her Profession ye 24 of November An° 1658 at ye age of 17. Died 1708.

1658 Dame Teresa Hyde

Dame Teresa Hyde* Daughter of Mr Antonie Hyde at ye woodhouse in ye Countie of South-Hampton was received into ye Monasterie the 13 of October An° 1656. Invested with ye holy Habit of St Benedict the 27 of August 1657, & made her Profession ye 24 of November 1658 at the age of 24. Died 1698.

1659 Dame Francis Goodier

Dame Frances Goodier daughter of M Thomas Goodier at Lantall-starkes in ye Countie of Heryford was received into the Monasterie the 31 of December An° 1657. Invested with ye holy Habit of St Benedict ye 25 of November 1658 & made her Profession ye 26 of November 1659 at ye age of 25. Died 1680.

1669 Dame Philip Garnons

Dame Philip Garnons† Daughter of Mr Roger Garnous of Amstry in ye Countie of Heryford was received into ye Monasterie the 5 of June An° 1659. Invested with ye holy Habit of St Benedict, and made her Profession on her death-bed ye 10 of September An° 1659 at ye age of 22. Died 1659.

1649 Dame Marie Bedingfeld

Dame Marie Bedingfield Daughter of Mr Mathew Bedingfield‡ in Bruxells was Invested with ye holy Habit of St Benedict in ye English Monasterie at Gant on ye 22 of Februarie An° 1648 & made her Profession there ye 13 of April 1649 & was afterwards by permission of Superiors translated to this Monasterie & received here ye 4 of September 1661. Died 1685.

1693 Dame Elizabeth Neale

Dame Elizabeth Naile Daughter of Sr Paule Naile§ in Lincolneshire was received into the Monasterie the 5 of June An° 1654. Invested with the holy Habit of St Benedict ye 19 of August 1663

* Baptized Anne.

† Gernon corrupted to Gernons, pronounced as in the text. Baptismal name Philippa.

‡ Matthew Bedingfeld is of the Redlingfield, Suffolk, branch of the family (*C.R.S.*, vii, 432-3).

§ Son of Richard Neale, successively Anglican Bishop of Rochester, Licheld, Lincoln, Durham and Winchester, and finally Archbishop of York.

& made her Profession ye 21 of August 1664 at the age of 18. Died 1673.

1665 **Dame Scholastica Gage**

Dame Scholastica Gage Daughter of S[r] Thomas Gage of Furle in ye Countie of Sussex was received into the Monasterie ye 5 of August An[o] 1662. Invested with the holy Habit of S[t] Benedict 23 of November 1664 & made her Profession on her death-bed the 28 of October 1665, at the age of 17.

1666 **Dame Marina Hunlock**

Dame Marina Hunlock Daughter of S[r] Henrie Hunlock of Wingorworth in ye Countie of Derby was received into the Monasterie the 11 of July 1663. Invested with the holy Habit of S[t] Benedict the 30 of December 1664, and made her Profession ye 7 of October 1666 at the age of 19. Died 1716.

1666 **Dame Marie Speare**

Dame Marie Speare Daughter of M[r] Cicill Speare was received into the Monasterie the 14 of June An[o] 1663. Invested with the holy Habit of S[t] Benedict the 30 of December An[o] 1664 & made her Profession the 7 of October 1666 at the age of 20. Died 1718

1666 **Dame Theodosia Waldegrave**

Dame Theodosia Waldegrave* Daughter of S[r] Henerie Waldegrave of Staninggill Hall in the Countie of Norfolk and of Catherine daughter of M[r] Rich[d] Bacon was received into the Monasterie the 8 of August An[o] 1663. Invested with the holy habit of S[t] Benedict the 30 of December 1664 & made her Profession the 7 of October 1666 at the age of 18. Died 1719.

1666 **Dame Magdalene Streete**

Dame Magdalene Streete Daughter of M[r] Richard Street of Gattertope in the Countie of Heryford was received into the Monasterie the 7 of December An[o] 1664. Invested with the holy Habit of S[t] Benedict the 6 of September 1665 & made her Profession the 7 of October 1666 at the age of 33. Died 1700.

1669 **Dame Scholastica Byron**

Dame Scholastica Byron Daughter of M[r] Gilbert Byron† of

* Dame Theodosia was baptized Joanna, and was the eighth abbess.

† Mr Burke, Norroy King of Arms, and Vice-President C.R.S., suggests that Gilbert, son of Sir John Byron of Newstead, by Anne, daughter of Sir Richard Molyneux, bart, is meant. His eldest brother, Sir John Byron, K.B., was created Lord Byron of Rochdale, 24 Oct. 1643, and died in 1652. Gilbert himself became a major-general in the royalist army and died of his wounds. His widow, Dorothy, whose maiden name has not been learned, petitioned the king in 1661 for a pension, stating that six of her husband's

Rufford Abbey in the Countie of Nottingham was received into the Monasterie the 10 of May An° 1666. Invested with the holy Habit of S[t] Benedict the 10 of Februarie 1667 & made her Profession the 22 of August 1669 at the age of 23. Died 1719.

1672 **Dame Marie Scrope**

Dame Marie Scrope Daughter of S[r] Adrian Scrope* of Cockerington of the Countie of Lincolne was received intc the Monasterie the 24 of June An° 1662. Invested with the holy Habit of S[t] Benedict the 23 of August 1671 & made her Profession the 13 of November 1672 at the age of 18. Died 1739.

1678 **Dame Marie Errington**

Dame Marie Errington Daughter of M[r] Raph Errington of Bingfield in the Countie of Northumberland afterwards of Markington in the Countie of York was received into the Monasterie the 3 of June An° 1676. Invested with the holy Habit of S[t] Benedict the 11 of July 1677, & made her Profession the 15 of August 1678 at the age of 21. Died 1741.

1682 **Dame Marie Benedict Collins**

Dame Marie Benedict Collins Daughter of M[r] John Collins of Dadmans in the Countie of Kent was received into the Monasterie the 16 of May An° 1680. Invested with the holy Habit of S[t] Benedict the 13 of Januarie 1681, & made her Profession the 22 of June at the age of 39. Died 1728.

1686 **Dame Mary Anne Udall**

Dame Mary Anne Udall Daughter to M[r] James Udall of Antwerpe descended from the family of the Udalls of Oxfordshire was invested with the holly Habit of S[t] Benedict Aprill 29 An°. 1685 and made her holly proffestion the 30 of Aprill 1686 at ye age of 35. Died 1738.

1687 **Dame Marie Crispe**

Dame Marie Crispe Daughter to M[r] Henry Crispe of Quaiks† in y[e] Isle of Thanet in Kent [and of Mary daughter of M[r] John

brothers fell in the cause of Charles I, and that her husband took part in most of the battles, defended Raglan Castle, but was taken prisoner in attempting to get to Colchester. She stated she had spent all her estate on him and her children, five in number. A pension of £200 per annum was granted to her. (*Kal. State Paper Dom.* 1660-2.)

* Sir Adrian Scrope, K.B., of Cockerington, co. Lincoln; mar. Mary, dau. of Sir Robert Carr, Baronet.

† The issue of Sir Henry Crispe of Quex, at the Visitation of 1619, is not continued in that of 1663-8. (*Harl. Soc.*, xlii, 74 and liv, 41.) The words within brackets are a later insertion.

Collins of Dadmans in Kent] was received into the Monastary the 16 of May 1680 An° and was invested with the Holly habit of St Benedict the 7 of May 1686 and made her Proffestion ye 5 of June 1687 at ye age ot 17. Died 1757. 9th Abbess.

1691 **Dame Elizabeth Chillton**

Dame Elizabeth Chillton Daughter to M r Christopher Chillton of Newcastle in the County of Northumberland and was received into ye Monastary ye 29 of May 1689, Invested with the Holly Habit of St Benedict October 1st An° 1689 & made her proffestion Novbr ye 4 An° 1691 at the age of 18. Died 1738.

1692 **Dame Marie Teresa Urancx**

Dame Marie Teresa Urancx daughter to Mr Guido Urancx of Brussels was received into the Monestary Octr of 1686, & was invested with The Holly Habitt of St Benedict May ye 1st 1691 and her made her Proffestion May the 4th An° 1692 att The age of 21. Died 1740.

1693 **Dame Augustina Ireland**

Dame Augustina Ireland Daughter to Thomas Ireland Esq. of Abrightowne * In. Shropshire was received into the Monestary Nov. 6 An° 1691 & invested with the Holly Habit of St Benedict Jan. 21 1692 and made her proffestion on the 23rd of January 1693 att the age of 19. Died 1743.

1694 **Dame Gertrude Chillton**

Dame Gertrude Chillton † Daugher to Mr Christopher Chillton of Newcasttell in the County of Northumberland was received into the Monestary Sepr 7 An° 1689 was invested with the Holly habit of St Benedict ye 5 of Aprill 1693, and Professd June ye 3rd 1694 att the age of 19. Died 1794.

1695 **Dame Lucy Ireland**

Dame Lucy Ireland Daughter to Thomas Ireland Esquire of Abrightown,* In Shropshire was received into the Monestary the 31 of May 1694 and invested with the Holly Habit of St Benedict the 21st of Novbr in ye year 1694 & made her proffestion The 22 of Novbr 1695 at the age of 21. Died 1750.

1697 **Dame Maria Beatrix Deeble (*call'd* Read)**

Dame Marie Beatrix Deeble Daughter to Mr John Deeble of —— in the County of Cornwall came to the Monestary Sepbr 21st An° 1686 & was invested with the Holly Habit of St Benedict the 8 of Sepbr 1695 and made her profestion the 14 of feb. 1697 at the age of 20. Died 1756.

* Albrighton.

† Baptized Henrietta.

1697 Dame Anastatia Mannock

Dame Anastatia Mannock* Daughter to Sir William Mannock Baronet of Giffords Hall in the County of Suffoulke was received into the Monestary Dechr ye 31 Ano 1694 & was invested with the Holly Habit of St Benedict Sepbr ye 8th 1695 and made her proffestion on ye 17 of March 1697 at the age of 23. Died 1746.

1697 Dame Xaveria Darell

Dame Xaveria Darell† Daughter to William Darell Esquire of Scotney in the County of Kent was received into the Monastary June ye 28th Ano 1693 and was invested with the Holly Habit of St Benedict Decbr 29 Ano 1695 and made her Proffestion feb ye 14 An 1697 att the age of 29. Died 1750.

1701 Dame Isabella Belligny

Dame Isabella Belligny Daughter to Mr Peeter Belligny of Brussells was received into the Monestary the 9th of Sepbr 1697 and was invested with the Holly Habit of St Benedict Sepbr 12 1700 and was proffesd Octbr 16 Ano 1701 at ye age of 21. Died 1737.

1701 Dame Mary Magdalen Mettham

1706 Dame Catherine Mettham

Dame Marie Magdeline and Dame Catherine Daughters of George Mettham Esquire of North Cave In Yorkshire were received into the Monestary Jun 30 Ano 1699 & were invested with the Holly Habit of St Benedict, Dame Marie Magdeline on Sepbr 12, 1700 proffesd Oct 16 Ano 1701 at ye age of 20. Died 1739. Dame Catherine invested with the Holly Habit ye 2 of June 1705 professed July 4 Ano 1706 att the age of 21. Died 1751.

1710 Dame Marie Josepha Darell

Dame Marie Josepha Darell‡ Daughter of William Darell Esq. of Scotney in the County of Kent was received into the Monestary on the 23 of Julie 1708 and invested with the Holly Habit of St Benedict ye 14 of Aprill 1709 and made Her Proffestion Nov ye 23 1710 att the age of 27. Died 1761.

1711 Dame Scholastica Erington

Dame Scholastica Erington§ Daughter to Nicholas Erington alias Stapleton Esquire of Carlton in Yorkshire was received into ye Monestary June ye 4th 1704 was invested with the Holly habit of

* Baptized Ursula.

† Baptismal name Elizabeth.

‡ Baptized Margaret.

§ Baptized Elizabeth.

St Benedict Novbr 24 1709 & made her profestion Julie ye 7 at ye age of 20 Ano 1711. Died 1765.

1711 **Dame Ursula Mannock**

Dame Ursula Mannock* Daughter to Sr William Mannock Barnt of Giffords Hall In the County of Suffoulke was received into the Monestary Jul 27 Ano 1707 and was invested with ye Holly Habit of St Benedict on the 24 of August 1710 And made her Profession on the 25 of August 1711 at the age of 19. Died 1732.

1711 **Dame Winifred Berkely**

Dame Winifred Berkely† Daughter to Thomas Berkely Esquire of Spechley In Worcestershire was received into the Monestary the 23 of Julie 1709 and was invested with the Holly Habit of St Benedict on the 24 of August 1710 and made her Profestion the 25 of August 1711 at ye age of 21. Died 1759.

1712 **Dame Alouiza Compton**

Dame Alouiza Compton‡ Daughter to Sr William Compton Barronet of Harpury Court in Gloucestershire was received Into the Monestary the 16 of August 1711, and Invested with the Holly Habit of St Benedict Novbr 21 and made her proffestion Novbr 22 Ano 1712 at ye age of 19. Died 1758.

1716 **Dame Maura Whettenhall**

Dame Maura Whettenhall Daughter to Henery Whettenhall Esquire of Peckham in the County of Kent [And of Lettice daughter of——Tichborne],§ was received into the Monestary the 27 of May 1705 and was invested with the Holly Habit Octbr 4 An 1712. and made her proffestion Jan the 7th 1716 att the age of 19 Died 1762.

1715 **Dame Marie Anne Bell**

Dame Marie Ann Bell Daughter to Mr Renaild Bell of the County of Northumberland was received into the Monestary ye 2nd of Julie 1711 and was invested with the Holly Habit of St Benedict the 4 of Octbr 1712 made her Proffestion the 16 of June 1715 at the age of 26. Died 1754.

1715 **Dame Agnes Carrew**

Dame Agnes Carrew Daughter to Antony Carrew Esquire of

* Baptized Faith.

† Baptized Margaret.

‡ Baptized Catharine.

§ Dame Maura's baptismal name was Catharine. She was the tenth abbess. Her maternal grandfather was Sir Henry Tichborne, third baronet. The words within brackets are in a later hand.

N

Shatterworth In the County of Somersite was received into the Monestary the 7 of Ocbr 1711 and invested with the Holly Habit of St Benedict the 4 of Ocbr 1712 made her Proffestion ye 25 of feb 1715 att ye age of 24. Died 1755.

1717 Dame Placida Waldegrave

Dame Placida Waldegrave* Daughter to M Edward Waldegrave of ye County of Norffollke was received into the Monestary the 1st of May 1715 and was invested with the Holly Habit of St Benedict ye 14 of May 1716 and made her Proffestion the 23 of May 1717 att the age of 17. Died 1774.

1717 Dame Barbara Jackson

Dame Barbara Jackson Daughter to Mr Nicholas Jackson of Bumpitt In the County of Kent was received into the Monestary the 9 of August 1710 and was invested with the Holly Habit of S Benedict the 7th of June 1716 and made her Proffestion the 10 of August 1717 att the age of 20. Died 1753.

1720 Dame Ignatia Collins

Dame Ignatia Collins Daughter to Christopher Collins Gent of Dadmans in the County of Kent was receiv'd into our Monastery ye 30th of Oct. 1718 Invested with the Holy Habit of St Benedict the 16th of November 1719 and made her Profession ye 17th of of ye same Month 1720 at the age of 24. Died 1770.

1723 Dame Stanisla Poole

Dame Stanisla Poole† Daughter of William Poole Esqr of Poole in the County of Cheshire was receiv'd into our Monastery the 29th May 1718 Invested with the holy Habit of St Benedict 8th November 1722 & made her Profession the 9th of the same month 1723 In ye 21st year of her Age. Died 1771.

1727 Dame Mary Angela Petre

Dame Mary Angela Petre‡ Daughter of William Petre Esqr of Bellhouse in the County of Essex was received into our Monastery 25th July 1725 Invested with the holy Habit of St Benedict 20th August 1726 & made her Profession 2nd September 1727 In ye 21st Year of her Age. Died 1762.

1731 Dame Ethelred Mannock

Dame Ethelred Mannock Daughter of Sr Francis Mannock Baronet of Gifford's Hall in the County of Suffolk was received

* Baptized Elizabeth.

† Baptized Philippa.

‡ Baptized Mary Anne.

into our Monastery 2nd September 1726 Invested with ye Holy Habit of St Benedict 3rd Janry 1730 & made her Profession 11th of same Month 1731 In ye 19th year of her Age. Died 1773. 11th Abbess.

1732 Dame Mary Benedict Plowden

Dame Mary Benedict Plowden Daughter of Mr Peter Plowden Gent. of Clarkenwell in the County of Hampshire, was receiv'd into our Monastery 25th November 1727 Invested with the Holy Habit of St Benedict 3rd January 1730 & made her Profession 24th February 1732 In ye 23rd Year of her Age. Died 1748.

1732 Dame Mary Francis Bodenham

Dame Mary Francis Bodenham* Daughter of Charles Bodenham Esqr of Rotherwas in the County of Hereford, was receiv'd into our Monastery 25th April 1726 Invested with the holy Habit of St Benedict 5th August 1731 & made her Profession on the 17th of the same month 1732 In ye 19th Year of her Age. Died 1792.

1733 Dame Marina & Dame Augustine Byerley

Dame Marina & Dame Augustine Byerley † Daughters of Beaumont Byerley Esqr of Bellgrave in the County of Leicester were receiv'd into our Monastery 30th August 1727, Invested with the Holy Habit of St Benedict 24th June 1732 & made their Professions 7th July 1733. Dame Marina in the 21st Year of her Age, & Dame Austine in ye 19th Dame Austine died 1738 and Dame Marina died 1762.

1733 Dame Mary Agnes Mannock

Dame Mary Agnes Mannock Daughter of Sr Francis Mannock Baronet of Giffords Hall in the County of Suffolk was receiv'd into our Monastery 2nd September 1726, Invested with the Holy Habit of St Benedict 24th June 1732, & made her Profession 7th July 1733 In ye 19th Year of her Age. Died 1774.

1733 Dame Clementina Simpson

Dame Clementina Simpson Daughter of Edward Simpson Esq of Barton in the County of Derby was receiv'd into our Monastery 28th December 1726, Invested with the Holy Habit of St Benedict 24th June 1732 & made Her Profession 7th July 1733 In ye 19th Year of her Age. Died 1754.

1737 Dame Mary Christina Stapleton

Dame Mary Christina Stapleton Daughter of Nicholas Stapleton Esqr of Carleton in the County of Yorkshire was receiv'd into our

* Baptized Mary Anne.

† Dame Marina was baptized Elizabeth, and Dame Augustine was Anne.

Monastery 5th June 1728, Invested with the Holy Habit of St Benedict 25th October 1735 & made her Profession 24th Febry 1737 In ye 22nd Year of her Age. Died 1797.

1737 Dame Henrietta Blount

Dame Henrietta Blount Daughter of Michael Blount of Mapledurham Esqr in the County of Berks was receiv'd into our Monastery 7th July 1734, Invested with the Holy Habit of St Benedict 25th October 1735 & made her Profession 24th Febry 1737 In ye 19th Year of her Age. Died 1740.

1738 Dame Cecily Mannock

Dame Cecily Mannock* Daughter of Sr Francis Mannock Baronet of Giffords Hall in the County of Suffolk was received into our Monastery 8th June 1736, Invested with the Holy Habit of St Benedict 27th August 1737 & made her Profession 19th October 1738. In ye 22nd Year of her Age. Died 1780.

1742 Dame Mary Teresia Collins

Dame Mary Teresia Collins Daughter of John Collins of London in the County of Middlesex was receiv'd into our Monastery 8th June 1736 Invested with the Holy Habit of St Benedict 10th Octbr 1741 & made her Profession 23rd of same month 1742 In ye 19th Year of her Age. Died 1802.

1742 Dame Ursula Pigott

Dame Ursula Pigott† Daughter of Ralph Pigott of Whitten in the County of Middlesex Gent was receiv'd into our Monastery 29th September 1741 Invested with the Holy Habit of St Benedict 10th October 1741 & made her Profession 23rd October 1742 in ye 19th Year of her Age. Died 1796.

1745 Dame Xaveria Pigott

Dame Xaveria Pigott sister to Dame Ursula was received, 1st June 1743 Invested with the holy Habit 7th July 1744, made her Profession Octr 12th 1745, aged 19. Died 1769.

1753 Dame Catherine *and* Dame Philippa Eccles

Dame Catherine & Dame Philippa‡ Daughters of Henry Eccles in the County of Lancashire were received into our Monastery

* Baptized Anna. Her mother was Frances Yates.

† Baptized Rebecca. She was the twelfth abbess. Her mother was Alethea, daughter of William, ninth Viscount Fairfax of Elmley. The family assumed the name of Fairfax on inheriting the Gilling estates.

‡ Henry Eccles of Meanfields, Winwick. The baptismal names were,—of Dame Catharine, Elizabeth; of Dame Philippa, Anne (*C.R.S.*, ix). The last became the thirteenth abbess.

30th July 1751, Invested with the Holy Habit of St Benedict 22nd August 1752 & made their Professions 28th of same month 1753 D. Catherine in ye 21st year of her age & D. Philippa in ye 19th D. Cat. died 1808. D. Phil. 1811.

1754 **Dame Mechtilda Dabord**

Dame Mechtilda Dabord* Daughter to Edward Dabord of Bishoprick in the County of Durham was received into our Monastery 27th August 1751 Invested with the Holy Habit of St Benedict 17th October 1752 & made her Profession 15th January 1754 in ye 23rd Year of her Age. Died 1813.

1754 **Dame Romana Foxe**

Dame Romana Foxe Daughter of Henry Foxe of Rheleskin† in the County of Mountgomory was received into our Monastery 25 April 1752 Invested with the holy Habit of St Benedict 17th October 1752 & made her Profession 15th January 1754 in the 22nd Year of her Age. Died 1791.

1754 **Dame Mary Benedict Reddy**

Dame Mary Benedict Reddy Daughter to Dudley Reddy Esqr of Brangenstone in the County of Kildare Ireland was receiv'd into our Monastery 6th January 1751, Invested with the Holy Habit of St Benedict 12th March 1753 & made her Profession 8th September 1754 in ye 32nd Year of her Age. Died 1792.

1754 **Dame Augustine *and* Dame Mary Bernard Tancred**

Dame Augustine & Dame Mary Bernard Tancred‡ Daughters of Sr Thomas Tancred Baronet of Brampton in the County of Yorkshire were receiv'd into our Monastery 16th September 1747, Invested with the Holy Habit of St Benedict 30th July 1753 & made their Profession 8th September 1754. Dame Augustine in the 20th Year of her Age, & D. Mary Bernard in ye 19th D. Augustine died 1797 & D. M. Bernard died

1768 **Dame Scholastica Rozer**

Dame Scholastica Rozer§ Daughter to Henry Rozer Esqr of Nottly Hall in Mary-Land was received into Our Monastery the 29 of January 1767, was invested with the Holy Habit of St Benedict 24 of November same year; made her holy Profession Decr the 8th 1768 at the Age of 22. Died 1791.

* Baptized Elizabeth.

† Rheleskin in Guilsfield parish. Henry Fox, Esq., appears as witness to a marriage at Welsh Pool by the Rev. Monox Hervey 26 Feb. 1750. His registers are in preparation for the *C.R.S.* xiv. See also Payne's *Non-jurors*, 188.

‡ Dame Augustine, who was elected fourteenth abbess, was baptized Margaret. Dame Mary Bernard was baptized Frances

§ Baptized Elizabeth.

1774 Dame Mary Anne Rayment

Dame Mary Anne Rayment Daughter to Mr Thomas Rayment of Worcester was receiv'd in our Monastery july ye 3rd 1768, was invested with the holy Habit of St Benedict ye 19 of November 1772 made her Profession ye 10 of February 1774, in ye 18 Year of her Age. Died Nov. 14th 1839.

1774 Dame Aloysia Witham

Dame Aloysia Witham (Baptiz'd Dorothy), Daughter of Henry Witham Esqr of Writtles in Yorkshire* enter'd our Monastery April ye 6 : 1772, was invested with the holy Habit of St Benedict April ye 27th 1773 & made her Profession ye 26 of July 1774 in ye 26 year of her Age. Died Feb. 24th 1818.

1780 Dame Ignatia Collins

Dame Ignatia Collins† Daughter of Mr Joseph Collins of London County Middlesex and of Elizabeth daughter of Mr Sterch. Received in our Monastery Invested with the Holy Habit of St Benedict July 13th 1779 Made her Profession Nov. 17 1780 at the age of 26. Died July 26 1814.

1781 Dame Mary Joseph Collins

Dame Mary Joseph Collins. Sister to Dame Ignatia Collins (Katharine) Received in our Monastery 1779 Invested with the holy Habit of Religion 1780. Made her Profession July 2nd 1781 At the age of 25. Died Febry 7th 1806.

1783 Dame Ursula Scoles

Dame Ursula Scoles‡ Daughter of Mr William Scoles. Received in our Monastery 1781. Invested with the holy Habit of Religion 1782. Made her Profession May 1st 1783. At the age of 25. Died January 16th 1801.

1793 Dame Maura Harper§

Daughter of John Harper. Invested with the holy Habit of St Benedict June 12th 1792. Made her profession Decbr 9th 1793 at the age of 25. Died 18 Oct. 1846.

1793 Dame Elizabeth Joseph Collingridge‖

Daughter of Mr William Collingridge & of Anne daughter of

* An extraneous note at the convent gives her mother as Elizabeth Pickering.

† Baptized Elizabeth.

‡ Baptismal name Elizabeth, her mother being Elizabeth Ehresbey.

§ Baptized Hannah, her mother being Mary Powell.

‖ Baptized Anne.

Mr John Reeve of Island Hill, Warwick. Invested with the holy Habit of St Benedict June 12th 1792. Made her Profession Dec. 9th 1793. Died 1845.

Last Profession at Brussels

WINCHESTER

First Profession in Winchester

Date of Profession

1796 **Dame Mary Benedict Macdonald***

Daughter of Mr Renald Macdonald. Received in our Monastery May 22nd 1794. Invested with the holy Habit of St Benedict August 11th 1795. Made her Profession Sep^{br} 8th 1796 At the age of 24 Chosen Abbess Sept 9th 1811. Blessed Abbess Oct 10th 1811 Resigned her office Feb 25 1848. Died May 17th 1854. Aged 82.

1802 **Dame Gertrude Veydt**

Daughter of M Ambrose Veydt of Antwerp Baptized Regina. Received in our Monastery 1793. Invested with the Holy Habit of St Benedict Nov 21st 1794. Made her Profession the 18th of May 1802 Died Feb^{ry} 27 1843.

1798 **Dame Anselm Edburga Collins†**

Daughter of Joseph Collins Esq & of Elizabeth daughter of Mr Sterck. Invested with the Holy Habit of St Benedict June 27th 1797. Made her Profession July 17th 1798 At the age of 35 years. Died July 19th 1839.

1803 **Dame Mary Francis Gabriellé**

Daughter to M Vincent Gabriellé of Leghorn & London (Teresa). Received in our Monastery January 1801. Invested with the holy Habit of St Benedict Jan. 19th 1802. Made her Profession January 25th 1803 At the age of 28. Died Feb^{ry} 17th 1841.

1807 **Dame Mary Magdalen Johnson**

Daughter of Mr Richard Johnson of Preston Lancashire & of Elizabeth daughter of Mr Edward Barrow of Lancashire (Mary). Received in our Monastery 1805. Invested with the Holy Habit of St Benedict July 15th 1806. Made her Profession August 18th 1807 At the age of 20. Died March 6th 1869.

1808 **Dame Mary Joseph Hutchinson**

Daughter of Matthew Hutchinson (Teresa). Invested with the holy Habit of St Benedict June 1807. Made her Profession July 5th 1808. At the age of 19. Died 1832.

* Baptized Elizabeth.

† Baptized Mary.

1809 **Dame Mary Agnes Whelan (*Oblate*)**

Daughter of Mr John Whelan, her Mother's name was Mc-Neale (Mary). Received in our Monastery April 23rd 1808. Made her Profession June 6th 1809 At the age of 28. Died May 21 1829.

1809 **Dame Mary Winefride Hutchinson**

Daughter of Matthew Hutchinson. Received in our Monastery 1807. Invested with the H. Habit of St Benedict September 8th 1808. Made her Profession September 10th 1809 At the age of 20. Died 1820.

1809 **Dame Mary Austin Witherington**

Daughter of M Thomas Witherington, her Mother's name was Johnson (Mary). Received in our Monastery 1807. Invested with the Holy Habit of St Benedict Sepbr 8th 1808. Made her Profession Sepbr 10th 1809 At the Age of 22. Died May 13th 1864.

1809 **Dame Mary Scholastica Lane**

Daughter of M Charles Lane of Wolverhampton Staffordshire and of Priscilla daughter of Mr Smith of Wolverhampton (Priscilla). Received in our Monastery September 10th 1807. Invested with the Holy Habit of S Benedict with the two former Sisters Sepbr 8th 1808. Made her Profession Sepbr 10th 1809 At the Age 23 years completed April 1809. Died April 4th 1877 at the age of 90.

1810 **Dame Mary Xaveria Bowman**

Daughter of Mr Charles Bowman, her Mother's name was Patrick (Anne). Received in our Monastery 1808. Invested with the Holy Habit of St Benedict June 13th 1809. Made her Profession July 3rd 1810 At the Age of 21. Died March 7th 1870.

1812 **Dame Mary Philippa Mitan**

Daughter of Mr William Mitan of London (Frances). Received in our Monastery 1810. Invested with the Holy Habit of St Benedict Febry 5th 1811. Made her Profession Febry 6th 1812 At the age of 28. Died May 12th 1839.

1814 **Dame Mary Benedict Sidden**

Daughter of Mr John Sidden, her Mother's name was Purseglove (Sophia). Received in our Monastery 1813 Invested with the Holy Habit of St Benedict Dec. 21 1813. Made her Profession February 17th 1814 At the Age of 19. Died July 9th 1826.

1818 **Dame Mary Teresa Howard**

Daughter of Mr John Howard of Warrington, her Mother's name was Howarden (Jane). Professed as a Bridgittine, and afterwards in our Monastery July 21st 1818. Died June 22nd 1861.

1819 Dame Mary Etheldred Nowlan

Daughter of Mr James Nowlan of Carlow (Mary). Received in our Monastery Nov^{br} 6th 1817. Invested with the holy Habit of Religion July 21st 1818. Made her Profession August 3rd 1819 At the Age of 23. Had been for several years a Novice with the Bridgetines at Peckham, London, Died May 6th 1881.

1821 Dame Mary Agatha Philips

Daughter of Charles Philips Esqre of Ruxley (Frances). Received in our Monastery June 6th 1819. Invested with the holy Habit of Religion June 13th 1820. Made her Profession August 21st 1821 At the Age of 31. She was a convert to the Faith. Died February 20th 1860.

1821 Dame Mary Aloysia Brenan

Daughter of Mr Charles Brenan of Kilkenny (Mary). Received into our Monastery June 20th 1818. Invested with the holy Habit of St Benedict June 13th 1820. Made her Profession Nov. 29th 1821 At the age of 21 years completed Nov^{br} 2nd 1821. In the year 1851 was Elected Abbess on the 26th of Feb^{ry}. On the Feast of the Glorious Assumption of the same year received her Benediction at the hands of his Eminence Cardinal Wiseman Archbishop of Westminster in our Convent of the Glorious Assumption then residing in the Ancient City of Winchester where the Community from Brussells settled July 14th 1794 when driven by the French revolution from their peaceful Monastery at Brussells. Removed to St Mary's Abbey East Bergholt June 15th 1857. Died October 11th 1870. 16th Abbess.

1822 Dame Mary Placida Kendal

Daughter of M John Kendal of Kensington London and of Mary daughter of Mr Morris of London (Catherine). Received into our Monastery July 11th 1820. Invested with the holy Habit of St Benedict Sep^{br} 11th 1821. Made her Profession October 24th 1822 At the age of 21. Died May 31st 1887.

1823 Dame Mary Catherine Molteno

Daughter of Mr Anthony Molteno of Como in Italy & of London and of Mary daughter of Mr Lewis (Eliza). Received into our Monastery April 30th 1821. Invested with the holy Habit of St Benedict Sep^{br} 3rd 1822. Made her Profession October 23 1823 At the Age of 21. Died Feb^{ry} 23rd 1839.

1831 Dame Mary Benedicta Brenan

Daughter of Mr Charles Brenan of Kilkenny (Margaret). Received into our Monastery January 1st 1829. Invested with the holy Habit of St Benedict Jan^{ry} 26th 1830. Made her Profession February 8th 1831 At the age of 26. Died September 28th 1865.

1832 **Dame Mary Mechtilda Mather**

Daughter of M Henry Mather of Lancashire (Adelaide). Received into our Monastery January 6th 1830. Invested with the holy Habit of St Benedict January 18th 1831. Made her Profession May 8th 1832 At the age of 26. Died 1866.

1832 **Dame Mary Bernard Molteno**

Daughter of Mr Anthony Molteno of Como in Italy and of London, and of Mary daughter of Mr Lewis (Emma). Received into our Monastery Novbr 6th 1830. Invested with the holy Habit of St Benedict Novbr 18th 1831. Made her Profession December 13th 1832 At the age of 32. Died September 1st 1860.

1834 **Dame Mary Eadburga Weathers**

Daughter of Mr William Weathers of Lambeth Southwark (Mary Anne). Received into our Monastery Sepbr 8th 1831. Invested with the holy Habit of St Benedict Octbr 6th 1833. Made her Profession January 14th 1834 At the age of 21. Died December 5th 1899.

1835 **Dame Mary Joseph Delaney**

Daughter of Mr Denis Delaney of Dunnow and of Anne Murray (Anne) Kilkenny. Received into our Monastery June 1st 1833 Invested with the holy Habit of St Benedict July 1st 1834. Made her Profession August 27th 1835 At the age of 30 years. Died Febry 26th 1877.

1840 **Dame Mary Agnes Corney**

Daughter of Mr James Corney of London Middlesex and of Mary Anne daughter of Mr Myrtle of Brighton (Mary Agnes). Received into our Monastry June 29th 1838. Invested with the holy Habit of St Benedict July 2nd 1839. Made her Profession August 11th 1840 At the age of 24 completed Decbr 30th 1839. Died Janry 7th 1888.

1841 **Dame Mary Francis Sales Woollett**

Daughter of Mr Henry Woollett, of London, Middlesex, and of Mary, daughter of Mr Bernard Macdonnall, Ireland, (Mary). Received into our Monastery August 13th 1839, Invested with the holy Habit of St Benedict September 24th 1840. Made her Profession October 5th 1841. At the age of 24 years completed, Febry 28th 1841. Was elected Abbess, Novbr 4th 1870. Blessed, Novbr 16th of the same year by Right Revd Dr Quinn Bishop of Brisbane Australia, in the place of Dr Amherst Bishop of Northampton. Died Octbr 6th 1888. 17th Abbess.

1843 **Dame Mary Joanna Weld**

Daughter of James Weld* Esqr, of Archer's Lodge Southampton,

* Seventh son of Thomas Weld of Lulworth Castle. His chil-

and of the Honble Julia daughter of Lord Petre (Agnes). Received into our Monastery Sepbr 4th 1841. Invested with the holy Habit of St Benedict Octbr 5th 1842. Made her Profession October 20th 1843. At the age of 22 years completed 22 July 1843. Died Febry 23rd 1883.

1845 **Dame Mary Stanislaus Corney**

Daughter of Mr James Corney of London Middlesex & of Mary Anne daughter of Mr Myrtle of Brighton (Barbara). Received into our Monastery, 10th of October 1843. Invested with the holy Habit of St Benedict Novbr 11th 1844. Made her Profession Novbr 18th 1845. At the age of 21 years completed Decbr 27th Died January 10th 1900.

1848 **Dame Mary Francis Lescher**

Daughter of Mr William Lescher and of Mary Anne daughter of Mr Copp, (Caroline). Received into our Monastery Sep. 29th 1846. Invested with the holy Habit of St Benedict, October 5th 1847. Made her Profession Novbr 7th 1848, At the age of 46. Died Octbr 22nd 1864.

1852 **Dame Margaret Mary Lescher**

Daughter of Mr William Jos Lescher* of London and of Mary daughter of Mr Wm Hoy, of Stoke by Nayland Suffolk (Monica). Received into our Monastery, August 5th 1850. Invested with the holy Habit of St Benedict August 15th 1851. Made her Profession August 17th 1852. Aged 21 years Janry 24 /52. Educated at our Monastery Winchester. Died March 16th 1898.

1855 **Dame Mary Walburga Leigh**

Daughter of Mr John Leigh of Moor Hall Lancashire and of Mary Anne daughter of Mr Michael Gibson of Eaton House Liverpool (Mary Anne). Received into our Monastery May 14th 1853. Invested with the holy Habit of St Benedict May 16th 1854. Made her Profession May 24th 1855. Aged 21 years April 1855. Educated at our Monastery Winchester. Died January 16th 1900.

1856 **Dame Mary Gertrude Lescher (Agnes)†**

Received into our Monastery Oct. 18th 1854. Invested with the holy Habit October 23rd 1855. Made her Profession Novbr 4th 1856 Aged 21. The last Professed at Winchester. Elected Abbess Oct. 13th /88. Blessed by the Right Rev. Dr Riddell, Nov 8th 1888. Died May 18th 1904.

dren were—(1) Henry, (2) Monsignor Francis J. Weld, (3) Philip, and (1) Anna Maria, (2) Dame Mary Joanna, (3) Catharine 4 Charlotte.

* His son, Edward, was superior of the Oblates of St Charles at Bayswater from May 1877 to May 1878. He resigned on account of ill health, and died 1 March 1897. Dame Margaret Mary Lescher was prioress for twenty years.

† Niece of Dame Mary Francis Lescher, and sister of Prioress Margaret Mary Lescher.

No. IV

ROSARY CONFRATERNITY LISTS

CONTRIBUTED BY THE REV. BEDE JARRETT, O.P.

THE lists here published are taken from two MSS. volumes in the possession of the English Dominican Province. The first is of paper 8×7 inches, and is really the conventual register of the Priory at Bornhem, where the English Fathers were reorganised by Cardinal Howard, O.P. It begins as a summary of rents and debts, and ends as a diary. Between these two parts is wedged in the list here published, written in a contemporary hand. Many of the names are of the boys (*students*) at the Bornhem College (cf. *Merry England, Bygone Colleges,* by the Rev. Raymond Palmer, O.P., Feb. 1889), and the rest are probably, for the most part, of those with whom the Dominican missionaries came in contact in England. This book is in the Archives at S. Dominic's Priory, London. The other is a smaller volume (4¼ inches by 2½) of white cardboard, covered by thin vellum. It is preserved at S. Peter's Priory, Hinckley. Within its cover is the following in F. Underhill's writing :—

'LIBER INSCRIPTORUM IN CONFRATERNITATEM SACRATISSIMI ROSARII A R.R.P.P.F.F.O.P.P. ANGLORUM.

Thoma Worthington (ab anno 1728 in annum 1753)
Antonino Hatton (ab. 1753 in 1783)
Edwardo Leadbitter (ab. 1783 in 1785)
Ambrosio Gage (ab. 1785 in 1796)
Alberto Underhill (ab. 1796.'

This volume, unlike the other, was kept in England. F. Worthington settled in 1727 at Middleton Hall, near Leeds, till his death in 1753. A year previously he was joined by F. Hatton who removed to Stourton Lodge, where he died in 1783. He was succeeded by F. Leadbitter, who left however in 1785 for Selby. In that year F. Gage took his place at Stourton Lodge till 1796. When he died, F. Underhill, to whom the book now passed, was then serving the missions of Roundhay and Hunslet near Leeds; and eventually added Selby to his field of labours. In 1802 he founded the mission in Leeds itself where his little chapel has become a stately Cathedral. In 1814 he removed to Hinckley, taking the book with him, where it still remains. The various places of its sojourn are evident also in the lists where the residence of each member of the Confraternity is given. It will be noted that the lists become almost wholly—towards the end—a register of the girls' school attached to the convent of Michelgate Bar at York. By this means the missing page of 39 names (mentioned in the *History of St Mary's Convent,* with a preface by H. J. Coleridge, S.J., 1887, London, p. 389) can be recovered by noting the dates 1750, June 3, to June 14, 1752.

BEDE JARRETT, O.P.

Nomina et cognomina eorum qui Conscripti sunt in Archi-Confraternitatem SSmi. Rosarii fratribus Predicatoribus Anglis ab anno 1706

1706 March 25. Soror Maria Ignatia Stanley,* Ord. St Augustini Brugis.
Soror Dorothea Stanley, Ord. St Augustini, Brugis.
Soror Maria Gertrude Stanley, Ord. St Augustini, Brugis.
Soror Placida Stanley, Ord. St Augustini, Brugis.
Agnes Stanley.
Catarin Stanley.

March 30. Thamer Roberts.
Thamer Martha Roberts. †
Elizabeth Brent. ‡
Ursula Brent.
John Brent.
John Brent.
Ursula Brent.
Robert Brent
Mary Gerder.
Soror Penelope Stanford, Ord. Prœd. Bruxellis, obiit 29th Sept. 1710. R. I. P.§

Dec. 10. Fr. P. Thomas Hunter,‖ Ord. Præd. Angliæ.
Francis Stanford. John Stanford.
William Stanford. John Stanford.
Dorothy Savage. Benjamin Parott.
Jane Stanford Parott. Robert Sigault.
Mary Sigault. Catharine Purcivile.

Dec. 25. Catharine Crosses *alias* Grinald.

1707 Soror Anna Catharina Johnston. }
Soror Maria Aurelia Crathorne. } Ord. St Augustini Lovanii
Soror Geneveve Tunstall. }

* Marwood's Diary, Sunday, 14 Nov. 1700 notes among Canonesses of S. Augustine at Bruges 'Mrs Stanlys.' (*C.R.S.* vii, p. 77.)

† Took her vows as a laysister with the Dominican Nuns at Brussels 21 Dec. 1706 and died 23 May 1755. (*MSS. Dominic's Priory, Carisbrooke*).

‡ A laysister at Brussels, professed 21 Dec. 1706, died 13 June 1752 (*MSS. at Carisbrooke*).

§ Daughter of Mr James Stanford, born 1680, took the vows at Brussels 20 April 1710. Her name in religion was Mary Clara (*Carisbrooke MSS.*).

‖ A native of Lancashire, born about 1679, took vows as a Dominican at Bornheim in 1700, laboured for a dozen years in London, dying 10 June 1723, at the age of 45 (*Palmer's Obits, p.* 10).

Oct. 15. Ord. Carmel. Liræ.
Margaret Teresia of the Immaculate Conception.
Mary of St Joseph.
Margaret of Jesus.*
Catharine of the Infant Jesus.
Lucy of the Holy Ghost.
Mary of the Incarnation.†
Teresia Francisca of Jesus.
Mary Anne of St Winnifried.
Mary Francis of St Anne.‡
Mary Catharine of the Bl. Sacrament.§
Teresia Maria of Jesus.
Mary Constantia of the Assumption.
Elizabeth Ursula of the Visitation.
Mary Delphina Joseph of the Annunciation.
Anne Maria of St Joseph.
Mary Winefried of Jesus.
Anne Teresia of the Presentation.
Joseph Teresia of the Purification.

1708 Feb. 2. Andreas Wynter, jam ordine professus.‖

July 28. Thomas Smith.¶ } ex amicis nostrarum
Eleonora Smith. } monialium.**

Simon Rabbits.	Jacobus Rabbits
Simon White. ‡‡	Sara Carter.
Thamar Rabbits.	Thamar Rabbits.
Simon Sheaperd.	Robertus Warner.
Elizabeth Warner.	Maria Hutchinson.
Catharina Hutchinson.	Isabella Newbutt.

* Her family name was Somerset, professed 1680, died 1745 (*C.R.S.* vii, 58).

† Sister to Sir Henry Bedingfield, professed 1673, died 1714 (*C.R.S.* vii, 58).

‡ Daughter of Elizabeth Bedingfield, who married W. Cobbe, professed 1671, died between 1709 and 1714. (*Ibid.*, 45).

§ Daughter of Mary Bedingfield who married T. Eyre, professed 1691, died 1729. (*Ibid.*, 45).

‖ Born 1691, studied at Bornhem, receiving the Dominican habit 25 Feb. 1710. He spent all his life in Flanders in various offices of the order and died at Louvain on 19 March 1754, at the age of 64.

¶ Perhaps this refers to Thomas Smith of Walworth Moor in County of Durham whose daughter (by his wife, Mary Salvin) became a Dominican Nun at Brussels in 1681. (*Carisbrooke MSS.*)

** Dominican nuns, then in the old Pin Mill (Spellekins) at Brussels, now at Carisbrooke, but originally founded by Card. Howard O.P. at Vilvord 1660 (Palmer. *Life of Card. Howard.* London, 1867, pp. 119 etc., 222 etc.)

†† Simon White of Wardour Castle, servant to Thomas, Lord Arundel, 1715, had estates at Plaitford, West-Wellow, etc. (*Payne. English Catholic Non-Jurors,* 81, 232, 286).

1710 Feb.	2.	R. P. Stephanus Shuttleworth.*
		Carolus Melvill, Studiosus.†
1711 Jan.	18.	Carolus Hannan.
		Thomas Carnforth.
April	5.	Robert Bruse,‡ Student.
May	3.	James Darbyshire.§
1712 July	31.	Margaret Polier.
1713 May	14.	Henricus Weyburn, Studiosus.
1714 Jan.	7.	B. Joseph Carr. ‖
1718 Sept.	4.	Pius. Jo Short. ¶
Oct.	2.	Maria Smith.

* John Stephen Shuttleworth, born 1676, took his vows as a Dominican at Bornhem 19 Sept. 1699. For some time was on the English Mission, principally in London, taught later at English Dominican College at Louvain, where he died of a slow fever 16 Nov. 1710 about 10 o'clock at night. He was buried among the Irish Dominicans there.

† 'Studiosus' or 'Student' (from references to the College Accounts) means studying at the English Dominican College of Bornhem. Melvill eventually received the Dominican habit 25 Feb. 1710 '*qui paulo ante hic ab eruditissimo et dignissimo admodum Rev. P. Thoma Worthington Provinciali ex Anglia Missus fuit.*' He took the name of Hyacinth, and left next day to make his noviciate at Ghent. On 5th April he gave up his habit and went away. (*MSS. at S. Dominic's Priory, Haverstock Hill.*)

Was as his name testifies a Scotchman, of the family of the Earls of Ailesbury. He served for some time as a dragoon under the Duke of Marlborough in the campaigns of the Low Countries. He received the Dominican habit at Bornhem 1 Jan. 1714, taking the name of Pius; though, 'whilst he became an excellent religious, he never lost his military comportment and precision.' Sent on the English mission he resided first with Mr Holland, Palm Street, in Matlock Street by Hanover Square; then with Mr Beesly, Panton Street, near Leicester Fields. He was subsequently Chaplain to Bp. Williams, O.P. Vicar Apostolic of the Northern District; was for some time at Felton in Northumberland with Mr Brandby; then at Aston Hall Farm, Aston-Flamville, and again in London. He returned to Bornhem in 1757 where he held the office of Prior and other charges. He died 23 Feb. 1768, worn out with old age aggravated by hernia, in his 81st year. (*Haverstock Hill MSS.*)

§ Received Dominican habit 1 Jan. 1714 taking the name of Dominic. After some years teaching at Bornhem went on the English mission. Stationed first at Standish Hall near Wigan, also at Borwich Hall, Wharton, seven miles from Lancaster, the other seat of the Standish family. In Jan 1728 he became Chaplain to Sir Francis Mannock of Gifford Hall, Suffolk; but seven years later he went to Lord Clifford of Chudleigh at Ugbrooke, Devonshire. Here he resided almost continually till his death, in his 68th year, 7 Jan. 1757. His remains still repose at the back of S. Cyprian's Chapel. (*Haverstock Hill MSS.*)

‖ Received laybrother's habit 3 Jan. 1712, was Procurator or Syndic of the Convent from 1716 to 1740, died 1747. (*Haverstock Hill MSS.*)

¶ Younger son of Thomas Short, M.D. of S. Edmund's Bury. His mother, Ursula, was daughter of John Daniel of Aston-Place, Suffolk, by Elizabeth, daughter of Sir Edward Waldegrave of Stansgrave, Norfolk. He was born in 1685, became a Dominican at Bornhem 14 Sept. 1718. He taught almost continuously in Flanders, dying at Louvain 3 April 1754 (*Haverstock Hill MSS.*)

1719 June 14. Francis Underwood,* Studiosus.
Nov. 5. James Pritchard.
1720 Oct. 6. Eduardus Hatton.† Matheus Leadbitter.‡ Johanne Tesdale.§ Radulphus Leadbitter } Studiosi.
1721 Sept. 8. Thomas Groves Fowler.
1722 July 17. Cudbert Clifton. Robert Wingate.
1724 Feb. 6. David Parson. March 12. William Lewis. } Studentes
Aug. 16. Frances Attmar. ‖
1726 Feb. 2. Edward Polehampton. ¶
Feb. 3. Jacobus Lee, Studens.
April 5. Franciscus Clifton, olim hic Studens.
June 7. Soror Theresia of Jesus *alias* Howard Ord. Carm. Antwerp.
9. Edward Elleker, Studens.** Mary Francis Farmer.

* Francis Underbord born 1701, educated at Bornhem, where he became a Dominican, 20 April 1718. His whole life was spent in teaching in Flanders. He closed his life at Bornhem 24 Jan. 1761, in the 60th year of his age. (*Haverstock Hill MSS.*)

† Born 1701, educated at Bornhem, taking Dominican habit there under name of Antoninus. Soon after his ordination, he served on the English mission, first as Chaplain to Jordan Langdale, then to Mr Tempest of Tong, to Mr Brandling at Felton; finally he was sent to Middleton Hall near Leeds. He removed his mission to Stourton Lodge, not many miles distant, and founded another at Hunslet. He died in his 80th year at Stourton Lodge. Several manuscript sermons and some amusing letters on the Catholic quarrels of the day are still preserved in the archives of the Province.

‡ Matthew Leadbitter, eldest son of John Leadbitter of Warnley, born 1702, educated at Bornhem, taking Dominican habit there 20 May 1723. Died of consumption at Louvain 4 Feb. 1735. (*Haverstock Hill MSS.*)

§ John Teasdale was born in 1703, educated at Bornhem, where became a Dominican under name of Vincent 15 Sept. 1722. His missionary districts lay in the North of England for he is mentioned as residing with 'Mr Crathorne of Ness in Yorkshire,' and he begged to be excused from the quadricunial Provincial Chapters held in London on the plea of lack of necessary funds for travelling. But no record has survived of his precise missions. After 17 years in England he retired to Flanders where he died 5 Jan. 1790. (*Haverstock Hill MSS.*)

‖ There was a Dominican nun, Sister Jane Agnes Atmore, whose father was Richard Atmore of Brindlymore in Tardigg Parish, Worcestershire. This may be a fanciful spelling of the same name. (*Carisbrooke MSS.*)

¶ Son of James Polehampton and Elizabeth Sarsfield, born 1709, took Dominican habit at Bornhem under name of Peter, 29 April 1728. He was an excellent musician, serving as organist in the conventual church. He died at Bornhem 1 Dec. 1740. (*Haverstock Hill MSS.*)

** Among the nuns at Spellekins mention is made of S. Margaret Elleker, daughter of Mr Elleker of Doncaster, Yorks. No doubt this was one member of her family. She was at the convent at this date (professed 1714, died 1737). (*Carisbrooke MSS.*)

1717 Sept. 13. Elizabeth Heaton.
16. Martha Robson.
19. Lucy Dormer.*
26. Mary Hilson. Ann Merson.
. Margaret Martin.*
27. John Brown.
} Ex Anglia

1726 Feb. 22. Mr Collingwood,† Nobilis Anglus passus morte pro rege Leverpool.
27. Item Richard Carnabi, John Selby. } in carcere defuncti pro Rege
29. William Radcliffe‡, Luke Gardiner } in carcere defuncti pro Rege
Sept. 2. Margaret Howard. Helen Mary Cory.
Dec. 25. Ann Prior.

1727. Oct. 4. Lawrence Barbour,§ jam ordinie nostro professus
James Shaw, John Adams } Studentes.

Occurrente anno 1734, 1735, 1736 etc.
Mr Elkins. Mr Brown.
Mr Dunkerley Mr Jones.
Mr Herbert‖ jam ordine nostro professus.
Mr Morphew¶ jam ordine nostro professus.
Mr Gouge Mr Lewis Alexander.
Mr George Alexander Mr James Grey.
Mr Rugge** jam ordine nostro professus.
Mr Bullock†† jam ordine nostro professus.

* Probably one of the Martins of Long Melford, to whom Lucy Dormer would be related. (*Payne's Records of English Catholics*, 16.)

† George Collinwood suffered on the scaffold for taking part in the rising of 1715 (cf. his widow's petition in the *Records of English Catholics*, 101.)

‡ A relation, it is said, of the Earl of Derwentwater.

§ James Lawrence Barbour entered the Dominician Order at Bornhem 30 May 1729. After serving in various offices of his Order in Flanders, he disappears from the Province's history. A letter speaks of him as 'for many months in the convent of Chanbery and is very well.' He died there to May 1752. (*Haverstock Hill MSS.*)

‖ William Herbert, born 1701, took religious name of James when he entered the Dominican Order on 11 Feb. 1716. He was known under his surname of Legge, but being sent to some foreign convent for his studies, his name disappears from history (*Ibid.*)

¶ Timothy Morphy, born 1698, describes himself as an Englishman, though the name sounds sufficiently Irish. He was professed 15 Feb. 1717, together with Herbert, served on the English mission at Stonecroft and London, where his work among the poor prisoners brought on his death 18 June 1746. (*Ibid.*)

** John Rugge took the Dominican habit under the name of Paul, 29 Oct. 1716. He was assigned with Herbert to some foreign convent for study, was in Bornhem in 1728, but after that is not mentioned again. (*Ibid.*)

†† William Bullock, called in religion Joseph, received Dominican habit at Bornhem 20 Jan. 1720. He was on English mission, as Chaplain

Mr Charles Rackel. Mr Robert Rackel.
Mr Bernard Rackel. Mr Benjamin Wyburn.
Mr Henry Wyburn. Mr Caffrey.
Mr Buttler,* jam ordine nostro professus.
Mr Clyfton Mr Madden.
Mr Catterel,† jam ordine nostro professus.
Mr Fothergill Mr Williams.
Mr Clarkson‡ jam ordine nostro professus.
Mr Tebay§ item ordine nostro professus.
3 Persons all Bridges, there names are forgot.
Mr Charlton Mr Gipson.
Mr Cottam.

1729. Sept. 6. Mrs Strickland.

1731.

Studiose Convictores:
- Dm̃s Franciscus Bulstrode.
- Dm̃s Joannes Wade.
- Dm̃s Richardus Wright.
- Dm̃s Jacobus Alexander.
- Dm̃s Joannes Firth.
- Dm̃s Georgius Turvile.
- Dm̃s Richardus Bellew.
- Dm̃s Mathœus Bellew.
- Dm̃s Joannes Tredwell.

Domicella Anna Carnforth. Guilielmus Granger.
Domicella Brigitta Andrews. Laurentius Welsh.
Fr. Josephus Carr, Conversus professus.
Maria Cook Dms Edwardus Wright.
Dms Radulphus Hansbie‖ Georgius Kearton.

first to Mr Crathorn at Ness, then to Mr Porter at Durham, where he died 31 Jan. 1730. (*Ibid.*)

* Richard Buttler was born 1701, entered Dominican Order 20 April 1718. After his studies he went to Civita Vecchia, worked on the parish there under the care of his Order and died there 1733. (*Ibid.*)

† John Catterel (or Cotterel) was born in Hexham, professed at Bornhem 27 April 1719 under name of Stephen. He studied at Louvain and Civita Vecchia; returned to Flanders; in Sept. 1737 sent on English mission. He served at Stonecroft till his death, 1765, while in office as Provincial. (*Ibid.*)

‡ John Clarkson, professed as a Dominican 11 Feb. 1716, served on the English mission as Chaplain to Francis Turvile of Aston-Flamville Hall, on whose death he returned to Flanders as Confessor to the Dominican nuns of Spellekins, Brussels. He occupied various posts of authority in his Province as Prior and Provincial. He returned to Aston-Flamville, but for the greater convenience of his scattered flock removed to Sketchly. He returned to Brussels, dying there 29 March 1763. (*Haverstock Hill MSS.*)

§ James Tebay, born 1695, professed as a Dominican 11 Feb. 1716, sent into France for parochial work, where he died seven years after ordination on Feast of S. Dominic, 1727. (*Ibid.*)

Hansbie of Tickill Castle near Rotherham, W. Riding of Yorkshire. He had a daughter a nun at Spellekins, professed 1682, died 1734. (*Carisbrooke MSS.*)

		Phillis Kearton.	Joseph Kearton.*
		Elizabeth Anderson.	Ruth Loftus.
		Jane Metcalfe.	Mary Peacock.
		Rosamunda Kearton.	Dorothy Close.
		Martha Close.	Elizabeth Peacock.
		Elis Holmes.	Jane Milner.
		Elizabeth Milner.	Antony Metcalfe.
		Agnes Metcalfe.	Mary Richardson.
		James Milner.	Jane Metcalfe.
		Marmaduke Graunger.	Simon Milner.
		John Clarkson.	Gulielmus Short.
		Margaret Clarkson.	Jacobus Lake.†
		Rosamunda Clarkson.	Mary Thornborough.
1731		Benedict Thomas.	Thomas Walker.
		Anna Rolfleet.	Joanna Marie Boots.
1735 July	3.	D. Joannes Strickland. D. Richardus Griffin.‡ D. Richardus Smith. § D. Elleker Stanfield.	Studentes.
		Gabriel Poultner.	
1737		Nicholas Leadbitter. ‖ William Robinson. David Fowler. Joannes Porter.¶	Studiosi.
		Richardus Bostock.	
		Gabriel Poultney.	
1742 Nov.	1.	Dms. Gulielmus Eyston.	Doms. Robertus Bullock.
1744 Sept.	1.	Joannes Boucher,** studiosus.	Samuel Ellis.

* The Keartons and Clarksons were related. Moreover, Loftus, Peacock, Metcalfe, Kearton were all Catholic families, then residing near Richmond. (*Old English Cath. Missions,* 64.)

† Professed at Bornhem 14 Sept. 1736, died there 21 Oct. 1749, aged twenty-nine. (*Haverstock Hill MSS.*)

‡ Richard Griffin was educated at Bornhem where he took the Dominican habit 9 Feb. 1740. He died there 24 April 1754. (*Ibid.*)

§ It is tempting, though the dates seem too far apart, to quote from *Records of English Catholics,* how Mrs Johnson of Crosby, 1 Nov. 1716, pays for the maintenance and schooling of Edward Molyneux of Altkar and of Richard Smith, the money being paid to 'some Popish College beyond seas to make the said youths priests.' (*Records of English Catholics,* 126.)

‖ Another member of the Northumbrian family, born 1722, received Dominican habit under name of Hyacinth 8 Aug. 1742. On English mission, he was stationed at Aston-Flamville, serving the neighbouring district, Sketchly, Hinckley, Market-Bosworth, Nuneaton, Belgrave. In 1754 he went to Hexham, returning 1762 to Bornhem where he died 15 Aug. 1768. (*Ibid.*)

¶ John Porter, born 1725, son of Joseph Porter of Durham, whose chapel was served by the Dominicans. Under the religious name of Peter he was professed at Bornhem 29 Oct. 1744 and died 14 Dec. 1759. (*Haverstock Hill MSS.*)

**Among the nuns in Spellekins at this date was Sister Mary Clare

1745 March 7. Nobillissima Dna Catharina Walmesley, Baronissa de Stourton.*
1747 Sept. 10. Jacobus Hely, Hybernus.
1748 D. Catharina Neale.
March 28. Henricus Segrave.† Helena Muller.
D. Petrus Mostyn. D. Petrus Josephus Smith Studiosus.
Domina Ethelreda Mannock, Ord. S. Benedicti, Bruxellis.
Domicella Winifreda Claverine.
Domicella Elisabetha Pawson.
Domicella Catherina Pawson.
R. Dominus Thomas Willis, Confessarius Monasterii Ord. S. Benedicti, Bruxellis.
Domina Maria Cusack.
1750 July 5. Franciscus Cornforth } Studiosi.
Franciscus Osbaldston‡ }
Oct. 4. Gulielmus Houghton,§ Studiosus.
1751 March 25. Dom. Josephus Turnhill, Studiosus.
Aug. 15. Georgius Mackneb.
Oct. 3. Matuœus Norton,‖ Studiosus.
Nov. 1. Joannes Chantrill, Studiosus.

Boucher, the daughter of Richard Boucher of Weston-Underwood, Bucks., and of Mary Wearring his wife. (*Carisbrooke MSS.*)

* In the 'Memorandum Præd. Bornhem': under 1742: 'Baronissa Petre dedit conventui ellemosynam decem librarum Anglicanarum ut feria sexta prima vacante solemni fieret sacrum de S. Cruce ad obtinendam sanitatem sui mariti Prœnobilis Domini Caroli Stourton Missa illa solemnis habita fuit 2dà Martü. Orate pro marito et uxore.' She was a constant benefactress. F. Benedict Short, O.P., was her chaplain in Grosvenor Square, 1762-1785. (*Haverstock Hill MSS.*)

† Francis Segrave of Scabborough, Dublin, had at this date a daughter a nun at Spellekins. (*Carisbrooke MSS.*)

‡ Educated at Bornhem, took Dominican habit 10 April 1753, professed 17 April 1754. After which he disappears from the records. (*Haverstock Hill MSS.*)

§ Educated at Bornhem, took Dominican habit 15 Oct. 1753, under the name of Hyacinth. His championship of the scientific theories of Des Cartes and Newton, in the public defensions of Louvain University created such opposition that he had to resign his professorship and retire to England. In Oct. 1780 he went to Fairhurst Hall near Wigan as Chaplain to the Nelson family, where he died 3 Jan. 1823, in his 87th year. He was an excellent classical scholar and no mean poet. (*Ibid.*)

‖ Born 1723 at Roundhay, near Leeds. He became a Catholic on a visit to Flanders and entered the Dominican noviciate at Bornhem 15 Oct. 1753 under the name of Thomas. He wrote several treatises on agriculture and the management of bees, published by the Imperial Academy of Brussels in 1776, etc. He was an indefatigable missioner, walking on one occasion 54 miles in one day on a sick-call. He is frequently mentioned as an authority in agricultural works of the Eighteenth Century. After a faithful discharge of his duties at Hinckley for 20 years, he died 7 Aug. 1800, and lies buried at Aston Flamvill. (*Ibid.*)

1752 Nov. 1. Theobaldus Dillon, Studiosus.
1753 March 4. Carolus Bone, Studiosus.
1754 Jan. 6. Antoninus Sheriff Novitius Conversus.
Sept. 30. I received Mr Henry Eyles into the Society of the Rosary——Fr. J. Clarkson.
Oct. 9. Jacobus Farleman,* Studiosus.
March 25. William Poole received into this confraternity.
1755 March 25. Dms. Owenus Kelly. Dominicus Philips. JoannesLeadbitter.† Thomas Yates. } Inscripti St Confraternitali SS. Rosarii per me F. T. Clarkson, Priorem.
Ab eodem inscriptus est in S. Confraternitati, Dms. Lucas Plunket.
Aug. 15. Receptus est in Confraternitati SS. Rosarii, D. Robertus Patient.‡
1761

William Ran.	Anne Fairfax.
James Pritchard.	Mary Hodgson.
Anne Soulby.	Barbara Bellasis.
Catharine Bellasis.	Richard Horner.
Elizabeth Fairfax.	Lancelot Foster.
Margaret Ratcliffe.	Mary Rose Brooke.§
Gerrard Dillon.	MaryTherese Brooke.§
Joanna Vicars.	Elizabeth Brook.‖
Mary Aloysia Spalding.¶	Mary Wilkinson.**

* Ferleman, or Fairlamb as he often subscribes himself, was born about 1740 in or near Hexham. Entered Bornhem Noviciate 14 Sept. 1758. In London was Chaplain to Neapolitan Embassy, then moved to Hexham for 17 years, returned to Flanders; he died at Louvain 5 Feb. 1796. (*Ibid.*)

† Second son of Mathew Leadbitter of Warden, by Elizabeth, daughter of John Heron of Paise, near Hexham; born 10 Jan. 1740, educated at Bornhem, became a Dominican 15 Oct. 1766; served Stonecroft mission, residing latterly at Whalley Grange where he died 25 April 1811. (*Ibid.*)

‡ Born in 1742. entered Noviciate 14 Sept. 1758, was Chaplain to Riddells of Cheeseburn Grange from 1774 till his death 7 Aug. 1783. (*Ibid.*)

After some years seafaring life, became a Dominican under name of Vincent at Bornhem 19 Sept. 1759. He taught in the College there till its removal to Carshalton, where he died 4 Dec. 1802. (*Ibid.*)

§ Daughters of Leonard Brooke and Ann Mud his wife, both of Maryland, U.S.A. They took their vows at Spellekins 1 June 1756; Mary Rose, the youngest, died within seven months, 21 Jan. 1757; Mary Theresa lived on till 5 Oct. 1789. (*Carisbrooke MSS.*)

‖ She is described in the Carisbrooke lists as the daughter of Edward Cole and Ann Neal. She took her vows under the name of Ann Dominica, 10 May 1757; was elected Prioress in 1783, 1789; fled with the rest into England 1794, dying at Hartpury Court, Gloucestershire, 1816. (*Ibid.*)

¶ Received Dominican habit in May 1756; professed on her death-bed, 22 Jan. 1757. (*Ibid.*)

** Daughter of William Wilkinson and Dorothy Purson, of the County of Durham. She took her vows 11 May 1758 as a Dominican Nun at Spellekins, dying there 27 Dec. 1788. (*Ibid.*)

Mary Clementina Paston.* Elizabeth Kitchin.†
Richard Gammond. Mary Kelly.
Elizabeth Wilkinson. Mary Smith.
Bridgit Lectonby. Mary Titchburn.
Joannes Burn. Maria Anna Windey.

1762 Oct. 20. Ignatia Collins. Thomas Wilkins.
Nov. 9. Joannes Buckingham.
1763 April 14. Eduardus Leadbitter.‡
Dec. 19. Thomas Underhill.§ Nathanael Macdonel.
Joannes Bullock.|| Nicholaus Dixon.¶
Robertus Robson.** Joannes Spencer.
1764 Jan. 24. Henricus Coleman.
Feb. 27. Maria Oswaldina Errington. Joanna Wilkinson.
Oct. 2. Jaspar Leadbitter.†† Gulielmus Coats.
Joannes Kelshaw. Daniel Morgan.
Thomas Potier. Petrus Potier.‡‡

* Daughter of Clement Paston and Mary Brown, professed at Spellekins 16 May 1758, dying 2 Aug. 1779. (*Ibid.*)

† Took vows as a Dominican laysister under the name of Jerome, 4 Jan. 1761. She came to England with the rest in 1794, died at Hartpury Court, 8 Feb. 1824. (*Ibid.*)

‡ Born in 1747, educated at Bornhem, clothed in Dominican habit 21 Nov. 1769. On the English mission he was at Leicester, at Stourton Lodge, finally at Selby where he died 6 Jan. 1788, and where he was buried in chancel of Selby Abbey. (*Haverstock Hill MSS.*)

Younger brother of Albert Underhill, born 1750, received to Dominican habit 16 Oct. 1766. After teaching many years was driven from Flanders by the Revolution, afterwards working in London, Carshalton, and Sutton Place near Guildford. In 1880 he became Chaplain to the Nuns at Micklegate Bar where Dr Oliver met him; he died there quite suddenly, 19 Jan. 1810. (*Ibid.*)

|| Belonged to a rich North Country family, born 1750, educated at Bornhem, became a Dominican 16 Oct. 1766; taught there in the College. Coming to England, served mission at Cale Hill, near Charing, Kent,—the seat of Edward Darell, who had married his niece. He died 25 June 1819. (*Ibid.*)

¶ Born in 1743, educated at Bornhem, professed as a Dominican 22 Oct. 1767. Transferred the Belgrave mission to Leicester, serving Hinckley from there. Later removed to Woburn Farm, near Chertsey, the residence of Mrs Southcote. On her death he moved to Lower Woburn Lodge where he died 4 Feb. 1788. (*Ibid.*)

** Born 1746, educated at Bornhem, received Dominican habit 21 Nov. 1769, under the name of Ambrose. He served mission at Tone, near Bertley, a little village on the coal-district north of Cobridge. Tone House was then the seat of William Sanderson, who resided abroad. He died there 13 April 1782. (*Ibid.*)

Fifth son of Mathew Leadbitter, younger brother of F. John Leadbitter; born 11 May 1749; educated at Bornhem, where he became a Dominican 20 May 1771, under the name of Dalmatius. He worked on the English mission at Hexham for fifty years, dying quite suddenly while kneeling at his bed-side on 1 July 1830. His tomb-stone notes, as he had wished, that he was 'the sixth Leadbitter of the Order of S. Dominick.' Five were priests, the sixth a nun of the Second Order. (*Haverstock Hill MSS.*)

‡‡ Born 23 Dec. 1750, educated at Bornhem, became a Dominican under

1765 Jan. 14. Carolus Bullock.*
Festo Purific: B.M. Fr. Gulielmus Blevin, Carthusianus.
1766 Thomas Brittain.†
1767 Feb. 21. Anna Hill. Anna Mathews.
Esther Errington.
Feb. 27. Gulielmus Greyson. Francisca Bond.
Maria Harris.
March 12. Sara Burnhem.
25. Helena Coope.
1769 Feb. 2. Franciscus Gillis. Dms Petrus Francis Carton.
D. Joannes Smith.‡ D. Mathæus Dixon.
Dmo Anna Dixon.
1768 Aug. 15. Fr. Thomas Carfoot, Carthusianus. } Ex
Soror Xaveria Patient Ord. } Neuport.
Heuricus Colemàn. Joannes Thoma Bulteel.
1770 Feb. 4. Domina —— Howard.
Petrus Smith. Joannes Cools, Studiosus.
Joannes Simons }
Petrus Josephus Simons. } Ex Hinghen.
Isabella Maria Thresia Simons. }
1771. Aug. 15. Richard Roche, studiosus
1773. April 8. Petrus Everard.
Nov. 7. D. Alexander Grange
D. Gulielmus Williams } Studiosi Bornhem,
James Doves } PP. Præd. Angliæ
1774. Post examen de moribus piis ceterisque vitæ Christianæ muneribus ritę cognitis et peractis: ut milites Beatissimæ Virginis Sociique Sanctissimi Rosarii, juvenes studiosi qui sequntur sunt admissi riteque instituit.
Js. Lincoln.§ Thomas Collingridge.

name of Philip 21 Oct. 1771. On the French invasion of Flanders, he came to England as Chaplain to Edward Meynell, the Fiiary, Yarm; then to Hales Place, Canterbury; finally to Weybridge where he began a mission and served it for 19 years. He wrote numberless articles to Catholic periodicals, died at Hinckley 18 Nov. 1846. (Ibid. Correct by this the reference to him as an 'unknown French Refugee'—*Old English Catholic Missions,* 39.)

* Younger brother to F. Raymond Bullock, born between Nov. 1751 and following April, educated at Bornhem, joined Dominican Order 15 Nov. 1768; chiefly employed in Flanders; died at Louvain 12 June 1794. (*Ibid.*)

† Born of Protestant parents near Chester, 1745. In 1761 he and his brother were converted to Catholic Faith; and 16 Oct. 1766 he took the Dominican habit at Bornhem. For 20 years he was head of the College there; then became Confessor to the nuns at Spellekins, fled with them to England, was their Chaplain at Hartpury Court, where he worked the mission, where he died 3 May 1827. His 'Rudiments of English Grammar' was highly spoken of by John Walker, whose complimentary letter to the author is still preserved in the Archives of the Province. (*Ibid.*)

‡ Educated at Bornhem, where took Dominican habit under name of Bernard 20 May 1771. He served on the English mission at Hinckley, Leicester, and Sawston Hall, the seat of the Huddleston family in Cambridgeshire. He died at Bornhem 16 March 1804. (*Ibid.*)

§ John Atkinson, *alias* Lincoln, born 1757, educated at Bornhem, pro-

	Rs. Compton.*	Joannes Fenwick.†
	Philips. Graves.	Joannes Heveringham.
	Josephs. Smith.‡	Samuel Wilson.§
	Carolus Hunt. ‖	Joannes Hunt.
March 5.	Joannes Anderton.	
1775.	Gulielmus Nibbs.	Phils. de Vaux.
	Dons. Macmahon.	Jos. Beaumont.
	Th. Nugent.	Rostan. Gamage.
	H. P. Nugent.	Pat. Forrest.
	J. Phillips.	Th. Puleston.
	J. Nugent.	Gul. Anderton.
1776.	J. Evans.	
March 25.	Sarah Ashton.	
1777. Aug. 4.	Mary Alexia Kitchen.¶	
1778. April 2.	Elizabeth Frances Catharine Hitchcock.	
	Mary Lewis Constania of St Joseph.	

[On the last page of the book and on the front page, the following addresses are scribbled :—]

Dominick Gwillns direct.

For Captaine Gwillns in S. Albans Street next dore to the Chyungraves Arms to be sent to Mr Jacops.

For Mr Willard Smith next door to the Golden Plow in Bloomsberry fish market.

To Mrs Smith Crossgate Durham recommended to the Post office London.

fessed as a Dominican there 11 Jan. 1773, under the name of Benedict. Taught chiefly at Bornhem and Carshalton; but in Oct. 1801 he went to Bruges as Chaplain to Augustinian Nuns there, where he died 16 Oct. 1826. (*Ibid.*)

* Just before this date there had been at the Spellekins Convent Sr. Margaret Joseph Compton. Her father is given as Edward Compton of Gersby, of the family of the Earls of Northampton. It is possible that this boy was a relation. (*Carisbrook MSS.*)

† An American, born in Maryland, U.S.A., in 1759; educated at Bornhem, received Dominican habit 14 Oct. 1777, taught for a short time at Carshalton, returned to his native county, died 1816. (*Haverstock Hill MSS.*)

‡ Born 1761; educated at Bornhem, where became a Dominican 14 Oct. 1777 under the name of Thomas. He entered into scheme for the foundation of the American Province of Dominicans, crossed the Atlantic in 1805, became one of the four founders of the Province of S. Joseph, U.S.A. He was superior of the Priory of S. Rose, Kentucky, where he died in 1824. (*Ibid.*)

§ Educated at Bornhem, professed as a Dominican 12 April 1784. He taught at Bornhem and Carshalton; thence to Stourton Lodge where he died somewhere between 1802 and 1806. (*Ibid.*)

‖ These two boys (from 14 Feb. 1772 to 30 Jan. 1774 at Bornhem) brought with them to school, says the Register of the Convent, 'two dogs and a monkey.' (*Ibid.*)

¶ Sarah Alexia Kitchen was a laysister in the Spellekins Convent. She was professed in Jan. 1763, and died 6 March 1789. (*Carisbrooke MSS.*)

For M[r] John Jacobs at the hon[able].
Resident of the grand Duke of Tuscany.
The haymarket London.
Mrs Anne Hodgkinson living with Mrs Clifton
at Mr Robert Stricklands in S. James's London.
In country Mrs Anne Hogkinson at Lytham nigh Preston in Lancashire.
For F. Dom Guanarra.
A Monsieur Albia Gentill homme a recommendé au Portier à l' Ambassadeur d' Espanys a Wilde House Londres.

LIBER CONFRATERITATIS ROSARII

1738. Jan. 21. Anna Widdrington.* Northumberland.
June 29. Elizbeth Sayer. York.
July. 7. Jane Lund. Haslewood.
Aug. 5. Approbavi, confirmavi, et de novo concessi R. Domino Potts O. S. B. licentiam admittendi et recipiendi in Rosario A.R.P.F. Littleton olim concessam.
Aug. 15. York:
Lady Mary Hungate. Mary Magdalen Davis.
Elizabeth Stanfield. Mary Hodshon.
Hester Mary Magdalene Conyers. Eleonora Clifton.
Elizabeth Mary Hodson. Dorothy Anne Lodge.
Anne Aspenal. Mary Magdalene Menard.
Ann Blackburn. Helena Holmes.
Helena Sexton. Isabella Laurenson.
Jane Dutchburn. Ann Darley.
Frances Beaumont. Catharine Brigan.
R. D. Thomas Willibrod Helmes† O.B.
Huic dedi licentiam recipiendi in Rosarium.
Nov. 1. Ann Jackson. Hooton, Cheshire.
17. Concessi licentiam recipiendi in Rosarium R. D. Eduardo Houghton, O.B.
Hoc anno verbabiliter approbavi et concessi de novo licentiam recipiendi in Rosario.
R. D. Placido Acton O.B.

* Anne Widdrington of Cheeseburn Grange, widow of William Widdrington and daughter of Caryl, Lord Molyneux. (*English Catholic Non-Jurors*, p. 203.)

† Weldon mentions a Thomas *Wilfrid* Helme, O.S.B., who is presumably the monk here intended. (*Weldon's Chronological Notes. Appendix*, 22.)

Concessi licentiam recipiendi in Rosarium.
R. P. Cardo Ecop S.J.

Dec. 8. Mary Scorie.*
Concessi licentiam recipiendi in Rosario.
R. D. —— Cass O.B.

1729. June 10. Ann Brandling.
Ralph Brandling Esquire. } Middleton, York.

1729 Aug. 15. John Clavering Esquire, cui etiam assignatur hora vigiliæ ab Hora 5a ad 6am Vespertinam die Assumptionis B.V.M. Mutavi Margaritæ Clavering Horam vigiliæ ab Hora 4a ad 5am Vespertinam die Circumcisionis D.N.J.C.

Sept. 8. John Knowles,† famulus Rmi Episcipi Tiberiopolis

Oct. Margaret Johnson.
William Johnson.
Robert Johnson. } Lancastriensis.

18. Concessi licentiam recipiendi in Rosario.
R.D. Gulielmo Champhey O.B. Lancastriæ.

Dec. 28. Item R.D. Briano Tunstal S.S. Yorkshire.

1730 Sept. 19. Item R.D. Laurentio Kirby O.B. Lancastriæ.

1831 April 11. Michael Hansbie. Yorkshire.

1832 Aug. 15. Jane Houseman.
Jane Bowron.
Dorothy Pearson. } Durham.

Oct. 28. Concessi licentiam recipiendi in Rosario.
R.D.——Bulmer O.B. Lancashire.

Nov. 1. Mary Thorp.
Ann Stringer. } Middleton. Yorkshire.

1734 Oct. 6. Elizabeth Tasker. York.
John Wade. Leeds.

1735 April 16. Francisca—— Halifax.

Aug. 4. Alexander Jameson.
10. Mary Thakston. } Huddelston. Yorkshire.

Nov. 30. Arnold Griffith.‡ Middleton.

1736. March 25. Ralph Brandling, Junior.
Elizabeth Thorpe.
Catherine Stringer.
Ann Royston, Junior. } Middleton.

June Concessi licentiam recipiendi in Rosario.
R.D. Georgio Kindale, alias Brown, D.D.S.S. Lancashire.

* Mary Scoray of Ossett, in W. Riding, Yorkshire. (*English Catholic Non-Jurors*, p. 311.)

† The servant of Bishop Williams, O.P. (*Merry England*, Dec. 1887, p. 485, 488.)

‡ Had been received into the Church by F. Worthington himself, 15 Aug. of the previous year. (*Old English Catholic Missions*, p. 56.)

	Aug.	26.	Thomas Worthington, Junior		Lancastriæ.
	Nov.	12.	Concessi licentiam recipiendi in Rosario R.D.——Gow O.B.		Bedal, Yorkshire.
1737.	Feb.		Concessi licentiam recipiendi in Rosario. R.D. Henrico Georgio Heddon, S.S.		Huddleston.
	Feb.	10.	Item R.D. Christophoro Graddell S.S.		Shefield.
	March	25.	Item R.D. Johanni Elston, S.S. R.D. JoannesElston.		Roundhay. Yorkshire.
	Aug.	14.	Maria Martial.		Middleton.
1738.	Feb.	28.	Ann Hatherley.		Middleton.
	Aug.	25.	Francisca Thompson, Junior.		Middleton.
1738.	Oct.	6.	Catharina Simpson.		Sherborn
	Oct.	8.	Maria Martial, Junior.		Middleton.
	Oct.	29.	Carolus Ireland.	prope	Wakefield.
		30.	Anne Helme.	prope	Halifax.
	Nov.	1.	Thomas Briggs		Middleton.
		5.	Josue Smith. Joseph Milthorp		Driglington.
			Maria Constable.		Middleton.
		19.	John Stephens.		Pot-Ovens.*
	Dec.	25.	Catharine Oti.		Leeds. Hib.
			Rachael Vivers.		Hounslet.
1739.	Feb.	22.	Elizabeth Aspenel.		Roundhay.
			Jane Gles.		Leeds. Hib.
	Oct.	27.	Grace Elleker.		Roundhay.
1740.	Dec.	28.	Sacheveral Sanders.		Halifax.
1741.	Feb.	2.	Maria Helmes.	prope	Halifax.
	March	22.	Maria Bayswater.		Rothwell.
	Oct.	9.	Thomas Horbery.		Hounslet.
		12.	Thomas Beans.		Hounslet.
	Dec.	20.	Maria Bullock.		Hounslet.
		22.	Elizabeth Stephens.		Pot-Ovens.
		25.	Paulus Thorp. Mathias Martial		Middleton.
1742.	Feb.	2.	Johannes Martial.		Chapeltown.
	June	8.	Maria Helmes Junior.		Middleton.
		20.	Judith Wilson.		Hounslet Cos.
	Oct.	3.	Francesca Thompson, Junior.		Middleton.
		1.	Anna Roberts.		Rothwell.
			Catherine Realton.		Leeds.
	Dec.	11.	Marie Realton.		Leeds.
		12.	Thomas Hatterley.		Middleton.
		25.	Catherine Rigglesworth.		Rothwell.
1743.	Jan.	2.	Johannes Hatterley. Johanna Hatterley		Middleton.
		6.	Petrus Realton.		Leeds.

* Pot-ovens is another name for the village of Wrenthorpe, formerly Warrenthorpe, in Wakefield parish, Yorkshire.

	Aug.	14.	Elizabeth Hool.	Rothwell.
	Oct.	1.	Maria Baron. p.m.	
1744.	Jan.	16.	Joanna Robinson.	Leeds.
	Feb.	18.	Martha Taylor p.m.	Leeds.
	July	1.	Mathias Martial, Junior.	Middleton.
			Anna Ronson, Senior.	Middleton.
		2.	Johannes Jackson, p.m.	Leeds.
	Aug	12.	Martha Cox.	Leeds.
		23.	Maria Nordos, Senior. Maria Nordos, Junior.	Leeds.
	Oct.	14.	Johannes Rayson.	Middleton.
		28.	Maria Cassade.	Hounslet.
1745.	Jan.	18.	Anna Crekill.	Leeds.
	March	30.	Anna Vivers	Hounslet.
	Aug.	15.	Maria Restrick.	Hounslet.
	Dec.	20.	Hugo Rogers.	Hib: Leeds.

These following were received into the Rosary by R. D. Nailer, O.B. in Lancashire.

1723.	March	5.	Ellen Coupe. Margaret Coupe.	Walton.
			Ellen Turner. Alice Tasker.	Houghton.
	July	26.	Mrs Mary Clifton. Grace Toutel. Margaret Gerard. Betty Toutel.	Brindle.
	Aug.	10.	Laurenence Maska.	Elizabeth Maska.
	Aug.	15.	Isabell Eastham.	Cuerdale.
			Alice Oram.	Brindle.
	Sept.	21.	Richard Bank.	Walton.
	Oct.	6.	Alice Smith.	Samsbury.
1724.	March	15.	Mary Singleton.	Katon.
	Sept.	20.	Richard Helme.	Wood Plumpton.
	Nov.	2.	Elizabeth Worsick.	Brindle.
	Nov.	4.	Anne Shuttleworth.	Preston.
		12.	Jane Gordon.	Brindle.
	Dec.	6.	Thomas Wells.	Walton.
1725.	Aug.	15.	Ellen Livesay. Mary Croak.	Brindle.
1726.	Feb.	2.	Jane Bleasdel.	Ribleton.
			Anne Leigh.	Preston.
	March	18.	Elizabeth Foster.	Charnock.
			Elizabeth Bleasdel, Senior.	
			Elizabeth Bleasdel, Junior.	
	Aug.	20.	Alice Ownsworh.	Preston.
	Sept.	29.	Jane Cuerdon.	
	Dec.	7.	Jane Shuttleworth.	Preston.
1727.	Jan.	4.	Ann Williamson.	Preston.
1727.	April	16.	Helen Charnley. Ginet Charnley.	Preston.

Hæc nomina ex R. D. Gulielmo Nailer, O.B.

1746.	April	26.	Mary Steel, Junior.	Hounslet.
	May	28.	Marmaduke Steel.	p.m. Rothwell.
	June	30.	Hanna Wilson.	p.m. Leeds.

Sept. 29. Thomas Beans. Mary Brigs. Hunslet.
Nov. 7. Thomàs Boperal. Rondo.
Nov. 16. Martha Hatherley. Middleton.
23. Alisia Lester. Middleton.
April 2. Received in York Castle.
John Catton. David Souter, Senior.
Dorothy Souter, Senior. David Souter, Junior.
Dorothy Souter, Junior. Mary Souter.
Emerentiana Souter. Ann Souter.
Jane Souter. John Souter.
Catharine Souter. Elizabeth Souter.
1746. July 14. Luke Potts. York Castle.
17. Margaret Manson.
Aug. 1. Neddy Hill. Betty Hill. York Castle.
Aug. 15. James Rivelet and his wife.
Edward Hill, Junior. Elizabeth Hill, Junior.
Aug. 20. Fancy Ingel. Ann Clarck.
Mary Baker.

Hæc nomina A. R. P. Joanni Green, O.P.

1747. Feb. 28. Carolus Kains. Beeston.
March 17. Ann Ody. Leeds.
April 2. Francis Ronson. Middleton.
27. Ann Barwick. Leeds.
June 7. Hugo Rogers. Leeds Hib.
Oct. 4. Susanna Handestine. Joannes Bocock. Leeds.
11. John Concannon. Hib. Leeds.
18. Maria Philips. Leeds.
1748. Jan Alisia Cottam. p.m Bradford.
Feb. 8. Jacobus Rice. Lancas.
16. Jane Hollins. Bruxells.
June 22. Elizabeth Overans. Rothwell.
Oct. 2. Ann Clark. John Clark. Leeds.
Thomas Hewet. Middleton.
Nov. 1. Dorothy Smith. Leeds.
Dec. 1. Michael felix Davill. Newcastle.
7. Johannes Briton. Rebecca Briton. Leeds.
25. Elizabeth Wharton ad instancias Dmi Marsch.
Hister Key. Glass House.
James Toogood. Leeds.
1749. Oct. 28. Anna Turner. Leeds.
Nov. 1. Ruth Scoley. Leeds.
12. Marie Butler. prope. Bradford.
1750. At the desire of Mrs Elizabeth Hodshon on Whitsunday at York.
June 3. Anna Taskers, mater. Eliza Stokel.
Anna Taskers, filia. Marie Smith.
Eliza Taskers. Henerieta Teate.
Maria Gaskon *(Gascoigne?)* Maria Gray.
Anna Bell. Elizabeth Lenny.

Grace Russell. Maria Lenny.
Helena Russell. Mary Hinsby.
At the desire of Mrs Clifton at York.
Elizabeth Hindley. Elizabeth Atkinson.
Mary Scott. Ann Gray.
Elizabeth Scott.
June 22. Sera Inskep. Leeds.
1751. Maria Roberts. Leeds.
Feb. 2. At the desire of Mrs Elizabeth Hodshon.
Maria Lynch. West Indys.
Jane Wirecle Maria Mallard } York.
Ann Hokele
Feb. 8. At the desire of Mrs Elizabeth Hodshon at York.
Jane Lodge. Maria Handsby.
Maria Mallard. Maria Handsome.
Johannes Smith. Robertus Smith.
Gulielmus Smith. Maria Scott.
Thomas Gasking. Maria Bobdorson.
May 3. Nicholas Edwards Hib. fire Engin.
At the desire of Mrs Elizabeth Hodshon at York.
May 16. Ann Smith. Elena Stokehold.
July 1. Ann Owst. York.
Aug. 15. At the desire of Mrs Mary Davis at York.
Barbara Singleton. Mary Farril.
Frances Fitzwilliam. Susanna Humble.
Elizabeth Farren. Elizabeth Edmundson.
Jane Charge. Mary Butler.
Margaret Messenger. Ann Bowdon.
Catherine Waterton
26. Mary Barker. Norton by Stubs.

The following were received into the Rosary by Mr Maire of Durham S.S.

1750. Dec. 8. Mrs Mildred. Mrs Catharine Rookby. Durham.
1751. July 5. Mary Kent. Durham.

Concessi licentiam recipiendi in Rosarium R. P. Carolo Liddle S.J. Yarm.

At the desire of Mrs Elizabeth Hodshon at York.
Nov. 12. Mrs Frances Radcliffe.
Dec. 25. Mary Urquhard. Ann Reynoldson.
Ann Stokeheld. Catharine Witham.
1752. March 26. Thomas More Esquire.
May 7. Mrs Ann Dale at the request of Mrs M. Davis, York.
June 14. Item at the desire of the Ladys at York.
Mary Stotkel. Isabella Sturdy.
James Tasker. Catharine Wetherid.
Mary Tasker. Mary Tait.

Ad instantiam R. D. Gulielmi Naylor ordinis Sancti Benedicti per litteras datas Brindle May 31, 1751, concessi licentiam recipiendi in Rosariam omnibus suis patribus in partibus Angliæ Borialibus viz:

In Northumbria.	D. Gregorio Selby at Beaufoart.
	D. Joanni Berry at Swinburn Castle.
	D. Gulielmo Hutton at Hesleyside.
	D. Evan Eastham at Capiheaton.
In Cumberlandia.	D. Roberto Daniel at Whitehaven etc.
In Episcopatu Dunelmensi.	D. Antonio Raffa at Chester le Street.
	D. Gregorio Walker at Tanfield.
In Comitatu Eboracensi.	D. Benedicto Staare at Parlington.
	D. Hugone Frankland at Huddleston.
	D. Ambrosio Davis at York.
	D. Antonio Hutchinson at Stalham Lodge near Ilckley.
	D. Joanni Carlton at Plumbton.
	D. Joanni Fisher at Holme.
	D. Laurentio Hardesty at Everingham.
	D. Launcelot Newton at Gilling.
	D. Joanni Rigby with Lady Gascoigne.
	D. Jacobo le Grand at Larkland near Settle.
In Lancastria.	D. Edwardo Houghton at Low.
	D. Thoma Hutton at Much-Woolton.
	D. Benet Shuttleworth at Woolston.
	D. Jacobo Keye at Sefton.
	D. Jacobo Price at Standish.
	D. Bertram Bulmer at Ormskirk.
	D. Thoma Simpson at Walton.
	D. Gulielmo Naylor at Brindle.
In Chestria.	D. Gregorio Mackay at Alderley.

His omnibus concessi licentiam vel confirmavi antea datam quibusdam ex eis.

These following were received into the Rosary by R. D. Beda Potts O. Benedicti in comitatu Eboracensi and sent to me to be enrowled, viz:—

1738. April 8. Everingham, Yorkshire

Robert Usher.	Elizabeth Jackson.
Mary Usher.	Jane Hare.
Mary Richardson.	Robert Mell.
Frances Smith.	Mary Mell.
Alice Catton.	Ann Mell.
Mary Jackson.	Ann Thompson.
Mary Turner.	Mary Jackson.
Elizabeth Turner.	Margaret Mell.
Magdalene Smith.	Catharine Blackburn.

Hæc nomina ex R. D. Beda Potts.

1752. Nov. 21. William Hartloc. George Addison. } Halifax
Elizabeth Thekar.

1753. Feb. 2. John Stevens. Mary Stevens. } Pot-
James Stevens. Ann Stevens. } Ovens.
Mary Auther [*Audaer*? *] at the desire of Mrs Hodshon. York.
March 19. John Nordos.
1753. March 19. John Nordos.
April 22. At the desire of Mrs Davis at York.
Ann Brigan. Ann Champney.
Frances Stamford. Elizabeth Witham.
Ellen Sherret.
May 5. Elizabeth Humble.
20. At the desire of Mrs E. Hodshen, Mary Bishoprick, York.
June 10. Agnes Pinder. Burwallis.
Ann Simpson. Sutton.
Oct. 7. At the desire of Mrs Davis at York.
Mary Daly. Barbara Watterton.
Margaret Witham. Bridget Champney.
Thomas Bell. Mary Rither.
Catherin Pinder. Isabella Hardcastle.
Jane Pinder. Emerentiana Coney.
Mary Tasker. Mary Graham.
Elizabeth White.
1751.† Dec. 25. Ann Galley. Tong.
1753. Dec. 25. Ralph Humble. Birkley.
1754. June 2. Mickie Gate Bar, York.
Mrs Mary Bishoprick. Peter Wilson.
Ann Sanderson. Hannah Watson.
Mary Saxton. David Young.
Mary Young.
Oct. 6. Catherine Champney. Grace Williams. York.
1755. Oct. 5. At the desire of Mrs Davis, York.
Mary Conquest. Elizabeth Harsnap.
Ann Dalton. Elizabeth Urquhart.
Sarah Harsnap. Mary Smith.
Mary Dalton. Jane Hutton
1756. Dec. 25. At the desire of Mrs Davis, York.
Penelope Shirwood. Ann Wood.
Elizabeth Knowles. Dorothy Exton.
Bridget Tasker. Ann Darley.
Ann Saxton. Ann Hinderson.
Mary Pecket. Isabella Hinderson.
Ann Spencer. James Wood.
Ann Hinderson. Ann Wood.
Hannah Spencer. Mary Evers.

* Both Audaer and Audas were the names of well-known Catholic families in Yorkshire. (cf. *Catholic Record Society*, iv, p. 369, 381.)

† Here begins the handwriting of F. Antoninus Hutton, O.P.

Mary Wilks. Ann Gerard.
Winifred Silvertop. Mary Bradshaw.
Bridget Silvertop. Mary Elerker.
Eleanor Barnard. Elizabeth Gibson.
Dorothy Hutton.

1758. At the desire of Mrs Davis, the following were inscribed

Aug. 15. Mary Taylor. Mary Taylor, Junior.
Winefred Tuite. Mary Witham.
Winefred Witham. Frances Dalton.
Ann Owst. Elizabeth Ella.
Jane Selbye. Elizabeth Lamb.
Ann Warburton. Grace Hamilton.
Ann Coney. Mary Pridgin.
Ann Hill. Mary Consit.
Alathea Smith. Ann Consit.
Mary Saxton. John Bean.
John Welbank. Mary Consit, Junior.

1761. April 30. At the desire of Mrs Aspinal at York.
Anastasia Lawson. Mary Ravenscroft.
Catharine Lawson. Elizabeth Acton.
Mary Sherret. Francis Acton.
Elizabeth Langdale. Alice Bowdon.
Eleanora Sherlock. Charlotte Bowdon.
Mary Caley. Bridget Lynch.
Susanna Caley. Dorothy Dalton.
Catharine Tully. Eleanora Chadwick.
Sarah Worthington. Frances Green.
Sarah Fergus. Margaret Debord.
Ann Bolton. Agnes Francis.
Elizabeth Bean. Mary Hodgshon.
Elizabeth Adamson. Catherine Stokel.
Ann Saxton. Agnes Stokel.

1762. At the desire of Mrs Aspinall at York.
Ann Hales. Mary Chaffers.
Mary Humble. Elizabeth Chaffers.
Ann Emerson. Mary Morley.
Mary Perkin. Susanna Ravenscroft.
Catherine Caley. Francis Trafford.
Ann Metcalf. Francis Witham.
Mary Smith. Ann Green.
Elizabeth Stonehouse.

1763. At the desire of Mrs Aspinall at York.
Margaret Dun. Jane Elliot.
Mary Massey. Clementina Lynch.
Elizabeth Paxton. Mary Swinburne.
Mary Hornyold. Teresa Charlton.
Mary Smith. Dorothy Witham.
Mary Browne. Elizabeth Hankesworth.

			Mary Langdale.	Catherine Briggs.
1764.			At the desire of Mrs Maxwell at York.	
			Elizabeth Witham.	Elizabeth Gerard.
			Elizabeth Bero.	Elizabeth Charge.
			Elizabeth Smith.	Elizabeth Saxton.
			Christina Brown.	Jane Eyre.
			Mary Clifton.	Jane Smith.
			Mary Evers.	Catherine Darrell.
			Mary Wheatly.	Catherine Saxton.
			Mary Owst.	Ann Leetch.
			Ann Champney.	Ann Ridley.
			Ann Wheatley.	Ann Owst.
1765.	Sept.	22.	Mary Wharton. Margaret Wharton. Heber House.	
	Oct.	5.	(Rosary Sunday) at the desire of Mrs Maxwell, Mickle Gate Bar.	
			Mary Rookwood Gage.	Mary Broomhead.
			Mary Bellasis.	Helen Bertwish.
			Priscilla Bellasis.	Barbara Talbot.
			Bridget Hutton.	Frances Gordon.
			Margaret Leetch.	Elizabeth Wildsmith.
			Ann Cooban.	Elizabeth Calvert.
			Ann Clifton.	Elizabeth Dalton.
			Catharine Gerard.	Jane Dalton.
			Catharine Howard	Mary Heppleston.
1768.	Oct.	2.	(Rosary Sunday) at the desire of Mrs Maxwell, York.	
			Catherine Rouby.	Elizabeth Lawson.
			Ursula Brigham.	Mary Syne.
			Elizabeth Witham.	Barbara Townley.
			Mary Haggerston.	Barbara Darell.
			Mary Smythe.	Agnes Sharp.
			Catharine Hodshon.	Ann Ball.
			Catharine Talbot.	Margaret Hay.
			Christina Gordon.	Elizabeth Hunt.
			Teresa Champney.	Ann Hotcham.
			Sarah Reddit.	Margaret Dale.
1769.	Aug.	3.	R. D. Gulielmus Wynter.	Roundhay.
1770.	Oct.	7.	Ann Grant.	Leeds.
1772.	Sept.	8.	(Nativity B.V.M.) at the desire of Mrs Maxwell, Mickle Gate Bar.	
			Amelia Ferguson.	Catharine Salvin.
			Jannet Robertson.	Frances Gordon.
			William Cottam.	Catharine Gordon.
			Mary Cottam.	Ann Gordon.
			Jane Cottam.	Mary Bean.
			Ann Blakey.	Francis Chicken.
			Rachel Winterbury.	Elizabeth Coyney.
			Susanna Humble.	Elinor Slater.

			Jane Gibbon.	Mary Hutchinson.
			Winifride Jones.	George Hill.
			Winifride Champney.	Edward Hill.
			Ann Hodgson.	Elizabeth Hill.
			Ann Worswick.	Elizabeth Hill.
			Ann Taylor.	Elinor Canvane.
1772.	Sept.	8.	Bridget Dalton.	Ann Selbye.
			John Dixon, Pater.	Ann Dixon, Mater.
			John Dixon, Filius.	Ann Dixon, filia.
			Hannah Beleby.	Mary Daile.
1773.	Aug.	15.	Miss Betzy Humble.	Middleton.
			Miss Anne Teresia Humble.	Birkley.
	Oct.	3.	Rosary Sunday at the desire of Mrs Maxwell, York.	
			Teresa Davis.	Teresa Talbot.
			Ann Robinson.	Ann Talbot.
			Ann Cliffe.	Mary Jump.
			Mary Westby.	Margaret Robertson.
			Frances Eastwood.	
	Oct.	8.	At the request of Mrs Elizabeth Hodshon, York.	
			Teresa Allason.	Mary Horberry.
			Mary Fletcher.	Apud me.
	Oct.	15.	Mistress Ann Smith.	Haigh-side.
1775.	Aug.	15.	Margaret Humble.	Catharine FitzGerald.
			Helen Fletcher.	Helen FitzGerald.
			Helen Caley.	Constantia Caley.
			Sarah Gillow.	Elizabeth Smith.
			Barbara Askew.	Elizabeth Smilter.
			Frances Seel.	Mary Smilter.
			Jane Cottam.	Ann Cottam.
			Ann Sherwood.	Elizabeth Calvert.
			Jane Williamson.	Apud me.
	Aug.	22	Dorothy Bradford.	
	Nov.	1.	Elizabeth Cliffe.	Jane Charlton. Mickle Gate Bar.
	Dec.	25.	Margaret Bentats. Catharine Moody.	Winefred Charlton } York.
1776.	June	29.	Margaret Seel.	York.
	Aug.	15.	Mary Young.	Ann Atkinson. York.
			Mary Galley.	Sudwick.
			At the desire of Mrs Maxwell, York.	
			Helen Houghton.	Ann Farquharson.
			Mary Collingwood.	Grace Sharp.
	Oct.	5.	Mary Bidenham.	Mary French.
			Agnes Gillow.	Mary Allen.
			Ann Young.	Esther Allen.
			Margaret Farquharson.	Ann Unsworth.
			Elenor Kirwan.	Alice Unsworth.
1779.	Oct.	3.	Rosary Sunday at the desire of Mrs Maxwell, Mickle-Gate-Bar.	

Martha French. Alice Seel.
Elizabeth Slade. Elizabeth Gardon.
Ann Parker. Ann Langley.
Mary Henry. Catharine Langley.
Mary Watt. Alice Talbot.
Francis Mathew. Henrietta Hinde.
Francis Tempest.

1779. Oct. 3. Joseph Holdforth. Leeds.

1780. Oct. 1. Rosary Sunday at the desire of Mrs Maxwell, York.

Elizabeth Sanderson. Mary Lee.
Elizabeth Unsworth. Mary Coyney.
Elizabeth Hodgshon. Mary Mountain.
Elizabeth Nason. Mary Wilkinson.
Elizabeth Gray. Mary Scoley.
Elizabeth Mountain. Mary Marshall.
Elizabeth Brown. Mary Gage,
Elizabeth Birdsall. Ann Allen.
Ann Knight. Ann Farall.
Ann Jefferson. Frances Bedingford.
Ann Priestman. Frances Gage.
Ann Johnson. Frances Walker.
Ann Brown. Sarah Roche.
Thomas Hill. Clementina Scroope.
Harriot Cliffe. Bridget Ferrall.
Hellen Hunt. Alice Lee.
Winefred Allen. Christina Brown.
Winefred Bourgess.

1781. Oct. 7. Rosary Sunday at the desire of Mrs Maxwell, Mickle-Gate-Bar.

Mary Young. Jane French.
Mary French. Jane Gordon.
Margaret Gordon. Esther Whetingdale.
Margaret Gerard. Anestasia Lawson.
Agnes Ball. Elizabeth Lawson.
Frances Barker. Elizabeth Knight,
Bridget Ansell. Elizabeth Blackledge.
Mary Lodge. Elizabeth Lomax.
Ann Brown. Elizabeth Wilcock.

1782. March 31. being Easter Sunday that year Mrs Carpfanger, Stourton Lodge.

Oct. 6. Rosary Sunday at the desire of Mrs Maxwell, York.

Mary Ward. Ann Meynell.
Mary Brown. Ann Riddell.
Mary Hardwick. Ann Walker.
Mary Richmond. Sophia Birdsall.
Elenor Mountain. Elizabeth Hanson.
Martha Scoley. Elizabeth Gerard.
Martha Hanson. Elizabeth Ashmall.
Judith Warren Elizabeth French.

Jane Allenson. Constantia Dalton.
Catharine Maynell. Isabella Salvin.
Andrew Gordon. Isabella Chalmers.
Margaret Talbot. Bridget Unsworth.
Alice Morgan. Alicc Unsworth.
Alice Gillow.

1783. May 24. Mary Winterburn. Jane Day.
Mickle-Gate-Bar.

*1784. Aug. 15. At the desire of the Ladies of Mickle-Gate-Bar, York.

Mary Ashmall. Mary Ann Ball.
Mary Weld. Martha Hippisley.
Mary Savage. Martha Mountain.
Mary Gerard. Teresa Hippesley.
Mary Unsworth. Elizabeth Young.
Mary Martin. Elizabeth Benson.
Mary Holdforth. Ann Carpere.
Ann Heatby. Ann Slayter.
Ann Cater. Ann Iveson.
Ann Hardwick. Ann Bulmer.
Ann Andear. Ann Darnell.
Monica Stapleton. Sophia Clifton.
Barbara Langley. Sarah Ashmall.
Sarah Smith. Helen Bedingfield.
Hannah Ryan. Helen Lawless.
Pamela Busby. Jane Gillow.
Jane Champney. Jane Day.
Isabella Darnell. Juliana Weld.
Isabella Atkinson. Elizabeth Scot.

Oct. 3. Rosary Sunday Mrs Pottgeisser.

†1787. Oct. 2. Mickle-Gate-Bar, York.

Isabella Bedingfield. Eleonora Lawless.
Ann Warren. Ann Lawless.
Ann Warburton. Ann Bird.
Bridget Langdale. Mary Gabb.
Jane Ferguson. Sarah Bray.
Elizabeth Gibson. Mary Silvertop.
William Headley. Mary Bullen.
Martha Headley. Mary Allen.
Jane Horsman. Elizabeth Snow.

1786. Aug. 15. Ann Harrison.
Middleton.

Oct. 1. Mary Hill. Frances Riveley.
Mary Rose. Frances Warburton.
Mary Jefferson. Ann Burges.
Mary Atkinson. Ann Rowes.
Elizabeth Steed. Rachel Rowes.
Catharine French. Helen Bushell.

* This is in the handwriting of F. Edward Leadbitter, O.P.

† Here begins the handwriting of F. Ambrose Gage, O.P.

		Jane Mountain.	Jannet Furniss.
		Margaret Smith.	Margaret Wharton.
		Sarah Lynch.	
1787. Oct.	6.	Mickle-Gate-Bar, York.	
		Mary Gledhall.	Teresa Wharton.
		Mary Moore.	Teresa Iveson.
		Mary Foggatt.	Margaret Iveson.
		Mary Ann Chew.	Esther Unsworth.
		Mary Bushell.	Dorothy Ball.
		Mary Gainsford.	Charlotte de Gandasequi.
		Elizabeth Gladhall.	Elizabeth Handby.
		Catharine French.	Ann Bushell.
		Ann Cockshott.	Anna Maria Clarkson.
1788. Oct.	5.	Anna Stoker.	Elizabeth Ashton.
		Ann Ashton.	Elizabeth Unston.
		Ann Blackoe.	Elizabeth Gibson.
		Ann Buckle.	Mary Cornforth.
		Ann Hall.	Mary Reilly.
		Ann Bramley.	Rachel Dawson.
		Ann Boland.	Henriette Clarkson.
		Ann Mountain.	Catharine Penswick.
		Margaret Clint.	Catharine Hutton.
		Margaret Mops.	Catharine Lidle.
		Frances Reynolds.	Jane Brown.
		Elizabeth Horner.	Jane Fawbert.
		Mary Gibson.	
1789. Oct.	4.	Mickle-Gate-Bar, York.	
		Mary Shaw.	Sarah Ball.
		Mary Bowyer.	Alice Ball.
		Mary Atkinson.	Ann Gibson.
		Mary Rose.	Ann Lunt.
		Mary Hopps.	Ann Furniss.
		Mary Dalton.	Ann de la Haye.
		Jane Kirkham.	Ann Liddle.
		Jane Gibson.	Hannah Dawson.
		Jane Snow.	Catharine Winter.
		Elizabeth Talbot.	Catharine Walton.
		Elizabeth Picket.	Catharine Thorpe.
		Winefred Nicholson.	Lucy Dalton.
		Winefred Steel.	Elizabeth Boland.
*1794. Oct.	30.	Micklegate Bar, York.	
		Jane Varley.	Frances Howard.
		Mary Liddle.	Sarah Hick.
		Christina Smith.	Robert Hewinson.
		Frances Taylor.	Mary Hobson.
		Mary de Strora.	Elizabeth Cockshott.
		Helen Caley.	Ann Booth.

* Here begins the handwriting of F. Albert Underhill, O.P.

Elizabeth Curr. Mary Werswick.
Barbara Warmsley. Margaret Wharton.
Ann Carter. Winifred Iveson.
Mary Carpue. Harriet Fox.
Elizabeth Morrogh. Mary Atkins.
Mary Yates.

1795. Leeds Blackwell Handy. John Sowerby.
Elizabeth Bushby. Miss Catharine Holdforth.
Miss Ann Humble. Miss Elizabeth Holdforth.
Miss Mary Tipping. Miss Dorothy Holdforth.
Miss Jane Tipping. Joseph Barraclough.
James Holdforth.

1796. York Nunnery. Mary Sowry. Mary Shires.
Mary Robinson. Mary Aspinall.
Hannah Goodman. Catharine Roe.
Jane Wharram. Mary Winter.
Mary Carpue. Ann Winter.
Mary O'Connor. Ann Denie.
Mary Costello. Ann Morrison.
Elizabeth Hobson. Ann Reavely.
Elizabeth Blundell. Ann Kaye.
Elizabeth Walton. Ann Gwillim.
Elizabeth Sandeman. Ann Fox.
Catharine Eyre. Jane Graham.
Catharine Jones. Jane Porter.
Catharine Newton. Josephina Costello.
Catharine Winter. Isabella M'Donell.
Mary Smith. Ann Christian.
Rose Byrne. Rosetta O'Reilly.
Leonile Beauregard. Frances Farmin.
Margaret Kaye. Catharine Knight.

1797. Mary Adamson. Miss Elizabeth Tipping. Leeds.
Margaret Basto. Mary Burkenshire. } Wetherley.
Martha Basto.

Knaresboro'. Margaret Cass. Elizabeth Marshall.
Jane Cass. Ann Pownder.
Ann Cass. Ann Douthwaite.
Dorothy Cass. Elizabeth Hornby.
Ann Robinson. Ann Powden, Junior.
Mary Spink. Winifred Lawson.
Ellen Dickinson of Spofford.

The names of the foregoing persons of Westherby, Knaresboro', and of Spofford were delivered to me (A.V.) by the Rev. Mr Appleton of Folifoot, 23rd May.

4th June being Whitsunday Michael Quin. }
Thomas Willie. } Leeds.
Elizabeth Willie. }

On the same day at the desire of Mrs Rouby, Superior of York Nunnery.

Alice Talbot. Elizabeth Smith.
Mary Chadwick.

6th June being Whitsun. Tuesday, York Nunnery.

Margaret Goodin. Helen Hansom.
Helen Audaer. Catharine Chasly.
Alice Clayton. Mary Seddal.
Jane Smith. Elizabeth Hargit.
Alice Duck. Mary Aspinal.

June 9th being Whitsun. Friday. Luke Ward. York Nunnery.

June 15th being Corpus Christi Louis Marie Josephine Gouyon Beaufort.

Elizabeth Bargh. Mary Saul.

Sept. 29. Grace Anderson. Mary Carpue.
Elizabeth Scanlen. Elizabeth Brown.
Catharine Worthy. Margaret Buckle.
Esmy Corr. Mary Gwillim.

Sept. 29. York Nunnery. Elizabeth Livington.
Teresa Young.
Harriet Reave.
Mary Byers.
Charlotte Barker.
Elizabeth O'Shea.
Mary Wake.
Margaret Wharton.

Christmas Day. Maria Studder.
Hannah Houlinshire.
Mary Consit.
Mary Wheelhouse.
} The Rev. Mr Appleton.

1798. Rosary Sunday at the request of Mrs Ruby of York Nunnery.

Mary Curr. Mary Gogin.
Mary O'Brien. Mary Wiseman.
Mary Blundell. Mary Champhey.
Mary Saul.
Blanche Hobson. Julia McCarthy.
Helen Wiseman. Catharine Stanley.
Frances Blundell. Jane Lacey.
Elizabeth O'Shea. Margaret Young.
Honble. Paulina and Lucy Southwell. Teresa Young.
Grace Anderson. Mrs Catharine McDonald.
Hellen Kerby. Elizabeth Pyle.
Agnes Aspinal. Catharine Worthy.
Ann Fisher.

1799. Rosary Sunday 6th Oct. Miss Sarah Humble.

1800. Feb. 8. Thomas Adamson.
At the request of Mrs Ruby, Superior of Nuns at York.

Mary Robertson. Sophy Newton.
Angelique Ponfilly. Ann Hanison.
Elizabeth Harrison. Elizabeth Harrison.
Joseph Harrison. Salvador Gordon.
Catharine Morrisey. Mary Christian.
Frances Winter. Celide Mannay.
Cecilia Addis. Ann Laing.
Mary Knight. Elizabeth Knight.
Helena Core. Mary Richardson.
Ann Core. Frances Claydon.
Mary Huison. Ann Aspinal.
Margaret Hoey. Elizabeth Smith.
Margaret Gibson. Elizabeth Siddal.
Ann Smith. Catharine Siddal.
Mary Johnson. Mary Wilson.
Ann Roe. Cicilia Hogart.
Ann Hogart. George Hogart.
Michael Snowden. Elizabeth Hodkinson.
Ann Going.

1803. Rosary Sunday, Leeds William Hoyle Margaret Chartterton.
Elizabeth Hoyle. Ann Barker.
Maria Mountain. Ann Varley.
Alice Heptenstall. Mary Barker.
Mary Heptenstall.

Eliza Weld. Margaret Morta.
Anna Maria Ball. Ann Cook.
M. Connolly. Jane Horseman.
Bartholomew Hoy. Ann Stocker.
Ann Richardson. Mary Moulds.
M. Darnley. Margaret Valentine.
Harr. Marshall. Margaret Modester.
Helen Gallen. Helen Blundell.
Isabella Ball. Ann Burges.
Mary Robertson. Mary Anderson.
Ann Smith. El. Reavely.
Eleanor Corr. Xaveria Glendouwyn.
Anna Maria Kelly. Ismene Glendouwyn.
Eliz. Cleaseby. Mich. Ellis, Senior.
Catherine Roberts. Mich. Ellis, Junior.
Elizabeth Rigg. Jane Snell.
Anne Witham. Teresa Curr.
Mary Housman. Mary Wilson.
Eliza Christian. Sara Hobson.
Sara Metcalfe. Teresa Michotte.
Caroline Deverish. Ann Pratt.
Mary Craggs. Dorothy Simpson.
Catharine Dodd. Mary Ashurst.
Martha Lamb. M. Ann Langley.
Anne Maria Hevy. Elizabeth Hartley.

Ann Cromvleholme. Ann Anderson.
Rosita Gordon. Eliza Tomkinson.
Mary Coyney. Catherine Stapleton.
Sara French. Margaret Leigh.
Helen Ashurst. Anna Maria Dobson.
Ann Nelson. Aloysia Addis.
Margaret Gordon. Cornelius Boardman.
Francis Porter. Helen Boardman.
Mary Kiernan. Christina Gordon.
Nicholas Gilbert. Mary Beaufort.
Ann Colbeck. James Swift.
Elizabeth Swift. Elizabeth Bell.
Rose Dunn. Clare Weld.
Ann Dunn. M. Wilkinson.
Mary Wilson. Elizabeth Robinson.
Mary Mitchell. Mary Kaseby.
Susan Hodchinson. Sophy Devenish.
Elizabeth Bouney.

1805. Dec. 1. Dorothy Grimstone. Jane Body. Helen Dickson. Alice Holkerself. } Broughton Hall.

Dec. 13. Ann Norris. Mary Emmerson. Leeds
Dorothy Eccles. Margaret Emmerson.
Annabella Porrit. Sarah Foster.
Sarah Wincop. Helen Norris.
Catharine Heptenstall. Frances Atkinson.
Jane Heptenstall. Catharine & Mary Cadogan.
Mary Ann Thornton. John Daniel.
Harriot Strodder. Mary Sowerby.
Charlotte Lawrence. Charlotte Alldred.
Ann Wincop. Elizabeth Chatterton.
William Wincop.

1806. Sept. 16. Mary Shepherd. Margaret Norris. Margaret Kemp. } of Broughton Congregation.

Mary Ann Champney. Ann Hey. Broughton.

1807. March 25. Peter Middleton. Isabella Glover. Broughton.

May Rachael Norris. Helen Walmesley.

1807. Carmelite Nuns near Durham.

Mary Ann Bernard of S. Theresa.
Euphrasia Maria of the Holy Angels.
Philippine of S. Teresa.
Mary Bernard of S. Joseph.
Mary Gertrude of the heart of Mary.
Teresa Maria of divine Providence.
Ann Teresa of Mount Carmel.
Mary Bridget of the Sacred Passion.

Mary Joseph of the Infant Jesus.
Mary Catharine of the Blessed Sacrament.
Teresa of Jesus.
Benedicta Teresa of our Blessed Lady.
Mary Martha of Jesus.
Alice Heyhurst.

1808. From the Carmelite nuns near Durham.
Mary Teresa of the mercies of God.
Anthony Corry.
Frances Xaveria of the Mother of God.
Mary Howard.
Mary Ann Bennet. Catharine Jeub.
Charles Tempest.

1809. Sept. 1. Catharine Worth. Mary Gerard. Grace Humble. Hannah Norton. } Leeds Congregation.

Oct. 1. Francis Middleton of Myddleton Lodge.
Catharine Prendergast. Leeds.
William Middleton of Mydleton Lodge. Catharine Goss.
Honourable Hugh Clifford. Stonyhirst.

1810. Sept. 1. Clara Wallis. York.
Valentine Prendergast. Mary Prendergast. John Prendergast. Margaret Prendergast. } Leeds.
John Stoner. Richard Ashurst. York.
Elizabeth Lock. Leeds.

Rosary Sunday Rosetta O'Reilly. Susanna Marshall. Ann Marshall. } York.
Mary Peacock. Isabella Cadogan. Leeds.
Ann Peacock. Mathew Tolson.
Jeremiah Barraclough. John Tolson.
Thomas Mullein. James Mac-Guin.
Henry Burkby. Samuel Glover.
John Sowerby.

Nov. 21. Mary Lee. York.

Dec. 4. Clarinda O'Reilly. Ellen O'Reilly.
Elizabeth Bray. Cecilia Coleman.
Emma Bray. Sarah Brown.
Helen Consitt.

1811. Feb. 2. Young Ladies of the Bar School.
Jane Fitzpatrick. Mary Davies.
Helen Turner. Mary Kyle.
Catharine Dick. Mary Dolores Anquibel.
Elizabeth Dowell. Mary Clark.
Frances Gibson. Henrietta Brown.
Emma Smythe. Alicia Browne.
Ann Latham. Ann Greenough.

Margaret O'Connor. Julia Browne.
Henrietta Curr. Mary Smith.
Ann Saul. Margaret Gibson.
Elizabeth Hooker.

1812. June 5. Young Ladies of the Bar School, York taken into the Rosary.

Champney. Tasker.
Fitzpatrick. Marshall.
Crombleholme. Hall.
Rogerson. Chamley.
Ann Brown. Eliza Simpson.
Coleman. Pochaine.
Byrne. Carthan.
Gradwell. McCarthy.
Mary Wilson. Trapps.
Kelly. H. Taylor.
Fitzwilliams. Lewis.
Coyney. Parry.
O. Taylor. Ashton.
O'Reilly. Eliza Wilson.
Smelter. L. Gibson.
M.Gibson. Langdale.
Tempest.

Sr. Sophia Teresa Himes for Rosaries both of the Name of Jesus, and of the Blessed Virgin.

" July 21. Henry Oxley. Joseph Seddon. Leeds.
John Baptist Gillis. Ricnard Procter.
Rosoland Grimshaw. Samuel Procter.
John Baines. Robert Adamson.
Elizabeth Reynolds. Mary Anderson.
John Clarke. Elizabeth Cooper.

" Oct. 4. Young Ladies at Heath Hall.

Marie Seton. Marie Leigh.
Marie Hutton. Ann Lynch.
Martha Hutton. Emelie Rapling.
Hannah Hutton. Josephine Monteiro.
Elizabeth Dowdwell. Emelie Monteiro.
Agnes Waterton. Catharine Waddell.
Matilda Waterton. Anne Waddell.
Henriette D'Alton. Ann Bould.
Susanne Winsor. Sarah Laver de la Nativité.
Catharine Cassin. Pauline Byrne.
Marie Pockrin. Elizabeth Byrne.
Elizabeth Dixon.

1813. July 2. Mary Bowden. Laura Mansabié. Heath.
Elizabeth Bowden. Catharine Lynch.
Elizabeth Dane. Martha Chambers.
Sarah Anslow.

NO. V

THE CATHOLIC REGISTERS OF CAPHEATON KIRKWHELPINGTON, NORTHUMBERLAND, A CHAPLAINCY OF THE SWINBURNES, 1769-85.

CONTRIBUTED BY CARLISLE J. S. SPEDDING.

HISTORICAL NOTES BY JAMES RAE BATERDEN.

THE Capheaton branch of the ancient Northumbrian family of Swinburne dates from 1274, when Alan de Swinburne purchased the estate from the Fenwicks. Alan being in holy orders had no issue and in 1284 he gave Capheaton to his brother Sir William de Swinburne in exchange for Chollerton on the North Tyne, where Swinburne Castle is situate.

The earliest chaplain we can trace to Capheaton is Dom Ralph Cuthbert Farnworth, O.S.B. He was one of the family of that name who lived at Runshaw Hall in the parish of Leyland, Lancs. Born in 1680, professed at St Lawrence, Dieulward in Lorraine in 1701, and afterwards went to St Gregory's, Douai; his brother John Jerome was also a Benedictine. Ralph Cuthbert was on the mission at Wetherby, Yorks., in 1726 and came to Capheaton in 1727. He became President-General in 1741 and so continued till 1753, about which time he resigned the chaplaincy at Capheaton, where he meanwhile had had assistants from about 1743. He died at Paris on New Year's Day, 1754. Fr. Farnworth's first assistant at Capheaton was—

Dom John Benedict Simpson, O.S.B., *alias* Daniel, who would be at Capheaton along with Fr. Farnworth. Fr. J. B. Simpson left in 1747 and afterwards spent twenty-two years till 1769 at Weston in Bucks. Finally in 1769 he became Vicar of the nuns at Cambrai, and died there 10th July 1775. He was succeeded by—

Dom Hugh Frankland, O.S.B., a native of York, professed at St Gregory's, Douai, in 1700 and ordained in 1705. He was sub-Prior of St Edmund in Paris in 1708, returned to St Gregory in 1709. He went to Yorkshire in 1713, and was at Middleton Lodge, close to Ilkley, for 26 years, 1719-1745, came to Capheaton in 1745, and probably stayed there until 1748 when he went to Huddleston Hall, a few miles east of Leeds, where he died 16th May 1755.

Dom John Placid Rigby, O.S.B., succeeded Fr. Frankland, and received faculties from Bishop Dicconson 5th March 1748-9. The Bishop elsewhere calls him John Daniel Rigby, so he was possibly a relation of Fr. J. B. Simpson, *alias* Daniel, as likewise of his successor, Dom Robert Daniel. He was a native of Lancashire, professed in 1725 at Dieulward, of which he became sub-Prior, was at Hanley, Co. Worcester, in 1736, and came north in 1746. When he left Capheaton in 1750 he became chaplain to Lady Gascoigne, subsequently, about 1755, returned to the south and died at Dieulward in 1764.

Dom Robert Daniel, O.S.B., succeeded Fr. Rigby in 1750. He was born at Whittingham, co. Lancaster, and was also professed at Dieulward in 1735, and coming to the mission in the north was stationed at Capheaton for part of the years 1750-1. He then removed to Whitehaven, thence to Birtley, co. Durham, in 1759, where he remained until his death 12th Sept. 1781. His successor at Capheaton was—

Dom Evans Anselm Eastham, O.S.B., a native of Walton-le-Dale, Lancs., an alumnus of St Gregory, Douai, professed at St Edmunds in 1731. His first mission was Whitehaven in 1750, which he exchanged with Fr. Daniel in the early part of 1751 for Capheaton, where he remained until 1754. He then went to Coughton in Warwickshire, thence to Low Strangeways, Lancs.; finally retired to St Edmund, Paris, in 1773, and died at La Celle 13th May 1774.

Dom Peter Dunstan Holderness, O.S.B., professed at St Lawrence, Dieulward, in 1741, appears to have come to Capheaton as assistant to Fr. Farnworth or Fr. Eastham in 1753, and remained here for 20 years, until probably about the middle of 1773. From Capheaton Fr. Holderness returned to his abbey at Dieulward, where he held the office of Prior until his death on 25th June 1782. Capheaton seems to have been his only mission. It was during the chaplaincy of Fr. Holderness that the new chapel at Capheaton was opened and the Register commenced.

In the first Register, a small book about 5 inches by 4 inches, of 40 leaves, which together with its successor is preserved at Swinburne Castle by Mr Cuthbert D. G. Riddell, there is a note as follows, 'This Chapel at Capheaton had prayers in it for the first time, St Ursula's day, ye 21 Oct. 1759.' 'Prayers' was the usual term for service, 'Mass' was a word rarely or ever used until well into the 19th century. The first Register runs from 24th Feb. 1760 to 25th Feb. 1774; it is apparently all in one handwriting, possibly that of Fr. Holderness, or more probably a member of the household, except the last two entries. These are apparently in a different hand, and the phraseology is somewhat different, and they were probably written, as one of them is signed by J. Naylor, Dom John Ambrose Naylor, O.S.B., who spent most of his life at Biddleston Hall, 1767 till his death there in 1821. But he was evidently staying at Capheaton for a short time, probably just after Fr. Holderness left. It could scarcely have been a casual visit, for these entries, one on 20th Nov. 1773 which is signed, and the other on 25th Feb. 1774 which is not signed, were baptisms which took place the day after birth. The book contains particulars of 48 baptisms, it also contains the names of candidates at two confirmations, one on 26th May 1764 by Dr Francis Petre, called 'Ld. Bishop Peters' in the book, when the name of Thomas Swinburne, Junr., appears in the list; the other on 'June ye 10th 1773,' by 'ye R. Bishop Walton' when 61 were confirmed, and amongst them four sons and one daughter, children of Sir Edward the 5th Bart. and Christina Dillon. It is somewhat curious that the eldest of these, John the future 6th Bart., was only 11 years of age, whilst Christina the youngest was only 5 years of age, when confirmed.

The second Register, an ordinary copy book of 18 pages, is inscribed, 'Baptized, Capheaton 1774,' and commences on 19th April that year, probably by Fr. Thomas Adrian Gurnal, O.S.B. This again is apparently all in one handwriting throughout, and the only signature is that in a very shaky hand of 'And. Riding,' which curiously enough is put three times to the last baptismal entry in the book, 8th June 1784. Whether this is Fr. Ryding's own signature is doubtful, as it is more like that of a very old man than of one in his 32nd year, but he came here about the time that the entry was made. This book contains particulars of one marriage, in May 1782, a confirmation by Dr Matthew Gibson in 1783, and a list of deaths commencing in 1774 and continuing down to June 1785. It would be about the middle period covered by these registers when the lady, who told the circumstance to the late Dr Charlton of Newcastle, used to be posted when a girl at the north windows of the hall, whilst Mass was being said, to give warning of strangers. There are two priest's hiding places in Capheaton Hall.

Dom Thomas Adrian Gurnal, O.S.B., born in London in 1742 and ordained in 1767 at Lambspring, succeeded Fr. Holderness at Capheaton in 1774, and he evidently started the second Register. He was only at Capheaton a short time, as he went to Beaufront the following year, and afterwards to Hesleyside. He retired to Everingham, the Constables' seat in Yorkshire, in 1781, and spent there the last 30 years of his life, dying 5th Jan. 1811.

Dom Alexander Benedict Catterall, O.S.B., succeeded him at Capheaton. Fr. Catterall was also a Lancashire man, born in 1724 and professed at St Edmund's in 1743. He was on the mission at Brandsby, Yorks., 1761-64, Whitehaven 1764-74, and in the latter year came to Capheaton where he remained until 1783. He then went as confessor to the nuns at Paris where he remained till his death 31st July 1791. A Dominican priest with the same surname, probably a relative, served Stonecroft, Northumberland, for many years a few decades earlier.

The last priest at Capheaton appears to have been Dom Andrew Bernard Ryding, O.S.B., born at Wigan in 1752, professed at St Gregory, and ordained in 1776. This appears to have been his first mission, and the Benedictine records place him here 1783-87. He then went to Warwick Bridge near Carlisle, was afterwards at Holme Hall, Lord Stourton's place in Yorkshire, Hindley in Lancs., 1792-97, back again to Warwick Bridge in the latter year, and in this pleasant locality he resided for 37 years, retiring in 1834 to Ampleforth, where he died 26th Sept 1841.

Sir Edward Swinburne died at Capheaton in 1786 and he was the last head of the family who adhered to the old faith, as his eldest son Sir John, 6th Bart. (who died so lately as 1860 at the patriarchal age of 98) became M.P. for Launceston in 1788 and High Sheriff of Northumberland in 1799, positions which could not be held by Catholics of that period. So the death of Sir Edward Swinburne practically coincides with the close of the Catholic mission at Capheaton, which had been in existence during the larger part of the 18th century, and probably earlier, and so far as our records shew was, like several adjoining missions, served wholly by members of the Benedictine Order.

J. R. B.

[*On Cover*].

This Ch. . . . . . . Capheaton had pray . . .
in it the first time St Ursula's Day
ye 21 Octo^r^
1759.

BAPTISMS

[1760]

1. Joseph Atkinson's Daughter Mary was baptiz'd here Feb^ry^ 24 1760. Willm Ekenside & Jane Urron Sponsors.

[1761]

2. John Dobson's Daughter Mary was baptiz'd here Jan^ry^ 20th 1761. John Cook Mary Brown Sponsores.

3. Matt^w^ Liddle's Daughter Mary was baptiz'd here Feb^ry^ 6th 1761. John Brown Mary Nevils Sponsores.

4. John Errington's Daughter Ann was baptiz'd here Septr 18th 1761. John Cook & Mary Brown Sponsores.

5. Joseph Atkinson's Son John was baptiz'd here Octr ye 6th 1761. John Atkinson & Ann Carrick Sponsores.

6. Thomas Dunn's Son Joseph was Baptiz'd here Novem^r^ ye 27th 1761. John Errington Mary Mawsen Sponsores.

[1762]

7. John Carrick's daughter Isabell was baptiz'd here April 21st 1762. John Brown Mary Nevils Sponsores.

8. John Dobson's Daughter Catharine was baptiz'd here Septr 25 1762. John Errington Catharine Brown Sponsores.

8. Walter Mahun's Daughter Mary was baptiz'd here Novemb^r^ 28 1762. Thos Wilthue & Mary Brown Sponsors.

[1763]

9. John Brown's Dr Hannah was baptiz'd here April ye 14th 1763. Thos & Mary Bron Sponsors. She died ye next Day.

10. Joseph Atkinson's Daughter Eleanora was Baptiz'd Septr 26 1763. John Miller & Mary Wilthue Sponsors.

[1764]

11. John Carrick's son Richard was baptiz'd here January ye 15th 1764. John Wilthue Junior & Margarite Hunter Sponsors.

12. John Brown's Daughter Ann was baptiz'd here March ye 26 1764. Mr Willm Kissop and Mrs M. Nevils Sponsors.

13. Robt Tomblin's Daughter Lucia was baptiz'd here June ye 1st 1764. John Tomblin Jun. & M. Wilthue Sponsors.

14. John Dobson's Son Patrick was baptiz'd here Octo^r^ 21 1764. Thos. Brown & Sarah Brown Sponsores.

[1765]

15. Thos Dunn's Daughter Hellen was Baptiz'd here Jan^ry^ ye 13 1765. John Dunn & Ann Carrick Sponsors.

16. Joh^{s} Atkinson's Son Joseph was Baptiz'd July ye 11st 1765. Parce Brown & Frances Miller Sponsors.

17. Sr^{r} Edward's Son Edward was Born at Capheaton Septr ye 3rd 1765 & was Baptiz'd on the 4th D^{o} John Brown & Mrs Charlton pro Sponsors.

[1766]

18. John Errington's Daughter Catharine was born January ye 6th 1766 & was baptiz'd the same Day. Thomas Wilthue & Ann Wilthue Sponsors.

19. John Carrick's Daughter Mary was born March ye 1^{s} 1766 and baptiz'd here the same Day. Ralph Sanderson pro quo Joseph Wilthue & Isabell Dikison Sponsors.

20. John Brown's Daughter Ellen was born at Capheaton Septr ye 15th 1766 & was baptiz'd here Septr ye 16th 1766. Thos Brown & Miss Ellen Swinburne Sponsors.

21. Robt Tomblin's Daughter Mary was born here Sept. ye 18th 1766 & was baptiz'd here ye same Day John Dunn & Ann Carrick pro Sponsors.

[1767]

22. Sir Edward Swinburne's Son Thomas was born at Capheaton January ye 23 1767 & was baptiz'd here ye same Day Mrs Charlton & John Brown pro Sponsors.

23. John Errington's Daughter Catharine was born at Capheaton March ye 7th & was baptiz'd here ye 8th D^{o} 1767. John Oard & Ellen . . . Sponsors.

24. Joseph Atkinson's Son Mathew was born at Westharle June ye 24th 1767 and was baptized here June ye 25th 1767. Thos. Todd& Isabell Wilthue Sponsors.

[1768]

25. Peter Todd's Daughter Catharine was Born & Baptiz'd at the Mill Jany ye 12th 1768 John Wilthue Junior & Margarte Hunter Sponsors.

26. Feby ye 27th 1768, John Dobson's Son Willm was born here & baptiz'd the same Day John Dunn & Isabell Dikison Sponsors.

27. Feby ye 26 1768 Robt Tomblin's Son Luke was Baptiz'd here John Wilthue & Isabella Dikinson Sponsors Born ye 25th.

[1769]

28. Jany ye 22 1769 John Carrick's Daughter Margarite was born & baptized ye 23^{d} J^{n} Miller and Margarite Brown Sponsors.

29. Jany ye 23^{d} 1769 J^{n} Carrick's Son John was born and baptiz'd ye same Day Mary Hunter & Ralph Saunderson Sponsors.

30. April ye 22^{d} 1769 Mr Leadbitter's Daughter Margarite was Born and baptized here on ye 23^{d} Thos Brown & Jane —— Sponsors.

31. June ye 25th 1769 Jos. Atkinson's Son William was

Baptiz'd at Westharle Thos. Miller and Mary Dunn Sponsors. Born ye 17 inst.

32. Octo^r^ ye 1st 1769 Thos Dunn's Daughter Jane was Born & baptiz'd here the same Day John Wilthue Jun. & Jane Mordue Sponsors.

[1770]

33. July ye 6th 1770 Robert Tumblin's Son John was born here & baptiz'd the same Day Thos Miller & Margarite Hunter Sponsors.

34. Peter Todd's Son was baptiz'd here by ye name of Thomas July ye 15th 1770 Thos. Gibson & Mary Foreman Sponsors.

[1771]

35. Jan. ye 6th 1771. John Millar's Son Francis was born & Baptiz'd here the same Day Thos Miller & Frances Miller Sponsors.

36. Jan. ye 24th 1771. Mr Leadbitter's Daughter Winifrid was born & baptiz'd here the same Day Thos. Brown & Jane Mordue Pro Sponsors.

37. Sepr ye 1st 1771 Jo^s^ Hutchison's Son Thos was Baptiz'd at Westharle Thos Hutchison & Mary Hotchison Sponsors.

38. Sepr ye 30 1771 Jo^s^ Dobson's Son Michael was Born & baptiz'd here Mrs Leadbitter & John Dobson Sponsors.

39. Septr D^o^ D^o's^ Son John was born & Baptiz'd Mary Errington & Charles —— Sponsors, he Died the next Day.

[1772]

40. John Carrick's Daughter Ann was born & Baptiz'd here Feby ye 6th 1772 John Oard and Jane Mordue Sponsors.

41. Mr Leadbitter's Daughter Jane was born & Baptiz'd here May ye 6th 1772 John Wilthue & Jane Mordue Sponsors.

42. Thos Harrison's Daughter Eliz. was born and Baptiz'd here Septem ye 12 1772 Math: Carnegy & Mary Dunn Sponsors.

43. John Miller's Son George was Born & Baptiz'd here Octo^r^ ye 23^d^ 1772 Thos. Brown & Jane Snowdon Sponsors.

44. John Errington's Daughter Mary was born and Baptiz'd here Novem^r^ ye 10th 1772 Thos Brown & Margarite Oard Sponsors.

45. Robt Tomblin's Daughter Jane was born & Baptiz'd at Capheaton Novem^r^ ye 23^d^ 1772 John Oard and Isabella Wilthue Sponsors.

[1773]

46. Mr Leadbitter's Son John was born & Baptiz'd here April ye 31 1773 John Wilthue & Mrs Mordue Pro Sponsors.

47. John Wilthue's Son Thomas was born & baptiz'd here the same Day viz. May ye 28th 1773 Thos Brown and Ellen Evereux Sponsors.

48. Elizabeth Atkison Daughter of Joseph & Elizabeth Atkinson was born at West-Harle ye 20th November 1773 & baptized

ye 21st of ye same month & year. The Sponsors were William Shaftoe & Jain Snowdon Catholicks.

J: Naylor: M: O: S: B.

49. Anna Harrison Daughter of Thomas & Elizabeth Harrison was born at Capheaton ye 24th of Feb: 1774 & baptized ye 25th of ye same month & year. The Sponsors were Thomas Hotchison & Margaret Hunter Catholicks.

CONFIRMATIONS

1764. May ye 26th.

The following persons were Confirm'd here by Ld Bishop Peters, viz.

Thos Swinburne Jun.
Mary Tomblin
John Dunn
Joseph Wilthue
John Dobson
Eliz. Wilthue
Jane Brown
Frances Miller
Mary Dunn
Matth. Carnagy
Ann Robson
Eliz. Gibson
Ann Dunn
Thos Gibson
Margarite Snawdon
Henry Robson
Mary Brown
Margarite Brown

all of Capheaton.

From Hesleside.

Michael Scott
John Charlton
John Wilthue
Jane Scott
Ann Charlton
Eliz. Charlton
Ann Scott

From ye Grange.

John Barns
John Barns
George Barns
Robt Bell
John Potts
Willm Bell

June ye 10th 1773.

The following Subjects were confirmed at Capheaton by ye R. Bishop Walton viz.

John Swinburne
Robt Swinburne
Edwd Swinburne
Thos Swinburne
5. Miss Christina Swinburne
Ellen Devereux
Thos Dunn
Margarite Hunter
Ann Simpson
10. John Dunn
Math. Leadbitter
John Leadbitter
Frances Leadbitter
Mary Leadbitter
15. Winefride Leadbitter
Jane Leadbitter
Eliz. Miller
Francis Miller
George Miller
20. Richd Carrick
John Carrick
Isabell Carrick
Margarite Carrick
Nancy Carrick
25. George Dunn
Joseph Dunn
Ellen Dunn
Jane Dunn
Luke Tumblin

30. John Tumblin
Lucy Tomblin
Mary Tomblin
Jane Tomblin
Thos Harrison Junior
35. Margarite Harrison
Eliz. Harrison
Ann Carnagy
Ann Brown
Ellen Brown
40. Ann Errington
Cath^{ne} Errington
Mary Errington
James Brown
John Brown
45. Isabell Dobson
Cath^{ne} Dobson
Mary Dobson
Michael Dobson
Mary Liddle
50. Eliz. Atkinson
Mary Atkinson
John Atkinson
Ellen Atkinson
Joseph Atkinson
55. Math^{w} Atkinson
Willm Atkinson
Thos Atkinson
James Scott from Simonburne
Thos Anderson
60. Robt Anderson
Willm Phillpson

IN SECOND NOTE BOOK

BAPTIZED CAPHEATON

In the year 1774

Thomas, ye Son of Joseph & Mary Dobson was Baptiz'd April 19th Thomas Dobson & Margaret Dobson being Sponsors.

William the Son of William and Mary Shaftoe was born June the 12th & Baptiz'd the 13th of the said Month Joseph and Elizabeth Atkinson being Sponsors.

Mary the Daughter of John and Ann Carrick was born and Baptized August 10th Thomas Brown & Mary Errington being Sponsors.

Elizabeth the Daughter of John & Mary Leadbitter was born & Baptized October 24th Nicolas Leadbitter & Mary Kirsop being Sponsors; Thomas Brown & Mary Errington standing as Proxies.

In the year 1775

Isabella the Daughter of John and Mary Wilthue was Born & Baptized January 23^{d} Joseph Wilthue & Jane Harrison being Sponsors.

John the Son John & Elizabeth Miller was born March 4th & Baptized the 5th of ye said Month, Joseph Wilthue and Mary Robson being Sponsors.

Sarah the Daughter of Robert and Mary Tumbling was born & Baptized June 29th George Dunn & Margaret Dobson being Sponsors.

Jane the Daughter of Thomas & Jane Dixon was born & Baptized at West Shaftoe July 11th Thomas Brown & Jane Dixon the Grandmother being Sponsors.

Elizabeth the Daughter of John and Mary Errington was born

& Baptized August 8th Thomas Brown & Mary Hodgson being Sponsors.

In the year 1776

John the Son of John & Mary Wilthue was born September 14th and Baptized the 16th of the said Month, George Dunn & Helen Tompson being Sponsors.

Matthew the Son of Thomas & Elizabeth Harrison was born & Baptized November 5th George Dunn and Ann Carnegy being Sponsors.

In the year 1777

Edward the Son of Thomas and Elizabeth Dobson was born & Baptized June 2d John Dobson & Sarah Atkinson being Sponsors.

Mary the Daughter of Joseph & Mary Dobson was born August 13th and Baptized the 14th of the said Month Thomas Brown & Jane Wilson being Sponsors.

In the year 1777

Elizabeth the Daughter of John and Mary Newton was born August 23d and Baptized the 24th of the said month. Thomas Brown & Mary Hodgson being Sponsors.

Jane the Daughter of John & Elizabeth Miller was born November 1st and Baptized the 2d of the said Month George Dunn & Ann Carnegy being Sponsors.

In the year 1778

Luke the Son of John & Mary Wilthue was born & Baptized January 31st Thomas Dunn & Ann Dunn being Sponsors.

Helen the Daughter of Helen Thompson & Fathered by her to John Scot the Groom was born at Capheaton April 15th & Baptized the said Day John Errington and Ann Dunn being Sponsors.

In the year 1778

Robert the Son of William and Mary Shaftoe was born & Baptized at Ladywell House July 15th Robert Cook and Mary Taylor being Sponsors.

John the Son of Thomas & Elizabeth Dobson was born July 14th & Baptized the 17th of the said Month, John Dobson & Catharine Dobson being Sponsors.

In the year 1779

Jane the Daughter of John & Jane Ambleton was born at the Frolic farm February 5th & Baptized the 7th of the said month, Robert Ambleton & Jane Snowden being Sponsors.

William the Son of Thomas & Elizabeth Harrison was born May 9th & Baptized the 10th of the said Month, John Miller & Sarah Atkinson being Sponsors.

In the year 1779

Catharine the Daughter of John and Mary Errington was born & Baptized July 15th George Dunn & Margaret Dobson being Sponsors.

Ann the Daughter of John & Mary Newton was born &

Baptized simply August 20th. The ceremonies were afterwards supplied Thomas Brown and Frances Leadbitter being Sponsors.

In the year 1780

Joseph the Son of John & Mary Wilthue was born & Baptized Jany 15th John Errington & Catharine Brown being Sponsors.

Thomas the Son of Joseph & Elizabeth Miller was born & Baptized February 4th John Ord & Isabella Carrick being Sponsors.

In the year 1780

Mary the Daughter of John & Ann Scot was born & Baptized February 10th. Thomas Dunn & Mary Liddal being Sponsors.

Robert the Son of Robert and Mary Tumbling was born & Baptized June 3d. Thomas Brown & Elizabeth Miller being Sponsors.

Thomas the Son of Thomas and Elizabeth Dobson was born July 18th and Baptized July 23d. Thomas Atkinson & Catharine Brown being Sponsors.

In the year 1781

Matthew the Son of John & Mary Newton was born & Baptized February 26th. Thomas Dunn & Catharine Hodgson being Sponsors.

George the Son of John & Mary Newton was born & Baptized February 26th. George Dunn & Frances Leadbitter being Sponsors.

Thomas the Son of William & Mary Shaftoe was born & Baptized at Ladywell House February 26th. Thomas Shaftoe & Elizabeth Shaftoe being Sponsors.

Isabel the Daughter of John & Ann Cruthers was born March 3d and Baptized March 4th. George Dunn & Ann Errington being Sponsors.

In the year 1781

Joseph the Son of Joseph & Mary Dobson was born & Baptized April 30th. Robert Ambleton & Catharine Dobson being Sponsors.

Mary the Daughter of Margaret Dobson & Fathered by her to a servant at Bavington was born June 6th and baptized June 8th. George Dunn & Isabel Carrick being Sponsors.

James the Son of John & Ann Scot was born & Baptized August 28th. James Brown & Helen Dunn being Sponsors.

Elizabeth the Daughter of William and Jane Hall was born October 27th and Baptized October 29th at Kirkharle. Robert Snowdon & Mrs Sarah Brown being Sponsors, represented by their Proxies.

In the year 1782

George the Son of John & Mary Wilthue was born February 24th and Baptized February 25th. James Brown & Jane Ambleton being Sponsors.

Martin the Son of Thomas & Elizabeth Dobson was born &

Baptized March 22^{d}. Robert Ambleton & Elizabeth Charlton being Sponsors.

Ann the Daughter of John & Mary Dobson was born & Baptized May 6th. Thomas Harrison & Catharine Dobson being Sponsors.

Matthew the Son of John & Elizabeth Miller was born November 27th and Baptized November 28th. Thomas Dunn and Jane Ambleton being Sponsors.

In the year 1783

Thomas the Son of Margaret Dobson and Fathered by her to James Brown one of the Grooms at Capheaton was born and Baptized July 23^{d}. Robert Ambleton & Ann Brown being Sponsors.

1784

Ann the Daughter of John & Mary Dobson was born & christened or baptized the 6th of June 1784. James Brown & Margaret Brown the Gardener's wife being Sponsors, Betty Charlton standing as Proxy for Margaret Brown.

ANDREW RYDING.

CONFIRMED

In the year 1783 July 10th. By the Revd Bishop Gibson.

John Brewse
Ann Harrison
Elizabeth Leadbitter
Thomas Wilthue
Hannah Dobson
Elizabeth Errington
John Miller

MARRIED

In the year 1782

May 21st. Thomas Brown was Married to Margaret Hunter both living at Capheaton.

DEAD

In the year 1774

M. Ann Carrick died August 10th.

Mary the Daughter of John & Ann Carrick died this Year, an Infant.

In the year 1775

Elizabeth Nevils died December 17th.

In the year 1777

Elizabeth Liddal died March 9th.

Old Catharine Errington died Novr 28th.

In the year 1778

John Ambleton Died at the Frolic Farm August 8th.

In the year 1779

Ann the Daughter of John & Mary Newton Died in August an Infant.

Catharine the Daughter of John & Mary Errington died in July an Infant.

In the year 1779

Catharine the Daughter of John & Mary Errington about 12 years old Died April 24th.

Elizabeth Robston Died at the Clock mill April 29th

In the year 1780

Helen Brown the Daughter of John & Sarah Brown died May 7th.

Mary Hodgson died May 14th.

In the year 1781

Matthew Liddal died March 26th.

Catharine Brown died December 31st.

In the year 1782

Old Mary Lamb died about the beginning of December.

In the year 1783

Mrs Mary Leadbitter, Wife of Mr John Leadbitter Died March 11th.

Ann the Daughter of John & Mary Dobson an Infant Died about the Month of June.

Thomas the Son of Margaret Dobson an Infant died about the beginning of November.

In the year 1784

Died Janry 18th at Newcastle & was buried at Whelpington Janry 21 Mary Leadbitter Daughter of John & Mary Leadbitter.

Died August 30 & was buried at Whelpington Septber 1st Margaret Brown Daughter of Henry & Mary Brown aged about 51 or 52.

In the year 1785

Ann Armstrong a child of about a month old & Daughter of Robert and Margaret Armstrong Died Jany 13th at Cambo & was buried Jany 15 at Whelpington.

Died Jany 16 & was buried at Whelpington Jany 18 Mary Wilthue Wife of John Wilthue aged

1785

Died June [*ends.*]

No. VI

THE CATHOLIC REGISTERS OF BIDDLESTON HALL, ALWINTON, NORTHUMBERLAND, THE SEAT OF THE SELBY FAMILY, 1767-1840.

CONTRIBUTED BY JOSEPH S. HANSOM

HISTORICAL NOTES BY JAMES RAE BATERDEN

THE registers are contained in two books, the first being a common paper note book of 44 pages 7⅛×4½ inches, covered in marbled paper. The second is 7¾×6¼ inches of about 136 original pages, and has been recently bound in half vellum, cloth sides. There is no pagination, which is supplied here. Both are in sound condition. They are now numbered Northumberland 8,I and 8,II amongst the non-parochial registers at Somerset House, where I was permitted by the Registrar-General to transcribe them.

The certificate is posted in the first book and signed 'George J : A : Corless, D :D·:,' and also 'Catherine Clauing' [?Clavering] as proprietor. Fr. Corless states on 28th Oct. 1840 that 'the Register Books of Biddlestone Hall of births, baptisms, deaths and marriages had been kept by him since June as 'Catholic Chaplain,' 'officiating for the time being.' He speaks of the chapel being 'founded about the year 1200.'

J. S. H.

HISTORICAL NOTES ON CHAPLAINCY

As Burke in his *Landed Gentry* truly says, the Selbys have been seated in Northumberland 'time out of mind.' An existing grant from Edward I in 1272, shows that they derive from Sir Walter de Selby who flourished in the reigns of Henry III and Edward I; the lands given to this Sir Walter have continued uninterruptedly in the family and are enjoyed by them to-day.

A Christopher Selby, son of Percival de Selby, one of the Commissioners of the Middle Marches in the 6th year of Edward VI married Eleanor, daughter of Sir William Ogle of Causey Park, Northumberland, a son of Ralph, Lord Ogle; their great grandson was the Sir William Selby, High Sheriff of Northumberland who was knighted by James I at Berwick in 1603. He married Eleanor, a daughter of Sir Thomas Haggerston of Haggerston. The issue of this marriage was three daughters, one of whom became a nun at Liege, and three sons.

Charles the third son, who succeeded, married Elizabeth Gillibrand of Chorley, Lancashire. Their eldest son and successor Thomas William Selby took to wife Barbara, daughter and heiress of Christopher Percehay of Ryton, Yorks, and would be living here about the beginning of the 18th century when we get the first records of the chaplaincy.

Biddleston Hall standing on the southern slopes of the Cheviots, about 750 feet above sea level, is said to be the Osbaldestone Hall of Sir Walter Scott's *Rob Roy,* and since the Reformation has been the centre of Catholic worship in Upper Coquetdale, that out of the way district of Northumberland.

Biddleston even to-day, is 8 or 9 miles from a railway station and a main road; its only connection with civilization in the 18th century was by a pack road from Rothbury passing through the hamlet of Alwinton, which led up, and still leads up Coquetdale, and over the Cheviots into Scotland. It must have proved a dreary residence for many a poor priest during the winter season. It had however the compensating advantage during penal times, of being far removed from the persecuting courts, and on the rare occasions when their officials did approach, the wild moors on the north and west, 200 square miles in area, afforded a safe refuge to the hunted priest until the danger was over. It is an historic neighbourhood. At Holystone, 3 miles south, may still be seen the spring or well where St Paulinus baptised 3000 converts in the 7th century. The old Border tower of Clennel, held for centuries by the family of that name, lies two miles to the west; Alnham another old tower, now a parsonage, lies a few miles north-east; still further east is Eslington, once the seat of the Collingwoods, who kept the faith, until fines, and attainders, and the scaffold, caused the extinction of the family soon after 1715. Callaly the seat of the Claverings for centuries, and Cartington the home in succession of the Cartingtons, the Radcliffes, the Widdringtons and the Talbots, are within a radius of six miles. Harbottle with its ruined castle where in 1515 Queen Margaret of Scotland gave birth to the future mother of Lord Darnley, held in the 17th century by Gascoignes and Widdringtons, lies two miles south-west. Of these old Catholic families, who formed the fighting race of the Borders, all are gone save Selby of Biddlestone, who still hold the old lands and the old faith.

The Selbys had been mixed up with all Border troubles for centuries, in the great civil war they espoused the cause of the king, and during the Jacobite rising of 1715 they were in the thick of it —they suffered on both occasions.

The family chapel was built probably about the beginning of the 19th century when the existing mansion was erected by Thomas Selby who died in 1816. It stands upon the foundation of the old 'Tower of Biddleston held by a John Selby in 1415,' and was thoroughly repaired in 1879.

The first record we get of a chaplain at Biddleston is by an inspection of the parish register at the ancient church of Alwinton, where for centuries the Selbys were buried. Under date 6th July 1725 is recorded the burial of 'Mr Thomas Durham, *alias* Collingwood, p. priest, Biddleston.'

Fr. Thomas Collingwood, junr., S.J., *alias* Durham, was the 4th son of George Collingwood of Eslington, and Agnes daughter of John Fleming of Ryedale, Westmoreland. Born in 1658 he entered the Society of Jesus in 1678, and was ordained 17 March 1680. His two younger brothers, Robert and Charles, as well as his uncle Thomas Collingwood, were also Jesuits; their cousin John Metcalfe was a secular priest. Foley says that Fr. Collingwood was in this Jesuit District of St John the Evangelist in 1701, so he was probably at Biddleston, close to his home, early in the 18th century. He would be here during the Derwentwater rising consequent on which his eldest brother George Collingwood of Eslington, 'a very pius gentleman and much beloved in his county' was executed in Liverpool in 1716. Foley gives the date of Fr. Collingwood's death, although he does not say where, 16 July 1725.

He was probably succeeded by Fr. Robert Widdrington, S.J., who was still here about 1736, as chaplain to William Thomas Selby. Dr Chandler, Bishop of Durham, in his 'Parochial remarks on his Visitation,' made about this time, says '28 papists meet at Biddleston about a mile from the church, at Mr Selby's, Rob. Widdrington, priest.' Fr. Widdrington was born in Northumberland in 1660, entered the Society 7th Sep 1679, spent his whole life in the north and was Superior of this district from 1720 to 1723. He probably left Biddleston in 1736, died at Durham, and was buried in St Oswald's churchyard there, 17th Jan. 1742, aged 82. Foley and other writers say that he was a brother of Henry Widdrington, S.J., and son of Lord Widdrington, but the latter statement does not appear to be correct. He was more likely one of the Widdringtons of Cartington, or of the other branches of this wide spread family, Catholic in all their lines. Foley says he appears to be identical with Robert Watson.

Rev. Lawrence Robinson, O.S.F. of the Recollect Order, went to Biddleston in 1736. He was then probably about 30 years of age. He was Preses of Hexham 1737-43, afterwards lived in the south of England, part of the time at Beckford, Gloucestershire, and died about 1760.

Alwinton church register records under 14th Feb. 1747 the burial of 'Mr Pennivim, priest, Biddleston,' but whether he was secular or regular we cannot trace.

His probable successor was the 'Mr Newton' whom Foley places here in 1750. This is evidently Rev. William Newton, S.J., junr., born in Lincolnshire 30th Oct. 1718 who entered the Society in 1736. He was at the penitentiary of Loretto in Rome 1747-49 and probably came direct from there to Biddleston, where he says he arrived after the partial completion of the Jubilee celebration of 1750. His report on this occasion states 'customers here between 50 and 60, salary £10 and diet.' He could only have stayed here a few years, as he died in the Oxfordshire district 16th Oct. 1755 at the age of 37.

Dom. John Anselm Bolton, O.S.B., the first of his Order we trace to Biddleston was in residence in 1764. Born at Brindle, Lancs., 1735 he was professed at the Abbey of St Lawrence at Dieulward, Lorraine, in 1753. Sent to south of England he was for some time stationed at Leighland, Somersetshire. He was only a short time at Biddleston as he went in 1764 as chaplain to the Hon. Anne Fairfax at Gilling Castle, Yorks., and remained with her until her death in 1793. Shortly before her death she built him a house at Ampleforth, close to Gilling, to which he removed about 1793, and lived there until about 1802. He then handed over this house to his own Community of Dieulward, who driven out at the French Revolution, had found shelter for some years in various houses in England. This house of Fr. Bolton's formed the foundation of the present Benedictine Abbey of Ampleforth, he retired to Birtley, co. Durham, in 1802, died there 22nd Dec. 1805 and was buried at Chester le Street. (Gillow, *Dict. Eng. Caths.*)

Dom. Joseph Lawrence Hadley, O.S.B., son of John Hadley and Mary Clements born in London 1739 and professed at St Gregory,

Douai, 1757, came to Biddleston as his first mission succeeding Fr. Bolton in 1764, and remained till 1767, when he went to Brindle, Lancashire. There he lived 35 years retiring in 1802 to Netherton in ill-health. He died in Liverpool 30 May 1805.

Dom. John Ambrose Naylor, O.S.B., succeeded in the summer of 1767, and commenced the Register the same year. This was during the ownership of Thomas Selby (1) whose five sons by his second wife, Eleanor, daughter and co-heiress of Nicholas Tuite, were all educated at St Gregory's Benedictine School, Douai. Born in Lancashire, the son of Louis Naylor of Rainford and Alice Smith, in 1738, Fr. Naylor was professed at St Gregory, Douai, in 1757. With the exception that we find his name in the Register of Capheaton on two occasions in 1773 and 1774, doing temporary duty there, his whole clerical life was spent at Biddleston. He commenced the Baptismal register, 29th July 1767, probably shortly after his arrival, and continued it in his own handwriting down to 11th Oct. 1820 the year before his death. He lived under three generations of Selbys, and five successive owners, under the rule of six Vicars Apostolic and their coadjutors, died 10th Nov. 1821 and was buried in Alwinton churchyard. He was Provincial of the Province from 1799 until his death.

The last few years of Fr. Naylor's life were fatal ones for the Selby family. Thomas Selby (2) who had married Catherine, the daughter and co-heiress of Ralph Hodgson of Lintz, co. Durham, died in May 1816, his eldest son Thomas died unmarried in June 1818, Edward the next in succession died abroad a few months afterwards, and the property passed to the fourth son Walter Selby (1), then in his 31st year. He had married in 1817, Alicia, daughter of Dr John Swarbreck.

During 1821, the last year of Fr. Naylor's life, temporary duty was done by Fr. Thomas Gillow from Callaly Castle who had been chaplain there 25 years. He left this same year to take charge of the new mission at North Shields, where he resided until his death 19th March 1857, aged 87. (See Registers of Callaly Castle, *C.R.S.*, Vol. 7.)

Dom. James Higginson, O.S.B., of Swinburne Castle, baptised a daughter of Walter Selby the squire in Aug. 1821. Born at Wrightlington, Lancashire, in 1764 and professed at St Gregory, Douai, in 1785, he had been chaplain to the Benedictine nuns of Cambrai, was imprisoned with them during the French Revolution, brought the community to England in May 1795 and shortly afterwards came as chaplain to Thomas Horsley Widdrington Riddell, at Swinburne Castle. He remained there until 1828, thence went to the old established Benedictine mission of Birtley, co. Durham. Whilst saying mass here on 13th Dec. 1835 he was taken suddenly ill and died in half an hour clad in his sacramental vestments.

Fr. Naylor's successor was Dom. Matthew Charles Fairclough, O.S.B., born at Wigan 1788, professed at St Lawrence, Ampleforth, in 1813 and ordained there in 1820. He evidently came here direct from college, soon after Fr. Naylor's death, but only stayed a short time and only makes one entry in the register, in Feb. 1822. He was afterwards at Bungay, Suffolk, 1826-7, the following year he went to the monastery of St Gery, Arras, in France, where he remained 50 years. Retired to St Edmund in 1878, and died at Douai 4th April 1880, aged 92.

After Fr. Fairclough left there was no resident chaplain for about 12 months. Temporary duty was done again in 1822-23 by Dom. James Higginson, O.S.B., who baptised Walter Selby (2) the heir, son of Walter Selby and Alicia Swarbreck, on 6th Nov. 1822. Also by Fr. Thomas Stout who at this time was in charge of the old mission of Thropton, Northumberland. A Northumbrian, educated at Douai, Fr. Stout left France in 1793-4 and was for a time at St George's Fields Chapel, Southwark, London. He went to Callaly Castle about Nov. 1796, remained there till the following September when he removed to Thropton. He lived there 30 years, died 26th July 1828 at the age of 62 and was buried in front of the altar rails of his chapel. (See Registers of Callaly Castle, *C.R.S.*, Vol. 7.)

Rev. James Albot, a young priest from Ushaw, came in the latter part of 1823, remained until June 1828 when he went to Thropton, where he died 28th Jan. 1837.

Rev. Thomas Middlehurst succeeded in the summer of 1828 and remained until September 1830. A native of Lancashire, born 11th Sep. 1802, he was educated and ordained at the English College, Lisbon. After leaving Biddleston he went to West Witton, Bedale. He was stationed at Malton about 1850 and died there 12th July 1880. (See Registers of Danby, West Witton and Leyburn, *C.R.S.*, Vol. 13.)

After Fr. Middlehurst left there was again no resident priest, and the duties were attended to by Fr. James Albot of Thropton from March 1831 to Jan. 1832.

After this there is a complete blank in the register until July 1836. The reason probably was that Walter Selby (1) dying in 1833, and his wife being already dead, the new owner was at this time only 11 years of age, and probably living with his aunt Mrs Clavering at Callaly, or at school. He afterwards became J.P. and D.L. and married Laura Anne, daughter of Henry Tempest of Broughton Hall, Yorks., died Sep. 1868 and was buried in the family vault in Alwinton Church. Henrietta, Abbess of Hammersmith and Teignmouth, was one of his aunts.

Rev. John Henry Fisher was chaplain during the summer of 1836. Born in Manchester 12th Sep. 1812, the 4th son of John Fisher, a merchant of that city, he was ordained at Ushaw 28th May 1836 and shortly after came to Biddleston. After a few months' stay he went to his native district where he spent the remainder of his life. He served St Mary's, Liverpool, 1837-8; Duckenfield, Cheshire, 1839-40; Birkenhead, 1840-41. He was President of St Edward's College, Liverpool, from Jan. 1842 until 30th June 1884, one of the first Canons of Liverpool in 1851, V.G. from 1868, he became 3rd Provost of Liverpool in 1879. He died at Southport, Monsignore and D.D., 3rd May 1889.

Rev. Joseph T. Howard, another young Ushaw priest, was chaplain from Sep. 1836 to August 1838, when he went to Callaly Castle and remained there until the end of 1839. He then left in ill health and died 7th June 1840.

Henry Sutton signs from Nov. 1839 to the end of register. This was Dom. Henry Ignatius Sutton, O.S.B., born at Liverpool 12th Oct. 1812, educated at Ampleforth and ordained priest there 20th May 1837. He was at Birtley, co. Durham, for a short time, 1838-39, before coming to Biddleston. Left here for Lawkland, Yorks., before Oct. 1840 and was there 1840-41. He spent most of his missionary life in the south of England and South Wales, was at Cheltenham 1876-84, and from thence retired to Ampleforth, where he died 28th Aug. 1886. He was once shot at by a fanatic whilst saying mass, but fortunately missed.

The succeeding priests were as follows:

Rev. George J. A. Corless, D.D., attended from Thropton for a time in 1840.

Rev. Thomas Hoggett, 1841 till death 29th June 1886.

Rev. Henry Cartmell, 1887-89.

Rev. William Drysdale, 1890-93, died at Scorton, Yorks., 27th Sep. 1912.

Rev. Robert Henry Kerr, 1894-1907.

Rev. Henry Walmesley, 1908-1909.

Rev. Joseph Fitzsimmons, 1910 to present time.

Pinned into the Biddleston register is a certificate of baptism dated London 7th Sep. 1787 of Thomas Selby, eldest son of Thomas Selby (2) and Catherine, daughter and co-heiress of Ralph Hodgson of Lintz, co. Durham, born 3rd Jan. 1780, signed 'Thomas Meynell Sac.' This refers to the baptism at Causey Park, Northumberland, on 3 Jan. 1780 by Thomas Meynell, S.J. He was the 2nd son of Richard Meynell of North Kilvington, Yorkshire, and Barbara Anne eldest daughter of Thomas William Selby of Biddleston, great-great-aunt of the child whom he baptized. Born 29 Sep. 1737, he entered the Society S.J. in 1756. He was chaplain to the Stapletons of Carlton, Yorks., 1768-73, afterwards resided with Fr. William Strickland, S.J., in London, where he died suddenly whilst in conversation with his friend Dr Nichols, 1 Feb. 1804. It is probable that the certificate was got at this time (1787) for legacy purposes as Thomas Selby, grandfather of this child, and then owner of the estates, died 31 May 1787.

J. R. B.

FIRST BOOK

Inside binding,—10 Northumberland I
[*and the 'Certificate or Statement' pasted in*]

[Page 1]. A list of those who have been married of the Congregation at Biddleston since the 28th of July 1767.

Percival **Clennell** of Rothbury, Protestant, to Mary **White** of Foxton the 30th of May [1868 *xd out*].

John **Avery** of Netherton to Margt **Dodds** of the Follions the 22d of November 1768.

Robert **Blacklock** of Callaly to Margt **Thomson** of Netherton the 19th of July 1772.

John **Dodds** of Netherton to Ann **Gray** of the same place the 24th of April 1774.

Willm **Brown** of Biddleston to Jane **Davidson** of Biddleston Edge 24th of April 177 [4 *over* 7].

J: Nay Miss: O: S: B:

[2]. Robert **Blacklock** of Yetlington to Jane **Rutherford** of Plainfield the 25th of June 1777.

[*Four lines referring to the following crossed out*]

Christopher **Davison** at Yeddon was married by me to Ann **Frizzel** of the same place, Protestant, the 10th of july 1786 &

promised to be married at Church the next day, but afterwards refused to be marryed to her, or own her for his Wife, he has since marryed another Woman with whom he lives at present & Ann Frizzel has married another Man at Alnwick.

J: Naylor Miss: O: S: B: 1791

[3]. Henry **Bollum** of Whittingham to Jane **Holmes** of Biddleston the 22[d] of November 1791.

Andrew **Murton** servant at Netherton to Mary **Turnbull** of the same place the 2[d] of May 1790.

Luke **Thorborne** of Biddleston to Mary **Barningham** of the same place the 18th of May 1797.

George **Bolam** of Biddleston to Barbara **Wallace** of the same place the 25 of August 1801.

John **Gray** of Woodhall to Marg[t] **Brown** of Biddleston the 23[d] of August 1810.

J: Naylor Miss: O: S: B: 1810.

[4]. Tho[s] **Davison** of Callaly to Dinah **Nicholson** of Biddleston the 13th of July 1812.

Rob[t] **Gray** servant to Tho[s] Selby to Elizabeth **Hickson** both of Biddleston the 11th of May 1813.

Tho[s] **Grundy** servant to M[r] Tho[s] Selby to Mary **Gallon** maid to M[rs] Selby, both of Biddleston the 14th of September 1814.

George **Best** servant to the late Tho[s] Selby Esq[r] to Rebecca **Clifton** nursery-maid 36 years in the family of the late M[r] Selby both of Biddleston the 7th of August 1816.

Tho[s] **Thorborn** son of Luke Thorborn of Biddleston to Elizabeth **Clark** of Screenwood Dec[r] [*no day*] 1821.

Thomas **Brown** of Biddleston village to Mary **Dixon** (alias **Richardson**) May 14th 1828.

[5] A.D. 1838

Feb. 23. John **Athey** of Harbottle Village was married to Elizabeth **Redhead** 2[1 ?] of Feb: 1838 not in the Catholic church, but in the Protestant Church, without leave and consent of his pastor

Jos. Haward, Miss App.

[*Here follow* 19 *blank pages before the end of reverse entries*]

[1 R]. T. R.* A Catalogue of the dead of Biddleston Congregation since the 29th of July 1767.

+ Frances **Moody** died at Allenton the 29th of february 1768.

+ Isabel **Fail** an infant died at Hazletonridge the 2[d] of february 1769.

+ George **Fail** an infant died at Hazletonridge the 5th of february 1769.

+ Jane **Grey** died at Netherton the 11th of December 1769.

+ Robert **Gallon** died at Cotewalls the 26th of may 1770.

+ Mary **Potts** died at Sharpèrton the 1st of may 1771.

+ Mathew **Dickison** died at Allenton the 10th of janury 1772.

* Initials of Thomas Rees, Commissioner.

+ Helen **Davison** died at Biddleston Edge the 28th of janury 1772.

[2 R]. Margaret **Dickison** died at yeldom the 6th of may 1773.
Elizabeth **Reed** died at Plainfield the 13th of april 1774.
Robert **Grey** died at Biddleston the 24th of July 1775.
Ann **Wealings** died at Borrowdon the 24th of July 1776.
George **Rutherford** died at Borrowdon the 21st of august 1771.
Jane **Elder** died at Cotewalls the 22d December 1776.
Ann **Scott** died at Allenton the the 18th of July 1778.
John **Turnbull** died at Netherton the 21st of September 1778.
Mary **Brown** died at Sharperton the 13th of March 1779.
Elizabeth **Rutherford** died at Borrowdon the 13th of december 1779.

Requiescant in pace.

[3 R]. Mary **Ilderton** died at yeldom the 28th of April 1780.
Mary **Davison** died at Cotewalls the 6th of march 1781.
Ann **Cariceaux** died at yeldom the 9th of September 1781.
Mrs Teresa Tuite **Selby** died at Biddleston the 12th of November 1781.
Andrew **Rutherford** died at Harbottle the 6th of September 1782.
George **Jordan** died at Harbottle the 18th of September 1782.
Mathew **Jordan** died at Harbottle the 24th of May 1783.
Barbara **Davison** died at Screenwod the 15th of august 1782.
Thos **Davison** died at yeldom the 26th of April 1784.
Dorothy **Brown** died at Netherton the 25th of July 1784.

Requescant in pace.

[4 R] 1785

Dorothy **Donce** died at yeldom the 24th of September 1785.
John **Davison** died at Biddleston the 5th of october 1785.

1786

Robt **Brown** an Infant died at Biddleston the 25th ofJanuary 1786.
Mary **Jordan** died at Harbottle the 28th of May 1786.
Mary **Smith** [an infant *above*] died the 14th of March 1784.
Aloisa Elizabeth **smith** an Infant died the 6th of july 1785.
Margt **Brown** Wife of Robt Brown died at Neitherton the 22d of August 1786.

Requiescant in pace.

[5 R] Barbara **Brown** Daughter of Robt Brown died at Netherton the 13th of September 1786.
Thos **Selby** Esqr died at Biddleston the 26th of May 1787.
Elizabeth **Rutherford** died at Burrowdon Mains the 25th of March 1788.
Thos **Rutherford** died at Burrowdon Mains the 4th of July 1788.
Robt **Brown** an Infant died at Borrowdon the 31st of August 1788.
Ferdinand **jordan** an Infant died at Harbottle the 21st of october 1789.
John **Scott** died at Allenton the 27th of August 1789.

Requiescant in pace.

1790

[6 R] Ann **Bollum** died at Biddleston the 13th of August 1790.

David **Gordon** died at Elilaw the 15th of December 1790.

Willm **Brown** died at Burrowdon the 15th of July 1791.

Isabel **Turnbull** died at Netherton the the 12th of December 1791.

Mary **Kirkup** died at Allenton the 23d of October 1794.

Helen **Robson** an Infant 3 years old died at Barrow Mill the 11th of November 1794.

James **Turnbull** an Infant died at Netherton the 24th of May 1797.

Mary **Elder** at Alnwick Novbi [4 ?]th 1796.

Requiescant in pace.

[7 R] 1798

Jane Thorborne Daughter of Luke & Mary **Thorborne** an Infant died at Biddleston of the small Pox the 15th of October 1798.

Robt **Stamp** died at Harbottle the 5th of October 1798.

1799

Sarah **Turnbull** an Infant [6 months ?] Daughter of Christopher & Sarah Turnbull died at Netherton the 30th of October 1799.

James **White** died at Burrow-Burn the 25th of December 1799.

Mary Turnbull an Infant 5 years old Daughter of Christopher [Turnbull *xd out*] & Sarah **Turnbull** died at Netherton the 26th of Decembr 1799.

Requiescant in pace.

[8 R] [1800]

Elizabeth **Potts** of Hallystone in the Parish of Allinton, Widow, was found dead on Hallystone Common the 24th of January 1800, was supposed to have perished on the 23d being a very stormy day. R: in P:

[1801]

Jane Murton an Infant 10 years old daughter of Andrew & Mary **Murton** died near Borrowdon the 23d of Jan. 1801. R. in P.

Isabel Turnbull Daughter of George **Fisher** & Isabel **Turnbull** died at Netherton the 29th of April 1801 aged 18. R. in P.

Thos **Brown**, an Infant one month old, son of Charles & Ann Brown, died at Biddleston the 3d of June 1801.

Mary Smith Daughter of Thos & Margt **Smith** died at Woodhall the 30th of January 1801.

[9 R] Robert **Brown** died at Biddleston in the Parish of Allenton the 27th of Novbr 1801. R. in P.

[1802]

Isabel Turnbull an Infant Daughter of Christopher & Sarah **Turnbull** died at Netherton in the Parish of Allenton the 29th of Jan: 1802.

Catherine **Stamp** died at Harbottle the 28th of August 1802. R. in P.

[1803]

Jane **Loraine** died at Woodhall the 5th of March 1803. R: in P:

Jane Thorborne an Infant 16 months old Daughter of Luke & Mary **Thorborne** died at Biddleston in the Parish of Alwinton the 15th of May 1803.

Requiescant in Pace.

[1804]

[10 R] Robert **Brown** of Biddleston in the Parish of Alwinton died on the 17th of February 1804 being kill'd by the fall of a Cart. R. in P.

Joseph **Thompson** of Screanwood in the Parish of Alnham died on the 14th of June 1805.

Thos **Stamp** of Burrowdon in the Parish of Alwinton died the 21st of August 1805. R. in P.

[1806]

James **Thornborne** of Biddleston in the Parish of Alwinton died the 29th of January 1806. R. in P.

Bartholomy **Franckland** of Biddleston in the Parish of Alwinton died the 7th of June 1806. R. in P.

[11 R]. Albert Selby son of Thos & Catherine **Selby**, died at Biddleston in the Parish of Alwinton on the 24th of July 1806 in the 15th year of his age. R. in P.

Christopher **Turnbull** of Netherton in the Parish of Alwinton died on the 30th of July 1806.

John Turnbull an Infant 15 [months *xd out*, weeks *above*] old son of Christopher & Sarah **Turnbull** died at Netherton the 5th of September 1806.

[1808]

Mary Athy an Infant son of John & Helen **Athy** died at Harbottle the 14th of May 1808. R: in P.

Sarah Turnbull an Infant 13 days old, Daughter of Christopher & Sarah **Turnbull** died at Netherton the 8th [?] of September 1808. R. in P.

[12 R] [1809]

Ann **Ferry** of Burrowdon in the Parish of Alwinton died the 22d of Jan. 1809. R. in P.

[1810]

Michael **Davison** of Sharperton in the Parish of Alwinton died the 24th of June 1810. R. in P.

Margaret **Stamp** of Borrowdon in the Parish of Alwinton died the 7th of March 1810. R. in P.

Dorothy **Best** of Biddleston in the Parish of Alwinton died the 18th of April 1810. R: in P.

Charles **Brown** of Biddleston in the Parish of Allenton died the 17th of July 1813 aged 57. R. in pace.

Christopher **Bollum** of Biddleston in the Parish of Allenton died the 4th of February 1815 aged 85. R. in pace.

[13 R]. Jane **Trumble** died at Netherton in the Parish of Allenton the 26th of April 1815. R: in p: 81.

Mary **Thornborne** died at Biddleston in the Parish of Allenton the 5th of September 1815. R. in P. aged 78.

Richard Selby 5th son of Thos & Catherene **Selby** died at Biddleston in the Parish of Allenton the first of November 1815. R. in P. aged 26.

Thomas **Selby** Esqr died at Biddleston in the Parish of Allenton the 15th of May 1816 aged 63. R. in P.

[14 R]. Helen Haughton Daughter of Mary **Haughton** died at Biddleston in the Parish of Allenton the 22d of October 1816. Aged . . . R. in P.

George Brown Son of John & Sarah **Brown** an Infant not 2 years old died at Biddleston in the Parish of Alwinton the 17th of March 1817.

Henrietta Turnbull Daughter of [*erasure*, James & *above*] Elizbh **Turnbull** an Infant died at Biddleston in the Parish of Alwinton the 23d of May 1817.

Isabel Turnbull Daughter of James & Elizabeth **Turnnbull** died at Biddleston in the Parish of Alwinton the 13th of June 1817 aged 18.

R. in P.

[15 R] Elizabeth Turnbull Daughter of James & Elizabeth **Turnbull** died at Biddleston in the Parish of Alwinton the 25th of July 1817 aged 13: 6 month.

Thomas **Harrison** many years Groom at Biddleston died [Nov. *xd out*, Dec. *in marg.*] 14, 1822. SS. munits oibs* aged 64.

James **Turnbull** aged 51, Labourer died May 12, 1823 oibs SS. munits at Biddleston. Harriett **Selby** aged 2 years died July 7, 1823.

Harriet **Selby** aged 2 years died July 7, 1823.

William **Graham** of Burradon in the Parish of Alwinton died on 18th of April 1824 [aged *xd out*] in [his 95th year *above*] oibs SS. munits. R.I.P.

[16 R] Robert **Hixton** many year Gamekeeper at Biddleston died July 15th 1825 aged 86. R.I.P.

Ann **Grey** in the 14th year of her age died 1st April 1826 at Wood-hall. R.I.P.

M[ary *xd out*, rs *above*] Selby the Lady of Walter **Selby** Esquire died on the 24th of May 1826 aged 33. R.I.P.

Mary **Grundy** died on the 7th of March 1827 aged 57. R.I.P.

Christopher **Turnbull** died 12th May 1827 aged 67. R.I.P.

Catharine **Selby** aged [9 *in pencil*] died July 7. 1828.

Mary **Wilson** of Burradon in the Parish of Alwinton died on the 25 August 1828 aged . . . oibus SS. munit. R.I.P.

Margaret **Turnbull** 10 July } [*in pencil.*]
Jane **Turnbul** 28 Septr }

[17 B] Margaret Turnbull daughter of Christopher and . . . **Turnbull** died at Netherton in the parish of Alwington July 10th 1828 aged . . . years oibus S.S. munita.

* Abbreviation for "omnibus sacramentis munitus."

Jane [Thorborne *x^d out*, **Turnbull** *above*] died 28 Sep^br 1829 at Netherton aged —.

Mr George **Best** died 17th Aug. 1830 aged 78 at Biddleston [*written over* Mr Best 17 Aug. 1830—78 *in pencil.*]

Jane **Thorborn**
Jane **Sproate** July 15, 1831 } [*in pencil.*]

[18 R] 1836

Ann **Simmonds** obiit apud Netherton Absolutione & sacri olei perceptione munita die 29 Augusti. J. H. Fisher. Miss App. R.I.P.

Maria [Bolam *x^d out*, **Jordan** *above*] obiit apud Hepple absolutione & sacri olei perceptione munita die 3 Novembris—J. H. Fisher Miss: App:—Requiescat in Pace.

1838

Anne **Brown** obiit apud Biddleston die 2 Martii 1838, sine absolutione & sacri olei perceptione per negligentiam illorum habitantium cum illâ.—Jos. Howard Miss App. [Aged 32 *below.*] R.S.P.

[19 R] Henricus Stourton, filius secundus Hon. Caroli & Luciæ **Stourton** obiit Collegii Stonyhurst, 24th Febuarii 1838. Absolutione & sacri olei perceptione munitus—R.S.P.

Gulielmus Stourton, filius primus Hon. Caroli & Lucæ **Stourton** obiit apud Biddleston 23 Martii 1838, absolutione & sacri olêi perceptione munitus—Jos. Howard Miss. App.—R.S.P.

Stephanus **Every** obiit apud Callaley die Maii 18, 1838, absolutione & sacri olei perceptione munitus—J. T. Haward—Biddleston—R.S.P.

[20 R] Edwin Stourton, filius tertius Hon. Caroli & Luciæ **Stourton** obiit apud Biddleston 21 Maii 1838, (ætate 5½).

John **Turnbull** of Netherton in the Parish of Alwington died March 7th 1840, (omnibus Sacramentis munitus) aged 87 years. R.I.P.—H. Sutton Miss: Ap:

We certify that this is one of the Registers or Records deposited in the General Register office, pursuant to the Act of the 4th Victoria, Cap. 92. John Bowring
Thos. Rees
John Shoveller } Comm^rs.

SECOND BOOK

[*On page 3 is the commissioners' certificate, followed by five blank pages*]

[Page 9]. A Catalogue of those that have been baptized in Biddleston Congregation since the 29th of July 1767. T.R.

Isabel Fail Daughter of Geerge **Fail** & Catharine **Moody** his Wife was born at Hazleton-ridge in Northumberland the 27th day of September 1767 & baptized the 29th of the same month & year, the Sponsors were George Davison & Helen Davison Catholics.*

* The spelling is usually 'Catholicks,' but the 'k' is crossed out.

Mary Turnbull Daughter of Christopher **Turnbull** & Jane **Henderson** his Wife was born at Netherton the first of November 1767 & baptized the 3[d] of the same month & year, the Sponsors were George Davison & Elizabeth Rutherford.

John Naylor Miss: O: S: B:*

1768

[10]. Ferdinand Jordan Son of George **Jordan** & Mary **Wallis** his Wife was born at Harbottle the 17th of May 1768 & baptized the 22[d] of the same month & year the Sponsors were James Thorborne & Jane Davison Catholics.

Mary Brown Daughter of Rob[t] **Brown** & Marg[t] **Scrowther** his Wife was born at Biddleston the 12th of June 1768 & baptized the same day, the Sponsors were David Gordon & Helen Davison Catholicks.

George Stamp Son of Tho[s] **Stamp** & Mary **Buddle** his Wife Protestant was born at Biddleston the 16th of October 1768 & baptized the same day, the Sponsors were Andrew Rutherford & Helen Davison Catholics.

J. Naylor Miss. O: S: B.

1769

[11]. Elizabeth Bollum Daughter of Christopher **Bollum** & Helen **Peary** his Wife was born at Biddleston the 2[d] of March 1769 & baptized the same day, the Sponsors were Christopher Peary & Mary Thorborne Catholics.

George Dodds Son of Christopher **Dodds** & Hanna **Dunn** his Wife was born at Netherton the 22[d] of April 1769 & baptized the same day, the Sponsors were George Dodds & Elizabeth Dodds Catholics.

Isabel Fail Daughter of George **Fail** & Catharine **Moody** his Wife was born at Ha—letonridge [*sic*] the 27th of June 1769 & baptized the 28th of the same month & year the Sponsors were Will[m] Moody & Frances Moody Catholics.

J. Naylor Miss. O: S: B.

[12]. Alice Greham Daughter of Will[m] **Greham** & Jane **Pringle** his Wife was born at Netherton the 4th of August 1769 & baptized the 5th of the same month & year, the Sponsors were John Thompson & Jane Grey Catholics.

1770

Christopher Turnbull Son of Christopher **Turnbull** & Jane **Henderson** his Wife was born at Hetherton the 20th of March 1770 & baptized the 22[d] of the same Month & year, the Sponsors were John Thompson & Ann Grey Catholicks.

Thomas Thorborne Son of James **Thorborne** & Mary **Grey** was born at Biddleston the 15th of April 1770 & baptized the 16th of that Month & year, the Sponsors were Rob[t] Grey & Mary Grey.

J. Naylor Miss. O: S: B:

[13]. Barbara Jordan Daughter of George **Jordan** & Mary

* F Naylor signs each page, not each entry

Wallis his Wife was born at Harbottle the 4th of September 1770 & baptized the 5th of the same Month & year, the Sponsors were John Scott & Margt Selby, Catholics.

1771

Ann Storer* Daughter of Edward **Storer*** Protestant & Mary **Robson** his Wife was born at Hally-stone the 27th of february 1771 & baptized the 28th of the same Month & year, the Sponsors were John Robson & Elizabeth Gibson Catholics.

Margt Brown Daughter of Robt **Brown** & Margt **Scrowther** his Wife was born at Biddleston the 3d of March 1771 & baptized the 4th of the same month & year. the Sponsors were Willm Grey & Helen Davison Catholic.

J. Naylor Miss: O: S: B.

[14] Thos Greham Son of Willm **Greham** & Jane **Pringle** his Wife was born at Netherton the 2d of July 1771 & baptized the 3d of the same Month & year. the Sponsors were John Turnbull & Ann Grey Catholicks.

Mary Bollum Daughter of Christopher **Bollum** & Helen **Peary** his Wife was born at Biddleston the 4th of September 1771 & baptized the same day. the Sponsors were Robt Peary & Agnes Unwing Catholics.

Christopher Dodds son of Christopher **Dodds** & Hanna **Dunn** his Wife was born at Netherton the 11th of october 1771 & baptized the 12th of the same Month & year. the Sponsors were John Dodds & Mary Scott Catholicks.

J. Naylor Miss. O.S.B.

1772

[15] Mary Avery Daughter of John **Avery** & Margt **Dodds** his Wife was born at Biddleston the 31st of April 1772 & baptized the same day. the Sponsors were Luke Avery & Dorothy Dodds Catholics.

Edward Fail son of George **Fail** & Catharine **Moody** his Wife was born at Quickningcote the 25th of June 1772 & baptized the 28th of the same Month and year. the the Sponsors were Edwd Selby & Mary Moody.

James Turnbull Son of Christopher **Turnbull** & Jane **Henderson** his Wife was born at Netherton the 23d of July 1772 & baptized the same day. the Sponsors were Willm Grey & Jane Scott.

J. Naylor Miss. O: S: B.

[16] Luke Thorborne Son of James **Thorborne** & Mary **Grey** his Wife was born at Biddleston the 27th of September 1772 & baptized the 28th of the same Month & year. the Sponsors were Luke Thorborne & Jane Grey Catholicks.

1773

John **Greham** Son of Willm **Gream** & Jane **Pringle** his Wife was born at Netherton the 3d of August 1773 & baptized the 4th of

* This may have been *Storrer*, some letter having been obliterated in the place of the second r.

the same Month & year the Sponsors were John Dodds & Jane Scott Catholicks.

Elizabeth Storer* Daughter of Edw[d] **Storer†** Protestan & Mary **Robson** his Wife was born at Haly-stone the 4th of August 1773 & baptized the 5th of the same Month & year. the Sponsors were Jasper Gibson & Helen Robson Catholicks.

J. Naylor Miss. O: S: B.

1774

[17] John Dodds Son of Christopher **Dodds** & Hanna **Dunn** his Wife was born at Netherton the 19th of January 1774 & baptized the same day. the Sponsors were John Thompson & Marg[t] Turnbull.

Rob[t] Brown Son of Rob[t] **Brown** & Marg[t] **Scrowther** his Wife was born at Biddleston the 13th of February 1774 & baptized the same day. The Sponsors were Will[m] Brown & Jane Davison.

Barbara Bollum. Daughter of Christopher **Bollum** & Helen **Peary** his Wife was born at Biddleston the 22[d] of September 1774 & baptized the 23[d] of the same Month & year. the Sponsors were Will[m] Snowdon & Barbara Collingwood.

J. Naylor Miss. O: S: B.

1775

[18]. Helen Brown Daughter of Will[m] **Brown** & Jane **Davison** his Wife was born at Biddleston the 15th of July 1775 & baptized the 16th of the same Month & year, the Sponsors were Will[m] Dodds & Barbara Brown.

Mary Storer* Daughter of Edward **Storer*** Protestant & Mary **Robson** his Wife was born at Newton the 14th of September 1755 & baptized the 15th of the same Month & year, the Sponsors were Tho[s] Rutherford & Mary Alder Catholicks.

Ann Greham Daughter of Will[m] **Greham** & Jane **Pringle** his Wife was born at Cote-walls the 17th of September 1775 & baptized the 18th of the same Month & year, the Sponsors were John Brown & Barbara Brown.

J. Naylor Miss: O: S: B.

[19]. Thomas Davison natural son of Rob[t] **Davison** Catholick & Isabel **Farguison** was born at Yelden the 28th of October 1775 & baptized the 29th of the same Month & year, the Sponsors were Tho[s] Davison & Elizabeth Davison Cath.

1776

Eleonora Davison Daughter of George **Davison** & Catharine his Wife was born at Borrowden Mains the 16th of June 1777 & baptized the 17th of the same month & year, the Sponsors were George Robson & Jane Scott.

Will[m] Brown Son of Will[m] **Brown** & Jane **Davison** his Wife was born at Biddleston the 26th of June 1777 & baptized the 27th of the same month & year, the Sponsors were Stephen Wilkins & Ann Avery.

J. Naylor Miss. O: S: B.

* 'r' in Storrer *crossed out.*

† A second 'r' crossed out.

[20]. Frances Turnbull Daughter of Christopher **Turnbull** & Jane **Henderson** his Wife was born at Netherton the 18th of July 1777 & baptized the 19th of the same Month & year, the Sponsors were Francis Scott & Frances Snowdon.

Christopher Bollum Son of Christopher **Bollum** & Helen **Peary** his Wife was born at Biddleston the 29th of September 1777 & baptized the same day, the Sponsors were Thos Smith & Rachel Bell.

1778

Jane Greham Daughter of Willm **Greham** & Jane **Pringle** his Wife was born at Cote-walls the 21st of January 1778 & baptized the 22d of the same month & year, the Sponsors were Willm Snowdon & Jane Elder.

J. Naylor Miss. O: S: B.

[21]. Thos Davison Son of Charle **Davison** Catholick & Mary **Potts** his his Wife, protestant, was born at Sharperton the 21st of may 1778 & baptized the 24th of the same month & year, the Sponsors were Thos Dodds Ann Hann Catholics.

1779

John Brown Son of Willm **Brown** & Jane **Davison** his Wife was born at Biddleston the 17th of January 1779 & baptized the 18th of the same Month & year, the Sponsors were John Davison & Dorothy Brown.

1780

Thos Selby Son of Thos **Selby** Esqr & Catharine **Hodshon** his Wife was born at Causey Park in North-land the 3d of January 1780 & baptized the same day by Thos Meynell, the Sponsors were Thos Selby Esqr & Mrs Scroope.

J. Naylor Miss. O: S: B.

[*A loose certificate reads*] Londini 7 Sep. 1787. Ego infrascriptus baptisavi Thomam filiam Thomæ et Catharinæ Selby, Conjugum natum 3d Jan. 1780, susceptores fuere Thomas Selby et Clementina Scroope. Thomas Meynell, Sac.

[22]. Elizabeth Feram Daughter of John **Feram** & Clare **Bulins** his Wif was born at Netherton the 27th of December 1780 & baptized the same day, the Sponsors were Willm Turnbull & Jane Turnbull.

1781

Ralph Simon Selby Son of Thos **Selby** Esqr Jun. & Mrs Catharine **Hodshon** his Wife was born at Etall the 26th of March 1781 & baptized the same day, the Sponsors were Simon Scroope Esq. & Mrs Eleonara Selby.

Margt Brown Daughter of Willm **Brown** & Jane **Davison** his Wife was born at Biddleston the 20th of April 1781 & baptized the 22d of the same Month & year, the Sponsors were Charles Brown & Isabel Grey.

J. Naylor Miss. O: S: B.

[23] 1782

[Charles *xd out*, Robert *above*] Brown Son of Charles **Brown**

& Ann **Robison** his Wife was born at Cote-walls the 11th of March 1782 & baptized the 12th of the same month & year, the Sponsors were James Thorborne & Elizabeth Brown.

Edward Storer* son of Edward **Storer*** Protestant & Mary **Robson** his Wife Catholick was born at Newton the 2d of April 1782 & baptized the 14th of the same Month & year. the Sponsors were —— Kelson & Jane Elder Catholicks.

Joseph Greham Son of Willm **Greham** & Jane **Pringle** his Wife was born at Cote-walls the 15th of July 1782 & baptized the 19th of the same month & year, the Sponsors were Robt Thorborne & Mary Watson.

J. Naylor Miss. O : S : B.

[24] Edward Selby Son of Thos **Selby** Esqr Jun. & Catharine **Hodshon** his Wife was born at Etall in North-land the 3d of August 1782 & baptized the 4th of the same month & year: the Sponsors were Edward Meynell Esqr. & Miss Mary Selby.

1783

Robt Kirkup Son of Thos **Kirkup** & Mary **Scott** his Wife was born at Harbottle the 31st of January 1783 & baptized the 2d of February the same year the Sponsors were John Turnbull & Jane Scott Catholicks.

Isabel Turnbull natural Daughter of George **Fisher** & Isabel **Turnbull** was born at Netherton the 14th of february 1783 & baptized the 15th of the same Month & year the Sponsors were Christopher Turnbull & Jane Turnbull.

J. Naylor Miss. O.S.B.

[25] Margt Davison Daughter of Christo **Davison** Catholick & Mary **Potts** his Wife Protestant was born at Sharperton the 6th of August 1783 & baptized the 10th of the same month & year. the Sponsors were John Turnbull & Elizabeth Snowdon Catholicks.

Robert Brown son of Willm **Brown** & Jane **Davison** his Wife was born at Biddleston the 13th of September 1783 & baptized the 14th of the same month & year, the Sponsors were Willm Dickison & Frances Patterson.

1784

Helen Pringle Daughter of Willm **Pringle** Protestant & Barbara **Pringle** his Wife was born at Ryal the 10th of March 1784 & baptized the 11th of the same Month & year. the Sponsors were Christopher Davison & Dorothy Snowdon Catholics.

J. Naylor Miss. O : S : B.

[26] Mary Smith Daughter of Thos **Smith** & Margt **Loraine** his Wife was born at Wood-hall the 14th of March 1784 & baptized the 15th of the same Month & year, the Sponsors were George Loraine & Mary Alder.

Joseph Brown Son of Charles **Brown** & Ann **Robison** his Wife was born at Cote-Walls the 19th of March 1784 & baptized the same day the Sponsors were Willm Turnbull & Sara Watson.

* A second 'r' crossed out.

1785

Elizabeth Smith Daughter of Thos **Smith** & Marg **Loraine** his Wife was born at Wood hall the 21st of May 1785 & baptized the 22d of the same Month & year. the Sponsors were John Smith & Mrs Margt Trevallian.

J. Naylor Miss. O: S: B.

[27] Walter Selby Son of Thos **Selby** Esqr & Catharine **Hodson** his Wife was born at Chesters in Northumberland the 27th of May 1785 & baptized the same day. the Sponsors were Mr Nicho Selby & Mrs Cay.

Mary Davison Daughter of Thos **Davison** Catholick & Mary **Scott** his Wife Protestant was born at Elilaw the 29th of July 1785 & baptized the 31st of the same Month & year, the Sponsors were John Brown & Margt Stamp Catholicks.

John Kirkup Son of Thos **Kirkup** Protestant & Mary **Scott** his Wife was born at Allenton the 19th of November 1785 & baptized the 27th of the same Month & year, the Sponsors were Francis Scott & Mary Dodds Catholicks.

J. Naylor Miss. O: S: B.

[28]. Thos Brown Son of Willm **Brown** & Jane **Davison** his Wife was born at Biddleston the 21st of December 1785 & baptized the 22d of the same Month & year, the Sponsors were John Brown & Dorothy Jordan.

1786

James Robson Storer* Son of Edwd **Storer*** Protestant & Mary **Robson** his Wife was born at Newton the 4th of May 1786 & baptized the 9th of the same Month & year, the Sponsors were Thos Smith & Margt Gibson Catholicks.

Jane Brown Daughter of Charles **Brown** & Ann **Robison** his Wife was born at Cote-walls the 11th of May 1786 & baptized the 14th of the same Month & year, the Sponsors were John Brown & Fortune Brown.

J. Nay Miss. O: S: B.

[29]. Margt Smith Daughter of Thos **Smith** & Margt **Loraine** his Wife was born at Woodhall the 27th of May 1786 & baptized the same day, the Sponsors were Roger Palms & Ann Smith Catholicks.

John Sample Son of Robt **Sample** of Hagdon Protestant & Sarah **Watson** his Wife Catholick was born at Borrowdon the 18th of September 1786 & baptized the 20th of the same Month & year, the Sponsors were James Thorborne & Ann Bollum Catholics.

Ann Davison Daughter of Christopher **Davison** Catholick & Ann **Frizzel** his Wife Protestant was born at Yeldom the 28th of October 1786 & baptized the 29th of the same month and year, the Sponsors were Thos Davison & Ann Dodds Catholicks.

J. Naylor Miss. O: S: B.

* A second 'r' crossed out.

[30]. N.B. Christopher **Davison** was maried to the said Ann **Frizzel** by me the 10th of July 1786 & promised to be married at Church the next day, but afterwards refused to be married to her, or own her for his Wife.

Jane Davison Daughter of Thos **Davison** Catholick & Mary **Scott** his Wife Protestant was born at Elilaw the 4th of November 1786 & baptized the 5th of the same month & year, the Sponsors were Willm Turnbull & Isabel Greham Catholics.

1787

Jane Davison Daughter of Charls **Davison** Catholick & Mary **Potts** his Wife protestant was born at Sharperton the 7th of January 1787 & baptized the 8th of the same Month & year, the Sponsors were John Jordan & Mary Turnbull Catholics.

J. Naylor Miss. O: S: B.

[31]. Catharine Mary Selby Daughter of Thos **Selby** Esqr & Catharine **Hodshon** his wife was born at Chesters in North-land the 4th of February 1787 & baptized the same day by Mr J: Taylor Priest of Hexham, the Sponsors were Mr John Selby & Mrs Henrietta Carr.

[*The last register is repeated with important variations on a piece of paper pinned on to the page, and is doubtless an original register. It reads as follows*:—Febr 4 1781.

Catharine Mary Selby Daughter of Thos & Cathr **Selby** was born at Chesters in Northumberland and baptized the same day by me John Taylor of Hexham—Patrinus John Selby—Duaci, Matrina Henrietta Carr—Eboraci.]

Eleonora Morralu Daughter of Robt **Morralu** Protestant & Jane **Blacklock** his Wife was born at Hatherwick the 26th of January 1787 & baptized the 30th of the same month & year, the Sponsors were John Blacklock & Ann Blacklock Catholicks.

Thos Smith Son of Thos **Smith** & Margt **Loraine** his Wife was born at Woodhall the 19th of July 1787 & baptized the 20th of the same month & year by Mr Potts Priest at Thropton, the Sponsors were John Smith & Mrs Radcliffe.

J. Naylor Miss. O: S: B.

[32]. Ann Smith Daughter of John **Smith** & Ann **Loraine** his Wife was born at Warton the 8th of September 1787 & baptized the same day, the Sponsors were George Loraine & Margt Smith.

Thomas Kirkup Son of Thos **Kirkup** Protestant & Mary **Scott** his Wife Catholick was born at Allenton the 13th of September 1787 & baptized the 16th of the same Month & year, the Sponsors were Willm Turnbull & Mary Thorborne Catholicks.

1788

Christopher Robson Son of [James *xd out*, Henry *above*] Witherington **Robson** & Ann **Bollum** his Wife was born at Rothbury the 27th of January 1788 & baptized the 28th of the same month & year, the Sponsors were Christopher Bollum & Margt Bollum.

J. Naylor Miss. O: S: B.

[33] Henrietta Eleanora Selby Daughter of Thos **Selby** Esqr and Catherine **Hodshon** his wife was born at Chesters in North-land the 12th of April 1788 & baptized the same day by Mr Thos Story Priest of Hexham the Sponsors were Mr Robt Selby & Mrs Catherine Selby.

Robt Brown Son of Willm **Brown** & Jane **Davison** his Wife was born at Borrowdon the 8th of August 1788 & baptized the 10th of the same Month & year the Sponsors were Robt Robson & Elizabeth Brown Catholicks.

Willm Dixon Son of Thos **Dixon** [Protes *above*] & Isabel **Greham** his Wife [Catholick *above*] born at Elilaw the 15th of September 1788 & baptized the 16th of the same month & year. The Sponsors were James Thorborne & Jane Holmes Catholicks.

J. Naylor Miss O: S: B.

[*Pinned to the previous, facing page is a slip as follows.*]

Marg^t^ Brown Daughter of Charles **Brown** & Ann **Robinson** his Wife, was born at Biddleston the 9th of December 1788 & baptized the 11th of the same Month & year, by the Revd Mr Himsworth of Thropton, the Sponsors were Henry Boldon & Jane Holmes Catholicks.

1789

[34] Gilbert Hetherington son of Willm **Hetherington** & Elizabeth **Oliver** his Wife was born at Cooper-hill in the Parish of Simonburn on the 20th of February 1789 & baptized the 2^d^ of March 1789 the Sponsor was Mary Oliver Catholick.

Barbara Brown Daughter of Willm **Brown** & Jane **Davison** his Wife was born at Borrowdon the 31st of August 1789 & baptized the same day the Sponsors were Robt Robson & Elizabeth Brown Catholicks.

Richard John Selby Son of Thos **Selby** Esqr & Catharine **Hodshon** his Wife was born at Chesters in the Parish of Warden, County of Northumberland, the 25th of September 1789 & baptized the same day. The Sponsors were John Weston Webb Esqr & Miss Frances Scroope Catholicks.

John Naylor Miss: O· S: B:

[35] Ferdinand Jordan Son of Ferdinand **Jordan** & Mary **Davison** his Wife was born at Harbottle the 20th of October 1789 & was baptized the same day the Sponsors were James Witherington Robson & Mary Bollum.

George Kirkup Son of Thos **Kirkup** protestant & Mary **Scott** his Wife [Cat: *above*] was born at Allinton the 17th of Decemb^r^ & baptized the 18th of the same month and year 1789 the Sponsors were Thos Robson & Barbara Ferry Catholics.

1790

James Robson Son of Hen: Witherington **Robson** & Ann **Bollum** his Wife was born at Barrow mill the 15th of Feb: 1790 & was baptized the 16th of the same month & year, the Sponsors were Robt Potts & Eleanor Potts, Catholicks.

John Naylor Miss: O: S: B:

[36] Jane Murton Daughter of Andrew **Murton** & Mary **Turnbull** his Wife was born at Borrowdon the 27th August 1790 & baptized the 28th of the same month and year, the Sponsors were James Turnbull & Mary Murton, Catholicks.

Eleonora Storer Daughter of Edwd **Storer** Protestant & Mary **Robson** his Wife was born at Newton the 20th of october 1790 & baptized the 26th of the same month & year. the Sponsors were John Gibson & Ann Gibson Catholicks.

[1791]

Mary Jordan Daughter of Ferdinand **Jordan** & Mary **Davison** his Wife was born at Harbottle the 13th of August 1791 & baptized the same day the Sponsors were John Jordan & Mary Davison Cath.

J. Naylor Miss: O: S: B:

[37] Elizabeth Smith Daughter of John **Smith** & Ann **Loraine** his Wife was born at Warton in the Parish of Rothbury Northld the 17th of September [1791 *above*] & baptized the 18th of the same Month & year. the Sponsors were James Champney & Jane Elder Catholi[cks.]

Charles Brown Son of Charles **Brown** & Ann **Robison** his Wife was born at Biddleston in the Parish of Allenton Northld the 19th of September 1791 & baptized the same day. the Sponsors were Wilm Snowdon & Mary Simmons, Cath.

Francis Kirkup Son of Thos **Kirkup** Protestant & Mary **Scot** this Wife was born at Allenton the 20th of October 1791 & baptized the 21st of the same month & year. the Sponsors were Thos Thompson & Margaret Stamp [?] Catholicks.

J. Naylor Miss: O: S: B.

[38] 1792 [*sic*]

Elizabeth Mary Hickson Daughter of Robt **Hickson** & Rachel **Frankland** his Wife was born at Biddleston in the Parish of Allenton the 18th of December 1791 [and baptized the same day *above*]. the Sponsors were Henry Bolam & Jane Bolam Catholicks.

[1792]

Helen Robson Daughter of Henry Witherington **Robson** & Ann **Bollum** his Wife was born at Barrow mill in the parish of Allenton the first of February 1792 & was baptized the same day the Sponsors were Christopher Bollum Jun. & Barbara Bollum Cat.

Albert Selby Son of Thos **Selby** Esqr & Catharine **Hodson** his Wife was born at Chesters in the Parish of Warden the 23d of March 1792 & baptized the same day the Sponsors were Mr Simon Scroope & Mrs Ann Stapleton Catholicks.

J. Naylor Miss: O: S: B:

[39] Isabel Murton Daughter of Andrew **Murton** & Mary **Turnbull** his Wife was born near Burrowdon in the Parish of Allenton the 16th of October 1792 & baptized the 17th of the

same month & year the Sponsors were John Turnbull and Frances Turnbull Catholicks.

[1793]

Willm Selby Son of Thos **Selby** Esqr & Catherine **Hodshon** his Wife was born at Chesters in the Parish of Warden North-land the 13th of October 1793 & baptized the same day, the Sponsors were Willm Mannock Esqr & Chariot Strickland, Catholicks.

John Brown Son of Charles **Brown** & Ann **Robison** his Wife was born at Biddleston the 12th of October 1793 & baptized the same day by the Rev^{d} Mr. Himsworth of Thropton, the Sponsors were John Brown & Helen Boyde Catholicks.

J. Naylor Miss: O: S: B:

[40]. 1794

Willm John Smith Son of Thos **Smith** & Margaret **Loraine** his Wife was born at Woodhall in the Parish of Allenton North-land the 14th of January 1794 & baptized the 15th of the same Month & year, the Sponsors were George Loriane & Elizabeth Champney, Cat.

Christopher Robson Son of Willm Witherington **Robson** & Anne **Bollum** his Wife was born at Barrow mill in the Parish of Allenton North-land the 13th of June 1794 & baptized the 15th of the same Month & year, the Sponsors were Christopher Bollum & Marg^{t} Whinhum Catholicks.

Marg^{t} Murton Daughter of Andrew **Murton** & Mary **Turnbull** his Wife was born at Burrowdon in the Parish of Allenton North-land the 15th of Nov^{br} 1794 & baptized the 16th of same month & year, the Sponsors were James Murton & Jane Turnbull Catholicks.

[41] 1796

[*The following certificate is pinned on p.* 41.]

Willm Brown Son of Charles **Brown** & Anne **Robbison** his Wife born at Biddleston the 5th of May 1796 in the Parish of Allenton North-land & baptized the same day, the Sponsors were Luke Thornborne & Mary Brown Catholicks. J: Naylor.

Henry Witherington Robson Son of Hen^{y} Witherington **Robson** & Anne **Bollum** his Wife was born at Barrow Mill in the Parish of Allenton North-land the 27th of September 1796 & baptized the 28th of the same month & year, the Sponsors were Luke Thorborne & Barbara Bollum Catholicks.

1797

James Turnbull Son of Christopher **Turnbull** & Sarah **Bolam** his Wife was born at Netherton in the Parish of Allenton North-land the 2^{d} of April 1797 & babtized the same day, the Sponsors were James Turnbull and Frances Turnbull Catholicks.

Willm Murton Son of Andrew **Murton** & Mary **Turnbull** his Wife was born near Burrowden in the Parish of Allenton Nor-land the 15th of April 1797 & baptized the 16th of the same month & year, the Sponsors were Robt Brown and Jane Murton Catholicks.

J. Naylor Miss: O: S: B:

[42] George Smith Son of Thos **Smith** & Marg^{t} **Loraine** his Wife was born at Woodhall in the Parish of Allenton North-land the 16th of July 1797 & baptized the 17th of the same Month and year, the Sponsors were George Loraine & Ann Snowdon Catholicks.

John Whinham Son of Henry **Whinham** & Marg^{t} **Bollum** his Wife was born at Burrowdon in the Parish of Allenton North-land the 20th of July 1797 & baptized the 21st of the same month & year, the Sponsors were Christopher Bollum & Mary Bollum Catholicks.

Frances Athy Daughter of John **Athy** Protestan & Helen **Boyde** his Wife was Born at Elilaw in the Parish of Allenton North-land the 2^{d} of November 1797 & baptized the 3^{d} of the same month & year, the Sponsor was Mary Jackson Catholick.

J. Naylor Miss: O: S: B:

[43] 1798

Maria Selby Daughter of Thos **Selby** Esqr & Mrs Catharine **Hodshon** his Wife was born at Biddleston the 2^{d} of March 1798 in the Parish of Allenton North-land, and baptized the 3^{d} of the same month & year, the Sponsors were the Hon. Charles Dormer & M^{rs} —— Blount Catholicks.

Jane Thorborne Daughter of Luke **Thornborne** & Mary **Barningham** his Wife was born at Biddleston in the Parish of Allenton North-land the 16th of March 1798 & baptized the 17th of the same Month & year, the Sponsors were John Thorborne & Helen White Catholicks.

Barbara Brown Daughter of Charles **Brown** & Ann **Robison** his Wife was born at Biddleston the 8th of July 1798 in the Parish of Allenton North-land & baptized the same day m^{r} sous verte a French Priest at Wooler, the Sponsors were Willm Brown & Hannah Brown Catholicks.

J. Naylor Miss: O: S: B.

[44]. Isabel Turnbull Daughter of James **Turnbull** & Elizabeth **Richardson** (Protestant) his Wife, was born at Netherton in the Parish of Allenton, North-land, the 21st of october 1798 & baptized the 22^{d} of the same month & year, the Sponsors were Christopher Turnbull & Sarah Turnbull Catholicks.

Frances Turnbull Daughter of Christopher **Turnbull** & Sarah **Bolam** his Wife was born at Netherton in the Parish of Allenton, North-land the 3^{d} of December 1798 & baptized the 4th of the same month & year, the Sponsors were James Blacklock & Frances Turnbull Catholicks.

Isabel Robson Daughter of Witherington **Robson** & Ann **Bollum** his Wife was born at Barrow Mill in the Parish of Allenton North-land the 2[4]th of December 1798 & baptized the 29th of the same Month & year, the Sponsors were Mark Selby & Helen Bollum Catholicks.

J. Naylor Miss. O: S: B.

[45] 1799

Sarah Turnbull Daughter of Christopher **Turnbull** & Sarah

Bolam his Wife was born at Netherton in the Parish of Allenton North-land the 7th of October 1799 & baptized the same day the Sponsors were Robt Blacklock & Frances Turnbull Catholicks.

Thos Thorborne Son of Luke **Thorborne** & Mary **Barmingham** his Wife was born at Biddleston in the Parish of Allenton North-land the 21st of December 1799 & baptized the 22d of the same month & year the Sponsors were George Bolam & Mary Gallon Catholicks.

[1800]

Jane Turnbull Daughter of James **Turnbull** & Elizabeth **Richardson** (Protestant) his Wife, was born at Netherton in the Parish of Allenton North-land the 23d of February 1800 & baptized the 24th of the same month & year, the Sponsors were John Turnbull & Frances Turnbull Catholicks.

J. Naylor Miss. O: S: B.

[46]. Margaret Athy Daughter of John **Athy** (Protestant) & Helen **Boyde** his Wife was born at Harbottle in the Parish of Allenton North-land the 24th of February 1800 & baptized the 25th of the same month & year, the Sponsors were George Robson & Sarah Elder, Catholicks.

Helen Whinham Daughter of Henry **Whinham** & Margaret **Bollum** his Wife was born at Burrowdon in the Parish of Allenton, North-land the 6th of April 1800 & baptized the same day, the Sponsors were Willm Curry & Margaret Smith Catholicks.

Jane Brown Daughter of Robt **Brown** [Jun. ?], & Barbara **Potts** (Presbyterian) his Wife, was born at Biddlestone in the Parish of Allenton North-land the 2d of September 1800 & baptized the same day the Sponsors were Robt Brown Jun: and Sarah Elder, Catholicks.

J. Naylor Miss O S B

[47] Mary Turnbull Daughter of Christopher **Turnbull** & Sarah **Bolam** his Wife was born at Netherton in the Parish of Allenton North-land the 7th of November 1800 & baptized the 8th of the same month and year, the Sponsors were James Turnbull & Rachel Hickson, Catholicks.

1801

Thos Brown Son of Charles **Brown** & Ann **Robison** his Wife was born at Biddleston in the Parish of Allenton North-land, the 30th of April 1801 & baptized the same day by Rachel Hickson, thought to be in danger of death, the rest supplied by me, the Sponsors were Willm Curry & Elizabeth Mills, Catholicks.

Isabel Snowdon Daughter of George **Snowdon** & Elizabeth **Hudspeth** his wife (Presbyterian) was born at Biddleston Edge in the Parish of Allenton, North-land the 26th of June 1801 & baptized the 27th of the same Moth and year, the Sponsors were Luke Thorborne and Rachel Hymers, Catholicks.

J. Naylor Miss: O S B

[48] 1802

Jane Thorborne Daughter of Luke **Thorborne** & Mary

Barmingham his Wife was born at Biddleston in the parish of Allenton North-land the 16th of January 1802 & baptized the same day, the Sponsors were Thos Thorborne & Jane Thorborne, Catholicks.

Edward Robson Son of Witherington **Robson** & Ann **Bollum** his Wife was born at Barrow mill in the Parish of Allenton North-land the 27th of March 1802 & baptized the 28th of the same month & year. the Sponsors were Robson Storer & Ann Storer Catholicks.

Margaret Turnbull Daughter of James **Turnbull** & Elizabeth **Richardson** his Wife (Presbyterian) was born at Netherton in the Parish of Allenton, North-land the 2d of April 1802 & baptized the same day, the Sponsors were Andrew Murton & Margt Turnbull Catholicks.

J. Naylor Miss: O S B

[49] Margaret Brown Daughter of Robt **Brown** & Barbara **Potts** (Presbyterian) his wife was born at Biddleston in the Parish of Allenton North-land the 16th of May 1802 & baptized the the 17th of the same month & year, the Sponsors were John Brown Susanha Welton, Catholicks.

Thos Bolam Son of George **Bolam** & Barbara **Wallace** his Wife was born at Biddleston in the the Parish of Allenton North-land the 2d of July 1802 & baptized the same day the Sponsors were Edward Simmons & Sarah Elder Catholicks.

Helen Athy Daughter of John **Athy** (Protestant) & Helen **Boyde** his Wife was bornt at Harbottle in the Parish of Allenton, North-land the 6th of November 1802 & baptized the 8th of the same month & year, the Sponsors were Charles Davison & Margt Stamp Catholicks.

J. Naylor Miss: O S B:

[50] 1803

Jane Whinham Daughter of Henry **Whinham** & Margaret **Bollum** his Wife was born at Sharperton in the Parish of Allenton North-land the 1st of January 1803 & baptized the 2d of the same Month & year the Sponsors were James Robson Stor[r *xd out*]er & Margt Smith Catholicks.

Thos Brown Son of Charles **Brown** & Ann **Robison** his Wife was born at Biddleston in the Parish of Allenton North-land the 27th of January 1803 & baptized the same day & Month the Sponsors were John Brown & Elizabeth Mills Catholicks.

George Snowdon Son of George **Snowdon** & Elizabeth **Hudspeth** his Wife ware born at Biddleston Edge in the Parish of Allenton North-land the 31st of August 1803 & baptized the same day, the Sponsors were John Brown & Rachel Hickson.

J. Naylor Miss: O S B.

[51] 1804

Elizabeth Turnbull Daughter of James **Turnbull** & Elizabeth **Richardson** his Wife (Presbyterian) was born at Netherton in the Parish of Alwinton Northland the 16th of January 1804 &

baptized the 17th of the same month & year, the Sponsors were Edward Simmons and Mary Murton Catholicks.

Matthew Bolam Son of George **Bolam** & Barbara **Wallace** his Wife was born at Biddleston in the Parish of Alwinton North-land the 12th of February 1804 & baptized the same day, the Sponsors were Thos & Catharine Rutherford Catholicks.

Mary Thorborne Daughter of Luke **Thorborne** & Mary **Barmingham** his wife was born at Biddleston in the Parish of Alwinton North-land, the 15th of Aprill 1804 & baptized the same day, the Sponsors were Luke Farrer & Mary Haughton Catholicks.

J. Naylor Miss : O : S : B.

[52] Margaret Turnbull Daughter of Christopher **Turnbull** & Sarah **Bolam** his Wife was born at Netherton in the Parish of Alwinton North-land the 1[6 ?]th of June 1804 & baptized the 17th of the same Month and year, the Sponsors were James Turnbull & Mary Murton Catholicks.

Barbara Brown Daughter of the late Robt **Brown** of [Biddleston *above*] & Barbara **Potts** his Wife (Presbyterian) was born at Netherton-Pike in the Parish of Alwinton North-Land the 7th of August & baptized the 8th of the same Month and year, the Sponsors were George Bolam & Rachel Hickson Catholicks.

Willm Robson son of Witherington **Robson** & Ann **Bollum** his Wife was born at Barrow mill in the Parish of Alwinton North-ld the 13th of August 1804 & baptized the [same day *xd out*] [15th of the same month and year *above*], the Sponsors were John Brown & Ann Coates Catholicks.

J. Naylor Miss : O : S : B :

[53] 1805

Jane Murton Daughter of Andrew **Murton** & Mary **Turnbull** his Wife was born near Burrodon in the Parish of Alwinton North-land the first of March 1805 & baptized the 2d of the same Month & year, the Sponsors were John Murton & Mary Murton Catholicks.

John Athy Son of John **Athy** Protestant & Helen **Boyde** his Wife was born at Harbottle in the Parish of Alwinton North-land the 30th of April 1805 & baptized the 3d of May year do the Sponsors were Robt Hickson & Diana Snowball Catholicks.

Alexander Bolam Son of George **Bolam** & Barbara **Wallace** his Wife was born at Biddleston in the Parish of Alwinton North-land the 8th of November 1805 & baptized the same day, the Sponsors were John & Ann Rutherford Catholicks.

J. Naylor Miss : O : S : B.

[54] Margt Whinham Daughter Henry **Whinham** & Margt **Bollum** his Wife was born at Sharperton in the Parish of Alwinton North-land the 30th of November 1805 & baptized the 2d of December the same year, the Sponsors were Thos Davison & Barbara Bollum Catholicks.

1806

Mary Rhode Turnbull Daughter of Willm **Turnbull** & Elizabeth **Richardson** his Wife (Presbyterian) was born at Netherton in the

Parish of Alwinton North-land the 22[d] of March 1806 & baptized the 23[d] of the same month & year, the Sponsors were Lawson Moffit & Jane Moffit Catholicks.

James Snowdon Son of George **Snowdon** & Elizabeth **Hudspeth** his Wife was born at Biddleston in the Parish of Alwinton North-land the 19th of April 1806 & baptized the 20th of the same Month & year the Sponsors were Joseph Brown & Mary Story Catholicks.

J. Naylor Miss: O: S: B.

[55]. John Turnbull Son of Christopher **Turnbull** & Sarah **Bolam** his Wif was born at Netherton in the Parish of Alwinton North-land on the 23[d] of May 1806 & was baptized on the 25th of the same month & year, the Sponsors were Rob[t] Blacklock & Helen Blacklock Catholicks.

1807

Ann Robson Daughter of Witherington **Robson** & Ann **Bollum** his wife was born at Barrow Mill in the Parish of Alwinton North-land on the 25th of January 1807 & was baptized the same day, the Sponsors were Rob[t] Gray & Mary Storer Catholicks.

James Turnbull Son of Christopher **Turnbull** & Sarah **Bolam** his wife was born at Netherton in the Parish of Alwinton North-land on the 9th of August 1807 & was baptized the same day, the Sponsors were John Turnbull & Frances Turnbull Catholicks.

J. Naylor Miss: O: S: B.

[56]. John Bolam Son of George **Bolam** & Barbara **Wallace** his Wife was born at Biddleston in the Parish of Alwinton, North-land on the 13th of August 1807 & baptized the same day, the Sponsors were Luke Farrell & Elizabeth Storer, Catholics.

Jane Elizabeth Thorborne Daughter of Luke **Thorborne** & Mary **Burmingham** his wife was born at Biddleston in the Parish of Allenton Northl-d on the 15th of November 1807 & baptized the same day, the Sponsors were Rob[t] Gray & Martha Hunter Catholicks.

1808

Mary Athy Daughter of John **Athy** [Protestant *above*] & Helen **Boyde** his Wife was born at Harbottle in the Parish of Allenton Northland on the 25th of February 1808 & baptized the 28th of the same month & year, the Sponsors were James Robson & Rachel Hickson, Catholicks.

J: Naylor Miss: O: S: B.

[57]. Frances Turnbull Daughter of James **Turnbull** & Elizabeth **Richardson** his Wife (Protestant) was born at Netherton Mill in the Parish of Allenton, North-land on the 7th of April 1808 & was baptized on the 8th of the same month & year, the Sponsors were John Turnbull & Frances Turnbull Catholicks.

Sarah Turnbull Daughter of Christopher **Turnbull** & Sarah **Bolam** his Wife was born at Netherton in the Parish of Allenton North-land on the 27th of August 1808 & was baptized on the 28th of the same month & year, the sponsors were James Turnbull & Jane Moffet Catholicks.

1809

Thomas Snowdon Son of [Henry *xd out*] [George *above*] **Snowdon** & Elizabeth **Hudspeth** his Wife was born at Biddleston in the Parish of Allenton North-land the 11th of April 1809 & baptized the 12th of the same month & year the Sponsors were Robt Brown & Elizabeth Snowdon, Catholicks.

J: Naylor Miss: O: S: B

[58] Mary & Frances Murton twin sisters Daughters of Andrew **Murton** & Mary **Turnbull** his Wife were born at Low trewitt in the Parish of Rothbury North-land on the 30th of April 1809 & baptized on the 1st of may of the same year, the Sponsors of Mary were John & Ann Dodds—of Frances James Turnbull & Margt Turnbull Catholicks.

1810

George Athy son of John **Athy** (Protestant) & Helen **Boyde** his wife, was born at Harbottle in the Parish of Allenton Northumberland on 19th of may 1810 & baptized on the 22d of the same Month & year. The Sponsors were John Gray & Rachel Hymers Catholics.

Mary Darling Daughter of Thomas **Darling** [Presbitn *above*] & Helen **Thompson** his Wife, was born at Borrowdon in the Parish of Allenton Northumberland on the 31st of august 1810 & baptized the same day, the Sponsors were George Robson & Jane Robson—Proxies Thos Smith & Elizabeth Brown, Catholicks.

J. Naylor Miss: O: S: B:

[59] 1811

Ann Gray Daughter of John **Gray** & Margt **Brown** his Wife was born at Woodhall in the Parish of Allenton North-land on the 10th of July 1811 & baptized the same day, the Sponsors were Robt Gray & Miss Catharine Selby Catholicks.

James Thorborne Son of Luke **Thorborne** & Mary **Barmingham** his Wife was born at Biddleston in the Parish of Allenton North-land on the 10th of November 1811 & baptized the 11th of same month & year. the Sponsors were John Morral[ee ?] & Henrietta Selby Catholics.

[1812]

Elizabeth Snowdon Daughter of George **Snowdon** & Elizabeth **Hudspeth** his Wife was born at Biddleston in the Parish of Allenton, North-land on the 15th of February 1812 & baptized the same day the Sponsors were Willm Selby & Catharine Selby Catholicks.

J: Naylor Miss: O: S: B:

[60] 1813

Willm Brown Son of John **Brown** & Sarah **Hunter** his Wife was born at Biddleston in the Parish of Allenton North-land on the 24th of January 1813 & baptized on the 25th of the same month & year; by the Rev. John Sharrock Pst of long Horseley, the Sponsors were Mr Richd Selby & Miss Catherine Selby Catholicks.

Jane Turnbull Daughter of Christopher **Turnbull** & Sarah

Bolam his Wife, was born at Netherton in the Parish of Allenton North-land on the 28th of February 1813 & baptized on the 2d of March the same year, the Sponsors were John Bolam & Elizabeth Mills [?] Catholics.

Eleanor Darling Daughter of Thos **Darling** (Presbyterian) & Helen **Thompson** his his Wife was born at the Pieles in the parish of Allenton North-land on the 24th of April 1813 & baptized on the 29th of the same month & year. The Sponsors were John & Helen Morallee, Catholicks.

John Naylor Miss: O: S: B:

[61] Catherine Gray Daughter of John **Gray** & Margt **Brown** his Wife was born at Woodhall in the Parish of Allenton North-land on the 28th of April 1813 & baptized on the 30th of the same month & year, the Sponsors were Robt & Jane Brown Catholicks.

Christina Turnbull Daughter of James **Turnbull** & Elizabeth **Richardson** his Wife (Protestant) was born at Allenton North-land on the 26th of July 1813 & baptized on the 27th of the same month and year, the sponsors were Christopher Turnbull Junr & Helen Morallee Catholicks.

1814

William Patrick Gray Son of Robt **Gray** & Elizabeth **Hickson** his Wife was born at Biddleston in the Parish of Allenton North-land on the 17th of March 1814 & baptized the same day, month & year, the Sponsors were Mr Willm & Miss Catherine Selby Catholicks.

J. Naylor Miss: O: S: B:

[62] Ann Bolam Daughter of Thos **Bolam** (protestant) and Mary **Snowdon** his Wife [Catholick *above*] was born at harbottle Studs in the Parish of Whittingham, Northumberland on the 25th of Jani 1814, baptized on the 26th of the same month & year, the Sponsors were John Brown & Frances Turnbull, Catholicks.

1815

George Brown, son of John **Brown** & Sarah **Hunter** his Wife was born at Biddleston in the Parish of Allenton, Northumberlan, on the 29th of March 1815 & baptized the same Day, the Sponsors were Willm Brown & Mary Pape, Catholicks.

William Gray son of John **Gray** & Margaret **Brown** his Wife was born at Wood Hall the Parish of Allenton, North-land on the 10th of April 1815 & baptized the 11th of the same month & year, the Sponsors were John Brown & Barbara Brown Catholicks.

Jn Naylor, Miss: O: S: B:

[63] Rachel Catharine Gray, Daughter of Robert **Gray** & Elizabeth **Hickson** his Wife was born at Biddleston in the Parish of Allenton, North-land, on the 23d of August 1815 & baptized the same Day, the Sponsors were Thos Gray & Elizabeth Mills, Catholicks.

1816

Henrietta Turnbull, Daughter of James **Turnbull** & Elizabeth **Richardson** his Wife (Protestan) was born at Biddleston in the

Parish of Allenton North-land on the first day of may 1816 & baptized the same day, the Sponsors were Luke Thorborne & Mary Pape, Catholicks.

Rob[t] Gray Son of Robert **Gray** & Elizabeth **Hickson** his Wife was born at Biddleston in the Parish of Allenton, North-land on the 21st of July 1816 & baptized the same day—the Sponsors were Rob[t] & Rachel Hickson, Catholicks.

J[n] Naylor, Miss: O: S: B:

[64] John Erington Bolam son of Tho[s] **Bolam** (Protestant) & Mary **Snowdon** his Wife, Catholick, was born at Biddleston Edge in the Parish of Allenton, North-land, the 11th of September 1816 & baptized on the 12th of the same month & year. the Sponsors were John & Isabel Snowdon, Catholicks.

[1817]

Mary Brown Daughter of J[n] **Brown** & Sarah **Hunter** his wife was born at Biddleston in the Parish of Allenton, North-land, on the 19th of January 1817 & baptized the same day the Sponsors were Tho[s] & Mary Grundy, Catholicks.

James Turnbull son Christopher **Turnbull** jun. Catholick & Jane **Hogg** his Wife (Presbyterian) was born at Burrowdon in the Parish of Allenton, North-land on the 15th of March 1817 & baptized the 16th of the same month & year, the Sponsors were James Turnbull & Dorothy Wilson, Catholicks.

J[n] Naylor, Miss: O: S: B.

[65] Margaret Gray, Daughter of John **Gray** & Marg[t] **Brown** his Wife was born at Wood hall in the Parish of Allenton, North-land, the 30th of June 1817 & baptized the first of July the same year, the Sponsors were John Snowdon & Jane Dickison, Catholics.

1818

Maria Gray Daughter of Rob[t] **Gray** & Elizabeth **Hickson** his Wife was born at Biddleston in the Parish of Allenton, Northumberland the 22[d] of April 1818 & baptized the 23[d] of the same month & year, the Sponsors were James Gray & miss Maria Selby, Catholics.

Will[m] Andrew Hogg-Gray, son of Tho[s] **Gray** & Frances **Hogg** his Wife, was born at Holystone in the Parish of Allenton, Northumberland, the 27th of November 1818 & babtized the 29th of the same month & year, the Sponsors were Rob[t] Gray & Elizabeth Dodds, Catholics.

J[n] Naylor, Miss: O: S: B.

[66] 1819

Tho[s] Rutherford son of Tho[s] **Rutherford** & Mary **Dixon** his Wife was born at Biddleston Edge in the Parish of Allenton, North-land, the 28th of January 1819 & baptized the 31st of the same month & year, the Sponsors were Rob[t] Croziar & Catharine Anderson, Catholics.

Elionora Henrietta Brown, Daughter of John **Brown** & Sarah **Hunter** his wife, was born at Biddleston in the Parish of Allenton,

Northumberland, on the 2[d] of August 1819 & baptized the same day, the Sponsors were George & Rebecca Best, Catholics.

Mary Selby 2[d] daughter of Walter **Selby** Esq[r] * & Alice **Swarbrick** his Wife was born at Biddleston in the Parish of Allenton, Northumberland, on the 4th of September 1819 & baptized on the 5th of the same month & year, the Sponsors were M[r] Ralph Selby & M[rs] Agnes Anderade, Catholics.

J[n] Naylor, Miss: O: S: B.

[67]. Christopher Turnbull son of Christopher **Turnbull** jun. Catholic & Jane **Hogg** his Wife (Presbyt[n]) was born at Barrowdon in the Parish of Allenton (now call'd Alwinton), Northumberland, on the first of December 1819 & babtisd the 3[d] of the same month & year. The Sponsors were Will[m] Brown & Ann Hinderson, Catholics.

[1820]

Charles Gray son of John **Gray** & Margaret **Brown** his wife was born at Woodhall in the Parish of Alwinton, Northumberland on the 3[d] of august 1820 & baptised the 4th of the same month & year, the Sponsors were Thomas & Mary Thorborne [Catholics *below*].

[*Here follows a six line entry, scored out, which seemed to be that of* Eleanor Selby, *repeated on the next page.*]

John Naylor Missi: O: S: B.

[68]. Eleanora Selby 3[d] Daughter of [? o] Walter **Selby** Esq[r] & Alice **Swarbrick** his Wife was born at Biddleston [Hall *above*] in the parish of Allenton, Northumberland, on the 9th of August 1820 & baptized the same Day, the Sponsors were Will[m] Selby Esq[r] & M[rs] Catharine Clavering, Catholics.

Will[m] Rutherford son of Tho[s] **Rutherford** & Mary **Dixon** his Wife was born at Burrowdon in the Parish of Allenton, Northumberl'd on the 29th of Septemb[r] [1820 *above*] & baptized on the first of October the same year, the Sponsors were Will[m] Rutherford & Elizab White, Catholics.

Tho[s] Bartholomew Gray, son of Robert **Gray** & Elizabeth **Hickson** his Wife was born at Biddleston in the Parish of Allenton, Northumberland, on the 10th of October 1820 & baptized the 11th of the same month & year, the Sponsors were Tho[s] Kirkley & Jane Dixon, Catholics.

J[n] Naylor, Miss: O: S: B.†

* After the ampersand there is something interlined above, perhaps meant for "Mrs." Walter Selby was fourth son of Thomas Selby, but had succeeded to the Biddleston estates in 1818, by the death of his eldest brother Thomas. Walter Selby married at St Peter's Catholic church, Lancaster, 13 April 1817, Alice (born 13 Jan. 1794) daughter of John Swarbreck, surgeon, of Poulton in the Fylde, Lancashire, by his first wife, Ann daughter of Thomas Worswick, of Lancaster and his wife Alice Gillow. Dr Swarbreck married secondly Susannah Darbieshire by whom he had issue,—Thomas, and Samuel Dukinfield Swarbreck. He moved to Sandhutton n[r] Thirsk in 1821, and eventually to Sowerby near Thirsk, where his son Thomas (father *inter alios* of our member, Edward Dukinfield Swarbreck) was already established as a solicitor, and died there in 1842.

† Fr. Naylor's last entry and signature.

[69] 1821

Sarah Brown, Daughter of Johnn **Brown** & Sarah **Hunter** his Wife was born at Biddleston in the Parish of Allenton on the 16th of April 1821 & baptized by Revd Thos * Gi-[llow] of Callaly on the 17th of the 17th of the same month & year, the sponsors were Willm & Anne Henderso[n].

Henrietta Selby fourth daughter of Walter **Selby** Esqr and Alice **Swarbrick** his wife was born at Biddleston in the parish of Alwinton, Northumberland, on the fifteenth day of August 1821, and baptized the sixteenth day of August 1821. The Sponsors were Thomas Swarbrick and Mrs Mary Clifford, Catholics.

James Higginson, Misso Apcus O.S.B.

1822

Sarah Turnbull daughter of Christopher **Turnbull** and his wife Jane **Turnbull** (formerly **Hogg**,) was born at Borrowdon on the 10th of February 1822 & baptised the 11th of February 1822. The Sponsors were John Turnbull & his Sister F. Turnbull, Catholics.

M. Fairclough, Missus Aposcus O.S.B.

[70] Luke Thorborne son of Thomas **Thorborne** and Elizabeth **Clark** his wife was born at Biddleston on the eighteenth day of September 1822 and baptized on the twentieth day of the same month by the Revd Mr Stout of Thropton. The sponsors were John Snowdon and Mary Thorborne.

Walter Selby son of Walter **Selby** Esquire and Alice **Swarbrick** his wife was born at Biddleston in the Parish of Alwinton, Northumberland on the second day of November 1822 and baptized on the sixth day of the same month. The Sponsors we Mr Robert Selby Junior and Mrs Julia Selby.

James Higginson, Miss Apo.—O.S.B

[71] 1823

8 Martii 1823.—Biddleston.—Die [9 *over* 2] Februarii 1823 nata et die 8 Martii 1823 baptizata fuit Margarita Brown filia Gulielmi et Aliciæ **Brown** (olim **Mills**) conjugum, Patrinus Joannes Snowdon, Matrina Maria Snowdon.—a me Thomâ Stout, Misso Apostlco: [*This is in a new hand, Fr. Stout's, as is the third following one*].

[1823]

Margaret Gray, daughter of Robert and Elizabeth **Gray** his wife, was born at Biddleston on the twelfth day of January 1823 and baptized on the twenty first day of the same month by the Revd Mr Stout. The Sponsors were Margaret Foster & John Athy.

[*The last and next are in the same hand, Fr. Higginson's.*]

John Brown son of John **Brown** and Sarah **Hunter** his wife was born at Biddleston in the Parish of Allwinton Northumberland on the twenty fourth day of March [1823 *above*] and baptized on

* Only 'Gi' are decipherable, the middle of the word is at the edge of the paper and the end is blotted. See however *C.R.S.* vii, 321. This is quite different to the other writing, and travels upwards to the right, quite an inch in six. It would have done more so, had the space on the paper allowed it. It is doubtless Mr Gillow's caligraphy.

the twenty eighth of the same month. The Sponsors were John Robson & Margaret Brown, James Higginson O.S.B., Miss. Apo.

[72] [Biddleston x^d *out*] Wood hall April 7, 1823. Die 27 Martii 1823, nata et die 7 Aprilis 1823 baptizata fuit Joanna Gray filia Joannis et Margaritæ **Gray** (olim **Brown**) conjugum, Patrinus Georgius Snowdon, matrina Isabella Snowdon.—a me Thomâ Stout, Misso. Apostlco.

[*The hand changes here, and continues the same with Fr. Albot's signatures.*]

William Henderson son of William **Henderson** and Catharine **Clark** his wife was born at Netherton in the Parish of Allwington Northumberland on the 18 day of December 1823 and baptized on the 22 day of the said month by me the undersigned Pastor at Biddleston. The Sponsors were John & Sarah Brown Catholics.—James Albot, Miss. App.

[73] 1824

Thomas Selby son of Walter **Selby** Esquire and of Alice **Swarbreck** his wife, was born at Biddleston in the Parish of Alwington Northumberland on the nineteenth day of January 1824 and baptized on the twenty-second day of the said month in the said year by me the undersigned Pastor at Biddleston. The Sponsors were Mr [Thom x^d *out*] Samuel Swarbreck and Mrs Alice McCartney.—James Albot. Miss. App.

Ann Gutterson the daughter of Robert **Gutterson** and of Bárbary **Brown** his Wife, was born at Borrowton Mains in the Parish of Alwington, Northumberland on the 2nd of April 1824, and baptized on the 4th day of the said month [74] by me the undersigned Pastor at Biddleston. The Sponsors were John Brown and Rudda Turnbull.—James Albot, Miss App.

John Rutherford the Son of Thomas **Rutherford** and of Mary **Dixon** his Wife was born at Burradon in the Parish of Alwington, Northumberland on the seventh day of July 1824 and baptized on the twelfth day of the said month by me the undersigned Pastor at Biddleston. The Sponsors were Mr William Forster and Miss Elizabeth Forster.—James Albot, Miss. App.

Die 18 Novembris 1824 natus et die 22 ejusdem mensis et anni Baptizatus fuit Richardus Douglas filius Richardi et Dorothea **Douglas** (olim **Wilson**) conjugum, Patrino Gulielmo Wilson, Patrina Mariâ Davidson. a me Jac. Albot, Misso Apco.

[*The last entry has been crossed over and is duplicated in English by the following one; but some differences are evident.*]

[75] Richard Douglass the Son of Richard **Douglass** and of Dorothy **Wilson** his Wife was born Burradon in the Parish of Alwington Northnd on the 18th day of Novbr 1824 and baptized on the 22nd day of the same month by me the undersigned Pastor at Biddleston. The Sponsors were Wm Wilson and Mary Davidson. James Albot, Miss. App.

1825

Anne Simmonds the Daughter of Edward **Simmonds** and of

Anne **Alexander** his Wife was born at Screnwood in the Parish of Alnham, Northumberland, on the 26th day of March 1825 and baptized on the 27th day of the said month by me the undersigned Pastor at Biddleston. The Sponsors were John Snowdon and Jane Dixon.—James Albot, Miss. App.

[76] Anne Brown the Daughter of Wm. **Brown** and of Alice **Mills** his Wife was born at Biddleston on the 29th day of March 1825 in the Parish of Alwington Northlnd and baptized on the 30th day of thc said month by me the undersigned Pastor at Biddleston. The Sponsors were Thos Brown and Margaret Turnbull.—James Albot, Miss. App.

1826

Elizabeth Johnson the Daughter of George **Johnson** and of Margaret **Tully** his Wife was born at Burradon in the Parish of Alwington Northlnd on the 13 day of Febry 1826 and baptized on the 20th day of the same month by me the undersigned Pastor at Biddleston. The Sponsors were Edward Simmonds and Anne Simmonds. James Albot, Miss. App.

[77] John Henderson the Son of William **Henderson** and of Catherine **Clarke** his Wife was born at Follians in the Parish of Alwington Northumberland on the 4th of April 1826, and baptized on the 19th of the said month by me the undersigned Pastor at Biddleston. The Sponsors were Thomas Henderson and Helen Henderson.—James Albot, Miss. App.

Elizabeth Selby the Daughter of Walter **Selby** Esqre and of Alice **Swarbreck** his Wife was born at Biddleston in the Parish of Alwington Northlnd on the 27th day of April 1826 and baptized on the 30th day of the said month by me the undersigned Pastor at Biddleston. The Sponsors were John Selby Esqre and Miss Maria Andrade. James Albot. James Albot, Miss. App.

[78] Ann Grey Daughter of John **Grey** and of Margaret **Brown** his wife was born at Woodhall in the Parish of Alwington, Northlnd the 15th day of June 1826 and baptized the same day by the said John Grey her Father, being thought in danger of death. The other ceremonies were supplied by me the undersigned Pastor at Biddleston. The Sponsors were Thomas Snowden and Frances Turnbull.—James Albot, Miss. App.

David Bolam the Son of Thomas **Bolam** and of Mary **Snowden** his wife was born at Planting House in the Parish of Alwington, Northlnd on the 1st day of July 1826 and baptized on the 3rd day of the said month by me the undersigned Pastor at Biddleston. The Sponsors were Thomas Snowden and Martha Williams.—James Albot, Miss. App.

[79] John Grey the son of Robert **Grey** and of Elizabeth **Hickson** his Wife was born at Biddleston in the Parish of Alwington [North-lnd *above*] on the 29th day of Novbr 1826 and baptized on the 30th day of the said month by me the undersigned Pastor at Biddlestone.—The Sponsors were Thomas Brown and Isabella Snowden. James Albot, Miss. App.

[1827]

Margaret Douglass the Daughter of Richard **Douglass** and of Dorothy **Wilson** his Wife was born at Burradon in the Parish of Alwington on the 7th day of March 1827 and baptized on the 16th of the said month by me the undersigned Pastor at Biddlestone.—The Sponsors were John Wilson and Isabella Dixon—James Albot, Miss. App.

[80] John Brown the son of William **Brown** and of Alice **Mills** his wife was born at Biddleston in the Parish of Alwington, Northumberland, the 14th day of July 1827 and baptized the 15th day of the said month by me the undersigned Pastor at Biddleston. The Sponsors were Robert Brown and Jane Brown.—James Albot, Miss. App.

Ann Brown daughter of John **Brown** and of Sarah **Hunter** his Wife was born at Biddleston in the Parish of Alwington Northumberland on the 7th day of August 1827 and baptized on the same day by me the undersigned Pastor at Biddleston. The Sponsors were William Brown and Jane Brown.—James Albot, Miss. App.

[1828]

James Simmonds, the son of Edward **Simmonds** and of Anne **Alexander** his wife was born at Screnwood in the Parish of Alnham Northumberland the 31st day of Decbr 1827, and baptized the 2nd day of Janry 1828 by me the undersigned Pastor at Biddleston. The Sponsors were John Simmonds and Margaret Simmonds.—James Albot. Miss. App.

[81] Andrew Todd Peary, the son of John **Peary** and of Mary **Todd** his wife (Protestant) was born at Harbottle in the Parish of Alnwington Northumberland the 25th day of January 1828 and baptized the 27 day of February, without the accustomed ceremonies, by me the undersigned Pastor at Biddleston.—James Albot, Miss. App.

Mary Johnson the Daughter of George **Johnson** and of Margaret **Tully** his Wife was born at Burradon in the Parish of Alwington Northumberland the 9th [day *above*] of March 1828 and baptized the 16th [day *above*] of the said month by me the undersigned Pastor at Biddleston. The Sponsors were John Brown and Margaret Simmonds—James Albot, Miss App.

[*The hand changes with the signatures.*]

Bartholomew Grey son of Robert [**Grey** above] and Elizabeth [**Hixon** *after erasure*] his wife was born at Biddleston in the Parish of Alwington Northumberland on the 18th day of October 1828 and baptized on the 19th of the same month by me the undersigned Pastor at Biddleston. The Sponsors were William Grey & Sarah Philipson.—Thomas Middlehurst, Miss: App:

[82] 1829

Robert Grey the son of John **Grey** & Margaret **Brown** his wife was born at Wood-Hall in the Parish of Alwington North-land the 6th day of February 1829 and Baptized the 9th day of the said month by me the undersigned pastor at Biddleston. The Sponsors were William Grey & Christina Turnbull.—Thomas Middlehurst, Miss: App:

James Simmonds the son of Edward **Simmonds** and of Anne **Alexander**, his wife, was born at Screnwood in the Parish of Alnham Northumberland on the 25th day of March 1829, and baptized on the 30th day of the said month by me the undersigned pastor at Biddleston. The Sponsors were Jane Brown & Wm Brown.—Thomas Middlehurst: Miss: App:

Elizabeth Douglass the Daughter of Richard **Douglass** and of Dorothy **Wilson** his wife, was born at Burradon in the Parish of Alwington Northumberland, on the 16th day of April 1829 and baptized on the 27th day of the said month by me the undersigned Pastor at Biddleston. The Sponsors were Henry Wilson & Mary Wilson.—Thomas Middlehurst, Miss: App:

[83] Charles George Brown the son of Thomas **Brown** and Mary **Dixon**, his wife, was born at Biddleston in the Parish of Alwington Northumberland the 30th day of April 1829 and baptized the 3d day of May by me the undersigned pastor at Biddleston. The Sponsors were Jane Dixon and Robert Brown.—Thomas Middlehurst, Miss: App:

Thos Bolam the son of Thomas **Bolam** and Mary **Snowden**, his wife, was born at Planting House in the Parish of Alwington North-land the 16th day of July 1829 and baptized the 19th day of the said month by me the undersigned Pastor at Biddleston. The Sponsors were James Snowden and Anne Bolam.—Thomas Middlehurst, Miss: App:

Margaret Johnson the daughter of George **Johnson** and Margaret **Tully**, his wife, was born at Burradon in the parish of Alwington, Northumberland, the 13th day of November 1829, and baptized the 15th day of the said month by me the undersigned Pastor at Biddleston. The Sponsors were William Brown and Jane Brown.—Thomas Middlehurst, Miss: App:

[84] 1830

John Thorborne, son of Thomas **Thorborne** and Elizabeth **Clarke** his wife, was born at Burradon in the Parish of Alwington North-land, the 5th day of July 1830 and baptized the 12th day of the said month by me the undersigned Pastor at Biddlestone. The Sponsors were James Thorborne and Mary Thorborne.—Thomas Middlehurst, Miss: App:

Mary Brown, daughter of Thomas **Brown** and Mary **Dixon**, his wife, was born at Biddleston in the parish of Alwington, North-land, the 24th day of September, and baptized the 26th of the said month by me the undersigned Pastor at Biddleston.—The Sponsors were John Snowdon and Barbara Gutturson.—Thos Middlehurst. Miss. App.

[85] 1831

James Grey Son of Robert **Grey** and of Elizabeth **Hickson** his wife was born at Biddleston in the Parish of Alington Northumberland on the thirteenth of March 1831 and baptized on the fourteenth day of the said month and year by me the undersigned Pastor at Thropton. The Sponsors were Andrew Evans and Rachel Hickson.—James Albot, Miss App.

William Brown Son of William **Brown** and of Alice **Mills** his Wife was born at Biddleston in the Parish of Alnington Northumberland on the 16th day of March 1831 and baptized on the same day by me the undersigned Pastor at Thropton. The Sponsors were John Brown and Barbara Gutterson.—James Albot, Miss App.

[86] George Johnson son of George **Johnson** and of Margaret **Tully** his wife was born at Burradon in the Parish of Alnington Northumberland the 3rd day of December 1831 and baptized the 5th day of the said month by me the undersigned Pastor at [Biddleston *x[d] out*, Thropton *above*]. The Sponsors were Thomas Thorborne and Catharine Anderson.—James Albot, Miss App.

1832

John Gray the son of John **Gray** and of Margaret **Brown** his Wife was born at Woodhall in the Parish of Alnwington Northumberland on the 18th day of January 1832 and baptized on the 23rd of the same month by me the undersigned Pastor at Thropton. The Sponsors were William Gray and Catharine Gray.—James Albot, Miss App.

[*It will be noticed that four years and a half are missing; but the book seems intact. Also that Fr. Albot had been supplying from Thropton for two years previously. The hand here changes again.*]

[87] 1836

Die 20 Julii 1836 natus & die 25 ejusdem mensis Baptizatus fuit Thomas Johnson filius Georgii & Margaritæ **Johnson** (olim **Tully**) conjugum a me infrascripto pastore apud Biddleston. Patrinus fuit Thomas Simmonds, Matrina Maria Foster.—Joannes Henricus Fisher: Miss: App:

Die 30 Augusti 1836 natus & die 5 Septembris Baptizatus fuit Thomas Peary filius Georgii & Saræ Peary (olim Thompson) conjugum, à me infrascripto pastore apud Biddlestone. Patrinus fuit Christopher Peary, Matrina Dorothy Clarke.—Joannes Henricus Fisher, Miss. App.

[88] Anno Domini 1837

Die 30 Augusti 1837 natus [apud Burradoni *above*], et die 10 Septembris hujusdem anni baptizatus fuit Rupertus Peary, filius Andri &. Mariæ **Peary** (olim **Eliot** prespeterian) conjugum, a me infrascripto pastore apud Biddleston, patrinus fuit Stephen Tayte, matrina Miss Joan Forster.—Josep hus Thomas Howard, Miss Ap.

Die 3 Novembris 1837 natus apud Biddleston et die 4 Novembris hujusdem anni baptizatus fuit Carolus-Papool Parsons, filius Jacobi & Mariæ **Parsons** (olim **Brooks**) conjugum, a me infrascripto pastore apud Biddleston. Patrinus fuit Josephus Stevenson.—

Matrina—Catherine *Daughty.—Josephus Thomas Howard. Miss. Ap°.

[89] Anno Domini 1838

Die 18 Januarii 1838 natus [apud Burradon, *above*] et die 20 ejusdem mensis 1838 baptizatus fuit Stephanus Tayte simpliciter, filius Stephani et Mariæ **Tayte** (olim **Smith**) prost†) conjugum:—Patrinus fuit Andreus Peary.—Matrina Maria Brown [*like* Brawn].

Die 1 Aprilis 1838 Supplendæ fuerunt ceremoniæ super dictum Baptizatum simpliciter.

Die 11 Aprilis [1838, *above*] apud Burradon, et die 12 ejusdem mensis 1838 baptizatus fuit Joannes Duglass simpliciter, filius Ricardi & Dorotheæ **Duglass**, (olim **Wilson**) conjugum.—Patrinus fuit Joannes Wilson.—Matrina Maria Wilson.

Die 27 Maii 1838, Supplendæ fuerunt cœremoniæ super dictum baptizatum simpliciter.

[90] Die 23 Maii 1838 natus apud Harbottle & die 8 Junii 1838 baptizatus fuit Joannes Athey, filius Joanni & Elizabeti **Athy** (olim **Redhead**. pros[t]) conjugum.—Patrinus fuit Georgii Athey.—Matrina Elen Athey.—a me Miss° Ap[co].—Thos[?] Howard.

Scrainwood --Die 9 Augusti 1838 nata et die 11 ejusdem mensis 1838 baptizata. Joanna Maria Forster, Thomæ et Esabellæ **Forster** (olim **Davison**) conjugum,—Patrinus Thoma Snowdon Storer.—Matria Maria Forster.—a me Miss Ap[co] Jos Howard.‡

[91] Anno Domini 1839

Die 7 Novembris 1839 [natus *above*] et die 8 ejusdem mensis 1839 baptizatus fuit Robertus Brown, filius Thomæ & Mariæ **Brown** (olim **Dixon**) conjug: Patrinus fuit Thomas Douglass: Matrina Margarita Brown, à me—Henrico Sutton.—Miss° Ap[co].

1840

Die 12 Januarii 1840 nata, et die 14 ejusdem mensis 1840 baptizata fuit Margarita Peary, filia Andreæ & Mariæ **Peary** (olim **Elliot**) Conjug: Patrinus fuit Christophorus peary, Matrina Francisca Turnbull, a me—Henrico Sutton.—Misso Ap[co].

[92] Die 27 Februarii 1840 natus et die 19 Martii 1840 baptizatus fuit Gulielmus Athey, filius Joannis & Elizabethæ **Athey** (olim **Readhead**) conjug: Patrinus fuit Gulielmus Brown, Matrina Sarah Peary, à me—Henrico Sutton.—Miss° Ap[co].

Die 16 Martii 1840 natus et die 20 Aprilis 1840 baptizatus fuit Robertus Nesbit Meehan, filius Thomæ & Isabellæ **Meehan** (olim **Lees**) conjug: Patrinus fuit Robertus Blacklock, Matrina Maria Selby à me Henrico Sutton

T. R. Miss° Ap[co]

* This may be Doughty, as Fr. Howard makes 'o' and 'a' similar at times, as 'Haward.

† Probably for *protestantis*.

‡ In addition to the spellings Fr Howard's writing gets very bad in his last two entries.

[*Here follow 17 blank pages bringing us to the end of notes written from the reverse end of the book as follows.*]

[*Reverse end of book, 6 blank pages*]

[7 R] A Catalogue of those that were confirmed by L[d] Bishop Walton the 14th of June 1773.

BIDDLESTON

Barbara Brown
Elizabeth Brown
Fortune Brown—Ann
John Brown
Mary Brown
Ann Bollum
Marg[t] Bollum
Elizabeth Bollm Smith
James Thorborne
Robert Thorborne—Joseph
John Thorborne
Tho[s] Thorborne
Marg[t] Stamp
[8 R] Mary Stamp
Tho[s] Stamp
George Stamp

YELDOM

Elizabeth Davison
Barbara Davison
Tho[s] Davison
George Dodds

NETHERTON

Ralph Gibson
Isabel Dodds
Mary Dodds
Hanna Dodds—Ann
George Dodds
Christopher Dodds
Mary Greham
Isabel Greham
Alice Greham—Elizabeth
Will[m] Greham—John
[9 R] Will[m] Turnbull—Joseph
Isabel Turnbull
Mary Turnbull
Jane Turnbull
Ralph Thompson—Peter
James Thompson
Mary Thompson

COTE-WALLS

Luke Downey
James Downey

BORROWDON

Luke Main

BIDDLESTON EDGE

Isabel Grey

HALLY-STONE

Jane Potts

HARBOTTLE

George Stamp
Tho[s] Stamp
[10 R] George Jordan

ALLENTON

James Selby
Barbara Selby—Mary

QUICKNING COTE

Isabel Fail
Elizabeth Fail

J. Naylor Miss O.S.B.

Confirmed by L[d] Bishop Mat.* Gibson the 27th of July 1783.

BIDDLESTONE

Luke Thornborne—Joseph
Mary Bollum

NETHERTON

Christopher Turnbull, John

NEWTON

Tho[s] Robson
Ann Storrer—Mary
J. Naylor, Miss: O: S: B.†

[11 R] HARBOTTLE

John Jordan

* The Christian name, Matthew, has been inserted later, to prevent confusion between the brothers Matthew and William, who confirmed in 1796 as below, having been consecrated.

† Fr. Naylor seems by mistake to have signed here not seeing to name at the top of p. 13 R.

Confirmed by L[d] Bishop Will[m] Gibson the 2[d] of September 1796.

BIDDLESTON	SCREINWOOD
Ann Brown—Mary	Helen Blac[k]lock
NETHERTON	NEWTON
James Turnbull	Elizabeth Storer
Frances Turnbull	Mary Storer—Monica
John Robson	Edward Storer
Robert Blacklo [c *above*] k	Mary Berningham—Elizabeth

J. Naylor, Miss: O: S: B.

[12 R] Confirmed by Will[m] Gibson. Bishop of Acanthos the 9[th] of September 1809.

BIDDLESTON *	Marg[t] Brown—Ann
Richard Selby—Tho[s]	John Brown
Maria Selby—Catharine	Martha Sunter—Elizabeth
Rob[t] Gray	NEWTON *
Tho[s] King—Jerome	Helen Storer—Theresa
Elizabeth Mills—Ann	Robson Storer—John
Helin Morlee—Mary	BARROW MILL *
Mary Pape	James Robson
Mary Bolam	Christopher Robson
Elizabeth Nickson—Mary	NETHERTON *
Elizabeth Snowdon	[13 R] Christophe Turnbull
Mary Snowdon	WOODHALL *
Rob[t] Brown	Tho[s] Gray

J Naylor, Miss: O: S: B:

Confirmed by the Rt Reverend Thomas Smith Bishop of Bolina, Vic. Apost. of Northern District.

June 15 1823

Baptism	Confirmation
Isabell Dixon	Mary
Frances Turnbull	Mary
Rhoda Turnbull	Mary
Margaret Brown	Elizabeth
Barbara Brown	Mary
Isabella Snowdon	Elizabeth
Mary Turnbull	Ann
Barbara Gutterson	Ann
Jane Thorborn	Elizabetn
Elizabeth Thorborn	Mary
Mary Thorborn	Elizabeth
Thomas Thorborn	Luke
William Brown	Charles
Thomas Brown	John
Thomas Kir[k *or* la]ley	James
[14 R] John Athy	Thomas
Helen Athy	Mary
Helen White	Mary

* Biddleston and other place names written at the side.

Baptism	Confirmation
Mary Rutherford	Ann
Margaret Turnbull	Mary
Margaret Brown	Mary
Sarah Brown	Mary
John Snowden	Joseph

Testa me Thomâ Stout Miss° Apostlco.

Part of Biddleston Congregation confirmed at Thropton by the Right Rev. Thomas Penswick Bishop of Europum and Vicar Apostolic of the Northern District. Oct. 23, 1831.

	Baptism	Confirmation
	Christina Turnbull	Elizabeth
	Jane Brown	Lucy
	Catharine Gray	Anne
	*William Gray Woodhall	Joseph
	*William Gray Holystone	Joseph
	*William Gray Biddleston	Joseph
	George Athey	Peter
	James Thorborne	Joseph
	Anne Bolam	Anne
	Maria Gray	Anne
	Mary Brown lately from Biddleston	Mary
[15 R]	Rachel Grey	Elizabeth
	Robert Grey	Peter
	Mary Brown [,] Netherton	Mary

Confirmed at the Biddleston Chapel by the Right Rev. John Briggs, Bishop of Trachensis V. Ap: of the Northern District and assisted by his Secretary, the Rev. J. Curr.

June the 21th 1837

No.	Baptismal Name	Surname	Confirmation Name	Residence
	Charles	Brown	Peter	Biddleston
	James	Parsons	Peter	Biddleston Hall
	Joseph	Simmons	John	Netherton
	George	Simmons	Michel	Netherton
	Thomas	Simmons	Joseph	Netherton
	Thomas	Duglass	Peter	Burradon
	Stephen	Taite	John	Burradon
	Luke	Thurburne	Michel	Netherton Burnfoot
10	John	Brown	James	Netherton
	Ann	Cass	Mary	Biddleston Hall
	Maria	Midcafth	Tereza	Biddleston Hall
	Helen	Wilson	Tereza	Biddleston Hall
[16 R]	Margaret	Grey	Ann	Biddleston
	Margaret	Brown	Ann	Biddleston

* Presumubly three William Grays; but there is no punctuation.

No.	Baptismal Name	Surname	Confirmation Name	Residence
	Ann	Gutterson	Mary	Biddleston
	Lucy	Cook	Mary	Biddleston
	Mary	Taite	Elizabeth	Burradon
	Margaret	Johnson	Elizabeth	Burradon
	Margaret	Grey	Mary	Wood-Hall
	Sarah	Brown	Mary	Netherton
12	Sarath	Turnbull	Mary	Netherton

Teste me Josepho Howard. Mis: Ap[os] at the Biddleston Hall.
[17-20 R *blank*].
[21 R] A list of the communicants of Biddleston congregation of the year 1837.

No.	Names	Surnames	Employment	Residence
1	M[r]	Stourton		Biddleston Hall
2	M[rss]	Stourton		ditto
3	Miss	Colds		ditto
4	Thomas	Prisby	Buttler	ditto
5	Joseph	Stephenson	Footman	ditto
6	James	Parsons	Coachman	ditto
7	Joseph	Gordon	Gardener	ditto
8	Miss	Abrill	Ladies maid	ditto
9	Miss	Birch	Nurse	ditto
10	Miss	Bone	Housekeeper	ditto
11	Catharine	Doughty	Servant	ditto
12	Mary	Midcufth	Servant	ditto
13	Mary	Brown	Servant	ditto
14	Helen	Wilson	Servant	ditto
15	An	Cass	Servant	ditto
16	Mary	Parsons	Wife of the Coachman	ditto
17	Robert	Grey senior	Gamekeeper	Biddleston Village
18	Elizabeth	Grey	his wife	ditto
19	William	Grey	his Son	ditto
		admitted in the church 1837		
20	Robert	Grey junior	Son	ditto
21	Rachel	Gray	Daughter	ditto
22	Maria	Grey	Daughter	ditto
23	Margaret	Grey	Daughter	ditto
	admitted in the church 1837			
24	Elizabeth	Dixon	the grandmother	ditto
25	Miss	Best	Old woman	ditto
26	Lucy	Cook		ditto
27	An	Broun	Old woman	ditto
28	Barbary	Gutterson		ditto
29	Maria Rudda	Fleak	Shop Keeper	ditto
30	Charles	Brown	admitted the church 1837	ditto

No.	Names	Surnames	Employment	Residence
31	William	Brown	Labourer	Biddleston Village
[24] 32	James	Brown	Husbandman	Biddleston Village
33	Robert	Brown	Labourer	ditto
34	John	Turnbul	Shopkeeper	Netherton Village
35	Francis	Turnbul	Shopkeeper	Netherton
36	Richard	Duglass	Hind	Scrinwood
37	Dorothy	Duglass	his wife	Screnwood
38	George	Snodon	very old	Burradon
39	Elizabeth	Thurnburne	Labourer	Netherton Burnfoot
40	Ann	Simmons		Netherton Village
41	Catharine	Anderson	labourer	Burradon Mains and husband protestant
42	Miss	Foster		Screnwood
43	Sarah	Brown		Netherton Village
44	Francis	Grey	Shop Keeper	Halystone
45	Helen	Athey senior		Harbottle
46	Helen	Athey junior		Harbottle
47	Mary	Peary	labourer	Burradon
48	Miss Elizbetha	Foster	Farmer	Burradon
49	Miss Joan	Foster		Burradon
50	Miss Mary	Foster		Burradon
51	Jane	Foster	married and husband prot.	Burradon
52	Margaret	Grey	girl 19 years and admitted in the church 1837	Woodhall
53	Mary	Brown	labour	Burradon
54	Sarah	Turnbul	girl 15 years	Burradon
55	Margaret	Grey	Senior	Woodhall
56	John	Brown	boy 15 years	Netherton Village admitted in the church 1837
57	Joseph	Simmons	boy 16 years and admitted into the church 1837	Netherton Village
58	William	Grey	Carpenter	Woodhall
59	John	Grey	Carpenter	Woodhall
[23 R] 60	Andrew	Peary	Blacksmith	Burradon
61	Thomas	Thurnburne	Labourer	Netherton Burnfoot
62	James	Thurnburne	Labourer	Netherton Burnfoot
63	Mary	Thurnburne		Burradon
64	Catharine	Grey	Servant	Burn mill
65	John	Brown sen.	Stone mason	Netherton village
66	John	Peary	Buttler	Harbottle
67	Ezabella	Dixon	very old woman	Burradon
68	George	Johnson	Joinner	Burradon
69	Margaret	Johnson	his wife	Burradon
70	Mr	Storrer	Farmer	Yllelar *
71	Mrss	Storrer	his wife	Illelar *

* Perhaps Elilaw meant ?

No.	Names	Surnames	Employment	Residence
72	George	Athey	Joinner	Harbottle
73	Mary	Bolam		Burradon
74	Edward	Simmons	Joinner	Netherton
75	Mrs Ann	Commons	publican	Harbottle
76	John	Athey	Joinner	Harbottle
77	Margaret	Browne	Girl 15 years	Biddleston taken into the church on Witsunday.
78	Mary	Duglass	Girl 19	Screnwood, taken into the church on Witsunday.
79	Stephen	Taite	Servant for Forster & Convert,	Borraden taken into the Church, Witsunday
80	Mary	Taite,	his wife, & Convert,	Borradon, taken into the Church, Witsunday
81	Thomas	Simmons	Joiner	Netherton, Received at Witsuntide, the reason is owing to circumstances.
82	——	Watson	Surveyor	Thropton, A convert and made his first communion on the 24th of Sept. 1837

[24 R] A list of the Communicants of Biddlestone congregation of the year 1838.

Easter April 15

No.	Names	Surnames	Residence	Employment
1	M^r	Stourton	Biddleston Hall	
2	M^rs	Stourton	ditto	
3	Miss	Coldes	ditto	Governess Servant
4	Miss	Clifford	ditto	
5	Miss	Ebril	ditto	Lady's maid
6	Miss	Birch	ditto	Nurse
7	Miss	Daughty	ditto	Lady's maid to Miss Cliffo[rd]
8	Miss	Bone	ditto	House Keeper
9	Ellen	Wilson	ditto	House maid
10	Ann	Cass	ditto	Kitchen maid
11	Julia	Wood	ditto	Servant
12	Ann	Bregg	ditto	Servant
13	M^r	Brisby	ditto	Butler
14	Joseph	Stephenson	ditto	Footman
15	James	Parsons	ditto	Coach-man
16	George	Simmons	ditto	Servant, First Communion
17	Mary	Parsons	ditto	Coach man's wife

No.	Names	Surnames	Residence	Employment
18	Robert	Grey	Biddleston village	Game Keeper
19	Elizabeth	Grey	ditto	his wife
20	William	Grey	ditto	young man
21	Maria	Grey	ditto	young woman
22	Margaret	Grey	ditto	young woman
23	Rachel	Hixon	ditto	Old woman
24	M^rs^	Best	ditto	Old woman
[25 R] 25	Lucy	Cook	ditto	Assistant to Mrs Best
26	Barbary	Gutterson	ditto	
27	Ann	Gutterson	ditto	Girl, First Communion
28	Rudda	Fleak	ditto	Shop Keeper
29	Robert	Brown	ditto	Hind
30	Margaret	Brown	ditto	young woman
31	Ellen, senior,	Athy	Harbottle	Old woman
32	Mary	Brown	Burradon	
33	Miss Joan	Forster	Burradon	Farmer
34	Miss Bessy	Forster	Burradon	Farmer
35	Miss Mary	Forster	Burradon	Farmer
36	Mrs Ellen	Storrer	Illelaw	Farmer
37	M^r^	Storrer	Illelaw	Farmer
38	Mrs Mary	Storrer	Coat-walls	
39	Mrs Isabella	Forster	Screnewood	Farmer
40	Mr Thomas	Forster	Screnewood	Farmer
41	James	Watson	Rothbery	Surveyor
42	Mary	Athy	Harbottle	
43	Ellen	Athy, junior	Harbottle	
44	Sarath	Turnbul	Netherton	young woman
45	John	Brown, sen.	Netherton	Stone-mason
46	William	Brown	Netherton	Stone-mason
47	Stephen	Tayte	Burradon	groom
48	Catharine	Henderson	Burradon mains	
49	Margaret	Grey, senior	Woodhall	
50	Ann	Simmons	Netherton	
[26 R] 51	Thomas	Simmons	Netherton	joiner
52	John	Turnbul	Netherton	shop-Keeper
53	Frances	Turnbul	Netherton	shop-Keeper
54	Elizabeth	Dixon	Burradon	Old woman
55	John	Snowdon	Burradon	Old man
56	Isabella	Snowdon	Burradon	Servant
57	William	Grey	Woodhall	Carpenter
58	Edward	Simmons	Netherton	Carpenter
59	Margaret	Johnson	Burradon	
60	John	Brown junior	Netherton	Stone mason
61	Sarah	Brown	Netherton	young woman
62	Margaret	Grey, junior	Woodhall	young woman

No.	Names	Surnames	Residence	Employment
63	George	Athy	Harbottle	joiner
64	John	Grey	Woodhall	Carpenter
65	Joseph	Simmons	Netherton	Carpenter
66	Andrew	Pery	Burradon studs	Black-smith
67	Francis	Grey	Haly-stane	Shop-Keeper
68	Mary	Tayte	Burradon	
69	Thomas	Duglass	Burradon	Servant
70	Mary	Duglass	Burradon	Servant
71	William	Brown	Biddleston	Hind
72	Dorathy	Duglass	Buradon	Servant
73	George	Johnson	Burradon	Joiner
[27 R]			1840	
1	M^{rs}	Clavering	Biddleston Hall	There were
2	Miss	Selby	Do Do	27 more but I
3	Miss E.	Selby	Do Do	have not the
4	Robert	Blacklock	Do Do	list at hand.
5	George	Rippon	Do Do	
6	Mary	Morton	Do Do	
7	Jane	Morton	Do Do	
8	Mary	Crisp	Do Do	
9	Sarah	Brown	Do Do	
10	Elizabeth	Lindsay	Do Do	
11	Willm	Brown	Biddleston Village	
12	Marg^{t}	Brown	Do Do	
13	Robt	Brown	Do Do	
14	Barbara	Gutterson	Do Do	
15	Anne	Gutterson	Do Do	
16	M^{rs}	Best	Do Do	
17	Lucy	Cook	Do Do	
18	Rhoda	Fleck	Do Do	
19	Robt	Grey	Do Do	
20	Maria	Grey	Do Do	
21	Rachel	Grey	Do Do	
22	Rachel	Hickson	Do Do	
23	Willm	Forster	Burradon	
24	Miss	Forster	Do Do	
25	Joan	Forster	Do Do	
26	Elizabeth	Forster	Do Do	
27	Andrew	Peary	Do Do	
28	Mary	Peary	Do Do	
29	Stephen	Tait	Do Do	
30	Mary	Tait	Do Do	
31	Dorothy	Douglass	Do Do	
32	Thom^{s}	Douglass	Do Do	
33	Mary	Brown	Do Do	

[*This last list is much more elegantly written and spelt than previous ones; but the omission of 27 names and many particulars make it very unsatisfactory.*]

No. VII

THE CATHOLIC REGISTERS OF PYLEWELL HOUSE, LYMINGTON, HAMPSHIRE, 1805-40, AND ROOK CLIFF, MILFORD-ON-SEA, HAMPSHIRE, 1813-15.

CONTRIBUTED BY JOSEPH S. HANSOM.

HISTORICAL NOTES BY JOSEPH GILLOW.

THESE registers are at Somerset House, where the certificate states they were sent by the Rev. William Waterton, S.J., on 13th of October 1840, who describes them as of Pilewell House (in the parish of Lymington), the mission being founded about the year 1800. He makes no reference to Rook Cliffe House which is the adjoining parish of Milford. They are contained in two books in the non-parochial registers, and numbered 27, i and ii of the Hampshire series. The first book relating to Pilewell House consists of twelve sheets of paper, or 48 pages 9¼×7¼ inches in a marbled cover. The second consists of three sheets of paper or 12 pages 7¼ by 4½ inches.* It contains four baptisms and one death relating to Rook Cliffe, with five certificates from registers relating to Lymington, at St Aloysius's Church, Somers Town, London, where the originals seem to have been transfered by one of the French clergy, the Abbé Fautrel.

They have been described as commencing in 1803; but this is a mistake, that year being inserted in a blank form only. This is pointed out at the beginning of the registers. J. S. H.

HISTORICAL NOTES

The mission appears to have originated on or before 1800 through a French emigré priest coming to attend to the spiritual wants of his countrymen taken prisoners during the wars and interned in Lymington, as well as to his compatriots who had sought refuge in the old seaport town at the time of the Revolution. A chapel was then opened at Pylewell House, in proximity to the town.

Pylewell House was a minor residence of Thomas Weld, Esq., of Lulworth Castle, Dorset, and after his death in 1810 was occupied by his widow, Mary eldest daughter of Sir John Stanley-Massey, 6th bart., of Hooton Hall, Cheshire; and there she died 1st August 1830. Their third son, Joseph, married in 1802 to the Hon. Elizabeth Charlotte Stourton, fourth daughter of Charles Philip, 16th Lord Stourton, and occupied Pylewell House until 1828, when his eldest brother, Thomas Cardinal Weld, handed over the Lulworth estates to him. Their third son Joseph (*William* Joseph in the registers), who had resided with his father, married in 1848 Flora Macdonnell, fourth daughter of Sir Joseph Pickford Radcliffe, of Rudding Pall, co. York, 2nd bart., eventually on the death of his father removed

* When I went to collate the proofs with the originals I found both books bound in one, with green cloth sides, half calf.

to The Lodge, Lymington, and died there in 1889 aged 74. After Pylewell was given up and finally sold, the chapel was removed to The Lodge till an independent one was built by him in the town of Lymington, from the designs of the brothers Joseph A. and Charles F. Hansom, architects, and opened in 1859.

George, eighth son of Mr Thomas Weld, senior (above), born in 1786, and married in 1812 Maria daughter of John Searle, Esq., of London, had succeeded in 1810 his father in the Legram estates in Lancashire, part of those inherited by alliance of the family with the Shireburns of Stonyhurst. On his marriage he went to reside at Rook Cliff or Rookcliff, Milford-on-the-Sea, about three miles from Lymington, then a seat of the Rivett-Carnac family, and now of Mrs Robinson, sister of Monsignor Kennard. His two eldest sons were born and baptized in the domestic chapel. The last of four baptisms was on 2 March 1815, and the tenancy probably expired shortly after. *Burke* gives the marriage of Mr James Rivett-Carnac, later created a baronet, on 3 June 1815. Mr George Weld probably went abroad, as he had a son (a second George, the first having died in 1818) born at Liège in 1819, and he did not reside at Leagram till 1822.

Two French priests appear in the Rook Cliff registers, both seeming to supply from Lymington :—

François Marian [?] le Tailleur, 8 Feb. 1813 till 20 May 1814.
Jean-Baptiste François Fautrel on 2 March 1815.

The record of the priests at Lymington is as follows :—

L'Abbé J. Blot, a French emigré, who appears from 1800-5.

Fr. John Alloway, S.J., born 3rd April 1743, third son of William and Catherine Alloway, of Henley, co. Oxon, was educated at the English colleges at St Omer and Bruges, whence he proceeded to that at Rome, were he entered 28th January 1755, and was placed by Fr. Henry Sheldon, the rector, on one of the free funds which did not require the *alumnus* to take that part of the oath of Alexander VII which prohibited him from entering any religious order. He remained till 9th October 1766, when, having received minor orders, he was admitted into the novitiate of the Jesuits at Monte Cavalla, and left Rome for Flanders 18th September 1769. Two years later he became confessor to the English Teresian nuns at Antwerp, and subsequently became chaplain to Sir William Stanley, 5th Bart., at Hooton Hall, where he resided till he came to Pylewell about 1805. Here he remained till he was transferred to Portico, near Prescot, co. Lancaster, in 1807, and there he died 15th March 1808, aged 65, and was buried in the old Catholic cemetery at Windleshaw, near St Helen's. (*Kirk Biog. Collns, M.S., Foley Records, S.J.*, vi and vii.) He was succeeded at Lymington by—

Rev. Thomas Tilbury, born 17th October 1780, son of Charles and Lydia Tilbury, of Midhurst, co. Sussex (*C.R.S.*, i, 252), who entered Stonyhurst College in March 1795, was ordained priest by Bishop William Gibson at Durham 28th May 1806, and became chaplain to Mr Joseph Weld at Pylewell on 29th October 1807. Upon the death of Fr. Thomas Lewis *alias* Culcheth, S.J., at Chideock 5th September 1809, Mr Weld requested Mr Tilbury as a favour to transfer his services to that larger field for exertion, and hence he left on 14th November 1809 for Chideock, and there remained for thirty-one years, till he removed on 20th November 1840 to Weymouth. He was made a canon of the chapter of Plymouth 6th December 1853, and continued at Weymouth till his death 9th June 1856, aged 75 (*Oliver, Collns,* p. 421). Upon his departure from Pylewell in 1809 the mission was served by a French emigré, who seems to have been settled in Lymington for some years previously.

L'Abbé François Marie Le Tellier de Brotonne, formerly vicaire de Saint-Paul, diocèse de Paris, whom de Plasse (*Le Clergé Français Réfugié en Angleterre,* ii. 420) says was in London in 1794. His entries in the registers are between June 1806 and May 1814. After this he would seem to have been followed by——

L'Abbé Jean Baptist François Fautrel, formerly of the diocèse d'Avranches, who according to de Plasse (*Ibid* 411) was at Winchester in 1795. His name appears in the registers in October 1814 and March 1815, and upon leaving Lymington he took with him some of the registers to St Aloysius', Somers Town, London, whence its founder l'Abbé Carron had just returned to France, and was succeeded by l'Abbé Jean Nérinckx, who signs a certificate of extract from the Lymington registers. Meanwhile the Welds obtained a resident chaplain at Pylewell House in succession to Mr Tilbury in the person of——

Rev. John Brown, a priest educated at the English College at Rome and at St Edmund's College, Old Hall, whose entries in the register range between 21st January 1812 and 11th May 1824, when he appears to have transferred his services to Jersey, where he died 23rd November 1833. He was succeeded at Pylewell by——

Fr. John Leadbetter, S.J., born 7th September 1795, at Wigan, co. Lancaster, who studied at Stonyhurst, entered the Society at Hodder, 7th September 1814, made his theology at Rome and Modena, and was ordained priest at Reggio in June 1823. He served Pylewell for nearly two years, till October 1826, when he was transferred to Norwich, where he erected a chapel and opened it on 8th September 1829. He was missioner at Stonyhurst in 1832, and was appointed to the mission of Clayton-le-Moors, co. Lancaster, derived from the chaplaincy at Clayton Hall, the ancient seat of the Andertons, in December 1833, and there remained till the mission was taken over by the Bishop of Salford in December 1873. Fr Leadbetter then retired to Stonyhurst, where he died 20th May 1876 aged 81. He was succeeded at Pylewell by——

Fr. William Waterton, S.J., who according to his own statement came as chaplain on 28th October 1826. He was the fourth son of Thomas Waterton, of Walton Hall, co. York, Esq., by Anne, daughter and eventually sole heiress of Edward Bedingfeld, of Oxton, and was born 9th December 1794. He studied at Stonyhurst, entered the Society at Hodder in 1815, and made his theology at Clongowes College, Ireland, where he was ordained priest by Archbishop Murray in December 1823. He first served Pontefract, co. York, came to Pylewell in 1826, and stayed till September 1841 when he went to Tunbridge Wells, but in the same year was appointed prefect of the secular philosophers at Stonyhurst. In November 1845 he went to Wardour Castle, co. Wilts, and remained there till 28th May 1848. Thence he went to Croft, co. Lancaster, till 1849, and subsequently was at Bedford Leigh for a time, after which he retired to Stonyhurst, where he died 18th January 1852, aged 58. (Oliver, *Collns.,* p. 433, *Foley Records, S.J.,* vii.) During the latter part of his time at Pylewell the Rev. Joseph Stapleton resided in Lymington till his death, 27th August 1839, aged 55. He was the second son of John Stapleton, Esq., M.D., third son of Nicholas Stapleton, of Carlton Hall, co. York, Esq., by his third wife Winifred, daughter of John White, Esq., and was sent in 1797 to Sedgley Park, whence in July 1802 he went to Old Hall, where he was ordained priest 23rd September 1809, and was retained in the college as a professor till November 1816, when he went to Burton Green, Hants, till 1837, after which he retired to Lymington till his death. Fr. Waterton was succeeded at Pylewell by——

Fr. James Clough, S.J., born near Liverpool 11th January 1803, who studied at Stonyhurst, entered the Society at Hodder in 1827, and thence was ordained priest at Oscott, 4th April 1835, and was sent to Yarmouth, co. Norfolk. Thence he came to Pylewell on 30th September 1841, and stayed till 1844, when he was recalled to Stonyhurst. In the following year he went to Croft, but in 1847 succeeded his brother Francis at Lydiate till 1848, when his delicate health, for he was consumptive, necessitated short visits to Hereford, Pylewell, and Wardour, where he died 3rd November 1848, aged 45. His successor at Pylewell was——

Fr. Francis Daniel, S.J., born near London 8th February 1798, educated at Stonyhurst, and having been ordained priest at the Roman College returned to England in September 1824, and taught in the school opened by the Society in London till August 1825 when he went to Lincoln till January 1830. He then supplied at Soberton, Hants, and served Courtfield, co. Hereford, the seat of the Vaughans, from 1831-4, when he went to Stonyhurst, of which he became rector 27th May 1839, subsequently served at St Ignatius', Preston, and came to Pylewell in 1841, but left in 1846 for Liverpool to be *socius* to the provincial, and in the same year went to Holywell, Flint, where he stayed till April 1849. He then rejoined the provincial as *socius*, and 6th January 1851 returned as superior to St Ignatius', Preston, till 1855, when he became rector of the College of the Holy Apostles and served Great Yarmouth. In 1865 he was appointed rector of the College of St Michael, and was chaplain at Broughton Hall, co. York, the seat of Sir Charles Robert Tempest, Bart., and there died 6th December 1869 aged 71. Meanwhile Pylewell House was vacated or sold by the Welds and a temporary chapel was established at East End, Pylewell, and Fr Daniel's successor was——

Fr. William O'Brien, S.J., of the Irish Province, born in Dublin 15th August 1795, who entered the Society at Hodder in 1814, and was at Clongowes from 1816 to 1843, when he came to England and was placed at East End, Pylewell, in 1845 till his death 1st October 1851, aged 56. His successors in the mission were——

Fr. Thomas Williams, S.J., who established himself at Elm Cottage, Lymington, till 1852, his chapel being dedicated to Our Blessed Lady.

Fr. John Rigby, S.J., at Elm Cottage, 1852-3.

Fr. Ralph Cooper, S.J., 1853-4.

Fr. John Milner, S.J., 1854-60, but in 1856 the chapel was removed from Elm Cottage to The Lodge, Lymington, the residence of Mr Joseph Weld, till a new church dedicated to Our Lady of Mercy and St Joseph was opened 18th May 1859.

Fr. Joseph Holden, S.J., 1860-5, being assisted by Fr. Thomas

Mockler, S.J., from 1860 till his death at Lymington 15th January 1862 aged 29.

Rev. John McDonald, 1865-8.

Rev. John Wallace, D.D., 1868-9.

Rev. Patrick O'Connell, 1869-1903, the mission having meanwhile been apportioned to the new diocese of Portsmouth formed 19th May 1882, by division of the old diocese of Southwark.

Rev. Cuthbert G. Winder, 1903 to date. J. G.

BAPTISMS

[*Outside the cover on a slip of paper*]. This book belongs to Pilewell House, near Lymington, Hants.

[*On another slip*]. I came to Pilewell as Chaplain on the 28th of October 1826, and from that time to the present day, 3[d] of November 1840—all the names in this book were duly entered by me. W. Waterton, S.J.,

Chaplain of Pilewell.

[*On fly leaf* *]. Pilewell house near Lymington, Hants.

hoc Registrum pertinet ad Capellam Domûs vulgò Dictæ Pilewell in Districtu Londinensi.

Registrum Capella Domûs vulgò Dictæ pilewell in Districtu Londinensi.

[*The next page is blank; but on it is affixed a piece of paper* $8\frac{1}{8} \times 6\frac{3}{8}$ *inches on which are a number of MS. blank forms to help in writing registers. The first having the date of Januarii* 1803 *has caused misapprehension that the registers began on that date.*

[Page 1] 1805

Maria filia Legitima Jacobi et annæ **haime** Conjugum, nata vigesimâ quartâ die januarii 1805 Ritè Baptisata fuit Die proximè sequenti a Me infra scripto; patrinus fuit Samuel Cope, Matrina verò elizabeth Woods, patre presente qui Mecum Subscripsit [*sign*] James Haime. j: Blot Sacerdos.

Hodiè trigesimâ primâ die Januarii 1805 ego infrâ scriptus, nullo impedimento Reperto, Conjunxi in Matrimonium Carolum **plunket** et henriettam **villebois** [sign] Harriet Villebois.

M. J. Enys

Henry Villebois

Ch[les] Plunket

J. Blot Sacerdos.

[2] Die tertiâ Maii 1805 ego infrâ scriptus Rité Baptizavi Carolinam, Die vigesimâ quintâ februarii 1804 natam, filiam Ludovici **Versturme** (e guillelmo Vesturme, et petronillá **De Bruyher** Conjugibus in oppido gandavensi † orti) Medicinæ

* The rebinding has upset the numbers of pages when the transcript was made, and it seems to be well to adhere to the old order. It may be said however, that—the fly leaf has been made (1) and (2) the piece of paper (3) and (4), whilst [Page 1] has been numbered (5); and so on.

† The city of Gand or Ghent.

Doctoris honorarii imperatori germaniæ, totiusque extraneorum Militiæ Regi Majoris Britanniæ inservientium Medici generalis, pro tempore in Civitate vulgó Dicta Lymington Commorantis, et hariettæ paillet uxoris ejus Legitimæ (filæ Clementis **paillet** et Leah **oldmeadow** Conjugum patriâ anglorum). patrinus fuit Ludovicus Bellamont Loco petri Jacobi Versturme, Matrina vero Carolina Eliza uxor Christopi Servaes, prior in oppido gandavensi, posterior vero in oppido alostano* (in flandria) orti, et illas Civitates inhabitantes. J: Blot Sacerdos.

hodie Decimâ octavâ Die Julii 1805, ego infrâ Scriptus, nullo impedimento Reperto, Conjunxi in Matrimonium **heraldum Blaise** et elisabeth **Ryall** [*sign*] Elizabeth Ryall, Blaise herauel [?]

J: Blot Sacerdos.

[3] henricus filius Legitimus Caroli **Warin** et annæ **Elmes** Conjugum, natus vigesimâ quartâ die Maii 1805, Rité Baptisatus fuit vigesimâ die julii ejusdem anni a Me infrâ scripto, patrinus fuit julius josephus Le Cordier de Roucourt, Matrina vero Josephina **pamar de** Roucourt qui unâ Mecum subscripserunt

Le[?ch[ev]] deroucourt.

J: Blot Sacerdos,

[1806]

Die 8va Junii 1806 circa horam [sex *x[d] out*, 5 *above*]tam mane natus, eodemq. die baptizatus fuit Eduardus Josephus Weld, filius Josephi† et Carolettæ **Weld** (olim **Stourton**) conjugum: Patrinus illustrissimus Dns Carolus Stourton, Matrina D[na] Maria Weld—(Infantis Avus et Avia).

a me J. Alleway, Mission[s] Apos[us].

[1807]

Ego infra Scriptus attestor Mariam [Cope *x[d] out*, **Haimes** *above*] filiam Jacobi & Annæ (conjugum) olim **Cope**, Natam & baptizam esse a R° D° Tellier Presbitero gallico, die 19[a] Jan: 1807. Patrinus fuit Gulielmus Slade vice Roberti Franklin, Matrina Eliza Smithson vice Mariæ Roberto.

Joannes Alleway Missionarius Apost[us].

1808

[4] Hodie 27ma die Julii [conjuncti sunt *x[d] out*, (Lymington) *above*]. Ego infra scriptus conjunxi in Matrimonium, nullo reperto impedimento, Ludovicum Franciscum Xaverium De Fennin, filium Roberti & Rosaliæ **Fennin** (olim **Dumonchau**) et Mariam Rosaliam Oreille, filiam Joannis et Rosæ **Oreille** (olim **De la Suz**). Testibus Ludovico Josepho Coutelier et Sebastiana Maria Gomés. Thomas Tilbury, Missionarius Apost[s].

Die 23[a] Septembris 1808, circa horam tertiam post meridiem natus, eodemque die baptizatus fuit Thomas Josephus Weld, ‡

* Aalst or Alost.

† Joseph Weld, who succeeded his brother Cardinal Weld, and was in turn succeeded by Edward Joseph, whose baptism is here recorded.

‡ He succeeded to the Ince Blundell estates, Lancashire, and added the name of Blundell to his own.

filius Josephi & Carolettæ **Weld** (olim **Stourton**) conjugum: Patrinus Dominus Thomas Weld, Jun. Matrina Domina Elizabeth Butler; Infantis avus & avia.

A me Thoma Tilbury, Missionario Apos[co].

[1810]

Die 28[a] Martii 1810 nata, die vero 29[a] ejusdem mensis & anni baptizata est Francisca Haimes, filia Jacobi & Annæ **Haimes** conjugum. Patrinus fuit Ludovicus Davis, Matrina Maria Law.

A Rev[do] Dn[o] Le Tellier Presb[o] Gal[o].
absente Tho[a] Tilbury Miss[o] Apos[co].

[5] [1812]

Die vigesima Januarii 1812 circa horam nonam post meridiem natus, die vero 21[a] ejusdem mensis & anni baptizatus est Gulielmus Haime filius Jacobi & Anne **Haime**, olim **Cope**, conjugum. Patrinus fuit Gulielmus Slade, Matrina Elizabetha Cope.

A me Joanne Brown Miss[o] Apos[co].

[1814]

Die 16 Martii 1814 natus, die vero 19 ejusdem mensis & anni baptizatus est Thomas Haimes, filius Jacobi & Annæ **Haimes**, olim **Cope**, conjugum. Patridus fuit Mo [y *over* i] ses Roberts. Matrina Teresia Roberts. A me Joanne Browne, Miss[o] Apos[co].

Die 16 Octobris 1814 Nata & die 22 Decembris Ejusdem anni Baptizata fuit, sacris precibus ac ceremoniis pretermissis Augustine Julia Aimée Tournefort, Filia Augustini **Tournefort**, et Sara **Bailey** (olim **Read**). A me Joanne Browne Miss[o] Apos[co].

[1815]

Die 19[a] Junii 1815, circa Nonam horam ante meridiem natus, eodemque die, in casu necessitatis a Sophia Hyde undulatus fuit, Gullielmus Josephus Weld*, filius Josephi et Carolette **Weld** (olim **Stourton**) conjugum: Patrinus fuit Gullielmus Stourton. Matrina Theresia Vaughan. Cui Puero supra dicto Gullielmo Josepho Weld Baptismi ceremoniæ die 8[a] Julii mensis suppletæ sunt a me. Joanne Browne, Miss[o] Apos[co].

[6] Die 17[a] Octobris 1815 natus, die vero 26[a] ejusdem mensis & anni baptizatus est Franciscus Mafre, filius Josephi & Lucie **Mafre**, olim **Thomas**, conjugum. Patrinus fuit Franciscus Mafre. Matrina Roza Carmine. A me Joanne Browne Miss[o] Apos[co].

Die 4[a] Novembris 1815 nata, die vero 6[a] ejusdem mensis et anni baptizata est Maria Carmine filia Josephi & Rozœ **Carmine**, olim [D *over* **R**]**ogeri**, conjugum. Patrinus fuit Josephus Mafre.

A me Joanne Browne, Miss[o] Apos[co].

[1816]

Die 11[a] Januarii 1816 Natus & die 12[a] ejusdem mensis & anni Baptizatus fuit Richardus Charles filius Richardi & Mariæ **Charles** (olim **Edward**) Conjugum: Patrinus fuit Jacobus Haimes, Matrina Lucia Roberts. A me Joanne Browne, Miss[o] Ap[co].

[*Nearly a third of the page blank.*]

* He was usually known as Joseph Weld of the Lodge, Lymington, where he built the church.

[7]
Die 15ª Januarii 1813 nata, die vero 25ª Junii 1816 Undulata fuit Anna Reightor filia Caroli & Susannæ **Reightor** (olim **Slack**) conjugum. A me Joanne Browne, Miss° Apos^co^.

Die 5ª Januarii 1815 natus, die vero 25ª Junii 1816 undulatus fuit Thomas Gulielmus Reightor, filius Caroli & Susanne **Reightor** (olim **Slack** *) Conjugum. A me Joanne Brown, Miss° Apos^co^.

Die 31 Augusti 1816 Nata & die 1 Septembris 1816 Baptizata fuit Elizabetha Haimes filia Jacobi & Annæ **Haimes**, olim **Cope**, conjungum. Patrinus fuit Aaron Roberts, Matrina Francisca Roberts. A me Joanne Browne, Miss° Apos^co^.

Die 4ª Augusti 1816 natus, die vero 5ª ejusdem mensis & anni Undulatus fuit Ernestius Reighter, filius Caroli & Susanne **Reighter**, olim **Slack**, conjugum.
A me Joanne Brown, Miss° Apos^co^.

[1817]

[8] Die 9ª Aprilis 1817 nata, die vero 11ª ejusdem mensis & anni baptizata fuit Roza Carmine filia Josephi & Rozæ **Carmine**, olim **Dogeri**, Conjugum. Patrinus fuit Ego Joannes Browne.
A me Joanne Browne, Miss° Apos^co^.

Die 22ª Aprilis 1817 natus, die vero 23ª ejusdem mensis & Anni Baptizatus fuit Joannes Ris, filius Michaeli & Mariæ **Ris**, olim **Randall**, Conjugum. Patrinus fuit Josephus Carmine.
A me Joanne Browne, Miss° Apos^co^.

[*A space for one or two entries left*]

[1818]

Die 18ª Februarii [1818 *above*] nata, die vero 19ª ejusdem mensis & anni Undulata fuit Maria Vertel, filia Josephi & Elizabeth **Vertel**, olim **Pack**, conjugum.
A me Joanne Browne, Miss° Apos^co^.

[9] Die 18ª Februarii [1818 *above*] nata, die vero 19ª ejusdem mensis & anni Baptizata fuit Maria Charles, filia Richardi & Marie **Charles**, olim **Edwards**, conjugum. Matrina fuit Helena Baker. A me Joanne Browne, Miss° Apos^co^.

Die 6ª Augusti 1818 natus die vero 16ª ejusdem mensis & anni Baptizatus fuit Robertus Gary filius Archerus [Gary *x^d^ out*] et Martha **Gary** olim **Paddick** conjugum. Matrinae fuit Anna Birch..
A me Joanne Browne, Miss° Apos^co^

[1819]

Die 9ª Januarii 1819 Nata & die vero 20ª ejusdem anni Baptizata fuit, sacris precibus ac ceremoniis pretermissis, Lucia Chiezer, Filia Bartholomæi **Chiezer**, et Saræ [Chiezer olim *below*] **Churchill**, conjugum. A me Joanne Browne, Miss° Apos^co^.

Die 25ª Martii 1819 Natus & eodem die baptizatus fuit Josephus Langdown filius Petri & Teresiæ **Langdown** (olim **Langford**) conjugum. Matrina fuit Teresia Langdown.
A me Joanne Browne, Miss° Apos^co^.

* This must be Slack with the second letter crossed in error, and making it into Stack. See the previous register, and the second following.

[10] Die 25[a] Junii 1819 nata & eodem die baptizata fuit Maria Ris, filia Michaeli & Mariæ **Ris**, olim **Randall**, Conjugum. Patrinus fuit Philippus Evers.

A me Joanne Browne, Miss° Apos[co].

Die 30ma Decembris 1819 natus, eodemque die baptizatus fuit Gulielmus Charles filius Richardi Charles, et Mariæ **Charles** (olim **Edwards**) conjugum. Matrina fuit Elizabetha Soper.

A me Joanne Browne, Miss° Apos[co].

[1820]

Die 3[a] Januarii 1820 Natus, die vero [5 *x[d] out*, 4 *above*][a] ejusdem mensis & anni baptizatus est Joannes Haimes filius Jacobi & Annæ **Haimes** (olim **Cope** [*or* Cape],) conjugum. Patrinus fuit Thomas Roberts, Matrina Elizabetha Soper.

A me Joanne Browne, Miss° Apos[co].

Die 12ma Julii 1820 nata, eodemque die baptizata fuit Maria Caroletta Weld*, filia Josephi, et Caroletæ **Weld** (olim **Stourton**) conjugum: Patrinus Humphredus Weld, Matrina Maria Stourton.

A me Joanne Browne, Miss° Apos[co].

[11] Die 3[a] Decembris 1819 natus, die vero 22[a] Julii [1820] undulatus fuit Jacobus Madden, filius Joannis & Mariæ **Madden** (olim **Preston**, Conjugum).

A me Joanne Browne, Miss° Apos[co].

Die 15[a] Septembris natus, die vero 16[a] baptizatus Henricus Ris filius Michaeli & Mariæ **Ris**, olim **Randall** Conjugum.

A me Joanne Browne, Miss° Apos[co].

[1821]

Die 7[a] Junii 1821 nata, die vero 28[a] Augusti ejusdem anni undulata fuit Anna Maria Madden, filia Joannis & Mariæ **Madden** (olim **Preston** Conjugum).

A me Joanne Browne, Miss° Apos[co].

Die 8[a] Septembris 1821 Nata, eodemque die Baptizata fuit Elizabetha Charles, filia Richardi, et Mariæ **Charles** (olim **Edwards**) Conjugum, Patrinus fuit Ludovicus Davies, Matrina Maria Roberts. A me Joanne Browne, Miss° Apos[co].

[12] [1822]

Die 3[a] Martii 1822 Nata, die vero 4[a] ejusdem Mensis & Anni Baptizata fuit Anna Maria Cot, filia Caroli et Annæ **Cot**, olim **Lune** [? **Lane**], Conjugum. Patrinus fuit Ludovicus Davis, Matrina Lucia Roberts.

A me Joanne Browne, Miss° Apos[co].

Die 16[a] Maji 1822 Nata eodem die Baptizata fuit Caroletta Maria Haimes, filia Jacobi & Annæ **Haimes**, olim **Cope**, conjugum. Patrinus fuit Georgius Bates, Matrina Maria Hunt.

A me Joanne Browne, Miss° Apos[co].

[1823]

Die 17[a] [?] Novembris [1823 *above*], die vero 18[a] ejusdem mensis & Anni baptizatus Thomas Charles filius Richardi &

* She became second wife of Colonel John Francis Vaughan of Courtfield.

Mariæ **Charles**, olim **Edwards** Conjugum. Matrina fuit Elizabetha Gray. A me Joanne Browne, Miss° Apos^co^.

[1824]

Die 10^a^ Maji 1824 Nata, die vero 11^a^ ejusdem Mensis et Anni Baptizata fuit Caroletta Cot, filia Caroli et Annæ **Cot**, olim **Lane**, Conjugum. Patrinus fuit Joanne Maud, Matrina Hannah Slade. A me Joanne Browne, Miss° Apos^co^.

[13] [*Hand changes*] 1825

Die 18 Februarii natus, die vero 22 Martii ejusdem Anni baptizatus fuit Guielmus Langdown filius Teresæ **Langdown**. Patrinus fuit Joannes Maud, Matrina Anna Haimes.
A me Joanne Leadbetter, Missionario Apostolico.

Die 29 Augusti nata, et die 30 ejusdem mensis baptizata fuit Anna Weld, filia Josephi et Carolettæ **Weld** (olim **Stourton**) Conjugum. Patrinus fuit Edwardus Stourton, Matrina Catherina Stourton. A me Joanne Leadbetter, Missionario Apostolico.

Die 3 Novembris natus, die vero 1 Decembris ejusdem anni baptizatus fuit Joannes Fitzgerald filius Richardi et Mariæ **Fitzgerald** (olim **Yarwood**) Conjugum. Patrinus fuit Joannes Maud, Matrina Lucia Roberts.
A Me Joanne Leadbetter, Missionario Apostolico.

[14] Die 24 Decembris natus eodemque die baptizatus fuit Henricus Charles filius Richardi et Mariæ **Charles** (olim **Edwards**) Conjugum. Patrinus fuit Joannes Maud, Matrina Hannah Slade.
A me Joanne Leadbetter, Missionario Apostolico.

[*Hand changes*] 1826

Die 2° Augusti nata et die 3° ejusdem mensis et anni baptizata fuit Elizabetha Cot, filia Caroli et Annæ **Cot** (olim **Lane**) conjugum. Patrinus Jacobus Bramble. Matrina Elizabetha Soper. a me Thoma Tilbury, Miss° Apos^co^.

[*Hand changes*] 1828

Die 26° Maii natus et die 30° ejusdem mensis baptizatus fuit Josephus **Charles** filius Ricardi et Mariæ (olim **Edwards**) conjugum. Patrinus Josephus Edwards. Matrina Elizabetha Barnes. a me Gulielmo Waterton, S.J.*

[15] Die 4° Septembris nata et die 5^a^ ejusdem mensis baptisata fuit Maria M^c^Donnell filia Jacobi et Carollettæ **M^c^Donnell** (olim **Lane**,) conjugum. Patrinus Ricardus Charles. Matrina Anna Cott. a me Gulielmo Waterton, S.J.

[*On a slip of paper pasted and sewn in opposite to the last, facing it and the other side being blank, is the following entry.*]

Die 4. Sep. 1828, natus, et die 29 Sep. ejusdem Anni baptizatus fuit Gulielmus Henricus Geary, filius Patricii et Mariæ **Geary** (olim **Massissy**) Conj. Patrinus Gulielmus Waterton. Matrina Ellen Lyons. a me Gulielmo Waterton.

* In the original a fourth line is given to the signature and a fifth & sixth to the sponsors. The order is here changed & all closed up. Fr. Waterton keeps his entries this way generally.

1829

Die 4° Maii natus et die 7° ejusdem mensis baptisatus fuit Gulielmus Taylor filius Caroli et Saræ **Taylor** (olim **Davy**) Conjugum. Patrinus Joannes Taylor. Matrina Sophia Collingridge. a me Gulielmo Waterton S.J.

Die 22ª Octobris nata, et die 8° Novembris baptista fuit Maria McCarthy, filia Gulielmi et Joannæ **McCarthy** (olim **Edwards**), conjugum. Patrinus Joannes Wood. Matrina Hannah Slade. a me Gulielmo Waterton, S.J.

[16] Die 21° Decembris nata et die 22° ejusdem mensis baptisata fuit Joanne Cott, filia Caroli et Annæ **Cott** (olim **Lane**) conjugum. Patrinus Gulielmus Haimes, Matrina Elisabetha Weeks. a me Gulielmo Waterton, S.J.

1831

Die 21° Februarii natus et die 25° ejusdem mensis baptisatus fuit Gulielmus Cott, filius Caroli et Anna **Cott** (olim **Lane**) Conjugum. Patrinus Joannes Wood. Matrina Maria Birt. a me Gulielmo Waterton S.J.

Die 26 Augusti 1828 natus, et die 22° Februarii 1831 baptisatus fuit Carolus Josephus Gilbert, filius Miles et Luciæ **Gilbert** (olim **Squirs**), Conjugum. Patrinus Carolus Weld. a me Gulielmo Waterton S.J.

[17] Die 22° Januarii nata, et die 22° Februarii baptisata fuit Lucia Matilda Gilbert, filia Miles et Luciæ **Gilbert** (olim **Squires**) Conjugum. Patrinus Jacobus Weld. a me Gulielmo Waterton, S.J.

Die 23° Martii nata et die 28° ejusdem mensis baptisata fuit Sara Taylor, filia Caroli, et Saræ **Taylor** (olim **Davy**) Conjugum. Patrinus Jacobus Taylor. Matrina Catharina Taylor. a me Gulielmo Waterton S.J.

Die 24° Maii nata et die 27° ejusdem mensis baptisata fuit Anna Charles, filia Ricardi et Mariæ **Charles** (olim **Edwards**) conjugum. Patrinus [*blank*], Matrina [*blank*]. a me Gulielmo Waterton, S.J.

[18] 1832

Die 4° Junii nata, et die 5° Julii ejusdem anni baptisati sunt Joannes et Jacobus **McDonnell** filii Jacobi et Carolettæ McDonnell, (olim **Lane**), Conjugum. Patrinus [Joannis *x^d^ out*, Jacobi *above*]; Gulielmus Waterton Matrina Maria Champ. Patrinus [Jacobi *x^d^ out*, Joannis *above*], Joannis Wilcox, Maria Birt. a me Gulielmo Waterton S.J.

1833

Die 26 Aprilis nata et die 12° Maii baptizata fuit Anna Amelia Taylor, filia Caroli, et Saræ **Taylor** (olim **Davy**) Conjugum, Patrinus Gulielmus Davy. Matrina Sara Taylor. a me Gulielmo Waterton S.J.

Die 27° Septimbris natus, et die 28° Octobris ejusdem anni baptisatus fuit Thomas Gilbert filius Miles, et Luciæ **Gilbert** (olim **Squire**) conjugum. Patrinus Thomas Weld. Matrina Sara Taylor. a me Gulielmo Waterton, S.J.

[19] Die 22° Novembris nata, et die 30° ejusdem mensis baptisa

fuit Brigitta Kelly, filia Joannis et Catharinæ **Kelly** (olim **Folan**) conjugum. Patrinus Thomas Whitty. Matrina Barbara Finlay.
a me Gulielmo Waterton, S.J.

1834

Die 4° Martii natus, et die 23° ejusdem Mensis baptizatus fuit Josephus Edward, filius Joannis et Elisabethæ **Edward** (olim **Cunningham**) conjugum. Patrinus Cornelius Murphy. Matrina Elizabetha Willis. a me Gulielmo Waterton.

Die 9° Decembris nata, et die 14° ejusdem mensis baptisata fuit Carolina Cott, filia Caroli et Annæ **Cott** (olim **Lane**) Conjugum. Patrinus Richardus Charles. Matrina Maria Champ.

[20] 1835

Die 3° Aprilis natus, et die 3° Maii ejusdem anni baptisatus fuit Josephus Crabb, filius Gulielmi, et Mariæ **Crabb** Conjugum. Patrinus Miles Gilbert. Matrina Dorothea Nind.
a me Gulielmo Waterton, S.J.

Die 2° Augusti natus est et die 16° ejusdem mensis baptisatus fuit Thomas Gregory, filius Thomæ et Elisabethæ **Gregory** (olim **Frewick**) Conjugum. Patrinus Thomas Gregory. Matrina Sara Gregory. a me Gulielmo Waterton, S.J.

Die 19° Augusti nata, et die 18° Octobris ejusdem anni baptisata fuit Sophia Patientia House, filia Joannis, et Joannæ **House** (olim **Crabb**) Conjugum. Patrinus Joannes Wilcox. Matrina Sophia Caddell. a me Gulielmo Waterton, S.J.

[21] 1836

Die 6° Maii nata, et die 12° ejusdem mensis baptisata fuit Elizabetha Taylor, filia Caroli et Saræ **Taylor** (olim **Davy**) Conjugum. Patrinus Miles Gilbert. Matrina Lucia Gilbert.
a me Gulielmo Waterton, S.J.

Die 14° Septembris natus, et die 26° ejusdem mensis baptisatus fuit, Gulielmus Aloysius Gilbert, filius Miles, et Luciæ **Gilbert** (olim **Squire**) conjugum. Patrinus Gulielmus Waterton. Matrina Cecilia Caddell. a me Gulielmo Waterton.

Die 6° Novembris natus, et die 4° Decembris ejusdem anni baptisatus fuit Joannes McBride, filius Alexandri et Margarettæ **McBride** (olim **Power**) conjugum. Patrinus Joannes Fergus Matrina Maria Fergus. a me Gulielmo Waterton.

[22] 1837

[*A line of dates similar to following crossed out*]

Die 10ª Novembris 1836 natus, et die 8ª Januarii 1837 baptisatus fuit, Carolus Taylor, filius Jacobi et Sophiæ **Taylor** (olim **Buckett**) conjugum. Patrinus Georgius Cott. Matrina Maria Champ. a me Gulielmo Waterton, S.J.

Die 10ª Januarii 1837 nata, et die 13ª ejusdem mensis baptisata fuit Paulina, Maria, Luisa Jerningham filia Arthurii,* et Sophiæ **Jerningham** (olim **Caddell**) Conjugum. Patrinus, Edmundus Jerningham. Matrina, Paulina Caddell.
a me Gulielmo Waterton, S.J.

* He became an Admiral in the Royal Navy.

Die 19[a] Aprilis 1837 [natus *above*] et die 14 Maii ejusdem anni baptisatus fuit Edmundus Molloy, fillus Joannis et Margaritæ **Molloy** (olim **Murphy**) conjugum. Patrinus Joannes Wilson. Matrina Elisabetha Mahony.

a me Gulielmo Waterton, S.J.

Die 22da Maii 1837 natus, et die 28 ejusdem mensis baptisatus fuit Joannis Canary, filius Davidis et Margaritæ **Canary** (olim **Cagan**) Conjugum. Patrinus Jacobus Mahony. Matrina Maria Murphy. a me Gulielmo Waterson, S.J.

[23] Die 20[a] Maii 1837, nata, et die 4[a] Junii ejusdem anni baptisata fuit Martha Gregory, filia Thomæ et Elizabethæ **Gregory** (olim **Treveak** *) Conjugum. Patrinus Thomas Gregory Senr. Matrina Paulina Caddell. a me Gulielmo Waterton S.J.

Die 3[a] Maii 1837, natus, et die 4[a] Junii, ejusdem anni baptisatus fuit Ricardus Driscoll, filius Joannis et Margaritæ **Driscoll** (olim **Errington**) Conjugum. Patrinus Gulielmus Campbell. Matrina Anna Campbell. a me Gulielmo Waterton S.J.

[*Dates crossed out*]

Die 16 Julii 1837 natus, et die 23[d] ejusdem mensis baptisatus fuit Thomas Wright, filius Thomæ et Bridgettæ **Wright** (olim [**Lane** *x[d] out*] **Tracy**) Conjugum. Patrinus Jacobus ONeil. Matrina Maria Davis. a me Guililelmo Waterton S.J.

Die 5[a] Novembris 1837 natus, et die 19 ejusdem mensis baptizatus fuit Joannis Mahony, filius Jacobi & Elisabethæ **Mahony** (olim **Harrigan** Conjugum. Patrinus David Kennedy. Matrina Margarita Organ. a me Gulielmo Waterton.

Die 31 Octobris 1837 nata, et die 26 Novembris ejusdem anni baptisata fuit Julia Francisca Walsh, filia Gulielmi et Joannæ **Walsh** (olim **Lane**) conjugum. Patrinus Thomas Culnane. Matrina Maria Fergus. a me Gulielmo Waterton S.J.

[24] 1838

Die 1° Februarii 1838 nata est Helen Gardener, Filia Josephi et Henriettæ. **Gardener** (olim **Smithen**) Conj. et baptisata die 18 Martii ejusdem anni. Patrinus Georgius Cott. Matrina Elizabeth Gibbs. a me Gulielmo Waterton S.J.

Die 25 Aprilis 1838 nata, et Die 13 Maii ejusdem anni baptisata fuit, Teresa Tayler, filia [Saræ *x[d] out*] Caroli et Saræ **Tayler** (olim **Davy**) Conj. Patrinus Robertus Damon. Matrina Helena Tayler

a me Gulielmo Waterton, S.J.

Die [2 *or* 3]o Aprilis 1838, natus et die 1° Maii [bapti *x[d] out*] ejusdem anni baptisatus fuit Georgius **Pape** [?] filius Caroli et —— **Pope** Conj. Patrinus Georgius Cott. Matrina Lucia Roberts.

a me Gulielmo Waterton S.J.

Die 22 Julii 1838 nata et die 4 Augustii ejusdem anni baptizata fuit Maria Flin, filia Morgan & Margaritæ **Flin** (olim **Grant**) Conj. Patrinus Gulielmus Campbell. Matrina Maria Fergus.

a me Gulielmus Waterton,

* This appears somewhat doubtful; but is not 'Frewick' as in 1835.

[25] Die 26 Octobris 1838, natus, et die 4° Novembris ejusdem anni baptisatus fuit Dennis **Kenelly** filius David et Margaritæ Kenelly (olim **Cogan**) Conj. Patrinus Gulielmus Campbell. Matrina Elizabeth Mahony. a me Gulielmo Waterton S.J.

1839

Die 14 Martii, 1839 natus, et die 25 Aprilis ejusdem anni baptizatus fuit Bernardus Whitren, filius Gulielmi et Mariæ **Whitren** (olim **Huggins**) Conj. Patrinus Georgius Huggins. Matrina Hanah Phillips. a me Gulielmo Waterton S.J.

Die 19 Aprilis 1839 natus, et die 5 Maii [ejusdem anni *above*] baptizatus fuit Jacobus Resden filius Dennis et Catharinæ **Resdon** (olim **Crowley**) Conj. Patrinus Gulielmus Welsh. Matrina Ellen Welsh. a me Gulielmo Waterton S.J.

Die Maii 29 1839 natus, et die 23 Junii ejusdem anni baptizatus fuit Joannes Kernan, filius Edwardi & Franciscæ **Kernan** (olim **Smith**) Conj. Patrinus Cornelius Driscoll. Matrina Margarita Kenelly. a me Gulielmo Waterton S.J.

[26] Die 2 Julii 1839 nata, et die 4 Augusti, ejusdem anni baptisata fuit Emely [Carpenter *above*] filia Gulielmi & Francisæ **Carpenter** (olim **Cutler**) Conj. Patrinus Carolus Slade. Matrina Anna Davis. a me Gulielmus Waterton S.J.

Die 10 Junii 1839 natus et die 14 Julii ejusdem anni baptizatus fuit Josephus Lane, filius Thomæ et Mariæ **Lane** (olim **Champ**) Conj. Patrinus Antonius Clark. Matrina Maria Clark. a me Gulielmo Waterton, S.J.

Die 27 Junii 1839 nata, et die 21 Julii ejusdem anni baptizata fuit Helena Driscoll, filia Cornelii & Bridgettæ **Driscoll** (olim **Pigott**) Conj. Patrinus Jacobus Fergus. Matrina Bridgetta Duhig. a me Gulielmus Waterton.

Die 18 Novembris 1839 [nata *above*] et die 1° Decembris ejusdem anni baptizata fuit Margarita Mahony, filia Jacobi et Elisabethæ **Mahony** (olim **Harrigan**) Conj. Patrinus Gulielmus Campbell. Matrina Anna Campbell. a me Gulielmo Waterton, S.J.

Die 23 Novembris 1839 [nata], et die 25 Decembris ejusdem anni baptizata fuit Ellen Walsh, filia Gulielmi [et] Joannæ **Walsh** (olim ——) Conj. Patrinus David Kenelly. Matrina Margarita McCarthy. a me Gulielmo Waterton, S.J.

1840

Die 12 Septembris [1840 nata *above*] et die 4 Octobris ejusdem anni baptizata fuit Anna Brown, filia Joannis, et Mariæ **Brown** (olim **Fergus**) conj. Patrinus Daniel McGinnity. Matrina Margarita Kempton. a me Gulielmo Waterton S.J.

[*Then follow the initials of John Bowring, the first of the three commissioners and their certificate completing the page. Sixteen* blank pages follow and the book is then used from the reversed end. The reverse page corresponding to* [1] *at the obverse end is used for the following marriages.*]

* Since rebinding I find when collating that only two blank pages remain.

MARRIAGES

James **Paxton** and Tamsen **Halsey** were married by me according to the rites of the Catholic Church May 26, 1832.

W[m]. Waterton, S.J

Witnesses. Robert Halsey—Thomas Halsey [*not signed*].

Thomas **Lane** and Mary **Champ** were married by me according to the rites of the Catholic Church. January 8th 1837.

W[m]. Waterton, S.J.

Witnesses. George Cott and John Wood.

William **Carpenter** and Frances **Cutler** ware married by me according to the rites of the Catholic Church February 12, 1837.

W[m]. Waterton, S.J.

Witnesses. George **Cott** and Jane **Cutler**.

Florence **McCarthy** and Margaret **Harrigan** were married by me according to the rites of the Catholic Church 23[d] of April 1837. W[m] Waterton.

Witnesses. Joanna Walsh & Mary Murphy.

[*Sewn in the same are three sheets of notepaper* = 12 *leaves including the covering ones as follows. Note however the certificates relating to Lymington at the end of Rook Cliffe.*]

[ROOK CLIFF, MILFORD, HANTS]

[*On Cover*] 1 Hants, No. II.

Registre / Des Baptêmes, Marriages, / et Sépultures / De La Chapelle Rook Cliff / Near lymington / hants [*The reverse blank*].

(1) J.B.

Die 7 februarii 1813 Natus Et Die 8 Ejusdem mensia Et Etiam anni Baptizatus fuit Joannes-Baptista Weld filius Georgii, Et Mariæ **Weld** (olim **Searle**) Conjugum: Patrinus fuit Joannes Searle, Matrina Maria Weld, Præsentibus R[do] Domino Brown Miss[o] apco pro patrino, Et Domina fréeman pro Matrina, a me francisco Mariano Le tailleur Miss[o] apco.

Ce jourdhui treizieme jour de mai mil huit Cent treize a Etée Baptisée par moi Prêtre soussigné, marie barbe, née d'heir du legitime mariage de philippe **pou**[**davigne** *over other letters**] (*selon sa déclaration *below*) et de rose (2) **Ximenez**, Le pere present, Le parrain jean Baptiste reanon [?], La marraine marie barbe Ribera Epouse du parrain avec nous Soussignés a l'Exception de la marraine que scachant pas Ecrire nous a laissée sa Croix. Poudavigne [?].

Croix de + la Marraine.

approvè le mot poudavigne, ligne Cinq, qui a Eté Corrigé, Et le Renvoi a la Vin de pay de d'autre Coté.*

* The spelling is by no means clear, in spite of—or perhaps by reason of—Monsieur Poudivigne's jocose approval of it, and the adjournment to the beer in the next apartment: And the registers are silent as to his feelings when his little Mary Barbara was, a few hours later, a bit of clay at his feet, and an angel pleading for him in heaven.

Le tailleur Prêtre Miss. apostol. de la Mission de Rook-Cliffe [*signature to entry on p.* 309].

Ce jourdhui seisieme jour de mai mil huit Cent trieze jái recité les prieres de la Sepulture de marie barbe **poudavigne** décedée d'hier, agée d'Environ deux jours. Le tailleur Prêtre Miss. Apostol.

(3) Die 18 maii 1814 natus, Et die vigesima ejusdem mensis Et Etiam anni Baptizatus fuit Georgius Thomas Weld filius Georgii, et Mariæ **Weld**, (olim **Searle**) Conjugum: Patrinus fuit thomas Weld, Matrina anna Searle; a me francisco mariano Le tailleur Miss° Ap^{co}.

Die vigesimo Secto februarii mensis, anno domini 1815, in parociâ dictâ de milford, provinciâ vero Simeniâ { vulgò* hampshire, natus, et die Secundâ mensis martii Sequentis in capellâ de Roocliff Baptizatus fuit Thomas Yeates, filius Thomæ **yeates**, et elizabeth Yeates { olim **Bradley** in Yorckshire comitatu nata } Conjugum. Patrinus fuit Thomas Roberts, matrina Maria Cox.

à me jb. f. fautrel, misso Ap^{co}.

Thomas Roberts [*signs*] J.B Maria Cox [*signs*]

[*There remain seven blank pages. The leaf at the extreme reverse end corresponding with the cover has been cut to form a guard for the following certificates pasted on to it.*

[*Certificate* A] [Certificats de Baptêmes—*in margin above official government embossed stamp of twopence.*]

Extractum á Registro Baptismale capellæ catholicæ De Lym ington in hampshire in Anglia.

Ego joannes Baptsta francis fautrel missionarius apostolicus in districtu Londinensi, attestor justà Baptismale registrum, joannem Baptistam Vertel filium jacobi **Vertel** oriundi ex urbe De L'isle en flandre, et elizabeth **Paque**† Anglicanæ Conjugum, natum die vigesimâ tertiâ Maii mensis 1806 Baptizatum fuisse Die decimâ mensis junii eodem anno, à Domno le Tellier presbytero capellano catholicæ capellæ de Lymington qui Subscripsit in Registro, patrinus fuit jean Baptiste jouette.

jnsupar attestor, josephum hectorem vertel filium jacobi **vertel**, et elizabeth **Pack**. natum Lymingtonii, Die vigesimâ Secundâ mensis Decembris, anno 1807, eodem anno, Die 26 decembris Baptizatum fuisse à dno le tellier presbytero. patrinus che^{lier} De Roucourt.

[*On the back*] Attestor quoque Annam elizabeth Vertel filiam jacobi [josephi *above*] **Vertel**, et Elizabeth **Paque** conjugum natam Lymingtonii Die Secundâ martii, anno domini 1812, à domino Le Tellier presbytero capello Baptizatam fuisse Die nonâ martii eôdem anno, patrinus fuit Louis Auguste de jousseaume, matrina francisca Lacan.

Quos quidem baptismales actus attestor esse conformes cum

* There is an oblique thick line across 'vulgo.'

† This looks like Payne, but the word appears later as Pack.

Registris in quorum fidem his testimoniis meâ manu Subscripsi, Londini, Die 25 maii mensis 1816.

j. B. f. fautrel missionarius apostolicus.

[*Certificate* B*] Extractum ex registro Baptismali Capellæ Catholicæ Lymingtoniensis, vulgò de Lymington in provinciâ Siméniâ vulgò hampshire in Angliâ.

Die Decimâ tertiâ mensis Aprilis, 1814, in loco dicto Lymington, provinciâ de hampshire in Angliâ natus fuit, et die Decimâ Septimâ ejusdem mensis et anni Baptizatus fuit josephus **Vertel** filius josephi, et elizabeth **Vertel**, olim **Pack** conjugum, patrinus Ambrosius Discalceati, matrina joanna La Rose, à me j. b. f. fautrel, missionario Apostolico, necnon in urbe Lymington, militaris Depositi capellano. Patrinus et matrina mecum Subscripserunt, in Registro.

[*On the back*] Extractum é registro baptismali capellæ catholicæ de Lymington.

Ego joannes Baptista franciscus fautrel missionarius Apostolicus, in districtu Londinensi attestor prædictum extractum in omnibus esse conforme cum Registro, in cujus fidem huic testimonio, mea manu Subscripsi, Londini Die mensis Maii, anno domini 1816.

j. B. fr. fautrel miss[s] Ap[cus] .

[*Certificate* C] Extractum è registro Baptismale Catholicæ Capellæ De lymington sub districtu Londinensi, in provinciâ vulgô hampshire.

Die Nonâ Maji Mensis 1814, propè Lymington, in districtu Londinensi Natus, et die decimâ ejusdem mensis et Anni Baptizatus fuit Jacobus Charles, filius Richardi Charles, et Mariæ **Charles** { olim **Edward[s]** Conjugum. Patrinus jacobus Edwards, Representatus per guillelmum Knight. Matrina Maria hunt.

à me j. b. fr. fautrel, miss[o] Ap[co].

[*On the back*] Ego Sacerdos Subscriptus, joannes Baptista franciscus fautrel, olim militaris depositi capellanus in urbe dictâ Lymington in hampshire provincia Sub districtu Londinensi, attestor prædictum extractum in omnibus esse conforme cum Registro, in cujus fidem huic testimonio meâ manu Subscripsi, Die decimâ octavâ mensis octobris, anno domini 1814, in urbe dictâ Lymington.

J. b. f. fautrel, missionarius Apostolicus. Lymington, Signed in my presence the 14th day of November 1814.

Cha. St Barbe, a magistrate for Hampshire.

[*Certificate* D] Maffré, né le 10 aout 1817, a 6 heures du Soir Rue Weselley N° 25 paroisse de St Pancras, fils de Joseph **Maffré** et de anne **Thomas** sa femme mariés à Limingthon 1814. Le pere fils de feu Barthelemy Maffré et de Cecile Ordi né à Bastia en Corse et baptisé sur les fonds de la Cathedrale de S[t] Omery en x[bre] 1794. Le parain . . . . Iouan. La maraine . . . . femme de [Del *x[d] out*] . . . . De la Vigne.

[*on the back*] Remember Call on—Mrs Curl, Lymington

* On stamped form.

D° —Mrs Compton, ashleys Lean, Lymington.

I shall be glad to hear you go to Jearsey—and ware [where] to Direct to you there too.

[*Certificate* E] Extractum e Registro Baptismali Cappellæ S[ci] Ludovici de Gonzaga, in Pago, vulgó Sommerstown,* in districtu Londinensi.

natus Die decimâ mensis Augusti, anni 1,817, et die duodecimâ ejusdem mensis & anni baptisatus fuit Josephus Ludovicus Maffre, filius Josephi & Luciæ **Maffre** (olim **Thomas**) conjugum: Patrinus fuit Marcus franciscus Jouan; Matrina Maria Gree dicta, La vigne, a me

J. Nevincka M.A.

Ego, claudius Guerry, Sacerdos, attestor prædictum Extractum in omnibus esse Conforme cùm Registro: in cujus fidem huic testimonio meâ manu Subscripsi.

Sommer's town, die Vigesimá Sectâ mensis Augusti, anni 1,817.

C. Guerry, Sacerdos.

[*The back is blank. This ends the contents of the book.*]

* The Chapel of St Aloysius de Gonzaga, Somers Town.

VIII

THE CATHOLIC REGISTER OF THE REV. MONOX HERVEY *alias* JOHN RIVETT *alias* JOHN MOXON

OXFORDSHIRE 1729-30, LONDON 1730-34, YORKSHIRE 1734-47, MONTGOMERYSHIRE 1747-52, and LONDON 1753-56.

CONTRIBUTED BY JOSEPH STANISLAUS HANSOM

THE registers can hardly be described as a book, or they make a very curious one. They consist of a bundle of paper sheets 13×8⅜ inches, folded to 8⅜×6½ inches. Instead of being made up in sections, the sheets are placed continuously one within the other, so that the inner ones protrude about an inch beyond the outer ones. The only way to bind them uniformly, and keep the proper sequence, would be to cut the sheets in two, and mount the parts on guards. There might be difficulties in this, as parts of writing might be covered. They had perhaps best be preserved as a sample of domestic book-binding, for to add to the grotesque appearance they have been sewn into an old brown leather cover, much too small, the sides being only 7½×5¼ inches, forming a poor protection to the paper which is dirty and frayed in consequence. Good substantial paper has been used, and each page is lined in red ink for dates, three columns of figures and head lines. Particulars of missing pages are given below, but these do not form gaps in the registers.

They are preserved in the archiepiscopal archives of Westminster, and I have been accorded permission to copy them at Archbishop's House, for which I have to thank his Eminence the Cardinal Archbishop and the archivist Monsignor Jackman.

The language used frequently proclaims the fact that the registers must have been written, as we see them, at a comparatively late period in Hervey's life. Although he gives numbers to his functions, in places he skips them, and puts down at the end a number as though dissatisfied with the total, and—perhaps his own memory. It would indeed have been difficult for him at times to have kept such registers. Nay more: it would have been dangerous to keep such palpable evidence of his priesthood. Especially the long imprisonment he underwent in York Castle militates against the possibility, or at least probability, of his being able to preserve even notes. Differences in the spelling of personal and place names may not go for much, with three provincial pronunciations and that of Londoners. The name of his 'Proditor' Ralph Pierceson, appears elsewhere as *Pearson*; but the latter could not write his own name, as will appear elsewhere. When we come to the question of dates, some seem improbable when tested by other evidence, and we may wonder how it could be otherwise, and how he could preserve so many in his mind with any approach to certainty.

It is intended to produce a number of documents and some information about Hervey and others in another paper. So we will now proceed with other particulars.

The date of Monox Hervey's birth is approximately shewn by the following certificate courteously supplied to me by the Rev. Forbes Phillips, Vicar of Gorleston, near Great Yarmouth, Suffolk, for which our thanks are rendered.

'Baptisings 1698
Elizabeth D[r] of Henry Hervey & Margaret May-17.
1699
Monox son of Henry Hervey and Margaret Sept[r] 22.

I Forbes Phillips, Vicar of Gorleston, do certify the above to be a correct copy of the Baptismal register of Gorleston Parish Church. Given under my hand this twenty seventh day of February 1913. (Signed) Forbes Phillips'

His mother was Margaret, daughter of Monox Rivett.

The interest in our work evinced by our Vice-President, Mr Burke, Norroy King of Arms, may enable us to print his pedigree on the distaff side, by which it appears that his maternal grandfather and one uncle bore the baptismal name of 'Monox.' He always writes it so, and out of twenty-three of his god-sons, he names fourteen Monox, several of them when he was passing under the *alias* of John Rivett. Mr Richard Thackeray Bedingfeld (who supplied so much interesting matter regarding his family to Volume vii.) has kindly supplemented this by a pedigree of the Herveys of Suffolk. The name has generally been given before as 'Harvey,' but this was before these registers, and other evidence now produced made it clear beyond all cavil. He abbreviates it as 'Her' and 'He.' The name is generally accounted as Norman in origin, and as Hervé pronounced easily in French, as our 'hare,' but like many other names in English pronounced Harvey, like 'hardy,' or else awfully as 'Hurvey' or 'hurdy.' So we have Barnard, Farmer, clark; or else Burnurd, Furmur, clurk; *never* Bernard, Fermor, clerk.

About 1713 he was converted to the Catholic Faith, and confirmed at London by Bishop Bonaventure Giffard, Vicar Apostolic of the London District.* Subsequently he is stated to have been at the English College, Lisbon.† He was admitted to the English College, Rome, 23 March 1724, aged 25, and ordained with Robert Constable, subdeacon and deacon in August and September, and priest 18 Sept. 1728 by Pope Gregory XIII.‡ He left for England with Nicholas Masson, *vere* Apthorpe, 6 April 1729.§ In the *College Diary* he is called John Moxon *vere* Harvey.‖ Following Hervey's autobiographical notes, we find he entered on his missionary work in England 12 June 1729, no place being named. He went to Bishop John Talbot Stonor, Vicar Apostolic of the Midland District, at Old Heythrop, Oxon, where he remained a whole year, presumably serving some distant chapel every fifth week at his own expense, if this is the

* Bro. Henry Foley's *Diary of the English College, Rome*, p. 474.

† Gillow's *Register of Lisbon College*, 211.

‡ *Diary of Eng. College, Rome*, p. 473.

§ *Ibid.*, p. 474.

‖ He is described as of Norfolk, probably referring to his father having been a merchant at Yarmouth.

ARMS OF HERVEY.—*Or, a chevron Gules, in chief two leopards' faces of the lo*
CREST 1 (false).—*A demi-leopard holding between his paws an increscent Ermi*
CREST 2 (true).—*A demi-leopard Argent, an increscent Ermine on mount held sinister paw, dexter paw on mount.*

...aster of ·

Nicholas Myn of Fransham Parva, Suffolk.

...ervey of Ey.

Nicholas Myn of Fransham Parva. Will dated 153 proved 1530.

John Hervey.

Edward Mynne of Fransham Parva.=Maud .... Will dated 1542; proved 1548.

...ge"). *next,*

Robert Mynne of Wolterton, Norfolk,=Ann, sister of William Gent., 1580. Will proved 1582. Guestwick, Norfolk, ye...

James Barber

Stephen Baxter of Suffolk.

Edmund=Susan Mynne Revett. Great Yarmo...

...argaret, dau. of Tho-...as Sicklemore and ...elict of William Cut-...r of Ipswich.

James Hervey of Eye,=Rachel Suffolk, Esq., in 1646; of Debenham, Gent., in 1664 ("Suffolk Visitation"). Baxter.

Christopher of Yarmouth

...ervey, ...bur. at ...lk, 27 ...).

Martha Hervey, 4th dau., 1664.

Mary Hervey, 5th dau., 1664.

...ey, 3rd

Monox Rivett,=Margaret, dau. of admitted Freeman of Yarmouth 1651. M.I. 1674, æt. 47. John Albertson *alias* Hendrick of Yarmouth. M.I. 1684, æt. 56.

Morley Revett of Yarmouth, merchant. Will 1683.

...pt. at Stoke Ash, Suffolk,=Margaret ...chant of Great Yarmouth ...ckham Skeith as "Henry ..." 4 Oct. 1701. Rivett.

Monox Rivett of Yarmouth, mariner, ob. 1698, s.p.

Samuel Rivett of Yarmouth, surgeon, ob. 1701.

B
R
Y

...enry Hervey, "Son of ...enry, Gent.," bur. at ...Vickham Skeith 9 Feb. ...702.

Elizabeth Hervey, bapt. at Gorleston, Suffolk, 17 May 1698.

Monox Hervey *alias* **John** priest, bapt. at Gorleston 1699; ob. in London 22 Dec.

...; articles before marriage dated 2 April 1743; ...7 Sept. 1791, aged 71.

tion about Hervey and others in another paper. So we will now proceed with other particulars.

The date of Monox Hervey's birth is approximately shewn by the following certificate courteously supplied to me by the Rev. Forbes Phillips, Vicar of Gorleston, near Great Yarmouth, Suffolk, for which our thanks are rendered.

'Baptisings 1698
Elizabeth D[r] of Henry Hervey & Margaret May-17.
1699
Monox son of Henry Hervey and Margaret Sept[r] 22.

I Forbes Phillips, Vicar of Gorleston, do certify the above to be a correct copy of the Baptismal register of Gorleston Parish Church. Given under my hand this twenty seventh day of February 1913. (Signed) Forbes Phillips'

His mother was Margaret, daughter of Monox Rivett.

The interest in our work evinced by our Vice-President, Mr Burke, Norroy King of Arms, may enable us to print his pedigree on the distaff side, by which it appears that his maternal grandfather and one uncle bore the baptismal name of 'Monox.' He always writes it so, and out of twenty-three of his god-sons, he names fourteen Monox, several of them when he was passing under the *alias* of John Rivett. Mr Richard Thackeray Bedingfeld (who supplied so much interesting matter regarding his family to Volume vii.) has kindly supplemented this by a pedigree of the Herveys of Suffolk. The name has generally been given before as 'Harvey,' but this was before these registers, and other evidence now produced made it clear beyond all cavil. He abbreviates it as 'Her' and 'He.' The name is generally accounted as Norman in origin, and as Hervé pronounced easily in French, as our 'hare,' but like many other names in English pronounced Harvey, like 'hardy,' or else awfully as 'Hurvey' or 'hurdy.' So we have Barnard, Farmer, clark; or else Burnurd, Furmur, clurk; *never* Bernard, Fermor, clerk.

About 1713 he was converted to the Catholic Faith, and confirmed at London by Bishop Bonaventure Giffard, Vicar Apostolic of the London District.* Subsequently he is stated to have been at the English College, Lisbon.† He was admitted to the English College, Rome, 23 March 1724, aged 25, and ordained with Robert Constable, subdeacon and deacon in August and September, and priest 18 Sept. 1728 by Pope Gregory XIII.‡ He left for England with Nicholas Masson, *vere* Apthorpe, 6 April 1729.§ In the *College Diary* he is called John Moxon *vere* Harvey.‖ Following Hervey's autobiographical notes, we find he entered on his missionary work in England 12 June 1729, no place being named. He went to Bishop John Talbot Stonor, Vicar Apostolic of the Midland District, at Old Heythrop, Oxon, where he remained a whole year, presumably serving some distant chapel every fifth week at his own expense, if this is the

* Bro. Henry Foley's *Diary of the English College, Rome,* p. 474.

† Gillow's *Register of Lisbon College,* 211.

‡ *Diary of Eng. College, Rome,* p. 473.

§ *Ibid.,* p. 474.

‖ He is described as of Norfolk, probably referring to his father having been a merchant at Yarmouth.

…, dau. and coheir of Roger Fotheringay. …wife. ╤ William le Hunte of Ashen, son and heir, ob. 9 Oct. 1551. = Alice, dau. of . . . . Bull of Herts. ╤ Thomas Knighton, Esq., of Little Bradley, Suffolk. 1st husband.

Lewes Hervey of Ey. ╤

Thomas le Hunte, living 1540.

Richard le Hunte, Esq. 20 Oct. 1540.

Will dated ╤ Anne Knighton, dau. and heir ╤ Thomas Soame of Betley, Norfolk, ob. 1569. 2nd husband.

Robert Hervey.

John Hervey. ╤

…unte, eldest son of Little Bradley, …k, Esq. ╤ Jane, dau. of Henry Colt of Colt's Hall in Cavendish.

William le Hunte, 2nd son.

John Day the printer. = Alice le Hunte. = William Stone, 2nd husband. = Edward Grimston, Esq. 3rd husband.

John Hervey (*vide* "Visitations of Cambridge"). *This John was possibly identical with the next, who bore the same arms.*

Rob… Gen…

dau. of Sir Ralph Shelton, Kt., of … Norfolk; mar. at St. Dunstan-in-… 27 Nov. 1597. 1st wife. ╤ Sir George le Hunte, Kt., of Little Bradley, Suffolk, High Sheriff of that county in 1610; ob. 1641. ╤ Elizabeth, dau. of Sir John Peyton and relict of Sir Anthony Irby.

John Hervey of Eye in com. Suff. (MS. D. 22, fo. 99.) ╤ Lettice, dau. of James Barber of Suffolk.

…Hunte, … and … Little

George le Hunte, 2nd son.

Mary le Hunte, ux . . . . Lukin of Cambridge.

Martha le Hunte, ux . . . . Talkarne of Hunts.

William Bramston, Esq., of Boxwell, Essex. 1st husband. = Jane le Hunt, eldest dau., bur. at Wickham Skeith 19 July 1644. ╤ Edmund Hervey of the Abbey in Wickham Skeith, Suffolk, Esq., where he took up his abode in the time of Charles I., and continued to reside there long after the King's death. He purchased Woodhall in Stoke Ash, said county, in 1646. As a J.P. he was much respected, and was elected M.P. for Suffolk in 1656, but was rejected by Cromwell, who had reason to expect opposition from such a man. Died 16 May 1664, aged 74, bur. 17 May at Wickham Skeith. = Margaret, dau. of Th…mas Sicklemore a… relict of William Cu…ler of Ipswich.

…Mary, …dau. …f . . . .

William Linstead, Gent., of Burlingham, Norf. = Barbara Hervey, bapt. at Wickham Skeith 13 May 1630; mar. there 26 Sept. 1653. She was the eldest dau.

Mary Hervey, bapt. at Wickham Skeith 8 Oct. 1632.

Jane Hervey, bapt. at Wickham Skeith 22 Oct. 1634; bur. there 14 Aug. 1638.

Henry Hervey, Esq., son and heir, resided at Wickkam Skeith; bapt. there 5 July 1631; bur. there 6 July 1664; died on the 4th, aged 33. Will dated 7 June 1664. ╤ Elizabeth, dau. of Benjamin Cutler of Ipswich, Gent.; mar. 1652.

Edmund Gardiner, son of Edmund Gardiner of Stoke Ash, Gent. = Bridget Hervey, bapt. at Wickham Skeith 4 Oct. 1636; mar. there 10 Sept. 1657.

James Hervey, son and heir, æt. 25 Ano. 1664.

Henry Richards, living 1664. = Dorothy Hervey, mar. *ante* 1665.

Rachel Hervey, 2nd dau., bur. at Eye, Suffolk, 27 April 1670.

Jane Hervey, 3rd dau., 1664.

Martha He… 4th dau., 1…

Mary Her… 5th dau., 1…

=Sarah, dau. of . . . . Hunt of Elmsett, Suffolk; living 1712 (Blois).

Barbara Hervey, bur. at Wickham Skeith 4 June 1664.

Elizabeth Hervey, bapt. at Wickham Skeith 16 June 1663.

Edmund Hervey of Norwich, Gent., 16 Feb. 1683, of South Burlingham, Norfolk, 1674, and of Wickham Skeith, Suffolk, 1695, 1697, and 1703. ╤ Anne, dau. of . . . . ; living 1692.

Henry Hervey, Gent., bapt. at Stoke Ash, S… 29 July 1661; was a merchant of Great Yar… 16 Feb. 1683; bur. at Wickham Skeith as "… Harvey of Yarm°, Gent.," 4 Oct. 1701.

…Vesey, Gent., of Sproughton, …lk, and of Hintlesham, where bur. 21 April 1736, aged 54 ╤ Elizabeth Hervey, born 16 July and bapt. at Wickham Skeith 29 July 1691; died 26 April 1716, aged 24. M.I. in Hintlesham Church.

Edmund Hervey, Gent., bapt. at Wickham Skeith 1 June 1689; bur. there 17 Dec. 1712 as "Edmund Hervey, junr., Gt." = ... dau. of . . . .

Thomas Hervey, Gent., bur. at Wickham Skeith 22 Nov. 1705.

Linstead Hervey.

Anne Hervey, bapt. at Wickham Skeith 2 Aug. 1692.

Barbara Hervey.

Henry Hervey, "So… Henry, Gent.," bur… Wickham Skeith 9 … 1702.

Rev. John Beaumont of Sproughton; mar. *circa* 1737. = Mary Vesey, eldest dau. and coheir. = John Vere, Esq., of Henley, Suffolk, and Thorpe, Norwich.

Rev. Charles Beaumont. ╤ Elizabeth Vesey, dau. and coheir; articles before ma… bur. at Witnesham, co. Suffolk, 27 Sept. 1791, aged 7…

Philip Bowes of Nacton ╤ Elizabeth Beaumont.

Amanda Beaumont.

meaning of 'gratis.' On the 7th July 1732 he went to London to supply for the Rev. Gerard Saltmarshe, chaplain to Lady Thomas Howard in Red Lion Square, Holborn, until 29 Sept. 1732. He says nothing about any special work after this, when he continued living in Red Lion Street, but an anonymous writer* credits him with starting a school there in 1733, and conducting it with considerable success. It will be noticed that his London baptismal registers practically stop on 13 Feb. 1733, which lends colour to the statement. If this is correct, it would be likely to attract the attention of the authorities, and he certainly moved nearly 250 miles to Ugthorpe, in the parish of Lythe, Cleveland, near Whitby, on 25 May 1734.

Before proceeding with that part attention may be called to special notices, in the Reconciliations, of houses where Hervey may have said Mass, seemingly in rooms of some size, as the functions are described as held *before the Congregation.* Such are,—twice at Mr Gendor's, at the Fleece and Dove in Drury Lane, 27 Dec. 1730, and 7 Feb. 1731. Twice at Mr Wynell's, the Muzzled Bear in Little Wyld Street, 28 Feb. and 4 April 1731. Twice at Mr Walker's, Great Queen Street, 20 April and 2 May 1731.† There is then more continuity,—Mr Blake's in Drury Lane being mentioned eight times from 17 June to 12 Sept. 1731, and, after two at his own lodgings in Red Lion Street, twice more at Mr Blake's, 13 Feb. and 1 May 1732. From 19 March 1732 until 1 April 1733 only 'my lodgings in Red Lion Street' are mentioned. On 8 April 1733 'Mr Blake's, Drury Lane,' is mentioned for the last time. On 17 and 21 April he officiates at Mr Richard Blevin's, at Kentish Town, seemingly reconciling two members of the same family in their private house, where he had baptized the Rev. James Blevin on the previous 6 Jan.

In Yorkshire he assumed the maternal *alias* of John Rivett, and seems to have preserved the secret of his proper name during 11½ years on the mission there, and 1½ as a prisoner in York Castle. He started a school at Ugthorpe, about the end of 1737, as he acknowledged at the end of 1745 when he had ten boys under his charge. They are stated to be gentlemen's sons, and one of them was a Clavering of Callaly, Northumberland. He would probably have continued his ministrations and school there, had it not been for the Stuart rising in 1745. The Duke of Newcastle ordered the detention of a number of priests in the north and midlands. He was arrested 11 Dec. 1746, and conveyed to York Castle, on the unfounded suspicion that he might be favouring the Young Pretender's cause. When arrested a payment for young Clavering's schooling and some bill transactions were found and construed into money being raised for that cause. Not only Hervey, but everybody having been party to the passage of the money, was suspected! The ostensible cause for his and other arrests was the priesthood, which was punishable by imprisonment for life. But he and the others acknowledged their priesthood and were liable to the penalty as Confessors. They could not have been acquitted of what they confessed. But they were acquitted; and this must have been on a treason charge, although he was still detained until 2 June 1747, and then only discharged under bail to leave Yorkshire. The registers

* *The Present State of Popery in England, etc.,* 1735.

† He married a couple at the same house, 24 Aug. 1731, James Wynell being a witness.

give no further account to make us imagine that he returned to Ugthorpe. Shortly before his arrest at Ugthorpe he had been at Scarborough, and reconciled a few to the Faith, including members of the Readhead family. On his release he repairs there again, and completes his task. And then—'Adieu to Bonny Yorkshire.'

On 29 July 1747 he went to Buttington Hall, Montgomeryshire, resuming his real name of Monox Hervey. We find his ministrations extending to Powis Castle and Welshpool, but no evidence of his keeping a school, or to whom he may have been chaplain.* He left there 24 Aug. 1752, and for nearly a year after he gives no account of himself. The next date is 7 Aug. 1753, when he lived in Oxford Road, London, his functions being with people in various parts of the Metropolis, both north and south of the Thames.

He notes that his entries were also made in the registers at Count Haslang's or the Bavarian embassy chapel in Warwick Street from 10 Aug. 1753 to 15 Feb. 1754; one at the Spanish embassy chapel, which seems to have been in Oxford Road (*now* Street), on 31 March 1754; at the French chapel, probably that of the embassy, in Grosvenor Square, 29 April 1754 to 26 June 1755; again at Warwick Street on 19 Aug. and 8 Sept. 1755; sixteen at the Neapolitan (embassy) chapel 28 Oct. 1755 to 30 April 1756; at the Spanish chapel, 28 Aug. and 12 Sept. 1756. There is one undated and unplaced after 16 Oct. 1756, which may be premonitory of his death about two months later. He was only fifty-seven years of age when he died. The Rev. John Shepherd recorded his death in the *Obituary of secular priests* (*C.R.S.*, xii., 9) 'Mr Monox Havey [*sic*] died in London ye 22 of December 1756.'

He is credited with being a zealous and successful preacher. We know him as a teacher of youth. His registers, perhaps incomplete, are before us as witness of his missionary work. We know him as a Confessor, enduring a long captivity, and scorning to abjure the Faith, or accept the liberty and worldly emoluments which would have been the usual reward of an apostate priest, especially when endued with talents, as Harvey must have been. He preferred to render back those talents to his Master, and not come empty-handed.

RETROSPECT OF UGTHORPE

King John gave Isabella, daughter of Robert de Turnham, in marriage to Peter de Mauley (de Malo Lacu), the murderer of Prince Arthur, together with Mulgrave Castle and extensive estates. Six of seven descendants in line, all called Peter, enjoyed the estates. The male line failing in 1415, one aunt of the last Peter, fourth Lord de Mauley, carried the Lythe part, including Mulgrave Castle, to the Bigod family, the lordship of Egton and property elsewhere going with another aunt to the Salvins or Salvains (Silvanus). From the Bigods† the estates passed by marriage to the Radcliffes.‡ Sir Roger Radcliffe of Mul-

* Fr. Henry Norbert Birt, O.S.B., gives the name of a Benedictine serving Buttington Hall as late as 1792. (*Obit-Book of the English Benedictines*, 1913.) Catherine Palmer, who died in 1730, held dower from the manor in 1717 (*Non-jurors*) Earlier it belonged to the Herberts of Powis.

† Also spelt Bigott, Bygod, etc.

‡ Also spelt Ratcliffe, Ratclyffe, etc. The spelling given above seems that generally used by the Ugthorpe family. The arms were,—argent, a bend engrailed sable, with a mullet argent for difference.

grave Castle, *jure uxoris* Dorothy Bigod, in 1584 granted the manor of Ugthorpe to Katherine their only daughter. Her brother Francis was heir to Mulgrave Castle, with Lythe, Hutton-Mulgrave, Ugthorpe, Mickleby, Barrowby, Barnby, Newton-Mulgrave, Ellerby, etc., which had passed about 1625 to Edmund Sheffield, Lord Sheffield of Butterwick, co. Lincoln, Lord President of the North 1602-19, who was advanced to the Earldom of Mulgrave 7 Feb. 1626. The Radcliffes had been ruined by the merciless fines for recusancy.

Katherine Radcliffe's name constantly appears in lists of recusants down to 1614 (*N. Riding Records*, ii., 65), when five other recusants are named as 'sojourners' with her at Ugthorpe, and also four 'servants' recusants.* Her will was proved 31 July 1615 (*Yorks. Arch. Rec.*, xxviii.). By it she left the manor of Ugthorpe to her half-brother William, eldest son of Sir Roger Radcliffe by his second wife, Margaret daughter of John Ryther of Ryther, co. York. He and other members of the family appear as recusants; but he conformed once, perhaps temporarily as he appears retaining recusants later.

Afterwards the most important families were the allied ones of Salvin of Newbiggin in Egton, and Fairfax of Dunsley in Whitby parish, scions of the Gilling and Walton family, who are omitted in all pedigrees that have come to my notice. Henry and Ralph sons of George Fairfax appear regularly as recusants; but that family seems to have died out during the Commonwealth. At the Visitation on 22 March 1665 (Dugdale's, *Surtees Soc.*, xxxvi., 230) descendants of Cuthbert Fairfax of Acaster-Malbys, a younger brother of George, are found to be of Dunsley.

The Smiths of Egton Bridge, a family still extant, but whose property is now alienated, were comfortably off; and also the Hodgsons and Piersons of Ugthorpe; but hardly able to maintain a chaplain; although at an early period the first seem to have been great harbourers of priests. Amongst those owning land in 1717 there were also Gabriel Dale† of Ugthorpe, Christopher Simpson of Huntehouse in Goathland, William Stangoe (not Stanger) of Ugthorpe and a few like Henry Harrison of Danby further afield. There were however a certain number of Catholic yoemen and tradesmen in the neighbourhood, who would take their share in the maintenance of priests mostly employed about Egton and Ugthorpe, one or two at a time.

The places disclosed by Hervey's registers stretch half way to Stokesley on the west, to Scarborough on the south-east, and indefinite miles inland to the south-west amongst the moors and dales. The same extent of mission work, centred about Ugthorpe and Egton, would seem to have existed long before his time, and also long after. Outside that area were Catholic families of position who maintained chaplains, as the Mayes at Yarm, the Eures and later the Piersons of Stokesley, Nunthorpe, Faceby and Forcett, the Crathornes of Crathorne, the Tunstalls of Lower Silton, near which the Franciscans

* The annual legal exactions for herself and retainers would be £1430. Many of the same names appear in Peacock's list in 1604. There would also be exactions of £260 against each of the nine recusant retainers.

† Robert Dayles [*sic*] had two thirds of his estate in Ugthorpe sequestered from 1644 to 1654 when he died. His sons Gabriel, Ralph and John sold it to Joseph Dayles and the sequestration was removed. (*Yorks. Arch. Rec.*, xx., 205.)

for some time maintained a monastery at Osmotherley, the Greens of Lanmouth, the Meynells of North Kilvington, the Saltmarshes of South Kilvington, the Fairfaxes of Gilling Castle, etc. The chaplains would have a fixed residence; but their ministrations would be able to narrow the field of the East Cleveland missioners. With the exception of Stokesley, all were outside of a circumference of twenty five miles struck from Whitby.*

It must have been a strenuous and well-sustained combination between priests and people that has handed down the Faith, without interruption, from generation to generation, to the present time. The stern resolution which enabled them to do this, may enable the Catholic people of Egton especially to look with some complacency on the bitter words of Hervey about their forefathers. The Stuart rising of 1745 must have raised a state of terror, and it is exceedingly doubtful whether the Egton Catholics could have protected him and his fellow priest. Although a large part of the English troops had been drawn away to meet the Scots' advance, there was quartered at Guisborough alone a regiment of Dutch mercenaries. † The Catholics of Egton were and still are a considerable minority of the people; but that would be the very reason why the Government would exercise a stricter surveillance over them, as it might suspect them of favouring the advent of a *de jure* Catholic King, in place of the Hanoverians, foisted on the nation for nothing but their Protestantism, who had in no way earned the affection, still less the enthusiasm, of the people.

Amongst some evidence to be produced, there seems no cause for suspicion to any general extent, like there might have been thirty years before, when the first Hanoverian was hardly seated on the throne. It shews however that,—(1) Mr. Thomas Liddell, the recent priest at Egton Bridge, had been taking some political action adverse to the Government of the day,—(2) that when Bishop Dicconson, who was resident at Wycliffe under the name of Eaton, appointed Mr Luke Potts *alias* Cowper to the mission, with authority to Hervey to induct him and introduce him to the Catholics there, he did so to remedy Liddell's offence,—(3) that Hervey dissuaded Potts from going to Egton Bridge, and persuaded him to remain at Ugthorpe, knowing of the damage attempted by Liddell.

If there were a danger in Mr Potts going there, it may be inferred that that danger would be accentuated by their both going, as they did later, failing to obtain the precarious shelter sought, on which he comments so bitterly, and—perhaps unjustly. There can be no doubt of Hervey's loyalty. He speaks of the highlanders as 'rebels.' Potts is sent by Bishop Dicconson as a suitable missioner after Liddell, and nearly all of the priests, arrested on suspicion, cleared themselves of disloyalty, the real cause of their arrest. ‡ This may be construed into an opposition to two loyal priests; but it is more likely that the Egton people, having had experience of Liddell, and little if any as to the views of Hervey and Potts (the latter being an utter stranger to them), may have thought that they were likely

* There was no mission at Whitby itself until 1794, when the registers begin Mass is reported to have been said in private houses from 1790.

† John Walker Ord's *History of Cleveland*, 228.

‡ The arrests were made on an order of detainer issued by the Duke of Newcastle, but the pretext for arrest is generally stated 'for being Popish priests,' etc. In a few cases disloyalty is stated as the cause See notes later.

to be embroiled in schemes, which would have plunged the whole nation in bloodshed, after a generation of settled government. 'Obedience to the powers that be,' is an injunction of the Church, which such staunch Catholics, generation after generation, could not fail to know. Only when the Government came between them and God came their firm refusal to comply. On that basis the name RECUSANT will always remain an honoured one amongst us. Those of Ugthorpe and other places occurring in Hervey's registers, although their precise positions in the families requires further detail, read like a list of recusants at times.

PRIESTS IN THE DISTRICT

That there were constantly priests about Katharine Radcliffe's house, we may be certain. It was probably Ugthorpe Old Hall, the manor house, where, some years ago, images of St Michael and St John the Baptist were discovered in one of the hiding places.* The names of priests seem little known.

Christopher Stonehouse of Dunsley (Xpofer Stonas in Peacock's list) is known to have been a great harbourer of priests from the time of his starting in business as a jet and amber worker about 1590 and during the rest of his life (*see* his will proved 1631, *C.R.S.*, vi.); and it is stated that not one of them was captured, his ambition for martyrdom in such an event being baulked by his own dexterity. He was probably, during the earlier period, residing at his farm at East Row. Its contiguity to the sea would render it a quiet landing place if Whitby had to be avoided, whilst the park of Mulgrave Castle and flanking valleys of East Row Beck and Sand's End Beck would have provided alternative means of escape. Besides this it is related that he had a house contrived with so many doors, as to be an embarrassment to the searchers. On one occasion the constables coming to apprehend him, his wife giving him warning, he slipped out at one door, as they came in at another, finding the place at which he had been working still retaining the warmth of his body. Such incidents come out in the *Annals of St Monica's, Louvain.* But how many incidents of a similar nature, and of other Catholics, are unrecorded?

His son Andrew, born at East Row, who became a priest at Rome in 1623, under the name of Stonas, joined the Jesuits in 1634, died in Yorkshire 31 August 1663, aged 66, according to Foley, who says his death is recorded as Andrew Town, and that he went on the Yorkshire mission in 1647. As John Fairfax he was a prisoner in York Castle from March 1657 to Sept. 1660, when freed by proclamation. Nothing seems to be known where his missionary life in the county was spent. One might expect him to have visited his relatives and the home of his youth, but conjecture is idle. Foley records another *alias,* John Cuthbert; but he falls into error by mistaking Stonas as Latin for Stone, instead of broad Yorkshire for Stonehouse.† There must be fifty spellings of the name.

* Her name appears as contributing £25 to the loan levied in 1589 to repel the Armada invasion.

† There is nothing, however, peculiar to the county in finding the 'h' silent in words with it in the middle. In names ending with 'ham,' 'hall,' 'hill,' 'house,' etc., it is not pronounced, and falls out, or gets misspelt and mispronounced by mixing with the previous letter. Our French-speaking ancestors would be largely responsible for this, and much more in modern English.

UGTHORPE AND SOME EGTON PRIESTS

A spy reported to the Privy Council in 1593 that the Rev. Cuthbert Crayford, a Douay priest, had been serving at Mrs Katherine Radcliffe's at Ugthorpe, in Blackamore, for a year, and also that Alexander Rawlins, Peter Gonne, Peter Snowe, Richard Parker *alias* Smith, Roger Redon, Thomas Jackson, Anthony Page, and John Wilton, all priests, had been seen at the house of John Hodgson, called Crowmonte [Grosmont, Growmond, &c.], in Blackamore.*

In Peacock's list of Yorkshire recusants in 1604 constant references are made to secret baptisms and marriages implying that these functions were by or before Catholic priests. On page 95 we read that Robert Warmworth and Margaret Harrison of Stokesley, his supposed wife, were suspected to be 'secretly marryed by a popishe preist *about Egton.*' Also that Bartholomew George of Stokesley, a pewterer, had a child born in January and secretly baptized† at Mr Barthram's‡ house 'with some popish preist, for two strangers were sene ther in the night tyme suspected to be preistes.' Christopher Hutchinson of Stokesley, a tannner, was 'a resetter [harbourer] of strange persons suspected.' Stokesley then had a Catholic recusant churchwarden, Thomas Morley,§ who 'refused to ioyne in the presentment because he knew more than the rest as is supposed.' At Guisborough three families have children secretly baptised, including Robert Hoggard's daughter Joan, 'by a popish preist, as is supposed for he confesseth there was water & salt used.' At Lofthouse 'William Sympson, (cordwainer) and Elizabeth Gibson his supposed wife marryed (as themselves confes) by a priest in York Castell.' Mr Peacock thinks that the priest had resorted to the Castle to marry them. But is it not equally likely that they had resort to the unnamed priest? Coming nearer, John Hogg and Joan his wife, John Ray and Jane his wife of Lythe were secretly married. The first had three and Robert Harland one child secretly baptized. Robert Sympson, a *turbulent Recusant,* of Hinderwell cum Roxby, and his wife Elizabeth were secretly married, and 'also had fower children baptized, not according to lawe.' Egton makes a brave show,—'Xpofer Conset, Ellis Knaggs; Chrofer Simpson, Dorothie Pearson; Henrie Lawson, Dorothy Marshall; George Knaggs, Ellis Dowson; Xpofer Tailler, Jane Burton; all thes lyve together as man and wife & suspected to be secretly marryed,' Edward Sympson, Henry Lawson, George Knaggs, Xpofer Consett, Jane Posgate widowe,

* This is from information supplied by Mr Gillow from the state papers *Dom. Eliz.* ccxlv, *n.* 24. In the printed *Calendar* Thomas Clarke, a renegade seminary priest has previously given information, putting the number of priests seen at Grosmont at fourteen. It is possible that Clarke was the spy?

† The Stokesley register has between Jan. 15 and 31 ' daughtr to Batholmew George not Bapt.' (*Yorks. Par. Reg. Soc.*, vii.) He married Margery Shawe 19 April 1593, and had three children baptized at the church before the above; but on the 27 Sept. 1609 they had a child and 'not baptysed at church.' (*Ibid.*)

‡ William Barthram or Bartram, pewterer, married at Stokesley 9 Aug. 1601 Meryall [? Muriel] Kirkbye, who appears with him as a recusant. (*Ibid.*)

§ Thomas Morley, cordwainer, married 10 May 1601 Ann Stainhouse [a variation of Stonehouse], who appears with him as a recusant; but may not have been as staunch as her husband, for 'she dare not communicate for [fear of] her husband.'

THE PARENTAGE OF NICHOLAS POSTGATE.

Being in York whilst the Index was being printed, I paid a visit to the Probate Office, and found correct my surmise that Margaret was the widow of James Postgaite. I therefore obtained the following copies (expanded from the abbreviated originals) of the two administrations. They lack the interest of wills, but tend to corroborate the tradition that the Venerable Nicholas Postgate was born at Kirkdale House in Egton chapelry or town. As a recusant in 1612, Margaret is described as of 'West Bankes,' in Egton. At the time she had a recusant servant, Anne Postgate (*N.R.Records*, iii, 79, 80). In 1614 she is given as 40 years of age, and a recusant 12 years [? minimum], having a servant, Thomas Calvert, aged 24, recusant 7 (*Ibid* ii, 65). Here are signs of continuous residence, servants, and means. For dates:—

1603-4: Jan. 30—Administration of James Postgaite's goods granted to his widow, Margaret.

1621: July 4—Nicholas admitted an alumnus at Douay College, where he assumed the *alias* of Whitmore—perhaps his mother's name? When arrested he bore that of his paternal grandmother, Watson (*C.R.S.* x, 185).

1624: Apr. 15—Administration of Margaret's goods granted to Matthew, her son.

JAMES POSTGAITE.

Cleveland, 30 *January* 1603.

Eisdam die et anno dictus Decanus [Dean of Cleveland] certificavit se commississe administracionem bonorum que fuerunt Jacobi Postgaite nuper de Kirkdaile Diocese Ebor defuncti Margarete Postgaite ejus relicte prius jurate, &c., Salvo jure cujus-cunque exhibitum fuit Inventarium Solutis Vs. Et predictam Margaretam et alios due prestiti sunt cauciones [bond].

MARGARET POSTGAITE.

Cleveland, 15 *April* 1624.

Eisdem die et Anno dictus decanus certificavit se commississe administracionem bonorum Margarete Postgaite nuper de Kirkedale Ebor diocese defuncte Mattheo Postgaite filio dicte defuncte prius jurate Salvo, &c., exhibitum fuit Inventarium ultra 40*li* et præstita est caucio.

To face p. 321.

John Roe & Raphe Harwood had children baptized privately. Finally in Whitby parish Xpofer Stonas (mentioned above) and his wife [Ursula, the second], George Marsingale and [Ellis] his wife, Henrie ffairfax and [Edith] his wife, were secretly married.* The parish registers are lost, but the records of the recusants' marriages stand, although 'not knowne where.' The canon law did not necessitate the presence of a priest, and the canon law was still the law in England. We may be sure however that those who suffered so much for the Church, did not fail to get the Church's blessing through its validly ordained priests.

Here are evidences of priests working about the district, and yet no names have been handed down. Good had to be done by stealth, and anything in the way of a fixed residence would sooner or later have led to apprehension and the shambles. And so the first priest, who can safely be said to have been a local missioner, was—

The Rev. Nicholas Postgate. The *Douay Diaries,* first made public by the Society, revealed some authentic information quite at variance with previous statements, and it was my privilege to add a few particulars.† The son of James Postgate, both parents having suffered much for the Faith, is described in Jan. 1615-6 as of Egton, where Margaret Postgate, a widow, was a recusant in 1614 and 1616, probably the same of Kirkdale (administration 15 April 1624).‡ It is certain that Nicholas was admitted to the English College, Douai, as an alumnus, for which he paid three hundred florins, 4 July 1621. He was aged 21, and assumed the name of Whitmore. He took the college oath 12 March 1623, was ordained priest 20 March 1628, and set forth for the English mission 29 June 1630 at the age of thirty. At this date the Diaries fail us, and the next dates we have are vague ones given by himself on 9 Dec. 1678, the day after his capture, when in his seventy eighth or ninth year, and possibly dazed after rough treatment. The examination is not his own statement, but such facts as could be extracted from him by magistrates, &c. He is put down as *'about eighty.'* Again *'About 40 years since* he lived at Saxton with the Lady Hungate until she died.'

Among Saxton recusants of 1604 appear the names of William Hungate, esq., (only a noncommunicate then) and his wife Margaret [daughter of Roger Sotheby of Pocklington], William Hungate, and Johanna his wife, who is given by Foster as ' . . . daughter of Sir John Gower, knt.' § The younger William was knighted at York

* The Christian names are supplied from later recusant lists in the North Riding Records.

† *C.R.S.,* x. and xi.

‡ *Yorks. Archæol. Rec.,* xxxii., 159. Whether this is Margery, wife of James Postgate of Ugglebarnby or not, requires elucidation by wills, etc. But since the *Douay Dairies* (*C.R.S.,* x. and xi.) were printed I noticed an administration of James Postgaite of Kirkedale (in Egton), 20 Jan. 1603 (*n.s.* 1604), who may be the husband of Jane Postgate of Egton, widow, a recusant in 1604 (E. Peacock's list, 97, 99). This is the earliest printed list of local recusants. It is worth noting that the signature of the martyr, in a book belonging to the Bishop of Middlesborough, is spelt Postgayt, not Postgate, Poskett, etc. Mr Peacock thought the relationships might 'for ever remain uncertain.' It would be pleasant to disprove this and print copies of wills, etc., shewing the pedigree. Not only indeed in this case, but in others, where the subject is one of veneration.

§ Sir William Hungate's wife is given alternatively as ' . . . daughter

11 April 1617, and his widow, Lady Joane, renounced administration of his estate 19 Dec. 1634.* Whether Postgate had been chaplain to Sir William Hungate, or to Lady Hungate, before this is not stated. The Rev. Cyril Ash, Vicar of Saxton, obligingly favours me with a copy of the faded post-entry in the parish registers of Saxton, which clearly reads† 'Memorandu the [ ] daye [ ]—Ladie Johan Hungate of Saxton dyed the 30th of Maye 1642.' Here we have a definite date, and Postgate's 'about 40 years' agrees with the middle term of Lady Hungate's widowhood, the last date being over thirty six years and a half only. There is no entry of Lady Hungate's burial at Saxton, but one would like to imagine that Postgate rendered the last rites privately in the Hungate chantry, which would be under control of the family.

The next statement however demonstrates the martyr's inability to fix dates at the time,—'And since he hath lived with the old Lady Dunbar, but *how long it is since he knoweth not.*' Mary, daughter of Sir John Tufton of Hothfield, Kent, was wife of Sir Henry Constable of Halsham and Burton-Constable, Holderness, who was created Viscount Dunbar 14 Nov. 1620, and died in 1645. On 18 Jan. 1653-4, she petitioned the sequestration commissioners to be allowed to compound for two thirds of her dowry of £200 and for two parts of East and West Halsham. I have not been able to ascertain the date of Lady Dunbar's death; but it is not so important as that of Lady Hungate's, Postgate's information being very vague.

Sir Philip Constable of Everingham, baronet, had probably learned to appreciate Postgate during this chaplaincy, when, on 20 Feb. 1664-5, he left 'to Mr Poskett (if living) 5*l*.' (*C.R.S., iv.*, 269).

The Rev. Peter Saltmarshe, who was born at (South) Kilvington Castle in 1658 stated that he was baptized by Postgate (Foley, *Records S. J.*, vi., 434).

Thomas Ward, states that Postgate dwelt in a thatched cottage on Blackamoor, a wide tract of moor-land. This eminent Catholic writer was born a Protestant at Danby Castle in 1652, was educated at Pickering, and was later a tutor.§ We may conjecture that he must have been at least 20 years of age when he became a Catholic, which would be about 1672, when Postgate was about 72 years old. Although he states that he knew Postgate well, that knowledge was hardly likely to be before he became a Catholic, and reduces the friendship to the last six years of the missionary life of the martyr. His statement may however be that of Postgate relating to a time previous to 1672, or his personal knowledge

of . . . Midleton of . . , co Lanc.' (Joseph Foster's *Yorks. Visitations*, 114-15.). The name is sometimes given as *Elizabeth*, which must be wrong from evidence given in the text.

* *Yorks. Archæol. Records*, xxxv., 45 and 185.

† The Rev. Cyril Ash describes it as hardly legible, but took the trouble to send what must have been a good facsimile, as it enabled me to give the above. Perhaps the blanks have always been blanks.

‡ *Royalist Composition Papers. Yorks. Archæol. Records*, xx., 114. This sequestration was for her recusancy, and the decision was that she was to have her full third part paid *in kind*.

* The Danby Registers (*Yorks. Par. Reg. Soc.* xliii.) contain no record of his birth or baptism.

later. We have however Postgate's examination on 9 Dec. 1678, saying,—'Of late he hath had no certaine residence, but hath travelled about among his friends.' The only names he revealed in the examination are those of the dead. Some martyrs had times of weakness. Postgate had none, and he compromised no living man. He names Mr Jowsie (mentioned later), and Mr Goodricke, both dead. The latter may have been a member of the Hovingham family. His heroic constancy has our veneration, and leaves us only the poorer in knowledge of his movements. It was reserved to two apostate women to state that they had heard Postgate say Mass at the houses of John Hodgson of Biggin House, near Ugthorpe, and of Thomas Pattinson of Ugthorpe. Matthew Lyth of Little Beck in the township of Ugglebarnby and parish of Whitby, in whose house Postgate was, and whom he attempted to save, shared the imprisonment. We find in these notes that he officiated in at least three houses, instead of people coming to him.

The Rev. John Jowsey was probably working about Egton before December 1678; but there is only the last date 8 Dec. to go by, when Andrew Jowsey was apprehended there as a priest. This was at the same time that Postgate was arrested a few miles away, and the intention must have been to capture the two simultaneously. A witness, Matthew Morgan of Egton, deposed that he had heard Andrew describe himself as a priest and say he came from Ireland. He denied the fact of his being a priest, but declined to take the oaths, including that of supremacy, being evidently a Catholic. The case is clearly that the wrong man had been arrested, for John Jowsey, the real priest, was dead, as appears from Postgate's examination; and the prisoner was acquitted.* Whether John Jowsey had been in Ireland or not, he was clearly a Cleveland man.

He went to Douay describing himself as son of Thomas Jowsey, of York diocese, and Jane his wife. His parents are described as of small means, who had endured much persecution, his father having suffered fetters and prison, and his mother hardships and losses in their home, as confessors of the Faith. Profiting by their example, and by the advice of pious priests, he turned his attention to literary studies, giving up the art of a currier or leather-dresser, which he had followed for some years with profit. Then he was animated to embrace the ecclesiastical state, and succour his afflicted country. On arrival at the College he gave himself to the study of humanities and philosophy, and acted as assistant to the administrator or procurator, but dwelling in the town at his own expense, and suffering many hardships. Nevertheless persevering in his intention, in his third year of theology, the President presented him for all the sacred orders including the priesthood. He was admitted to the College as a convictor 29 Dec. 1646; went to receive orders 13 March 1647 at 'Maurontis Villam.'† and returned 2 April, singing his first Mass on the 22nd. On 2 June he had again to seek a home in the town. On 30 July 1648 he wrote an acknowledgement that he had only been admitted to the college on condition that, after receiving priest's orders, he was to live in the town at his own expense. On the same

* Surtees Society, xl., 232.

† Dr Burton thinks this probably Bac St Maur. There is Mauron near the western coast of Brittany, but this is too remote. Perhaps there may be an error in the original, as for Wavrans?

day he was examined as to his fitness for the English mission, and on 18 Aug. he set forth by way of Holland, presumably for Yorkshire, as on 12 July following he turned up with two Yorkshire boys, Matthew Lockwood *alias* Atkinson and Marmaduke Beckwith *alias* Thomas Nateby. On 10 Dec. 1651 he came back to the college to take back the second boy, leaving again three days later, also taking charge of Nicholas Tempest *alias* Wilmot, who had to leave on account of his health.

Matthew son of Robert Lockwood, of Sowerby by Thirsk, petitioned to have the sequestration on his father's estate taken off, 26 June 1655. After his father's death in 1646 he had been put to a Protestant school; but when 14 years of age and 'beyond sea,' had been summoned to take the oath of abjuration, and not since his coming of age. The sequestration was discharged.* If Marmaduke Beckwith was of the Ackton family, they had some property at Thirsk.† There were also Beckwiths of Handale Abbey in Loftus parish, Cleveland. The enquiry seems to suggest that Jowsey was working at or near Thirsk.

The recusant lists are sufficiently clear as regards the family in spite of the spellings. They all refer to Guisborough, the capital town of Cleveland, about ten miles from Ugthorpe. In 1604 Thomas Jolsey, carpenter, was one of nine *old recusants,* whilst Jane Gradon, servant to Thomas Jolsey, was one of 22 *obstinate recusants* since Easter Anno 1603. Whether she became his wife is not certain. Tho. Jocy and Jane his wife recusants in 1607. Tho. Jocie and Jane his wife, rec. iii. years, in Jan. 1607-8. Tho. Jowsie, carpenter, and Jane his supposed wife, rec. 8 years in 1609.‡ Tho. Jocy, carpenter, and Jaine his wife, in 1611. Tho. Jowsie (aged 60), carpenter, and Jane (34) his wife, in 1612. Tho. Jowsie, carpenter, in 1616. The will of Thomas Jowise of Gisbrough, carpenter, is dated 25 Jan. 1620 (o.s.) and proved 19 April 1621.§ His son, the priest, as the Douay Diaries shew, appears,—'John Jowsie of Gisburgh, currier,' was presented and proclaimed a recusant at Thirsk sessions, 5 Oct. 1636, and convicted at Helmesley on 10 Jan. 1636-7. It is likely that he assumed *aliases* on the mission; but no other information is now at my disposal. Thomas Jowsie or Jorosie the shoe-maker and infirmary servant at Douay College was doubtless a relative.

The Rev. George Smith had evidently been on the Ugthorpe mission sometime previous to 24 July 1684, and there was a stipend attached to the work, as appears from Franciscan archives. A proposal had been submitted to the Franciscan Chapter 'whether the province would accept the incumbency of Ugthorpe in Yorkshire, now held by the Rev. Father George Smith, of the Order of Hermits of St Augustine, who receives twelve pounds per annum for his services; with this condition—that our [Franciscan] missionary shall receive two pounds annually during Father Smith's lifetime, and

* *Yorks. Archæol. Rec.,* xx., 208. His mother Dorothy ——, a recusant, had two thirds of her dower sequestered. This is however only quoted to fix the locality of Jowsey's labours.

† *Ibid.,* p. 180.

‡ The terms of years and ages vary in much greater degree in many cases. The *supposed wife* is a common term used where couples were married before a priest privately but validly. (*North Riding Records.*)

§ *Yorks. Rec. Series,* xxxii, 54.

after his death ten. On the understanding, however, that those ten pounds shall revert to the Augustinian fathers, if they obtain from the Holy See faculties for the English mission. * The proposal is said to have been accepted; but no further particulars are given. The Franciscans may have served the mission from Osmotherley.

The Rev. John Marsh, educated at St. Omers and Valladolid, where he was ordained, returned to England in 1660. His early labours are said to have been in the South of England; and during the Oates plot he was banished from London by the machinations of Thomas Dangerfield, the informer. For a time he was in Lancashire, and 'then humbly betook himself to the most desolate and laborious place in Yorkshire, that is to assist a great multitude of poor in the Moors, where, at one Easter, he had near 900 communicants, and these scattered at great distances. His abode was chiefly at Egton Bridge.' He is described as a priest 'of excellent wit, parts, and zeal.'† The Rev. Bernard Kelly gives the year 1685; but Mr Gillow thinks he was there about 1590.

Mr Anderton is the first mentioned by Hervey as forced to leave the place [*sic*]; but whether he refers to Ugthorpe, or Egton, or the Moors generally, is not clear. He gives no date, and leaves us in the dark as to whether it was due to the government, local authorities, or privations. Whether he was the Thomas Salkeld, *alias* Whalley, *alias* Anderton, suggested in a foot-note, remains doubtful; but if so he went on mission work 16 Dec. 1694, and died in 1708.‡

Mr John Danby is said by Hervey to have been cast into York gaol as the evil action of the poor penitent Ursula Hawkswell about 1710; but a quotation from an official document, embodied in a foot-note, shews the warrant for his apprehension was dated 13 July 1708, and he is described as 'of Egton Bridge'; and on 5 Oct. 1708 the Treasurers were directed to pay the chief constable of the Langbarugh (Cleveland) 32s. 6d. charges in taking up some Roman Catholics at Egton and elsewhere. § If Hervey's date is right Danby must have escaped apprehension for a considerable time. It is significant that he talks of houses and grounds being betrayed as though in some secluded position, that there was a fixed domicile for the priest. It must however be noted that what he heard occured a quarter of a century before he went to Ugthorpe, and so was hearsay, put down in writing many years later. Mr Danby was ordained at Lisbon College 11 Dec. 1689, left for England 2 Jan. 1693, and was only known to be somewhere on the mission in Yorkshire before.

Mr Bostock is said by Hervey to have 'died of cold in hiding himself from the constables'; yet on another page he says that he 'was forced to fly.' These statements are so clearly at variance with one another as to raise further and stronger doubt as to his memory. If the incident refers to the same period as that to John Danby, one might surmise that this one being of Egton Bridge, Hervey's 'Mr Bostock' might have been missioner of Ugthorpe. There are 'grounds and houses belonging to the priest of the place'; yet

* Fr. Thaddeus's *Franciscans in England*, 181-2.

† Kirk's *Biographies of English Catholics*, 159.

‡ Kirk's *Biographies*, 204; *C.R.S.*, iv., 375.

§ *N.R. Records*, vii., 213 and 215.

|| Gillow's *Lisbon College Register*, 192.

immediately after he speaks of 'the house and chapel.' He goes even further, saying that Ursula Hawkswell 'betrayed all the grounds and houses [plural] belonging to the priest [one] of the place [one] and sold them.' Besides the question of date it is matter of wonder what authority this woman had to sell. Was she trustee? No one would be likely to buy without a proper title. Perhaps he means that her action caused the alienation of the property; but it is loose writing.

It is quite possible that the event may have been years later during the apostacy of Ursula Hawkswell. Kirk and Foley give the names of two priests named Bostock, both named George; but they were not aware of either of them being at Ugthorpe or Egton Bridge. There are some suggestive words about the infirmity of George Bostock *alias* Baron, son of Roger and Eliza (Kirk says Alicia) Bostock of . . . Lancs. Admitted to the English College, Rome, 18 Oct. 1695 at the age of 23, and ordained priest 5 June 1700, he left for England 12 April 1701.* Placed at Hathersage soon after his arrival, not later than Ladyday 1702. *Long disabled before death* which took place 28 Dec. 1727, aged about 55.† There is however Bostock *alias* West, son of Thomas and Anne B., of co. Denbigh, admitted to the English College, Rome, 1 Oct. 1683, aged 19. Ordained priest 12 June 1688, he left for England 1 July 1690.‡ He is said to have lived in Staffordshire or Derbyshire, and his death is given 17 Sept. 1728,§ aged about 64. If the dates here given are correct, and if there was no other Mr Bostock, the incident mentioned by Hervey must apply to the second George Bostock, priest at Egton Bridge, between May and September 1728. For in May Bishop Williams, O.P., held confirmations at four gentlemen's houses in Cleveland, as shewn by the following table supplied to me by the Rev. Bede Jarrett, O.P., from the Dominican archives at Haverstock Hill. It will be noticed that no reference is made to Ugthorpe, unless it be in the words 'et prope'; but the few local people would be more likely to resort to Mr Richard Smith's at Egton Bridge, rather than to that of Mr Zachary Steward More at North Loftus. The letters 'S.S.' stand for *Sacerdotes Seculares.*

1728 *Dmni*	*Sacerdotes.*		*Confirma*
Maie Smith [of Egton]	Bostock [George]	S.S.	84
More [of Loftus]	Hunt		59
May(e)s [of Yarm]	Tunstal [Peter Bryan]		57
Crathorn [of Crathorne]	Lodge [John].		89

The Rev. Thomas Smith is named by Hervey as banished, without date. One of the name, born 30 June 1674, of Chester diocese, took the college oath at Douay 8 Sept. 1696. He may be the same who died at Oulston, near Esingwold, 2 Nov. 1755.‖ Mr Gillow says that Bishop Dicconson inserted in the list of his clergy in 1741 'Tho: Smith at Oulston wth La Falc. Do[uay priest].' He would thus be chaplain to Catherine daughter of John Betham of Rowington, co. Warwick, and wife of Thomas Belasyse, Viscount Fauconberg, created

* Foley, vi., 434.
† Kirk's *Biographies,* 32, and *C.R.S.*, xii.
‡ Foley, vi., 434.
§ Kirk's *Biographies,* 32, and *C.R.S.*, xii.
‖ *C.R.S.*, xii., 8.

Earl Fauconberg 16 June 1756. Lady Fauconberg died 29 May, and was buried at Coxwold 12 June 1760. (J. W. Clay, *Extinct Northern Peerage*, 10.) Thomas Smith is sometimes described as of Angram Grange, which is (like Oulston) a township in the parish of Coxwold.

Francis, son of Thomas Hodgson and Mary Simpson of the diocese of York, born 2 Feb. 1682 (o.s.), known as Simpson at Douay, took the college oath 4 Oct. 1704.* He lived at Cliffe, N.R. York, with Mr George Witham, and assisted the poor Catholics on the Moors and in Cleveland. Later he was in the Bishopric, but in 1692 returned into Yorkshire, and died 24 May 1726.†

Monox Hervey's appointment at Ugthorpe from 25 May 1734 till his arrest 11 Dec. 1745, is recorded by himself. *See above.*

The Rev. Thomas Liddell, ordained at Lisbon 21 Jan. 1742, and sent to England 16 Jan. 1743,‡ was evidently the one at Egton, to which he must have gone very soon. It would seem that he had given offence to the government, presumably by political propaganda in favour of the Stuart dynasty. This appears in the examination of Mr Potts, who was sent to replace him. He does not belong to Ugthorpe; but is inserted here on account of his association with the subject. He is probably son of William Liddell of Wycliffe, gent., who by will left 'to my son Thomas Liddell £20 per annum during his natural life, provided he quitt and renounce all claim or right to what may have been left him by my brother Thomas Liddell.'§ He leaves the residue of manors, &c., in Ravensworth, Farnacres, Winton, Newsham, &c., in cos. Durham and York to 'my sons Cuthbert and William (executor) and my daughter Mary Farray,' with remainder to 'my dear cousin Marmaduke Tunstall (executor) of Wycliffe, esq.,' and names 'my cousin Adam Dale (executor) of Girklington.' The will is dated 9 May 1742, inrolled 17 Jany 1744-5. (*N. Riding Rec.*, ix., 164.) The brothers William, in 1717 of West Middleton, co. York, Henry and Thomas, held equal shares of £25 4s. 1½d. in Whickham, co. Durham, in 1747, and allowed their father, Henry Liddell £18 yearly (Payne's *Non-jurors*, 55 and 57). The Rev. Thomas Liddell died at Liverpool, 12 May 1775 (*C.R.S.*, xii., 13, 18).

The Rev. Luke Potts *alias* Cooper was appointed to the Egton mission by Bishop Dicconson, Vicar Apostolic of the Northern District, by letter to Hervey dated 12 Nov. 1745, delivered the following day. Hervey thought however it would not be wise for Potts to go to Egton after what had taken place, and advised his remaining at Ugthorpe. This was done; but, when the news had leaked out that the arrests were to be made, both tried to obtain shelter amongst the Catholics at Egton; failing which they wandered about the moors, until exhausted they returned to Ugthorpe, and were arrested on 11 Dec., as shewn elsewhere. He was resident at Ugthorpe, but must be accounted one of Egton's missioners; his incarceration however precluded further connection. Kirk relates that on his acquittal (on 21 Dec. 1746 as Hervey says) he rode sixty miles to Wycliffe,

* *First Douay Diary*, 54, 87, 89.

† Kirk's *Biographies*, 120. There is possibility of confusion as Kirk names another Francis Hodgson who died — April 1733, a year before Hervey went to Ugthorpe.

‡ Gillow, *Lisbon College Register*, 226.

§ This Thomas Liddel was also a priest. The uncle and nephew appear as Lisbon priests, although not so associated (Gillow's *Lisbon Col. Reg.* 226).

and that, when called the next morning, he was found booted and spurred, kneeling as he knelt exhausted to say his prayers the night before.* He was born at Throckley, near Newcastle-on-Tyne, and ordained priest at Douay.

After the arrests of Hervey and Potts difficulty may have been experienced in making appointments to Egton and Ugthorpe.

The Rev. Thomas Shepherd had been in charge of Ugthorpe some time previously to August 1747, probably after Hervey's release from prison on 2 June, on condition of his leaving Yorkshire, but owing to the troubles of the time had to leave soon. The son of William Shepherd and Mary Blundel of Chester diocese (who are stated by Gillow to have been of Croxteth, Lancashire,) he took the college oath at Douay on 28 Dec. 1741, when aged 21. He would thus be only lately ordained on his appointment, and probably died in Holderness on 19 Jany 1774. Having seen a statement that he became later the missioner at Egton Bridge, serving Ugthorpe at times, the following statement seems called for.

The Rev. John (?) Shepherd is stated to have gone to Egton Bridge in 1750. In a return made to the Archbishop of York (dated 26 Nov. 1767, but probably compiled in the previous year, as witness the case of James Parkinson below) he is described as 52 years of age, and resident at Egton Bridge 16 years. If the date of the document is 1766, this would tally with the John Shepherd born in London 19 Feb. 1714, who has not hitherto been known to be at Egton, calling for notice here as he supplied at Ugthorpe during vacancies. *Kirk's Biographies* (p. 207) gives him as son of John Shepherd and Brigitta Wilkinson, his wife, both Catholics. After studying four years and a half at Douay, he was admitted to the Roman College 6 Aug. 1731, leaving 17 April 1732, and proceeding to Lisbon College. Gillow (*Records of Lisbon College,* p. 250) says he was ordained priest there, sent to England 16 July 1637, and stationed at Cowdray, Sussex, in 1745. Kirk surmises that he lived there many years; but his advent to Egton would be dated about 1750, as shewn above, and he must have remained there at least 16 years, although Kirk says he settled at the Convent at Hammersmith in 1758. It is possible that he was there in that year for a time, or that the year is wrong, or that another of the name (1678-1761) may be mistaken for him, and who died at London. Our John Shepherd, like the other, became a member of the Chapter, its Secretary, and in 1781 Dean. He died at London 11 March 1789, aged 75 (*C.R.S.*, xii., 31, where his name is given as *Sheppard*†). Mr Gillow says that Bishop Dicconson gives his baptismal name as *Thomas;* but Bishop Gradwell supplied the name to Kirk as *John,* although he connects the name with Lancashire.

The Rev. Edward Ball, *alias* Worthington, who took the college

* Kirk's *Biographies,* 188. It must be pointed out that the evidence produced shews that Kirk is wrong about Potts being actually in office at Ugthorpe and Scarborough.

† This spelling agrees with that in Cowdray registers, (*C. R. S.* i, 244) where he signs the first entry. Fr Willaert says all the entries before 1757 are in the same handwriting, the assumption being that he was at Cowdray all the time. It is quite likely that they are all *copies*, it being more certain that the man who wrote the last wrote the first. The first four entries carefully give the parentages; but then they are laxly omitted. Mr —— Redford baptized once in 1749, and the 'Rev. Lord, the Lord —— O'Donell' in 1752, perhaps an Irish bishop.

oath at Douay 3 Nov. 1735 when aged 18,* was a professor there till 6 Aug. 1747 after which he was appointed to Ugthorpe, but left in 1750,† and then there seems no appointment for several years, during which the mission may have been dependent on Mr Shepherd at Egton Bridge.

The Rev. Peter Phillips *alias* Pessell or Purshall took the college oath at Douay 12 April 1690. He had been at Egton Bridge in 1741, and in 1743 went to Leyburn, coming to Ugthorpe about 1757 (*C.R.S.*, xiii., 233), and died there 23 Nov. 1761 (*C.R.S.*, xii., 10). Mr Gillow says Bishop Dicconson describes him as a priest of the English College at Rome.

The Rev. James Parkinson (confused with James Parkinson, a Douay priest, who died in Lancashire, 26 Jan. 1766), ordained 2 April 1758 at Lisbon, and left 13 May, he is said to have come to Ugthorpe about the end of 1761. In a return made to the Archbishop of York, dated 26 Nov. 1767, 'Mr Parkinson' is given at Ugthorpe without the usual further particulars. He died at Ugthorpe 13 Nov. 1766, which may account for the omissions.‡

The Rev. Christopher Hodgson, son of William and Elizabeth Hodgson of Ugthorpe, born 1729, admitted to Lisbon College 1 June 1745, and ordained priest 7 April 1753, left for England 1762, was stationed at Ugthorpe till his death 25 Dec. 1765, aged 36. If his term at Ugthorpe is covered by that of Mr Parkinson (*ut supra*), we may assume he returned home an invalid, perhaps doing some work, as he died so young. The mission could not have supported two priests.

The Rev. John Bradshaw came from Douay in 1767 and in the following year opened the new chapel, which occupied the space over his rooms, and under the thatched roof.§ It sounds the reverse of magnifence, but this had to serve its purpose for 42 years. At Bishop William Walton's visitation in Oct. 1773 the communicants of the congregation were returned at 173. Mr Bradshaw left Ugthorpe for Cliffe in 1777, but he died at Ugthorpe 30 April 1790.‖

The Rev. Thomas Ferby succeeded about 1774. The son of Thomas F. and his wife Dorothy Lumsden, born 25 March 1740. Ordained at Rome 17 Dec. 1763, and left for the mission in May 1764.¶

The Rev. John Marsland, ordained at Douay in 1763, was at Scarborough in 1773, returned to Douay 4 Jan. 1775, and left again 18 Apr. 1776. He came to Ugthorpe in 1777.** He took the college oath at Douay, 27 Dec. 1760, being described as of Lancashire (*First Douay Diary*, 72), and died 9 Aug. 1817 (*C.R.S.*, xii., 135). Mr Gillow thinks that there has been a confusion between *Marsland* and *Morland*, and kindly supplies me with the following memoir.

'The Rev. James Wilson *alias* Morland, son of James Wilson and his wife Agnes Morland, born in Lancashire, May 23, 1726, took the oath at Douay College June 3, 1748, and after ordination served in

* First *Douay Diary*, 63.

† *Ibid.*, 216, and *C.R.S.*, xii., 31., xv, 52.

‡ Gillow, *Lisbon College Register*, 237, and *C.R.S.*, xii., 11.

§ Gillow, *Haydock Papers*, 220-1.

‖ *C.R.S.*, iv., 249; xii., 34.

¶ Kirk's *Biographies*, 81.

** Gillow, *Lisbon College Register*, 229.

Lancashire. In 1767 he was at Stydd Lodge near Ribchester where he was known as Morley or Morland. Subsequently he was at Alston Lane, near Preston; Greystoke Castle, the seat of the Howards; and would appear to have come to Ugthorpe in or after 1777. After some time he became insane, and was removed to an asylum in York, where he died May 20, 1808, aged 82.'

The Rev. Henry Dennett succeeded in 1788, but remained only a year, and after this brief tenure termed Ugthorpe,—'The Purgatory of the Mission.'*

The Rev. Thomas Talbot took charge of both Ugthorpe and Egton in 1788 until 1803. In 1794 the Abbé Nicolas Alain Gilbert started the Whitby mission, which remained in his charge until 1815. A note in the registers states that the communicants at Whitby in 1774 were not above 15, whereas in 1815 the number had risen to 184.† The second son of James Talbot of Wheelton, Lancashire, he was born 27 June 1736, and admitted to the English College in Rome 14 Jan. 1752, ordained 10 April, and sent on missionary labour 25 May 1762. His brother John, born in 1737, who died at Rixton in 1801, became a Jesuit. Another, Richard, born in 1738, was also ordained in Rome in 1762, was for some time at Bishop Thornton, near Ripon, and died 1 August 1823 (*Com. by* Mr Gillow, and *C.R.S.*, xii.).

The Rev. George Leo Haydock was appointed to Ugthorpe in Feb. 1803. The income of the mission was shortly after augmented by £10, the bequest of Rowland Conyers, esq., and £5 from the Rev. Mr Tootell. Mr Haydock found the chapel in a very dilapidated condition. In October he replaced the old thatch by a tiled roof and renovated the place. In 1808 he was contemplating a new chapel and house, which were opened in 1810. When the Abbé Gilbert left Whitby for France on 20 Aug. 1815, Mr Haydock had to serve that growing mission from Ugthorpe, but was ordered to reside at Whitby from July 1816.‡ In 1822 the Rev. Richard Gillow was appointed to Ugthorpe, with charge of Scarborough, but could not stand the strain, and resigned after seven months, and the work again devolved on Mr Haydock.§

On 23 June 1827, the Rev. Nicholas Rigby was appointed to Egton Bridge, and took over the care of Ugthorpe, to which he moved in 1835. He died 7 Sept. 1886 at Ugthorpe aged 86, having retired two years before. To his energy is due what is to be seen now,—a new church and presbytery and a prosperous middle-class school, such as his predecessors could only have dreamt of. He was a fellow collegian at Ushaw of the illustrious Cardinal Wiseman, who opened the new church in September 1857. Cardinal Manning opened the schools in 1870, and in a short time they contained over seventy students.

His curate from 1883, the Rev. Edmund Hickey, succeeded him. The heads of the establishment since have been the Revv. Henry Reynolds, 1891; Richard Lewis, 1893; and Patrick M'Kernan, 1904 to date.

* Gillow, *Haydock Papers*, 220.

† J. Orlebar Payne's *English Cath. Missions*, 78. Our member Mr James Rae Baterden informs me that he finds the names of Jabal, Fallis and Batteau, French *emigrés* priests, working in the district.

‡ Gillow, *Haydock Papers*, 220-2.

§ Gillow, *Haydock Papers*, 226.

[THE REGISTERS]

[Only traces of pages 1-15ª exist. 15ᵇ to 18ª are blank. The pages are duplicated, facing one another, and not on the same leaves.]

[18ᵇ] Libellus
Functionem Parochalium
Exercitarum
Jn
Missione Anglicanâ A M. H.
Collegij Anglorum
De Urbe
Alumno &
Sacerdote
A
Primo Missionis ejusdem
Anno
Annoque Domini
1729
Usque ad Mortem
Illius
*

(19ª *blank*)

(19ᵇ) Junij 12 Anno † 1729 M : H. entred the Mission : July the fourth following he went to Bishop Stoner at Old Heathrope‡ in Oxfordshire, Staid there a § whole Year, during which time he had to ride fourscore Miles Every five Week, twenty-two of which he was obliged to ride Gratis.

On the seventh of July, Anno 1730, he went to London, to Supply for Mʳ Gerrad Saltmarsh,‖ at the Lady Thomas Howard, Mother to his Grace Thomas Duke of Norfolk, in Red Lion Square. He left that place, 29 of September 1732. Staid in London, till he went into the North.

On the 25 of May 1734 He went to Ugthorpe in the¶ North Riding of (20ª) of Yorkshire : where lived by the Town of Whitby, till yᵉ Year 1745.

* This is left open for his own death on the 22nd of December 1756 at the age of fifty seven. It may be well to say that the English College 'de Urbe' is that at Rome.

† Something like 174 scored out.

‡ The Rt. Rev. John Talbot Stonor, Bishop of Thespiæ, and Vicar-Apostolic of the Midland District, had formerly resided at Watlington. Later he went to Old Heythrop, a house belonging to the Stonors. New Heythorp, the seat of the Earls of Shrewsbury, is mentioned in these registers. (The Hon. Mrs Bryan Stapleton's *Oxfordshire Missions.*) They are east of Chipping Norton.

§ Written 'an,' but the last letter scored out.

‖ The Rev. Gerard Saltmarshe *alias* Ireland died 26 Jan. 1732-3 over eighty years of age. (Gillow's *Dict. Eng. Caths.*, v., 471.)

¶ 'We' scored out.

On December the 18th 1745 he was sent to York Castle, & continued there 18 months, & was on the second of June* 1747, set at Liberty.

On the 29 of July 1747, he went to Buttington Hall near Welch Pool & Powis Castle in Montgomeryshire, North Wales, where He† Staid till August 24th Anno 1752.

On the Seventh of August 1753 He was admitted into ye London District, and [*ends*]

(20b) The forme of a Marriage Certificate.

To Day were joind in Matrimony N. N. Of the County N, & ‡ of the Parish N. And Martha N. of ye § County N, & Parish N. According to the Rites and Ceremonys of our Holy Mother the Catholick Church.

In the Presence of N. N. as Wittnesses thereto. N. N. & N. N.

A forme of Baptismal Certificate.

N. N, the Son, or Daughter of N. N, & N N, born 10 of this Month, was baptized & the Godfather was N N, of N. & Godmother was N N, of N.

(21a blank)

(21b.) Marriages in Oxfordshire ||

November the first, 1729, were Marrid at Old
Upton Heathrope, in Oxfordshire, James **Upton** of Cherr- 1
& ington in Warwickshire, and Frances **Leadbeatter**
Leadbeater of Long Compton, in the same County, by M: H:
before these Wittnesses.

William Hollis
Robert Thurlwind
Winifrede Smith.

Partridge April the 19. Anno 1730, were married John 2
& **Partridge** & Elizabeth **Hubball** at New Heathrope
Hubball ye Earl of Shrewsberry's Seat, in Oxfordshire,
before, before these Wittnesses by M.H.

Francis Baskervile,
John Smith Senior
John Smith Junior,

John Partridge, being a Protestant made the following Promise before the above mentioned Wittnesses—

[22a] Marriages in Oxfordshire **

I John Partridge, do in the Presence of God, swear, protest, &

* '1746' scored out.

† Part of word scored out.

‡ 'N.N.' scored out.

§ 'Pa' scored out.

|| 'Marriages' repeated and all in four lines. Samples of the two first entries are given; but the marginal names are omitted later, the parental sirnames being given in heavy type instead. The signatures, as they seem, are not autographic.

** Each page is similarly headed.

promise, that I never will trouble, or molest Elizabeth Hubball my wife, Either directly, or Indirectly about Religion: but will always give her ful Liberty to Exercise her own Religion: I do likewise in the Presence of God, swear, protest and promise, that all the children both Male and female, I shal have by her, not one Excepted, shall be brought up Roman Catholicks; And if they come not to the y[e] Years of Discretion, before my wife Dies, In case I shal survye her, they shall be brought up Roman Catholicks: In case I turn before her Death a Roman Catholick. But if my Wife should before my children come to y[e] Years of Discretion of knowing their Religion, & I then still a Protestant, then shall my Children be brought up Protestants unless, I shall promise my Wife (22[b]) on her Death Bed otherwise.

So help me God.

Wittness my Hand John Partridge, of Bloxham in Oxfordshire: And Elizabeth Hubball of Churchly Parish in Worcestershire, his Wife, and William Hollis his Master. this John Partridge was a Joiner Journy Man, & she was a Servant at New Heathrope.

3. April 23, Anno 1730, were Married at Old Heathrope, Richard **Widdrington** of Steeple Barton in Oxfordshire, a Protestant, and Frances **Clemens** of Kiddington the same County: by M. H., before these Wittnesses—Charles Arrowsmith, Winifrede Smith, Hanna Smith, Bridgett Durham.

The Husband promised that all Children should be brought up Roman Catholicks, & that he would give his Wife no trouble or Molestation about her Religion.

(23[a]) Marriages at London

4. December the 27, Anno 1730, were married Thomas **Nightingale**, and Mary **Northcote** of S. Andrew Parish, Holborn, by M. H. before these Wittnesses—Adam Worbridge, Dorothy Fram, John Kendall.

Anno 1731

5. January the 7th 1730-1 * were married Joseph **Dean** of Cinnington in Cheshire & Hannah **Ecorell** [**Escorell** *in margin*] of Deansborough in Lincolnshire at M[rs] David's Lodgings. In Earl's Court, at M[r] Pain at the Golden Key, by M. H: before these Wittnesses—James Prichard, Dorothy Davis, Ann Chatt.

The Husband being a Protestant, made the following Promise before the Said Wittnesses.

I Joseph Dean do promise in the Presence of God, that I never will directly or Indirectly molest my Wife about her Religion; (23[b]) & that all the Children I shall have by her, shal be breed up Roman Catholicks, wittness my hand, Joseph Dean.

6. February the 10th 1730-1 were married at M[r] Penn's at the two black Posts in great Wild† Street in the Parish of S. Giles in

* Seems corrected from 1701-2.

† Called from the site of Weld House, where the Weld family resided.

the fields, Matthew **Schoever** of Brussells in Flanders, & Elizabeth **Careless** of the City of Worcester, Worcestershire, by M H, before the Wittnesses.—John Beils, Perpabull Jackson.

July y[e] 18th 1731, M. H gave away in Marriage Miss Margarett **Mings**, to M[r] Henry **Burdett**, who were married by M[r] John Smith S. J. at y[e] Sarardinian Envoy's Chapple, Lincoln Inn Fields. [*In margin* Nota Bene]*

7. August the 24. 1731. were married Michael **Warner** and Elizabeth **Unwin**, at the Muzzle Bear in little Wild Street by (24[a]) Lincoln Inn Fields, by M H, before these Wittnesses.—James Wynell, James Heylan.

8. September the 29, 1731. were married John **Barns**, & Ann **Jackson** both of y[e] Parish of Stepney in Bengnal† Green, by M H, before these Wittnesses—Edward Potter, Thomas Baldin, Ann Baldin, Elizabeth Dove.

9. October the 11th 1731, were married Michael **Moor** & Mary **Haslamb**, of the Parish of Saint Andrew Holborn, in Balding's Gardins, Grey's Inn Lane, by M H, before these Wittnesses,—Margarett Wembell, Ann Orme.

Anno 1732.

10. February the 7th 1831-2 were married att the lodgings of M H, Emmanuel **Hendrick**‡ & (24[b]) Elizabeth **Walter**, by M H, before these Witnesses,—Mary Jobourn, Patrick Nash, Mary Wheat, Mary Spencer, Mary Willot.

11. February the 17th 1731-2 were married at M[r] Warner in New Bond Street, M[r] Peter **Butcher** of the Parish of S[t] Martin in the Fields, & Miss Sarah **Ayliffe**, of the Parish of S[t] Ann Westminster, by M. H, before these Witnesses,—Richard Mills, Michael Warner, Elizabeth Warner, Ann Mills,
the aforesaid Witnesses saw the married Couple between the Sheets Just after y[e] Marriage Ceremonys were over, in order to say, the Marriage was Consummated.

(25[a]) 12. February the 22[d] 1731-2 were married at M H, Lodgings, John **Anthony** & Sarah **Berry**, both of the Parish of S. Giles in the fields, by M H, before these Wittnesses,—Patrick Nash, Ann Orme, Thomas Stringer, Alice Holland.

13. April y[e] 15th 1732, were Married at M. H Lodgings, Richard **Hackett**, & Isabell **Sturdy**, by M H. before these Wittnesses.—Thomas Rope, Ann Lawson, Ann Orme.

14. April the 28, 1732, were married at M H Lodgings, Thomas **Browning** & Mary **Fifefield**, by M H, before these Witnesses,—John Edsaw, Ann Johnson, Rebecca Painter.

(25[b]) 15. June the 11th 1732, were married at M H Lodgings,

* No marginal number is given to this wedding, probably as not the Rev. Monox Hervey's celebration.

† Probably Bethnal Green, which prior to 1669 was part of Stepney parish.

‡ This may have been a relation of Hervey's, his maternal grandmother being a Hendrick. His spelling the name, in the baptism of 24 December 1732, as *Endrick* is opposed to such conjecture however.

Christiphor **Sturdy**, & Ann **Lawson** by M H, before these Wittnesses,—Thomas Rope, Catharine Hill, Richard Hackett, Isabel Hackett.

16. October the 17th 1732, were married Thomas **Hall** & Mary **Wood**, by M H. before these Wittnesses—John Hindle, Catharine Banister.

17. December the 24, 1732. were married at M H Lodgings, Thomas **Merrye**, & Hanna **Burnell**, by M H, before these Wittnesses,—John Hervey, Alice Holland, Hanna Twates.

(26a) 18. December 24—1732. were married Richard **Well**, & Mary **Proudlove**, att ye Sardinian Chapple in Lincoln Inn Fields, by M H, before these Wittnesses—Mary Martin, Gertrude Banister.

1733

19. On the 17th of february anno 1732-3 were married Robert **Fleming** & Decy **Bell** of ye Parish of S. Sepulcher, near New Gate, by M H, before these Witnesses—James Fleming, [Mary *xd out*, Eliz. *above*] Fleming, Mary Bradley.

20. February the 18—1732-3, were at Mrs Ann Marshall in great Queen Street, near Lincoln Inn Fields, Collin **Graham**, and Ann **Saunders**, by M. H, before (26b) these Wittnesses—Mary Marshall, Ann Saunders, Adam Worlich.

21. March the 20th 1732-3 were married Henry **Sayer**, & Ann [? Grant *xd out*] **Trant**, by M H, before these Wittnesses—Mary Trant, Adam Worlich.

22. On the 27th of March 1733 were married Christiphor **Armstrong**, & Dorothy **Obrian** by M H. before these Wittnesses, —James Bushell, Mary Bushell.

23. On the 10th of June 1733 were married Thomas **Hunt**, & Martha **Mitchell**, by M. He. before these Wittnesses—Frances Cheeseman, James Hunt.

(27a) 24. December 26—1733, were married James **Jefferson**, and Helen **Dwyer** by M. H. before these Wittnesses. Ann Orme, Alice Holland.

[1733-4]

25. On January 27. 173-4 [*sic*] were married Robert **Drabwell**, and Catharine **Uptebeck** by M H, before these Wittnesses—John Frith of New Inn, Richard Blevin, John Gee, Joseph Uptebeck, Ed*: Chapman Junior.

(27b) Marriages in Yorkshire

Anno 1734

24.† On the 22d of December at Ugthorpe, by Whitby, were married John **Knaggs** ‡ of Stone-Gate,§ & Isabel **Sturr** of East

* There are two crossings out here, something like 'Ed' in both cases.

† The numbers do not run consecutively after the marriages in London marked '25.'

‡ Eighteen named Knaggs appear in a list of recusants in 1690, all resident within a few miles of, or in Ugthorpe.

§ Stonegate in the parish of Glaisdale.

Barnby,* Yorkshire, by J. R. *alias* M H, before the whole Congregation, but particularly before the Wittnesses—Richard Smith Senior of Mulgrave Castle, Robert Stephenson of Ugthorpe.

Anno 1736

25. On the 14th of January 1735-6 were married, att Ugthorpe William **Burrell** of Bishoprick & Elizabeth **Allely** of Tranmire † by J R. alias M H, before these Wittnesses—Ann Pearson, Ann Stonehouse, Jane Sommersett, John Hodgson of Biggin House. ‡

(28[a]) 26. on the 26 of July, at Ugthorpe were married John **Daile** of Glassdale§ in the Parish of Danby near Ugthorpe, and Ann [H &c *x[d] out*] **Hill** of Leith [Lythe], they were third Cousins, yet by Virtue of a Dispensation from Doctor Carnaby Vicar for the North,‖ they were married by J R. alias M H, ann 1736, before

* East Barnby and West Barnby are in the parish of Lythe. They are also spelt Barmby.

† Tranmire in the parish of Lythe.

‡ The Hodgsons were probably the most important Catholics of Ugthorpe at the period. In 1717 the following papists registered their estates. Francis Hodgson of Foggithwaite, yeoman, son of John H. of Growmond, deceased, and Elizabeth his widow who had an annuity of £2, whilst another son, John, had a charge of £50 (*N.R. Yorks. Rec.*, viii., 29). John Hodgson of Bigginthorpe, yeoman (*Ibid.*). William Hodgson of Ugthorpe, yeoman, grandson of Cuthbert H. (*Ibid.* 20.). There is also Elizabeth, widow of George Hodgson of Ugthorpe, yeoman (*Ibid.*). But as there is a statement of further relationships concerning the sale of part of the same estates in 1734 (*Ibid.*, ix., 126), it may be well to amalgamate the two as below. John Hodgson, of St Paul's, Covent Garden, Middlesex, perriwig-maker, is named in the second paper. Cuthbert Hodgson of Whitby, gentleman, and Christopher Simpson of Hunt House, in Goathland, malster, are named as trustees; and John Maire and Thomas Smith, gentlemen, both of Gray's Inn, were probably the notaries. Elizabeth Hodgson mentions as relations of her deceased husband, Cuthbert Hodgson of Stakesby, William Hodgson of Ugthorpe and Gabriel Dale of Ugthorpe.

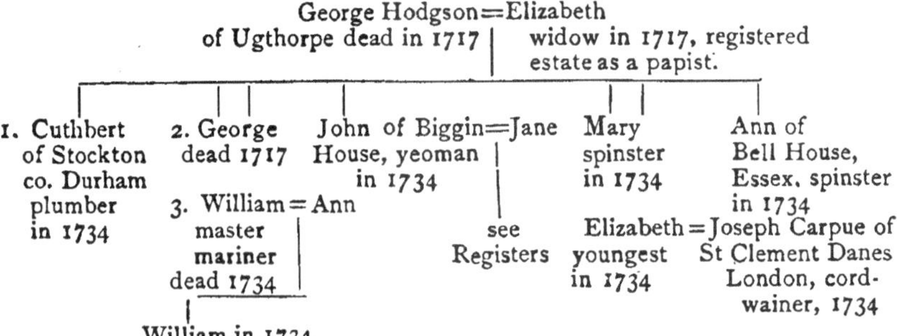

§ Glaisedale.

‖ Luke Gardiner *alias* Robert Carnaby, born 20 June 1683. Son of John Gardiner of the diocese of Chester, and his Wife Catherine Midford, he took the college oath at Douay 25 Sept. 1703; but proceeded to Paris, where he was ordained 23 Sept. 1713, and made D.D. in 1715. Before August 1717 was chaplain to Lady Mary Radcliffe at Old Elvet, Durham, till her death 3 March 1724. Was at York some years, but returned to Durham, and died there 2 Oct. 1740. Hervey must mean that that he was Vicar to Bishop Williams for the Northern District, which seems justified by the dispensation and other circumstances (*First Douay Dairy*; *Kirk's Biographies*, 40; *C.R.S.* xii, 5.)

these Wittnesses, Dorothy Stephenson Senior, Ann Hodgson senior.

Anno 1737

27. On November 10-1737. were married Andrew **Jousy** of Ugthorpe, and Sarah **Saunderson** of Easington, by J R. alias M H. before these Wittnesses—Luke Gallilee, Dorothy Gallilee Senior, Dorothy Gallilee Junior.

Anno 1738

28. August the 21. 1738, were married Peter **Garbutt**, & Dorothy **Gallilee**, both of Ugthorpe, by J R. alias M H. before these Wittnesses (28[b]) Ralph Pierceson, Thomas Garbutt, John Atkinson, William Burrel.

29. On October the 29th 1738 were married Jonas **Garbutt** of Ugthorpe, & Martha **Bellwood** of Whitby, at Ugthorpe by J R. alias M. H, before these Wittnesses—Jane Garbutt, Ann Garbutt, Ralph Pierceson, Margaret Kell, Thomas Garbutt.

1839.*

30. November the 15, 1739* George **Shiming** of Sorefoot† in the Parish of Leith [Lythe], and Ann **Garbutt** of Ugthorpe were married by J R: alias M H, before these Wittnesses—(29[a]) Mary Shiming, Jane Garbutt.

31. On June the 10th 1739 were married at Ugthorpe, Kenneth **M[c] Kensie**, & Elizabeth **Atkinson**, both of Sands End by Whitby,‡ by J R, alias M. H, before these Wittnesses—William Unthunkt,§ William Attkinson, Grace Woods, Thomas Hodgson, Ann Smelt, John Leith.‖

32. October the 10th 1739, were married at North Lofthouse, by Gisborough, Richard **Taylor** & Mary **Easilby** both of Steathes,¶ by J R, alias M H, before these Wittnesses,—John Sayer, Mary Suggett.

(29[b]) 33. November the 30th 1739, were married John **Attkinson** of Ugthorpe, & Elizabeth **Pierceson** of Mickleby, both of the Parish of Leith [Lythe], by J. R. alias M. H, before these Wittnesses—Elizabeth Adamson, Robert Attkinson.

1740

34. On the 12th of february 1739-40 were married John **Harrison** of Green Houses, in the Parish of Danby, & Helen **L[y** *over* **ei]th** of Cockwouldnuke in y[e] Parish of Leith, by J R, alias M H, before these Wittnesses att Ugthorpe—Mary Harrison, John L[y *over* ei]th, Matthias Booth.

* In both cases '9' is written over '8.' '1739' is written clearly in the margin.

† May have been 'Soreford' changed.

‡ Sands End is in Lythe parish, close to Whitby parish, but three miles from the town of Whitby.

§ Unthank, a personal name assumed from places in the north.

‖ As Mr Hervey misspells the place, he probably also writes the personal name of Lyth or Lythe—Leith. He corrects himself a few lines later.

¶ Staithes in Hinderwell parish.

(30[a]) 35. On the 19th of february 1739-40 at Ugthorpe were married Henry **Stonehouse**,* & Winifrede **Wall**. He of Hinderwell, & She of Gisborough, by J R. alias M. H, before these Witnesses.—Elizabeth Adamson, Mary Knaggs.

36. March the 2[d] 1739-40 were married at Ugthorpe, Thomas **Eldwin** & Mary **Alenson**† both of the Parish of Ingleby Green How by Stoxley [Stokesley], by J R, alias M. H, before these Wittnesses,—Thomas Garbutt, Jane Garbutt, Paul Garbutt.

1741

37. January the Seventh, 1740-1, were married William **Lyth** ‡ of Cockwoodnuke, & Ann **Booth** of Dunsly, at Ugthorpe, by J R, alias M H, before these Wittnesses—(30[b]) Thomas Lyth, Richard Lyth, Dorothy Gallilee, Robert Stephenson, Ann Meller, John Batty Esquire.

38. January the 17th. 1740-1 — were married, at Ugthorpe, Thomas **Taylor** of Steathes, & Sarah [P&c *x[d] out*] **Porrit** of Liverton, § by J R. alias, M H, before these Wittnesses—John Batty

* Henry, son of Rodger (Roger) Stonehouse, was baptized at Hinderwell, 12 Dec. 1714 (*Orig. Registers*); his mother being Mary Hutchinson, married 30 Nov. 1704 (*Ibid., see note C.R.S.*; iv., 378). Henry was uncle of Elizabeth (baptized there 16 April 1793) who married Richard Hansom of York. She handed down the tradition to her grandson (my father) that the family had been always Catholic, and that some ancestors used to go to Stokesley, with the ladies Radcliffe, to be fined for recusay. I thought this meant *Ladies* Radcliffe, until studying recusant lists I found the Radcliffes of Ugthorpe and Stonehouses (Stonas, etc.) in the same lists, summoned to the sessions held at several places. My father used to look on Christopher Stonehouse of Dunsley (and East Row as appears by his will in *C.R.S.*, vi., 73-4) in Morris's *Troubles of our Catholic Forefather*, i., 222, as a direct ancestor. The *Annals of St Monica's, Louvain,* have been published since his death. Christopher does not appear in the roll of recusants as one in 1592-3, because he was a prisoner in York Castle, and escaped 23 Aug. 1593 after 20 months imprisonment. This was for sending crosses, etc., to Catholic prisoners, asking for prayers for his wife in her first confinement, and refusing to attend Protestant worship. The name of his first wife, Frances Smith, is left blank. It is very likely that his second wife appears as, Ursula wife of George Fairfax? If this is so, Christopher's son Andrew, a priest of the English College at Rome, and later a Jesuit, assumed the *alias* of Fairfax from his step-mother's name in her earlier marriage. At York there is an administration of the estate of George Fairfax of Dunsley, 4 Oct. 1598; perhaps a son of George Fairfax who married Frances, daughter of Sir Francis Salvin of Newbiggin.

† It is likely that this couple secured registration by a subsequent parochial marriage, for Thomas Elden and *Anne* Alleson both of this parish;' were married 'by virtue of Bans published,' on 26 Aug. 1740. The following burials occur,—23 May 1761, Susanna dau. of Thos. Eldin; 4 Apr., 1763, Thomas Eldin, householder; 23 Dec. 1773, Ann Eldin, widow. Tho. Eldin appears as witness to a church terrier in 1754. Very few of the name appear in the registers. (Rev. John Blackburne's *Registers of Inglebye juxta Greenhow.*)

‡ It would have been of interest to know whether he was related to Matthew Lyth, who attempted to save the martyr, Nicholas Postsgate, when arrested in his house, and who was committed to York Castle with the martyr.

§ 'One low room in the east end of a house belonging to Mary Torrett in Liverton set apart for the religious worship of the people called Quakers." (*N.R. York. Records,* vii., 233.) Mr Hervey would seem to have got the

Esquire, Elenora Meller, Ann Meller, Marmaduke Langdale Esquire, Dorothy Gallilee, Thomas Alanson.

NB. The Woman was a Quaker but turnd & was baptized before she was married.

(31[a]) 39. On May the second, 1741, were married Robert **Saunderson** & Elizabeth **Duck** of Easington by North Lofth[ouse], at Ugthorpe, by J R. alias M: H, before these Wittnesses—Elizabeth Adamson, Helen Daile.

40. May the 28. 1741, were married at Ugthorpe, John **Lyth** of Cockwoodnuke, & Mary **Ward**, by J R. alias, M. H. before these Wittnesses.—Ambrose Lyth, Richard Lyth.

1742 ✱

41. January 12. 1741-2 were married Robert **Attkinson** and Barbara **Harrison**, at Ugthorpe, by J R, alias M. H. before these (31[b]) Wittnesses—John Harrison, Joseph Harrison.

42. August the 2[d] 1741[?] were married James **Edwards** & Elizabeth **Tompson** of North Lofthouse, at Ugthorpe, by J R, alias M. H, before these Wittnesses — John Hill, Elizabeth Adamson.

43. October the 20th 1741, were married Ralph **Pierceson** & Elizabeth **Daile** of Ugthorpe, by J R, alias M H, before these Wittnesses — Ralph Daile, Helen Daile, Elizabeth Adamson, Henry Conyers.

(32[a]) 44. November the 7th 1741, were married William **Roe**, and Elizabeth **Garbutt** of Ugthorpe, at Ugthorpe, by J R. alias M H, before these Wittnesses.—Elenora Meller, Ann Meller.

Anno 1742[?3] †

45. March the 31. 1742[?], were married att Ugthorpe, William **Page** & Jane **Consitt**, both of Ugthorpe, by J R, alias M. H, before these Wittnesses—Dorothy Stephenson, Elizabeth Stephenson, Alice Stephenson.

46. August the 5th 1742[?], were Married John **Carter**, & Ann **Umphrys** both of [North Lofthouse *x[d] out*] the Parish of Skelton near Gisborough; at Ugthorpe, by J R, alias M H, before these Wittnesses — Elizabeth Adamson, Ann Stephenson, Henry Conyers—obijt.

Anno 1745

47. April the 22[d] 1745, were married Robert **Milburn** and Phillis **Saunderson** of Whitby, at Ugthorpe, by J. R, alias M. H, before these Wittnesses,—William Price alias Smith Esquire, obijt, Ann Wilford, Thomas Gallilee.

name wrong, perhaps from trusting to memory. Licences to private houses were granted by Act 1 William and Mary for dissenters; but not for Catholics.

✱ After several amendments between 41 and 42 it has been finally put down as 1742 distinctly. It seems to make all the following years' registers doubtful.

† See note to heading of previous year, which if 1742, would make this year 1743 or even 1744, as 1745 follows. This affects also the two registers, which are queried.

48. November the Seventh 1745, were married att Ugthorpe by J R, alias (33[a]) M H, William **Barton** of Westsenby, and Mary **Coats** of Egton Bridge, both of the Parish of Egton, before these Wittnesses—Luke Potts, alias Cooper, Michael Barton of Barton Hold.

The December following the Said M[r] Luke Potts alias Cooper, thô sent to be at Egton Bridge, and the Said J. R. alias M H, thô so many years among the Moors, were denyd shelters, by the Unchristian Catholics, and after playing hid & seek, were forced to return to Ugthorpe; & there were taken by [the *x[d] out*] three Constable, a Sargient, (33[b] *) & twelve Souldiers, att ten at Night on Wednessday, the 11th of December 1745. carried the next day to Whitby, & were there Assaulted & Abused by the Mob; kept there till Sunday morning Under Strict Guard, then carried to Gisboroug[h *above*], where they arrived on Monday following, where four [Ju *x[d] out*] Justices of the Peace, viz. Esquire [of K *x[d] out*] Turner of Kirk Leatham, Consit, Robertson, & Scotta, who Committed them to York Jail or Castle, upon refusing to take the Oaths; on the 18th of December 1745 they arrived there; M[r] Luke (34[a]) Potts, alias Cooper, was kept Prisoner till y[e] 21 of December 1746.

As for J R alias M H, He was Jndited, & brought to the Bar, along with Sir William Anderson† of Crathorne, July 26, 1746, they were Jndited on their Sacred functions: they pleaded for time: which was granted till y[e] next Lent Assizes; viz, March y[e] 30, 1747, when again they appeard at the Bar, were Acquitted of the Jndictment, & brought in not Guilty by the Jury: yet they were at y[e] Bar obliged to give a Bond of a hundred pound Each, for security, of their Leaving Yorkshire, within six Week after they were to be sett a Liberty; which was not till the second of June following, 1747.

(34[b]) These four more, viz. M[r] John Green,‡ who had been Prisoner 15 Months, M[r] Martin Hounsel§ 15 Months, & M[r] Thomas Wilson¶ [& ther *x[d] out*] for [15? *x[d] out*] 14 Months: But they

* Pages 33[b], 34[a], 34[b], and 35[a] are headed 'Nota Bene.'

† A note about him appears elsewhere; and he has been dealt with in the last paper in this volume.

‡ John Green was committed from West Riding Sessions, 10 Oct. 1745, to York Castle, as a 'Popish Priest and one disaffected to his Majesty.' This looks as though some real evidence existed as to political action or language.

§ Martin Houns[h]ill was at Roundhay near Leeds and committed to York Castle 18 Nov. 1745. Son of Martin Hounshill of Ringwood, Hants, brazier, a Catholic Non-Juror in 1717, and his wife Elizabeth Hunt. Born 8 March 1718, he was educated at Twyford Catholic School, Hants, and the English College, Lisbon, where he was ordained 27 March 1742, and went to Roundhay. After his release he went to Arundel Castle, and later to Lisbon where he was chaplain to the Bridgettines. Ill health caused his return, and he died in London, a few days later, 9 Aug. 1783.

¶ Thomas Wilson was at Hathersage, co. Derby, and sent to York Castle

[were] set at Liberty all along with Mr Potts alias Cooper,* on the 21 of December 1746 aforesaid.†

A
Memorandum for
the Moors of Ugthorpe
In
Perpetuam Rei Memoriam.

Mr Nicholas Postgate was martyred at York.
Mr Anderton was forced to leave the place. ‡
Mr John Danby was cast into York Jail. §
Mr Bostock ‖ dyed of a Cold in hiding himself from the Constables.
Mr Thomas Smith was banishd.
J. R, alias M H, was denyd Shelter, taken & cast in Jail, as above.
And Mr Potts, alias Cooper, they would not receivd at Egton Bridge, and therefore was taken along with the said J R. alias M H.

From the Moors in
Yorkshire Good Lord deliver
us—Amen.

The Chiefe Evidence against J. R. alias M. H. was Ralph Pierceson a Weaver, a fallen Catholick, to whom J R, alias M H, had for many years been a father, to him & his poor family.

The Lord Convert and Pardon him: I freely forgive him, & all my Enemys.

(36b) A Marriage in York Castle, Yorkshire.

49. On the Ninth of June 1746 were married in York Castle, Edward **Clavering**, & Elizabeth **Grant** by J R, alias M: H. before Ralph Atkinson, a Debtor: the Said Mr Edward Clavering was Executed Novem. the first following—1746. & his Wife Elizabeth Clavering, was transported with several Rebels, the April following, 1747.

5 Nov. 1745, as a reputed Popish Priest and dangerous to the peace of the Kingdom. After his release he returned to Hathersage, and died there 12 Dec. 1779.

* It is intended to produce some details about him in another paper.

† Hervey's longer detention may be due to his keeping the school?

‡ Perhaps Thomas Salkeld, *alias* Whalley, *alias* Anderton, born 1624, ordained at Rome 1652, who was at York in 1691. (*C.R.S.*, iv., 375.)

§ A warrant for the apprehension of John Danby of Egton Bridge was directed 13 July 1708 (*N.R. Yorks. Rec.*, vii., 213). This was for 'saying Mass.' He was probably the Lisbon priest ordained 21 Dec. 1689, sent to England 2 Jan. 1693.

‖ There are two priests called George Bostock in Obituaries of secular priest (*C.R.S.*, xii., 2, 3) who died 28 Dec. 1727 and 17 Sept. 1728. It must be matter of regret that Hervey did not give more particulars of the four names, presumably at Ugthorpe, between Nicholas Postgate, arrested in 1678, and his own going to Ugthorpe in 1734.

N.B. This Marriage made a great Noise, & J R, alias M H, was might[i]ly blamed: but It was done ad Melius Bonum, In order to prevent Sin: & out of two Evils the less, in that Case, was to be Chosen: & sin att all times should be, If possible, Prevented.

(Page 37[a] *blank.*)

(37[b]) Marriages in Montgomeryshire.

1747

50 and 1.* October the 18[th] 1747, were married at Buttington Hall, near Welch Pool, Samuel **Evans** & Elizabeth **Meredith**, both of Welch Pool Parish, before these Wittnesses—Michael Jones Senior, Elizabeth Evans.

51 & 2. October y[e] 30th 1748 were married at Welch Pool, by M H, John **Langdale** of Powis Castle, & Catharine **Williams**, Widow, before these Wittnesses.—Susanna Ruffe, Penelopy Lindsey, Michael Jones Junior, all three of Welch Pool. (£01. 00*s.* 00*d*, *in margin.*)

(38[a]) Anno 1750

52 & 3. On the 26 of february 1750, were married by M H. at Welch Pool, Thomas **Lloyd** & Mary **Plowden** of Crowder's Copy† in the Parish of Gillsfield, before these Wittnesses.—Henry Fox Esquire, Matthew Du Bawffe, & Mary Bellis.

53 & 4. On Saturday the 10th of March 1750 were married Terence **Conell** of Kells in the County of Meath in the Kingdom of Ireland, & Susanna **Griffith**, of welch Pool, montgomeryshire, by M. H, att Buttington Hall, before these wittnesses,—Francis Reynolds [*signs*]; Eliz. ○ Hannis, her mark; Mary + Bellis, her mark; Mary + Griffith, her mark. (£00. 02*s.* 06*d*, *in margin.*)

(38[b]) 53 & 5. On Easter Monday April 16. 1750 were married at Buttington Hall, before the Altar & Congregation, by M. H., Edward **Glover**, of S. Julian Parish of Salop, & Sarah [Bt ? *x[d] out*] **Banner** of the same parish & same Town Shropshire, Before these under-written Wittnesses.—Edw[d] Philpott; W. Prichard; Marg[t] Aubin; Sus: Ruff Senior. (£00. 05*s.* 00*d. in margin.*)

Anno 1751

54 & 6. On [Whit Sunday *x[d] out*] White Tuesday May 28, 1751. Were married [att *above*] Buttington Hall, before the Altar, by M. H. [Nicholas *above*] **Pinnet**, and Margaret **Tudor**, Both of Welch Pool, before these Witnesses—Ann + Pinnet of Welch Pool, her mark; (39[a]) Elizabeth + Hannis, [at *x[d] out*, hired to my *above*] L[d] Visc. Hereford, her Mark; Mary + Griffith of Buttington Hall, her mark; Mathew De Balfe of Powis Castle.

Anno 1752

55 & 7. June the 15th were married at Dreewmraig near Welch-

* At this point Hervey adds above each register the number celebrated at his new post in Wales.

† Crowther's Coppice formerly the forest of Coed y Mynach, as stated in H. Payne's *Welshpool Almanack* 1906, kindly lent me by Mr Robert Owen of Welshpool.

Junior branch of Plowden Family.

Francis Plowden of Plowden, ob. 1652. = Mary, dau. of Thomas Fermor of Somerset, sister to Sir Richard Fermor, Knt.

Edmund Plowden of Waustead, co. Southampton, styled in his will (July 20, 1655) Sir Edmund Plowden, Lord Earl Palatine, Governor and Captain-General of Province of New Albion in America. = Mabel, dau. of Peter Marriner, Esq., of co. Hants.

Francis Plowden, eldest son.

Thomas Plowden, 2nd son. =

James Plowden, eldest son. =

A quo Protestant branch, CHICHELE-PLOWDENS.

Francis Plowden, 3rd son, killed in North America. = Frances, dau. of James Gamons.

1. Thomas Plowden of Buttington, died in Inverness in 1729. = Hannah, dau. of . . . . Pritchard of Buttington.

2. John Plowden. — 3. Charles Plowden.

Floretta. — Ann.

1. Benjamin Plowden. — 2. Thomas Plowden.

3. Francis Plowden. = Mary, dau. of John Davies of New Quay.

4. James Plowden of Crowder's Copy or Crowther's Coppice.

Ann.

Mary, mar. Thomas Floyd or Lloyd. — A . . . . Plowden.

Teresa Plowden of Crowder's Copy.

1. Thomas Plowden of New Quay, born Nov. 23, 1750.

2. William Plowden, born 1754, kept "The Barge Inn," Salop, of which his grand-nephew William John Plowden-Pugh was the licensee in 1887.

3. Francis Plowden.

4. John Plowden, born 1763; said to have been of Park Cottage, Lydbury. He was agent to Squire Plowden, and died at Plowden. — 5. Charles Plowden, born 1766.

Mary, born 1748. — Elizabeth, born 1756. — Winifred.

Mitchell Hughes and Clarke, 140 Wardour Street, W.

Poole. By M H, John **Pinches** of Plowden in the Parish of Lidbury North, Shropshire, And Elizabeth **Powel**, Native of y[e] Forge at Powis Castle, but Servant at Esquire Plowden of Plowden,* before these Wittnesses—John Harding near Plowden; Elizabeth Hannis, Matthew Debalfe.

Nota Bene—Solemnly declared before the Above mentioned Wittesses, that He would give his Wife Elizabeth Pinches the full Liberty of her Religion; & that all the Children Both Boys & Girls should be Baptizd & brought up in her Religion.

Marriages in London District† Anno 1753
Anno 1753.

51 & 1.‡ August 27-1753—were married at the Spainish Chaple (Oxford Road, *above*) by M Hervey; (In Oxford§ Road *above*) James **Gregson** & Sarah (? **M**) **oor** *above*) Spinster, She granting that all the Children both Male & female shall be breed up Catholicks—Before these—William Worden, Mary woolls senior, Stephen Woolls, John Woolls senior, John Woolls Junior, Mary Woolls Junior.

57 & 2. October the 6th 1753. Were married by M H, (in Oxford Road *above*), Richard **Lewthwaite**, & Elizabeth **Ricks**, according to the Rites of the Holy Church, before these Wittnesses—Antony Hanford, John Prichard, Mary Prichard.

Nota Bene—This is register'd at his Excellency Count Haslang's Chaple, in Warwick Street.‖

(41) 58 & 3. October 11 1753 were Join'd in Wedlock by M. H, at his Excellency Count Haslang Chaple in Warwick Street, William **Proctor** & Elizabeth **Sinott**, according to the Holy Rites of the Catholic Church, before these Wittnesse—Valentine Hover & Mary Bradey.

59 & 4. December 4. 1753. were married by M H, at M[rs] Obrian, in Lamb Conduits Passage, Red Lion Square, Henry Michael **M[c] Kee**, & Ann **Mowbray**, before these Wittnesses,—John Mowbray, her son; John Obrian Junior; Sir William Anderson; Elizabeth Obrian.

(*In margin*) N.B. this is Register'd in Warwick Street Chaple.

60 & 5. December the 9th 1753 were married by M H, in Oxford Road, John **Bateman** & Ann **Kendal**, of the Parish of S. Giles in

* The squire of Plowden at this period was William Plowden, who had succeeded to father, Colonel William Plowden, 5 March 1740-1, and married Frances dau. of Sir Charles Dormer. (Burke's *Commoners*, iii., 254.)

† The word 'District' is written above.

‡ Hervey here starts in addition numbers for London.

§ Oxford Street, as now called, may be meant, *i.e.* commencing west of Tottenham Court Road. The Rev. Bernard Kelly, in his *English Catholic Missions*, says the Spanish Chapel was in Ormond Street in 1736, which does not comply with this; but that about 1767 it was in the Spanish ambassador's house, without giving any locality. The chapel in Baker Street did not exist.

‖ The chapel of the Bavarian embassy.

the fields, before these Wittnesses.—John Obrian, Elizabeth Obrian.

(*In margin*) N.B. Registerd in Warwick Street Chaple.

[Two sheets, or four pages, have been torn out here; but the sequence of register numbers is consecutive. The following register, No. 61, is very badly blotted, as though liquid had been spilled on it. The next following is partially so.]

61 & 7. December 10. 1753 were Join'd in Matrimony by M^x H, Joseph **Upteback** & Margaret **Pierce** before these Wittnesses—Mary Upteback, Catherine Rome.

(*In margin*) Registerd in Warwick Street Chaple.

Anno 1754

62 & 8. March 4. 1754. were Join'd in Matrimony by M^x H, John **Macdonald** and Lewisa **George**, before these Wittnesses.—Stephen Woolls, Joseph Christie, & Jane Christie.

(*In margin*) Registerd in Warwick Street Chaple.

63 & 9. March 24, 1754. were Married by M^x H. John **Obrian**, & Helen **Worlick**, before these Wittnesses—Adam Worlich, Henry Mackee, Ann Mackee, Miss Ann Widdrington, & Sarah Meigham. (*In margin*) Registred in Warwick Street Chaple.

[Duplicate facing pages 44 to 76 are blank.]

(77^a) M H—God's Children.*

[In Oxfordshire]

1.* Monox Durham, the Son of Richard & Bridgett **Durham**, by Denthrope, near Old Heathrope in Oxfordshire: October ye 19th 1729.

[In London]

2. Monox Perkins, the Son of Edward & N. **Parkins**, in Lamb's Conduitt Passage, Red Lion Square: January the 24—1731.

[*In margin*] Mortuus Est 1742.

[In Yorkshire]

3. Henry Harrison, the Son of Joseph & Mary **Harrison**, of Ugthorpe near Whitby, Yorkshire: November the 19. Anno 1734.

4. Monox Carter, the Son of Thomas & Elizabeth **Carter**, of North Lofthouse, Yorkshire: December the 2^d Anno [174 *x^d out*] 1734.

5. John Hodgson Son of John and Jane **Hodgson** of Biggin House near Ugthorpe, [Yorkshire *above*] May the 16. 1735. The Child [died *above*] on ye 3^d of June following.

6. Sarah Hill, five years Old, the Daughter of Michael & Mabel **Hill**, near Ugthorpe. April the 24th 1736, in Yorkshire.

(77^b) 7. Thomas Taylor, of Thomas and Margaret **Taylor** of great Moorsome, Yorkshire. April 28th 1736.

8. Alice Hill, Daughter of Michael & Mable **Hill**, near Ugthorpe: May the 2^d 1736. Yorkshire.

* Each page is headed 'M.H.—God Children.' 's' has however been added to the two first of 6 pages. Presumably he accepted sponsorship of all. The numbers in the original are all in the margin.

9. William Atkinson, the Son of Stephen & Jsabell **Atkinson** of Whitby, Yorkshire, October the 6th 1736.

10. Mary White, Daughter of Miles & Elizabeth **White**, of Court Houses near Whitby, Yorkshire. October the 16th 1736. The Child is since dead.

11. Monox Pierceson, Son of Ralph (Ecce Proditor, O Cœli, *in margin* *) & Ann **Pierceson** of Ugthorpe, Yorkshire, July ye 21. 1737.

12. Monox John McKensie, the Son of Keneth [Mc *xd out*] & Elizabeth **McKensie**, of Sands End, near Leith: Yorkshire: September the 23d 1740.

(78a) 13. Dorothy Harrison, Daughter of John & Helen **Harrison** of Green Houses in the Parish of Danby; near Ugthorpe; Yorkshire: April the first—1741.

14. John Monox Lyth, Son of John & Helen **Lyth** of Cockwoodnuke, April the Eight, 1742. Yorkshire.

15. John Cole, the Son of Cornelius & Ann **Cole** of Staiths by Hinderwell, in Yorkshire: Jan: 30th 1743.

16. Monox Duck † the Son of John & Ann **Duck**, of Easington near North Lofthouse, Yorkshire Jan: 19th. 1745.

17. John Harrison the Son of John & Helen **Harrison** of Green Houses, near Ugthorpe, in the Parish of Skelton, or Danby, Yorkshire. June 24. 1745.

(78b) 18. William Corbett, the Son of William & Mary **Corbett** of Whitby; Yorkshire. July the first 1745.

19. John Sotro Son of David & Dorothy **Sotro** of Upsill, ‡ near Gisborough, Yorkshire, December 26. 1741.

[In London]

20. Mr Adam **Worlich's** Daughter [Helen *above*] Anno 1733—May the first at ye Pilgrims Ale House, facing King Gate Street—Holborn—London.

[In Montgomeryshire]

21. Monox [Edwards *xd out*, **Matthews** *above*] the Son of Edward & Elizabeth Matthews of Welch Pool, Mongomeryshire—November 15th 1747.

[In London]

22. Charles Monox [Perkinson *above*] the Son of Nicholas and Margarett **Perkinson** of Maiden Lane in the Parish of S. Saviour, Southwark, October 24. 1752.

[In Montgomeryshire]

23. Thomas Clement Plowden the Son of Francis & Mary **Plowden** at the Key in Guilefield Parish, Mountgomeryshire, November 23—anno 1750.

* The Rev. Monox Hervey states that this Ralph Pierceson, a weaver, was the chief witness against him.

† John Frank and Mary Duck, both of Danby, were married there, 6 Dec. 1764. the witnesses were Robert Duck and *Manax* Duck (Yorks. *Par. Reg. Soc.* xliii, 217.)

‡ East and West Upsall in Ormsby parish.

24. Monox Matthews, the Son of Edward & Elizabeth **Matthews** of Welch Poole, Montgomeryshire; November 15. 1747.

25. Monox Posle the Son of Samuel & Mary **Posle** by Welch Poole, Montgomeryshire, April 13. 1748.

26. Monox Davis the Son of Edward & Mary **Davis** of Montgomery, April 20, 1750.

27. Monox Pugh the Son of David and Mary **Pugh**, by Powis Castle, Mongomeryshire. August 20. 1750. [*In margin*, Dead.]

28. Elizabeth Conell the Daughter of Terence & Susanna **Conell** of Welch Poole, Montgomeryshire; October 11—1750 [*In margin*, Dead.]

29. James Barnaby Ruffe the Son of Susanne **Ruffe** Junior, of Welch Poole, Montgomeryshire. June 11. 1753.

[In London]

30. Martha Smith the Daughter of John and Ann **Smith** of Bedford Court, Hosier, by East Street, Theobald's Row, & Red Lion Street, Holborn, London. July 11. 1753. [*In Margin*, Dead July 13. 1753].

31. Charles Monox Perkinson, the Son of Nicholas & Margarett **Perkinson** of y[e] Parish of S. Mary Overe, Southwork, in Gardiners Lane by Mason's Stairs, born October 17. 1752, & baptiz'd on the 24 of the same month. [*In Margin*, died Jan. 2, 1754.]

(79^b) 32. Winifride Tomins [**Tommins**], born feb: 10. 1754, & baptiz'd by M H, the 15th of y[e] same month.

[The remainder of the page, corresponding with seven entries on the facing page (79a) is blank, as well as the three following pages.]

(82^b) Christenings in Oxfordshire.

1729

1. On the 15th of August, 1729. The Daughter of Edward and Mary **Fell**, at Chipping Norton, In Oxfordshire, was baptized by M H, by the names of Mary Clare, born on the 12. of the same Month: The Godfather was Charles Arrowsmith; and Godmother was M[rs] Ann of Weston.

1730

2. On the 19th of March 1729-30. The Son of Richard & Bridgett **Durham**, at the New Farme house by Dunthrope, in the Earl of Shrewsbery's Estate, was baptized by M. H, by the Name of Monox, the Godfather was M H, & the Godmother Winefride Smith, of Old Heathrope.

(83^a) Christenings in London.

1730

3. On the 5th of August 1730, the Son of William & Mary **Hodgson**, In Bloomsbury Market in the Parish of S. Giles in the Fields, was baptized by M. H, by the name of William. the Godfather was Henry Green, & the Godmother Teresy Brown: the Child dyed the same year.

4. On the 16th of November 1730. The Daughter of John & Catharine **De Matt**, in Cock Alley in the Parish of S. Martin Le Grand, by M: H, by the name of Catharine: the Godfather was Jasper Hopkins & the GodMother, Mary Hopkins.

5. On December the 7th 1730, [was *xd out*] the Son off N.N. & N. N., no questions to be askd, by the Name of Monox, by M: H. the Godfather was Thomas [Grimes *above*] & the GodMother was Mrs Grimes, Aunt to ye said Child.

(83b) 6. On the 13th of December, 1730, the Daughter of Patrick & (Mary *xd out*) Sara **Gardiner**, in Hart Street, in the Parish of S. Giles in the fields, was baptized by M H, by the Name of Mary: the Godfather was Thomas Mason, & the Godmother was Mary Smith;—N B. The Child afterwards was baptized by a Parson.

7. On the 21 of December, 1730, the Son of George & Margarett **Pottbery**, in the Old Change, Cheap Side, by M H, by the Name of Thomas; the Godfather was N. Walker, & the Godmother was Mary Thorpe.

1731

8. On the 10th of January 1730-1. The Son of N. & N **Bellarmine** at the Gold fleece, Drury Lane, was baptizd by the Name of John, by M H: the Godfather was N Gendor, & the Godmother was Mary Earnell.

(84a) 9. On the 24th of January 1730-1. The Son of Edward & N. **Perkins**, in Lamb's Conduit Passage, Red Lion Square, was baptized by M H, by the name of Monox, the Godfather was M H, & the Godmother Frances Allen.

10. On the same day also, the Daughter of Joseph, & N **Dudley**, in Golden Ball Court, Great Wild (Street ?), near Drury Lane, was baptizd by M H, by the Names Mary Joseph; the Godfather was Francis Kelly, & the GodMother Catharine Gibbons.

11. On the 16th of february 1730-1. The Daughter of Raymund and Mary **Jouret**, in the Wood Yard in Long Acre, was baptized by M H, by the Name of Mary, the Godfather John Transecu Aviere, & the Godmother was Catherine De Jardin.

12. On March the 9th 1730-1 the Son of John & N. **Bearwall**, at Mrs Mundy's in Essex Street in the Strand, was by M H, baptized, (By the name of John *below*) the Godfather was N (84b) Bourn & Godmother was N. Turner.

13. On the 14 of March 1730-1, the Son of John & Mary **Brittain**, in Great Kirby Street, by Hatten Gardin in the Parish of S. Andrew, Holborn, at my own Lodgings (was baptized by M H, *above*) by the Name of Joseph, by M H: the Godfather was George Greeswell, & the Godmother was Helen Dwyer.

14. On the 16th of March 1730-1. The Daughter of John & Darkiss (? Dorcas) **Rigalls**, Jn Vine Court, in Harp Alley, Shoe Lane, in the Parish of S. Bridgett, Fleet Street, was baptized by the Name of Esther, by M H: the Godfather was Robert Rigalls, but there was no Godmother, Ratio Sine qua non.

15. April the 28, 1731, The Daughter of Thomas (C *xd out*) &

Mary Cecil of the Parish of S. Giles in the fields, was baptiz'd by M H, by y[e] Name of Mary, the Godfather was Thomas Grimes, & the Godmother was Elizabeth Gale.

(85[a]) 16. On May the 29-1731. was the Daughter of Richard & Elizabeth **Parr**, by the Coal Yard in Holborn, in y[e] Parish of S. Giles, was baptized by M H, by the Name of Elizabeth, the Godfather was James Hulett & the Godmothers were Mary Hulett & Barbara Warden.

17. On the 6th of June 1731, the Son of George & Susanna **Limas**, at y[e] King's Head in James Street by Covent Gardin, was baptizd by M H, by the Name of Barnaby; the Godfather was Brian Mahonny & the Godmother N.

18. On the 22[d] of August 1731, the Daughter of James (Macm *x[d] out*) & Mary **Macmollen**, next door to y[e] Griffin & Parrott in Drury (Lane *above*) over against Parker's Lane, in y[e] Parish of S[t] Giles in the Fields, was baptizd by M H, by the Name of Ann; the Godfather was Terence Obrian, & the God Mother was Bridget Obrian.

(85[b]) 19. On the 2[d] of September 1731, was baptized by M H, the Daughter of John & Mary **Ffloid**, of y[e] Parish of Christ's Church, Southwark, by the Name of Penelope, the Godfather was John Aleworth, & y[e] GodMother Mary Garensiers.

20. On the 6th of October 1731 the Daughter of John & Mary **Lane**, in Bull head Court, Great Queen Street, in the Parish of S[t] Giles in the fields, was baptizd by M H, by the Name of Ann, the Godfather was James Rigg, & the GodMother was Elizabeth Parker.

21. On the 16th of October 1731, the Daughter of N, & N **Holden** was baptized by M H, by the Name of Sarah: the Godfather was James Sibsey, & the Godmother N.

(86[a]) 22. On the 19th of October 1731, the Daughter of N & N **Bandlow**, in S. Bartholmew's Close, in the Parish of S. Bartholomew the Great was baptized by M H, by the Name of Mary, the Godfather was N Walker, & the Godmother Ann Robinson.

23. On the 28 of December 1731 was the Son of John & Jane **Lamb**, at M[r] Hogan's a Baker in Great Wild Street, in the Parish of S. Giles in the fields, was baptized by M H, by the Name of Christiphor. the Godfather was William Hugan, & the Godmother was M[rs] Elizabeth Suttleworth.

Anno 1732

24. On the 17 of January 1731-2 was the Daughter of N & N (Macd's in the *x[d] out*) **Maccuoy**, in the Parish of S. James, Poultney, was baptizd by M H, by y[e] N of Mary, the Godfather was James Maccuoy, and the Godmothers Mary Step, & Jane Holland.

(86[b]) On January the 24th 1731-2. The Daughter of Michael & Elizabeth **Brady**, next Door to the Pillgrimes Ale house, Holborn, in the Parish of S. Giles in the fields, was baptizd by M H, by the

Name of Sarah: the Godfather was Martin Murphey, & y[e] God-Mother Elizabeth Hunt.

26. On March the 2[d] 1731-2, the Daughter of Fremundo, & Mary **Jourett** at the Wood Yard in Long Acre, of the Parish of S. Martin in the fields, was baptiz'd by M H, by the Name of Mary, the Godfather was Antony Fonterbeya & the GodMother Mary Dath.

27. On the 15th of March 1731-2, the Son of John & Sarah **Holland**, Jn Dean Court, Eagle Street, in the Parish of S. Andrew, Holborn, was baptized by M H, by the names of John Gabriel, the Godfather was B* Benjeman Holland, & the GodMother Penelope Aston.

(87[a]) 28. On the 11th of September 1732 the Daughter of Antony, & Isabella **Askew**, was baptizd by M. H, by the Name Catharine, the Godfather was Christiphor Wallis, & the Godmother margarett White.

29. On the Same day, also, 1732 the Daughter of William & Mary **Lane**, was baptiz'd by M. H., by the name Ann; the Godfather was Richard Hignett & the GodMother, Blanch Wolverton.

30. On the 24 of September, 1732, the Son of Michael & Mary **Moore**, Jn Queen's Head Yard, Gray's Jnn Lane, Holborn, was baptiz'd by M H, by the name Michael: the Godfather was James Robinson, & the Godmother Frances Hobthorow.

(67[b]) 31. On 25 of September 1732, The Son of Thomas & Mary **Fling**, in Charles Court in the Strand, in the Parish of S. Martin in the fields, was baptized by M H, by the Name William; the Godfather was James (Mullineux *x[d] out*) Whitnall, & the Godmother was Jane Mullineux.

32. On the 26 of September 1732 the Daughter of John and Dorothy **Wilkinson**, in Long Lane West Smithfield, was baptizd by M H, by the Name Mary, the Godfather was John Reeves, & the Godmother, Ann Hullett.

33. On the 27 of September 1732. The Daughter of James & Dina **Cavanage**, was baptized by M H, (at M[r] *x[d] out*) by the Name Catharine, the Godfather was James Doiles, & the Godmother Ann Blake.

(88[a]) 34. On the 3[d] of October 1732, the Son of Thomas & Mary **Hooker**, in Long Acre, was baptized by M H, by the Name Thomas: The Godfather was John Gardyner, and the Godmother, mary Chester.

35. On the 27 of October 1732, the Son of (Richard Williamson, *x[d] out*) John and Sarah **Rippon**, in Tagk† Court, Gray's Inn Lane, Holborn, was baptized by M: Hervey‡ by the Names

* This may be a letter crossed out.

† It is possible that this is 'Task' Court, with a long 's,' in lieu of 'g.'

‡ This is the first time he gives his sirname. Practically the first syllable is, unlike 'here,' unpronouncable, and is sounded like Harvey—not Hurvey.

Richard Williamson, the Godfather was James Shirley Senior, & the Godmother Elizabeth Kilby.

36. On the 26 of November 1732, The Daughter of Edward & Ann **Perkins** was baptized by M H, by the Name Catharine, The Godfather was Richard Talboise, & the Godmother Mary Talboise.

On the 27 of November 1732, the Daughter of Richard & mary (88[b]) **Walker** in Nelson's Court, Drury Lane, was baptiz'd by M H, by the Name Catharine: The Godfather was James Conor, & the Godmother Ann Blake.

38. On the 24 of December 1732 was the Daughter of Emanuel & Elizabeth **Endrick** baptizd by M H, by the Name Sarah: In Vinegar Yard, Drury Lane: the Godfather was Benjeman La Assen, & the Godmother Sarah Flemings.

Anno 1733.

39. On the 4th of february 173$\frac{2}{3}$ the Daughter of Robert & Ann **Holden** was baptizd by M H, by the Name Mary: the Godfather was James Sipsey, & the Godmother was Mary Marshall.

40. On the 13th of february 173$\frac{2}{3}$ the Daughter of Laurence and Ann **Fling**, in Newton's Lane, in the Parish of S. Giles in the fields, was baptizd by M H, by the Name Bridgett; the Godfather was John (89[a]) Eggin, and the Godmother (G *x[d] out*) Susanna Lee.

Anno 1734.

41. On the Sixth of January 173$\frac{4}{3}$, The The Son of Richard & Jane **Blevin**, at Kentish Town, in the Parish of S. Pancratius, Middlesex, near London, was baptizd by M H. by the Name James*: the Godfather was John Dalton, & the Godmother, Catharine Aston.

Christenengs in Yorkshire
since Anno 1734
under the Name of J R alias M H.

42 & 1. † On the 22[d] of October 1734. The Daughter of John & Christina **Danby**, at Leith (Lythe) near Whitby, was baptiz'd by J R, alias M H, by the Name Ann, the Godfather was George Harrison, & the God Mother, was N Danby.

43 & 2. On the 19th of November 1734 the Son of Joseph & Jane **Harrison** of Ugthorpe near Whitby, was baptiz'd by J R, alias M H, by the name Henry: the Godfather was J R, alias M H, and the (89[b]) Godmother Mary Hodgson, Aunt to the said Child.

44 & 3. On the (11 ? *x[d] out*; 2[d] *above*) of December 1734, The Son of Thomas & Esther **Carter** of North Lofthouse, was baptized by J R, alias M H, by the name Monox, the Godfather was J R, alias M H, and Godmother Mary Suggett.

45 & 4. On the 11th of December 1734, the Daughter of William & Elizabeth **Boijs** of Stanehacre,‡ by Whitby, was baptizd by

* This looks very like the James, son of Richard Belvin and his wife Jane Amerston, the Lisbon priest, said to have been baptized by Rev. Robert Morgan, 18 Sept. 1732. See the Cowdray registers (*C.R.S.*, i).

† Hervey begins with an additional number for his Yorkshire functions.

‡ Probably Stainsacre.

J R, alias M H, by the Name Elizabeth, The Godfather was Francis Wagewood, & the Godmother Elizabeth (Daile *x*[d] *out*) White.

46 & 5 & 6. On the Same Day also 1734. The two Sons, Twins, of John & Catharine **Atkinson** of Sand's End, near Leith,* were baptizd by J R, alias M H: the Eldest by the Name Peter, to whom Stood Godfather Robert Atkinson, & the Godmother was Mary Atkinson: The Youngest was baptizd by the Name Paul: to whom Stood Godfather Francis Wagewood, & the God=(90[a])= Mother was Elizabeth Atkinson.

47. On the 24th of December 1734. The Son of Ambrose & Elizabeth **Lyth** at Cockwoodnuke near Ugthorpe: (*letters x*[d] *out*) was baptized by J R, alias M H: by the Name of William, the Godfather was Robert Stephenson, & the Godmother Helen Pierceson.

Anno 1735.

48. On January the 23[d] $173\frac{5}{4}$ The Daughter of John & Ann **Duck** of Easington, near North Lofthouse, was baptized by J R, alias M H: by the Name Esther, the Godfather was John Ward, & the Godmother Margarett Crosby.

49. On the 16th of May 1735. The Son of John & Jane **Hodgson** of Biggan House, near Ugthorpe, was baptized by J R, alias M H, by the Name John, the Godfather was J R, alias M H, & the God Mother was Ann Hodgson the Widow, of Ugthorpe.

(90) Anno 1736.

50. On the 29 of february $173\frac{6}{5}$ the Son of Francis **Wagewood** & Mary **Stephenson**, was baptized by J R, alias M H, before the whole Congregation at Ugthorpe; the Godfather was William Wilks, & the Godmother Jane Sommersett.

51. On the second of April 1736, The Son of William & Winifride **Wall**, of Gisborough, was baptized by J R, alias M H, by Name William: the Godfather was Thomas Taylor, and the God Mother Mrs Elizabeth Metcalfe.

52. On the 24th of April 1736, The Daughter of Michael & Mabel Hill, near Ugthorpe, was baptized by J R. alias M H, by the name Sarah, the Godfather was J R. alias M H, & the Godmother was Ann Stonehouse. the father was a Quaker, & the mother a Catholick: And the Child was five years Old.

53. On the 28 of April 1736, The Son of Thomas & Margarett **Taylor**, of Great Moorsome, was baptized (91[a]) by J R. alias M H. by the Name Thomas, the Godfather was J R, alias M H, & the Godmother Susanna Sayer of little Moorsome.

54. On May the second, 1736, The Daughter of Michael & Mabel **Hill**, near Ugthorpe, was baptized privately, the Godfather was J R. alias M H. &c by the name Alice.

55. On the 6th of October 1736. The Daughter of Miles & Elizabeth

* Sand's End is in the parish of Lythe, on the sea coast, and close to the border of Whitby parish.

White of Court Houses, near Whitby, was baptized by J R, alias M H, by the name Mary, The Godfather was J R. alias M : H, and the GodMother was Jane Sommersett.

56. On the 16th of October 1736. The Son of Stephen & (Esab *xd out*) Jsabell **Atkinson**, of Whitby, was baptized by J R. alias M H : by the Name William, the Godfather was J R. alias M H : & the Godmother Grace Wood of Mulgrave Castle.

57. On the 30th of (September *xd out*, October *above*) 1736 the Daughter of John & Ann **Duck** of Easington near North Lofthouse (91b) was Baptized by J R, alias M : H, by the Name Zebora, the Godfather was Martin Adamson of Rouseby, & the Godmother (Elizäbeth *xd out*; Mary *in margin*) Easilby of Steathes.

58. On the 31st of October 1736. The Son of Cornelius and Ann **Cole**, of Staiths, by the sea side, near Ugthorpe, was baptized by J R, alias M H, by the Name John, the Godfather was William Watson, & the Godmother Mary Easilby. the Child dyed.

Anno 1737

59. On the 13th of January 173$\frac{6}{7}$ the Daughter of Ambrose & Elizabeth **Lyth**, of How House near Egton, was baptized by J R, alias M H: the Godfather was George Nellis, & the Godmother was Mary Harrison of Green Houses; the Child's Name, was Mary.

(92a) 60. On the 27th of february 173$\frac{6}{7}$ the Daughter of William and Esther **Carter** of North Lofthouse, was baptized by J R : alias M : H, by the Name of Elizabeth : the Godfather Michael Grimstone & the Godmother Elizabeth Watson.

61. On the second of May 1737, the Daughter of William & Elizabeth **Boijs** Stanchacher by Whitby, was baptized by J R, alias M : H. by the Name Ann : the Godfather was John Lyth, of Cockwoodnuke, & the Godmother was Agnes Bartin of Whitby.

62. On the 21th of May 1737, the Daughter of John & Ann **Daile** of Glassdale in the Parish of Danby, was baptized by J R : alias M H. by the Name Mary; the Godfather was Robert Stephenson, of (92b) Ugthorpe, & the Godmother was Elizabeth Harrison of Egton.

N.B. This Child was born, with a Thumb & a little finger on her left Hand, occasiond by a fright of the Mother, whilst she was with Child of her : In a fright the Mother tookt hold of (her *xd out*) three of her fingers on the left hand, & the Child was born so.

63. On the first of June 1737, the Daughter of William & Alice **Hoggard**, at East Stray,* by Sands End, was baptized by J R, alias M H: by the Name Ann; the Godfather was John Lyth of Cockwoodnuke, & the GodMother was Elizabeth Atkinson of Sand's End.

64. On the 9th of June 1737, the Daughter of Stephen & Elizabeth **Atkinson** of Whitby, was baptizd by J R, alias M H. by the Name

* Probably East Row is intended. It is referred to in the will of Christopher Stonehouse (*C.R.S.*, vi., 73-4).

Mary; the Godfather was Robert Atkinson of Sand's End; & the Godmother was Elizabeth Franklynn of Whitby.

(93^a) 65 & 66. July the 14th 1737. The Son & Daughter of Gideon & Elizabeth [ ], Quakers of Whitby, deceased, at the Earnest Request of M[rs] Margarett Lawson, of Sand's End, (where the Children were), who firmely Believd the said Children would not live, having a very bad Distemper then on them: of which both their father & * dyed: The Boy was baptized by J R, alias M H, by the Name George: and the Girl, by the Name Debora: The Godfathers were William Unthunkt, & William Atkinson, both of Sands End.

67. On the 21th of July, 1737, The Son of Ralph, & Ann **Pierceson** of Ugthorpe, was baptized by J R alias M. H, by the Name Monox, the Godfather was J R. alias M. H, and the Godmother was Jane Garbutt, of Ugthorpe.

(93^b) 68. On the 14th of October 1737, the Daughter of Francis and Elizabeth **Unthunkt**, of Robin-hood's Bay, but then at Lyth, was baptized by J R, alias M H, by the name of Elizabeth; the Godfather was William Unthunkt, and the Godmother was Elizabeth Atkinson both of Sand's End.

69. On the 21th of November 1737, the Son of William & Elizabeth **Watson** of North Lofthouse, was baptized by J R, alias M H; by the Name William, the Godfather was Cuthbert Hodgson of Stockton in Bishoprick, & the God Mother was Helen Lyth of Cockwoodnuke.

Anno 1738.

70. On the 26 of March 1738, The Son of John & Margarett **Camplin**† of Steaths in the Parish of Hinderwell, was baptized by J R, alias (94^a) M H, by the Name John: the Godfather was Luke Galilee of Ugthorpe, and the Godmother was Ann Hodgson, Widow, of the same place.

71. On the 13th of April 1738. The Daughter of John & Elizabeth **Knags** of Stonegate, near Ugthorpe, was baptized by J R. alias M H, by the Name Mary: the Godfather was William Knag of Yackley side: & the Godmother was Ann Garbutt of Ugthorpe.

72. On the 13th of May, 1738, the Daughter of John & Priscilla **Cole** of Steaths, was baptizd by J R alias M H: by the Name Elizabeth, the Godfather was Cornelius Cole, & the God Mother Mary Easilby, both of Steaths.

73. On the 27th of August 1738: The Daughter of John & Ann **Duck** of Easington, was baptizd by J R alias M H, by the name of (94^b) Mary: the Godfather was Thomas Sayer of little Moorsome, & the Godmother was Mary Duck of Rouseby.

74. On the 29th of August 1738, The Daughter [of] James &

* Presumably the 'mother' has been omitted by oversight, as also the family name above.

† In searching local registers some years ago I came to the conclusion that Camplin might be a corruption of Campion.

Jane **Shaw** of Yarm, was baptized by J R. alias M H, by the Name Ann: The Godfather was George Simpson, & the God Mother was Ann Horsley: both of Yarm:

N.B. neither M[r] Siddle, of Yarm, or M[r] Anderson of Stockton on the Tees, being at home, J R alias M H, being then on that side of y[e] Country was forced to be the Operator.

Anno 1739

75. On the 7th of January 173$\frac{9}{8}$ the Daughter of Martin and Margarett **Adamson** of Rousby,* was baptized by J R, alias (95[a]) M H, by the Name of Ann, the Godfather was Martin Adamson of Ugthorpe, & the God Mother Ann Duck of Easiton [Easington].

76. On the 15th of Aprill 1739. The Son of (Taylor *x[d] out*) Thomas and Margaret **Taylor** of great Moorsome in the parish of Skelton, was baptizd by J R, alias M H, by the Name of Tobias: the Godfather Tobias Taylor of Skelton, & the Godmother was Elizabeth Daile of Great Moorsome.

77. On the 17th of April 1739. The Daughter of Cornelius and Ann **Cole**, of Steaths, was baptized by J R, alias M H: by the Name of Mary. The Godfather was John Garnett of Cowburn, & the Godmother was M[rs] Mary Suggett of North Lofthouse.

(95[b]) 78. On the Eight of July 1739. In the Chaple of Ugthorpe, was baptized the Daughter of Peter & Dorothy **Garbutt** of Ugthorpe, by J R. alias M H. by the Name of Dorothy: the Godfather was M[r] Thomas Hodgson, & the Godmother was M[rs] Ann Meller.

79. On the 31th of December 1739 was baptized the Daughter of George & Ann **Shiming** of Ugthorpe: by J R, alias M H, by the Name Jane: the Godfather was Paul Garbutt, and the Godmother was Alice Garbutt.

Anno 1740

80. On the 21th of January 1740. The Son of William & Elizabeth **Boijs** of Stanchacker by Whitby, was baptiz'd by J R, alias M: H, by the Names of William and Sylvester: The Godfather was Thomas Wagewood; and the (96[a]) Godmother was Mary White.

81. On the 8th of May, 1740, was baptized the Daughter of Thomas & Ann **Eldin**, of the Parish of Inglleby How (by *x[d] out)* near Stoxeley, by J R. alias M: H, at Ugthorpe by the Name Elizabeth: the Godfather was William Eldin, & Godmother was Alice Garbut.

82. On the 15th of May, 1740. The Daughter of Ralph & Ann **Pierceson** of Ugthorpe, was baptized by J R. alias M H, by the Name of Mary: the Godfather was Francis Pierceson, & the Godmother was Jane Consitt.

83. On the 18th of July 1740, was the Daughter of Henry and Winifride **Stonehouse** of Gisborough baptized by J R alias M H

* Rousby or Roxby is a chapelry in Hinderwell-cum-Roxby parish.

by the Name Elizabeth: the Godfather was Richard Taylor of Steaths, & the GodMother was Mrs. Mary Metcalfe.

84. On the 20th of July 1740. The Son of Thomas & Jane **Wagewood**, (of *xd out*; near *above*) Robin Hood's Bay; by J R. alias M H: by the Name John: the Godfather was Francis Wagewood of Sorefoot, & the Godmother was Elizabeth Harrison of Egton Banks.

85. On the 18th of August 1740. The Daughter of Richard and Mary **Taylor**, of Steaths, was baptized by J R, alias M H, by the Name of Ann: the Godfather was Cornelius Peerceson, & the Godmother was Ann Cole.

86. On the 31st of August 1740' was the Son of John & Ann **Duke** of Easington, baptized by J R, alias M H, by the Name (97a) Christiphor, the Godfather was John Hill, & the Godmother was Mrs Mary Suggett, both of North Loftus.

87. On the 23d of September 1740. The Son of Keneth & Elizabeth **Mckenzie**, of Sands End near Leith, was baptiz'd by J R, alias M H, by the Names Monox John; the Godfather was J R, alias M H: and the Godmother was Grace Wood of Mulgrave Castle.

Anno 1741

88. On the 11th of January 1741 (S . . . r *xd out*) was baptized Sarah **Porrit** a grown up Woman, a Quaker, of the Parish of Liverton, near North Loftus, by J R. alias M H: She answerd for herself before these Wittnesses:—Elenora Meller, Ann Meller, Marmaduke Langdale, and Thomas Alenson.

(97b) 89. On March the 23d 1741. The Daughter of Francis & Elizabeth **Unthunkt**, of Leith, was baptiz'd by J R, alias M H, by the Name of Winifride; the Godfather was Robert Atkinson of Ugthorpe: & the Godmother was Anne Stangoe of Sands End.

90. On the first of April 1741. The Daughter of John and Helen **Harrison** of Green Houses, in the Parish of Danby, was baptiz'd by J R, alias M H, by the Name Dorothy: the Godfather was J R alias M H: and the Godmother was Mary Harrison.

91. On the 7th of April 1741. The Son of Thomas & Elizabeth **Sayer** of North Loftus, was baptized by J R, alias M H, by the Name John: the Godfather was William Turpin, & the Godmother was Elizabeth Sayer.

92. On the 13th of October 1741. The Daughter of Peter & Dorothy **Garbutt** of Ugthorpe, was baptized by J R alias M H, by the Name Ann, the Godfather was Thomas Galilee, & the Godmother Mrs Ann Meller.

93. On the 21st of December 1741. The Son of Robert & Elizabeth **Saunders(on** *inserted*) of Easington Moore side, was baptized by J R, alias M H. by the Name John: the Godfather was John Duck, and the Godmother was Sarah Saunders.

Anno 1742.

94. On the (fort *xd out*) fourth of february 1742. The Daughter of (98b) Henry & Winifride **Stonehouse** was baptized by J R,

alias M H, by the Name Ann; the Godfather was Tobias Taylor of Skelton: & the Godmother was Dorothy Stephenson, Junior, of Ugthorpe: the Child was Christen'd at Gisborough.

95. On the Sixth of february, 1742. The Daughter of David & Dorothy **Sotro** of Upsill, near Gisborough, was baptiz'd by J R. alias M H, by the name Elizabeth: the Godfather was Joseph Sayer of Hutton Rudby; & the Godmother was Everit Sayer. Ibidem

96. On the 8th of April: 1742. The Son of John & Helen **Lyth**, of Cockwoodnuke, near Ugthorpe, was baptiz'd by J R, alias (99[a]) M H, by the names John Monox, the Godfather was J R, alias M H, & the Godmother was Jane Ward of North Loftus.

97. On the 6th of June 1742. The Son of Robert & Barbara **Atkinson** of Ugthorpe, was baptized by J R. alias M H, by the Name of Robert: the Godfather was M[r] Thomas. Hodgson of Biggin House: & the Godmother was Alice Stephenson of Ugthorpe.

98. On the 7th of June 1742. The Son of George & Ann **Shiming**, of Ugthorpe, was baptiz'd by J R, alias M H: by the Name Thomas. The Godfather was Christiphor Simpson Senior, of Hunt Houses; & the Godmother, was Ann Camplin of Mickleby.

(99[b]) 99. On the 29th of July 1742 was the Daughter of William & Elizabeth **Boijs** of Stanchacher near Whitby, baptizd by J R alias M H: by the Name Jane: the Godfather was John Reynoldson of York, & the Godmother was Ann Wagewood, of Sorefoot.

100. On the 5th of August 1742. The Son of John & Ann **Duck** of Easington, was baptized by J R, alias M H: by the Name Joseph: the Godfather was William Duck, & the Godmother was Elizabeth Saunders.

101. On the 8th of August 1742. The Daughter of John and Helen **Harrison** of Green Houses, in the Parish of Danby (100[a]) was Baptiz'd by J R, alias M H, by y[e] Name of Mary: The Godfather was Thomas Lyth of Cockwoodnuke, and Godmother was Helen Daile of Ugthorpe.

102. On the 10th of August 1742. The Son of Tobias & Isabell **Taylor** of Skelton in the Parish of Skelton near Gisborough, was baptizd by J R, & M H. by the Name John; the Godfather was John Taylor (of *above*) Kilden, & the Godmother Helen Daile.

102.* On the 16th of September 1742. The Daughter of Wil iam & Elizabeth **Roe**, was baptiz'd by J R alias M H: by the Name Elizabeth; the Godfather was (Pierceson *x[d] out*) Ralph Pierceson of Ugthorpe: & the Godmother was Grace Grace Pierceson of Egton, The Child was born at Cockwoodnuk near Ugthorpe.

103. On the 20th of October 1742. The Daughter of Keneth &

* 102 is duplicated. There is a marked change in the writing, with a mistake over Pierceson's name, who although forgiven, seems hardly forgotten.

Elizabeth **McKensie**, of Sands End was baptized by J R, alias M: H, by the Name Mary: the Godfather was William Atkinson (100[b].) of Sands End: & the Godmother was Ann Stangoe, Ibidem.

104. On the 21th of October 1742. The Daughter of Thomas & Sarah **Taylor** of Steaths, in the Parish of Hinderwell, was baptiz'd by J R, alias M H, by the Name Mary: the Godfather was Richard Taylor, & the Godmother was Margarett Camplin, both of Steaths.

105. On the 25th of October 1742. The Daughter of Thomas and Elizabeth **Sayer** of North Loftus, was baptized by J R, & M H, by the name of Mary: the Godfather was Michael Snawdon & the Godmother was Susanna Sayer.

Anno 1743.

106. On the Ninth of January 1743. The Daughter of Thomas & Jane **Wagewood** of Farling Dales in the Parish of Robin Hood's Bay, was baptiz'd by J R, alias M H: the Godfather was Keneth McKensie of Sands End (101[a]) & the Godmother was Phillis Saunderson of Bolby.

107. On the 30th of January 1743. The Son of Cornelius & Ann **Cole** of Staiths in the Parish of Hinderwell was Baptiz'd by J R alias M H, by the name John: the Godfather was J R. alias M H, & the Godmother was Sarah Saunderson of Bolby.

108. On the 27th of february 1743. The Son of William & Ann **Lyth** of Dunsly in the Parish of Whitby, was baptiz'd by J R alias M H, by the Name Thomas; the Godfather was Thomas Lyth, & the Godmother Dorothy Stephenson of Ugthorpe.

109. On the 22[d] of March 1743. Was baptized the Daughter of Richard & Mary **Taylor** of Staiths, in the Parish of Hinderwell, by J R, alias M H, by the name Mary: The Godfather was Thomas Taylor of Ugthorpe, & the Godmother Ann Pierceson of Staiths.

(101 b) 110. On May 20th 1743. The Son of John & Jsabell **Daile** of Skelton by Gisborough was baptized, by J R, alias M H, by the Name John: the Godfather was Robert Daile of Thornborough, & the Godmother was Isabell Taylor of Skelton.

111. On the 8th of December 1743. The Son of David & Dorothy **Sotro** of Upsill near Gisborough, was baptiz'd by J R, alias M H, by the Name David, the Godfather was Robert Rose of Middleton & the Godmother was Elizabeth Mennell of Crathorne.

Anno 1744

112. On January the first—1744. The Son of Robert & Elizabeth **Saunderson**, of Easington Moore Side, was baptiz'd by J R, alias M. H by the Name Robert, the Godfather was Mr Robert Suggett of North Loftus, & the Godmother was Ann Coles of Staiths.

(102[a]) 113. On the 27th of february 1844. The Daughter of John & mary **Lyth** of Cuckwoodnuke near Ugthorpe, was baptized by J R, alias M H, by the name Mary: the Godfather was M[r] Thomas Hodgson of Biggin House, and the Godmother was Hanna Harland by the Moore side.

114. On March the 7th 1744. The Daughter of John & Helen **Harrison** of Green Houses in the Parish of Danby, was baptiz'd by J R, alias M H. by the Name Elizabeth; the Godfather was Ambrose Lyth of How House, & the GodMother was Elizabeth Harrison of Trann Mire.

115. On the third of May, 1744. The Son of Thomas & Sarah **Taylor** of Ugthorpe was baptiz'd by J R, alias M H, by the Name of Thomas; The Godfather was Thomas Galilee, of Ugthorpe; & the Godmother was Ann Hodgson of Biggin House.

(102[b]) 116. On the 11th of May 1744. The Daughter of John & Elizabeth **Hodgson** of the Wall Slack in Fryup, in the Parish of Danby, was Baptized by J R, alias M H, by the Name Mary: the Godmother [*sic*] was Francis Pierceson of Mockerr side, & the Godmother was Elizabeth Proddum of Hankton.

117. On the 10th of July 1744. The Daughter of Henry and Winefride **Stonehouse** of Gisborough was baptized by J R, alias M H, by the Name Sarah, The Godfather was m[r]. Robert Strictland of Richmond, in Richmondshire, Yorkshire, and the Godmother was Ann Pierceson of Gisborough.

118 and 119. On the 27th of August 1744. The Son & Daughter of Robert & Barbara (Harrison *x[d] out*, **Atkinson** *above*), by Ugthorpe, Twins, were baptized by J. R, alias M H: The Boy by the Name (103[a]) John, his Godfather was John Harrison of Green Houses: & his Godmother was Helen Pierceson of Foggot Foot. The Girls Name was Dorothy: and her Godfather was John Lyth of Cuckwoodnuke, & her Godmother was Dorothy Smith of Egton.

120. On the 18th of November 1744. The Son of George & Ann **Shiming**, of Ugthorpe, was baptized by J R, alias M: H, by the name George: The Godfather was Thomas Galilee, & the Godmother was Helen Daile, both of Ugthorpe.

Anno 1745

121. On the 19th of January 1745. The Son of John & Ann **Duck**, of Easington, was baptized by J R alias M H, by the Name (103[b]) Monox, the Godfather was J R. alias M: H, & the Godmother was Elizabeth Ward of North=Lofthouse.

122. On the 3[d] of february 1745. The Son of William & Elizabeth **Roe** of Ugthorpe, was baptized by J R, alias M H, by the Name William: the Godfather was Richard Lyth of Cuckwoodnuke, & the Godmother was Elizabeth Harrison of Tranmire.

123. On the 31st of March, 1745. The Son of Cornelius and Ann **Cole** of Staiths in the Parish of S Hilda's Well, commonly call'd Hinderwell, was Baptized by J.R, alias M H, by the Name of Robert, the Godfather was m[r] Robert Suggett of North Lofthouse, & the Godmother was Elizabeth Saunderson of Easington.

(104[a]) 124. On the 15th of Aprill 1745. The Son of Peter & Dorothy **Garbutt** of Ugthorpe, was baptized by J R, alias M H, by the Name Peter, the Godfather was Luke Galilee Junior, & the

Godmother was Margarett Camplin Unckle & Aunt to ye Child.

125. On the 24th of June 1745. The Son of John & Helen **Harrison** of Green Houses, near Ugthorpe in the Parish of Skelton (or Danby) was baptized by J R, alias M H, by the Name John: the Godfather was J R, alias M H: & the Godmother was Elizabeth Smith of High Hall at Egton Bridge.

126. On July the first, 1745. The Son of William & Mary **Corbutt** of Whitby, was baptized by J R, alias M H, by the Name (104b) William; the Godfather was J R, alias M H. & the Godmother was Jane Garbutt of Ugthorpe.

127.* On the 25th of August 1745. The Son of Ralph & Ann **Shaw**, of Lodge Hill, upon Egton Bridge in the Parish of Egton, was baptizd by J R, alias M H, by the Name Thomas. The Godfather was Thomas White, & the Godmother was Mary White: Both of Egton Bridge.

finis In Yorkshire

[*Mr Hervey starts* '128' on Friday the' & *smudges it out. The rest of the page, and the following one* (105a) *are blank.* '127' *had been originally a duplicate* '126,' *and corrected, probably after the following ones had started* 127.]

(105b) Baptisms & Christenings
Jn
Montgomeryshire
Anno
1747

127. On the 8th of October 1747. The Son of Alexander and Mary **Burnett** of Welch Pool, was baptized by M H, by the Name John: The Godfather was mr William Prichard of Powis Castle; And the Godmother was mrs Catharine Williams, Widow, of Welch Pool. Baptizd at Powis Castle. (1†)

128. On the 11th of November 1747. The Daughter of Samuel **Evans** & Margaret [now unjustly Mary, *in the margin seems to refer to her*] **Walter** of Welch Pool, was baptized by M H, at Powis Castle, by the Name Elizabeth; the Godfather was Edward Matthews, and the (106a) Godmother was Elizabeth Evans, both of Welch Pool. (2)

129. On the 15th of November 1747. Before the Congregation att Buttington Hall. The Son of Edward & Elizabeth **Matthews** of Welch Pool, was baptiz'd by M H, by the Name Monox—the Godfather was M H, and the Godmother was Mrs Margarett Aubin, of the Cross, by Welch Pool. (3)

130. On the 30th of December 1747. At the Dairy by Powis Castle. The Daughter of Thomas and Mary (**Meredith** *above*) of

* '126' has been written and crossed out as a duplicate, evidently after the Montgomeryshire baptisms were started, as they commence with '126.'

† Mr Hervey begins to number his baptisms in Wales in the right hand margins, continuing the serial numbers in the left.

Galva, by Powis Castle, was baptized by M H, by the Name Ann: the Godfather was John Meredith, & the Godmother was M[rs] Catharine Williams, Widow, both of Welch Pool. (4)

(106[b]) Anno 1748

131. On the 26th of January 1748. At Powis Castle, the Son of John & Grace **Meredith** of Welch Pool, was baptizd by M H, by the Name of John: the Godfather was John Meredith, Senior of Galva: & the God Mother was m[rs] Mary Worley, Senior, of the Dairy. (5)

132. On the thirteth (*sic*) of April 1748 I baptized the Son of Samuel & Mary **Possel**, of Welch Pool (by *x[d] out*) was baptized at Buttington Hall by M H, by the Name Monox, the Godfather was M H, & the Godmother, was Margery Jones of Welch Pool. Montgomeryshire. (6)

(107[a]) 133. On the 27th of June 1748, the fifth Son of Thomas & Mary Teresa **Price** of the Hall, in the Town & Parish of LLanfilling, & vulgò pronounced Clanvuckling in the County of Montgomery, (now of the Citty of London *x[d] out*) Esquire, was baptized by M H, of Buttington Hall, by the Name of William, William Hill Esquire of Peperhill in the Parish of [Albrighton] in the of Staffordshire [Salop], was Godfather M H being his Proxy, and the Godmother was Miss Betty Price, Aunt of the said Child, now of the City of London, m[rs] Catharine Williams, Widow, of Welch Pool in y[e] Said of Montgomery being her Proxy. (7)

(107[b]) 134. July 17th 1748, was baptized the Daughter of Edward, & Mary **Owen**, of Welch Pool, by M H, by the Name of Mary: the Godfather was Thomas Morgan, Unkle of y[e] Child, of Welch Pool, & the God Mother was Mary Williams Junior, of y[e] same place. the Child was baptized at Buttington Hall. (8)

135. July 21th 1748, was baptized att Buttington Hall, the Daughter of Samuel & Elizabeth **Evans**, by Powis Castle near Welch Pool: the Godfather was Robert Clarkson of Powis Castle, & the God Mother was Elizabeth Anderton of Welch Pool: the Child's Name was Catharine: baptized by M H. (9)

136. October the 30th was baptized att Buttington Hall, the Daughter of David & Mary **Pew** (by Powis Castle *above*) by M H, by y[e] Name of Catharine; the Godfather was Michael Jones Junior Dregum Reg, & the Godmother was Mary Griffith, of Welch Pool. (10)

(108[a]) 137. On November the third, was baptized 1748, by M H, the Son of Alexander & Mary **Burnett** of Welch Pool by the Name of James, the Godfather was m[r] Christiphor Aubin of Powis Castle, & the GodMother was m[rs] Elizabeth Anderton of Welch Pool. (11)

138. On the 26th of November 1748 was baptized by M: H, the Daughter of Francis & Mary **Plowden** by the Key in Gillsfield Parish, by y[e] Name of Mary, The Godfather was Michael Jones Junior of Dregum Reg, near Welch Pool & y[e] Godmother was Teresy Plowden Aunt to y[e] said Child. (12)

139. On the 28th of August, 1749, was baptized at Welch Pool, The Son of John & Penelope **Lindsey**, by the Name of Henry Augustine, the Godfather was Henry Fox of Retesking Esquire, & ye Godmother was mrs Catharine Langdale; by M H. (13) (5 shill: *in right margin*).

(108b.) Anno 1750

140. On the first of January 1750, at Buttington Hall was baptized the Son of John & Grace **Meredith** of Welch Pool, by M: H, by ye Name of Jinkin, the Godfather was mr William Winn of Myvod, The Godmother was miss Susanna Ruffe, Junior of Welch Pool, in Comitatu Montg.—(14)

141. On the 25 of february 1750 at Welch Pool was baptized by M H. the Daughter of Alexander & Mary **Burnett**, by the Name of Ann, the Godfather was Robert Clarkson of Powis Castle, & the Godmother was Ann Pinnett. (15)

142. On the 11 of March 1750, at Buttington Hall was baptized by M H, the Son of Samuel & Elizabeth **Evans** of Powis Castle; by the Name of Joseph, the Godfather was mr William Prichard of Powis Castle, & the Godmother was [Mary *xd out*] mrs Susanna Ruffe Senior of Welch Pool. (16)

(109a) 143. On the twenty seventh of March 1750 was baptized by M H, the Son of Thomas and Mary **Floyd** of Crowder's Copy, In the Parish of Gillsfield, at Buttington Hall, the Godfather was James Plowd [*sic*] of Crowder's Copy, Unkle to the same Child, & the God Mother was Teresy Plowden of Crowder's Copy, Aunt to the same Child: the Child baptized by the Name of Thomas. (17) [*In margin*—Mortuus est die 3io April 1750]

144. On the first of Aprill 1750 att Buttington Hall, was baptized by M H, the Daughter of Edward & Elizabeth **Matthews** of Welch; the Godfather was Matthew Debalf of Powis Castle, & the Godmother was Ann Pinnet of Welch Pool aforesaid. (18)

145. On Friday the 20th of Aprill 1750, the Son of Edward & Mary **Davis** of Montgomery was Baptized by the Rd mr J. P. S. J,* by the name of Monox; the Godfather was M H, of Buttington Hall in the County of Montgomery, & the Godmother was Margery Jones of Freewmraig by Welch Pool. (19)

(109b) 146. June 19th 1750 was Baptized att Buttington Hall, the Son of Thomas & Mary **Meredith**, of Welch Pool, by M H, by the Name of Thomas, the Godfather was Thomas Ruffe, of Welch Pool (who stood for John Meredith *above*), & the Godmother was Mary Williams Junior of ye same Town. (20)

147. August 24. (1750 *above*) was Baptized the Son of David & Mary **P[ew** *xd out*, **ugh** *above*] of Castle Cryrion by Powis Castle, by M H, by the Name of Monox, the Godfather was M Hervey; & the Godmother was Margery Jones of Freewmraig. (21) (*In right margin*—Dyed Oct 29, 1750).

* Mr Gillow suggests that this is the Rev. John Parker, S.J., who was chaplain at Plowden Hall.

148. September the Eight, 1750 at Welch Pool was Baptized the Daughter of Richard & Margaret **Bellow** of the Parish of Beru, by M H. by ye Name of Judith; the Child was born on the tenth of february, 1750: the father is an Irishman, & the Mother a (? Shrop *x^d^ out*) a Shropshire Woman—the Godfather was Terrence Conorll* of (*letters x^d^ out*) (110^a^) Welch Pool: & the Godmother was Martha Beaton of New Town. (22)

149. October the 24th 1750. att Buttington Hall was Baptized by M H, the Daughter of Terence & Susanna **Conell** of Welch Pool, by the Name of Elizabeth. The Godfather was M H: & the Godmother was Margery Jones, of Freewmraig. (23) (*In left margin,*—Born 22^d^ of October. Died ye 28th of Nov: 1749—*sic.*).

150. November 23^d^ S. Clement, Pope & Martyr, Anno 1750, The Son of Francis & Mary **Plowden** of Guilsfield Parish, near y^e^ Key, was there baptized by M H, by the name of Thomas Clement; the Godfather was M H. of Buttington Hall; the Godmother was Teresy Plowden of the Copy—Aunt to the same Child. (25) (*In left margin,* born Nov. 23^d^)

150. December y^e^ 12: Anno 1750. The Son of Thomas & Jane **Morgan** of Welch=Pool, was there baptized, by M. H, by the Name of Thomas, the Godfather was Humphry Morgan Grandfather to the Child, and the Godmother was Mary Griffith, both of Welch Pool. (24) (*In left margin,*—Born Decem. 7th)

(110^b^) Anno 1751

151. April the 12th 1751. The Son of Alexander & Mary **Burnett** of Welch Pool was Baptized by M H, privately at the Dairy by Powis Castle, by the name of Alexander,—And on y^e^ 13th the Ceremonys of Holy Baptisme were performed on the Child, at Michael (John *x^d^ out,* Jones in *right margin*) of Dre=cwmraig, near Welch Pool, the Godfather was William Owens of Welch Pool: & the Godmother was Martha Beaton of New=Town—of y^e^ same County. (26) (*In left margin,*—born April 11th? Died the 23: of September 1751).

152. May the 17th 1751, the Daughter of Edward & Mary **Owens** of Welch Pool, was baptized at Buttington by M H—by the Name of Helen; the Godfather was Matthew Debaulfe of Powis Castle & the Godmother was Jane Morgan of Welch Pool, Grand Mother of y^e^ said Child. (27) (*In left margin,*—Born May 7th).

153. August 8th 1751. The daughter of Samuel & Elizabeth **Evans** in Powis Park, in the Parish of Guilesfield, was there by M H baptized, by the Name of Ann: the Godfather was Christiphor Aubin of Powis Castle, & the God=Mother was m^rs^ Catharine Langdale of Welch=Pool. (28)

(111^a^) 154. September 2 [4 *over* 3]^th^, The Daughter of Nicholas & Margaret **Pinet** of Welch Pool, was there Baptized by M H, by the Name of Margaret. The God=father was Terence Conell, &

* This may read also Conodl; but in face of the following entry—No. 149—it would seem a mistake.

the Godmother was [? Ann Pinet x^d *out*, Grace Meredith *above*], both of Welch Pool. (29) [*In left margin*,—born 23 of 7 ber]

155. November the first 1751. The Son of Terrence & Susanna **Conell** of Welch Pool, [was baptized *above*], By M Her at Buttington Hall, by the Name of Richard—the Godfather was John Lindsay, & the God=Mother was Ann Pinnet both of Welch Pool. (30) [*In left margin*,—born October 30.]

Anno 1752

156. April the 5th—The Son of John & Grace **Meredith** at Welch Pool, was baptizd by M H: at Buttington Hall, by the Name of Edward, the Godfather was Humphry Morgan & the Godmother was Mary Williams both of welch Pool. (31) [*In left margin*,—born March 31. Dyed May 21, 1752.]

(111b) 157. June the Eleventh, the Son of Susan **Ruffe** Junior, of Welch=Pool, was by M H. at Buttington Hall, by the Name of James. Barnaby—the Godfather was M: Hervey, & the God-Mother was Mary Bellis of Buttington. (32) [*In right margin*,—Born ye same day, about 9 in the morning.]

[*Preparations have been made to add* '158' *and* '33'; *but the rest of this page and all of* p. 112a *are blank. These numbers however equalize for the error at the beginning. Some sheets have been removed up to and including 128a, the continuation of the registers being practically continuous.*]

(128b) Christenings in London District Anno 1753

159. On August the 19th 1753, was baptisd by M H, at his Excellency Count Haslang's Chapple, Warwick Street, the Son of Richard & Catharine **Clark** of the Parish of S. James, by the Name of Edward—the Godfather was William Goldly, & the Godmother was Mary Gilbert, (1 *)

160. On the 30th of September 1753 was baptiz'd by M H, at his Excellency Count Haslang's Chaple, Warwick Street, the Daughter of James & Jane **Dooling**, of the Parish of St Mary Over, Southwork, by the Name of Elizabeth: the Godfather was Christophor Flanagan & the Godmother was Susanna Macdonald. (2)

161. On the Seventh of October, was Baptiz'd at his Excellency Count Haslang's Chaple in Warwick Street, by M H. the Son of John & Mary **Mason** of the Parish of S. Martin in the fields, by the Name of Zachary,—the Godfather was John Monk, & the Godmother was Elenor Fielding. (3)

162. On the Ninth of October 1753, was Ann Sarah the Daughter of William & Elizabeth **Talboys** of the Parish of S. Andrew, Holborn, In Liquorpond Street in Cow Yard, baptiz'd by M H, the God father was Edward Perkin Senior, & the Godmother was Ann Mowbray. (4) [*In right margin*, — Died March 10th 1754.]

* Mr Hervey starts a new series in the right hand margins of his baptisms in the London District.

(129[a]) 163. October 14-1753 was baptiz'd at his Excellency Count Haslang's Chaple, in Warwick Street, Sarah the Daughter of Daniel & Mary **Sullivan**, by M H, of the Parish of S. Martin in the Fields—the Godfather was Patrick Macdonoth, & the Godmother was Sarah Conor. (5)

164. October 20, 1753 was baptizd at his Excellency Count Haslang's Chaple in Warwick Street—Teresia Ann born y[e] 14 of the same month, the Daughter of William & Mary **Standish**, of the Parish of S. George, Hanover Square—The Godfather was Thomas Rome, & the GodMother was Elizabeth Wheeler. (6)

165. November 22, 1753, was baptiz'd by M H. of the Parish of S. James, Mary the Daughter of George & Hannah **Daws**, born y[e] 20th of y[e] same Month—The Godfather was Thomas Murphy, & y[e] Godmother was Mary Carlow — N.B. this is Registerd in warwick Street Chaple.

166. December 3rd 1753. Was baptized in Lincoln Inn fields Chapble Duke Street, by M H, Joseph the Son of William & Mary **Appleby** of y[e] Parish of S. Martin in y[e] Fields—The Godfather was William Moore, & the Godmother was Mary Hoare. (8) [*In left margin*,—born of 25 Nov :]

(129[b]) Anno 1754.

167. February 15th 1754. was baptiz'd by M. H, [the *x[d] out*] Winifride, born feb: 10. The Daughter of George & [Mary *x[d] out*, Ann *above*] **Tomins**,* of y[e] Parish of S. James, Piccadilly, in Edmund's Court, Rupert Street, Soho. The Godfather was M. Hervey, & y[e] Godmother Mary Aires. (9) [*In margins*,—Born [March 24] *smudged out*, feb. 10th. NB. Registered in Warwick Chaple.]

168. March 31. 1754. was baptiz'd by M H, In Tottenham Court Road, in the Parish of S. Pancratius Margarett [D *over* B] oran Champion, the Daughter of Francis & Margarett **Champion**; the Godfather was Michael Doran, & the Godmother was Elizabeth Goran. (10) [*In margins*, Born March 24. N B. Registerd in the Spanish Chaple, Oxford Road.]

169. April 29-1754. was Baptiz'd by M H at the French Chaple Grovesnor's Square, Catharine the Daughter of Timothy & Catharine **Allen**, in the Parish of S. George Hanover† Square; the Godfather was Patrick Jordan; & y[e] Godmother was Helen Walker. (11) [*In margins*,—born April 23. NB. Registerd in the French Chaple, Grovesnour's Square.]

170. June 30, 1754. was baptiz'd [at the french Chaple *above*] by M H, William the Son of William & Mary **Reed**, of y[e] Parish of S. James; The Godfather was Francis Vinn, & y[e] Godmother, was Margarett Musson. (12) [*In margins*, June 30, born 16 of May. NB. Registerd in the French Chaple.]

* For particulars of Rev. Robert Tommins, son of George T. and Anne Gray, *see* vol. xiii, 301.

† Seems written like Hanour.

171. July the 2d 1754, was baptiz'd by M H, John the Son of John & Mary **Ha** [**rv** *or* **w**]**ay**, of ye Parish of S. Giles in the fields: The Godfather was Denis Dunawin, and God [*sic*] was Catharine Kenny. (13) [*In margins,*—July 2d, born May 16. NB. Registerd in the french Chaple.]

(130a) 172. July 17th 1754, was baptizd by M H, Thomas the Son of Matthew & Mary **Rosthorn**, of the Parish of S Luke, burn [hill *above*]* Row by Moor fields. The Godfather was Noah Nason, & ye Godmother was Sarah Bruce. (14) [*In margins,*—born June 15th. NB. Registerd in the french Chaple.]

173. September 13. Anno 1754; was baptiz'd by M H, Charles the Son of James & Elenor **Roberts**, born ye 2d of June eodem Anno, of the Parish of S. Gregory, by S. Paul's Cathedrall, London: The Godfather was Michael Obrian, grandfather to ye said Child: and the Godmother was Ann Smith. (15) [*In right margin,*—Registerd in the french Chaple.]

174. September 28. Anno 1754. was Baptiz'd by M. Hervey Edward Son of Edward, & **Conell**, born ye same Day: of ye Parish of Ann Soho, the Godfather was M. Hervey, & the GodMother was Mrs Lion. (16) [*In left margin,*—obijt Octobris 2do 1754.]

175. October ye 25—Anno 1754. was baptiz'd by M Hervey, Mary Lloyd, the Daughter of William & Hanna **Lloyd**, born on ye 24 of the same Month: of the Parish of S. George, Hanover Square: the Godfather was Antonio Ver [cl *or* d], & the Godmother was Harriott Mussen. (17) [*In r. margin,*—NB. tis Registerd in the french Chaple.]

(130b) 176. November ye 12. 1754. was baptiz'd by M Hervey, Henry Martin Vearpijl, the Son of John & Martha **Vearpijl**, of ye Parish of S. Giles in the fields, born ye 11th of the same Month, the Godfather was Henry Buxton, & the Godmother was Mary Morris. Died Decem 14 following. (18) [*In r. margin,*—NB. Registerd in the french Chaple.]

at London Anno 1755

177. April 15, 1755, was Baptiz'd by M H, Mary the Daughter of Thomas and Mary **Bell**, in New Bond Street, Oxford Road, in the Parish of S. George Hanover Square; the Godfather was Mr Britton of Carnaby Markett, & the Godmother was Jane Williamson, of Shepherd Street, Oxford Road. (19) [*In r. margin,*—Bell. Born April 13. Registerd in the french Chaple.]

178. April 16, 1755. Was Baptizd Brian the son of Brian & Ally **Maguaran**, in Dean Street, Soho; the Godfather was James Twidle & the Godmother was Bridgett Bridge—mortuns est Eodem Die. (28) [*In r. margin,*—Maguaran. Registered in the french Chapel. Born April 16.]

(131a) 179. April 27. 1755. Was Baptizd Mary the Daughter

* Probably Bunhill Row.

of James & Susanna **Twidle**, by M H, the Godfather was Brian Maguaran, & the Godmother was Jane Doyne in Dean Street, Soho. (21) [*In r. margin*,—Twidl. Born April 26. Registerd in the french Chaple.]

180. May 18, 1755. Was Baptizd by M H, Catharine, the Daughter of Michael & Margarett **Lutterell**, in Grey's [Im *x*[d] *out*] Inn Lane, in y[e] Parish of S. Andrew, Holborn—the Godfather was Richard Nowland, & the Godmother was Margarett Hurly. (22) [*In r. margin*,—Lutterell born May 17. Registerd in the french Chaple.]

181. May 20, 1755. was Baptized by M H, Elizabeth, the Daughter of Elizabeth **Winkle**, & **Clavering** — the Godfather was M H, & the Godmother was Jane Elsnere — In Piccadilly in S. James Parish. (22) [*In margins*,—N.B. Registerd in y[e] french Chapel. Winkle Born May 20.]

(131[b]) 182. May 26, 1755. Was baptiz'd by M H, William the Son of William and Elizabeth **Talboys**, in Liquorpond Street, of y[e] Parish of S Andrews Holborn, the Godfather was M H, & the Godmother was Mary Willis. (23) [*In r. margin*,—Talboys, born May 25. Registerd in the french Chapel.]

183. June 13, 1755, was Baptized Richard the Son of Christian **Flinn** & Richard **Byrn**, of Crown Court, King Street, S. James Square. The Godfather was Richard Edwards, The GodMother was Jane Elsner, the Midwife. (24) [*In r. margin*, N.B. Registerd in the french Chaple.]

184. June the 15, 175 [4 *x*[d] *out*, 5 *above*], was Baptized Elizabeth, the Daughter of Terrence & Elizabeth **Lawless**, in Exeter Street by the Strand, the Godfather was Daniel Moore, & y[e] GodMother Elizabeth Creton. (25) [*In r. margin*,—N.B. Registerd in the french Chaple.]

185. June 26, 1755, was Baptized Thomas Monox, the Son of Thomas & Ann **Prime** of Bedford Court, Theobalds. The Godfather was Edward Perkins senior & y[e] Godmother m[rs] Catharine Sloye. (26) [*In r. margin*, — N.B. Registerd in the french Chaple.]

(132[a]) 186. August 19-1755. Was baptiz'd—Sarah the Daughter of Francis Ignatius & Elizabeth **Roberts** in Vine Street by Piccadilly. The Godfather was m[r] John Lewis Cheneley, & the God [*sic*] was m[rs] Sarah La Fountaine. (27) [*In r. margin*,—Registerd in Warwick Street Chaple.]

187. September 8th 1755, was Baptized William the Son of Thomas & Dorothy **Webster** of y[e] Parish of S. Mary La Bone: the Godfather was m[r] John Williamson, & the Godmother m[rs] Ann Bell. (28) [*In r. margin*,—N R, Registered in Warwick Street Chaple.]

188. September 29, 1755, was Baptized Monox the Son of John & Martha **Verpijl** of S. Giles. The Godfather was M[r] Hervey, & the Godmother m[rs] Mary Fowler. (29)

189. October 28, 1755, was Baptized [John *x*[d] *out*] Charles the

Son of John and Winifride **Dod**, the Godfather was William Russel, & Rose Rinkly. (30) [*In r. margin*,—NB. Registerd in the Neapolitan Chaple.]

(132[b]) 190. December 29-1755—was Baptized Clemintina the Daughter of William & Mary **Palmer** — the Godfather was Charles Corbett, & the GodMother was m[rs] Jsabella Cornwell. (31) [*In r. margin*, — NR. Registerd in the Neapolitan Chaple.]

Nota bene all these [four *above*] following till the beginning of January are Misplaced. *

191. December 21-1755—was Baptiz'd Helen the Daughter of Daniel & Mary **Currel**, the Godfather was [*space left*] (32) [*In r. margin*,—NR. Registerd in the Neapolitan Chaple.]

192. On the same also, was Baptized [Maria x^d *out*] Mary the Daughter of Thomas & Mary **Saunders**—the Godfather [*space left*] (33) [*In r. margin*,—NB. Registerd in the Neapolitan Chaple.]

(133[a]) 193. December 23, 1755, was Baptized Charlotta, the Daughter of Charles & Mary **Jackson**, the Godfather was Andrew Moore, & y[e] Godmother was Hanna Vinn. (34) [*In r. margin*.—NB. Registerd in the Neapolitan Chaple.]

194. December 17, 1755, was Baptiz'd Mary Ann, the Daughter of Thomas **Dorson**—the Godfather was Joseph Brown & Mary Colligan. (35) [*In r. margin*,—Registerd in the Neapolitan Chaple.]

[*Blank space for about two more entries.*]

(133[b])† Christnings at London. 1756.

195. January 11. anno 1756—Was Baptized [? Ann x^d *out*] Ann the Daughter of James & Sarah **Madden**—the Godfather [? Th x^d *out*] Timothy Mulbeahy, & the Godmother, Ann Goodess (36) [*In r. margin*,—Registerd in the Neapolitan Chaple.]

196. January 18-1756 was Baptized Catharine the Daughter of Luke & Elizabeth **Plunkett**, the Godfather was James Cod, & y[e] Godmother Martha Cod. (37) [*In r. margin*,—Registerd in the Neapolitan Chaple.]

197. February the first 1756 was Baptizd Bartholomew, the Son of Charles & Elizabeth **Connor**, the God father was Francis Dow[l]and, the Godmother was Catharine Dowland. (38) [*In r. margin*,—Registerd in the Neapolitan Chaple.]

198. February 27-1756, was Baptiz'd Dorothy the Daughter of John & Mary **Smith**, the Godfather was James Maclean, & Godmother was Susanna Blackburn. (39) [*In r. margin*,—Registerd in the Neapolitan Chaple.]

(134[a]) 199. March the first, 1756—was Baptiz'd, Ann, the

* This is written before the four following baptisms, not interlined, ample space being given to the note. There is also space for two more on the following page.

† Pages 133b and 134a (obverse and reverse of one another) are specially blotted, the ink having run through the paper in many cases.

Daughter of James & Catharine **Swaddell**,* the Godfather was Peter Lane, & the Godmother Sarah Sloy. (40) [*In r. margin*,—Registerd at y[e] Neapolitan Chaple.]

200. March 10th 1756—was Baptiz'd Catharine the Daughter of James & Mary **Murphy** the Godfather was Joseph Macdonald, & the Godmother was Elizabeth [*blot*] Murphy. (41) [*In r. margin*, —Registerd at the Neapolitan Chaple.]

201. April the first, 1756—was Baptized Mary the Daughter of William & Ann **Schafs**. The suretys were William Georgij & Ann [K]incend. (42) [*In r. margin*,—Registerd in the Neapolitan Chaple.]

202. April the first, 1756, was Baptized Clementina the Daughter of John & Mary **Craven**—the suretys were Richard Hussey, & Catharine Daly. (43) [*In r. margin*,—Registerd in y[e] Neapolitan Chaple.]

(134[b]) 203. April 2[0 *or* 6] [1756 *above*] was Baptiz'd William the Son of John & Helen **Jrwin** (born 18 of y[e] same Month.) The Suretys were Patrick Savage & Margarett Reiding. (44) [*In r. margin*,—Registerd in the Neapolitan Chaple.]

204. April 30, 1756, was Baptiz'd Alice, the Daughter of Patrick & Alice **Flannigan**. These suretys were—James Tompson & Margarett Standing. (45) [*In r. margin*, —Registerd in the Neapolitan Chaple.]

205. August 28, 1756, was Baptized Ann Tomins (the Daughter of George & Ann **Tomins**) born the tenth of the same Month—The Suretys were—Thomas Drenn & Ulenthy Mackey. (46) [*In r. margin*,—N.B. Registerd in the Spainish Chaple.]

206. September y[e] first 1756 was Baptized Margarett Macdonald (born this day) the Daughter of Alexander & Mary **Macdonald**. The suretys were—John Kenny & Margarett Moore. (47) [*In r. margin*,—NR. Registerd in the Spainish Chaple.]

(135[a]) 237.† September 13, 1756, was Baptized Thomas Lutteral (born August 22 before) the Son of Michael and Margarett **Lutteral**—The Suretys were—Joseph SweetMan & Helen Rauney. (48) [*In r. margin*,—NB. Registerd in the Spainish Chaple.]

[*This ends the baptismal registers of the book, the remainder of the page and pages* 135[b]—176[a] *being blank, but one register on a loose piece of paper* $7\frac{1}{4}$ × 6 *inches, and containing nothing else, is inserted.*]

[n.d] October 1756

Was Baptiz'd; Ann Pennythorne (born 16 of y[e] same Month) of y[e] Parish of S. James, the Daughter of Peter & Elizabeth **Pennythorne**—The suretys were Thomas Pennythorne & Ann Patterson.

* The sirnames commence to be repeated in the left hand margins.

† This number should be 207 following the general series; but 30 numbers are omitted in this last baptismal entry; and curiously enough the number following it to which no entry is made skips 50 more numbers and is 288, whilst the serial number for London—49—is correct.

(Page 176[b])

A
Catalogue
of those reconciled
to the Church
Jn
Oxfordshire
District
by M H
Anno
1729

1. On the 29th of November 1729 M[rs] Sarah **Soul**, of Aston on the Wall Northamptonshire, was re reconciled to the Church, by M H, befor m[r] William Soul, her husband, & Sarah Soul her Daughter.

2. On the 14th of December 1729 Sarah **Hopkins** of Cherrington in Warwickshire, at Chippingnorton in Oxfordshire, was reconcild to the Church by M H, before the whole Congregation of Old Heathrope—Oxfordshire.

(177[a]) Anno 1730.

3. On the 21th of June 1730 M[rs] **Kesketh**,* wife of M[r] Matthew **Hesketh**, of Stonor, was reconciled to the Church by M H, before the whole Congregation at Wattlington Park, in Oxfordshire.

4. On the same Day, & at the same place, was reconcil'd to y[e] Church by M H, John **Willcott** of Britwell, by [Wallingt *x[d] out*] Wattlington Town: Oxfordshire.

Reconciled at
London
1730

5. On the 27th of December 1730 m[rs] Mary **Nightingale**, of London, was reconciled to the Church by M H, before the Congregation at m[r] Gendor's at the fleece & Dove, going into Short's Gardins Drury Lane.

(177[b]) Anno 1731.

6. On the Sixth of January, 173[1 *over* 0], m[rs] Ann **Tuzer** an [a *over* e]ntient Gentlewoman, at m[r] Moor's [,] Gilder, near the Globe Tavern, Fleet Street, was reconciled to the Church, by M: H, on her Death Bed

7. On the 23th of January, 1731, m[r] Joseph **Buckingham** at Essex Stairs in the Strand, was reconciled to the Church, by M H, on his Death Bed.

8 & 9. On the 7th of february 1731 M[r] George & Frances **Creswell** his Wife were reconcil'd to the Church, at m[r] Gendor at the Fleece & Dove in Drury Lane—by M H.

10 & 11. On the 28th of february, 1731, m[r] William **Adams** & m[r] Abraham **Matthews** were reconcil'd to the Church at m[r] Wynell in Little Wild Street—before the Congregation by M H.

* The name is so spelt, but the later spelling of the husband's name seems more likely to be right. Most likely Haskey.

12. On the 4th of April [1731 *above*] was reconciled by M H. to the Church, mr Francis **Sharpe** at mr Wynell in little Wild Street, at ye Muzzled Bear, before ye Congregation.

(178a) 13 & 14. On the 20th of Aprill [1743? *xd out*] 1731 were reconciled by M H, mr **Sterick**, & mrs Ann Talboys, at mr Walker in great Queen Street before the Congregation.

15. On the 24th of Aprill 1731. was reconciled [to the Church *above*] on his Sick Bed, Richard **Warwick**, by M H, at the Last & Hoop Petty Coat, in new Cloath Street Fair, by West Smith.*

16. On the second of May 1731 was reconciled to the Church, Ann **Satchell**, mr Rawlinson's Maid, before the Congregation at mr Walker in Great Queen Street—by M H.

17. On the 17 of June 1731, was reconcild to the Church, Catharine **Coltson** before ye Congregation at mr Blake, Drury Lane—by M H.

18th. On the 18th of June 1731, was reconciled to the Church by M H—mrs **Corbutt** on her Sick Bed, at mrs Salisbury in Cockpitt Ally, & afterwards publickly before the Congregation at mr Blake, on ye 11th of July.

(178b) 20.† On the 27 of June 1731 was reconciled by M H. to the Church Mary **Toopling**, before the Congregation at mr Blake's.

21. On the 14 of July 1731 was reconciled by MH, Alice **Jngram** before the Congregation at mr Blake's.

22. On the 26 of July, [1731 *above*] was reconciled by M H, Elenor **Walter**, at mrs Dudley in Golden Ball Court, Drury Lane on her Sick Bed, which she on the first of August following ratifyd ye same, before ye Congregation at mr Blake's.

23. On the first of August 1741 was reconciled by M H, to ye Church Mary **Willer**, mrs Joburn's Nice [*sic*], before the Congregation at mr Blake's

24. On the 3d of August 1731 was reconcil'd to the Church by M H, on his Death Bed, Alexander **Tompson**, att mr Matthews Peruke maker near Pall Mall—who receivd all ye Holy Rites of the Church.

(179a) 25. On the 5th of September 1731 was reconciled to the Church by M H, Elizabeth **Linniceps**, before the Congregation at mr Blake.

26. Also on the same Day, & same place, was reconciled to ye Church by M H, Elizabeth **Wheeler**.

27. On the 12th of September 1731 was reconciled to ye Church by M H, Mary **Moore**, before the Congregation at mr Blake's.

28. On ye 29 of September 1731, was reconciled, to the Church by M H, at my Lodgings in Red Lion Street, High Holborn, Edward **Potter**, before mrs Orme, mrs Baldwin, & mr Hodges. P.‡

* Query West Smithfield.

† Number 19 does not appear.

‡ P. perhaps for priest.

29. On the 12 of October 1731 was reconciled to the Church, att my Lodgings, mr Robert **Holden.**

(179b.) 30. On the 27 of November 1731 was reconciled to the Church by M H, on his Sick Bed, John **Kelly,** in Bedford Court, by the White Yard, Drury Lane.

Anno 1732.

31. On the [? second x^d *out*], thirtenth of February 1732 was reconciled to the Church by M H, Mrs Margarett **Kennet**, own Daughter to the famous Doctor **Brett**, & Nonjuror Bishop, before the Congregation at mr Blake's. Aged 32, born June ye Eight anno 1700. [*In margin*,—now of 13th of feb.] *

32. On the first of March 1732 was reconciled to ye Church by M H, Richard **Walker**, before the Congregation at mr Blake's.

33. On the 19th of March [now the 30th of March *in margin*] 1732, was reconciled to the Church, by M H, Thomas **Lewis**, at my Lodgings in Red Lion Street.

(180a) 34. On the 30th of Aprill 1732, was reconciled to the Church by M H, Peter **Hulett**, at my Lodgings in Red Lion Street.

35. On the 14th of May 1732, was reconciled to the Church, by M H, John [? E x^d *out*] **Jngram**, an Engraver, at my own Lodgings in Red Lion Street.

36. On the 16th of May 1732, was reconciled to the Church by M H, Margaret **Peg**, at my Lodgings, before Mrs Alice Holland & mrs Ann Trant

37 & 38. On the 17th of July 1732 was reconciled to the Church by M H, John **Elett**, & Elizabeth Elett his Wife at my Lodgings in Red Lion Street.

39. On the 28 of July, 1732, was reconciled to the Church by M H. Elizabeth **Mills**, at my own Lodgings, Red Lion Street.

(180b) 40. On the 29 of July, 1732, was reconciled to the Church by M H, Sarah **Grant**, at my Lodgings in Red Lion Street.

41. On the 18 of September 1732 was reconciled to the Church by M H, mrs Diana **Caverner** att her own Lodgings in Cock Pitt Alley in Drury Lane.

42. On the 11th of December 1732 was reconciled to the Church by M H, on her Death Bed, mrs Ann **Hemings** in S. Bartholomew's Close, mother in Law to mr Bandlow.

43. On the 20th of December 1732 was reconciled to the Church by M H. mrs Susanna **Lee** on her Death Bed in Chancery Lane.

44 & 45. On the 25 of December 1732 were reconciled to the Church by M He, at my Lodgings in Red Lion (181a) Street Mrs **Saunders** & her Daughter, who lived at mr Marshall Cabinet Maker in great Queen Street.

Anno 1733

46. On the first [Now ye 12th *in margin*] of January 1733 was

* The marginal note shews the change means only the eleven days to suit the calendar. Dr Thomas Brett (1667-1743) married Bridget, dau. of Sir Nicholas Toke (*Dict. Nat. Biog.*, vi, 285).

reconciled to the Church by M H, m[r] [James *above*] **Christy**, at my own Lodgings—in Red Lion Street.

47. On the first of february 1733 was reconciled, on her Death Bed, to the Church, by M H, m[r] **Westbrook's** Sister, in great Ormand Street.

48. On the 23[d] of March, was reconciled to the Church by M H, Josias **Bartram**, at my own Lodgings.

49. On the first of Aprill 1733 was reconciled to the Church by M H, Rebecca **Cheshire**, at my own Lodgings.

(181[b]) 50. On the Eight of Aprill 1733 was reconciled to the Church by M H, m[rs] Ann **Bone**; at m[r] Blake's, Drury Lane.

51. On the 17 of Aprill 1733 was reconciled to the Church, by M H, at m[r] Richard Blevin's House in Kentish Town, m[rs] Sarah [? Fris *x[d] out*] **Tristam*** of Bootle in Lancashire, before Rich: Blevin & Jane Blevin his Wife.

52. On the 21 of Aprill, 1733, was Reconciled to the Church by M H, [m[rs] *above*] Susanna **Howard**, at m[r] Blevin's in Kentish Town before M[r] Rich: Blevin, & John [Fri *x[d] out*] Firth of New Inn.

Laus Deo—
Amen

182[a]

Reconciled in Yorkshire.
Now for the
Northern Mission.
Jn nomine Domini

53. On the 16 of June 1734, was reconciled to the Church by J R, Alice **Hoggard**, of Sand's End, near Whitby in Yorkshire, before the Congregation of Ugthorpe.

54. On the 15 of December 1734 was reconciled to the Church by J R, before the whole Congregation at Ugthorpe, Yorkshire, Ursula **Hawkswell**;† who had 24 years before turn'd Protestant, Prosecuted the Priests, viz. M[r] Danby, & m[r] Bostock. the first she gott into York Castle, & the second was forced to fly. She Betrayd all the Grounds & Houses belonging to the Priest of y[e] place & sold them: Made away with all the Altar Stuffe, Goods & furniture of the House and Chaple, & made her Husband (182[b]) turn also Protestant, & breed up her Children in the same way. Yett after all this Mischiefe, Jnjustice & Jll Example, God was so

* Tristram, *see C.R.S.*, vols. vi and ix. In the latter volume some of the Blevins also appear.

† It would be difficult to ascertain how many of the 1755 North Riding Recusants of 1690 (*Hist. MSS. Com.*, ix, part i) survived when Hervey went to Ugthorpe 44 years later. But from Ursula's great age, it may be safe to identify Frank Hawkeswell and Ursula his wife of Ugthorpe. Ursula, wife of Fr. Hawkeswell, was a recusant in Jan. 1680-1 when they were described as of Roxby. Her apostacy and bad conduct must be assigned to an earlier date, before 13 July 1708. If this is not loosely written, it may imply that there were priests' houses (? and chapels) at Egton and Ugthorpe, and that later he refers, in the singular, to one only, *i.e.* to the house and chapel at Ugthorpe.

gracious as to touch her Heart—and on this Day, the third Sunday of Advent, she stood with a Lighted Torch & openly confessing her faults & great Evils, humbly desired to be reconciled to the Catholic, which was done before the People, they crying for Joy, & she for Sorrow of her Crimes & Scandals: she died on the 25th of May following, having receivd all the Holy Rites of the Church: aged four scoare & three. Requiescat in Pace. Amen.

Anno 1735.

55. On the fourth of Aprill 1735 on a Good Friday, was reconciled to the Church by J R, before the Congregation of Ugthorpe, William **Boys**, of Stanekaker ∗ by Whitby.

56. On the 18th of May, 1735, was reconciled to the Church by J R, before the Congregation of Ugthorpe William **Burrel** of [*letters x^{d} out*] Hartipole† in Bishoprick of Durham.

57. On the 19th of May, at Mulgrave Castle,‡ by Leith [? Pi *x^{d} out*] near Whitby, was reconciled to the Church by J R, Catharine **Attkinson**, wife of John Attkinson, of Sands End.

58. On the 18th of July 1735, was reconciled to the Church by J R, before Dorothy Galilee senior at Ugthorpe, & Ann Stonehouse, Jane **Johnson** of Mickleby near Ugthorpe.

59 & 60. On the 7th of August [*figures x^{d} out*] 1735 was reconciled, by J R, Mable **Hill**, Wife of Dyer Hill, a Quaker, of High Ale house, near Ugthorpe.

And also on the same Day at Ugthorpe, was reconciled to the Church by J R, Catharine (183b) **Kell** of Eastraw—Wife of John Kell.

61. On the 17th of August 1735, was reconciled to the Church by J R, Jane **Adamson**, Wife of Martin Adamson senior, of Ugthorpe, before these Wittnesses, Ann Hodgson Widow of Ugthorpe, & Jane Sommersett.

62. On the 19th of October 1735, was reconciled to the Church, by J R, William **Dalton** of Oaklake, before the Congregation of Ugthorpe.

Anno 1736

63. On the 4th of January 1736, was reconciled to the Church, by J R. Mary **Stephenson**, alias **Butterick**, before Ann Stonehouse, & Elizabeth Adamson. On this Woman's account J unjustly was persecuted by some Wicked and Loose Catholicks, whom God forgive.

64. On the twelveth of December 1736, was Reconciled to the Church by J R, before the Congregation of (184a) Ugthorpe Ralp **Pierceson**, (Pray good Reader take notice of this Yorkshire Chap) Late Constable of Ugthorpe, from this time to December

∗ Probably Stainsacre.

† Hartlepool.

‡ Mulgrave Castle, as a castle, had been destroyed by the parliamentarians; but there would be some habitable parts, and I understand a number of more or less poor persons dwelt there. The name of Thomas Smith is mentioned elsewhere as a resident.

1745, he behaved himself Exceedingly Well, & was very good & Regular, & not singular. His Wife dyed in Childbirth, & left him five small Children, I tookt one Boy from him, named Jacob, & breed him up: gave both the Boy & father Cloaths, & mony to keep him from starving, & married him for nothing to a good Careful Catholick. But in the year, 1745, when the troubles happened in Scot Land, this my Saint turnd Tail, & swore against me: & became y[e] main Evidence against [me] at York Castle. He swore Enough to hang all the Priests in the Kingdom: as to their functions: and all this in hopes of getting a Reward, which was at Last but Shame and Confusion. God Pardon him: I freely forgive him.

(184[b]) 65. On the same Day y[e] 12th of December 1735, at Ugthorpe was reconciled to the Church, by J R, Elizabeth **Burrell*** of William Burrell; before y[e] Congregation of Ugthorpe.

66. On the 19th of December 1736 was reconciled to the Church by J R, before the Congregation of Ugthorpe, Robert **Saunderson** of Easington Parish by North Lofthouse.

67. On the 27th of December 1736 was reconciled to the Church by J R, Mary **Saunderson**, of Easington Parish, and Sister to Robert Saunderson, before the Congregation, at North Loftus.

Anno 1737

68. On the 12th of Aprill, was reconciled to the Church, by J R, Catharine **Leith**, of Whitby, before the Congregation of Ugthorpe.

(185[a]) 69. On the fifth of June, att North Lofthous, was reconciled to the Church, by J. R, m[rs] Ann **Coulson** of Billsdale by Stoxley, whom the fallen & Apostate Franciscan Fryer Watson of Osmotherly had preverted, and deluded under Pretence of Piety: But after three Years Wandering, she on this Day, before the Congregation of North Lofthouse, returned to the Sheepfold of Jesus Christ, & was by me received into the Bosome of the Catholick Church.

70. On the 12th of November 1737, was reconciled on his Death Bed, by J R, William **Carter**, Miller, & Constable of North Lofthouse, before his Wife, & father in Law, Carter.

71. On the Seventh of December 1737, was reconciled to the Church, by J R, at Stockton, Bishoprick (185[b]) of Durham, m[rs] Elizabeth **Grainge**, Wife of m[r] Ralph Grainge, Brewer & Maltster, at his own House, before M[r] William (now Sir William†

* An omission is evident.

† A Catholic priest was most unlikely to be knighted in those days! The remaining implication is that Mr Anderson had succeeded to a baronetcy. After a fruitless search, I consulted Mr Burke, Norroy King, who solves the point by saying,—'The baronetcy of Anderson of Penlay, co. Herts, created in 1643, became extinct in 1699; but was assumed by several people of the name of Anderson up to the middle of the eighteenth century, and your Sir William may have been a member of this family of claimants.' This paper shews that he had not assumed the title in 1747 when the priests were liberated, but his death is recorded

Anderson, & her husband m[r] Grainge: when she made this Profession of Faith.

I Elizabeth Grainge, do with a firme Faith, & Steadfast Beliefe, Confess, Acknowledge, Receive and Believe all the Articles of Faith of the Holy, Apostolick, & Catholick Church, which have been taught in all Ages, & which She now teaches: And I do renounce, reject & Condemne all Heresys & Schismes [to the *x[d] out*] Contrary to the said Faith; And in this faith, God willing, I will live & dye. So help me God, & these Holy Gospells. Amen:

On the tenth of December, she made to me a general Confession, & received from me the Blessed Eucharist. Deo Gratias.

(186[a]) Anno 1738.

72. On the 26th of March 1738 was [received *x[d] out*] reconciled to the Church, by J R, Francis **Pierceson** * of Common Dale Side, in Danby Parish, before William Wilks, Margaret Crosby, Charles Attkinson & James Atkinson att Ugthorpe.

73. On the 27th of June 1738 [I brought *x[d] out*] was reconciled to y[e] Church by J R, Kennet **machezie** of Sand's End, before these Wittnesses, William. Unthunkt senior, William Atkinson, Elizabeth Atkinson, & Mary Atkinson.

74. On the 29th of June 1738 was reconciled to the Church by J R, Dorothy **Souter** of Upsill, near Gisborough, before [? Alban *smudged*, Alban *in margin*] Sayer, & [Bridgett Lune *smudged*, Bridgett Lane *above*].

(186[b]) 75. On the 29th of October 1738 was Reconciled to the Church by J R, George **Shiming**, of Ugthorpe, before these Wittnesses, Ralph Pierceson, Thomas Garbutt, Jane Garbutt &c.

Anno 1739.

76. On the 17th of June 1739, was reconciled to the Church, by J R, Thomas **Wagewood** of Falling Row, † by Robin Hood's Bay, before William Wilks, & William Boys. Trinity Sunday.

Anno 1740

77. On y[e] 16th of Aprill, Easter Sunday, was reconciled to the Church by J R, M[rs] Ann **Eldin**, Wife of Tho: Eldin of Ingleby Green How, by Stoxley, before the Congregation of Ugthorpe.

78. On the 20th of July 1740, was reconciled to the Church by J R, Jane **Wagewood** of Fareland Dales, ‡ By Robin Hood's

as Sir William in *C.R.S.*, xii., 9, on 28 Aug. 1759, and in *Mugrave's Obituaries*, i., as a baronet, on the previous day. A material point to these registers would be fixed by the time of assumption, as they must have been written, in their existing form, after it.

Mr Gillow says this William Anderson was a native of York diocese, and came to the mission in Yorkshire from Valladolid in 1733.

* Peason, Pairson, Peirson and Person are indexed in Danby registers (*Yorks. Par. Reg. Soc.*, xliii.); but never as given by Hervey. Pearson is given in connection with Francis about the time.

† Probably Row, a hamlet, in Fylingdales parish. See second entry following.

‡ This must be Fylingdales parish. See second entry above.

Bay, before (187[a]) these Wittnesses, Thomas Wagewood her Husband, Francis Wagewood, & Elizabeth Harrison of Egton Banks.

79. On the second of November 1740 was reconciled by J R, m[rs] Ann **Meller** of Scarborough, before these Wittnesses, Christiphor Simpson [of *x[d] out*] senior, And Ann Hodgson, Widow, both of Ugthorpe.

Anno 1741

80. On the 6th of January 1741 was reconciled to the Church by J R, m[rs] Elenora **Meller** of Scarborough, before her Daughter Ann Meller, and Elizabeth Adamson, at Ugthorpe.

81. On the 3[d] of february 1741 was reconciled to the Church, by J R, Elizabeth Daughter of (187[b])* **Clerk** of Northlofthouse, before the Wittnesses, m[rs] Mary Suggett & George Nellish. At North Lofthouse.

82. On the same Day, & at the same Place, & before the same Wittnesses was reconciled to the Church by J R, George **Battersby** of NorthLofthouse.

83. On the first of October 1741 was reconciled to the Church by J R, at Ugthorpe, m[r] William **Cotterell**, Peruke Maker & Hair Cutter, Curler & Dresser at Scarborough.

Anno 1742.

84. On May the second 1742 was reconciled to the Church by [the *x[d] out*] J R, on his Death Bed, George **Harland** of the Moorside by Egton Town: before John Leith.

Anno 1745.

85. On the 18th of March 1745 was reconciled to the Church by J R. [*letters x[d] out*], m[rs] Jane **Readhead** (188[a]) of Scarborough, before these Wittnesses, m[rs] Readhead her Mother, M[r] Henry Readhead, & m[r] Stephen Readhead her brothers—at Scarborough.

86. On y[e] 19th of March 1745, was reconciled at Scarborough, Madam **Fowler**, before m[rs] Maltby of y[e] same Place—by J R.

87. On the same Day, & att y[e] same Town of Scarborough was reconciled to the Church by J R, m[rs] Ann **Dobby**, Daughter to m[rs] Readhead, Widow, before her Mother, & sister Jane Readhead.†

Now Adieu to the Wild & ungrateful Moors of Yorkshire, where the Catholicks wuuld not shelter their Priests; & so he was forced

* Presumably the Christian name omitted. I treat *Clerk* as a sirname, not as *a clerk* or *the clerk*.

† At the Quarter Sessions held at Brompton, 8 Sept. 1746, it was 'Ordered that Henry Readhead, Stephen Readhead, mercers, John Loveday, bookseller, Lovel Readhead, inholder, William Cockerill, barber, all of Scarborough, and Thomas Dunning of Goathland, yeoman, be discharged of their recognizances, which they undertook, they being all Papists; Ordered that Christopher Maltby of Scarborough, barber, recognizances be estreated, as also George Masterman's one of his manucaptors, unless the said Christopher Maltby be and appear at the next Sessions at Thirsk.' (*N.R. Yorks. Records,* viii., 258.) These bail taken for the appearance of the above may almost certainly be ascribed to Monox Hervey's attendance at Scarborough.

to be taken on ye 10th * of December 1745, & sent to York Jail or Castle, where

Anno 1746

88. On the 18th of January 1746. Thomas **Wells**, a Debtor Prisoner was on his Death Bed reconciled to the Church, by J R, before these Witnesses, Ralph Atkinson, & Matthew Ibetson.

Anno 1747

89. On ye 18th of Aprill, 1747, was reconciled in York Castle to the Church, by J R, Daniel **Ross**, one of the HighLanders, before John Beatton & William Crosby, the said Daniel Ross was soon after transported with 39 other HighLanders.

And now out of that terrestial Purgatory, after 18 Months Jmprisonement, J R, fell to work again & therefore—

90. On the 26th of June 1747, was m^r Lovel **Readhead** of Scarborough, reconciled to the Church, by J R, before his Mother, Brothers & Sister Jane: at Scarborough.

Now farewell Bonny
Yorkshire.

(189^a) Montgomeryshire 1749.

91. On the 25 of May 1747, James **Parker** of Shrewsbury, was reconciled to the Church by M H, on Corpus Christi Day: before these

Wittnesses—Michael Jones, junior; mary bellis; Elizabeth + Hannis her Mark; Jerom + Whitefield his Mark.

92. On the 14th of August 1749, was Martha [? Bet *x^d out*] **Beatton** was reconciled to the Church by M Hervey, before these Wittnesses,—Mrs Cecily Worley of Welch Pool; Mrs Prudence Lewis [,] Ibiden]; Mrs Frances Aubin, Buttington Hall.

Mrs Beaton then lived at New Town, in Montgomeryshire.

Anno 1750

(189^b) 93. April the 13th on a Good Friday, 1750, Mary **Plowden**, wife of Francis Plowden of the Key,† was reconcild to the Church by M H, before these Wittnesses—mary bellis; Francis Reynolds.

94. On Easter Tuesday April 17-1750, Richard **Bellis** of Powis Castle, was reconciled to the Church by M H, before these Wittnesses‡—Francis Reynolds & Elizabeth Hannis &c.

95. On the 24th of June 1750. Mary **Troy** of the Township of Meesbury in the Parish of Oswestry in Shropshire, was reconciled to the Church, by M H, before these Wittnesses†—Elizabeth Hannis, & James Powel &c.

[96 *is written in the left margin but nothing against it and nearly half the page and* 190^a *are blank.*]

* This is given elsewhere more circumstantially as the eleventh.

† Probably New Quay or Pool Quay.

‡ These witnesses do not sign.

(190[b]) Reconciled in London District
Anno 1753

97. October the second [1753 *above*], was Reconcil'd to the Church Elenor **Clarkson** [**Clark** *in margin*] by M H. at her Lodgings in Turk head Yard, in Tumble Street, by Clarkenwell, before his Husband William Clarkson—Natali Jpsius. (1)*

98. October the third, 1753, was Reconciled to the Church, by M H, Jane **Dooling**, at her house in Fountain Ally by Horse Shoe Stairs, in the Parish of S. Mary Over,† Southwork, before her Husband James Dooling & Phebe [*letter x[d] out*] Kenyson. (2)

99. October 26. 1753, was reconciled to the Church by M H, at his Lodgings in Oxford Road, Elizabeth **Talboys**, of y[e] Parish of S. Andrew's, Holborn, Cow Yard Liquor pond Street; before these Wittnesses‡ John Wools Junior & Stephen Woolls. (3)

100. November 5th 1753 was Reconciled to the Church by M H. John **Willis** of Ward's Rent by Hatten Wall, before these Wittnesses—Matthew Debalfe,§ Jane Christie, & Mary Willis. (4)

101. December 10—1753 was Reconciled on his Death-Bed, John **Bowdenser** a Swiss, in Short Gardins, by Drury Lane, by M H,—before this Wittness—Thomas Rome. (5)

(191[a]) 102. January 20—1754. Receivd into y[e] Church by M Hervey, at her Lodgings in Warwick Street, Golden Square, Margarett **Hover**, before these Wittnesses: Valentine Hover, her Husband & Mary Deginn. (6)

103. January 30. 1754. Receivd into the Church by M H, Martha **Moore**, at her House in Ward's Rents by Hatton Wall, before—Mary Willis, her Mother. (7)

104. February 24. 1754. Richard **Nixon** was Received into the Church by M H. at his Lodgings in Oxford Road, before Elizabeth Nixon his own sister. (8)

105.‖ March 24. 1754. Were Receiv'd by M Hervey, M[rs] Rhoda **George**, and M[rs] Jane [*two attempts x[d] out*] **Bawdon** own Sisters, of Church Lane, by Saint Martin's in the field. (9 & 10)

106. September the 23. Anno 1754. was Receiv'd into the Church by M Hervey, Mrs Margarett **Daugherty**, at Whittengton & Cat, in Cross Lane, by Newton Lane, Holborn. (11)

(191[b]) 107. October the 16th 1754 was Receiv'd into the Church by M H, Ann **Parsons** one of Mrs Vendercome's Boarders. by Barwick Street, Soho—Ætatis 13. (12)

108. October 21. Anno 1754 was Receiv'd into the Church by M H, Ann **Schaffe** in Shepherd Street, Oxford Road. (13)

* Serial number for London.

† St Mary Overy, Southwark.

‡ Witnesses do not sign here or afterwards.

§ Perhaps the same who appears at Powis Castle earlier.

‖ Hervey only gives one number in the full series.

109. November 12. 1754—Was Receivd into the Church by M H, Susann **Coshone** before Margaret Huebert. (14)

110. December 22[d] 1754. was Receiv'd into Chureh, by M H, Charlotta **Langley**, before Valentine & Margarett Huebert, & Antonetta Tompson. (15)

111. December the Ninth, 1754. Was Received into the Church by M H, Elizabeth **Tye**, before m[r] Tye her Husband & m[r] Richard Freeman. [*In margin*,—NB. Omitted in its Proper Place] (15)

Anno 1755.

112. February 18th 1755, Eshter **Pentony** was brought into the Church by M H, of Great Wild Street, Drury Lane, before Ann Dougherty and Jane Dougherty. (16)

(192[a]) 113. March the 10th 1755. Elizabeth **Culheth** was Reconcilied & brought into the Church by M H, in Swallow Street, Piccadilly, before William Culheth her husband. (17)

114 & 115. March the 16, 1755, were brought into the Church by M H, m[r] Thomas **Prime**, & mrs Ann **Prime**, of Bedford Court, Theobald's Row: before mr Edward Perkins. (118 & 119)

116.* March 20th—1755, was brought into the Church by M H, Richard **Rook**, before mrs Sarah Heneritta Ann Bruce. (20)

176. May 4th was brought into y[e] Church by M H, Phillis **mitchell** before mr Richard Freeman & Ursula Beesly. (21)

177. May the 15, 1755, was brought into the Church by M H, Margarett **Flannigan** of Prince's Square, near Little Queen Square, before Mary Woolls, Senior & Jane Williamson, Senior. (22)

(192[b]) 178. May 16. 1755. was brought into the Church by M H, Hanna Mary **Mobbison**, of New bond Street—before mrs Jane Williamson Senior. (23)

179. May y[e] 30, 1755, was brought into the Church, by M H, michael [? Bourke *x[d] out*, **Bourn** *above*] at y[e] Hanch of Venison, Oxford Road. (24)

180. July y[e] first, 1755—was Reconcilied by M H, Sarah **Levy**, at m[rs] Fannigan's, Cavendish Street, Oxford Road. (25)

181. August 10th 1755, was Reconcilied by M H, Ann **Forester**, of New Street, by great Russel Street, before these Wittnesses, Dominick Fannin, Edward Fullum, & Mary Harbin. (26)

182. September 29 [*figures x[d] out*] 1755, was Reconcilied by M H, Ann **Conor** of S. Martin's Lane, before Charles Conor her Husband, & mr Chaple. (27)

183. December 15, 1755, was Reconcilied by M H, m[rs] Elizabeth **Holden**—before M[r] Buxton & his servant. (28)

(193[a]) Reconcilied in London 1756

184. January the 24th 1756 was Reconcilied Elizabeth **Anson**, before m[rs] Anson her Mother in Law.† (29)

* This may have been 176 but it will be noticed that the next number is certainly 176 shewing 59 numbers left out.

† The first *Douay Diary* (p. 78) records the birth of the Rev. Joseph Anson of the London diocese on 10 June 1753, his parents being Joseph Anson and Mary Blackburn. The omission of Christian names above is often unfortunate.

185. March 11. 1756. was Reconcil'd Ann **Miles**, before David Might. (30)

186. March 15. 1756. was Reconcilied Mary **Ward** senior, before Mary Smith by Aldergate. (31)

187. March 16, 1756, was Reconcilied Henry **Ash** before Helen Obrian. (32)

188. March 18, 1756, was Reconcilied Dorothy **Davis**, before Richard Cooper her Master. (33)

189. April 4. 1756. was Reconciled Agnes **Miles**, before David Might, & Thomas Rome. (34)

(193[b]) 190. April 11. 1756, was Reconcilied Jane **Bateman**, before M[rs] Beesly. (35)

191. April 19, 1756, was Reconcilied Mary **Ward** senior. (36)

192. September 7th 1756, was Reconcilied Mary **Ward** Junior. (37)

193. October the 20-1756—were Reconcield Mother & Son, Ann & John **Maijs**. (38 & 39)

[*Half the page is blank, as well as* 194[a] –136[a], *which complete the book, except the following written in the book reversed.*]

(235[a]) A / List of my Penitents—att & in London / 1753 / In Alphabetical Order. / A [*ends*]

(229[a]) M[r] James **Gregson**, in three Tun Court, in Red Cross Street, Cripple Gate—London—the first who came to me August 19—1753.

No. IX

OFFICIAL DOCUMENTS SUPPLEMENTING REV. MONOX HERVEY'S REGISTER

CONTRIBUTED BY JOSEPH S. HANSOM

THE following documents are from the North Eastern circuit records at the Record Office, London, and were selected to illustrate the register of the Rev. Monox Hervey, or as he appears in Yorkshire—John Rivett. The letters are not complete, but I could find none of the other fourteen mentioned in Hervey's examination, and there would seem to have been some of Anderson's beside those produced.

They consist of depositions or informations, and examinations relating to Hervey, Anderson and Potts; whilst some refer to the two Misses Metcalfe of Guisbrough, compromised by being the vehicle for passing school money to Hervey; and an account of Edward Clavering's marriage in York Castle, by his wife, &c. The index will give the necessary references between the documents and the registers.

The arrangement has not been easy, some overlapping others, chronological order not being always possible or advisable. An endeavour has been made to group them. J. S. H.

(1) THOMAS DAWSON'S INFORMATION AGAINST REV. MONOX HERVEY

The Information of Thomas Dawson Master & Marriner of Lythe in the County of York.

This Deponent saith, that about ten days ago Robert Stango of Ugthorpe said in [his house *x^d-out*, Whitby *above*] that there had been lately at divers times with Mr Rivett at his house in Ugthorpe several persons well dress'd & suppos'd to be Gentlemen, and that divers other persons had frequented the house of the said Rivett from 10 till 12 a clock at night suppos'd to be papists living in that Neighbourhood, And this Deponent further saith that he was informed in his own house last night that four Gentlemen dress'd in Lac'd Cloths had been lately seen at the House of the above said Mr Rivett.

Sworn at Whitby in the North Riding of the County of York 11th of Decr 1745 before me Robert Linskill — Tho Dawson

[*Endorsed*] Tho: Dawson's Deposition against Rivet Dec. 11 1745 before R. Linskil Esq.

(2) THOMAS BIRKETT'S INFORMATION AGAINST REV. MONOX HERVEY.

North Riding Yorkshire — Thomas Birkett of Whitby in the parts aforesaid mercer one of ye people comonly called Quakers Deposeth that he knows the person living at Ugthorp in the said parts who is comonly called Mr Revit Saith that he hath received several Letters from the said Mr Revit and y^{t} Indorsements on three several Letters now produced and shewn to this Deponent in the words and figures following to wit, November 13th 1745 Apud Jnsulam patmos [& marked Luke Cooper *above*], November ye 5th 1745 Apud Jnsulam patmos &—November 26. 1745 Apud Jnsulam patmos, all wch said three Jndorssments this Deponent has compared with one of the Letters which this Deponent lately received from the said Mr Revit and according to Deponents Judgement from comparing the said Jndorsements with the said Letter now in this Deponents custody he believes the said several Jndorssments to be all of the said Mr Revits hand writing

Affirmed at Whitby aforesaid T. Birket
ye 14th December 1745 Before
me— R[obt] Linskill

[*Endorsed*] Birkits Deposition ag^{t} Rivet—Dec. 14. 1745 before R: Linskil Esq.

(3) THE EXAMINATION OF REV. MONOX HERVEY

North Riding of the County of York } The Examination of John Rivet of Ugthorpe in the said Riding taken this 16th day of December 1745.

This Examinant saith, That he this Examin^{t} is a Priest in Orders of the Roman Catholic Religion, and that he hath for about the Space of Eight years kept and Still keeps a Boarding School at Ugthorpe afores^{d} for the Education of Children of the Romish Religion, and that he this Examin^{t} hath at this time Ten Boys of the said Religion boarded in his House for the purpose afores^{d}—Also this Examin^{t} doth Acknowledge, that the ffourteen Several Letters now shewn to him, and mark'd or numbred as follows, to wit, (N° 1) (N° 2) (N° 3) (N° 4) (N° 5) (N° 6) (N° 7) (N° 8) (N° 9) (N° 10) (N° 11) (N° 12) (N° 13) (N° 14) were all found in this Examin$^{t's}$ Custody, and that the words indorsed on the said Several Letters, purporting to be the Several dates thereof, with this addition (apud Insulam Patmos) are respectively of his this Examin$^{t's}$ own Handwriting. And upon being asked whether he would take the Oaths to the Governm^{t} or subscribe the Declaration against Transubstantiation, he this Examin^{t} Said, that he could not upon account of his Religion.

This Examination taken John Rivett
the day and Year aboves^{d}
Before us Cho: Turner
M: Consett
Ra: Robinson
Tho: Skottowe

[*Endorsed*] Mr Rivet's exam^{n} Dec. 16, 1745, York Castle

(4) ROBERT SUGGETT TO REV. MONOX HERVEY

Sr Lofthouse—4th Novemb. 1745

Yo^{rs} J Rec^{d} at 10° Clock as J was going to Gisbrough.

J did not see David Souter this day he was gone before J got in but I sent a line or two to him to desire him to go as soon as possible after Wednesday to M[r] Witham * to Stockton to get what money he can for you, and to bring or send it to you or me out of hand; but as for the horses there is nothing to be done about them yet until there be some blows struck. Which is expected in a small time; for all our forces are Drawing down to face them †—J am told this day by one that hath been down in Northumberland that they have had several Catholick Gentlemen up there, and would have had them to have Promised [not *above*] to take up Arms Against George but they would not, so that its thought they be imprisoned.

R.S.

[*Endorsed*] November y[e] 5th 1745. Apud Jnsulan Patmos. (N° 7)—M[r] Sugits letter — Nov[r] 5th 1745

(5) ROBERT SUGGETT TO REV. MONOX HERVEY

S[r] Gisbrough 25th 9[br] 1745

This day I have Rec[d] at M[rs] Metcalfs five pounds thirteen shillings and six pence which J have sent you by Jane Pinder which J hope will Come Safe to hand. Also you have M[r] Withams Lett[r] Jnclosed so that you[l] see what he sayth about the Rest. J fear you[l] not be able to read it wh[ch] is all in haste‡ from

S[r] Yo[r] Most Humbl Ser[t]
Rob[t] Suggett

[*Endorsed*] November 26, 1745. Apud Jnsulam Patmos. M[r] Suggets Lre to M[r] Rivet, 25 Nov. 1745 (N° 8).

[*Addressed*] To M[r] Rivet.

(6) BISHOP DICCONSON TO REV. MONOX HERVEY

Sir Wycliff 12 Nov: 1745

This is only to acquaint you that the bearer hereof Mr Luc Potts is to be your neighbor at Egton in the Place of Mr Liddell. You are desired to introduce him there, and acquaint him with particulars; and to let him know, what moveables are there for his use, and what may be there still, belonging to the said Mr Liddell. You will find great satisfaction in so good a person near you, w[ch] is a pleasure to

D[r] Sir

Your most humble servant
Ed Eaton

[*Endorsed*] Ed: Eaton to M[r] Revet, No. 1° 1745. (N° 9) [*and*] November 13th 1745. Apud Insulam Patmos. The same Day came M[r] Luke Cooper.

[*Address* outside] To / M[r] Rivett at / Ugthorp.

* The Rev. William Witham of Stockton-on-Tees.

† This reads like facetlem, but I think *h* and *e* have been run into one another.

‡ There is nothing to call for this remark, the writing being quite legible.

(7) REV. WILLIAM WITHAM TO ROBERT SUGGETT

Mr Suggett Stockton Novr 25th 1745

Sr J Reced yrs & a bill for Ten pounds on Mr Calvert wch J fear will be a hard Matter to get at Present, but have Sent ye bill to a Frd & if it can be gote he will gete it. J had Sent a letter to gete ye Eight pounds but J beleave it Never gote to his hand as yete. J have Send to Mrs Metcalfe 5l 13s 6d, wch came from Mrs Maire last Wednesday and Shall Send [*torn*] as it comes to hand. my Service to Mr Rivet [*torn*].

Sr y most Hum Serv
Wm Witham

[*Endorsed*] W. Witham to Mr Sugit about M Calverts Bill, Nov. 25, 1745—November 26, 1745. Apud Jnsulam Patmos. (No 10)

[*Addressed*] To Mr Robert Suggett at Loftus to be left wth mrs Metcalfe. In Gisbrough with 5lb. 13. 6.

(8) JOHN CORNFORTH TO REV. MONOX HERVEY

Mr Revitt Stokesly Novr 8th 1745

Sr

As J have not heard from you since J wass att Ugthorp J have made bold to give you the trouble of these Jnclosed in one for Mr Suggett. J Could have been glad to have heard whether the Chappell Clock be as Yett free from the damp, and Jf so; Could order my man to Call to Sett her Striking Parts to work. I design to send him to Lofthouse next week, not being allowd to go so far from home My self.* I have all the materells belonging to the oven Reddy and only waite your Orders for sending them not knowing whether you would have them directed in your *name or not.*

Sr I desire you would be so kind as to send me 5£ or 6£ pound att the first opportunity Jf you Possibly can —for as J am debar'd from going from home to look after buisiness and our Neighbouring Gentlemen are So malicious against Catholicks that Where J Use'd to get much Buisiness is at Prisant Jntirely turn'd out and where J have Bills due instead of having them answer'd, Meets with no other Return but the Vilest Redicule—Which has Jnfors'd me to desire the above favour and hopes as you are of a better way of thinking to meet with a friend which at this time will be a great Relief—to Sr Your Most humh servt

John Cornforth

[*Endorsed*] November 13, 1745. Apud Jnsulam Patmos. (No 4). Cornforth's lre to Rivet.

[*Addressed*] To / Mr Revitt / Ugthorp.

* John Cornforth, clockmaker, seems to have had illness in his family at this time as the parish registers of Stokesley shew he buried a son John on 16 May 1746, his wife Mary on 15 July 1747, and a daughter Mary on 17 July 1747. (*Yorks. Par. Reg. Soc.*, vii, 242, 246.) It is clear that was a Catholic, and so precluded from going five miles from his house, whereas he might send a Protestant workman.

(9) RALPH PEARSON'S OR PIERCESON'S INFORMATION AGAINST REV. MONOX HERVEY

North Riding of the County of York } The Information of Ralph Pearson of Ugthorpe Weaver taken upon Oath before me the 7th Day of July 1746.

This Jnformant saith that he has known M[r] John Rivitt Ten years and upwards, that y[e] said John Rivit was a popish priest and officiated as such at a Chappel in Ugthorp kept for that purpose in the parish of Ugthorp in this Riding, where he this Informant (being [then *x[d]-out*] a papist) frequently Resorted with Several other Roman Catholicks, and that the said M[r] John Rivit having a Book before him, did read to the Congregation in an Unknown Tongue, at least unknown to this Informant. He further saith that at times when y[e] said John Rivit administred y[e] Sacrament to them, in the said Chappel, he has seen him take what they Call the wafer in both Hands with his back to y[e] people and held it Above his head, And after that a Cup, in the Same manner [at y[e] same time *x[d]-out*, presently after *above*] Speaking a few words in Latin or some other Language that this Informant does not understand. He further saith that after the Elevation of the wafer in the manner he has declared, he has Seen the said John Rivit take of the said wafer, and Drink of the Cup to the best of his knowledge, and has also seen him give the wafer to the people, that his Custom was to lay it upon the Comunicants Tongue, Speaking Some words at the Same time, but not understood by this Informant, He further saith that during y[e] time of administring the Sacrament the said M[r] John Rivet had sometimes one sort of Cope or Vestment upon his Sirplice and Sometimes another, and that he this Informant did Receive the Sacrament at y[e] hands of the said M[r] John Rivit in the manner aforesaid at Easter in 1745 in the said Chappel, and was at prayers there when y[e] said M[r] Rivit officiated about Latter Lady Day w[h] is the 8th* of September, or about that time, being the last time that this Informant was at y[e] said Chappel; and that at Diverse times before he has Received the sacrament after y[e] aboves[d] manner from y[e] said John Rivit, This Informant saith that it has been the Common Report in his Neighbourhood that the s[d] M[r] Rivit Came from Yarmouth or a place near it, Call'd Goulston,† and saith that of his own Knowledge he has Kept a School for y[e] Education of youth, and that they were said to be children of Roman Catholicks, And further saith not.

Taken and Sworn the day & year above s[d] before me
Cho Turner

The Mark of
Ralph × Pearson

[*Endorsed*] 7 July 1746 Ralph Pearson's Informac'on ag[st] Rivett.

* The Nativity of Our Blessed Lady. This description seems unusual, or is at any rate new to me.

† Gorlestone. It was this clue which enabled me to obtain the baptismal certificate of baptisms of Monox Hervey and his sister Elizabeth.

(10) PRESENTMENT BY JURY AGAINST REV. MONOX HERVEY

July 21st 1746 putts not guilty

Yorkshire to wit—The Jurors of our Lord the King upon their Oath present that John Rivet late of Ugthorpe in the County of York Gentleman being a Popish Priest and little regarding the Laws and Statutes of this Realm and not fearing the pains and penalties therein contained After the Twenty ffifth day of March which was in the year of our Lord One thousand and Seven hundred to wit on the Eighth day of September in the nineteenth year of the Reign of our Sovereign Lord George the Second now King of Great Britain with fforce and Arms within this Realm to wit at Ugthorpe aforesaid in the County of York aforesaid did say Mass and the Office and Function of a Popish Priest did use and Exercise In Contempt of our said Lord the King and his Laws Against the peace of our said Lord the King his Crown and Dignity And against the form of the Statute in such Case lately made and provided etc Knottesford

[*In margin*] Misdemeanor.

[*Endorsed* i.e. *witnesses.*] Ralph Pearson
Thomas Fletcher
James Kempley
John Mathews
Thomas Morgan
Sworn in court.

[A similar presentment in the same bundle appears against 'William Anderson late of Crathorne' on the same date, is endorsed 'A true bill/Wm Milner.' The witnesses named on the dorse are 'Thomas Fletcher, James Kemplay, Thomas Weatherill, John Dicxon, Francis Richard,' who are 'Sworn in Court.' The words are added 'Granted Copy,' no doubt to the defendant.]

(11) ELIZABETH CLAVERING'S (*alias* GRANT) INFORMATION ABOUT HER MARRIAGE TO EDWARD CLAVERING

The JNformation of Elizabeth Clavering Wife of Edward Clavering of the Said Castle of York Gentleman taken this one and twentieth Day of June in the year of our Lord 1746 upon Oath before me Charles Cowper Clerk one of His Majesty's Justices of the peace for the North Riding of the County of York.

This Jnformant Saith that about Christmas last past she was with Several others comitted a prisoner to the Castle of York on Account of the present rebellion—that then She was a Widow and her name Elizabeth Grant—by which name She was comitted and Saith that When She was comitted to the Said Castle She found the Said Edward Clavering her present Husband a prisoner there and further Saith both Her Husband and She have been prisoners there ever Since and Saith that Her Said Husband and She are both papists—Saith that soon after this Informant was comitted to the Said Castle the Said Edward Clavering Sollicited this Jnformant to be His Wife to wch She at last consenting on

Monday the ninth Day of this instant June the Said Edward Clavering and She This Jnformant were married at the Castle of York by one Mr John Rivett a priest of the Church of Rome and then and now a prisoner in the Said Castle on that account as this Jnformant hath heard and believes—Saith that upon his being applied to by the Said Edward Clavering and this Jnformant to marry them He gladly would have declined the same on account of their being in the said Castle but upon the said Edward Clavering and this Jnformant insisting upon his marrying them and telling him that according to the Rules of the Church of Rome He As a priest thereof must do it he did marry them on the Day and year abovesaid and this Jnformant further Saith that one Ralph Atkinson then & now a prisoner for Debt in the Said Castle and a papist was by and present at the Said Marriage, and Saith that they were married according to the usage of the Church of Rome.

Taken upon oath the twenty first day of June 1746 before me—Chas Cowper — Elisebeth * c Lawering

[*Endorsed*] Yorkshire 21 July 1746.

(12) THOMAS FLETCHER'S INFORMATION AGAINST REVS. WILLIAM ANDERSON, MONOX HERVEY, MATTHEW COLLINGRIDGE, O.S.F., SIDDELL, AND PETER OF ALCANTARA GORDON, O.S.F.

North Riding of the County of York } The Information of Thomas Fletcher of Stoxley in the said Riding. Taken before Cholmley Turner, Timothy Mauleverer, Ralph Robinson and Thomas Skottowe Esquires, Justices of the peace for the said Riding ye 9th Day of July 1746.

This Informant upon his Oath Saith that when he was about Nine years of age, his Mother marrying a Roman Catholick, brought [him] up afterwards in that Communion, And that he Continued a papist till about Michaelmas last, during which time he went to hear Mass at Several Chappels, And said that he has heard one Mr Anderson Say Mass at a Chappel in Stockton [in ye County of Durham *above*] about five years agoe, and he observ'd at the said Time that he held up a wafer with both his hands, And immediately after a Cup in the same manner, saying something at that instant in a Language unknown to this Informant, And further saith that he had on at the same time a Surplice, And a Red Stole about his Neck, hanging down before, with a Cross wrought in it at Each End. And that the said Mr Anderson did then Eat of the wafer and Drank of the Cup, and after gave the Sacrament to a man and a woman in ye said Chappel. This informant saith that he has been at a Popish Chappel in Craythorn in this Riding Several times and has heard the said Mr Anderson say Mass in the like manner, only at Certain times when there

* A name has been written after 'Elisebeth' which may be Rivett, but it is scored out.

are prayers for the Dead, he had on a black Vestment and Stole upon y[e] Surplice, He further Saith that he did hear one M[r] Rivit Say Mass on a Latter Lady Day about Nine years agoe in a Popish Chappel at Osmotherly in this Riding after the same manner and form as M[r] Anderson did, And that he had with him several young Gentlemen, said to be Scholars and Boarders with him, And he Saith that the said M[r] Rivit came that night to his Fathers, who lived in a House in Stoxley made use of as a Chappel till M[r] Pierson* built his, And said Mass to his Mother and him and y[e] family. This Informant likewise upon his Oath saith that he knows one M[r] Collingdriget† a Popish Priest and has heard him say Mass in a Chappel at Silton in this Riding once, And at diverse times at Stoxley in M[r] Pierson's Chappel, where he Constantly Attended Once a Month for Two or three years last past, And that he perform'd the said Service in the form and after the Same manner as above described, He further Saith that he has heard one M[r] Siddell a Popish Priest Say Mass in a Room in M[r] Mayes House [at Yarm *above*] (whilest the Chappel there was building) after the Same manner & in the form as M[r] Anderson did as is above mention'd, And further That he has heard One M[r] Gordon‡ late of osmotherly a Popish Priest say Mass at Osmotherly afors[d] Several times and at Stoxley, in the Manner and form abovesaid, and that he has heard him say he was a Scotch Man & that y[e] Duke of Gordon was his Unkle—

Taken & Sworn the day & year
aboves[d] before us— The Mark of
Cho: Turner Thomas + Fletcher
Tim[o] Mauleverer
Ra. Robinson
Tho[s] Skottowe

[*Endorsed*] 9th July 1746. Thomas Fletchers Informac'on ag[t] Anderson & Rivett.

(13) JOHN DICXON'S INFORMATION AGAINST REV. WILLIAM ANDERSON

North Riding Yorkshire } To wit

The Examination [& information *above*] of John Dicxon of Castle Leavington in the said Riding taken before Cholmley Turner

* Bradshaw, son and heir of William Peirson of Forcett, lord of the manor of Stokesley, by Anne his second wife, daughter of Constable Bradshaw of Nunthorpe. Bradshaw Peirson was born at Stokesley 18 Dec. 1692, and buried there 13 March 1746-7, unmarried, and left his estate to a cousin. (John Walker Ord's *History of Cleveland*, 397-8; *Yorks. Par. Reg. Soc.*, vii.; J. Orlebar Payne's *Cath. Nonjurors*, 1715.) The chapel was wrecked by a mob in 1746.

† The Rev. Matthew Collingridge, O.S.F., was preses of Mount Grace, Osmotherly, 1740-49, and died in 1764. (Fr. Thaddeus, *Franciscans in England*.)

‡ The Rev. Peter of Alcantara Gordon is given as preses of Osmotherly 1732-38. (Fr. Thaddeus, *Franciscans in England*.)

Ralph Robinson Timothy Mauleverer and Thomas Skottowe Esq[rs] Justices of the peace for the said Riding this Ninth day of July 1746.

This Examinant upon his oath saith that he and one William Stonehouse being on the Twenty sixth day of December last appointed to keep watch within the Constablry, of Castle Leavington aforesaid betwixt the Hours of Six and Seven of the Clock in the Evening of the same day a Man came up to them whom they stoped and Examined and finding him to be one William Anderson of Crathorn in the said Riding a Reputed Roman Catholic priest they carryed & Delivered him to the Care of Thomas Weatherell Constable of Castle Leavington aforesaid And saith that at the time he and the said William Stonehouse took the said William Anderson as aforesaid he was very much Disguised in his Dress and when he found that this Examinant and the said Stonehouse knew him he Confessed his name was Anderson and that he was a Roman Catholic priest.

Sworn at Stokesley in the said Riding the day & year first above written before us— John Dicxon

Cho: Turner
Tim[o] Mauleverer
Ra: Robinson
Tho[s] Skottowe

[*Endorsed*] 9th July 1746—John Dixons Information ag[t] Anderson.

(14) JAMES KEMPLEY'S INFORMATION AGAINST REV. WILLIAM ANDERSON

North Riding of the County of York } The Information of James Kempley of Middleton in this Riding taken upon Oath the 9th Day of July 1746.

This Informant Saith that about Two years ago in February last He was marryed to Mary Mennel by M[r] William Anderson a Papist Priest According to the form and usage of the Church of Rome, in M[r] Andersons own Room at Craythorn in this Riding

Taken & Sworn the Day & Year aboves[d] before us—Cho: Turner
Tim[o] Mauleverer
Ra: Robinson
Tho[s] Skottowe

The Marke of James + Kempley

[*Endorsed*] 9th July 1746. James Kempley's Information ag[t] [Rivett *x*[d] *out*] Anderson

(15) THOMAS WETHERELL'S INFORMATION AGAINST REV. WILLIAM ANDERSON

North Riding Yorkshire } To wit

The Examination [& Information *above*] of Thomas Weatherell *

* Changed from Weatherill.

Constable of Castle Leavington * in the said Riding taken before Cholmley Turner Ralph Robinson Timothy Mauleverer & Thomas Skottowe Esq Justices of the peace for the said Riding this ninth day of July 1746.

This Examinant saith that William Stonehouse and John Dickson on the Twenty Sixth day of December last being appointed to keep Watch within the Constablry of Castle Leavington aforesaid on the Evening of the Same Day brought and Delivered to this Examinant one William Anderson a Reputed Roman Catholic priest whom this Examinant the Day following Carryed before the said M[r] Robinson and Mathew Consett Esquire another of his Majestys Justices of the peace for the said Riding. And Severall papers of the said William Anderson having been before Seized and Delivered to the Care of the said M[r] Turner or his Clerk, This Examinant was ordered by the said M[r] Robinson to goe to the said M[r] Turner's for the same and after this Examinant returned from the said M[r] Turner's and the said M[r] Robinson & M[r] Consett had signed a mittimus for this Examinant to Carry the said Anderson to York Castle, the said William Anderson Desired and very much Intreated this Examinant to let him know if any Writing was found amongst the said papers relating to any moneys being Collected by him for the pretender's use. And this Examinant further Saith that During the time the said William Anderson was in this Examinants Custody he severall times acknowledged himself to be a Roman Catholic priest and Declared that he then and for several years past Exercised the Function of a Roman Catholic priest at Crathorn in the said Riding.

Sworn the day and year first above written at Stokesley before us— Tho[s] Wetherell

Cho: Turner
Tim[o] Mauleverer
Ra: Robinson
Tho[s] Skottowe

[*Endorsed*] 9th July 1746 Tho[s] Weatherill's Information ag[t] Anderson.

(16) BISHOP DICCONSON TO [? REV. WILLIAM ANDERSON].

[The addressee, probably the Rev. William Anderson then chaplain at Crathorne, had consulted the Bishop as to accepting the position of spiritual adviser of a member of the Thornborough family of Leyburn. Like many of the county gentry they were at times resident in York, the 'Parish, where there are so many priests,' in the Bishop's words. In 1767 Mr Thomas Daniel, then aged 50, had been resident 25 years in that city. He died there 25 Aug. 1770. In 1769 there were nine priests resident there. Lop Lane, as shewn in Gent's *History of York*, 1730, leads from the southern end of Mint Yard towards the Minster, coinciding with Little Blake Street where two successive chapels stood, on the site of the present theatre.

* In Kirk-Levington parish, three miles S.E. of Yarm, and about three N.W. of Crathorne.

As extended it is now known as Duncombe Street, where St Wilfrid's church now stands. There is thus some historical continuity associated with the neighbourhood, if not with one actual site.]

Sir Wylliff [Wycliffe] 28 Feb: 174¾

Your's of the 19th J have, concerning what the daughter of Mrs Agnes Thornburgh desired. My advise is, that you would do well to make your excuse to her: and decline all such Visits; which if not necessary are very chargeable. If it be her inclination to be directed by you in matters of conscience, it will be no ways proper for you to meddle there (contrary to the general use of all others) in so great a Parish, where there are so many Prtts *. Besides she living in a Family where one is kept†; your medling that way may as I forsee, bring complaints to me on that head. If she have difficulty to make use of the Gent: kept by Lord; she may safely adress her self to Mr Daniel in Lop-Lane, who has sufficient prudence to give her the best advice. You may truly alledge that your own Parish concerns require your residence at home, which being your Duty, the other not so, you desire her to excuse you from so long and improper Journey. This is the advice of

Your very humble servant
Ed. Eaton‡

I suppose Mr Pierson has set all matters right between you and the Farmer, since you say nothing of it.

[*Endorsed*] Mr Eaton: N° 12 +

(17) BISHOP DICCONSON TO REV. WILLIAM ANDERSON.

Mr Anderson Wycliff 28 Apr: 1745

Sir

By the last poste, J received your's of the 23d Jnstant. The 2d payment to Mr Talbot will not become due till after the end of May; nor can J be sure of procuring it for him till then. As to his Debts to your neighbors, you will please to give me *an account* § (the best you can) to whom they are owing, and *how much to each one*; and also on what account. This as soon as you possibly can oblige me with. You will also let him know, that before J can pay anything on his account, it will be necessary to *send me in a Letter from himself* a like *Account* and list of Debts. For I must have *proper Vouchers* that they have been duly and fully payed, and he *discharged of them*. Jn such occurences those precautions are necessary for *his security* as well as mine: wherefore J must expect it from him His *desiring* me to pay those Debts, and the *Proper Acquittances in full* from each Party will make all secure.

* The small letters are doubtful; but *Priests* is intended.

† The Rev. Peter Phillips *alias* Purshall was chaplain at Leyburn at the time. (*C.R.S.*, xiii., 233.)

‡ The paper has been cut, perhaps nearly half gone, as there remains part of endorsement 'ton,' say for 'Eaton.'

§ Words in italics are underlined in the original.

His deceased Brother having been so great a Confectioner in the Pall-Mall; 'tis likely something may have fallen to him, which may make him easy; if no children be left to succeed thereto. Jf so J shall be glad, for his sake, to hear it. J wish him in better Circumstances than it is in my power to put him. Jn doing what is herein desired you will very much oblige

Your very humble servant
Ed Eaton

[*Endorsed*] Mr Eaton: N° 5

(18) REV. THOMAS DANIEL OF YORK TO THE REV. WILLIAM ANDERSON OF CRATHORNE.

[This letter—No. 10—is evidently one of those seized amongst the Rev. William Anderson's papers. The Rev. Thomas Daniel, described as of Lop Lane by Bishop Dicconson, is the writer, and evidently had some financial responsibilities. It would perhaps be taken as evidence of money passing illegally; but the object is clearly about Mr Anderson's stipend as chaplain at Crathorne. It fixes some dates and particulars of interest.]

Dr Sr York Feb: 20 $174\frac{3}{4}$

J have now a little time to answer yours of ye 17th Jnst. that you may understand what yr fund is, & how your Accts which J suppose you keep, should stand at present you will please to take notice yt the Annual Fund for Crathorn is 30ll ꝑ An: including the three guineas from the Yorkshire Fund, or 26ll: 17: ꝑ Annu abstracting from the three guineas from ye Yorkshire Fund. ye Fund is payable half yearly viz at ye 24th of june & ye 24th of 10br. you went to Crathorn about the 24th of Feb: $174\frac{2}{3}$. from thence to the 24th of June 1743. 4 month's pension was due to you viz 10ll. from ye 24th of June 1743 to ye 24 of Decr 1743 6 months pension was due viz 15ll. Now you have rec'd as follows as appeared by yr own receipts

	ll s d
Jn prim: Aug: 31, 1743 from me by Mr Holden 8: 3 & from me by pay'd Mr Hildyard for books for you 1: 17	10 : 00 : 00
i.e. for 4 months pensio due June 24	10 :
Jtem Aug: 31, 1743 from me by Mr Holden for 2 months pension in part of ye half years pension [which will be *above*] due Dec. 24, 1743	05 : 00 : 00
Jtem Jan: 5th 1743 from me by Mr Hartley ye remainder of ye half years pension due Dec: 24, 1743	10 : 00 : 00

You may Easily imagin twou'd be endless trouble to me to have often to send particulars to each in this manner. [*ends*]

[*Endorsed*] Mr Thom: Daniel. N° 10

(19) REV. EMIR GRIMBALSTON TO REV. WILLIAM ANDERSON.

[This is another letter of Mr Anderson's about a payment of money, the real object being for masses. Mr Grimbalston abbreviates his first name. In the first *Douay Diary* it is spelt 'Emir' as above, and has been thought to be *Emerich;* but in the will of John Grimbalston of Coughton Court, co. Warwick (14 July 1739, prob. 16 Feb. 1742), he speaks of his brother *Amor* and nephew *Amor*. (J. O. Payne's *Records of English Catholics*, 27.)]

S[r] May y[e] 7th 1745

M[rs] Tunstall of Newsham died on y[e] 4th of this Month. you'll be pleas'd to say prayers for her & desire M[r] [*letters scored out*] Siddell to do the same. give him him a Crown & I'll answer the same to you.

Adieu in haste
Em: Grimbalston

[*Endorsed*] M[r] Grimalstone. N° 3

(20) EXAMINATION OF REV. LUKE POTTS ALIAS COOPER

North Riding of y[e] County of York } The Examination of M[r] Luke Potts otherwise Luke Cooper taken before us the 16 Day of December 1745.

This Examinant saith that he was brought up a Roman Catholick from his Infancy and lived Lately at Throckley in Northumberland—And upon the 13th of November last came to Ugthorp by the Order of M[r] Edw[d] Eaton a Bishop of the Romish Church, who lives at Wycliff, That he was to perform the Office of a popish priest at Egton [that being his profession *above*] in the place of M[r] Liddal, He saith that he never came into y[e] possession of that Cure, upon the Acc[t] of a Report of M[r] Liddals Misbehaviour with Respect to the Government—And therefore on M[r] Rivetts Advice that it would be more prudent to Stay privately with him till y[e] troubles were over, He did so—And was there till he was taken up.

Upon his being Ask'd if he would take the Oaths to the Government, He answer'd he could take none that were not Consistant with his Religion as a Roman Catholic—Upon being Ask'd his Name he saith that his Real Name is Luke Potts, that he took upon him the Name of Cooper when he came to Ugthorpe, with intent to go by that Name during his Stay at Egton.

This Examination taken the Day & Year abovesd[d] before us— Luke Cooper

Cho: Turner
Tho' Skottowe
Ra: Robinson
M: Consett

[*Endorsed*] Luke Cooper, als Potts, Exam[n]—Dec[r] 16. 1745—York Castle.

(21) COUNCIL'S INSTRUCTIONS ON BEHALF OF MARY AND CATHARINE METCALFE OF GUISBROUGH

The King ag[t] M[rs] Mary & M[rs] Catharine Metcalfe
Brief for Def[ts]

Defend[ts] Case—That M[rs] Ann Maire of the County of Durham maintained one Francis Clawering A young bo[y] (her

Nephew) at School at Ugthorpe nigh Whitby in Yorks: wth one Mr Revett (a Popish Priest) who de[ ]pt Sev^l Gentlemens Sons as Boarders at his hous[e], And Mrs Maire thereby became indebted to Revett 5^lb 13^s 6^d for boarding & Schooling wch She Sent to Mr Wm Withams at Stockton in the County of Durham in order to Send to Revett, who desired one Mr Suggett (a papist & Stew^d [to M^r] Moore of Lofthouse to call upon Mr Witham for the money—Which he did, And Witham at Suggetts request promis'd to send the money to Mrs Metcalfes (who are papists) at Guisbrough in Yorks:—Witham in Novr last rec'ed the money of Mrs Maire and he sent it to M^rs [Mary *above*] Metcalfe by a man of Stockton who frequents Guisbrough Markett, and she p^d it to Suggett on or ab^t 25 Novr last—And Revett being a Popish Priest some short time before Xmas last all his papers were Searched & Examined & himself App^rhended by a Warr^t from Mr Cholmley of Whitby & Sent to York Castle where he now is, And a letter to him from Suggett was found in his house wherein Mrs Metcalfes & this money were so mentioned, That Some of the Justices wou'd then [have *above*] it So understood that it was to be p^d to Revett for the Pretend^rs use, Whereupon Suggett and Mrs Metcalfes were App^rhended & Obliged to enter into Recognizances wth Sureties for their Appearances at the present Assisses, and were bound Over by Mr Cholm: Turner & others who are not so well Satisfied that the money was for Clawerings board & Schooling, That Mr Turner has Ordered his Clerk to acquaint the Court therew^th And none is bound to prosecute nor is any prosecution intended herein, And Mrs Cath: Metcalfe was no way concern'd either in receiving or paying this money or otherwise herein, And is in So bad a State of health that she cannot travel to York or elsewhere So far abroad—And Def^ts are not in Duke of Newcastles War^t of detainer.

Wherefore move to have Def^ts discharged paying their Fees.

The Annex'd Affidav^t proves Mrs Cath: Metcalfes indisposition To prove Mr Turner is satisfied of both Def^ts innocency—Call Mr Richardson.

If the Judge will not discharge but have Def^ts bound Over to next Assizes—Mrs Mary Metcalfe and two sufficient Sureties will be bound for that purpose.

Copy of Suggetts letter to Rivett wherein Mrs Metcalfe is named.

Guisbrough 25th Novr 1745—I have this day rec'ed of Mrs Metcalfe 5^lb 13^s 6^d wth the inclosed letter from Mr Witham, and have sent it to you by Jane Pindor, and hope it will come Safe to hand, but I am in Such a hurry I fear you won't be able to read it—I am S^r Y^r most hble Servant—Robt Suggett.

NB—Mrs Metcalfes are not named in any other letter at all.

[*Endorsed*] York Assises 10th March 1745[6]. The King ag^t Mrs Metcalfes. Def^ts Brief. Move to have Def^ts discharged—paying their Fees. Geo: Perrot, York 10 March 1745[6]—Preston Soll^r

(22) BAIL FOR KATHERINE AND MARY METCALFE

North Riding of the County of York Katherine Metcalfe of Guisbrough in the said Riding, Spinster, doth acknowledge herself Indebted to Our Sovereign Lord King George the Second in the Sum of Fifty pounds of Lawful Money of Great Britaine £50

George Dickinson of the same place, Yeoman, Doth acknowledge himself likewise to be Indebted to our Said Lord the King in the Sum of Twenty five pounds of like money £25

Joseph Danby of the same place doth likewise acknowledge himself indebted to his said Majesty in the Sum of Twenty five pounds £25

To be levyed upon their several Goods and Chattels Lands and Tenements, to and for y[e] use of his said Majesty his heirs and Successors if failure be made in y[e] following Condition.

The Condition of this Recognizance is such that if the above bounden Katherine Metcalfe shall and do personally appear before his Majesty's Judges of Assize to be holden at y[e] Castle of York, in and for this County upon the Tenth of March next, Then and there to answer such matters as shall be laid to her Charge touching her being suspected of Transmitting of money from One papist to another—Supposed to be employ'd against his Majesties person and Government in the time of this wicked Rebellion and further to do and Abide by, what shall be enjoyn'd her by the said Court, Then this Recognizance to be Void, or else to be and Remain in full force— Taken and Acknowledged the 15th Day of December 1745 before me

Cho: Turner

[*Endorsed*] M[rs] Katherine Metcalfe—Recognisance to Answer, Yorks[r]—10 Mar: 1745[6]—Discharged

[The same almost identically, with one for her sister Mary Metcalfe, of the same, spinster, in the same amounts and with the same sureties.]

(23) EVIDENCE AS TO MARY METCALF'S INABILITY TO ATTEND.

[*Two embossed sixpenny stamps*]

John Johnson of Guisbrough in Cleveland in the County of York, yeoman, And Mary Metcalfe of Guisbrough afores[d], Singlewoman, Jointly and Severally make Oath That Catharine Metcalfe, of Guisbrough afores[d] Singlewoman has for above ten years last past been so weak & in[fir]m That she has not for all that time travelled ten miles from the Town of Guisbrough afores[d] And is weak & infirm a State of health That She is not at this Season able to travel from Guisbrough afores[d] to the City of York or elsewhere So farr from home without thereby extremely endangering her health, And the said John Johnson for himself maketh Oath That he is the better enabled to depose as afores[d] being he hath known & been very well acquainted with the said Catharine Metcalfe & hath lived at Guisbrough afores[d] for above twenty years last past And the said Mary Metcalf for herself maketh Oath That She is the better enabled to depose as afores[d] being She hath lived in the Same house with the said Catharine Metcalfe at Guisbrough afores[d] for the greatest part of twenty years last past.

Both Sworn at the Judges Lodgings in the City of York this twefth day of March 1745 Before me

The marke of
John + Johnson
Mary Metcalfe

T[ ]buey [?]

[*Endorsed*] Yorkshire March 10th 1745[6].—R. ag[t.] Metcalfe —Affid[t]—To be discharged.

INDEX

OF PERSONS AND PLACES

COMPILED AND CONTRIBUTED BY

MRS. T. E. MARTIN

* An asterisk signifies more than one entry on a page.
n Signifies a note on the page.
Ped. f. Signifies Pedigree facing page .

338, 345, 352-355 *pass.*, 357*, 358*

No Family Names.

Lightning Source UK Ltd.
Milton Keynes UK
UKHW041111311218
334816UK00013B/1262/P

9 781527 808713